June 26–30, 2017
Washington, DC, USA

I0054755

**Association for
Computing Machinery**

Advancing Computing as a Science & Profession

HPDC'17

Proceedings of the 26th International Symposium on

High-Performance Parallel and Distributed Computing

Sponsored by:

ACM SIGARCH and University of Arizona

In-cooperation with:

SIGHPC

Supported by:

Intel, Seagate Government Solutions, NSF, & US Department of Energy

Association for
Computing Machinery

Advancing Computing as a Science & Profession

The Association for Computing Machinery
2 Penn Plaza, Suite 701
New York, New York 10121-0701

ISBN: 978-1-4503-4699-3 (Digital)

ISBN: 978-1-4503-5590-2 (Print)

Additional copies may be ordered prepaid from:

ACM Order Department
PO Box 30777
New York, NY 10087-0777, USA

Phone: 1-800-342-6626 (USA and Canada)
+1-212-626-0500 (Global)
Fax: +1-212-944-1318
E-mail: acmhelp@acm.org
Hours of Operation: 8:30 am – 4:30 pm ET

Printed in the USA

Welcome Message by the General & Program Chairs

It is a great pleasure to welcome you to the 26th ACM International Symposium on High-Performance Parallel and Distributed Computing (HPDC 2017), and with it to the historical city of Washington D.C., the capital and seat of government of the United States of America. This year's HPDC continues its nearly three-decade tradition as the premier annual conference for presenting the latest research on the design, implementation, evaluation, and the use of parallel and distributed systems for high-end computing.

As in the previous years, HPDC 2017 focuses on defining and expanding the state-of-the-art of the field, by having the best work selected by and for our community, and by bringing together high-profile and rising researchers and industry practitioners to present their work and discuss existing and emerging challenges in the field. Overall, we had 100 high quality submissions, from which we have selected a set of 19 excellent articles (19% acceptance ratio for 2017, in line with the past decade's 15-20% acceptance rate). Our decisions have been made through a rigorous two-round review process with over 350 reviews, online discussion of second-round 45 candidates for acceptance, and a face-to-face program committee meeting. This year we have opted for full-papers only and the accepted articles have benefited from careful monitoring and shepherding. From among the best articles, after careful consideration we have awarded a Best Paper Award. The program is further enriched by our keynote speakers, invited panelists, and you, the attendees of the conference.

This year, we have also analyzed the performance of our reviewers, both quantitatively and qualitatively, and will be awarding a Best Reviewer Award. To facilitate the comparison among the many strong submissions, the reviewers followed a review format that encourages focus on innovation, on quality of the proposed research and of the technical content, and does not forget the problem statement and the quality of the presentation. Although quantity does not equate quality, we are happy to count over 35 reviewers with written reviews of on average 500 words of longer, and 13 reviewers who have written over 4,000 words in total (the rough equivalent of a workshop paper!). We thank the Program Committee members for their effort, expertise, and dedication to the lasting reputation of HPDC, acknowledging also the additional reviews completed upon request. We also thank the tens of additional reviewers without whom the selection of a conference program would have been much more difficult.

The entire Organizing Committee has been of great support and able to perform in parallel and distributedly, while delivering high performance. We would like to thank them all, and in particular the Workshops Chairs Rich Wolski (University of California at San Diego, USA) and Ana Lucia Varbanescu (University of Amsterdam, the Netherlands), the Poster Chair Radu Prodan (University of Innsbruck, Austria), the Publications Chair Antonino Tumeo (Pacific Northwest National Laboratory), the Sponsorship Chair Dean Hildebrand (IBM Almaden Research Center), the Travel Grant Chair Patrick Bridges (University of New Mexico, USA), the Publicity Co-Chairs Torsten Hoefler (Eidgenössische Technische Hochschule Zürich, Switzerland), Shuaiwen Leon Song (Pacific Northwest National Laboratory, USA), and Kenjiro Taura (The University of Tokyo, Japan), and the Web Chair Zach Leidall (University of Minnesota, USA).

We thank our sponsors, ACM, through its SIGARCH branch, the University of Arizona, Intel, Seagate, and the NSF. Without their generous contribution to science, and in particular to the parallel and distributed systems community, this event and many scientific breakthroughs would not take place.

On behalf of the whole organizing committee, we welcome you to Washington, D.C. Making HPDC 2017 a success is now in your hands!

Welcome,

General Chairs

Howie Huang
George Washington University, USA

Jon Weissman
University of Minnesota, USA

Program Chairs

Adriana Iamnitchi
University of South Florida, USA

Alexandru Iosup
Vrije Universiteit Amsterdam and Delft
University of Technology, the Netherlands

Table of Contents

Session: Fault Tolerance

Session: Performance Modeling and Analysis

Keynote 3

Session: Performance and Concurrency

Session: Data Partitioning

Author Index

HPDC 2017 Conference Organization

General Chairs: Howie Huang, *George Washington University, USA*
Jon Weissman, *University of Minnesota, USA*

Program Chairs: Adriana Iamnitchi, *University of South Florida, USA*
Alexandru Iosup, *Vrije Universiteit Amsterdam and Delft University of Technology, NLD*

Publication Chair: Antonino Tumeo, *PNNL, USA*

Workshop Chairs: Rich Wolski, *University of California at San Diego, USA*
Ana Lucia Verbanescu, *University of Amsterdam, NLD*

Poster Chair: Radu Prodan, *University of Innsbruck, AUT*

Sponsorship Chair: Dean Hildebrand, *IBM Almaden Research Center, USA*

Travel Grant Chair: Patrick Bridges, *University of New Mexico, USA*

Pubblicity Co-Chairs: Torsten Hoefler, *ETH Zurich, CHE*
Shuaiwen Leon Song, *PNNL, USA*
Kenjiro Taura, *The University of Tokyo, JPN*

Program Committee: David Abramson, *The University of Queensland, AUS*
Samer Al-Kiswany, *University of Waterloo, CAN*
Gabriel Antoniu, *INRIA, FRA*
Henri Bal, *Vrije Universiteit, NLD*
Michela Becchi, *University of Missouri, USA*
Patrick Bridges, *University of New Mexico, USA*
Ali Butt, *Virginia Tech., USA*
Franck Cappello, *Argonne National Laboratory, USA*
Abhishek Chandra, *University of Minnesota, USA*
Zizhong Chen, *University of California, Riverside, USA*
Andrew A. Chien, *University of Chicago and Argonne National Laboratory, USA*
Frederic Desprez, *INRIA, FRA*
Peter Dinda, *Northwestern University, USA*
Dick Epema, *Delft University of Technology, NLD*
Renato Figueiredo, *University of Florida, USA*
Liana Fong, *IBM T. J. Watson Research Center, USA*
Ian Foster, *University of Chicago and Argonne National Laboratory, USA*
Ada Gravilovska, *Georgia Tech, USA*
Haryadi Gunawi, *University of Chicago, USA*

Salim Hariri, *University of Arizona, USA*
Dean Hildebrand, *IBM Research, USA*
David Irwin, *University of Massachusetts Amherst, USA*
Adwait Jog, *College of William and Mary, USA*
Tevfik Kosar, *University at Buffalo, USA*
John (Jack) Lange, *University of Pittsburgh, USA*
Adrien Lebre, *INRIA/Mines de Nantes, FRA*
Jay Lofstead, *Sandia National Laboratories, USA*
Arthur Maccabe, *Oak Ridge National Laboratory, USA*
Satoshi Matsuoka, *Tokyo Inst. Technology, JPN*
Alberto Montresor, *University of Trento, ITA*
Christine Morin, *INRIA, FRA*
Bogdan Nicolae, *IBM Research, IRL*
Sangmi Pallickara, *Colorado State University, USA*
Manish Parashar, *Rutgers University, USA*
Radu Prodan, *University of Innsbruck, AUT*
Matei Ripeanu, *University of British Columbia, CAN*
Martin Schulz, *Lawrence Livermore National Laboratory, USA*
Yogesh Simmhan, *Indian Institute of Science, IND*
Evgenia Smirni, *College of William and Mary, USA*
Shuaiwen Song, *Pacific Northwest National Laboratory, USA*
Michela Taufer, *University of Delaware, USA*
Kenjiro Taura, *University of Tokyo, Japan*
Douglas Thain, *University of Notre Dame, USA*
Ana Lucia Varbanescu, *University of Amsterdam, NLD*
Rich Wolski, *University of California Santa Barbara, USA*

Additional Reviewers: Engin Arslan, *University at Buffalo, USA*
Kevin Brown, *Tokyo Institute of Technology, JPN*
Oliver Cairncross, *University of Queensland, AUS*
Jake Carroll, *University of Queensland, AUS*
Jin Chao, *University of Queensland, AUS*
Ryan Chard, *Argonne National Laboratory, USA*
Nathanael Cheriere, *ENS Rennes, FRA*
Alexandru Costan, *INRIA Rennes, FRA*
Helene Coullon, *INRIA, FRA*
Vincenzo de Maio, *TU Vienna, AUT*
Luigi Di Tacchio, *University at Buffalo, USA*
Minh Dinh, *University of Queensland, AUS*
Aleksandr Drozd, *Tokyo Institute of Technology, JPN*
Mark Endrei, *University of Queensland, AUS*
Yuanwei Fang, *University of Chicago, USA*

HPDC'17 Sponsor & Supporters

Sponsor:

In cooperation with:

Supporters:

ASCR DOE

Building Secure Platforms for Research on Human Subjects: The Importance of Computer Scientists

Julia Ingrid Lane
New York University
Wagner Graduate School of Public Service
Julia.lane@nyu.edu

ABSTRACT

Businesses and government are using new approaches to decision-making. They are exploiting new streams of (mostly) digital personal data, such as daily transaction records, web-browsing data, cell phone location data, and social media activity; and they are applying new analytical models and tools.

Social science researchers, who are not trained in the stewardship of these new kinds of data, must now collect, manage and use them appropriately. There are many technical challenges: disparate datasets must be ingested, their provenance determined and metadata documented. Researchers must be able to query datasets to know what data are available and how they can be used. Datasets must be joined in a scientific manner, which means that workflows need to be traced and managed in such a way that the research can be replicated(Lane, 2017).

Computer scientists' expertise is of critical value in many of these areas, but of greatest interest to this group is the facilities in which data on human subjects are stored. The data must be securely housed, and privacy and confidentiality must be protected using the best approaches available. The access and use must be documented to meet the needs of data providers. Yet the technology currently used to provide access to sensitive data is largely artisanal and manual. The stewardship restrictions placed on the use of confidential administrative data prevent the use of best practices for research data management. As a result, links between data sources are rarely validated, results often are not replicated, and connected datasets, results, and methods are not accessible to subsequent researchers in the same field

This is where computer scientists' expertise can come to play in building approaches that will enable sensitive data from different sources to be discovered, integrated, and analyzed in a carefully controlled manner, and that will, furthermore, allow researchers to share analysis methods, results, and expertise in ways not easily possible today.

Author Keywords

Privacy; confidentiality; secure data; social science

BIOGRAPHY

Julia Lane is a Professor at the NYU Wagner Graduate School of Public Service, at the NYU Center for Urban Science and Progress, and a NYU Provostial Fellow for Innovation Analytics. Julia has led many initiatives, including co-founding the UMETRICS and STAR METRICS programs at the National Science Foundation. She conceptualized and established a data enclave at NORC/University of Chicago. This provides a confidential, protected environment within which authorized researchers can access sensitive microdata remotely and provides data producers with a secure dissemination platform. She also initiated and led the creation and permanent establishment of the Longitudinal Employer-Household Dynamics Program at the U.S. Census Bureau. She is co-leading the development of the Administrative Data Research Facility at NYU, joint with the University of Chicago and the US Census Bureau.

Julia is the recipient of the 2014 Julius Shiskin award and the 2014 Roger Herriot award. She is an elected fellow of the American Association for the Advancement of Science and a fellow of the American Statistical Association. She has been the recipient of over $50 million in grants and has published many articles in leading journals, including Nature and Science.

HPDC'17, June 26–30, 2017, Washington, DC, USA.
ACM ISBN 978-1-4503-4699-3/17/06.
DOI: http://dx.doi.org/10.1145/3078597.3091518

REFERENCES

Lane, J.I., 2017. A call to action to build research data infrastructure. Nat. Hum. Behav. 1, 75.

Enabling Workflow-Aware Scheduling on HPC systems

Gonzalo P. Rodrigo*, Erik Elmroth, Per-Olov Östberg, Lavanya Ramakrishnan+

Dept. Computing Science, Umeå University, SE-901 87, Umeå, Sweden
+Lawrence Berkeley National Lab, 94720, Berkeley, California
{gonzalo,elmroth,p-o}@cs.umu.se
lramakrishnan@lbl.gov

ABSTRACT

Scientific workflows are increasingly common in the workloads of current High Performance Computing (HPC) systems. However, HPC schedulers do not incorporate workflow-specific mechanisms beyond the capacity to declare dependencies between their jobs. Thus, workflows are run as sets of batch jobs with dependencies, which induces long intermediate wait times and, consequently, long workflow turnaround times. Alternatively, to reduce their turnaround time, workflows may be submitted as single pilot jobs that are allocated their maximum required resources for their entire runtime. Pilot jobs achieve shorter turnaround times but reduce the HPC system's utilization because resources may idle during the workflow's execution. We present a workflow-aware scheduling (WoAS) system that enables existing scheduling algorithms to exploit fine-grained information on a workflow's resource requirements and structure without modification. The current implementation of WoAS is integrated into Slurm, a widely used HPC batch scheduler. We evaluate the system using a simulator using real and synthetic workflows and a synthetic baseline workload that captures job patterns observed over three years of workload data from Edison, a large supercomputer hosted at the National Energy Research Scientific Computing Center. Our results show that WoAS reduces workflow turnaround times and improves system utilization without significantly slowing down conventional jobs.

1 INTRODUCTION

In recent years, analyses of large scientific datasets, high-throughput processing, and large communication-intensive tightly-coupled jobs have become increasingly important components of HPC workloads. Thus, scientific workloads increasingly consist of scientific workflows with complex dependencies. However, existing HPC batch schedulers have job-centric designs and cannot account for the complexities of workflows. This inability to adapt to the characteristics of workflows adversely affects both performance and utilization. Scientific workflow tools used in HPC centers often run workflows as chained jobs (jobs with dependencies) or pilot jobs (a single job containing the entire workflow).

However, workflows run as chained jobs have very long and unpredictable turnaround times because each job in the critical path may have a lengthy intermediate wait time. Workflows run as pilot jobs are likely to have shorter turnaround times because the intermediate tasks need not wait for resources. However, their resource allocation is set to the maximum required by any task within the workflow, even though other tasks may have significantly lower resource requirements. This can lead to resource wastage.

For scientific workflows, it is possible to obtain detailed information about the dependencies between tasks, which can be used to improve efficiency. We present the design and implementation of a workflow-aware scheduling system (WoAS) that takes advantage of such information to achieve short turnaround times without wasting resources. WoAS modifies the scheduler's job waiting queue to make existing scheduling algorithms aware of the workflow's fine grained resource requirements and structure without requiring any modification of those algorithms. Thus, it can be easily integrated into current HPC centers.

We implement WoAS within Slurm, a common HPC workload manager, to demonstrate the benefits of workflow-aware scheduling. The system was evaluated by executing diverse workflow workloads using a simulated model of a real system. Our simulator uses workloads from Edison a supercomputing system at the National Energy Research Scientific Computing Center/NERSC) [22], [21]. Our analysis compares the performance achieved with WoAS to that for the chained and pilot job approaches. The experiment set comprises 271 scenarios, covering different workflow types and submission patterns. The simulated time represents 253,484 hours (29 years) of system time and 3.8 million compute core-years.

Our experimental results show that for majority of the evaluated workloads, workflows run under WoAS do not waste resources and achieve significantly shorter turnaround times than are possible with the chained job or single job approaches. Moreover, the impact on conventional jobs was minimal except for workloads heavily dominated by very large workflows. The scheduling in very large workflows is adversely affected by performance optimizations made during the implementation of the backfilling algorithm.

The specific contributions presented in this paper are:

- A design of a workflow-aware scheduling system and associated algorithms that achieve short turnaround times with almost no intermediate wait times or wastage of resources.
- An implementation of a WoAS system and its integration with Slurm.
- A comparative simulation-based evaluation of the performance and system impact of the WoAS, pilot job, and chained job approaches for diverse workloads.

---

* Work performed while working at the Lawrence Berkeley National Lab.

HPDC '17, June 26-30, 2017, Washington , DC, USA
© 2017 Association for Computing Machinery.
ACM ISBN 978-1-4503-4699-3/17/06...$15.00
DOI: http://dx.doi.org/10.1145/3078597.3078604

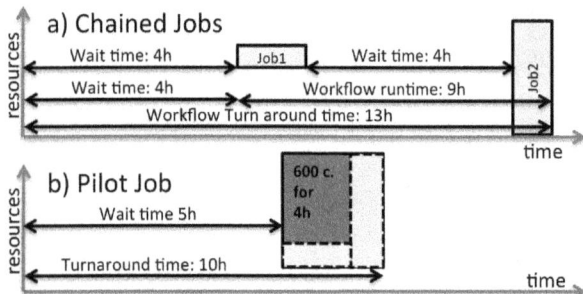

Figure 1: Resource usage and turnaround times for a Cybershake workflow executed using the chained and pilot job approaches. The chained jobs approach (a) results in longer execution time due to the intermediate wait times. The pilot job approach (b) eliminates intermediate wait times but wastes 600 cores for 4h.

We present the life-cycle of workflows and current scheduling approaches in Section 2). The Workflow-Aware Scheduling technique (WoAS) is discussed in Section 3. The methodology and our experimental results are detailed in Sections 4 and Section 5. Finally, we present our conclusions in Section 6.

2 BACKGROUND

This section describes the state-of-art and current challenges in scientific workflow management, and discusses related work.

2.1 Life-cycle of a workflow

Workflows are represented as Directed Acyclic Graphs (DAG) in which each vertex corresponds to a task (i.e. a work unit) and the edges correspond to control or data dependencies between tasks. The first step involved in running a workflow on an HPC system is to map its DAG onto one or more batch jobs in a way that respects the data and control dependencies indicated by the edges. Users perform this task manually or using a workflow manager [30], which typically automates the submission and control of the workflow tasks as jobs. Workflow mapping techniques are governed by objectives such as minimizing costs [31], minimizing runtime and turnaround time [4, 29], or tolerating faulty, distributed resources [19]. Once the mapping is complete, the resulting execution plan can be submitted with the aim of minimizing resource consumption (in which case the workflow is submitted as a *chained job*) or the turnaround time (in which case the workflow is submitted as a *pilot job*). Figure 1 illustrates the effect of these two strategies for a Cybershake workflow ([2]) used to simulate geological structures in order to characterize earthquake hazards in a region.

Chained job. In this approach, one batch job is submitted for each job in the execution plan, specifying the dependencies between them. This ensures that no job can start before its predecessors are completed. Each job receives the precise resource set required to run, and no allocated resources are intentionally left idle. However, the workflow's runtime will be extended by the wait time of each job in its critical path. Moreover, as described in Section 2.2, job priority systems keep jobs at the bottom of the waiting job queue until their dependencies are resolved. This extends the wait time of each workflow job, further increasing the workflow's overall turnaround time.

Figure 1a shows the Cybershake workflow's execution plan when submitted as a chained job. Even though both jobs are submitted at the same time, *Job2* must wait four hours after the completion of *Job1* because its priority (and thus its position in the waiting queue) cannot be increased from its initial value until its dependencies are resolved. The result is that the workflow's runtime (i.e. the time from the start of the first job to the end of the second) is nine hours. In this case, the wait time is four hours which is 44% of the runtime. The workflow turnaround time (i.e., from job submission to completion) is 13 hours with eight hours (61%) of wait time.

Pilot job. In this approach, the workflow is submitted as a single pilot job. The job's time limit is set to the expected runtime of its critical path in the absence of intermediate job wait times. The pilot job's resource request corresponds to the maximum resource allocation required by any one of the workflow's constituent tasks. While this minimizes the workflow's runtime, it presents the risk that some of the allocated resources may be idle (and thus wasted).

Figure 1b show the Cybershake workflow's execution plan when submitted as a pilot job. The workflow's wait time is greater than when using the chained job approach. However, the runtime is minimized because there is no intermediate wait time. In this case, the wait time for the pilot job to start is smaller than the wait time for the two jobs in the chained job approach. However, during the first four hours of its runtime, the workflow is allocated 600 CPU cores that remain unused, giving rise to 2400 idle core hours. This is the main drawback of the pilot job approach- it improves job turnover but increases the resource cost for a given quantity of work. This approach works well for workflows with small differences between their minimum and maximum widths.

Dynamic and static workflows. The workflow-aware technique presented in this work is designed for static workflows because it requires advance knowledge of the workflow structure. However, some workflows are dynamic, i.e. their structure is determined at runtime depending on the results obtained as individual tasks are completed. WoAS can improve the performance of the static sections of a dynamic workflow because during these sections the workflow's structure is known.

2.2 Classic HPC scheduling systems

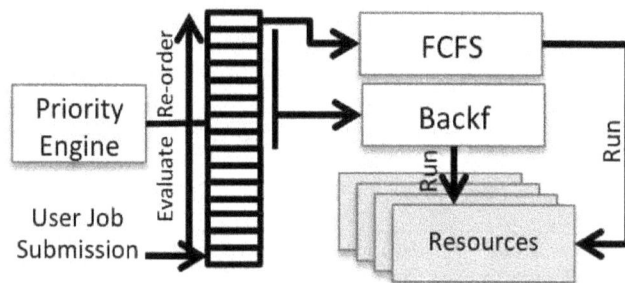

Figure 2: A classical batch scheduler with a central waiting job queue in which jobs are ranked by the priority engine and scheduled by FCFS and backfilling.

Figure 2 depicts a conventional HPC scheduler architecture with a central queue of waiting jobs. In this architecture, jobs are inserted into a queue when submitted by users, and scheduling algorithms select jobs from this queue to be extracted and run. Typical HPC

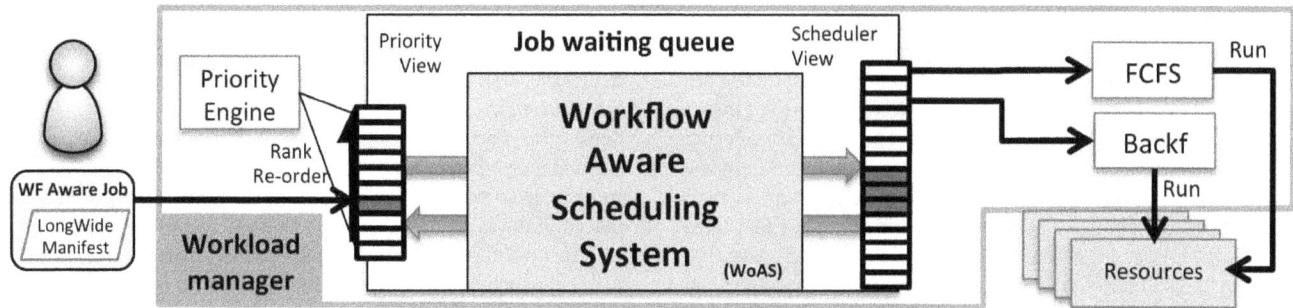

Figure 3: Progression of a workflow in the WoAS scheduling model from submission to the start of execution.

batch schedulers incorporate at least two scheduling algorithms. The FCFS (First-Come, First-Served) [7] algorithm runs the first job in the queue if sufficient resources are available. The backfilling algorithm [13] scans the other jobs in the queue and runs them if sufficient resources are available and they will not delay the start times of jobs ahead of them in the queue. Together, these two algorithms allow conventional schedulers to maintain high utilization and reasonable job turnaround times in HPC systems.

Schedulers also include internal prioritization engines to manage turnaround times by ranking waiting jobs according to some administrator-set policy. Backfilling algorithms take job priority ratings into account when scheduling. Batch schedulers also understand job dependencies (relationships between jobs). Dependencies can be used to express the structure of the jobs within a workflow. However, we have found that in existing HPC schedulers, dependencies affect job priority calculations. For example, job age priority engines consider that a job does not start aging until its dependencies are resolved. Consequently, the submission time assigned to a dependent job is the moment when its prerequisite job finishes, even if it is part of a workflow that was submitted much earlier.

2.3 Related work

Scientific workflows, i.e. collections of tasks structured by control and data dependencies [30], are increasingly used to capture complex dependencies in scientific computing and data processing. Workflows with location-specific or large resource requirements may be distributed [18], i.e., their tasks are run and their data are stored in different compute centers. The execution of such workflows depends on user inputs, specific resource characteristics, and variations in run-time resource availability [11]. Other workflows known as single site or HPC workflows are run entirely in a single compute facility.

Scheduling, automation, and execution systems for scientific workflows have been studied extensively. Pegasus [4], Askalon [6], Koala [16], and VGrADS [19] are examples of Grid workflow managers that incorporate different approaches to workflow mapping, meta-scheduling, execution, task management, monitoring, and fault tolerance. However, they all rely on current batch schedulers and do not offer specific solutions for scheduling the jobs of a workflow in a single site.

Efforts have also been made to develop Grid workflow scheduling algorithms, including *Myopic* [29], *Min-Min* [15], *Max-Min* [15], *Sufferage* [15], the Heterogeneous-Earliest-Finish-Time (*HEFT*) algorithm [28], and *Hybrid* [24]. These algorithms use different

strategies and objective functions to schedule tasks. However, they rarely schedule regular jobs and workflow jobs together, which is the main focus of this work.

Scientific workflow management systems for high throughput applications have become popular in recent years. Fireworks [9], QueueDO (QDO) [1], Falkon [17], and Swift [33] offer tools for workflow composition and management, execution, and monitoring. These systems deploy their own execution frameworks or run their tasks in workers packed inside HPC jobs, which are submitted as a pilot job or chained jobs.

Frameworks such as Hadoop [26], Spark [32], or Heron [12] offer tools for workflow composition, management, and automation for large-scale data processing. Cloud clusters increasingly support batch jobs and services over the same resources, forcing schedulers to compare applications with different performance metrics and objectives (e.g. turnaround vs. response time). Multi-level workload managers are designed to allow independent schedulers to manage different workloads: (e.g., Mesos [8], Omega [25], A2L2 [23]). Such systems could support workflow awareness by including a workflow-specific scheduler that would minimize intermediate wait times. Similarly, cloud cluster schedulers use different degrees of decentralization to achieve resilience and fast scheduling, and to address workload heterogeneity. For instance, Apollo [3] is fully distributed: each job includes its own scheduler and cluster information is shared through a loosely coordinated mechanism. Mercury [10] is a hybrid scheduling framework that supports dynamic resource division between a centralized scheduler and many distributed ones (depending on configuration and workload demand). Finally, Hawk [5] addresses workload heterogeneity (i.e. workloads with large and small jobs) by using a centralized scheduler for long running jobs and deploying distributed ones to perform opportunistic placement of numerous shorter less-critical jobs. These frameworks manage cloud workflows with dynamic resource allocations (e.g. MapReduce), and incorporate mechanisms that allow jobs' resources to be increased or reduced during their runtime. In contrast, WoAS provides the scheduler with an estimate of the workflow's future resource demands, enabling efficient FIFO and backfill scheduling.

3 WORKFLOW-AWARE SCHEDULING

Figure 3 illustrates the operation of the Workflow-Aware Scheduler (WoAS). The user interacts with WoAS by submitting a *workflow-aware job*, i.e. a batch job that includes a manifest describing the workflow's internal structure. This workflow-aware job is stored in the system's waiting queue and three mutually exclusive threads operate on it - WoAS, the scheduler, and the priority engine.

WoAS acts in between the actions of the scheduler and the priority engine, allowing these two components to perceive the queue in different ways. The two views supported in WoAS are referred to as the *scheduler view* and the *priority view*. The scheduler view exposes all the workflow tasks to the scheduler, enabling them to be scheduled individually. Conversely, the priority view preserves the characteristics of the original large workflow job, ensuring that the priority (and derived order) of the jobs corresponding to the workflow's tasks are based on those of the original workflow job when the queue is processed by the priority engine.

The system operates in a continuous cycle: a) the job priorities are (re)calculated based on the priority view of the queue, b) the queue is transformed into the scheduler view, c) a scheduling pass is performed, allowing the remaining workflow tasks to be scheduled appropriately, and d) the queue is converted back to the priority view. This section describes the two views and the steps of this process in more detail.

3.1 Workflow-aware job submission

In WoAS, users submit a workflow as a *workflow-aware job*. Users submit a job request for the maximum resources required in the workflow and the minimum duration of its critical path, as in the pilot job approach. In addition, a manifest describing the workflow is attached to the batch script.

Figure 4 presents an illustrative workflow description in JSON format for the LongWide workflow (defined in Table 2). It provides definitions of all the tasks within the workflow, including its resource requirements (i.e. CPU cores to be allocated for an estimated runtime). It also includes the command or application to be executed (cmd), and lists each task's dependencies on other tasks using the tag *deps*. In the example, SWide depends on the completion of SLong. This information is used by WoAS to transform a workflow-aware job (priority view) into its constituent task jobs (scheduler view).

```
1  {"tasks": [
2    {"id": "SLong", "cmd": "./SLong.py",
3     "cores": 48, "runtime": 14400.0},
4    {"id": "SWide", "cmd": "./SWide.py",
5     "cores": 480, "runtime": 3600.0,
6     "deps": ["SLong"]}]}
```

Figure 4: The LongWide workflow manifest in JSON format.

3.2 Workflow-Aware Scheduling system

The Workflow-Aware Scheduling system (WoAS) is a job waiting queue model designed to make HPC schedulers workflow-aware by offering different job lists (views) to different scheduler components as they interact with the queue. This multi-view model enables WoAS to enforce scheduling behaviors without requiring changes to the code of the scheduler elements that interact with the queue. The views offered by WoAS are:

Priority view: In this view, each workflow-aware job is presented as a single job (that submitted by the user). This view is the one presented to the priority engine. As a consequence, the priority and queue position of each workflow is based on the characteristics of the submitted workflow-aware job (i.e. its submission time and geometry). All tasks belonging to a given workflow receive the same priority.

Scheduler view: In this view, each workflow-aware job in the waiting queue is represented as a collection of jobs corresponding to its internal tasks (with the associated dependencies), which are placed in the same queue position as the original workflow-aware job. This is the view presented to the scheduler algorithms, so they can schedule the jobs corresponding to workflow tasks individually.

Algorithm 1 Algorithm for generating the scheduler view.

```
1  def woas_show_scheduler_view ():
2    global waiting_queue
3    for job in list(waiting_queue):
4      if is_workflow_aware_job(job):
5        remove_job(waiting_queue, job)
6        for task_desc in job.manifest["tasks"]:
7          new_job = create_job(task_desc)
8          new_job.prio.geometry = job.prio.geometry
9          new_job.prio.age = job.prio.age
10         new_job.submit_time = job.submit_time
11         new_job.copy_wf_job = job
12         insert_job(waiting_queue, new_job)
```

3.3 Workflow awareness in WoAS

This section discusses the impact of the multi-view model on the scheduler. Briefly, the multi-view approach produces three desirable behaviors. First, workflow task-level job scheduling ensures that the minimum necessary resources are allocated to the workflow at all times. Second, intermediate wait times are minimized to avoid the problem encountered under the chained job approach. Third, this approach minimizes system gaming because users don't have to modify their resource requests to ensure that all tasks within a workflow are given similar priorities.

Workflow task-level job scheduling. In WoAS, the scheduling algorithms assign each task within a workflow exactly the resources it requires. This is possible because the scheduling algorithms act on the scheduler view of the waiting queue. Unlike the pilot job approach, even though workflows are submitted as single jobs, WoAS ensures that the scheduling algorithms consider the individual tasks. This allows WoAS to minimize resource wastage when running workflows though they are submitted as single jobs.

Minimization of intermediate wait times. In WoAS, when the first job of a workflow is started by the scheduler, the remaining jobs remain related by their dependencies in the waiting queue. This situation is similar to the way that jobs remain in the queue in the chained job approach. However, in the chained job approach, intermediate wait times can be very long. Classical schedulers do not consider jobs with unresolved dependencies to have been "submitted", so their priority does not increase as they wait, and they remain at the bottom of the queue.

WoAS reduces intermediate wait times by propagating the priority attributes of the original workflow-aware job to all its tasks. All the jobs thus have the same geometry (requested runtime and CPU cores), priority factor, and submit time as the original workflow-aware job. Consequently, in the scheduling view, all tasks in a workflow are in adjacent positions in the waiting queue. Once the first job is completed, the next one will be in the same position as its predecessor was, and will begin at the earliest opportunity.

Propagation of priority information is performed by the operations within WoAS that make it possible to display different views of the waiting queue. A workflow-aware job's priority information is set during the priority calculation, which is based on the priority view of the waiting queue. In our system, a job's priority depends on two factors. First, the job geometry factor (smaller jobs receive higher priorities) is calculated only once in a job's lifetime, during the first priority calculation process to encounter that job. The job age factor (older jobs receive higher priorities) is recalculated during each priority calculation process. It depends on the job's time of submission.

The priority information of the workflow-aware job is propagated to its task jobs by the operation woas_show_scheduler_view, which generates the scheduler view of the waiting queue. The steps involved in this process are specified in Algorithm 1, which assigns the same workflow-aware job geometry factor, age factor, and submit time to each of the workflow's tasks. This propagation has three effects on future priority calculations for the workflow's task jobs. First, future task job age factor calculations will be based on a workflow's submit time. Second, the geometry factor of a job is fixed, so the priority engine does not recalculate it. Therefore, future task job priority calculations are based on the workflow-aware job's geometry rather than that of the individual task jobs. Finally, all task jobs belonging to the same workflow receive the same priority because they all have the original workflow's geometry factor and submit time. This ensures that all task jobs have the same priority and occupy similar positions in the waiting queue, minimizing intermediate wait times.

Priority propagation for workflows that haven't yet started is managed by the woas_show_priority_view operation. As it transforms the queue into the priority view, it consolidates jobs belonging to workflows that have not yet started into single workflow-aware job that retains the job submission times and priority factors of the corresponding original workflow-aware jobs.

Minimizing system gaming. The priority propagation mechanism described above has a beneficial side effect: because a job's priority factors are the same as those of the original workflow-aware job, the waiting time of the first job is equivalent to that for a job with the geometry and submission time of the original workflow-aware job. Therefore, users get the benefits of alternative approaches such as chained or pilot jobs without having to try to manually work around the system.

3.4 Batch Scheduler integration

WoAS was incorporated into the scheduler by modifying the core batch scheduling loop. Algorithm 2 provides a simplified representation of this process. Briefly, a phase in which job priorities are recalculated (line 4) alternates with another in which the scheduling algorithms act (lines 8-11). In this model, introducing WoAS does not necessitate any changes in the behavior of the priority

Algorithm 2 Simplified classical scheduler algorithm with WoAS calls to enable the multi-view model.

```
1  def scheduling_loop_with_WoAS():
2    while True:
3      if time_to_check_priority():
4        do_priority_calculations()
5      if (time_to_do_fifo() or
6          time_to_do_backfilling()):
7        woas_show_scheduler_view()    // WoAS specific
8        if time_to_do_fifo():
9          do_fifo_scheduling()
10       if time_to_do_backfilling():
11         do_backfilling_scheduling()
12       woas_show_priority_view()      // WoAS specific
```

engine or the scheduler. Two actions were added to the loop to modify the behavior of the scheduling system:

woas_show_scheduler_view: A call to a function (line 7) that converts the waiting queue into the scheduler view for scheduling.

woas_show_priority_view: A call to a function (line 12) that converts the waiting queue back into the priority view, so that any actions performed by the priority engine will be based on that view.

In Slurm, the priority and scheduling components run concurrently, and exclusive access to the queue is enforced through a lock. WoAS is integrated by adding the woas_show_scheduler_view call just after the scheduling code acquires the queue lock. It then calls woas_show_priority_view immediately after the scheduling code releases the lock.

4 METHODOLOGY

The performance of the workflow-aware system was evaluated by performing experiments with a Slurm simulator and analyzing the resulting scheduling logs. This section describes our simulator setup and the metrics used to evaluate performance, and presents details of the experiments.

4.1 System

We emulated NERSC's Edison as our reference system and used it to model the baseline workload. Edison is a Cray XC30 supercomputer that was installed in 2014. It has 6,384 nodes and 24 cores per node, with 133,824 cores and 357 TB of RAM in total. It uses an Aries interconnect and can produce a peak of 2.57 PFLOPS/s. Edison's hardware and workloads are representative of systems and applications used in many high performance computing facilities.

4.2 Simulation framework

Experiments were performed in the modified Slurm using our Scheduling Simulation Framework (ScSF) [20]. ScSF takes data on real HPC systems, users, and workloads as inputs and generates a model of the system with equivalent synthetic workloads. It then simulates the submission of the workloads over an instance of Slurm that runs on the emulated resources, and provides tools to analyze and compare the resulting scheduling logs. The Slurm simulator in ScSF is based on previous work by the Barcelona Supercomputing Center (BSC) [14] and the Swiss Supercomputing Center (CSCS)

[27]. ScSF improves the simulator, making it possible to run experiments up to 20× faster than real time and to perform multiple (up to 200) simulations in parallel.

ScSF Configuration In all experiments, the Slurm scheduler was configured similar to the Edison system, with FIFO and backfilling. However, to reduce the complexity of the experiments and facilitate analysis, differentiated queues and QoS levels were not configured in our simulator. These features provide user-level convenience but do not affect the scheduling approach. Slurm was configured to use the chained jobs, pilot jobs, or workflow-aware scheduling approach as required for the experiment at hand.

Each experiment was defined by its workload characteristics, the chosen scheduling method, a simulated system configuration, a target simulated time, and a random seed. Experimental workload traces were generated based on the characteristics of the experiment's workload. Workflow characteristics included the characteristics of the real HPC system's workload after the regular jobs were modeled, along with a list of specific workflows present in the workload and their submission patterns.

Experiments were initiated by submitting the appropriate workload trace to Slurm after starting it with ScSF. The scheduling process was run for a configured simulation time (5 days plus an extra day for cold start stabilization), and the scheduler logs were registered in a MySQL database for later analysis. Each experiment was repeated using six different random seeds (producing different workloads) and their results were aggregated.

Workload generation details Each experiment had a workload composed of regular (i.e. non-workflow) synthetic jobs and workflow jobs modeled on the experiment's configuration. The regular jobs in our workload traces were modeled using ScSF based on historical traces gathered over three years of operation of the NERSC's Edison system [21, 22].

The experiment configuration defines the specific workflows present in the workload, the resource configuration for the workflow run (a pilot job, chained jobs, or a job including a workflow manifest), and the submission pattern. Our simulator supports two workflow submission patterns - *workflow periodic* and *workflow share*. In the periodic pattern, a workflow is submitted once per user-specified period. In the share model, workflows are submitted at a uniform pace so the core hours allocated to workflows represents a user-specified share of the workload's total core hours.

The workload generator also includes a mechanism for pre-filling the system to capture a typical state of a supercomputer system. The length of each of the jobs in the pre-fill stage were configured to establish a baseline job wait time of four hours. There is also a job pressure control mechanism that adjusts job and workflow submissions to keep the workload job pressure (i.e. the ratio of submitted core hours to system capacity over a time period) slightly above 1.0. This ensures that the simulated system will have have enough pending work to maintain the baseline wait time without significantly increasing job wait times as workload scheduling progresses. In addition, the simulator used a system cold-start stabilization period of one day. The cold-start workload is artificial and not representative of modern workloads, so the corresponding logs were excluded from subsequent analyses.

Finally, the workload generator uses a random number generator that can be initialized with a seed. Running the generator with a given seed will always produce the same set of regular jobs and workflow submission times, independent of the selected workflow scheduling system. This ensures a fair comparison between different scheduling techniques for a given experimental configuration.

4.3 Evaluation metrics

This section presents the metrics used to evaluate our experimental results. We use three workflow (wait time, run time and turnaround time) and two system (system utilization and job slowdown) performance metrics to compare the pilot job, chained job, and WoAS approaches.

Workflow wait time (w^W) is the time between the submission of the first workflow job and its execution start. Shorter wait times are preferred. Wait times depend on the system's load, the job's geometry (smaller jobs tend to wait less due to backfilling), and the job's priority (higher priorities tend to imply shorter wait times).

Workflow runtime (r^W) is the time between the execution start of the workflow's first job and the completion of the last. It includes the runtimes of the jobs in the plan's critical path and their intermediate wait times. Shorter workflow runtimes indicate shorter waits between the job's tasks. The minimum possible workflow runtime is the sum of the runtimes of the jobs in the critical path (because they run back-to-back).

Workflow turnaround time (t^W) is the time between the submission of the first job and the execution completion of the last job of the plan. Smaller values are better. It is obtained as the sum of w^W and r^W.

Actual utilization during a time period (t) is $\frac{\sum corehours_i^J - \sum waste_i^W}{cores^S * t}$, where $corehours_i^J$ are the core hours allocated by jobs and workflows that are executed, $waste_i^W$ is the number of core hours allocated to a workflow that are not assigned to an internal task or job, and $cores^S$ is the compute system's total number of cores. This metric is a variant of the classical utilization metric that accounts for the possibility that workflows may be allocated resources that are not used at all points during their runtime. It measures the actual work done relative to the system's capacity rather than just the allocation of resources. This is important because pilot job workloads could potentially achieve a high theoretical utilization based on the classical metric while still having a high proportion of idle resources.

Job slowdown is measured as $\frac{r^J + w^J}{r^J}$, i.e., a job's turnaround time divided by its runtime. This metric allows us to compare the wait times for jobs with different runtimes. We use this metric to measure the impact of different workflow scheduling techniques on non-workflow jobs. The non-workflow jobs were divided into three groups based on their job sizes ([0, 48], [48, 960), and [960, ∞) core hours), and separate slowdown values were calculated for each group. The median values of this metric for each job group are used for the comparisons.

All the metrics used in this work are computed from the aggregated results of experiments that are repeated several times. Different aggregation methods are used for each metric to maintain semantic correctness and ensure the same number of workflows were compared for all scenarios. The actual utilization for an experiment was calculated as the mean of the observed utilization in

Group	A: Workflow critical path length.	B: Allocated cores, overall vs 1st job.	C: Allocated cores and rtime, overall vs 1st job.
Geometry Usage/Waste	n jobs/rtime:n h/max 240 core 240n core-h / 0 core-h.	2jobs/rtime:2n h/max 240n cores $240 + (n) * 240$ core-h. / $(n - 1) * 240$ core-h	2jobs/rtime:2n h/max 240n cores $240 + n(2n - 1) * 240$ core-h. / $n(n - 1) * 240$ core-h.
Profile			

Table 1: **Workflow characteristics for synthetic workflow groups including critical path size, pilot job geometry (rtime and max cores), core-hours consumed by workflow tasks (usage), potential wasted resources (waste), and a time-based profile of the allocated resources if the critical path is run with no intermediate waits.**

six runs. For the aggregated calculation of the job slowdown, all the non-workflow job slowdown values in the repetitions are read and used to perform the percentile calculation.

4.4 Experiment sets

We performed two sets of experiments simulating real and synthetic workloads to analyze the impact of WoAS on various workflows and workloads. In total, around 271 experimental configurations were tested. Each individual experiment consisted of five days of simulated scheduling of the workload plus an extra initial day for the system's cold start.

4.4.1 Workflow characteristics experiments. In this experiment set, we analyzed the effects of different scheduling techniques on the chosen workflow metrics using collections of workflows with different internal characteristics. A workflow group was established for each workflow characteristic of interest. Within each group, workflows were defined by a parameter, n, that controlled the effect of the characteristic in question; a larger n implies a larger effect.

These experiments allow us to understand expected wait times, runtimes, and turnaround times for some basic workflow characteristics. The workflow groups used in these experiments are listed in Table 1. The studied workflow characteristics include:

The workflow's critical path length (Group A): This group of workflows allow us to study the effect of the number of tasks (n) in the workflow's critical path on the workflow metrics. All workflows in this group were chained lists of n tasks of the same size (240 CPU cores and 1h runtime). Thus, if $n = 3$, the workflow would have three tasks, with the second depending on the first and the third on the second. In this scenario, we expected that workflows with longer critical paths would exhibit: a) larger differences between the runtimes of the pilot job and the first job under the chained job and WoAS approaches, b) more intermediate waits between the tasks in the chained job and WoAS approaches (which would affect workflow runtimes), and c) lower priorities for the pilot job and workflow-aware job relative to that of the first job in the chained job approach (which would affect workflow wait times).

The number of CPU cores allocated to the first job relative to the workflow's maximum core allocation (Group B): Group B was used to determine how the workflow metrics responded to changes in the difference between the number of cores allocated to the first job and the maximum number of cores allocated during the workflow. Here, n is a difference multiplier controlling the

workflow's breadth. All workflows in this group consisted of two jobs: the first was allocated 240 cores for one hour and the second was allocated $n * 240$ cores for one hour. Increasing the value of n should have two effects on workflow wait times. Under WoAS and chained jobs workflow scheduling approaches, it should increase the difference between the number of cores allocated to the pilot job and the first job. Additionally, it should reduce the priority of pilot jobs and workflow-aware jobs relative to that of the first job when using the chained job approach. These priority differences result from differences in resource allocation rather than workflow runtimes (Group A).

Allocated CPU cores and runtime of the first job relative to the workflow's maximum (Group C): This group was used to determine how the workflow metrics responded to changes in the number of cores allocated to the first job relative to the workflow's maximum core allocation when paired with changes in the minimum critical path runtime. In this group, n was a difference multiplier controlling both the length and breadth of the workflows. All workflows in this group consisted of two jobs i.e., the first was allocated 240 cores for one hour and the second was allocated $n * 240$ cores for $2n - 1$ hours. When combined with workflow scheduling techniques, a higher value of n should have two workflow wait time-related effects: (i) it should increase the difference between the allocated cores and runtime for the pilot job and the first job in the chained jobs and WoAS approaches, and (ii) it should reduce the priority for the pilot job and the workflow-aware job relative to that of the first job in the chained job approach. This expected difference in priority results from differences in both resource allocation and workflow runtime.

In this experiment set, six workflows were defined for each workflow group ($n \in \{1, 2, 4, 8, 16, 32\}$, except for group C, where $n > 8$ yielded very large workflows that caused system overflows. For each individual workflow (16 in total - six in Group A, six in Group B and four in Group C), we create a workload in which a workflow was submitted with fixed inter-workflow time. Each experiment was run using the pilot job, chained jobs, and WoAS techniques to enable comparisons of the resulting metrics across techniques and values of n.

4.4.2 Performance comparisons. In this experiment set, we compared the performance of the different workflow scheduling techniques for two synthetic and four real workflows drawn from real systems, which are presented in Table 2. The synthetic workflows

Workflow	LongWide	WideLong	Floodplain
Geometry	2jobs/rtime: 3h/480 max cores	2jobs/rtime: 3h/480 max cores	7jobs/rtime: 32.5h/512 max cores
Usage/Waste	672 core-h / 1728 core-h	672 core-h / 1728 core-h	5624 core-h / 11016 core-h
Profile			
Workflow	Montage	Cybershake	Sipht
Geometry	5jobs/rtime: 7.6h/960 max cores	5jobs/rtime: 4.5h/721 max cores	9jobs/rtime: 1.2h/384 max cores
Usage/Waste	375 core-h / 6920 core-h	1145 core-h / 2077 core-h	185 core-h / 395 core-h
Profile			

Table 2: Workflow characteristics for individual workflows including critical path sizes, pilot job geometries (rtime and max cores), core-hours consumed by workflow tasks (usage), potential wasted resources (waste), and a time-based profile of the allocated resources if the critical path were run with no intermediate waits.

(LongWide and WideLong) are representative of common patterns found in real workflows (i.e. a serial phase followed by a parallel one and vice-versa). The real workflows allow us to test our technique against more realistic workloads with diverse characteristics, including workloads consisting of fixed jobs with a complex profile (Floodplain) or many small grouped tasks (Montage), a large workflow with two large parallel stages (Cybershake), and a small workflow with a complex profile shape and many small jobs (Sipht).

Workflows were submitted using the workflow share approach with seven share percentages: 1%, 5% 10%, 25%, 50%, 75%, 100%. The experiments with lower workflow percentages (1% to 25%) provide insight into the performance of the techniques under realistic scenarios with workflows constituting an increasing minority of the total workload. The higher share values (50%, 75%, 100%) provide insight into systemic effects that occur with workloads dominated by workflows rather than regular jobs. The resulting 42 experiments were run using the pilot job, chained jobs, and WoAS techniques.

Similar experiments were performed using periodic workflow submission with periods of 1/12h, 1/2h, 1/h, 2/h, 6/h. This made it possible to compare workflow metrics in situations where the workflow component of the workload would not significantly alter the system's behavior.

5 RESULTS

This section presents the results and analyses of our simulation experiments. Our evaluation focuses on the two sets of experiments discussed above. The first set was performed to evaluate the impact of workflow characteristics on our chosen workflow metrics when using different workflow scheduling techniques (Section 5.1). The second set was performed to compare the performance of the different scheduling techniques (Section 5.2) across workflow types.

5.1 Workflow characteristics study

Figures 5, 6, and 7 show the observed median workflow wait times, runtimes, and turnaround times for the experiments with workflows from Groups A, B, and C (described in Section 4.4.1). Each horizontal block corresponds to a different workflow group. Inside each block, adjacent bars represent the measured median value for the same

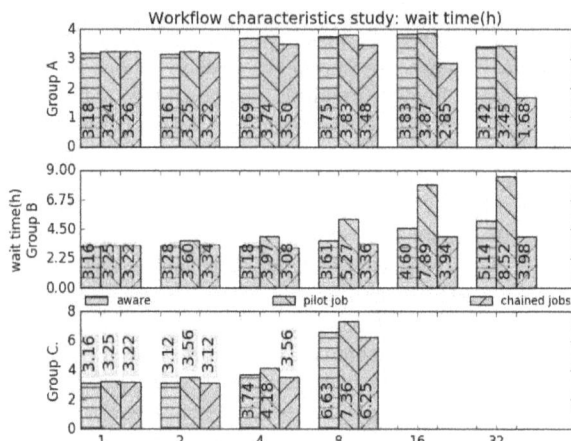

Figure 5: Median wait time as a function of the parameter n for workflow groups A-C.

experiment configuration with the three scheduling approaches (workflow-aware/WoAS, pilot job, and chained jobs). The x-axis corresponds to n, a value that defines the actual workflow used in each workflow group (see Section 4.4.1 for details). In each group, a higher value of n indicates a more pronounced effect of the special characteristic of the workflow group in question.

5.1.1 Workflow wait time. For **group A workflows** (results shown in the topmost block of Figure 5), the median wait times observed for the WoAS and pilot job approaches are similar, with those for WoAS being slightly shorter at all workflow sizes (n). Any differences in workflow wait time in these cases relate to differences in backfilling eligibility because the priority and CPU core allocations of the pilot and the first job in the workflow are identical.

In contrast, the chained job workflow has the same FIFO and backfilling eligibility as WoAS (both first jobs have the same geometry) but a higher priority because the job used in the priority calculation under WoAS is larger than that used in the corresponding calculation under the chained jobs approach. Thus, workflows run as chained jobs have much shorter wait times (by a factor of

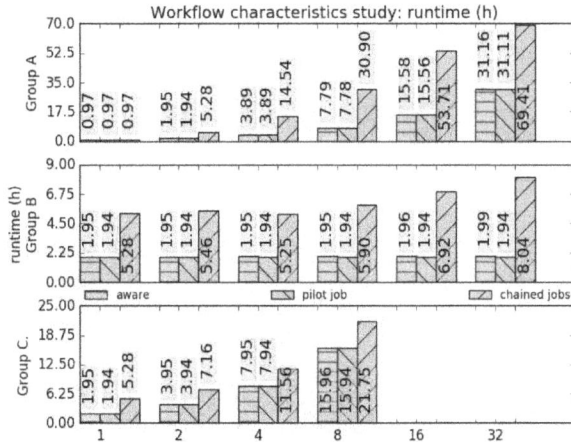

Figure 6: Median runtime evolution as a function of the parameter n for workflow groups A-C.

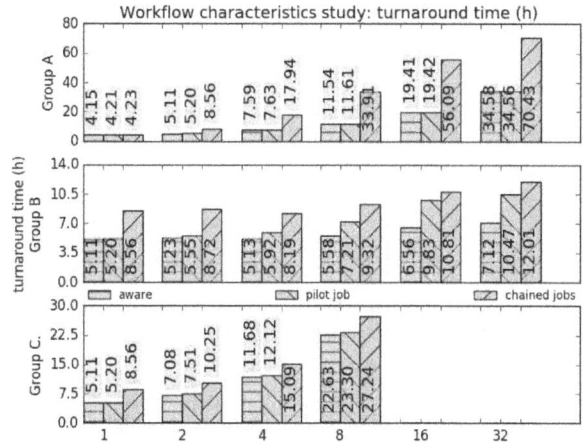

Figure 7: Median turnaround time as a function of the parameter n for groups A-C.

almost 0.5 when $n = 32$) as n increases and the difference in priority becomes larger.

Similarly, workflows in groups B and C (the middle and bottom blocks of Figure 5) exhibit the shortest wait times when run as chained jobs, and much longer wait times (especially for $n \geq 16$) when run as pilot jobs. The WoAS wait times fall between these extremes. The differences are due to the priority and backfilling eligibility of the first job of the workflow in each group. The chained jobs approach yields smaller first jobs that receive higher priorities, WoAS generates small first jobs with low priorities, and the pilot job approach generates large jobs with substantially lower priorities.

5.1.2 Workflow runtime. Figure 6 shows that all workflows run under WoAS or as pilot jobs exhibit very similar median workflow runtimes that are close to the expected minimum runtime for each value of n. This is expected for the pilot job approach because every task in each workflow is run within a single job with no intermediate wait times. WoAS offers good performance, similar to the pilot job approach, with negligible intermediate wait times between jobs. For example, workflows in group A where $n = 32$ consist of 32 jobs (see Table 1) but the median of the 31 intermediate wait times per workflow is only three minutes, corresponding to 0.1% of the total runtime.

Group A workflows, when run as chained jobs, show longer accumulated intermediate wait time as the number of jobs in the workflow's critical path increases. This matches the observation that most schedulers do not consider a job to have been submitted until its dependencies are resolved. Each extra job in the critical path thus adds an extra wait time to the workflow's total runtime.

Similarly, the workflows in groups B and C exhibited the lowest possible runtimes when run as pilot jobs, and near-minimum runtimes when run under WoAS. When run as chained jobs, the effect of the second job's wait time on the overall runtime becomes readily apparent - as n increases, the geometry of the second job grows (more slowly for group B than group C), and the wait time increases accordingly.

5.1.3 Turnaround time. Figure 7 shows that the WoAS approach provides the shortest turnaround times for all workflow groups, followed by the pilot job approach and then the chained job approach.

The workflow-aware approach provides bigger gains in turnaround time than the pilot job approach because it generates significantly shorter wait times. This is especially apparent in the results for group B where $n \geq 4$.

5.1.4 Summary. We observe that running workflows as chained jobs yields the shortest wait times but the longest runtimes. Conversely, running them as pilot jobs produces the shortest runtimes but the longest wait times. Meanwhile, WoAS yields intermediate wait times with near-minimal runtimes. Our results also show that WoAS produces the best turnaround time in every tested scenario. Moreover, the workflow-aware approach can be considered to offer significantly better performance than the pilot job approach even when they provide similar turnaround times because the former does not waste resources when applied to resources with widely varying resource requirements.

5.2 Performance comparison

In this section, our evaluation focuses on workflow turnaround times and the impact of the scheduling techniques on the system as a whole (i.e. its actual utilization) and non-workflow job (slowdown) performance. In the second experiment set, workflow jobs were submitted based on a workflow share approach (described in Section 4.2) in which the proportion of workload core hours devoted to workflows was set manually.

5.2.1 Workflow performance. Figure 8 shows the median workflow turnaround time speedup achieved with WoAS relative to the chained jobs and pilot job approaches. The x-axis shows the percentage of workload core hours allocated to workflows. When the speedup factor is one, the median turnaround time for WoAS and the compared approach are identical, whereas a speedup factor > 1 indicates the median turnaround time for the compared approach is X times that achieved with WoAS.

Comparision with the chained job approach. WoAS achieves very large speedups for long complex workflows such as Cybershake ($\approx 2\times$) and Sipht ($\approx 3\times$) compared to the chained job approach. The other workflows, which have shorter critical paths, exhibited smaller but clear speedups in most cases (e.g $\approx 1.4\times$ for WideLong, and $\approx 1.9\times$ for Montage). Floodplain has relatively

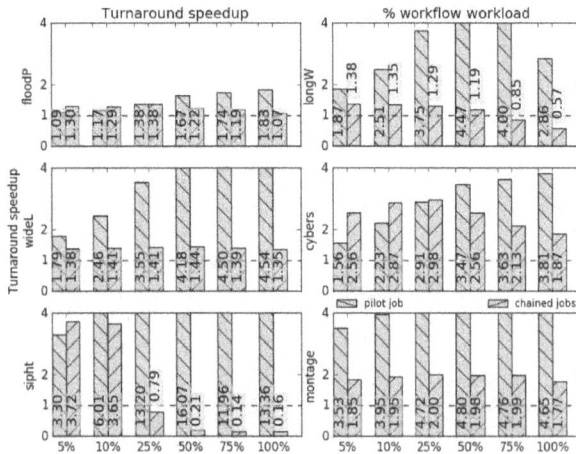

Figure 8: Workflow turnaround time speedup factors achieved with WoAS relative to pilot (blue) and chained job (pink) scheduling for six different workflow share values and six different workflows. Values > 1 indicate that WoAS achieves better performance.

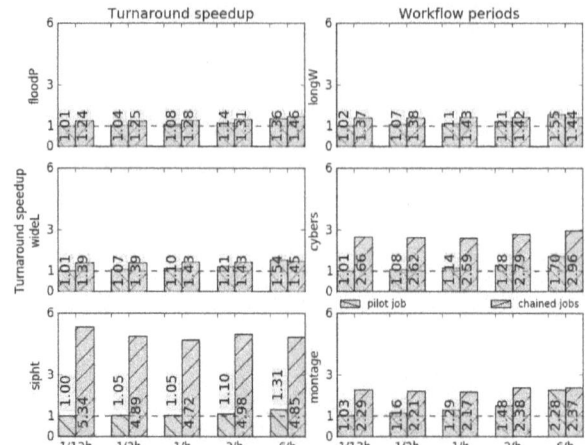

Figure 9: Workflow turnaround time speedup factors achieved with WoAS relative to pilot (blue) and chained job (pink) scheduling for six different workflow periods and six different workflows.

small jobs, reducing the impact of the intermediate wait times and speedups of 1.2×-1.3× were achieved for this workflow.

LongWide workflows exhibited shorter turnaround times when run as chained jobs than when run under WoAS in the 75% and 100% scenarios (< 1.0 speed ups). Analyses of the system's actual utilization and overall wait time in these cases revealed that using WoAS increased the baseline wait time and reduced utilization (by 20% and 30%, respectively). This is probably related to the workflow's shape. The LongWide workflow consists of one long job (48 cores, 4 hours runtime) and one wide job (480 cores, 1 hour runtime), and the long job can become a barrier that cannot start until a number of previous jobs end. The long job also stops other jobs from being backfilled since they would delay its start. This wait creates unused free resources, leading to low utilization. Such a scenario is very unlikely in a real system with a workload that includes a mix of different types of workflows and regular jobs, which facilitates efficient backfilling.

For workflow shares over 25%, the Sipht experiments yielded turnaround speedups below unity, which decreased as the workflow share increased. These turnaround times were not representative in all cases. In these scenarios, the chained jobs approach achieved lower utilization values (by ≈10-20%) and significantly fewer workflows were completed than under WoAS, invalidating the corresponding turnaround measurements. Sipht is a workflow with comparatively large numbers of jobs that have very small resource allocations. When workflows dominate the workload, the scheduler manages a large number of active jobs, affecting its performance and thus its capacity to utilize the system. WoAS is able to better handle the situation since all workflows that have not yet started are represented as single jobs in the scheduling view. As a consequence, in these experiments the job waiting queue under WoAS is shorter than under the chained jobs approach.

Comparison with the pilot job approach. WoAS achieved turnaround times that were orders of magnitude smaller compared to the pilot job approach (see Figure 8). The long pilot job turnaround times were due to their long wait times. This was an artifact of the

workload generation process, which was designed to produce the same amount of work for a given seed value (i.e. workloads containing the exact same jobs and workflows, submitted at the same time). This process was intended to produce a job pressure of ≈1.0 over the system when using the chained jobs approach. However, when using the pilot jobs approach, a given workload produced a much greater allocation of core hours because of resource wastage, greatly increasing the job pressure. For example, when the workload share was 100%, the job pressure when running workflows as pilot jobs was $1.0 + k$, where k is the percentage of wasted core hours in the chosen workflow. In summary, for a given amount of work, the pilot job approach yields much greater turnaround times and loads the system significantly more heavily than the WoAS or chained jobs approaches (more discussion in Section 5.2.3).

A final set of experiments was performed in which the contribution of workflows to the overall workload was reduced by only submitting one workflow job per time period. As shown in Figure 9, WoAS achieved similar or shorter turnaround times than the pilot job approach under these conditions. This trend confirms that for isolated workflows, both the pilot job approach and WoAS provide short turnaround times.

5.2.2 Job fairness. Figure 10 presents the observed median slowdowns for small jobs (under 96 core hours) at various workflow shares (x-axis). A value of one means that the median slowdown for conventional jobs is the same as in the case where no workflows are present; It is important to note that adding workflows changes the workload's composition, and so small variations in the slowdown are probably unavoidable.

The figure shows that the presence of workflows affects the slowdown of regular jobs. The experiments using the pilot job approach consistently yielded the largest slowdowns (up to 10×), followed by WoAS (up to 8×) and chained job scheduling (up to 2×). This difference is especially pronounced for Montage workflows run as pilot jobs, where a workflow share of just 1% triples the median slowdown, and a 5% workflow share increases the median slowdown almost ten-fold. These slowdowns result from increases

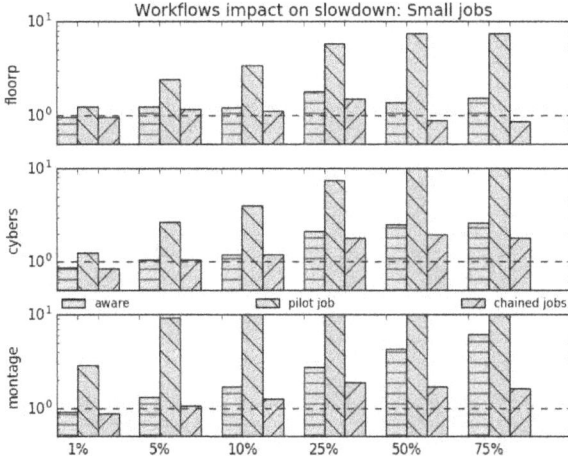

Figure 10: Relative differences in slowdown (*slowdownWithWorkflows/slowdownNoWorkflows*) **for jobs allocating** $[0, 48)$ **core hours. Tests were performed with three real workflows and different workflow shares.**

in the baseline wait time, which are due to the > 1.0 job pressure of the pilot jobs. In contrast, when the workflow jobs were scheduled with WoAS, a 1% share of Montage workflows had no effect on conventional jobs.

The experiments run with the chained job approach yielded the smallest changes in slowdown; the greatest slowdowns observed in this case were only 2×, and even these comparatively low values were only observed when the workflow share was above 50%. The chained job scenarios provide the greatest possible fairness for each workflow and workflow share because workflows are handled as regular jobs. It is significant that the slowdown of the regular jobs seemed to stop increasing once the workflow share rose above 25%, and actually decreased at higher workflow shares in experiments with the floodplain job. This can be explained by the lower priority of the floodplain jobs, which are significantly larger than many of the conventional workload jobs.

When using workflow-aware scheduling, the job slowdown in experiments with smaller workflow shares ($\leq$ 10%) was almost identical to that observed in the absence of workflow jobs. In the other experiments (with the exception of those involving Montage workflow shares above 25%), WoAS yielded only slightly greater slowdowns (< 2x) than the chained job approach. The large slowdowns (over 4×) observed with the Montage workflow at large workflow shares (> 25%) indicate that WoAS may have a significant impact on smaller non-workflow jobs when confronted by workloads that are dominated by workflow jobs with large resource allocations. This suggests that the scheduler may assign relatively little importance to regular jobs in systems dominated by workflow jobs. This is a consequence of limiting the queue processing depth when backfilling, which is a widely used technique for performance optimization. If the queue processing depth limit is hit before reaching these small conventional jobs, the only way they can move up the queue is by waiting even if they could be run without impacting the wait times of other jobs. This problem could be alleviated by adopting a method for filtering queued jobs that are not ready to be run before initiating the scheduling processes. Finally, a slowdown

Gain(%)	1%	5%	10%	25%	50%	75%	100%
floodP	1.80	5.22	14.46	29.29	44.53	51.64	64.47
longW	2.30	8.33	18.93	30.84	40.25	31.99	27.18
wideL	0.33	10.64	19.74	32.35	48.22	57.19	66.16
cybers	1.66	7.72	13.92	25.58	36.72	44.45	52.83
sipht	2.55	11.41	18.16	34.85	42.77	37.27	35.83
montage	12.36	44.90	60.30	72.34	80.13	82.14	85.26

Table 3: Differences in actual utilization with WoAS compared to the pilot job approach for different workflow shares.

analysis was performed for all the workflows listed in Table 2 with medium ($[96, 480)$ core hours) and large ($[480, \infty)$ core hours) jobs. The results showed similar trends as above and figures are omitted due to space constraints.

5.2.3 System utilization. We finally compared the actual utilization values obtained when running the same experiments using workflow-aware scheduling, pilot jobs, and chained jobs. Our results show that experiments using WoAS and the chained jobs approach both exhibited utilization values above 90%, and the results for the two approaches differed by $\leq$ 5%. As discussed in Section 5.2.1, the only exceptions were the experiments with the LongWide workflows and workflow shares of 75% and 100%, for which chained jobs scheduling achieves ¿90% utilization while WoAS achieved only ≈70% and ≈60%, respectively. Compared to the pilot job approach, WoAS achieved much higher actual utilization values as the workflow share increases. Thus, we see that WoAS avoids wasting resources while still achieving good turnaround times (Section 5.2.1), clearly demonstrating the benefits of workflow-aware scheduling.

5.2.4 Summary. For workloads with moderate workflow contents (< 50% of total core hours) WoAS offers the shortest workflow turnaround times, maintains high system utilization values (over 90%), wastes no resources, and offers best-case regular job slowdown. For workflow-dominated workloads, WoAS achieved the shortest turnaround and high utilization levels in all cases other than the LongWide experiments. The slowdown of regular jobs was greater than when using chained job scheduling for LongWide workflow scenarios.

Scheduling algorithms limit the number of jobs considered for scheduling using a configurable queue depth threshold k. It is possible that WoAS might perform better in workflow-dominated scenarios if the construction of the scheduler view was preceded by a filtration step to exclude jobs with unresolved dependencies, increasing the proportion of eligible jobs in the first k queue positions. Ideally, WoAS would also offer better performance for workloads with greater levels of workflow diversity. However, such optimizations are beyond the scope of this paper.

6 CONCLUSIONS

This paper presents Workflow-Aware Scheduling (WoAS), a new model for a batch queue scheduler. WoAS enables unmodified existing scheduling algorithms to take advantage of a workflow's fine grained resource requirements to achieve short turnaround times without wasting resources. We implemented WoAS and integrated it into Slurm. We evaluated it using our Scheduling Simulation

Framework (ScSF) by simulating NERSC's Edison supercomputer and its workload, basing our model on three years of real job traces.

Our results show that using WoAS reduces the turnaround times of workflows significantly relative to the chained job and pilot job approaches, and avoids wasting resources. In particular, in traces with moderate workflow contents (< 50% of total core hours), using WoAS, FCFS and backfilling yields turnaround times as short or shorter than submitting workflows as single jobs, and much shorter than as chained jobs (up to 3.75× speedup), while keeping the system highly utilized (over 90% with *no allocated idle resources*). It also produces utilization gains relative to the single job approach (e.g., 60% for Montage workflows with a 10% workflow share) and has negligible impact on the slowdown of non-workflow jobs. Finally, in workloads dominated by workflows (i.e. with workload shares of ≥ %50), it offers comparable workflow performance to established workflow scheduling approaches. Overall, our results indicate that WoAS workflow scheduling offers significantly better performance than current workflow scheduling approaches used in HPC systems and does not have any significant drawbacks.

7 ACKNOWLEDGMENTS

This material is based on work supported by the U.S. Department of Energy, Office of Science, Office of Advanced Scientific Computing Research (ASCR) and we used resources at the National Energy Research Scientific Computing Center, a DOE Office of Science User Facility, supported by the Office of Science of the U.S. Department of Energy, both under Contract No. DE-AC02-05CH11231. Financial support has been provided in part by the Swedish Government's strategic effort eSSENCE and the Swedish Research Council (VR) under contract number C0590801 (Cloud Control).

REFERENCES

[1] Stephen Bailey. 2016. (01 2016). https://bitbucket.org/berkeleylab/qdo
[2] Shishir Bharathi, Ann Chervenak, Ewa Deelman, Gaurang Mehta, Mei-Hui Su, and Karan Vahi. 2008. Characterization of scientific workflows. In *2008 Third Workshop on Workflows in Support of Large-Scale Science.* IEEE, 1–10.
[3] Eric Boutin, Jaliya Ekanayake, Wei Lin, Bing Shi, Jingren Zhou, Zhengping Qian, Ming Wu, and Lidong Zhou. 2014. Apollo: Scalable and Coordinated Scheduling for Cloud-Scale Computing.. In *OSDI*, Vol. 14. 285–300.
[4] Ewa Deelman, James Blythe, Yolanda Gil, Carl Kesselman, Gaurang Mehta, Sonal Patil, Mei-Hui Su, Karan Vahi, and Miron Livny. 2004. Pegasus: Mapping scientific workflows onto the grid. In *Grid Computing.* Springer, 11–20.
[5] Pamela Delgado, Florin Dinu, Anne-Marie Kermarrec, and Willy Zwaenepoel. 2015. Hawk: Hybrid Datacenter Scheduling.. In *USENIX Annual Technical Conference.* 499–510.
[6] T. Fahringer, R. Prodan, R.Duan, J. Hofer, F. Nadeem, F. Nerieri, S. Podlipnig, J. Qin, M. Siddiqui, H.-L. Truong, A. Villazon, and M. Wieczorek. 2007. ASKALON: A Development and Grid Computing Environment for Scientific Workflows. In *Workflows for e-Science,* I. Taylor and others (Eds.). Springer-Verlag, 450–471.
[7] Dror G Feitelson, Larry Rudolph, and Uwe Schwiegelshohn. 2005. Parallel job scheduling, a status report. In *Job Scheduling Strategies for Parallel Processing.* Springer, 1–16.
[8] Benjamin Hindman, Andy Konwinski, Matei Zaharia, Ali Ghodsi, Anthony D Joseph, Randy H Katz, Scott Shenker, and Ion Stoica. 2011. Mesos: A Platform for Fine-Grained Resource Sharing in the Data Center.. In *NSDI*, Vol. 11.
[9] Anubhav Jain, Shyue Ping Ong, Wei Chen, Bharat Medasani, Xiaohui Qu, Michael Kocher, Miriam Brafman, Guido Petretto, Gian-Marco Rignanese, Geoffroy Hautier, and others. 2015. FireWorks: a dynamic workflow system designed for high-throughput applications. *Concurrency and Computation: Practice and Experience* 27, 17 (2015), 5037–5059.
[10] Konstantinos Karanasos, Sriram Rao, Carlo Curino, Chris Douglas, Kishore Chaliparambil, Giovanni Matteo Fumarola, Solom Heddaya, Raghu Ramakrishnan, and Sarvesh Sakalanaga. 2015. Mercury: Hybrid Centralized and Distributed Scheduling in Large Shared Clusters.. In *USENIX Annual Technical Conference.* 485–497.

[11] William TC Kramer and Clint Ryan. 2003. Performance variability of highly parallel architectures. In *International Conference on Computational Science.* Springer, 560–569.
[12] Sanjeev Kulkarni, Nikunj Bhagat, Maosong Fu, Vikas Kedigehalli, Christopher Kellogg, Sailesh Mittal, Jignesh M Patel, Karthik Ramasamy, and Siddarth Taneja. 2015. Twitter heron: Stream processing at scale. In *Proceedings of the 2015 ACM SIGMOD International Conference on Management of Data.* ACM, 239–250.
[13] David A Lifka. 1995. The ANL/IBM SP scheduling system. In *Job Scheduling Strategies for Parallel Processing.* Springer, 295–303.
[14] Alejandro Lucero. 2011. Simulation of batch scheduling using real production-ready software tools. *Proceedings of the 5th IBERGRID* (2011).
[15] Muthucumaru Maheswaran, Shoukat Ali, HJ Siegal, Debra Hensgen, and Richard F Freund. 1999. Dynamic matching and scheduling of a class of independent tasks onto heterogeneous computing systems. In *Heterogeneous Computing Workshop, 1999.(HCW'99) Proceedings. Eighth.* IEEE, 30–44.
[16] Hashim H Mohamed and Dick HJ Epema. 2005. The design and implementation of the KOALA co-allocating grid scheduler. In *European Grid Conference.* Springer, 640–650.
[17] Ioan Raicu, Yong Zhao, Catalin Dumitrescu, Ian Foster, and Mike Wilde. 2007. Falkon: a Fast and Light-weight tasK executiON framework. In *Proceedings of the 2007 ACM/IEEE conference on Supercomputing.* ACM, 43.
[18] Lavanya Ramakrishnan and Dennis Gannon. 2008. A survey of distributed workflow characteristics and resource requirements. *Indiana University* (2008), 1–23.
[19] Lavanya Ramakrishnan, Charles Koelbel, Yang-Suk Kee, Rich Wolski, Daniel Nurmi, Dennis Gannon, Graziano Obertelli, Asim YarKhan, Anirban Mandal, T Mark Huang, and others. 2009. VGrADS: enabling e-Science workflows on grids and clouds with fault tolerance. In *Proceedings of the Conference on High Performance Computing Networking, Storage and Analysis.* IEEE, 1–12.
[20] Gonzalo Rodrigo, Erik Elmroth, Per-Olov Östberg, and Lavanya Ramakrishnan. 2017. ScSF: A Scheduling Simulation Framework. In *Workshop on Job Scheduling Strategies for Parallel Processing.* Accepted, Springer.
[21] Gonzalo Rodrigo, Per-Olov Östberg, Erik Elmroth, Katie Antypas, Richard Gerber, and Lavanya Ramakrishnan. 2016. Towards Understanding Job Heterogeneity in HPC: A NERSC Case Study. In *2016 16th IEEE/ACM International Symposium on Cluster, Cloud and Grid Computing (CCGrid).* IEEE, 521–526.
[22] Gonzalo Rodrigo, P-O Östberg, Erik Elmroth, Katie Antypass, Richard Gerber, and Lavanya Ramakrishnan. 2015. HPC System Lifetime Story: Workload Characterization and Evolutionary Analyses on NERSC Systems. In *The 24th International ACM Symposium on High-Performance Distributed Computing (HPDC).*
[23] Gonzalo Rodrigo, Lavanya Ramakrishnan, P-O Östberg, and Erik Elmroth. 2015. A2L2: an Application Aware flexible HPC scheduling model for Low Latency allocation. In *The 8th International Workshop on Virtualization Technologies in Distributed Computing (VTDC).*
[24] Rizos Sakellariou and Henan Zhao. 2004. A hybrid heuristic for DAG scheduling on heterogeneous systems. In *Parallel and Distributed Processing Symposium, 2004. Proceedings. 18th International.* IEEE, 111.
[25] Malte Schwarzkopf, Andy Konwinski, Michael Abd-El-Malek, and John Wilkes. 2013. Omega: flexible, scalable schedulers for large compute clusters. In *Proceedings of the 8th ACM European Conference on Computer Systems.* ACM, 351–364.
[26] Konstantin Shvachko, Hairong Kuang, Sanjay Radia, and Robert Chansler. 2010. The hadoop distributed file system. In *2010 IEEE 26th symposium on mass storage systems and technologies (MSST).* IEEE, 1–10.
[27] Massimo Benini Stephen Trofinoff. 2015. Using and Modifying the BSC Slurm Workload Simulator. In *Slurm User Group.*
[28] Haluk Topcuoglu, Salim Hariri, and Min-you Wu. 2002. Performance-effective and low-complexity task scheduling for heterogeneous computing. *IEEE transactions on parallel and distributed systems* 13, 3 (2002), 260–274.
[29] Marek Wieczorek, Radu Prodan, and Thomas Fahringer. 2005. Scheduling of scientific workflows in the ASKALON grid environment. *ACM SIGMOD Record* 34, 3 (2005), 56–62.
[30] Jia Yu and Rajkumar Buyya. 2005. A taxonomy of scientific workflow systems for grid computing. *ACM Sigmod Record* 34, 3 (2005), 44–49.
[31] Jia Yu, Rajkumar Buyya, and Chen Khong Tham. 2005. Cost-based scheduling of scientific workflow applications on utility grids. In *First International Conference on e-Science and Grid Computing (e-Science'05).* IEEE.
[32] Matei Zaharia, Mosharaf Chowdhury, Michael J Franklin, Scott Shenker, and Ion Stoica. 2010. Spark: cluster computing with working sets. *HotCloud* 10 (2010).
[33] Yong Zhao, Mihael Hategan, Ben Clifford, Ian Foster, Gregor Von Laszewski, Veronika Nefedova, Ioan Raicu, Tiberiu Stef-Praun, and Michael Wilde. 2007. Swift: Fast, reliable, loosely coupled parallel computation. In *2007 IEEE Congress on Services.* IEEE, 199–206.

Parallel Stream Processing Against Workload Skewness and Variance

Junhua Fang[†] Rong Zhang[†] Tom. Z. J. Fu[§◇] Zhenjie Zhang[◇] Aoying Zhou[♯] Junhua Zhu[¶*]

[†]MOE International Joint Lab of Trustworthy Software, School of Computer Science and Software Engineering, East
China Normal University, China, jf.fang@ecnu.cn, rzhang@sei.ecnu.edu.cn
[♯] School of Data Science and Engineering, East China Normal University, China, ayzhou@dase.ecnu.edu.cn
[◇]Advanced Digital Sciences Center Illinois at Singapore Pte. Ltd., Singapore, zhenjie@adsc.com.sg
[§] Faculty of Computer Guangdong University of Technology, China, fuzhengjia@gmail.com
[¶] Shannon Lab Huawei Technologies Co., China, junhua.zhu@outlook.com

ABSTRACT

Key-based workload partitioning is a common strategy used in parallel stream processing engines, enabling effective key-value tuple distribution over worker threads in a logical operator. It is likely to generate poor balancing performance when workload variance occurs on the incoming data stream. This paper presents a new key-based workload partitioning framework, with practical algorithms to support dynamic workload assignment for stateful operators. The framework combines hash-based and explicit key-based routing strategies for workload distribution, which specifies the destination worker threads for a handful of keys and assigns the other keys with the hash function. When short-term distribution fluctuations occur to the incoming data stream, the system adaptively updates the routing table containing the chosen keys, in order to rebalance the workload with minimal migration overhead within the stateful operator. We formulate the rebalance operation as an optimization problem, with multiple objectives on minimizing state migration costs, controlling the size of the routing table and breaking workload imbalance among worker threads. Despite of the NP-hardness nature behind the optimization formulation, we carefully investigate and justify the heuristics behind key (re)routing and state migration, to facilitate fast response to workload variance with ignorable cost to the normal processing in the distributed system. Empirical studies on synthetic data and real-world stream applications validate the usefulness of our proposals.

CCS CONCEPTS

• **Computing methodologies** → Self-organization; Vector / streaming algorithms; Massively parallel algorithms;

---

*Rong Zhang is the corresponding author.

HPDC '17, June 26-30, 2017, Washington, DC, USA
© 2017 Association for Computing Machinery.
ACM ISBN 978-1-4503-4699-3/17/06...$15.00
https://doi.org/http://dx.doi.org/10.1145/3078597.3078613

KEYWORDS

Distributed stream processing, Stateful operation, Workload variance, Load balance, Adjustment

1 INTRODUCTION

Workload skewness and variance are common phenomena in distributed stream processing engines. When massive stream data flood into a distributed system for processing and analyzing, even slight distribution change on the incoming data stream may significantly affect the system performance. Existing optimization techniques for stream processing engines are designed to exploit the distributed processor, memory and bandwidth resource based on the computation workload, but potentially render suboptimal performance when the evolving workload deviates from expectation. Unfortunately, workload evolution is constantly happening in real application scenarios (e.g., surveillance video analysis [5, 10] and online advertising monitoring [17]). It raises new challenges to distributed system to handle the dynamics of data stream while maintaining high resource utilization rate at meantime.

In distributed stream processing system, abstract operators are connected in form of a directed graph to support complex processing logics. Traditional load balancing approaches in distributed stream processing engines attempt to balance the workload of the system, by evenly assigning a variety of heterogenous tasks to distributed nodes [2, 3, 15, 28, 29]. Such strategies may not perform as expected in distributed stream processing systems, because of the lack of balance on the homogeneous tasks within abstract operators. In Fig. 1, we present an example to illustrate the potential problem with such strategies. In the example, there are three logic operators in the pipeline, denoted by rectangles. There are three concrete task instances running in *operator 2*, denoted by circles. The number of incoming tuples to the first task instance is two times of that to the second and third task instances, due to the distribution skewness on the tuples. Even if the system allocates the tasks in a perfect way to balance the workload when allocating task instances to computation nodes, the processing efficiency may not be optimal. Because of the higher processing latency in the first task instance of *operator 2*, *operator 1* is forced to slow down its processing speed under backpushing effect, and *operator 3* may be suspended to wait for the complete intermediate results from *operator 2*. This example shows that load balancing among task instances within individual logical operators is more crucial to distributed stream processing engines, to improve the system stability and guarantee the processing performance.

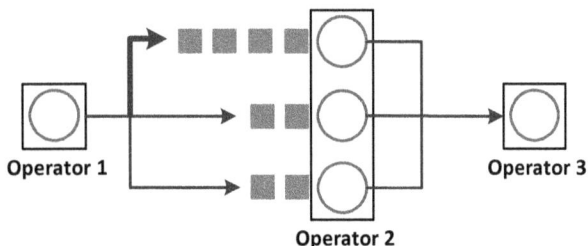

Figure 1: The potential problem of workload imbalance within operators in real distributed stream processing engines.

There are two types of workload variance in distributed stream processing engines, namely *long-term* workload shift and *short-term* workload fluctuation. Long-term workload shifts usually involve distribution changes on incoming tuples driven by the trends in physical world (e.g., regular burst of tweets after lunch time), while workload fluctuations are usually short-term and random in nature. Long-term workload shifts can only be solved by applying heavy-weight resource scheduling, e.g., [9], which reallocates the computation resource based on the necessities. Computation infrastructure of the distributed system may request more (less resp.) resource, by adding (removing resp.) virtual machines, or completely reshuffling the resource among logical operators according to computation demands. Such operations on the infrastructure level are inappropriate for short-term workload fluctuations, usually too expensive and render suboptimal performance when the fluctuation is over. It is thus more desirable to adopt lightweight protocols within the operators, to smoothly redistribute the workload among task instances, minimize the impact on the normal processing, and achieve the objective of load balancing within every logical operator. This paper focuses on such dynamic workload assignment mechanism for individual logical operators in a complex data stream processing logic, against short-term workload fluctuations. Note that existing solutions to long-term workload shifts are mostly orthogonal to the mechanisms for short-term workload fluctuations, both of which can be invoked by the system optionally based on the workload characteristics.

Our proposal in this paper is based on a mixed strategy of key-based workload partitioning, which explicitly specifies the destination worker threads for a handful of keys and assigns all other keys with the randomized hash function. This scheme achieves high *flexibility* by easily redirecting the keys to new worker threads with simple editing on the routing table. It is also highly *efficient* when the system sets the maximal size of the routing table, thus controlling the memory overhead and calculation cost with the routing table. Workload redistribution with the scheme is *scalable* and *effective*, by allowing the system to respond promptly to the

short-term workload fluctuation even when there are a large number of keys present in the incoming data stream. To fully unleash the power of the scheme, it is important to design a monitoring and controlling mechanism on top of system, making optimal decisions on routing table update to achieve intra-operator workload balancing. Recent work PKG [20, 21] performs well with stateless operator, e.g. Counting, but introduces new bottleneck and significant transmission cost with stateful operator, e.g. Join. Readj in work [11], although employing similar workload distribution strategy, only considers migration of *hot* keys with high frequencies, which may have difficulty on load balancing by manipulating bulky workload with hot keys only. We break the limit in this paper with a new solution for distributed systems to explore a much larger optimization space with all candidate keys for routing table, thus maximizing the resource utilization with ignorable additional cost. Specifically, the technical contributions of this paper include:

- We design a general strategy to generate the partition function under different stream dynamic changes at runtime, which achieves scalability, effectiveness and efficiency.
- We propose a lightweight computation model to support rapid migration plan generation.
- We present a detailed theoretical analysis for proposed migration algorithms to justify its usefulness.
- We implement our algorithms on Storm and give extensive experimental evaluations to our proposed techniques by comparing with existing work using abundant datasets.

The remainder of this paper is organized as follows. Section 2 reviews a wide spectrum of related studies on stream processing, workload balancing and distributed systems. Section 3 introduces the preliminaries of our problem. Section 4 presents our balancing algorithms to support our mixed workload distribution scheme. Section 5 describes our proposed algorithms and shows the implementation of our proposal. Section 6 presents empirical evaluations of our proposal. Section 7 finally concludes the paper and addresses future research directions.

2 RELATED WORK

Different from batch processing and traditional distributed database [6, 18, 24, 25, 30], the problem of load balancing is more challenging on distributed stream processing systems, because of the needs of continuous optimization. There are two common classes of strategies to enable load balancing in distributed stream processing systems, namely *operator-based* and *data-based*.

Operator-based strategies generally assume the basic computation units are operators. Therefore, load balancing among distributed nodes is achieved by allocating the operators to the nodes. In Borealis [29], for example, the system exploits the correlation and variance of the workloads of the operators, to make more reliable and stable assignments. In [28], Xing et al. observe that operator movement is too expensive for short-term workload bursts. This observation motivates them to design a new load balance model and corresponding algorithms to support more resilient operator placement. System S [26], as another example, also generates scheduling decisions for jobs in submission phase and migrates jobs or sub-jobs to less loaded machines on runtime based on complex statistics, including operators workload and the priority of the applications. Zhou et al. [32] presents a flow-aware load selection strategy to minimize communication cost with their new dynamic assignment strategy adaptive to the evolving stream workloads. In order to improve system balance property, [4] presents a more flexible mechanism by using both online and offline methods under the objective of network traffic minimization. A common problem with operator-based load balancing approaches is the lack of flexible workload partitioning. Our proposal in this paper generally enables highly flexible workload partitioning within streaming operators.

Data-based strategies allow the system to repartition the workload based on keys of the tuples in the stream, motivated by the huge success of MapReduce system and its variants. It is strongly related to elastic stream processing, which is a hot topic in both database and distributed system communities. Such systems attempt to scale out the computation parallelism to address the increasing computation workload, e.g., [12, 27]. By applying queuing theory, it is possible to model the workload and expected processing latency, which can be used for better resource scheduling [9]. When historical records are available to the system, it is beneficial to generate a long-term workload evolution plan, to schedule the migrations in the future with smaller workload movement overhead [7]. Note that all these systems and algorithms are designed to handle long-term workload variance. All these solutions are generally too expensive if the workload fluctuation is just a short-term phenomenon. The proposal in this work targets to solve the short-term workload variance problem with minimal cost.

A number of research work focus on load balancing in distributed stream join systems. [8] models the join operation with a square matrix, each side of which represents one of the input streams. One of the stream distributes its tuples by rows, while the other distributes its tuples by columns. Each cell contains the computation logic calculating the partial join results of tuples from the streams. To enable better elasticity, [19] proposes a join-biclique model which organizes the clusters as a complete bipartite graph for joining big data streams. It proposes to deal with load imbalance by using different join algorithms. All these techniques are designed for join operator only, therefore not directly extensible to general-purpose distributed stream processing.

In the rest of the section, we discuss limitations of four alternative solutions to intra-operator parallelism in distributed streaming processing.

Flux: Shah et al. [22] design a widely adopted load balancing strategy for traditional distributed streaming processing systems. It simply measures the workload of the tasks, and attempts to migrate workload from overloaded nodes to underloaded nodes. One key limitation of Flux is the lack of consideration on the routing overhead. In traditional stream processing systems, the workload of a logical operator is pre-partitioned into tasks, such that each task may handle a huge number of keys but processed by an individual thread at any time. The approach proposed in this paper allows the system to reassign keys in a much more flexible manner.

Consistent hash: Karger et al. [13] first discuss the dynmaicity of hash function, when the output domain is extensible. They show that it is likely to build such hash function that the number of tuples moved across target bins of the hash outcome reaches the minimal lower bound in theory. This technique is now widely used in distributed systems, especially for data-intensive computation scheme with high overhead on workload reassignment. We argue that consistent hash may not be an optimal option to intra-operator parallelism in distributed stream processing. When the key domain is small or the number of target instance is large, randomized hash may not distribute the workload evenly, because of the existence of relatively heavy keys. This phenomenon is demonstrated in our experimental results in Fig. 5.

Readj: Gedik et al. [11] propose to resolve the stateful load balance problem with a small routing table, which is the most similar work to our proposal. It introduces a similar tuple distribution function, consisting of a basic hash function and an explicit hash table. However, the workload redistribution mechanism used in Readj is completely different from ours. The algorithm in Readj always tries to move back the keys to their original destination by hash function, followed with migration schedules on keys with relatively larger workload. Their strategy might work well when the workload of the keys are almost uniform. When the workloads of the keys vary dramatically, their approach either fails to find a reasonable load balancing plan, or incurs huge routing overhead by generating a large routing table. The routing algorithms designed in this paper completely tackle this problem, which presents high efficiency as well as good balancing performance in almost all circumstances.

Partial Key Grouping: Nasir et al. [20, 21] design a series of randomized routing algorithms to balance the workload of stream processing operators. Their strategy is based on the theoretical model and its variant of power-of-two, which evaluates two or more randomly chosen candidate destinations for each tuples and chooses the one with smaller workload estimation. Their approach performs well for stateless operators in streaming processing, and a wide class of stateful operators by introducing an aggregator to combine results of tuples sent to different working threads, e.g., counting. For some stateful operators, e.g., join and median, the partial result is insufficient for simple aggregation, almost all original tuples must be forwarded to aggregator for processing.

3 PRELIMINARIES

A distributed stream processing engine (DSPE) deploys abstract stream processing logics over interconnected computation nodes for continuous stream processing. The abstract stream processing logic is usually described by a directed graphical model (e.g., Storm [23], Heron [16] and Spark Streaming [31]), with a vertex in the graph denoting a computation operator and an edge denoting a stream from one operator to another. Each data stream consists of key-value pairs, known as *tuples*, transmitted over network between computation nodes. The computation logic with an operator is a mapping function with an input tuple from upstream operator to a group of output tuples for downstream operators.

To maximize the throughput of stream processing and improve the utilization rate of the computation resource, the workload of a logical operator is commonly partitioned and concurrently processed by a number of threads, known as *tasks*. The upstream operator is aware of the concrete tasks and sends the output tuples to the tasks based on a global partitioning strategy. All concrete tasks within an operator process the incoming tuples independently.

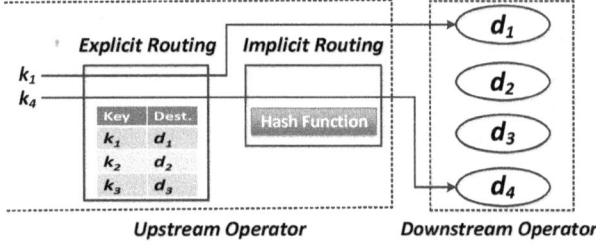

Figure 2: The scheme of mixed routing with a small routing table and a hash function.

Key-based workload partitioning is now commonly adopted in distributed stream processing engines, such that tuples with the same key are guaranteed to be received by the same concrete task for processing. An operator is called *stateful operator*, if there is a memory space used to keep intermediate results, called *states*, of the keys based on the latest tuples. Basically, a *state* is associated with an active key in the corresponding task in a stateful operator, which is used to maintain necessary information for computation. The state, for example, can be used to record the counts of the words or recent tuples in the sliding window. Because of the tight binding between key and state, when a key is reassigned to another task instance, its state must be migrated as well, in order to ensure the correctness of computation outcomes.

The workload partitioning among concrete tasks is the model as a mapping from key domain to running tasks in the successor operator. A straightforward solution to workload partitioning is the employment of mapping function (e.g., by consistent hashing), which chooses a task for a specific key in a fixed manner. As discussed in previous section, despite of the huge advantages of hashing on memory consumption and computation cost, such scheme may not handle well with workload variance and key skewness. Another option of workload distribution is to explicitly assign the tuples based on a carefully optimized routing table, which specifies the destination of the tuples by a map structure on the keys. Although such an approach is more flexible on dynamic workload repartitioning, the operational cost on both memory and computation is too high to afford in practice.

In this paper, we develop a new adaptive workload partitioning framework based on a mixed routing strategy, expecting to balance the hash-based randomized strategy and key-based routing strategy. In Fig. 2, we present an example of the strategy with one data stream between two operators. A routing table is maintained in the system, but contains routing rules for a handful of keys only. When a new output tuple is generated for the downstream operator, the upstream operator first checks if the key exists in the routing table. If a valid entry is found in the table, the tuple is transmitted to the target concrete task instance specified by the entry, otherwise a hash function is applied on the key to deterministically generate the target task id for the tuple. By appropriately controlling the routing table with a maximal size constraint, both the memory and computation cost of the scheme are acceptable, while the flexibility and effectiveness are achieved by updating the routing table in response to the evolving distribution of the keys. Workload balancing between tasks from the same logical operator is crucial and it is

the major problem we aim to deal with. With the mixed routing strategy, we can solve the problem by focusing on the construction and update of the routing table with the constrained size, without considering the global structure of processing topology and workload. Therefore, our discussion in the following sections focuses on one single operator and its routing table, while the techniques are obviously applicable to complex stream processing logics, as evaluated in the experimental section.

In our model, the time domain is discretized into intervals with integer timestamps, i.e., $(T_1, T_2, \ldots, T_i, \ldots)$. At the i-th interval, given a pair of upstream operator U and downstream operator D, we use $\mathcal{U}$ and $\mathcal{D}$ to denote the set of task instances within upstream operator U and downstream operator D, respectively. We also use $N_U = |\mathcal{U}|$ and $N_D = |\mathcal{D}|$ to denote the numbers of task instances in U and D, respectively. A tuple is tuple $\tau = (k, v)$, in which k is the key of the tuple from key domain $\mathcal{K}$ and v is the value carried by the tuple. We assume N_U and N_D are predefined without immediate change. The discussion on dynamic resource rescheduling, i.e., changing N_U and N_D, is out of the scope of this paper, since it involves orthogonal optimization techniques on global resource scheduling (e.g., [9]).

A key-based workload partitioning mechanism works as a mapping $F : \mathcal{K} \rightarrow \mathcal{D}$, such that a tuple (k, v) is sent to task instance $F(k)$ by evaluating the key k with the function F. Without loss of generality, we assume a universal hashing function $h : \mathcal{K} \rightarrow \mathcal{D}$ is available to the system for general key assignment. A routing table A of size N_A contains a group of pairs from $\mathcal{K} \times \mathcal{D}$, specifying the destination task instances for keys existing in A. The mixed routing strategy shown in Fig. 2 is thus modelled by the following equation:

$$F(k) = \begin{cases} d, & \text{if } \exists \, (k, d) \in A, \\ h(k), & \text{otherwise.} \end{cases} \tag{1}$$

Therefore, workload redistribution is enabled by editing the routing table A with an assignment function $F(\cdot)$. In the following, we provide formal analysis on the general properties of the assignment function $F(\cdot)$.

Computation Cost: We use $g_i(k)$ to denote the frequency of tuples with key k in time interval T_i, and define the computation cost $c_i(k)$ by the amount of CPU resource necessary for all these tuples with key k in time interval T_i. Generally speaking, $c_i(k)$ increases with the growth of $g_i(k)$. Unless specified, we do not make any assumption on the correlation between $g_i(k)$ and $c_i(k)$, both of which are measured in the distributed system and recorded as statistics, in order to support decision making on the update of $F(\cdot)$. The total workload with a task instance d in downstream operator D within time interval T_i is calculated by $L_i(d, F) = \sum_{\{k|F(k)=d, k\in\mathcal{K}\}} c_i(k)$.

Load Balance: Load balance among task instances of the downstream operator D is the essential target of our proposal in this paper. Specifically, we define the balance indicator $\theta_i(d, F)$ for task instance d under assignment function F during time interval T_i as $\theta_i(d, F) = \frac{|L_i(d,F)-\bar{L}_i|}{\bar{L}_i}$, where $\bar{L}_i = \frac{1}{N_D} \sum_{d\in\mathcal{D}} L_i(d, F)$ is the average load of all task instances in $\mathcal{D}$. As it is unlikely to achieve absolute load balancing with $\theta_i(d, F) = 0$ for every task instance d, an upper bound $\theta_{\max}$ is usually specified by the system administrator, such that the workload of task instance d is approximately balanced if $\theta_i(d, F) \leq \theta_{\max}$.

Memory Cost: For stateful operators, the system is supposed to maintain historical information, e.g., statistics with the keys, for processing and analysing on newly arriving tuples. We assume that each operator maintains states independently on individual time interval T_i and only the last w time intervals are needed by any task instance. It means that the task instance erases the state from time interval T_{i-w} after finishing the computation on all tuples in time interval T_i. This model is general enough to cover almost all continuous stream processing and analytical jobs (e.g., stream data mining over sliding window). The memory consumption for tuples with key k in T_i is thus measured as $s_i(k)$, and the total memory consumption for key k is the summation over last w intervals on the time domain, as $S_i(k, w) = \sum_{j=i-w+1}^{i} s_j(k)$.

Migration Cost: Upon the revision on assignment function F, certain key k may be moved from one task instance to another. The states associated with key k must be moved accordingly to ensure the correctness of processing on following tuples with key k. The migration cost is thus modelled as the total size of states under migration. By replacing function F with another function F' at time interval T_i, we use $\Delta(F, F') = \{k \mid F(k) \neq F'(k), k \in \mathcal{K}\}$. The key state migration includes all the historical states within the given window w. Thus, the total migration cost, denoted by $M_i(w, F, F')$, can be defined as $M_i(w, F, F') = \sum_{k \in \Delta(F, F')} S_i(k, w)$.

Based on the model of data and workload, we now define our dynamic workload distribution problem, with the objectives on (i) load balance among all the downstream instances; (ii) controllable size on the routing table; and (iii) minimization on state migration cost. These goals are achieved by controlling the routing table in the assignment function, under appropriate constraints for performance guarantee. Specifically, to construct a new assignment function F' as a replacement for F in time interval T_i, we formulate it as an optimization problem, as below:

$$\min_{F'(\cdot)} \quad M_i(w, F, F')$$
$$\text{s.t.} \quad \theta(d, F') \leq \theta_{\max}, \forall d \in \mathcal{D}, \qquad (2)$$
$$N_A \leq A_{max},$$

in which F is the old assignment function and F' is the variable for optimization. The target of the program above is to minimize migration cost, while meeting the constraints on load balance factor and routing table size with user-specified balance bounds $\theta_{\max}$ and $A_{\max}$ which is the maximum constrained size of A. It is worthwhile to emphasize that the new assignment function is constructed at the beginning of a new time interval T_i. The optimization is thus purely based on the statistical information from previous time interval T_{i-1}. The metrics defined in previous subsection are estimated with frequencies $\{g_{i-1}(k)\}$ over the keys, the computation costs $\{c_{i-1}(k)\}$ and the memory consumption $S_{i-1}(k, w)$.

The problem of initializing the keys in $\mathcal{K}$, with the task instance set $\mathcal{D}$ and load balance constraint θ_{max}, is a combinatorial **NP-hard** problem, as it can be reduced to Bin-packing problem[14].

Even worse, our optimization problem also puts constraints on the maximal table size and migration cost.

4 THEORETICAL PRINCIPLE

Since the optimization problem is NP-hard, there is no polynomial algorithm to find global optimum, unless **P=NP**. In the rest of the section, we describe a general workflow for a variety of heuristics, such that all algorithms based on these heuristics follow the same operation pattern.

4.1 Basic Steps

Generally, the system follows the steps below when constructing a new assignment function F'.

Phase I (Cleaning): It attempts to *clean* the routing table A by removing certain entries in the table. This is equivalent to moving the keys in the entries back to the original task instance assignment, decided by the hash function. Different algorithms may adopt different cleaning strategies to shrink the existing routing table in F. Note that such a temporary removal does not physically migrate the corresponding keys, but just generates an intermediate result table for further processing.

Phase II (Preparing): It identifies candidate keys for migration from overloaded task instances, i.e., $\{d|L(d) > L_{\max}\}$, where $L_{\max} = (1 + \theta_{\max})\bar{L}$. Different selection criteria, such as keys with highest computation cost first, and largest computation cost per unit memory consumption first (concerning about migration cost), and etc, can be applied by the algorithm to select keys and disassociate their assignments from the corresponding task instances. These disassociated keys will be temporarily put into a candidate key set (denoted by C) for processing in the third step of the workflow.

Phase III (Assigning): It reshuffles the keys in the candidate set by manipulating the routing table, in order to balance the workloads. In particular, all algorithms proposed in this paper invoke the Least-Load Fit Decreasing (LLFD) subroutine, which will be described shortly, in this phase.

4.2 Least-Load Fit Decreasing (LLFD)

In this part of the section, we introduce *Least-Load Fit Decreasing* (LLFD) subroutine, which will be applied by all the proposed algorithms in Phase III, based on the idea of prioritizing keys with larger workloads. The design of LLFD is motivated by the classic First Fit Decreasing (FFD) used in conventional bin packing algorithms. The pseudo codes of LLFD are listed in Algorithm 1.

Generally speaking, LLFD sorts the keys in the candidate set in a non-increasing order of their computation costs and iteratively assigns the keys to task instances, such that (i) it generates the least total workload (Line 4); and (ii) it tries to adjust the key assignment, if the new destination task instance is overloaded after the migration (Line 5). If such key-to-instance pair is inconsistent with default mapping by hashing (Line 6), an entry (k, d) is then added to the routing table A (Line 7). After each iteration, LLFD updates the total workload of the corresponding instance d and removes k from the candidate set (Line 8). The iteration stops and returns result routing table, when the candidate set turns empty (Line 9).

algorithm 1 Least-Load Fit Decreasing Algorithm

input: key candidate C, task instances in $\mathcal{D}$, imbalance tolerance factor θ_{max}, key selection criteria ψ

output: A'

1: **foreach** d in $\mathcal{D}$ **do**
2:     Initialize estimation $\hat{L}(d) = L_{i-1}(d)$
3: **foreach** k in C in descending order of $c_{i-1}(k)$ **do**
4:     **foreach** d in $\mathcal{D}$ in ascending order of $L_{i-1}(d)$ **do**
5:         **if** $\text{Adjust}(k, d, C, \theta_{max}) = \text{TRUE}$ **then**
6:             **if** $h(k) \neq d$ **then**
7:                 Add entry (k, d) to A'
8:             Update $\hat{L}(d)$; remove k from C; **break**;
9: **return** A'
10: **function** $\text{Adjust}(k, d, C, \theta_{max})$
11:     $L_{max} \leftarrow (1 + \theta_{max})\bar{L}_{i-1}$
12:     **if** $L_{i-1}(d) + c_{i-1}(k) < L_{max}$ **then**
13:         **return** TRUE
14:     **else if** $\exists\, \mathcal{E}$ selected by ψ and satisfying (i)-(iii) **then**
15:         **foreach** $k \in \mathcal{E}$ **do**
16:             Disassociate k from d
17:             Add k to C
18:         **return** TRUE
19:     **else**
20:         **return** FALSE

Basically, the algorithm moves the "heaviest" key to the task instance with minimal workload so far, which may generate another overloaded task instance (referred as "re - overloading" problem), if this key is associated with extremely heavy cost. Consider the toy example on the left side of Fig. 3. There are two instances: d_1 is responsible for keys k_1, k_2 and k_5 with costs 7, 4 and 5 respectively, generating $L(d_1) = 16$, and d_2 is associated with keys k_3, k_4 and k_6 with cost 2, 1 and 1 respectively, generating $L(d_2) = 4$. Suppose $\theta_{max} = 0$, meaning that the total workloads on both instances are required to be equal (i.e., average workload $\bar{L} = 10$). It is clear that d_1 is overloaded and k_1, which incurs the largest computation cost, is expected to be disassociated from d_1. Although $L(d_1)$ decreases to 9, it is still larger than $L(d_2)$. Based on the workflow of LLFD, k_1 is assigned to d_2, only to overload d_2 as a consequence. To tackle the problem, we add a new function, called *Adjust*, to avoid the happening of such conflicts.

Specifically, if re-overloading does not happen after an assignment, i.e., $L_{i-1}(d) + c_{i-1}(k) \leq L_{max} = (1 + \theta_{max})\bar{L}_{i-1}$, this assignment is acceptable and *Adjust* immediately returns a TRUE (Lines 12-13). Otherwise (Lines 14-20), *Adjust* attempts to construct a nonempty key set (called *exchangeable* set and denoted by $\mathcal{E}$), by applying the selection criteria ψ (e.g., highest workload first). The *exchangeable* set must satisfy the following three conditions: (i) $\mathcal{E} \subseteq \{k' | F(k') = d\}$; (ii) $\forall k' \in \mathcal{E}, c_{i-1}(k') < c_{i-1}(k)$; and (iii) $L_{i-1}(d) + c_{i-1}(k) - \sum_{k' \in \mathcal{E}} c_{i-1}(k') \leq L_{max}$. Basically, (i) means that only keys originally associated with d are selected for disassociation. (ii) tries not to choose a key with larger computation workload for disassociation, ensuring the decrease of the total workloads on instance d. Finally, (iii) ensures that instance d does not become overloaded, after the assignment (Lines 15-17).

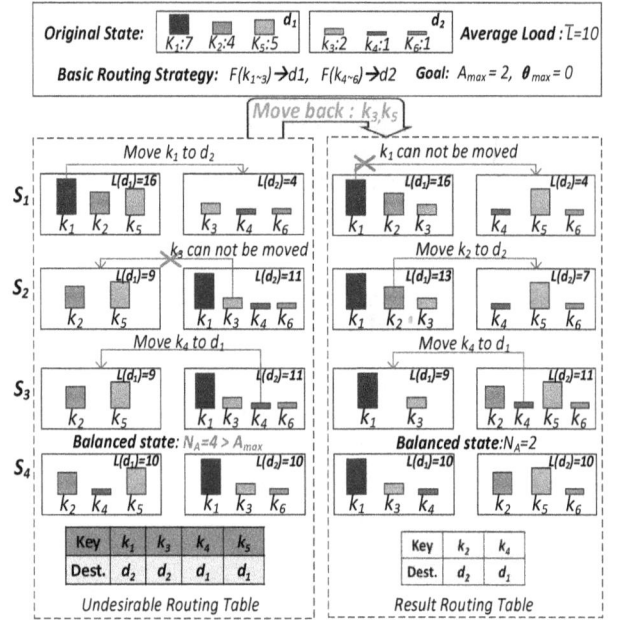

Figure 3: Running examples for LLFD and MinTable, in which the heights of the bars indicate the workloads of the corresponding keys. Each S_j with $j = \{1, 2, 3, 4\}$ is a running step in the algorithms. The items in original routing table are $\{(k_5, d_1), (k_3, d_2)\}$, and the result routing tables are listed at the bottom. The left dotted box reflects the result by LLFD and right one is the result generated by LLFD and MinTable.

Recall the running example in which LLFD tries to assign k_1 to d_2, which makes d_2 overloaded. A TRUE is returned by *Adjust* because there exists an $\mathcal{E} = \{k_3\}$ satisfying constraints (i) - (iii). Therefore, k_1 is assigned to d_2, while k_3 is disassociated from d_2 and put into C. Next, LLFD attempts to assign k_3 to d_1, because d_1 has less total workload at this moment. However, a FALSE (a red cross shown on left side of S_2 in Fig. 3) is returned by *Adjust* because overloading occurs (since $L(d_1) + c(k_3) = 11 > L_{max}$) and no valid $\mathcal{E}$ exists, when neither of the two keys associated with d_1 (k_2 and k_5) has smaller computation workload than that of k_3, violating constraint (ii). After this failure, LLFD is forced to consider another option, by keeping k_3 to d_2. Luckily, a TRUE is returned this time, because a valid *exchangeable* set $\mathcal{E} = \{k_4\}$ exists. After disassociating k_4 from d_2 and putting it into C, d_2 is responsible for k_1, k_3 and k_6 only, the keys with d_1 remains unchanged, and k_4 is now in C. The algorithm does not terminate until C becomes empty, after k_4 is assigned to d_1, finally reaching perfect balance at $L(d_1) = L(d_2) = 10$.

In order to derive theoretic results about the LLFD algorithm, we first look at a more simplified key assignment algorithm, namely the Simple algorithm. We next derive a serious of theoretic results based on the Simple algorithm. Lastly, we show how these results are applicable to the LLFD algorithm. The *Simple* algorithm works in the following way, at first, it disassociates and puts all the keys into the candidate set C. Secondly it sorts these keys in a descending order of the computation cost $c(k)$. Finally it sequentially assigns each key to the instance with the least total workloads so far.

LEMMA 4.1. *Given the instance set $\mathcal{D}$ of size N_D, key set $\mathcal{K}$ of size K and computation cost of each key $c(k)$, where keys are in a non-increasing order of their computation costs, i.e., $c(k_1) \geq c(k_2) \geq \cdots \geq c(K)$, if the perfect assignment exists, we have:*

$$c(k_{qN_D+1}) \leq \frac{1}{q+1}\bar{L}, \quad q = 1, 2, \ldots, \lfloor \frac{K-1}{N_D} \rfloor. \quad (3)$$

PROOF. Assuming $c(k_{qN_D+1}) > \frac{1}{q+1}\bar{L}$, then we have $c(k_1) \geq c(k_2) \geq \cdots \geq c(k_{qN_D+1}) > \frac{1}{q+1}\bar{L}$. This means that for keys from k_1 to k_{qN_D}, each instance can at most be associate with q of them. In result, any instance that is associated with the $(qN_D + 1)$-th key will generate workloads larger than $\bar{L}$, which contradicts the assumption of the existence of the perfect assignment. □

LEMMA 4.2. *Given the instance set $\mathcal{D}$ of size N_D, key set $\mathcal{K}$ of size K and computation cost of each key $c(k)$, where keys are in a non-increasing order of their computation costs, i.e., $c(k_1) \geq c(k_2) \geq \cdots \geq c(K)$, if the perfect assignment exists and $c(k_1) < \bar{L}$ (the computation cost of any individual key is smaller than the average workload of task instances), we have $K \geq 2N_D$.*

PROOF. This is straight forward given (a) the perfect assignment exists and (b) the computation cost of any individual key is smaller than $\bar{L}$, because for each instance, there must be at least two keys assigned to it. □

LEMMA 4.3. *Given the instance set $\mathcal{D}$ of size N_D, key set $\mathcal{K}$ of size K and computation cost of each key $c(k)$, where keys are in a non-increasing order of their computation costs, i.e., $c(k_1) \geq c(k_2) \geq \cdots \geq c(K)$, if the perfect assignment exists and $c(k_1) < \bar{L}$, we have:*

$$\theta_{max} \leq \frac{1}{3} \cdot (1 - \frac{1}{N_D}), \quad (4)$$

where $\theta_{max} = \max_{d \in \mathcal{D}} (\frac{L(d) - \bar{L}}{\bar{L}})$.

PROOF. We prove by considering the worst case (in terms of load balance) where (a) the $(2N_D + 1)$-th key has the largest possible computation cost $c(k_{2N_D+1}) = \bar{L}/3$, according to Lemma 4.1 and Lemma 4.2; (b) Keys after the $(2N_D + 1)$-th have equal amount of computation costs, denoted by ε, which are very close to zero; (c) The remaining workloads, i.e., $\sum_{k \in \mathcal{K}} c(k) - \frac{1}{3}\bar{L} - \varepsilon(K - 2N_D - 1)$, all concentrate on the first $2N_D$ keys and are evenly distributed, summarized as follows:

$$c(k_i) = \begin{cases} \frac{N_D\bar{L} - \frac{1}{3}\bar{L} - \varepsilon(K-2N_D-1)}{N_D} & \text{for} \quad i = 1, 2, \ldots, 2N_D; \\ \frac{1}{3}\bar{L} & \text{for} \quad i = 2N_D + 1; \\ \varepsilon & \text{for} \quad i > 2N_D + 1. \end{cases}$$

When $\varepsilon \to 0$, we have:

$$L_{\max} = \max_{d \in \mathcal{D}} L(d) = c(k_i) + c(k_{2N_D}) \leq \frac{4}{3}\bar{L} - \frac{\bar{L}}{3N_D},$$

where $i = 1, 2, \ldots, 2N_D$. Note $L_{\max} = c(k_i) + c(k_{2N_D})$ is because according to the Simple algorithm, keys $k_i, i > 2N_D + 1$ will never be assigned to the instance with $L_{\max}$. This completes the proof according to our definition of $\theta_{\max}$. □

---

algorithm 2 MinTable Algorithm

1: Phase I: *Move back* all keys in A.
2: $\psi \leftarrow$ highest computation cost $c(k)$ first
3: Phase II: According to ψ, select and disassociate keys from each of the overloaded instances, put them into C
4: Phase III: $A' \leftarrow$ LLFD $(C, \mathcal{D}, \theta_{max}, \psi)$
5: **return** A'

THEOREM 4.4. *Given the instance set $\mathcal{D}$ of size N_D, key set $\mathcal{K}$ of size K and computation cost of each key $c(k)$, where keys are in a non-increasing order of their computation costs, i.e., $c(k_1) \geq c(k_2) \geq \cdots \geq c(K)$, if the perfect assignment exists and $c(k_1) < \bar{L}$, LLFD always finds a solution resulting with balancing indicator $\theta(d, F)$ no worse than $\frac{1}{3}(1 - \frac{1}{N_D})$ for any task instance d.*

PROOF. According to Algorithm 1, it has a larger search space than that of the Simple Algorithm, and is devoted to finding the assignment with more balanced workloads among instances, i.e.,

$$\theta(d, F) \leq \theta_{max} \leq \frac{1}{3} \cdot (1 - \frac{1}{N_D}),$$

which is proved in Lemma 4.3. □

Furthermore, LLFD can produce a well-balanced adjustment because the load for the **long tails** in skew data distribution is significant.

5 ALGORITHM & IMPLEMENTATION

In this section, we discuss a number of heuristics with objectives on both routing table minimization and migration minimization. A mixed algorithm is introduced to combine the two heuristics in order to accomplish the constraints in the optimization formulation with a single shot. Then, we describe the overall workflow of those algorithms.

5.1 MinTable and MinMig Heuristics

The general workflow described above is essentially effective in guaranteeing load balance constraints, e.g., the LLFD sub-prodedure. To address the optimizations on routing table minimization and migration cost minimization, we discuss two heuristics, namely MinTable and MinMig in this sub-section.

The pseudocodes of MinTable is shown in Algorithm 2. In order to minimize routing table size, in Phase I, all entries in routing table A are erased. The highest computation workload first criterion, which emphasizes on the computation cost, is used for the second and third phases, so that minimal number of entries are added into the new routing table A' during the key re-assignment and load rebalance process.

The two toy examples in Fig. 3 demonstrate how MinTable helps to achieve a smaller routing table while keeping load balance constraints fulfilled. The example on left side of Fig. 3 initially has two entries in routing table, i.e., (k_3, d_2) and (k_5, d_1). LLFD is directly applied to achieve absolute load balance $L(d_1) = L(d_2)$, but resulting in a routing table with four entries at the end. In contrast, before applying LLFD, the example on right side of Fig. 3 moves back k_3 and k_5 (i.e., cleaning the routing table). Finally, it results in a routing table with only two entries. The pseudo code of MinMig is shown in Algorithm 3. Although the removal of keys from the routing is *virtual* only, it increases the possibility of key migrations. Therefore, there is no cleaning run in the first phase at all.

---

algorithm 3 MinMig Algorithm

1: Phase I: Do nothing.
2: $\psi \leftarrow$ largest $\gamma_i(k, w)$ first, where $\gamma_i(k, w) = \frac{c_i(k)^\beta}{S_i(k, w)}$
3: Phase II: According to ψ, select and disassociate keys from each of the overloaded instances, put them into C
4: Phase III: $A' \leftarrow$ LLFD $(C, \mathcal{D}, \theta_{max}, \psi)$
5: **return** A'

To characterize both computation and migration cost, we propose the *migration priority index* for each key, defined as $\gamma_i(k, w) = c_i(k)^\beta S_i(k, w)^{-1}$. Its physical meaning is straightforward, that is, a key with larger computation cost per unit memory consumption has the higher priority to be migrated. The weight scaling factor β is used to balance the weights between these two factors under consideration. Consider k_1 and k_2 in Fig. 3 and assume window $w = 1$. We have $c(k_1) = S(k_1, w) = 7$ and $c(k_2) = S(k_2, w) = 4$. If we give equal weights to both $c(k)$ and $S(k, w)$, i.e., $\beta = 1$, then $\gamma(k_1, w) = \gamma(k_2, w) = 1$. When we assign more importance to migration cost, i.e., $\beta = 0.5$, k_2 gains higher priority for migration. In addition, β also affects the size of the result routing table, i.e., the larger β, the smaller size of routing table. The largest $\gamma_i(k, w)$ first criterion, which is aware of both computation and migration cost, is used during both key re-assignment (Phase II) and load balance process (Phases III), in order to minimize the bandwidth used to migrate the states of keys (e.g., the tuples in sliding window for join operator).

5.2 Mixed Algorithm

Based on the discussion on the heuristics, we discover that there are tradeoffs between routing table minimization and migration cost minimization. Therefore, we propose a mixed algorithm to intelligently combine the two heuristics MinTable and MinMig, in order to produce the best-effort solutions towards our target optimization in Eq. 2.

The basic idea is to properly mix MinTable (Phase I) and MinMig (Phases II and III). In the first phase, the mixed strategy *moves back* n keys, which are selected from A, based on the smallest memory consumption $S_{i-1}(k, w)$ first criteria. The rest two phases simply follow the procedure of MinMig, in which the largest $\gamma_i(k, w)$ first criteria is used to initialize candidate key set C and applied by LLFD in the last phase. For the Mixed algorithm, the most challenging problem is how to pick up the number of keys for back moves, i.e., $n \in [0, N_A]$ during the cleaning phase. Actually, MinTable and MinMig works on two extremes of the spectrum in this step, such that $n = N_A$ in MinTable and $n = 0$ in MinMig.

Obviously, brute force search (named as $Mixed_{BF}$) could be applied to try with every possible $n = 1, 2, \ldots, N_A$, with the optimal n^* returned after evaluating the solution with every n. Alternatively, we propose a faster heuristic in Algorithm 4. It only tries a small number of values, which are the amount of table entries overused in the last trial (Line 10). The trial starts from $n = 0$ (Line 3, same as MinMig), and stops when it results in an updated A'

---

algorithm 4 Mixed Algorithm

1: $\eta \leftarrow$ smallest memory consumption $S_i(k, w)$ first.
2: $\psi \leftarrow$ largest $\gamma_i(k, w)$ first, where $\gamma_i(k, w) = \frac{c_i(k)^\beta}{S_i(k, w)}$
3: $n \leftarrow 0$
4: $A_{backup} \leftarrow A$
5: **do**
6:      $A \leftarrow A_{backup}$
7:      Phase I: According to η, select n keys from A and *move back* them
8:      Phase II: According to ψ, select and disassociate keys from each of the overloaded instances, put them into C
9:      Phase III: $A' \leftarrow$ LLFD $(C, \mathcal{D}, \theta_{max}, \psi)$
10:      $n = N_{A'} - A_{max}$
11: **while** $n > 0$
12: **return** A'

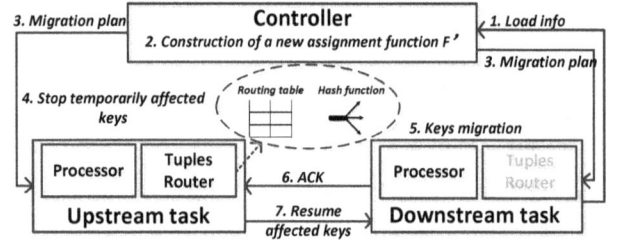

Figure 4: Overall workflow.

of acceptable size, i.e., $N_{A'} \leq A_{max}$ (Lines 11-12). Note that the efficiency of the algorithm is much better than $Mixed_{BF}$, although it may not always find the optimal n^* as $Mixed_{BF}$ does. Obviously, the size of the result routing table by the mixed algorithm is no smaller than that of MinTable approach. Similarly, the migration cost of the result assignment function is no smaller than that of the MinMig approach. However, mixed algorithm is capable of hitting good balance between the heuristics, as is proved in our empirical evaluations. Furthermore, for Mixed takes LLFD algorithm as its basic idea, the balance status generated by the Mixed is not worse than the balance status produced by the LLFD algorithm.

5.3 Implementation

The overall working mechanism of the rebalance control component is illustrated in Fig. 4. In the figure, each operation step is numbered to indicate the order of their execution. At the end of each time interval (e.g., 10 seconds as the setting in our experiments), the instances of an operator report the statistical information collected during the past interval to a *controller* module (step 1). The information from each instance d includes the computation cost $c_{i-1}(k)$ and window-based memory consumption $S_{i-1}(k, w)$ of each key assigned to it. On receiving the reporting information, the controller starts the optimization procedure (step 2) introduced in Section 4. It first evaluates the degree of workload imbalance among the instances and decides whether or not to trigger the construction of a new assignment function F' to replace the existing F. If the system identifies load imbalance, it starts to execute Mixed algorithm (Algorithm 4) to generate new A' and F'. After calculating the keys in $\Delta(F, F')$ for migration, the controller broadcasts both F' and $\Delta(F, F')$, together with a Pause signal to the instances of upstream operator for them to update the obsolete F, and temporarily stop sending (but caching locally) data with keys in $\Delta(F, F')$ (steps 3 and 4). Meanwhile, the controller notifies the corresponding downstream instances (step 3). Finally, the instances of downstream operator begin migrating the states of keys after the notification from the controller (step 5) and acknowledge the controller when migration is completed (step 6). As soon as the controller receives all the acknowledgments, it sends out a Resume signal to all instances of the upstream operator, ordering the tasks to start sending data with keys in $\Delta(F, F')$, since all the downstream instances are equipped with the new assignment function (step 7). It is worth noting that during the key state migration, there is no interruption of normal processing on the data with keys not covered by $\Delta(F, F')$.

6 EVALUATIONS

In this section, we evaluate our proposals by comparing against a handful of baseline approaches. All of these approaches are implemented and run on top of *Apache Storm* [1] under the same task configuration N_D. To collect the workload measurements, we add a load reporting module into the processing logics when implementing them in *Storm*'s topologies. Migration and scheduling algorithms are injected into the codes of *controllers* in *Storm* to enable automatic workload redistribution. We use the consistent hashing[13] as our basic hash function and configure the parallelism of spout at 10. The *Storm* system (in version 0.9.3) is deployed on a 21-instance HP blade cluster with CentOS 6.5 operating system. Each instance in the cluster is equipped with two Intel Xeon processors (E5335 at 2.00GHz) having four cores and 16GB RAM. Each core is exclusively bound with a worker thread during our experiments.

Queries and Dataset: We experiment on three queries and three datasets (**QD-1~3**), namely one join operation for real workload and two aggregation operation for synthetic and real workload. **QD-1)** We first use the synthetic skewed data for aggregation operation to test load skewness phenomenon(Sec. 6.1) and the impact of algorithm parameters(Sec. 6.2). By controlling the latency of tuple processing, we force the distributed system to reach a saturation point of CPU resource for the N_D number of processing tasks with the requirement of absolute load balancing ($\theta_{max} = 0$). Our synthetic workload generator creates snapshots of tuples for discrete time intervals from an integer key domain K. The tuples follow Zipf distributions controlled by skewness parameter z, by using the popular generation tool available in Apache project. We use parameter f to control the rate of distribution fluctuation across time intervals. At the beginning of a new interval, our generator keeps swapping frequencies between keys from different task instances until the change on workload is significant enough, i.e., $\frac{|L_i(d) - L_{i-1}(d)|}{\overline{L}} \geq f$. **QD-2)** We do the Top-K operation on social network to test the throughput and scalability of each approaches (Fig. 10(a) in Sec. 6.3 and Fig. 11(a) in Sec. 6.4). The *Social* data is come form chinese twitter (Weibo)data[1] and we take the topic keywords as our distribution keys. This workload includes 5-day feeds

from a popular microblog service, in which each feed is regarded as a tuple with words as its keys. There are over 5,000,000 tuples covering 180,000 topic words as the keys and the distribution of topics is unpredictable skewness. Each tuple is a piece of Weibo with size 2.5KB approximately. We run word count topology on *Social* data, which continuously maintains current tuples in memory and updates the appearance frequency of topic words in social media feeds. **QD-3)** We run self-join on *Stock* data over sliding window, used to find potential high-frequency players with dense buying and selling behavior (Fig. 10(b) in Sec. 6.3 and Fig. 11(b) in Sec. 6.4). This workload includes 3-day *Stock* records on buying and selling stocks, consisting of over 6,000,000 tuples with 1,036 unique keys (Stock ID) for stock transactions. Each record contains 20 columns, including account id, date, time, price, stock id, and etc.

Baseline Approaches: We use *Mixed* to denote our proposed algorithm mixing two types of heuristics. We also use $Mixed_{BF}$ to denote the brute force version of *Mixed* method, which completely rebuilds the routing table from scratch at each scheduling point. We use *MinTable* to denote the algorithm always trying to find migration plan generating minimal routing table. Finally, we also include *Readj* and *PKG* as baseline approaches, which are known as state-of-the-art solutions in the literature. *Readj* is designed to minimize the load of restoring the keys based on the hash function, implemented by key rerouting over the keys with maximal workload. The migration plan of keys for load balance is generated by pairing tasks and keys. For each task-key pair, their algorithm considers all possible swaps to find the best move alleviating the workload imbalance. In *Readj*, σ is a configurable parameter, deciding which keys should take part in action of swap and move. Given a smaller σ, *Readj* tend to track more candidate keys and thus finding better migration plans. In order to make fair comparison, in each of the experiment, we run *Readj* with different σ's and only report the best result from all attempts. *PKG* [20] is a load balancing method without migration at runtime. It balances the workload of tasks by splitting keys into smaller granularity and distributing them to different tasks based on randomly generated plan. Here, we only use *PKG* approach for simple aggregation processing in the experiments, because it is not appropriate to complex stateful operations, such as join, as explained in Sec. 2(*For this reason, we do not include* PKG *in Fig. 10(b) in Sec. 6.3 and Fig. 11(b) in Sec. 6.4*). Due to the unique strategy used by *PKG*, aggregation topologies deploying *PKG* must contain a special downstream operator in the topology, which is used to collect and merge partial results with respect to every key, from two independent workers in the upstream operator. Moreover, in the open source version of *PKG*[2], there is a parameter p controlling the time interval between two consecutive result merging. After careful investigation with experiments, we find a larger p prolongs the response time of tuple processing, reduces the additional computation cost and limits the maximal number of live tuples (known as maximal pending tuples in *Storm*) under processing in the system. We finally chose p at 10 milliseconds and set maximal pending tuples at 50, which are verified to be the best option to maximize the throughput of *PKG* in all settings. Note that we do not include *LLFD* and *MinMig* algorithms in the experiments,

---

[1]http://open.weibo.com/wiki/2/statuses/user_timeline

[2]*https://github.com/gdfm/partial-key-grouping*

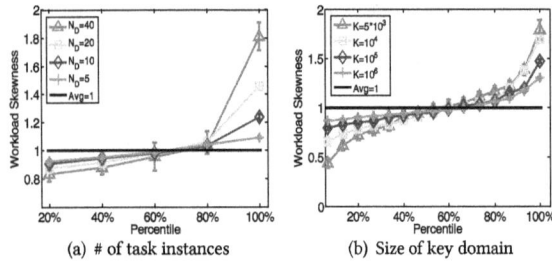

(a) # of task instances   (b) Size of key domain

Figure 5: Cumulative distribution of workload skewness under hash-based scheme.

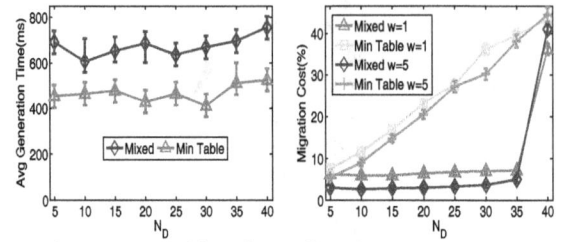

(a) # of instances *vs* scheduling efficiency (b) # of instances *vs* migration cost

Figure 6: Performance with varying number of task instances.

because both of them can not control the size of routing tables, therefore blowing off the memory space of the tasks in some cases.

Evaluation Metrics: In the experiments, we report the following metrics. **Workload skewness** (i.e., $\frac{\max L(d)}{\bar{L}}$), is the ratio of maximal workload on individual task instance to the average workload. **Migration cost** reveals the percentage of states associated with the keys involved in migration over the states maintained by all task instances. **Throughput** is the average number of tuples the system processes in unit second. **Average generation time** is the average time spent on the generation of migration plan in Storm controller.

6.1 Load Skewness Phenomenon

To understand the phenomenon of workload skewness with traditional hash-based mechanism, we report the workload imbalance phenomenon on the task instances by changing the number of task instances and the size of key domain, respectively. The results of load imbalance in Fig. 5 are presented as the cumulative distribution of average workload among the task instances over 50 time intervals. Fig. 5(a) implies that the skewness grows when increasing the number of task instances. When there are 40 instances (i.e., $N_D = 40$), the maximal workload at 100% percentile is almost 2.5 times larger than the minimal workload. Fig. 5(b) shows that the workload imbalance is also highly relevant to the size of key domain. When there are more keys in the domain, the hash function generates more balanced workload assignment. In Fig.5(b), the maximal workload for $K =5,000$ is around 4 times larger than the minimal one and is much larger than the maximal load under larger key domain size (e.g., $K =1,000,000$). Therefore, workload imbalance for intra-operator parallelism is a serious problem and cannot be easily solved by randomized hash functions.

6.2 Impact of Algorithm Parameters

We test the algorithm parameters on synthetic datasets using two window sizes (i.e., $w = 1$ and $w = 5$), in order to understand their impacts for short and long term aggregation over stream data. When $w = 1$, migration decisions are made based on the current stateful and instantaneous workload. When $w = 5$, more state information in the last five intervals are included in the decision making procedure.

Although the increase on N_D produces more workload imbalance, our migration algorithm *Mixed* performs well, by generating excellent migration plan, as shown in Fig. 6. *Mixed* costs a little additional overhead over *MinTable* algorithm for balancing, but its migration cost is much lower than *MinTable* when $N_D \leq 35$ for both $w = 1$ and $w = 5$, as presented in Fig. 6(b). The cleaning step in *MinTable* algorithm also leads to even higher skewness and much more migration cost in order to achieve load balancing. When $w = 5$, *Mixed* keeps more historical tuples which can be used as the migration candidates. This makes the migration easier and less expensive, when compared to the case with $w = 1$. When $N_D > 35$, however, the migration cost of *Mixed* jumps, almost reaching the cost of *MinTable* when $N_D = 40$. This is because the outcome of *Mixed* algorithm degenerates to that of *MinTable* algorithm, when the minimal routing table size needed for target load balancing exceeds the specified size of the table in the system.

Fig. 7 displays the efficiency of migration plan generation and the corresponding migration cost with varying workload balancing tolerance parameter $\theta_{\max}$. As expected, Migration scheduling runs faster on synthetic dataset with larger $\theta_{\max}$ in Fig. 7(a). When $\theta_{\max} \geq 0.2$, the efficiency of *Mixed* catches that of *MinTable*. If stronger load balancing (i.e., smaller $\theta_{\max}$) is specified, system pays more migration cost as shown in Fig. 7(b), basically due to more keys involved in migration. But *MinTable* incurs three times of the migration cost of *Mixed* under the same balance requirement. Even for strict $\theta_{\max} = 0.02$ (almost absolutely balanced), the algorithm is capable of generating the migration plan within 1 second. Moreover, migration cost with larger window size (i.e., $w = 5$) shrinks, as the historical states provide more appropriate candidate keys for migration plan generation.

In Fig. 8, we report the results on varying key domain size K. By varying K from 5,000 to 1,000,000, *Mixed* spends more computation time on migration planning but incurs less migration cost than *MinTable*. As shown in Fig. 5(b), the smaller the key domain is, the more skewed the workload distribution will be. But our proposed solution *Mixed* shows stable performance, regardless of the domain size, based on the results in Fig. 8(a). In particular, migration cost decreases for both *MinTable* and *Mixed* algorithms, when the window size grows to $w = 5$.

Since *Readj* is the most similar technique to our proposal in the literature, we conduct a careful investigation on performance

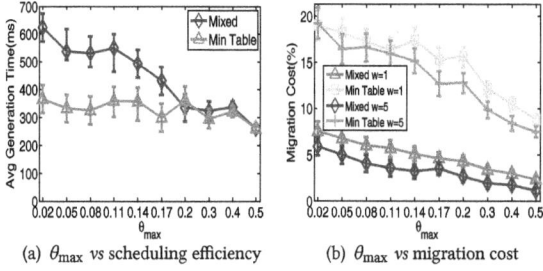

Figure 7: Performance with varying $\theta_{\max}$.

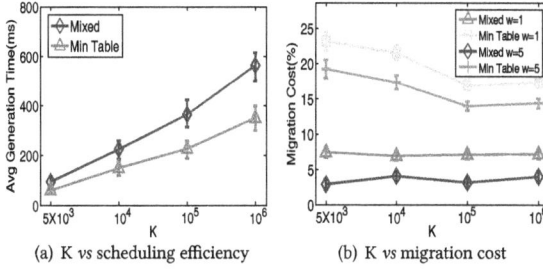

(a) Stream dynamics *vs* efficiency   (b) Stream dynamics *vs* MC

Figure 9: Scheduling efficiency and migration cost with varying distribution change frequency.

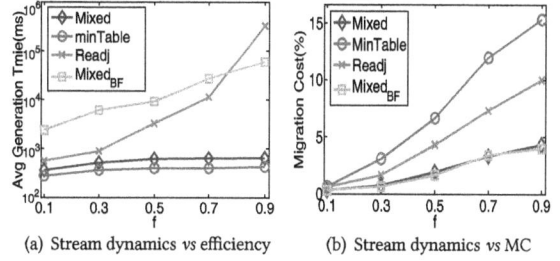

Figure 8: Scheduling efficiency in terms of average generation time and migration cost under different key domain size, K

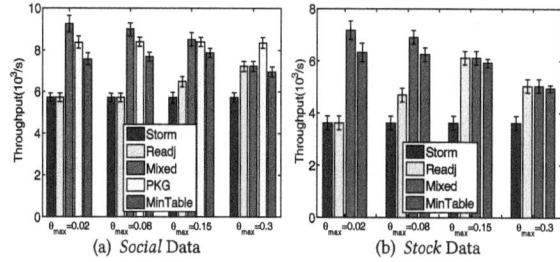

(a) *Social* Data   (b) *Stock* Data

Figure 10: Throughput with different balance demand.

comparison to evaluate the effectiveness of our proposal. To optimize the performance of *Readj*, we adopt binary search to find the best δ for *Readj*. Fig. 9 shows the performance on dynamic stream processing with imbalance tolerance $\theta_{\max} = 0.08$, by varying distribution change frequency f. When increasing f, *Readj* presents less promising efficiency when generating migration plan, since it evaluates every pair of task instances and considers all possible movements across the instances. Instead, *Mixed* makes the migration plan based on heuristic information, which outperforms *Readj* by a large margin. The results also imply that brute force search with *Mixed$_{BF}$* is a poor option for migration scheduling. When variances occur more frequently (i.e., with a higher f), migration cost of *Mixed* grows slower than that of *Readj*, while *Mixed$_{BF}$* performs similarly to *Mixed*.

6.3 Throughput

On *Social* data, we implement a simple word count topology on Storm, with upstream instances distributing tuples to downstream instances for store and aggregation on keywords. On *Stock* data, a self-join on the data over sliding window is implemented, which maintains the recent tuples based on the size of the window over intervals. The result throughputs are presented in Fig. 10. The most important observation is that the best throughput, on both of the workloads, is achieved by running *Mixed* with $\theta_{\max} = 0.02$, implying that strict load balancing is beneficial to system performance. *Mixed* also presents huge performance advantage over the other two approaches, with throughput about 2 times better than *Storm*

and *Readj* at smaller $\theta_{\max}$ in Fig. 10(b). The performance of *Readj* improves by relaxing the load balancing condition, catching up with the throughput of *Mixed* at $\theta_{\max} = 0.3$ ($\theta_{\max} = 0.15$ resp.) on *Social* (*Stock* resp.) This is because *Readj* works only when the system allows fairly imbalance among the computation tasks, for example $\theta_{\max} = 0.3$. *MinTable* does not care about migration cost and then it incurs larger migration volume, which reduces the throughput of system during the process of adjustment. *PKG* splits keys into smaller granularity and distributes them to different tasks selectively. Therefore, throughput of *PKG* is independent of the choice of $\theta_{\max}$, validated by the results in Fig. 10(a). The throughput of *PKG* is worse than *Mixed*, because its processing involves coordination between two operators. Despite of its excellent performance on load balancing, the overhead of partial result merging leads to additional response time increase and overall processing throughput reduction. Overall, as shown in Fig. 10(a), when $\theta_{max} = 0.02$, our method outperform *PKG* on throughput by 10% and on response latency by 40%. Moreover, we emphasize that *PKG* cannot be used for complex processing logics, such as join, and therefore is not universally applicable to all stream processing jobs.

6.4 Scalability

To better understand the performance of the approaches in action, we present the dynamics of the throughput over time on two real workloads, especially when the system scales out the resource by adding new computation resource to the operator. The results are available in Fig. 11. In order to test this kind of scale-out ability of different algorithms, we run the stream system to a balance status, and then add one more working thread (instance) to the system

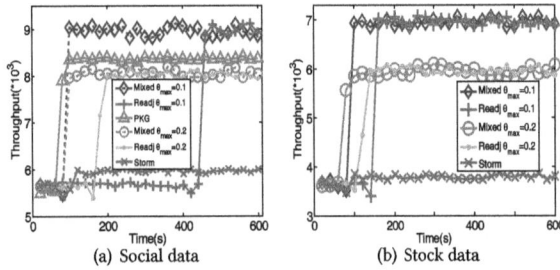

(a) Social data (b) Stock data

Figure 11: Performance during system scale-out.

starting the balance processing algorithms. The results show that our method *Mixed* perfectly rebalances the system within a much shorter response time than that of *Readj*. Though *PKG* is θ_{max} insensitive, it produces a lower throughput than *Mixed* while $\theta_{max} = 0.1$. Following the explanation of Fig. 10(a), *PKG* needs to keep track of all the derived data from a spout until it receives ack response and this action exacerbates its processing latency. On *Social data* with $\theta_{max} = 0.10$, *Readj* takes at least 5 minutes to generate the migration plan for the new thread added to the system. Such a delay leads to huge resource waste, which is definitely undesirable to cloud-based streaming processing applications. Similar results are also observed on *Stock*. The quick response of *Mixed* makes it a much better option for real systems.

7 CONCLUSION AND FUTURE WORK

This paper presents a new dynamic workload distribution mechanism for intra-operator load balancing in distributed stream processing engines. Our mixed distribution strategy is capable of assigning the workload evenly over task workers of an operator, under short-term workload fluctuations. New optimization techniques are introduced to improve the efficiency of the approach, to enable practical implementation over mainstream stream processing engines. Our testings on Apache Storm platform show excellent performance improvement with a variety of workload from real applications, also present huge advantage over existing solutions on both system throughput and response latency.

In the future, we will investigate the theoretical properties of the algorithms to better understand the optimality of the approaches under general assumptions. We will also try to design a new mechanism, to support smooth workload redistribution suitable to both long-term workload shifts and short-term workload fluctuations.

ACKNOWLEDGMENTS

This work is partially supported by National Science Foundation of China (NSFC) under grant (No.61232002), National High Technology Research and Development Program of China (863 Project) under No. 2015AA015307, and National Science Foundation of China under grant (No.61672233). Fu and Zhang are supported by the research grant for the HCCS Programme at the Advanced Digital Sciences Center from Singapore's Agency for Science, Technology and Research (A*STAR), and also by Science and Technology Planning Project of Guangdong under grant (No. 2015B010131015).

REFERENCES

[1] Apache Storm. In *http://storm.apache.org/*.
[2] D. Abadi, Y. Ahmad, M. Balazinska, and et al. 2005. The Design of the Borealis Stream Processing Engine. In *CIDR*. 277–289.
[3] Y. Ahmad and U. Cetintemel. 2004. Network-aware Query Processing for Stream-based Applications. In *VLDB*. 456–467.
[4] L. Aniello, R. Baldoni, and L. Querzoni. 2013. Adaptive Online Scheduling in Storm. In *DEBS*. 207–218.
[5] T. P. Chen, H. Haussecker, A. Bovyrin, and et al. 2005. Computer Vision Workload Analysis: Case Study of Video Surveillance Systems. *Intel Technology Journal 9*, 2 (2005).
[6] D. Dewitt and J. Gray. 1992. Parallel Database Systems: The Future of High Performance Database Systems. *Commun. ACM 35*, 6 (1992), 85–98.
[7] Jianbing Ding, Tom Z. J. Fu, Richard T. B. Ma, Marianne Winslett, Yin Yang, Zhenjie Zhang, and Hongyang Chao. 2015. Optimal Operator State Migration for Elastic Data Stream Processing. *CoRR* abs/1501.03619 (2015).
[8] M. Elseidy, A. Elguindy, A. Vitorovic, and C. Koch. 2014. Scalable and Adaptive Online Joins. *VLDB 7*, 6 (2014), 441–452.
[9] Tom Z. J. Fu, Jianbing Ding, Richard T. B. Ma, Marianne Winslett, Yin Yang, and Zhenjie Zhang. 2015. DRS: dynamic resource scheduling for real-time analytics over fast streams. In *Proceedings of the IEEE 35th International Conference on Distributed Computing Systems (ICDCS)*. 411–420.
[10] Tom Z. J. Fu, Jianbing Ding, Richard T. B. Ma, Marianne Winslett, Yin Yang, Zhenjie Zhang, Yong Pei, and Bingbing Ni. 2015. LiveTraj: Real-Time Trajectory Tracking over Live Video Streams. In *Proc. of ACM Multimedia, Demo*. 777–780.
[11] B. Gedik. 2014. Partitioning Functions for Stateful Data Parallelism in Stream Processing. *VLDBJ 23*, 4 (2014), 517–539.
[12] B. Gedik, S. Schneider, M. Hirzel, and K. Wu. 2014. Elastic Scaling for Data Stream Processing. *IEEE Trans. Parallel Distrib. Syst. 25*, 6 (2014), 1447–1463.
[13] David Karger, Eric Lehman, Tom Leighton, Rina Panigrahy, Matthew Levine, and Daniel Lewin. 1997. Consistent hashing and random trees: Distributed caching protocols for relieving hot spots on the World Wide Web. In *STOC*. 654–663.
[14] Narendra Karmarkar and Richard M Karp. 1982. An efficient approximation scheme for the one-dimensional bin-packing problem. In *Foundations of Computer Science*. 312–320.
[15] R. Khandekar, K. Hildrum, S. Parekh, D. Rajan, J. Wolf, K. Wu, H. Andrade, and B. Gedik. 2009. COLA: Optimizing Stream Processing Applications via Graph Partitioning. In *Middleware*. 308–327.
[16] S. Kulkarni, N. Bhagat, M. Fu, and et al. 2015. Twitter Heron: Stream Processing at Scale. In *SIGMOD*. 239–250.
[17] Mahendra Kutare, Greg Eisenhauer, Chengwei Wang, Karsten Schwan, Vanish Talwar, and Matthew. Wolf. 2010. Monalytics: Online Monitoring and Analytics for Managing Large Scale Data Centers. In *ICAC*. 141–150.
[18] Y. Kwon, M. Balazinska, B. Howe, and J. Rolia. 2012. Skewtune: Mitigating Skew in Mapreduce Applications. In *SIGMOD*. 25–36.
[19] Q. Lin, B. C. Ooi, Z. Wang, and C. Yu. 2015. Scalable Distributed Stream Join Processing. In *SIGMOD*. 811–825.
[20] M. Nasir, G. Morales, D. Garciasoriano, N. Kourtellis, and M. Serafini. 2015. The Power of Both Choices: Practical Load Balancing for Distributed Stream Processing Engines. In *ICDE*. 137–148.
[21] Muhammad Anis Uddin Nasir, Gianmarco De Francisci Morales, Nicolas Kourtellis, and Marco Serafini. 2016. When two choices are not enough: Balancing at scale in distributed stream processing. In *ICDE*. 589–600.
[22] M. Shah, J. Hellerstein, S. Chandrasekaran, and M. Franklin. 2003. Flux: An Adaptive Partitioning Operator for Continuous Query Systems. In *ICDE*. 25–36.
[23] A. Toshniwal, S. Taneja, A. Shukla, K. Ramasamy, J.M. Patel, S. Kulkarni, J. Jackson, K. Gade, M. Fu, J. Donham, and et al. 2014. Storm@ twitter. In *SIGMOD*. 147–156.
[24] B. Ufler, N. Augsten, A. Reiser, and A. Kemper. 2012. Load Balancing in MapReduce Based on Scalable Cardinality Estimates. In *ICDE*. 522–533.
[25] C. Walton, A. Dale, and R. Jenevein. 1991. A Taxonomy and Performance Model of Data Skew Effects in Parallel Joins. In *VLDB*. 537–548.
[26] J. Wolf, N. Bansal, K. Hildrum, S. Parekh, D. Rajan, R. Wagle, K. Wu, and L. Fleischer. 2008. SODA: An Optimizing Scheduler for Large-scale Stream-based Distributed Computer Systems. In *Middleware*. 306–325.
[27] Y. Wu and K. Tan. 2015. ChronoStream: Elastic Stateful Stream Computation in the Cloud. In *ICDE*. 723–734.
[28] Y. Xing, J. Hwang, U. Cetintemel, and S. Zdonik. 2006. Providing Resiliency to Load Variations in Distributed Stream Processing. In *VLDB*. 775–786.
[29] Y. Xing, S. Zdonik, and J. Hwang. 2005. Dynamic Load Distribution in the Borealis Stream Processor. In *ICDE*. 791–802.
[30] Y. Xu, P. Kostamaa, X. Zhou, and L. Chen. 2008. Handling Data Skew in Parallel Joins in Shared-nothing Systems. In *SIGMOD*. 1043–1052.
[31] M. Zaharia, T. Das, H. Li, T. Hunter, S. Shenker, and I. Stoica. 2013. Discretized Streams: Fault-tolerant Streaming Computation at Scale. In *SOSP*. 423–438.
[32] Y. Zhou, B. Ooi, and K. Tan. 2005. Dynamic Load Management for Distributed Continuous Query Systems. In *ICDE*. 322–323.

Caches All the Way Down:
Infrastructure for Data Intensive Science

David Abramson
University of Queensland
david.abramson@uq.edu.au

ABSTRACT

The rise of big data science has created new demands for modern computer systems. While floating performance has driven computer architecture and system design for the past few decades, there is renewed interest in the speed at which data can be ingested and processed. Early exemplars such as Gordon, the NSF funded system at the San Diego Supercomputing Centre, shifted the focus from pure floating-point performance to memory and IO rates.

At the University of Queensland we have continued this trend with the design of FlashLite, a parallel cluster equipped with large amounts of main memory, flash disk, and a distributed shared memory system (ScaleMP's vSMP). This allows applications to place data "close" to the processor, enhancing processing speeds. Further, we have built a geographically distributed multi-tier hierarchical data fabric called MeDiCI, which provides an abstraction of very large data stores across the metropolitan area. MeDiCI leverages industry solutions such as IBM's Spectrum Scale and SGI's DMF platforms.

Caching underpins both FlashLite and MeDiCI. In this I will describe the design decisions and illustrate some early application studies that benefit from the approach. I will also highlight some of the challenges that need to be solved for this approach to become mainstream.

Author Keywords

Caching; memory; IO; big data science

BIOGRAPHY

David has been involved in computer architecture and high performance computing research since 1979.

He has held appointments at Griffith University, CSIRO, RMIT and Monash University.

Prior to joining UQ, he was the Director of the Monash e-Education Centre, Science Director of the Monash e-Research Centre, and a Professor of Computer Science in the Faculty of Information Technology at Monash.

From 2007 to 2011 he was an Australian Research Council Professorial Fellow.

David has expertise in High Performance Computing, distributed and parallel computing, computer architecture and software engineering.

He has produced in excess of 200 research publications, and some of his work has also been integrated in commercial products. One of these, Nimrod, has been used widely in research and academia globally, and is also available as a commercial product, called EnFuzion, from Axceleon.

His world-leading work in parallel debugging is sold and marketed by Cray Inc, one of the world's leading supercomputing vendors, as a product called ccdb.

David is a Fellow of the Association for Computing Machinery (ACM), the Institute of Electrical and Electronic Engineers (IEEE), the Australian Academy of Technology and Engineering (ATSE), and the Australian Computer Society (ACS). He is currently a visiting Professor in the Oxford e-Research Centre at the University of Oxford.

HPDC '17, June 26-30, 2017, Washington , DC, USA
© 2017 Copyright is held by the owner/author(s).
ACM ISBN 978-1-4503-4699-3/17/06.
http://dx.doi.org/10.1145/3078597.3091525

NICE: Network-Integrated Cluster-Efficient Storage

Samer Al-Kiswany[*], Suli Yang[+], Andrea C. Arpaci-Dusseau[+], Remzi H. Arpaci-Dusseau[+]

[*] University of Waterloo, alkiswany@uwaterloo.ca

[+] University of Wisconsin-Madison, {suli, dusseau, remzi}@cs.wisc.edu

ABSTRACT

We present NICE, a key-value storage system design that leverages new software-defined network capabilities to build cluster-based network-efficient storage system. NICE presents novel techniques to co-design network routing and multicast with storage replication, consistency, and load balancing to achieve higher efficiency, performance, and scalability.

We implement the NICEKV prototype. NICEKV follows the NICE approach in designing four essential network-centric storage mechanisms: request routing, replication, consistency, and load balancing. Our evaluation shows that the proposed approach brings significant performance gains compared to the current key-value systems design: up to $7\times$ put/get performance improvement, up to $2\times$ reduction in network load, $3\times$ to $9\times$ load reduction on the storage nodes, and the elimination of scalability bottlenecks present in current designs.

KEYWORDS

Key-value storage, software-defined networks, network-system co-design, distributed storage

1 INTRODUCTION

The end-to-end design principle [38] pervades the design of virtually every modern distributed system [1, 3, 4, 11, 17]. In its extreme form, critical functionality is implemented solely in end hosts, with a relatively dumb and fast network to connect them.

One locale that closely adheres to the end-to-end principle is distributed storage, including distributed file systems [15, 20, 22, 24, 39, 45] and scalable key-value stores [6, 9, 12, 18, 26]. In these widely-deployed and increasingly important systems, the network is used as a point-to-point communication medium, while storage logic and protocols are implemented entirely in client libraries and server code.

Unfortunately, such Network-Oblivious (NOOB) storage systems are fundamentally inefficient. Consider, for example, the simple task of replicating a block. To do so, a node first sends the

HPDC '17, June 26-30, 2017, Washington , DC, USA

© 2017 Association for Computing Machinery.

ACM ISBN 978-1-4503-4699-3/17/06...$15.00

http://dx.doi.org/10.1145/3078597.3078612

block to one server, and then another, and then another; as a result, the same data redundantly traverses some number of network links and switches, increasing load on the network significantly. Even the simple task of locating a data item presents a significant challenge; for example, in protocols such as Chord [40], a logarithmic number of nodes must be contacted simply to discover the location of a particular key.

In this paper, we propose an alternative approach in which we co-design storage logic and networking support to realize more efficient, scalable, and reliable distributed storage. Such Network-Integrated Cluster-Efficient (NICE) storage harnesses recent advances in Software-Defined Networks (SDNs) [19, 30] to optimize key aspects of modern distributed storage architectures. For example, NICE storage systems can replicate a block while generating the least possible network load, and it can forward a request to the proper node in a single hop.

Two recent developments provide a unique opportunity to address NOOB inefficiencies and indicate that a network-integrated design paradigm that co-designs network and end-point functionality has a much higher chance of being successful today. First, recent advances in software-defined networks (SDNs) provide a standard interface for implementing in-network application specific optimizations, and for building a control mechanism that can orchestrate network and storage operations. The second development is the wide adoption of data centers as the main cloud computing platform. Having a single administration of the entire hardware/software stack and the ability to compartmentalize the infrastructure facilitates adopting custom solutions for different applications or subsystems.

NICE uses SDN technology to virtualize the storage system. The client accesses a virtual storage system deployed on a range of virtual IP addresses. The NICE network controller modifies client packets and forwards them to the proper storage node. Having a network controller that is informed of the storage system metadata and has full control of the network decisions enables optimizing packet paths to improve four essential storage mechanisms, including: request routing, which directs requests from clients to storage nodes; replication, for preventing data loss when nodes or storage devices fail; load balancing, which dispatches client requests across replicas to handle workload variation. Finally, NICE virtualization enables building a new fault tolerance mechanism: consistency-aware fault tolerance. This mechanism simplifies building consistency protocols by making failed nodes, or nodes with inconsistent data, inaccessible.

To demonstrate the efficacy of the NICE approach, we design and implement a key-value storage prototype, NICEKV. Our empirical evaluation with synthetic and real workload benchmarks shows that the NICEKV prototype realizes significant performance gains compared to a broad set of NOOB storage configurations. Membership maintenance in NICEKV is highly scalable and eliminates the maintenance operations overhead. NICEKV request routing achieves single-hop routing without requiring extra resources. NICEKV replication is network and storage optimal (discussed in detail in section 4.2), effectively halving the network-generated load and reducing storage load by 3× to 9×, depending on replication level. The NICEKV two-phase commit consistency protocol uses the consistency-aware fault tolerance mechanism to tolerate failures without increasing operation overhead. NICEKV load balancing effectively spreads client requests across servers without deploying dedicated load-balancing machines. The combination of these optimizations is powerful; the NICEKV prototype can achieve up to 7× put/get performance improvement as compared to the traditional network oblivious approach.

The rest of this paper is organized as follows. In Section 2, we present an overview of the current NOOB storage design, and the recent advances in software-defined networks. We then present the proposed NICE approach in Section 3, detail the system design 4, present the implementation of the NICEKV prototype in Section 5, and present our empirical evaluation in Section 6. We discuss related work in Section 7, and conclude in Section 8.

2 BACKGROUND AND RELATED WORK

In this section, we present an overview of a typical network-oblivious storage systems design, and summarize the recent advances in software-defined networks.

2.1 NOOB Storage System Design

Current distributed key-value storage systems are network-oblivious: the network is only used as a point-to-point communication medium without storage system control over its operations. NOOB storage systems typically implement storage logic and protocols within end hosts; this approach is fundamentally inefficient as many core storage system operations are, in principle, network-level operations, e.g., replication or request routing.

Many NOOB storage systems adopt a design based on consistent hashing [25]. In the original consistent-hashing design, the object hashing space represents a circular ring, all storage nodes are placed on the ring, and each node coordinates access to the objects in its part of the ring. Pastry [37] and Chord [40] were among the first to use consistent hashing to build a scalable peer-to-peer object storage system. They use, with high probability, $O(log\ n)$ hops to route a request, while only storing $O(log\ n)$ routing information on each node. While this approach scales well, it imposes additional latency.

To reduce the latency of request routing, prominent NOOB storage systems adopt a full-membership model [6, 9, 12, 18, 26], in which every node maintains complete knowledge about all the nodes in the system and their contents; hence, nodes can route any request directly to the responsible node. When a node joins or fails, all the nodes in the system need to be updated. This update happens through contacting every node and updating its information using $O(N)$ connections and messages [6], or through an epidemic protocol entailing $O(log\ n)$ steps and over $O(N)$ messages [41].

Access Mechanism. To access the system, current systems adopt one of the following three techniques to route client requests to the node maintaining the object. The first technique, which we refer to as the Replica-Oblivious Gateway (ROG), uses a generic off-the-shelf load balancer that forwards client requests to a storage node selected in a random or a round-robin fashion. This approach is common in production systems [6, 9, 18, 26] due to its ease of deployment and use of existing load balancers. This approach imposes two extra hops for routing a request.

The second approach we call the Replica-Aware Gateway (RAG). This approach uses a load balancer or a proxy access node [6] that is aware of replica placement, and imposes one extra hop for routing a request.

In the third approach, known as the Replica-Aware Client (RAC), the clients cache the metadata of previously accessed objects [33], and use it to route subsequent requests. This approach only works for deployments in which clients are collocated with the storage system and are allowed to know detailed data placement and replication information. For deployments in which the clients do not have access to storage internal information or are located behind a NAT [23] (e.g., shared cloud storage like Amazon S3), this approach is not an option. Finally, this approach hinders deploying load balancers.

2.2 Software-Defined Networks

The SDN architecture divides the network into two planes: data and control. The data plane is a traffic forwarding plane that uses the information in the switch forwarding tables to forward messages. The control plane is an external software-based logically-centralized component that controls one or more switches by altering the entries in switch forwarding tables. The communication API between the controller and the switches is based on the widely adopted OpenFlow standard [19].

The OpenFlow standard [30] facilitates external control of a single-switch forwarding table. It allows inserting or deleting forwarding rules. Each forwarding entry includes a matching rule and an action list. If a packet matches a rule, the actions in the actions list are performed in order on the packet. OpenFlow has a rich set of matching rules including wild cards for matching IP and MAC addresses, protocol or port numbers. The actions include packet forwarding to a specific switch port, dropping the packet, sending the packet to the controller, or modifying the packet. The possible modifications include changing the source/destination MAC/IP addresses. To avoid the need for switches to contract the controller on every packet, forwarding rules are stored on switches and have an expiry period that is set by the controller. Controllers can update, delete, or extend the validity of the existing rules at any time.

These capabilities enable fine-grained control of network operations and facilitate application-optimized traffic engineering.

3 NICE SYSTEM ARCHITECTURE

NICE leverages the programmability and fine-grained control of network operations provided by recent advances in software-defined networks [19, 30] to co-design network and storage operations. The NICE design virtualizes the storage system. The client accesses a virtual storage system deployed on a range of virtual IP addresses. The metadata service (detailed next) maps the virtual storage system to the physical one. The NICE design optimizes this mapping to achieve low-latency routing, efficient multicasting, load-balancing, and improved fault tolerance.

This section presents the system architecture and details the two core techniques that NICE proposes: storage virtualization, and consistency-aware fault tolerance. The following section details how we extend these techniques to optimize replication, consistency, and load-balancing mechanisms.

3.1 System Architecture

Similar to the NOOB storage, NICE uses consistent hashing to partition the object space among the storage nodes. Nodes are placed in a consistent hashing ring, such that each node serves part of the ring. We call this the *physical ring*. Every storage node is the primary replica for one or more partitions, and can serve as a secondary replica for other partitions.

The system is composed of three components (Figure 1): storage nodes, client nodes, and a metadata service, all connected with an OpenFlow-enabled switching fabric. The storage nodes serve put and get requests and implement the replication, consistency, and load-balancing protocols. The storage nodes send periodic heartbeats to the metadata service. The metadata service maintains storage system metadata. The metadata includes information about which storage nodes are participating in the system, and which range of the hash space (partition) each storage node is serving. The metadata service does not maintain per-object metadata.

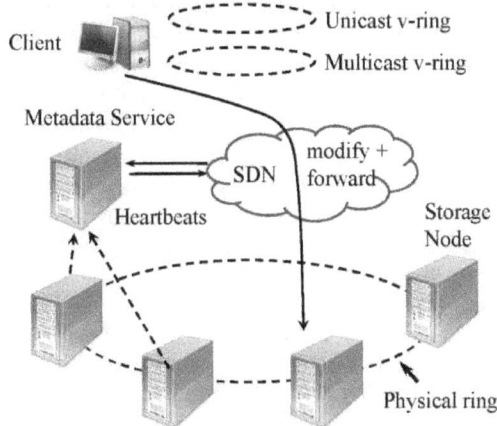

Figure 1. System Architecture. The client sends the requests using two virtual rings (vrings). The requests are rerouted in the network to the responsible storage node. The metadata service

receives heartbeats from the nodes and maintains the mapping information in the forwarding tables.

3.2 NICE Storage Virtualization

The first goal of virtualizing the storage system is to enable storage-aware routing of client requests; that is, to have a routing technique that can route a client request to the proper storage node (i.e., routing based on the key hash value). Building a storage-aware routing mechanism is challenging. While OpenFlow provides control over switch forwarding decisions, it only supports matching packets using information found in the packet headers (e.g., Ethernet, IP, UDP or TCP), not the packet payload data. Consequently, routing packets based on the key hash carried in the payload is not possible. Alternatively, allowing the client to know the physical-ring mapping and replica-placement inherits the NOOB RAC limitations.

The NICE approach virtualizes the storage system; the client accesses a virtual storage system deployed on a set of *virtual nodes (vnodes)*. The virtual addresses are organized in a *virtual consistent hashing ring (vring)*. For instance, all the IP addresses in the range of 10.10.0.0 to 10.10.255.255 can be virtual nodes in a vring. The number of vnodes and their addresses are configurable and do not correspond to the physical ring configuration. To access the system, the client hashes the object name and finds the vnode responsible for serving the object. The client sends the put/get request to the vnode address using UDP.

The metadata service maps the virtual ring to the physical ring. It maps a subset of virtual addresses to a single physical node address. While different mapping techniques are possible, we use simple prefix IP matching: we divide the virtual ring addresses into subgroups such that the number of vnodes per subgroup is a multiple of 2 (e.g., all vnodes in 10.10.1.0/24 form a subgroup). The metadata service maps any packets sent to a particular subgroup to a particular physical node. To this end, the switch will *modify* the destination IP and MAC addresses in the packet headers to be the IP and MAC addresses of the primary replica, then *forward* the packet to the switch port of the primary replica.

This mapping technique achieves three benefits. First, it achieves low-latency single-hop routing, as the client requests are directly routed in the network to the responsible node at switching speed. Second, by decoupling the virtual ring from the physical ring this technique simplifies deployment, as clients never need to change their virtual ring configuration, even when the physical ring configuration changes. Finally, this approach allows for multiple vnodes to be mapped to a single physical node, improving performance and load balancing [40]. Compared to NOOB request routing, NICE routing achieves the optimal routing latency of the RAC approach without suffering from its limitations.

3.3 Consistency-Aware Fault Tolerance

To guarantee sequential consistency NOOB storage systems use complex consistency protocols like two-phase or three-phase commit [41], Paxos [27], or Raft [32]. We illustrate in Figure 2 the put operation using the two-phase commit protocol (2PC), as a representative of these protocols to simplify our discussion. 2PC is among the early proposed protocols that are still widely used [5, 8, 13, 15].

Failure handling is a main differentiating factor between consistency protocols. The 2PC commit protocol is brittle in face of node failures during the put operation and may block if the primary node fails. To overcome the 2PC problems, Paxos and Raft use majority-based (i.e., quorum) design, in which at least the majority (but not all) of the nodes need to participate in the put operation. The drawback of this approach is that failed nodes (or disconnected nodes) may have stale data when they join back; consequently, it is necessary to access the majority of the nodes during the get operation as well to guaranty consistency. This approach creates unnecessary high overhead during get operations.

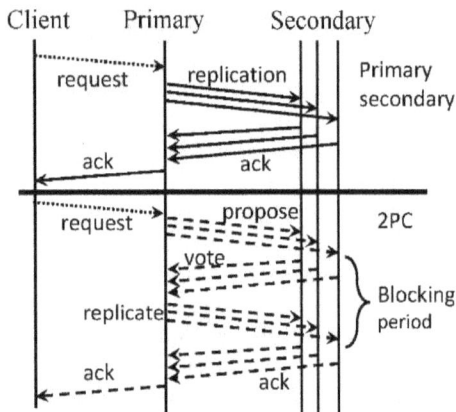

Figure 2. Put protocol alternatives. The figure shows the primary-secondary and 2PC put protocols. In the primary-secondary design (solid arrows) the primary replica serves all put and get request, hence no consistency protocol is necessary. In the two-phase commit (2PC) design (dashed arrows), two rounds of the 2PC protocol are needed to guarantee consistency.

We propose a consistency-aware fault tolerance mechanism. This mechanism solves the inefficiency problem found in current protocols by presenting inconsistent nodes as failed nodes to the client. The mechanism hides failed nodes, and newly-joining, but still inconsistent nodes, until they have a consistent version of the data. To this end, when a node fails it is removed from the switch mapping, rendering the node inaccessible from the client's point of view. When a node restarts, it joins the system in two phases. First, it is made accessible to other storage nodes and to client put requests only. During this phase the rejoining node will receive new objects and will fetch consistent versions of the objects that have been changed while the node was offline. Second, when the node has consistent data, it is made accessible for clients' get requests.

Unlike fail-stop failure model, which may allow returning nodes to receive client requests, the proposed mechanism *deterministically* only routes client requests to consistent nodes. Inconsistent nodes can communicate with the other consistent nodes to update their data set. This approach simplifies building

fault-tolerant consistency protocols (as we will see next) by guaranteeing that clients can only access consistent nodes.

4 SYSTEM DESIGN

In this section we first detail the design of system metadata service (i.e., metadata for mapping objects to nodes), then we extend the core techniques of NICE to build an efficient replication mechanism, improve the consistency protocol fault tolerance, and provide in-network load balancing.

4.1 Metadata Service Design

The metadata service is the only component that maintains the system membership and metadata, i.e., it has complete knowledge of all storage nodes in the system and the physical ring partitions they serve. The metadata service is composed of two modules: the membership module and the SDN controller. The membership module monitors storage nodes via heartbeats and detects membership changes (joins and failures), while the SDN controller controls the OpenFlow switches and updates the forwarding tables on membership changes. The SDN controller implements a layer 3 learning switch; it learns which storage node is connected to which switch port and uses this information to build unicast and multicasting forwarding rules.

Storage nodes maintain partial membership information related to the ring partitions of which they are part. Every node only knows the secondary replicas for the partition it is the primary replica for, and knows the primary replicas of every partition it is serving as a secondary replica; resulting in only $O(R)$ information maintained at every node where R is the replication level.

When a node fails, the metadata service selects a handoff node to serve in lieu of the failing node (we detail the fault tolerance mechanism later). The metadata service updates the switch forwarding rules to correctly route requests destined to the failed node to the selected handoff node. The metadata service also informs the affected replicas of the membership change.

On a node join, the metadata service selects which ring partitions the new node will serve as a primary or secondary replica. Similar to handling failures, the metadata service updates the switch and informs the affected replicas of the membership change.

This membership maintenance design is scalable; regardless of the number of storage nodes, the membership service needs $O(S)$ messages to update the switch's forwarding table, where S is the number of switches in the platform, and only $O(R)$ messages to inform the affected replicas of the membership change. Note that each storage node only knows about the replicas it shares data with (which is O(R) of nodes). R, the replication level, is independent of the total number of nodes and is typically small (3 or 5).

While our current metadata service is centralized, it can radially adopt well-known designs for building a highly reliable distributed metadata services. One approach we are currently investigating is having a hot standby replica of the metadata node. Two workload characteristics make this design feasible: the stored metadata is small and changes infrequently, and the load on our metadata service is low as it is mainly invoked on node or network failures. These two characteristics make maintaining a hot standby server feasible.

4.2 Replication

Storage systems should not lose data when a node fails. The main data reliability approach adopted by the majority of NOOB storage systems is replication [6, 9, 12, 18, 26, 33] (with the other popular technique being erasure coding).

Challenge. On a put request, a single node (known as the primary replica or the coordinator node) replicates the new object on R-1 different storage nodes through R-1 unicast TCP connections, enabling the system to tolerate R-1 replica failures without losing data.

This approach, in principle, is network non-optimal as the same data will traverse some links multiple times, especially those close to the node replicating the object. Further, this approach creates a high load on the node replicating the object as it needs to send/receive R-1 copies of the data on every put.

To alleviate the load on the replicating node Renesse et. al. proposed chain replication [43]. In chain replication, nodes are organized in chains, and each node replicates the new object to the next node in the chain until the required number of replicas is created. While this approach may distribute the replication load across the nodes, it significantly increases the operation latency, and is equally network non-optimal.

NICE Design. NICE builds network- and storage-optimal replication mechanism by leveraging network-level multicasting. The consistency mechanism discussed next requires to precisely identify and control which nodes are part of a given multicast group. While one may consider using traditional IP-multicasting, the fact that it requires every node to separately join/leave any multicast group makes it significantly harder (if not impossible) to build and maintain hundreds of multicast groups in face of node join and failure and to *precisely* identify when a particular multicast group has converged. OpenFlow helps solve these issues by allowing direct and centralized control of all groups.

NICE design divides storage nodes into overlapping replica sets; every physical node is, typically, a primary replica in one replica set and a secondary replica in at least R-1 other sets.

To realize single-hop replication, NICE storage follows the virtual-storage approach discussed earlier. The client has two virtual rings: a unicast ring (discussed in the previous subsection) and a multicast ring. Each ring uses a separate IP address range (e.g., 10.10.0.0/16 for the unicast vring, and 10.11.0.0/16 for the multicast vring). As the name indicates, messages sent to an address in the multicast ring are multicasted to all object replicas, while the messages using the unicast ring are sent to one of the replicas of the object (the primary replica unless load balancing is used). The multicast ring is only used to send the put request and data.

Similar to the unicast vring, the multicast vring is divided into subgroups with each subgroup mapped to a replication set. For

any packet targeting a virtual multicast address, the switch will *modify* the destination IP address to be the IP multicast address of the target replication set, and *forward* the packet to all the switch ports of the target replicas.

The proposed replication mechanism is optimal: first, it uses a single hop to route the put request; second, it uses optimal network paths for data replication (considering data center tree topology, the optimal path is equivalent to link-layer multicasting paths); third, it offloads the replication overhead from the primary replica to the network switch, achieving high performance and scalability. This approach is also optimal in terms of storage node load as each storage node only receives the data once. Finally, this replication approach is load balanced by design; the primary and secondary replicas send/receive an equal amount of data.

4.3 Consistency Mechanism

Sequentially consistent storage systems should guarantee data consistency across replicas, even when nodes fail or are disconnected and later join back with inconsistent data.

NOOB consistency protocols either face the possibility of blocking on node failure or require getting the object from the majority of nodes to resolve data inconsistency.

NICE proposes a consistency-aware fault tolerance mechanism. Here we demonstrate how NICE uses this mechanism to improve 2PC fault tolerance. The NICE-2PC mechanism (shown in Figure 3) follows the 2PC protocol design with two main differences. First, it leverages multicast-based replication to load balance and efficiently replicate an object. Second, it improves the 2PC fault tolerance without requiring quorum-like protocols.

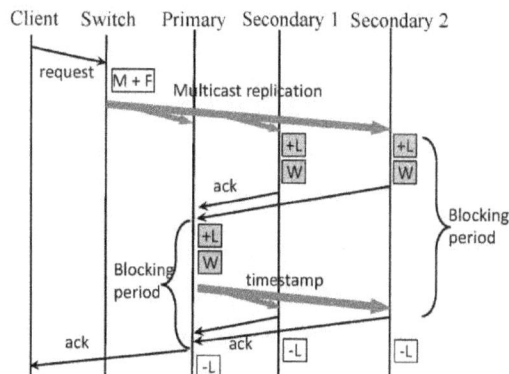

Figure 3. Consistency Mechanism. Timeline of the message sent in put operation in NICE storage. The switch performs modify and forward (M+F) for client packets to map the virtual address to the multicast group. (+L) is when a node logs the operation. (-L) is when the log entry is deleted. (W) is when the node writes the new object to the persistent storage. Gray boxes denote forced writes, and bold arrows denote multicasting. Object locks are maintained in memory only.

During the put operation, the client request is multicasted by the switch to all of the replicas. Upon receiving a complete object, the secondary replicas lock the object, log the operation, store the object to persistent storage, and acknowledge the operation to the primary replica. The primary replica, upon receiving an acknowledgment from all secondary replicas, generates a time stamp and multicasts the time stamp to all replicas. The timestamp contains the following quadruplet: primary address, primary timestamp, client address, and client timestamp,. The timestamp creates an order between put operations to the same object, even between retrials of the put operation by the same client. The secondary replicas release the lock on the object and acknowledge the end of the operation to the primary replica, which in turn acknowledges the operation to the client. We detail the fault tolerance mechanism next.

4.4 Fault Tolerance

Failure Model. NICE adopts a fault model assumed by current NOOB systems in which all node failures are assumed to be transient, with permanent failures being handled by administrator intervention [6, 9, 18] (The procedure for permanently adding or removing nodes is discussed at the end of this section). Consequently, when a node fails or is disconnected, the system does not automatically re-replicate the objects stored on that node, as these objects are still durably fully replicated.

Failure Detection. Node failure (include disconnected nodes) is detected through two techniques: the metadata service will declare the node failed if it misses three heart beats from the node, or if a node reports to the metadata service that another node is irresponsive (e.g., if a node time-outs twice while waiting for a reply from a particular node in the 2PC protocol). Node failure causes two main problems: First, when a failing node recovers/rejoins, it often contains old (inconsistent) versions of the objects, if any of the stored objects have changed while the node was offline/disconnected. Second, newly stored objects will be under-replicated. Next we discuss how we handle these two problems.

Failure Hiding. To handle the inconsistency problem of the failing nodes, on failure detection, the metadata service removes the failing node from the switch unicast and multicast vring mappings and informs the affected replicas. This effectively renders the node non-existent from the client point of view. When the node recovers, the switch mappings are updated only after the node is deemed consistent, as we will see next.

Maintaining Replication Level during Temporary Failures. When a node failure is detected the metadata service selects a handoff node to serve as a secondary replica in the hash region of the failing node [18]. Any storage node in the system that is not already part of the effected replication set can serve as a handoff node. The handoff node temporarily serves the object range until the failing node comes back. To simplify recovery, the handoff node stores the newly stored objects in a separate directory. If the handoff node receives a get request for an old object that it does not have, the handoff node will forward the request to the primary replicas. After selecting the handoff node, the metadata service updates the switch forwarding tables for both virtual rings and informs the affected replicas. When the original node comes back, it will discover the handoff node through contacting the metadata service and retrieve all the new objects. Primary node failure is discussed below. The system can handle multiple failures as long as at least one node in every region is an original node (not a handoff node) in the region.

Node Recovery. When a node recovers from failure, it contacts the metadata service to rejoin the system. Rejoining the system takes three steps: First, the metadata service adds the rejoining node to the multicast vring mapping. This makes the node receive and participate in the put operations but not serve get requests. Second, the recovering node contacts the handoff node to get all the objects stored during its failure. Finally, the node informs the metadata service that it has consistent data. The metadata service will add the node to the unicast vring mapping, remove the handoff node from all mappings, and inform the affected replicas.

Failures during Put Operation. If a node fails during a put operation the operation will fail and the client will retry.

If a secondary node fails during a put operation (i.e., before sending the last ack to the primary replica in Figure 3), the primary node will detect the failure through missing either of the two ack messages from the node. The primary node will abort the operation and inform the client. The primary node will also inform the metadata service of the failure, starting the process for hiding the failure as detailed above.

If the primary node fails before sending the final acknowledgment to the client, the client will time-out and retry the operation. If the primary node fails before sending the "timestamp" message in the 2PC protocol in Figure 3, the secondary nodes will detect the failure by timing out on the replication message and will inform the metadata service starting the failure-handling process detailed above. When a primary node fails, the metadata service selects one of the secondary nodes to act as a primary node. The new primary will contact the secondary nodes to identify all the objects that are locked on any secondary node. If an object is locked on any node, this means that node did not receive the timestamp message from the old primary. For locked objects, the primary does the following: if the object is committed on any secondary node, then this means the object was committed by the old primary and could have been served to subsequent get requests. The primary will commit and unlock the object. If an object is locked on all secondary nodes, then the new primary will abort the operation. In case of a complete cluster failure, in which all in-memory locks are lost, the persistent logs on the nodes will identify the latest put operations. The new primary will check them all using the rules above.

Ring Re-Configuration. Occasionally the administrator needs to reconfigure the system to add new nodes or remove nodes that permanently failed. To permanently remove a node, the administrator informs the metadata of the node removal. The metadata in its turn updates the forwarding rules related to the leaving node and informs all effected nodes of the membership change. Adding a new node to a replica set follows a procedure similar to rejoining a node after a temporary failure. The node is added first to the put vring to receive new updates and the primary node is informed of the new node. The node contacts the primary node to retrieve all keys stored in the hash range. Once the new node has consistent data it is added to the get vring and is made visible to get operations.

4.5 Load Balancing

While consistent hashing distributes the objects evenly across storage nodes, objects' popularity rarely follows a uniform distribution, leading to a skewed distribution in which a subset of objects is highly popular [14, 16]. In this case, storage systems use load balancing to distribute the get/put load on all the replicas of a given object.

Challenge. In current systems, a load-balancing node is deployed as a gateway to the system to forward client requests using the ROG or RAG approach (§2). This approach increases operation latency and requires provisioning load-balancers to avoid creating a system choke point. Alternatively, to avoid these drawbacks and to avoid the complexity of consistency protocols, latency-sensitive systems eschew load balancing and adopt the primary-secondary design [33, 42]. Alternatively, if a weaker consistency is an option, a client-side load balancing can be adopted (e.g., the client can randomly pick one of the replicas).

NICE Design. The NICE metadata service implements a workload-informed consistency- and replica-aware load balancer. Unlike the NOOB storage design, our multicast-based put operations are load balanced by design; consequently, our load-balancing technique focuses only on get requests. While previous effort explored SDN-based load balancing [21, 44] our approach advances the previous approaches by using the storage metadata to build consistency- and replica-aware load balancer.

To perform workload-informed load-balancing, the metadata service collects, through heartbeats, periodic workload statistics, including the range of client IP addresses accessing each partition.

The metadata service divides the client address space into R divisions, such that each division size is a multiple of 2. Requests coming from each division will be forwarded to a different replica. The metadata service alters the switch forwarding rules to match both the packet source and destination IP addresses. The destination IP determines which physical ring partition the request is targeting, while the source IP determines which replica to forward the request to. For requests coming from IP addresses that are not covered by these divisions, the metadata service forwards them to the primary replica. When an administrator adds a new node to a replica set the metadata server reparations the client address space to utilize the new replica for get requests.

Compared to NOOB load balancing, NICE builds an in-network load balancing without increasing the latency or deploying extra resources, as is the case in NOOB systems.

This approach increases the number of forwarding entries per partition of the unicast vring from 1 to R entries, each forwarding a subset of the clients to one of the replicas. Our future work will investigate more intelligent load-balancing techniques.

4.6 Switch Scalability

The proposed approach requires, for each physical partition, one entry in the switch forwarding table for the unicast vring mapping and one entry for the multicast vring mapping, if no load balancing is used. This leads to a total of *2N* entries in the forwarding table. Where N is the number of storage nodes. If load balancing is enabled, it uses R entries per partition (Where

R is the replication level), leading to a total of *(R + 1)N* entries. Given this requirement, current switches can support large-scale storage systems with thousands of nodes. Current switches support tables with 128K or more entries; they can easily support storage systems with up to 64K storage nodes without load balancing. With load balancing enabled and with a replication level of 3 they can support up to 32K storage nodes.

5 IMPLEMENTATION DETAILS

We implemented the NICEKV prototype following the NICE design. The NICEKV prototype is implemented in 14K lines of C++ code. The controller is implemented using 1K lines of python using the Ryu [10] framework.

The rest of the section discusses implementation details of the network centric operations, and summarizes our experience with the state-of-the-art switches.

Mapping Service. The SDN controller implements a layer 3 learning switch. If the controller receives a packet destined to a not-yet-seen IP address, the controller will check if the address is a vnode address and update the switch to map the address to its physical counterpart, else the controller will buffer the packet and broadcast an ARP request for the unknown address. On receiving an ARP reply, the controller will update the forwarding tables and forward the buffered packets. The controller keeps a list of recently ARPed addressed to avoid flooding the network with ARP requests. While NICEKV implements a single node mapping service, the service can be easily partitioned on multiple nodes.

Request Routing. We use UDP to send client requests and TCP for all other communications, i.e., the client sends the put/get request to the vnode IP address using UDP and waits for the reply on a client-side TCP socket. This design decision allows mapping multiple vnode addresses to a single physical address without worrying about handling the reverse mapping required for TCP, i.e., mapping the physical node address to multiple vnodes. Further, UDP is required for IP multicasting.

Replication. For large objects, replication requires a *reliable* transport for data dissemination. NICEKV builds a simple reliable UDP-based multicast transport layer that uses primitive flow and congestion control techniques. Data is divided into multiple chunks, each less than a single network MTU (1400 bytes). The protocol uses NACKs to inform the client of missing packets, and the client sends the missing packets using a unicast connection. ACKs are used for flow control.

We implemented a version of the reliable multicast protocol for quorum protocols. We optimized the quorum implementation by pushing the quorum design down to the multicast transport layer. To this end, we designed a reliable any-k multicasting protocol. For flow control, the protocol tracks a window of transmitted packets and advances the window when any k of the recipients acknowledges receiving the packets. The protocol returns when any k of the nodes fully receive the data. After returning, the protocol keeps supporting straggling nodes until they finish or timeout.

5.1 Deployment Experience

NICE exploits the latest capabilities of OpenFlow-enabled switches. Unfortunately, through examining three platforms with OpenFlow-enabled switches, we found that the current switches lag in terms of the supported OpenFlow features. Efficiently modifying packet headers, in particular, was rarely supported. Only one switch supported this feature, but in software, resulting in three orders of magnitude slower switching speed.

The CloudLab [2] Utah cluster, which we use, provides partial support for OpenFlow features; in particular, it supports forwarding the packets to multicast addresses but does not support modifying the packet IP destination address. Modifying the packet IP destination addresses is necessary for mapping virtual addresses to physical addresses.

To address this challenge, we deployed Open vSwitch [7] on every client machine. Open vSwitch is a software-based OpenFlow-enabled virtual switch. Further, we extended the NICEKV SDN controller to control multiple switches (i.e., multiple Open vSwitches and a single hardware switch). The controller installs the rules to modify packet headers (mapping virtual to physical addresses) on the client side Open vSwitches, and installs forwarding and multicasting rules on the hardware switch. Our evaluation shows that our new deployment leads to less than 4% performance loss of the switching speed.

6 EVALUATION

Our evaluation demonstrates the performance benefits brought by NICE. This section first compares the performance of NICE and NOOB storage, then evaluates the two systems using the Yahoo benchmark [16]. In addition to the NICEKV prototype, we have implemented a NOOB storage prototype with rich configuration options. The NOOB system implements the three common access mechanisms: RAC with client side caching, RAG with a replica-aware load balancer, and ROG with a randomized load balancer. NOOB prototype implements two consistency mechanisms: 2PC and Primary-backup designs. The NOOB prototype allows us to compare NICEKV to range of NOOB designs and configurations. Finally, to verify the NOOB performance, we ran a synthetic single client put and get workloads to compare the NOOB-RAG performance to the OpenStack Swift key-value store [6]. In both workloads NOOB-RAG performance was equivalent or slightly better than Swift storage.

Platform. We use a cluster of 30 nodes on the Cloud-Lab [2] Utah site. Each node has an 8-core ARMv8 2.4 GHz processor, 64GB memory, 120GB SSD disk and 1 Gbps NIC. The nodes are connected to an OpenFlow enabled switch that supports OpenFlow 1.3.1. While the evaluation uses a single hardware switch the controlled switching topology (including Open vSwitches software switches) is much more complex. Further, NICE can radially support multi-switch platforms, as the controller will install the same rules on all participating switches.

Deployment Configuration. Unless otherwise specified, we deploy the systems on 16 nodes (one mapping node and 15 storage nodes), 14 nodes for clients and load balancers, and configure the system with replication level of 3 and sequential consistency.

6.1 Request Routing Evaluation

We compare the request routing performance of the NICEKV prototype, and three NOOB storage configurations: ROG, RAG, and RAC. We measure the performance of get requests issued from a single client. The evaluation shows the average of 1000 get operations while varying the object's size from 4 bytes to 1 MB.

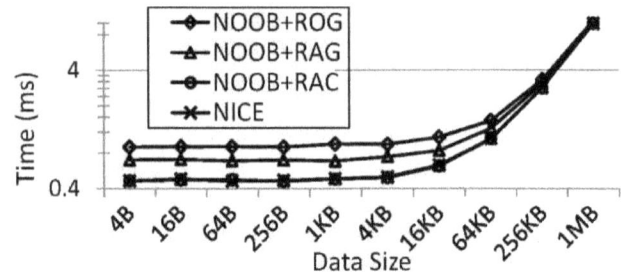

Figure 4. Request Routing Performance. The average time of the get operation. Note the log scaled y-axis. NICE and NOOB-RAC completely overlap.

Figure 4 shows the performance of the get operation on the four systems. NICE and NOOB+RAC systems achieve comparable performance as both achieve single-hop request routing. For small data sizes (less than 64KBs) NICE and NOOB+RAC systems achieve 2× and 1.5× performance improvement compared to NOOB+ROG and NOOB+RAG systems, respectively. This improvement is due to the delay added by the request routing mechanism. The benefits are not as pronounced with large data sizes, as transfer time dominates.

6.2 Replication Evaluation

We compare the replication performance of the NICE design and three configurations of the NOOB storage primary-only design: ROG, RAG, and RAC. The experiment measures the put performance of one client. The evaluation shows the average of 1000 put operations with objects sizes ranging from 4 bytes to 1 MB. The experiment measures replication performance in terms of operation time, generated network load, and load ratio between the primary and secondary replicas.

Replication time. Figure 5 shows the put operation time on the four systems. NICE storage achieves significant and consistent performance improvement across object sizes: up to 4.3× compared to NOOB+ROG, up to 3.4× compared to NOOB+RAG, and up to 2.6× compared to NOOB+RAC. The other systems lag NICE storage due to the extra effort needed for request routing and replication, while NICE storage uses optimal multicast-based replication.

Network load. Figure 6 shows the total link load generated by the put operation. NICE storage achieves, regardless of the object size, significant reduction in network load. NICE storage generates between 1.7× to 3.5× less network load compared to the other systems.

Storage Load Ratio. Figure 7 shows the ratio of the primary replica load to the secondary replica load. While all NOOB storage system configurations impose 3× more work on the primary compared to the secondary (this load imbalance is proportional to the replication level), NICE load balances the load evenly across the primary and secondary replicas.

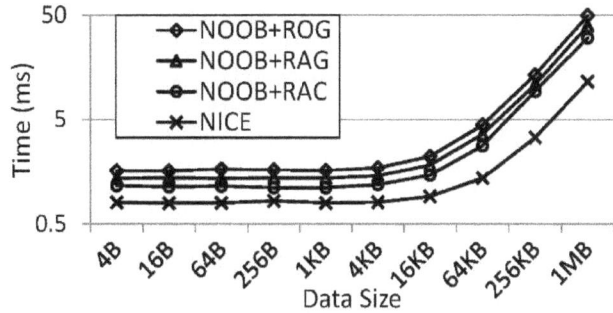

Figure 5. Replication Performance. The average time of the put operation. Note the log scaled y-axis

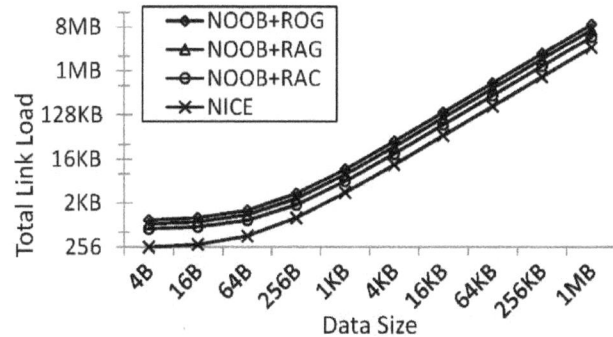

Figure 6. Network Link Load. The total network link load of the put operation.

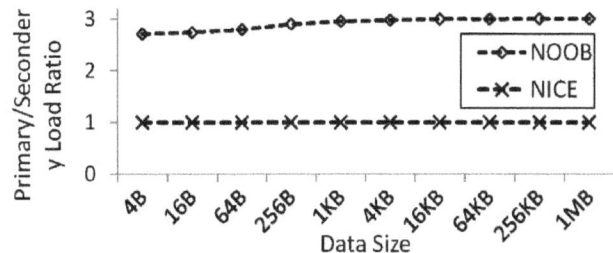

Figure 7. Storage Load Ratio. The ratio of the primary replica to secondary replica load in terms of amount of data sent/received during the put operation.

6.3 Quorum-based Replication Evaluation

This experiment compares NICE and NOOB storage quorum-based replication. The quorum design is appealing due to its ability to avoid slow or failed nodes. The experiment puts 1000 1MB objects

using a replication level of 7, while varying the quorum write-set size (quorum size for short). To emulate slow nodes we configured the network connection of 3 replicas to be 50Mbps, while the rest of the nodes enjoy a 1Gbps connection.

Figure 8 shows (a) the put operation time and (b) achieved bandwidth when varying the quorum size. While the performance of both systems suffer with quorum sizes of 5 and 7 (as it is not possible to avoid slow nodes), we note that NICE storage achieves up to 5.6× better performance with quorum sizes of 1 and 3. While the primary replica in NOOB storage is waiting for the first quorum-size of nodes to finish, it is concurrently replicating the object to all replicas, including the slow ones, creating high contention on the primary link.

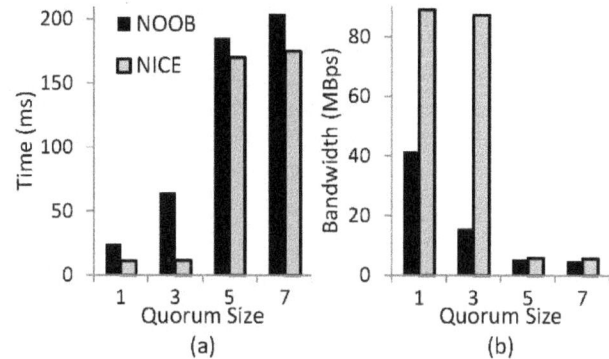

Figure 8. Quorum-based Replication Evaluation. Put operation performance using the quorum design. The experiment uses a replication level of 7 while varying the quorum size. The figure shows the put operation time (a) and bandwidth (b).

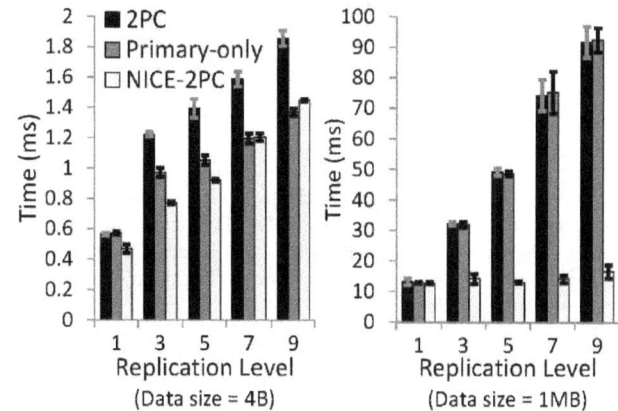

Figure 9. Consistency Mechanism Performance. The put performance while varying the replication level, with 4-byte (a) and 1MB (b) objects. Error bars represent standard deviation.

6.4 Consistency Mechanism Evaluation

We compare NICE storage to two NOOB storage configurations: primary-only and 2PC. To efficiently support highly popular objects, storage systems often create multiple replicas. This experiment evaluates the efficiency of the put operation while varying the replication level. NOOB storage use RAC request routing. We show the results for the two ends of the spectrum of object sizes, small 4-byte objects and large 1MB objects.

Figure 9.a shows the put operation time with 4-byte objects. NICE achieves up to 1.3× better performance than NOOB-2PC. NICE achieves comparable performance to NOOB primary-only replication, although it has an extra phase of communication. This is because of the multicast-based replication that reduces not only the data transfer time but also the overhead of creating and maintaining up to 8 TCP connections. We note that the performance of all systems degrades with higher replication levels, due to the increased overhead of the consistency protocol that dominates small object performance. The primary-only design achieves better performance than NOOB-2PC due to 2PC protocol overheads.

Figure 9.b shows the put operation time with 1MB objects. NICE achieves up to 5.5× better performance than NOOB systems. The primary-only and 2PC achieve comparable performance since, with large objects; performance is dominated by replication cost. While NOOB performance degrades considerably: by 7× when increasing the replication from 1 to 9, NICE performance degrades slightly when increasing the replication level (by 17% when increasing the replication from 1 to 9).

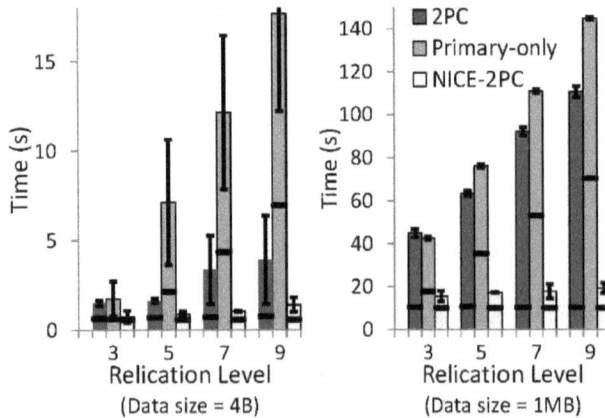

Figure 10. Load Balancing Evaluation. The three systems performance under the load balancing workload while varying the replication level and number of clients. The figure shows results with (a) 4-byte objects and (b) with 1MB objects. Bold markers show the performance of the get-only workload. Error bars represent standard deviation.

6.5 Load Balancing

This experiment measures the performance of NICE storage and two NOOB storage configurations (primary-only and 2PC) when serving highly-popular frequently-updated objects. We design a weak scaling experiment: we increase the number of clients proportional to the replication level. In each configuration 1 client puts the same object 1000 times, while R-1 clients get the same object 1000 times.

Figure 10 shows performance with 4-byte objects (a) and 1MB objects (b). NICE storage achieves better performance than NOOB storage systems: up to 7.5× better than the primary-only configuration, and up to 5.5× better than the 2PC configuration in both object sizes. The line markers on the bars in Figure 10 show the performance of the workload without updating the shared key (i.e., without the put client). The marker shows that NICE and 2PC

are able to load balance the get requests across replicas, while the primary-only design performance degrades with the increased workload as no load balancing is used. The figure also shows the significant overhead added by 2PC consistency mechanism (the difference between the marker and the top of the bar).

NOOB storage system performance degrades considerably when increasing the replication level and the number of clients, with primary-only performance degrading by 10× with small objects and 3.5× with 1MB object, and the 2PC configuration degrading by 2.6× with both sizes. This performance degradation is testimony that NOOB storage designs are not weakly scalable, i.e., NOOB is unable to meet the increasing demand despite the proportional increase in the allocated resources. Significant replication costs (dominant in large objects) and consistency-protocol overhead (dominant in small object) are the reason why. NICE storage performance degrades slightly when increasing the replication level and the number of clients (only by 20% with 1MB objects and by 80% with 4-byte objects).

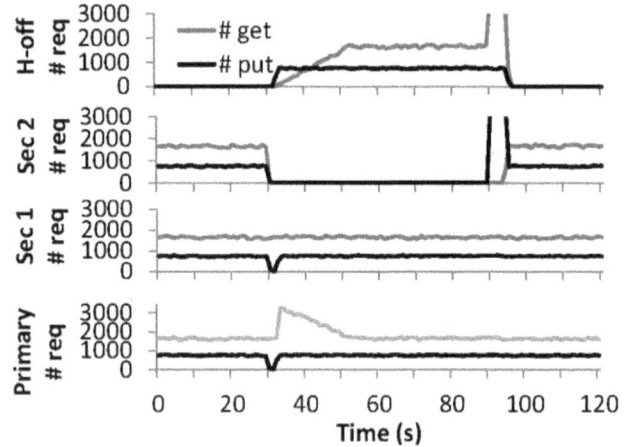

Figure 11. Fault Tolerance Evaluation. Secondary node 2 fails at 30s mark, triggering the fault tolerance mechanism, and 90s the node recovers, retrieves the missed objects from the handoff node, and starts serving client requests.

6.6 Fault Tolerance Evaluation

This experiment demonstrates the system fault tolerance mechanism. Three clients access the system with 20/80 put/get ratio and key size of 1KB. All objects are in the same partition. Figure 11 shows the number of put and get requests served per second. At the 30s mark, the secondary node 2 fails. The primary node detects the failure and informs the metadata service. The metadata service removes the failed node from the switch mappings and adds the handoff node to the replica set. This process makes the partition unavailable for put for less than 2 seconds (Figure 11 second 31). Client put requests during this period will fail and the client will retry after waiting for 2 seconds, in which case the operations will succeed. We are working on shortening this down time through allowing put operations to succeed if one node fails (i.e., having R-1 replicas) and by creating, in the background, one more replica on the handoff node when it joins the replica set.

For get operations, the client selects, in a uniform random fashion, one of the recently put objects to get. When the handoff node starts serving client requests (second 31), it does not have any of the requested objects. In this case, it forwards all get requests to the primary replica. As the handoff node stores more objects less get requests are forwarded to the primary node.

At 90s mark, the failed node joins back, and starts retrieving the objects it missed. This is represented by the spike in put requests (and gets requests at the handoff node). Once the node has a consistent set of objects (second 95), the metadata service adds the node to the unicast switch mapping and removes the handoff node.

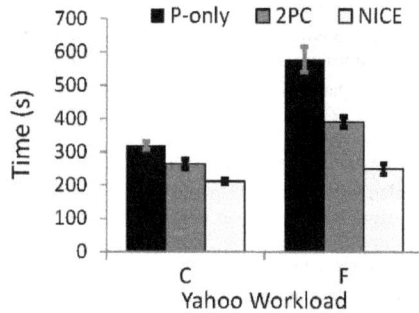

Figure 12. Yahoo Benchmark Evaluation. The three systems performance under two Yahoo benchmarks: read-only (C), and read-modify-write (F). Error bars represent standard deviation.

6.7 Real Workload Evaluation

To evaluate the system with real workloads we use the Yahoo benchmark (YCSB) [16]. YCSB includes workloads with a variety of get-to-put ratios. We use two workloads: C, the read-only workload, and F, the read-modify-write workload which generates the highest ratio (50%) of puts in YCSB. As in the majority of the Yahoo workloads, these two have a zipf popularity distribution.

The experiment compares the performance of NICE storage and two NOOB storage configurations (primary-only and 2PC). The system is accessed by 10 clients, each issuing 20K operations. We use the default YCSB configuration with 1KB objects.

Figure 12 shows the yahoo benchmark results. NICE achieves the best performance under the two workloads. Nice achieves 1.6× and 2.3× better than primary-only configuration under workload C and F, respectively. This improvement is due to the lack of load balancing in the primary-only configuration. Compared to 2PC configuration, NICE achieves 1.25× and 1.5× better performance under workload C and F, respectively. 2PC configurations lags NICE due to the added load-balancing latency and consistency-protocol overhead.

7 OTHER RELATED WORK

Request Routing. Beehive [35] proposes a different approach for achieving, on average, single-hop request routing for special workloads: workloads with highly skewed power-law popularity distribution. Beehive replicates each object based on its popularity, with the extremely popular objects replicated on every node, hence accessible in a single-hop. Due to the network and storage

overheads, this approach is only feasible for highly skewed workloads of infrequently updated objects.

SDN Optimized Systems. Recent research projects utilize SDN capabilities to provide load balancing [21, 36, 44], access control [31], seamless VM migration [29], and to improve system security, virtualization and network efficiency [28]. These systems still use the network as a separate entity and use SDN to optimize its operations. Unlike current efforts, we co-design network operations with system operations and protocols to achieve significant benefits.

The MOM [34] and SwitchKV [46] projects are the closest in spirit to our project. MOM builds an SDN-optimized Paxos protocol by building an ordered multicast layer. Unlike MOM, we propose a new complete system architecture that co-designs network and storage support for higher performance and efficiency. SwitchKV [46] builds a key-value storage with a tier of caching nodes. SwitchKV uses the SDN-capability to optimize request routing for get requests from the cache. Unlike NICE, SwitchKV does not use the SDN capability to optimize data replication and consistency mechanisms.

8 CONCLUSION AND FUTURE WORK

We present network-integrated cluster-efficient (NICE) storage, which co-designs storage logic and networking support to realize a more efficient, scalable, and reliable distributed storage. Our prototype evaluation shows that this approach can realize significant benefits: up to 7× performance improvement, substantial network-load reduction (up to 50%), and improved load balancing and scalability. While we focus the discussion on key-value storage systems, the proposed techniques for virtualization and consistency-aware fault tolerance are widely applicable. Our future work will investigate building SDN-enabled storage systems that implement a more intelligent approaches to load balancing and a better support for more complex key-value queries.

ACKNOWLEDGMENT

We thank our shepherd Dean Hildebrand for his guidance and insightful comments, and thank the anonymous HPDC '17 reviewers for their feedback. We thank Thanumalayan S. Pillai for his help with the Yahoo benchmark experiment, and Robert Ricci and the CloudLab team for their support at CloudLab. This material was supported by funding from NSERC, NSF grants CNS-1419199, CNS-1421033, CNS-1319405, and CNS-1218405, as well as donations from EMC, Facebook, Google, Huawei, Microsoft, NetApp, Samsung, Seagate, Veritas, and VMware. Any opinions, findings, and conclusions or recommendations expressed in this material are those of the authors and may not reflect the views of NSERC, NSF, or other institutions.

REFERENCES
[1] Amazon elastic compute cloud (ec2). https:// aws.amazon.com/ec2. Accessed: 2015.

[2] Cloudlab. http://www.cloudlab.us/. Accessed: 2015.

[3] Google app engine. https://appengine.google.com. Accessed: 2015.

[4] Microsoft azure: Cloud computing platform and services. https://azure.microsoft.com/. Accessed: 2015.

[5] Mongodb. https://www.mongodb.org/. Accessed: 2016.

[6] Openstack swift. http://docs.openstack.org/developer/swift/overview_architecture.html. Accessed: 2015.

[7] Openvswitch: Production quality, multilayer open virtual switch. http://openvswitch.org/. Accessed: 2015.

[8] Postgresql. http://www.postgresql.org/. Accessed: 2016.

[9] Riak cloud storage. http://basho.com/riak-cloud-storage/. Accessed: 2015.

[10] Ryu sdn framework. http://osrg.github.io/ryu/. Accessed: 2015.

[11] Spark lighting fast cluster computing. http://spark.apache.org/. Accessed: 2015.

[12] Voldemort project. http://www.project-voldemort.com/voldemort/design.html. Accessed: 2015.

[13] Marcos K. Aguilera, Arif Merchant, et al., Sinfonia: A new paradigm for building scalable distributed systems. Symp. on Operating Systems Principles (SOSP), 2007.

[14] Berk Atikoglu, Yuehai Xu, Eitan Frachtenberg, Song Jiang, and Mike Paleczny. Workload analysis of a large-scale key-value store. International Conference on Measurement and Modeling of Computer Systems (SIGMETRICS), 2012.

[15] Brad Calder, Ju Wang, Aaron Ogus, Niranjan Nilakantan, et. al., Windows azure storage: A highly available cloud storage service with strong consistency. Symposium on Operating Systems Principles (SOSP), 2011.

[16] Brian F. Cooper, Adam Silberstein, Erwin Tam, Raghu Ramakrishnan, and Russell Sears. Benchmarking cloud serving systems with ycsb. Symposium on Cloud Computing (SoCC), 2010.

[17] Jeffrey Dean and Sanjay Ghemawat. Mapreduce: Simplified data processing on large clusters. Symposium on Operating Systems Design and Implementation (OSDI), 2004.

[18] Guiseppe DeCandia, Deniz Hastorun, et al.,Dynamo: Amazon's Highly Available Key-Value Store. Symposium on Operating Systems Principles (SOSP), 2007.

[19] The Open Networking Foundation. Open networking foundation: Openflow switch specification. Version 1.3.0.

[20] Sanjay Ghemawat, Howard Gobioff, and Shun-Tak Leung. The Google File System. Symposium on Operating Systems Principles (SOSP), 2003.

[21] Nikhil Handigol, Mario Flajslik, et al., Aster* x: Loadbalancing as a network primitive. GENI Engineering Conference (Plenary), pages 1–2, 2010.

[22] J. H. Howard, M. L. Kazar, et al., Scale and performance in a distributed file system. Technical report, Information Technology Center, Carnegie-Mellon University, Pittsburgh, PA, August 1987.

[23] Javvin Technologies Inc. Network Protocols Handbook (2Nd Edition). Javvin Technologies Inc., 2005.

[24] R. Jain, P. Sarkar, and D. Subhraveti. Gpfssnc: An enterprise cluster file system for big data. IBM Journal of Research and Development, 57(3/4):5:1–5:10, May 2013.

[25] David Karger, Eric Lehman, et al.,.Consistent hashing and random trees: Distributed caching protocols for relieving hot spots on the world wide web. Symposium on Theory of Computing (STOC), 1997.

[26] Avinash Lakshman and Prashant Malik. Cassandra: A decentralized structured storage system. SIGOPS Oper. Syst. Rev., 44(2):35–40, April 2010.

[27] Leslie Lamport. The part-time parliament. ACM Trans. Comput. Syst., 16(2):133–169, May 1998.

[28] A. Lara, A. Kolasani, and B. Ramamurthy. Network innovation using openflow: A survey. Communications Surveys Tutorials, IEEE, 16(1):493–512, First 2014.

[29] Ali Jos´e Mashtizadeh, Min Cai, et al., Xvmotion: Unified virtual machine migration over long distance. USENIX Annual Technical Conference (ATC), 2014.

[30] Nick McKeown, Tom Anderson, et al.,Openflow: Enabling innovation in campus networks. SIGCOMM Comput. Commun. Rev., 38(2):69–74, March 2008.

[31] Ankur Kumar Nayak, Alex Reimers, Nick Feamster, and Russ Clark. Resonance: Dynamic access control for enterprise networks. Workshop on Research on Enterprise Networking, 2009.

[32] Diego Ongaro and John Ousterhout. In search of an understandable consensus algorithm. USENIX Annual Technical Conference (ATC), 2014.

[33] Diego Ongaro, Stephen M. Rumble, et al., Fast crash recovery in ramcloud. Symposium on Operating Systems Principles (SOSP), 2011.

[34] Dan R. K. Ports, Jialin Li, Vincent Liu, Naveen Kr. Sharma, and Arvind Krishnamurthy. Designing distributed systems using approximate synchrony in data center networks. Symposium on Networked Systems Design and Implementation (NSDI), 2015.

[35] Venugopalan Ramasubramanian and Emin G¨un Sirer. Beehive: O(1) lookup performance for power law query distributions in peer-to-peer overlays. Conference on Symposium on Networked Systems Design and Implementation (NSDI), 2004.

[36] Brendan Cully, Jake Wires, et al., Strata: scalable high-performance storage on virtualized non-volatile memory. Conf. on File and Storage Technologies (FAST). 2014.

[37] Antony I. T. Rowstron and Peter Druschel. Pastry: Scalable, decentralized object location, and routing for large-scale peer-to-peer systems. International Conference on Distributed Systems Platforms (Middleware), 2001.

[38] Jerome H. Saltzer, David P. Reed, and David D. Clark. End-to-end arguments in system design. ACM Transactions on Computer Systems, 2(4):277–288, November 1984.

[39] Russel Sandberg. The Design and Implementation of the Sun Network File System. USENIX Summer Technical Conference, June 1985.

[40] Ion Stoica, Robert Morris, et al., Chord: A Scalable Peer-to-Peer Lookup Protocol for Internet Applications. SIGCOMM '01, August 2001.

[41] Andrew S. Tanenbaum and Maarten van Steen. Distributed Systems: Principles and Paradigms (2Nd Edition). Prentice-Hall, Inc., Upper Saddle River, NJ, USA, 2006.

[42] Douglas B. Terry, Vijayan Prabhakaran, et al., Consistency based service level agreements for cloud storage. Symposium on OS Principles (SOSP), 2013.

[43] Robbert van Renesse and Fred B. Schneider. Chain replication for supporting high throughput and availability. Symp. on OS Design & Implementation (OSDI), 2004.

[44] Richard Wang, Dana Butnariu, and Jennifer Rexford. Openflow-based server load balancing gone wild. Conference on Hot Topics in Management of Internet, Cloud, and Enterprise Networks and Services, Hot-ICE'11.

[45] Sage A. Weil, Scott A. Brandt, et al., Ceph: A Scalable, High-Performance Distributed File System. Symposium on OS Design and Implementation (OSDI), 2006.

[46] Xiaozhou Li, Raghav Sethi, et al., Be fast, cheap and in control with SwitchKV. Conference on Networked Systems Design and Implementation (NSDI). 2016.

MaDaTS: Managing Data on Tiered Storage for Scientific Workflows

Devarshi Ghoshal
Lawrence Berkeley National Lab
1 Cyclotron Road
Berkeley, California 94720
dghoshal@lbl.gov

Lavanya Ramakrishnan
Lawrence Berkeley National Lab
1 Cyclotron Road
Berkeley, California 94720
lramakrishnan@lbl.gov

ABSTRACT

Scientific workflows are increasingly used in High Performance Computing (HPC) environments to manage complex simulation and analyses, often consuming and generating large amounts of data. However, workflow tools have limited support for managing the input, output and intermediate data. The data elements of a workflow are often managed by the user through scripts or other ad-hoc mechanisms. Technology advances for future HPC systems is redefining the memory and storage subsystem by introducing additional tiers to improve the I/O performance of data-intensive applications. These architectural changes introduce additional complexities to managing data for scientific workflows. Thus, we need to manage the scientific workflow data across the tiered storage system on HPC machines. In this paper, we present the design and implementation of MaDaTS (Managing Data on Tiered Storage for Scientific Workflows), a software architecture that manages data for scientific workflows. We introduce Virtual Data Space (VDS), an abstraction of the data in a workflow that hides the complexities of the underlying storage system while allowing users to control data management strategies. We evaluate the data management strategies with real scientific and synthetic workflows, and demonstrate the capabilities of MaDaTS. Our experiments demonstrate the flexibility, performance and scalability gains of MaDaTS as compared to the traditional approach of managing data in scientific workflows.

KEYWORDS

Data management; scientific workflows; multi-tiered storage; burst buffer

ACM Reference format:
Devarshi Ghoshal and Lavanya Ramakrishnan. 2017. MaDaTS: Managing Data on Tiered Storage for Scientific Workflows. In *Proceedings of HPDC '17, June 26–30, 2017, Washington, DC, USA, ,* 12 pages.
DOI: http://dx.doi.org/10.1145/3078597.3078611

1 INTRODUCTION

Large amounts of data from simulations and data analyses is now processed on High Performance Computing (HPC) machines as

HPDC '17, June 26–30, 2017, Washington, DC, USA
© 2017 Association for Computing Machinery.
ACM ISBN. 978-1-4503-4699-3/17/06. . . $15.00
DOI: http://dx.doi.org/10.1145/3078597.3078611

complex workflows. Workflows are critical for the management of scientific applications on current and future systems.

Storage and workflow systems have evolved independent of each other, creating a disconnect between the two. Today, scientific workflows largely rely on applications to manage their file-based communication which presents performance challenges when moving to future HPC systems. Simultaneously, the memory storage hierarchy on HPC systems is getting deeper, driven by new technologies and the need to minimize I/O costs. The memory-storage hierarchy in future systems will have different performance and cost points. There is a need for workflow tools to explicitly and efficiently manage data on HPC systems.

The increasing amount of data in scientific workflows results in greater I/O demands from the memory/storage subsystem on HPC systems. Additional storage layers composed of flash devices (e.g., 'Burst Buffer') have recently shown to improve I/O performance of many HPC applications [18, 28]. Applications need to explicitly manage the staging of data to storage layers prior to execution [20, 33]. The global knowledge of data dependencies enables workflow tools to optimize data movement. Workflow tools also need to resolve and manage data dependencies, minimize overheads of data movement, and manage storage space efficiently [7].

The goal of this paper is *to explore the software ecosystem that is needed to manage data for data-intensive complex workflows on the multi-level storage hierarchy on HPC systems*. We describe the design and implementation of MaDaTS (Managing Data on Tiered Storage for Scientific Workflows) that provides an integrated data management and workflow execution framework on HPC resources. MaDaTS coordinates, tracks and manages the lifecycle of data in a science workflow on an HPC system with multi-tiered storage.

In the context of MaDaTS, we propose and develop an abstraction called virtual data space (VDS) that captures the intermediate representation of the data in the workflow. VDS is managed to capture the data elements of the entire workflow based on user provided "hints" and preferences. The complexities of the underlying storage and filesystem are hidden from the user and users can operate on the data space through an Application Program Interface (API). A workflow is often represented as a directed acyclic graph (DAG) and VDS provides a data-centric view of the workflow akin to a *data DAG*. The nodes in the graph represent data elements with their properties and the edges represent the processes that derive the relationship between the data elements.

We demonstrate the operation of MaDaTS with current HPC systems and an existing workflow tool. MaDaTS can be easily configured to work with future systems and tools as well. We evaluate MaDaTS and study the various properties of workflows and policies that influence the data management within workflows using a mix of science and synthetic workflows. Our evaluation is performed on Cori, a Cray XC40 supercomputer at NERSC (National Energy Research Scientific Computing Center). Cori is an exemplar machine that captures the storage hierarchy of future systems through its tier of Burst Buffers. Our experiments show that MaDaTS scales upto 1024 cores on Cori and is only limited by specific workflow characteristics.

Specifically, our key contributions are:

- We present the design of MaDaTS in the context of batch queue systems and an existing workflow tool.
- We describe the concept, design and API of the virtual data space (VDS) to manage data objects in a workflow.
- In the context of MaDaTS, we evaluate different data management strategies and show the capabilities of MaDaTS, comparing the results to the traditional approach of managing data in workflows.

The rest of the paper is organized as follows. We present the background and related work in Section 2. We present the design and implementation of MaDaTS in Section 3. We present our results in Section 4. Finally, we present the conclusions in Section 5.

2 BACKGROUND

In this section, we provide an overview of scientific workflows on HPC systems, the memory/storage hierarchy and related work.

2.1 Scientific Workflows

In HPC environments, workflows are widely used to execute simulations and data analyses for scientific discovery [27]. Today, workflows are written as ad-hoc scripts and/or using workflow tools and they chain together a series of tasks with inputs and outputs in a pipeline. Existing workflow tools [8, 29] do not provide mechanisms to implicitly manage data on HPC resources. Current user methods are less than optimal in performance and effectiveness. For example, users often 'stage' the input data to a storage layer prior to executing the workflow. However, some of this data can be asynchronously staged as the workflow executes. Also, selective staging of data might be sufficient for improving performance while balancing costs. Additionally, scientists face challenges in automating these due to the possible wastage of compute hours, file system user quota limits, etc. Thus, there is a need to automate or semi-automate the data management steps in workflows, which is the goal of our work.

The execution of a workflow in an HPC environment depends on the mapping of workflow tasks to job scripts that are submitted to a batch scheduler. Single-job execution mode (also called Pilot job [19]), consolidates workflow tasks into a single batch job. Multijob execution mode creates distinct batch jobs for each task in a workflow. Single- and multi-job modes have trade-offs in wait time and utilization of resources and are preferred for different workflow types. For MaDaTS, we use the Tigres workflow library for managing workflows through job scripts on HPC resources and our evaluation tests both approaches.

2.2 Tigres Workflow Library

Tigres [12] is a programming library that allows users to compose large-scale scientific workflows and execute them on HPC environments. Tigres provides *"templates"* that enable scientists to easily compose, run and manage computational tasks as workflows. These templates define common computation patterns used in analyzing data and running scientific simulations. Currently, Tigres supports four templates – sequence, parallel, split and merge. Tigres can run on a variety of different platforms including desktops, clusters and supercomputers.

Tigres allows workflows to be composed from existing executable scripts and binaries. Tigres workflows are Python programs that are submitted as jobs to the batch scheduler directly. It manages workflow execution from within the job scripts, where resources are managed via different batch schedulers like Slurm, Torque, SGE etc. In this paper, we use Tigres as the workflow library to implement and evaluate MaDaTS.

2.3 Memory and Storage Hierarchy

Fast storage class memory devices are being added to the storage subsystem on current and future HPC systems. These devices (solid state drives or SSDs) currently use flash memory that is one form of non-volatile random-access memory (NVRAM). SSDs have added one more layer to the storage hierarchy in HPC systems in the form of Burst Buffer [18, 28]. It resides between compute nodes and the high-capacity parallel file system (PFS).

Current research on NVRAM technologies are also looking into alternate solutions that may add additional layers to the memory and storage hierarchy in future HPC systems. In this paper, we address the issue of data management across the tiered storage hierarchy in HPC systems. We use NERSC's most recent supercomputer Cori that provides a 'Burst Buffer' based on Cray DataWarp [13] for our evaluation. Cori's storage hierarchy is representative of the storage hierarchy that is expected in future systems. *MaDaTS has been designed to be generic and can be configured to be used with future HPC systems that have deeper storage tiers.*

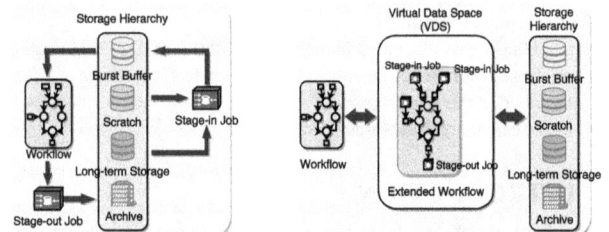

(a) Traditional workflow execution.

(b) MaDaTS workflow execution.

Figure 1: Traditional versus MaDaTS workflow execution. Today, in the traditional model of running workflows users manage the data stage-in and stage-out process at the beginning and end, independent of the execution. VDS provides a way to map the data of a workflow to the multi-tiered storage system. The data is managed with data movement tasks that are part of the workflow enabling greater efficiency throughout the workflow.

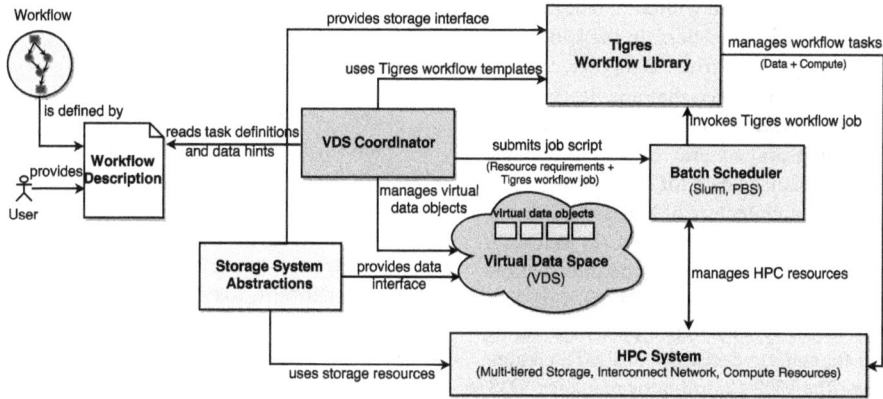

Figure 2: MaDaTS architecture: VDS Coordinator creates a data management plan (i.e., an extended workflow DAG). The DAG includes data movement tasks abstracted by virtual data objects. Virtual data objects are mapped to file system data objects through storage system abstractions. The tasks in the extended workflow are managed by Tigres and the resources are managed by a batch scheduler like Slurm.

2.4 Related Work

Data management for large data-intensive science workflows on HPC resources is an active area of research, and is getting increased attention due to the evolving memory and storage hierarchy. We detail work related to the multi-tiered storage, and the various data abstractions and approaches for managing scientific data.

Multi-tiered Storage. Multi-tiered storage has shown to improve I/O performance across various domains [16, 22] However, the improvements are still limited by the data movement costs between the storage tiers, and the underlying limitations of the storage and the network subsystems. MaDaTS uses storage and data properties, along with the structure of the workflow to generate an efficient data management plan that minimizes the cost of moving the data between the storage tiers. Deadline-based [32] and I/O-aware [14] data migration techniques have been proposed to move data efficiently between SSDs and HDDs. In contrast, the focus of MaDaTS is on the efficient execution of scientific workflows on multi-tiered memory storage hierarchy in current and future HPC systems. MaDaTS's current focus is on three data management strategies - storage-aware, workflow-aware and user-controlled/passive. MaDaTS's extensible design makes it possible to explore other strategies relevant to HPC workflows in the future.

Data Abstractions. Franklin et al. [11] propose a concept of dataspaces that provides a data management abstraction for application developers hiding the underlying differences of the data sources through a common set of services.Docan et al. [9] define DataSpaces as a data exchange framework that is used to access whole or part of the data through a shared address space. Previous works have also proposed memory abstractions [21] including more recently the Resilient Distributed Datasets [30]. The concept of abstracting data objects into 'virtual data' has been earlier used in Grid environments and data catalogs [10, 17]. VDS abstractions in MaDaTS is similar to these abstractions but is more focused on capturing the data-centric view of the workflow, that is necessary for managing the data efficiently on the complex memory-storage hierarchy.

Data Management. Previous works have focused on the challenges [7] for data management of scientific workflows in HPC

environments. Various aspects of distributed data management have been considered in the context of grid environments including tools for optimized wide area data transfer [2], replica management [5], and metadata catalogs [23]. Workflow systems managing data over a wide-area network [15, 26] make data management decisions based on network and storage parameters, and focus on strategies for efficiently transferring the data. These works address issues orthogonal to MaDaTS since they target distributed systems. MaDaTS's focus is on HPC systems and our focus is on determining appropriate storage layer for each data item in the workflow while allowing users control and hiding the complexities of the storage layers.

In-situ execution of workflows provide an alternative way to manage data and execute workflows by reducing the data movement costs [25, 31] or using resources on dedicated I/O transfer nodes [34]. While MaDaTS can address problems related to in-situ, our focus is more widely on workflows that have explicit I/O operations between stages of the workflow. Active Burst Buffer [4] proposes using a file system interface to minimize data movement between the Burst Buffer and parallel file system based on workflow patterns. MaDaTS operates at the middleware layer and will be able to work with technologies like the Active Burst Buffer.

3 MADATS DESIGN AND IMPLEMENTATION

Figure 1a shows the traditional way of executing workflows in an HPC environment. Users explicitly stage the input data to a storage layer (e.g., scratch), and then execute the tasks using the staged data. Finally, the output data is staged out to some persistent storage for long-term storage and analysis. The data movement between the storage layers is often constrained to the beginning and at the end of workflow execution.

We have designed MaDaTS to provide data management that works with existing workflow frameworks. MaDaTS generates a data management plan for moving the data between storage layers. It works in concert with workflow frameworks to execute the workflow and managing its data at run time in accordance to the data management plan. MaDaTS provides different strategies and policies that allow varying levels of control over the data management and movement during workflow execution without modifying the existing workflows and/or the batch schedulers. In the context of MaDaTS, we propose the concept of a Virtual Data Space (VDS) (Figure 1b). VDS is an abstract workspace that enables implicit data management for scientific workflows in a multi-tiered storage. It hides the complexities of the storage hierarchy and provides a simple and flexible interface to manage data for a workflow.

Figure 2 shows the high-level architecture of MaDaTS, with the Virtual Data Space (VDS) as its central component. In MaDaTS, users submit a workflow description containing the information about the workflow tasks and appropriate "hints" for the workflow data. For example, a user might specify that a particular input data set's size can be used for staging decisions. MaDaTS creates a VDS for every workflow. The VDS Coordinator manages VDS through virtual data objects that represents the data elements of a workflow and maps them to the underlying file systems. MaDaTS uses the hints and data management policies to create data tasks that orchestrates the movement of data across the memory-storage hierarchy. Next, an extended workflow consisting of compute and data tasks is created. The extended workflow is submitted through a job script to submit the workflow through a batch scheduler like Slurm. Once the job is submitted and resources are allocated, Tigres manages the execution of the workflow tasks on HPC resources. The data tasks in the workflow interact with the storage system to move data between the storage layers.

3.1 Workflow Description and Data Hints

MaDaTS uses a workflow description to derive data dependencies within a workflow, and generate policies to manage data during workflow execution. MaDaTS's workflow description extends current descriptions that specify the tasks and their dependencies by including their resource requirements (including number of CPUs, walltime etc.), and their input/output data sets. The workflow description may contain "hints" on the data that help MaDaTS to select the storage layer where the data can be moved during workflow execution. These hints can be provided by the users as additional annotations to a workflow description, describing various properties about the data. The hints provide information about the storage and quality of service requirements for workflows. For example, a data hint `persist = true` suggests that the data needs to be persisted for long-term storage and MaDaTS needs to stage the data out to a persistent storage. Similarly, a user might specify a data size that helps MaDaTS decide the appropriate storage layer for the workflow data. In addition to the data hints, MaDaTS uses different data management strategies - storage aware, workflow aware and passive (more details in Section 3.5) to decide if and when to move the data. In the absence of data hints, if the data management strategy requires the data to be moved, MaDaTS always moves the data to the storage layer with the highest throughput. Thus, users can skip specifying the data hints and MaDaTS still tries to aggressively optimize the I/O performance of the workflow.

Figure 3 provides a partial example of a workflow description, annotated with data hints. In this workflow description, a task `task1` is defined with certain inputs and outputs. Each input and output of the workflow task maps to a unique virtual data object which has an identifier. Each task definition contains information

```
task_definitions = ({
    task = 'task1';
    inputs = ['vdo_in1', 'vdo_in2'];
    outputs = ['vdo_out1'];
    cpus = 1024;
    walltime = '00:30:00'; ...}, ...);
data_properties = ({
    name = 'vdo_out1';
    size = '1G';
    persist = true; ...}, ...);
data_management_strategy = 'STRATEGY';
```

Figure 3: A workflow description contains task definitions, hints to the data elements and a data management strategy for MaDaTS.

about resource requirements for executing the task. In this example, the size and persistence hints are specified for vdo_out1. Our initial implementation accepts hints about the data-size, persistence and replication. These hints help MaDaTS to select the appropriate storage layer for accessing the data in the workflow. The existing set of hints are identified by our use cases, where workflows have both small (in KBs) and large (in GBs) data sets and where only part of the output data needs to be preserved for long-term storage. However, this is extensible to include other properties/hints since the data hints are specified as name-value pairs.

3.2 VDS Coordinator

The VDS Coordinator in MaDaTS manages virtual data objects and hides the complexities of managing data between the storage layers. The VDS Coordinator is responsible for managing the data on the memory-storage hierarchy and prepare a data execution plan. Its goal is to minimize data movement by keeping the data 'alive' in the selected storage layer throughout the lifetime of their associated tasks. Essentially, it copies and keeps the data in a selected storage layer until all the associated tasks of the virtual data object finish execution. Based on the data management strategy (described in Section 3.5), VDS Coordinator creates data movement tasks and associates them with the corresponding virtual data objects. Next, the VDS Coordinator generates an extended workflow consisting of compute and data tasks. It creates a directed acyclic graph (DAG) of the extended workflow and generates an execution order of the workflow tasks. Finally, it creates and submits a job script, consisting of a Tigres workflow, to the batch scheduler.

Tigres workflow library is used to execute the directed acyclic graph (DAG) generated by the VDS Coordinator. Since MaDaTS submits the workflow through a batch scheduler, it currently supports two job execution modes – i) single-job, which uses a single resource allocation for the entire workflow, and ii) multi-job, which uses separate allocation of resources for each task of the workflow. In the single-job execution mode, the VDS Coordinator creates a single job submission script for the entire workflow and uses Tigres to manage the execution of tasks on the allocated HPC resources. In the multi-job execution mode, VDS Coordinator creates a separate job submission script for each task of the workflow which is managed by the batch scheduler.

In order to maximize task throughput and resource usage, MaDaTS uses a *binning* technique to combine independent parallel

---

Algorithm 1 Task binning and deferring for just-in-time staging.

Input: Workflow DAG, W and task bins bin

1: Initialize $bin_j = 0 \; \forall \; j \in jobs_W$
2: **for** j in $jobs_W$ **do**
3:     **for** d in $dependents_j$ **do**
4:         **if** $bin_d < bin_j + 1$ **then**
5:             $bin_d = bin_j + 1$
6:         **end if**
7:     **end for**
8: **end for**
9: **for** j in $jobs_W$ **do**
10:     $bin_{min} = n_{bins}$
11:     **for** d in $dependents_j$ **do**
12:         $bin_{min} = Min(bin_d, bin_{min})$
13:     **end for**
14:     $bin_j = Max(bin_j, bin_{min} - 1)$
15: **end for**

---

tasks of the workflow into a single bin. First, MaDaTS determines the execution order of the tasks within a workflow by topologically sorting the DAG to combine tasks into bins. This step ensures that the order of the workflow tasks is based on their dependencies. MaDaTS then puts the tasks into separate bins by doing a breadth-first search (BFS) on the DAG. Hence, each bin ends up with workflow tasks that are independent of each other. The bins are sorted and executed in sequence from lower to higher, corresponding to starting and ending tasks of a workflow respectively. MaDaTS further optimizes the execution order of the tasks by *deferring* some tasks to a higher bin such that each task executes just prior to its dependent task. This minimizes the wait time between the subsequent tasks in the workflow and enables *just-in-time* data staging.

Algorithm 1 is used for binning and deferring workflow tasks to higher bins. Lines 1-8 finds the earliest (minimum) bin of each dependent task. Lines 9-15 then assigns the task to the bin that is just before the lowest bin of its dependent tasks. This ensures that the data staging occurs just prior to executing the tasks using it. Line 14 defers the stage-out tasks to higher bins. This is to ensure that in case of synchronous stage-out, the compute tasks do not unnecessarily wait for their completion.

The workflow tasks and bins are executed by Tigres. Each bin, consists of independent parallel tasks, is executed using the *parallel* template. The bins themselves, on the other hand, are executed in sequence. In the multi-job mode, MaDaTS manages the execution order of bins by specifying job dependencies through the batch scheduler. Each bin of the workflow is executed as a single batch job and all the bins are submitted at the same time through Slurm using the dependency specifier `--dependency=afterok:<job-id>`. The dependency specifier explicitly notifies Slurm not to execute a job until all of its dependencies have finished execution.

3.3 Virtual Data Object

A virtual data object is an abstract entity in VDS that is uniquely identified by an object identifier. Each object identifier is a combination of a storage identifier and path to the data object relative to the storage mount point. Figure 4 shows the mapping of a data object in the storage system to a virtual data object in VDS. The example maps the data object `/global/scratch/sample/foo` to a virtual data object `scratch:sample/foo`. Since `/global/scratch/sample/foo` represents the absolute path of the data object `foo` on the `scratch` storage (mounted on `/global/scratch`), the corresponding object identifier for the virtual data object in VDS is `scratch:sample/foo`. The storage identifier uniquely identifies the storage layer in the multi-tiered storage hierarchy. Storage system abstractions (more details in Section 3.4) resolve the virtual data object identifier to the corresponding physical location of the data object on the file system.

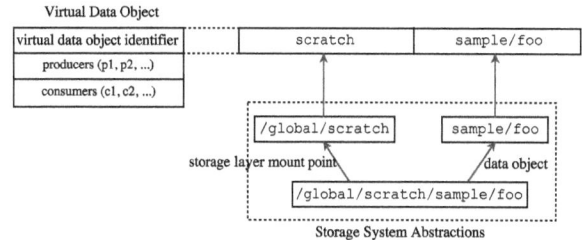

Figure 4: Example virtual data object in VDS that corresponds to a data object in the storage system.

In addition to the virtual data object identifier, each virtual data object consists of *producer* and *consumer* tasks. Hence, a collection of virtual data objects within a VDS provides a **data-centric** representation of workflows, where each data object is a node and the tasks are its edges. Producers are the tasks that generate the data object and consumer tasks use the data object. Using the data object from a different storage layer in a workflow now simply means replacing the storage layer for the virtual data object. Hence, this provides a simple abstraction for managing the data on multiple storage tiers without explicitly modifying the tasks.

VDS supports the data-centric model of workflows. In the era of big data and multi-tiered hierarchical storage, we need to move towards the data-centric model of workflows [1]. Data management is going to be the principal challenge with increasing volume and rate of data. Performance and efficiency of workflows now depend on efficiently utilizing the storage resources to manage data during execution. The data-centric model of workflows allows us to make data management decisions by examining each data object over the lifecycle, rather than just looking at individual tasks. In the data-centric model of a workflow, data objects are treated as first-class parameters to the workflow tasks. This results in a data-driven workflow execution, where a task can be executed as soon as the data it uses becomes available.

3.4 Abstractions

MaDaTS provides a two-level abstraction – at the VDS and system levels. The abstractions provide flexibility for managing workflow data in tiered storage. VDS provides different operations on virtual data objects to abstract the data management across multiple storage layers. These abstractions hide the complexities of data management and yet provide users control to manage data for scientific workflows in a tiered storage. Storage system abstractions hide the low-level complexities of the multi-tiered hierarchical storage system. These abstractions also provide the interface to connect different workflow engines and tools.

Abstraction	Description
create()	creates a virtual data space (VDS)
destroy()	deletes the VDS for a workflow
add(V)	adds virtual data object *V* to the VDS
copy(V,s)	copies virtual data object *V* to storage layer *s*
delete(V)	removes virtual data object *V* from the VDS

Table 1: Data abstractions in MaDaTS.

Data Abstractions. MaDaTS provide data abstractions to manage a virtual data space (VDS) and to manage virtual data objects within the VDS. Table 1 lists these abstractions to manage a VDS through two simple interfaces – i) create and ii) destroy. Once a VDS is created, it provides three basic operations on virtual data objects to abstract data management across the storage layers using – i) add, ii) copy, and iii) delete. The add and delete are used to create and remove the virtual objects from VDS. The copy operation on a virtual data object creates a new virtual data object on a specific storage layer and copies all the producers and consumers of the original virtual data object to the new one. These operations provide the foundation for the VDS Coordinator to implement different data management strategies through VDS. Although these operations are sufficient for managing the workflow data across the storage layers, new operations can be added to VDS when MaDaTS interfaces with other storage systems and workflow engines. Once the workflow execution ends, the associated VDS and its virtual data objects are deleted.

Algorithm 2 Creating data tasks to manage virtual data objects in VDS.

Input: A virtual data object v, destination storage layer s, and associated virtual data space *VDS*

1: $v' = VDS.copy(v,s)$
2: **if** v has no *producers* and has *consumers* **then**
3:     $task = T(v \rightarrow v')$
4:     $producers_{v'} = [task]$
5:     $consumers_v = [task]$
6: **else if** v has no *consumers* and has *producers* **then**
7:     $task = T(v' \rightarrow v)$
8:     $producers_v = [task]$
9:     $consumers_{v'}.append(task)$
10:    $consumers_v = []$
11: **else**
12:    $VDS.delete(v)$
13: **end if**

VDS Coordinator manages the virtual data objects in VDS through the data operations. The VDS Coordinator creates and adds a virtual data object to a VDS, using the add operation. Based on the data management strategy, it creates a data task (Algorithm 2) that copies the data between storage systems. The data task abstracts the data movement between storage systems from the user. It creates a data task corresponding to each data movement that is introduced by MaDaTS. It copies the source virtual data object to the destination storage system using the copy operation (Line 1). If data needs to be moved, it creates a data task for both stage-in (Lines 2-5) and stage-out (Lines 6-10) operations. If no data needs

to be moved, it simply deletes the old virtual data object using the delete operation and replaces it with the new data object (Line 11-12). This corresponds to intermediate workflow data that need not persist beyond the workflow execution.

Storage System Abstractions. Storage system abstractions provide interfaces to access data objects across multiple layers in the storage hierarchy. They provide translation of virtual data objects into file system data objects through various file system interfaces over the multi-tiered storage. They provide different mount points corresponding to the different storage layers in the hierarchy. A data object in the storage layer is accessed via the file system path relative to the mount point of the storage layer.

Our initial prototype implementation provides storage system abstractions through a storage configuration, which maintains the hierarchy of storage systems. Storage tiers can be added with hints on its properties or removed from the configuration file and MaDaTS moves the workflow data between the storage tiers specified through the configuration file. MaDaTS implements a hashtable mapping of the storage identifiers to the corresponding mount points in the storage system. For example, if /global/scratch is the mount point of the scratch file system, then the hashtable contains the mapping scratch → /global/scratch. This mapping is used to create virtual data objects in VDS corresponding to data objects in the file system. There can be multiple file system interfaces to a storage system. In the future, we envision that a tighter protocol between storage systems, file systems and VDS can be developed which would further improve the performance and hide the complexity.

Workflow Plug-ins. MaDaTS is implemented in C and Python, and prepares the data management plan through a description of a workflow provided by the user. The description is a set of key-value pairs describing the tasks and the data for the workflow. This provides a simple interface to represent different workflows into a format that MaDaTS understands. Standard workflow engines have workflow description formats and XML schemas that can be easily translated into the workflow description that MaDaTS uses by parsing the description files. The description also contains resource requirements pertaining to a workflow and the HPC system. This allows for an easy adaptation of the workflow and data management strategies on different HPC systems, without modifying the underlying architecture of MaDaTS.

The workflow DAG that is generated by the VDS Coordinator provides a workflow execution and data management abstraction to Tigres. Tigres templates are used to execute the workflow DAG that includes the data management tasks through a Tigres workflow script. MaDaTS currently provides different interfaces to optimize the execution order of the workflow DAG by binning and deferring task executions. Other workflow engines can be plugged into MaDaTS by including translators. First, we would need a translator that takes the user provided workflow DAG and translates it to MaDaTS's workflow description format. Second, a workflow engine could translate MaDaTS's data plan and convert it to its workflow description format. In previous work, Tigres workflows have been converted to other formats [3].

Type	Criteria	Strategy	Effectiveness
Storage-aware (VDS-STA)	storage and data properties	data for which the I/O performance improves	data caching
Workflow-aware (VDS-WFA)	structure of the workflow	only if data movement can be overlapped	data staging
User-driven (VDS-Passive)	user-defined rules	explicit data movement	application-specific
Traditional	-	explicitly move data before and after execution	-

Table 2: Data management strategies: the first three highlight the features of MaDaTS strategies. The traditional approach highlights managing data manually through separate scripts or tools that move data before and after running workflows.

3.5 Data Management Strategies

The VDS Coordinator in MaDaTS manages the data in a workflow by creating data tasks and each data task is created based on selected data management strategy. MaDaTS currently provides three data management strategies that provide varying levels of control – i) storage-aware (VDS-STA), which uses data hints and storage layer properties to define data management policies, ii) workflow-aware (VDS-WFA), which considers the structure of the workflow to optimize the data management policies, and iii) user-driven (VDS-Passive), which lets users describe the policies for managing the data. Table 2 summarizes the three data management strategies that MaDaTS supports. MaDaTS has been designed such that other strategies can be implemented as needed.

Storage-aware (VDS-STA). MaDaTS uses a storage function to select the appropriate storage layer based on certain properties, for each data object in the workflow. The storage function selects the 'lowest' storage layer for a data object that satisfies the properties. These properties consist of storage capacity read-write throughput, data-size, persistency etc. VDS-STA generates data movement tasks only if the storage layer satisfying the data requirements is different from the original data object storage. This strategy is useful when the workflow will benefit from 'caching' the data on a faster storage.

Workflow-aware (VDS-WFA). MaDaTS considers the structure of a workflow to define the 'when' and 'where' of the data movement. With VDS-WFA, VDS coordinator overlaps data movement with workflow tasks. If there are preceding tasks to the consumers of a virtual data object, then a data task is created that copies the virtual data object to a faster storage layer. A data task can also be created if there are succeeding tasks to the producers of a virtual data object, which copies the data out from a fast storage to a specific persistent storage. If no overlap is possible, then no data is moved between the storage layers. VDS-WFA is useful when data staging is part of the workflow execution. This data management strategy optimizes the I/O performance by selectively moving the data, thereby reducing the overheads of data movement.

User-driven (VDS-Passive).: MaDaTS directly maps the virtual data object to the workflow data. Data is moved, only when specified by the user. Users can use virtual data objects to create data tasks and explicitly move data between storage layers. All the data objects are generated and used from the storage layer specified by the user, for a workflow task. When users need to explicitly place the data based on application choices, VDS-Passive is the best choice.

4 EVALUATION

In this section, we evaluate the performance and resource usage of scientific workflows using MaDaTS. We compare our results against the traditional approach of executing workflows and managing data, where data is explicitly moved before and after the workflow execution using ad hoc scripts or data movement tools.

4.1 Evaluation Setup

We evaluated our system on Phase I of NERSC's Cori supercomputer. It is a Cray XC40 supercomputer with 1630 compute nodes. Each node has 32 cores and has 128 GB DDR4 2133 MHz memory and four 16 GB DIMMs per socket. Each core has its own L1 and L2 caches, with 64 KB and 256 KB, respectively.

For compute jobs, Cori provides multiple storage options with three different file systems that provides different throughput, storage space, and period for data retention. The GPFS based 'project' file system has a peak performance of 40 GBps and typically used for longer term storage of frequently accessed files. The filesystem used for I/O during job execution is 'scratch' which is a Lustre file system with peak performance of approximately 700 GBps. Cori's 'Burst Buffer' architecture is built upon discrete *Burst Buffer nodes* (BB nodes), each containing two Intel P3608 SSDs that deliver 6.4 TB of usable capacity and 5.7 GBps of bandwidth. Currently, Cori has a total of 144 BB nodes with over 800 GBps of peak performance. The BB nodes are managed by the Cray Datawarp API. Through a job script users can either specify datawarp directives or use Linux commands to move the data between the Burst Buffer and other parallel file systems. The job scripts are submitted and scheduled to run through the Slurm batch scheduler. MaDaTS uses the DataWarp API to manage data on BB nodes on Cori.

4.2 Workloads

We evaluate VDS Coordinator using synthetic and real I/O intensive science workflows. Figure 5 shows the different data and execution patterns of the workflows. The workflows use data sets of varying sizes, accessed at different stages in the workflows. Each workflow has a different data placement and access requirement, where data can be either shared or distributed across the workflow tasks. The workflows also cover fairly different execution patterns that can be composed using the basic templates in Tigres.

Science Workflows. We use three science workflows with varying I/O and execution characteristics and are a combination of one or more of the basic workflow patterns (i.e., sequence, parallel, split, merge). *CAMP* is an I/O and metadata intensive workflow. We use an optimized version of the CAMP workflow, where each computation task builds its own sqlite database (builddb) and a subsequent task reprojects the input data (set of 1-2 MB HDF4 files) from a coordinate system to a tiling system (reproject). The workflow processes one month's input data of size approx. 54 GB. CAMP has three stages of parallel tasks (Figure 5a). Each task in

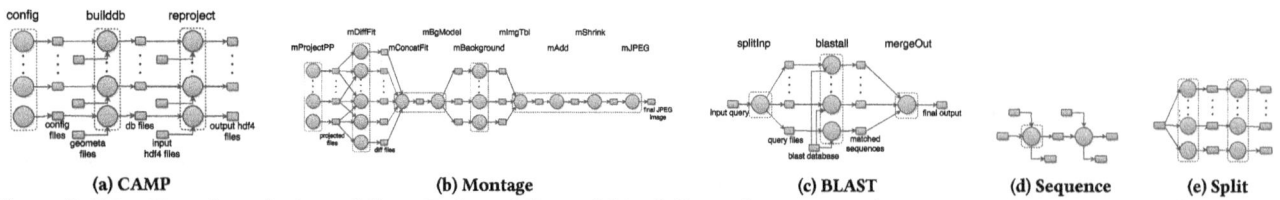

(a) CAMP   (b) Montage   (c) BLAST   (d) Sequence   (e) Split

Figure 5: Scientific and synthetic workflows: Each workflow exhibits different data access and execution pattern. CAMP transforms NASA MODIS satellite data from a coordinate system to a tiling system. Montage assembles an image for survey M17 on band j from 2mass Atlas images. BLAST performs protein sequence matching using a shared large protein database. Sequence and split workflows are synthetic I/O intensive workflows where each task reads and writes files using the 'dd' utility.

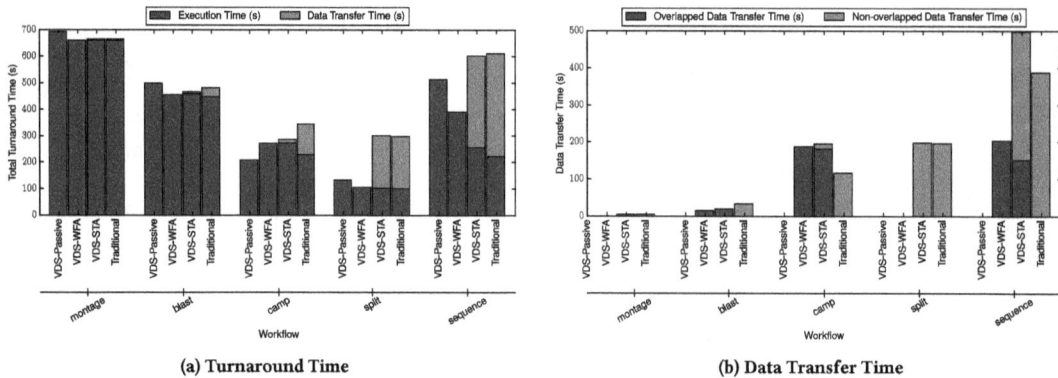

(a) Turnaround Time   (b) Data Transfer Time

Figure 6: Comparison of workflow performance under different data management strategies: VDS-WFA performs better than the other data management strategies for all the workflows except CAMP. For CAMP, VDS-Passive performs better than VDS-WFA because CAMP is dominated by data transfers, and not the computation tasks.

the subsequent stages use the data from the previous stage and some additional input files, which are used only during that stage.

Montage is a data-intensive workflow that assembles a jpeg image from sky survey data (fits files). Montage is combination of sequential and parallel tasks (Figure 5b) and requires all the input data in a single directory prior to executing the workflow. Each fits file is 1 MB in size, and a total of 23 GB of data is processed for degree 5.0 of the Montage workflow.

BLAST is a compute-intensive workflow that matches protein sequences against a large database (> 6 GB). BLAST splits an input file (7500 protein sequences for our tests) into multiple small files (a few KBs) and then uses parallel tasks to compare the data in those files to that of a large shared database (Figure 5c). It finally merges all the outputs from the parallel tasks into a single file.

Synthetic Workflows. The synthetic workflows are based on the basic workflow patterns as described in [24]. We use *sequence* and *split* synthetic workflows. In the sequence workflow the output of one task is used as an input to another task. In addition to previous task's inputs, each task also uses an independent external input. A split workflow has a single task that sets up parallel tasks. Each task of the synthetic workflow uses dd to read and write files. The workflows also correspond to different file I/O patterns in scientific workflows. The sequence workflow corresponds to sequential read and write pattern. The split workflow uses a shared and parallel read write pattern.

Metric (unit)	Description
Execution time (s)	Time to complete all the tasks in a workflow
Data transfer time (s)	Time to move data between the storage layers
Turnaround time (s)	Workflow execution time + Data transfer time
Total space used (GB)	Amount of space used on a storage layer
Total CPU time (hrs)	Task execution time * Number of cores allocated to task

Table 3: Metrics for evaluation.

Table 3 lists the metrics used for our evaluation. The metrics include execution time, data transfer time, turnaround time, space used, resources used, measure the performance and efficiency of the workflows with respect to the run time and storage space requirements.

4.3 VDS Coordinator Data Management Strategies

In this section, we evaluate the three MaDaTS data management strategies (Table 2). We compare the results against the traditional approach of managing data and executing workflows that enables data movement through job scripts outside of the actual workflow

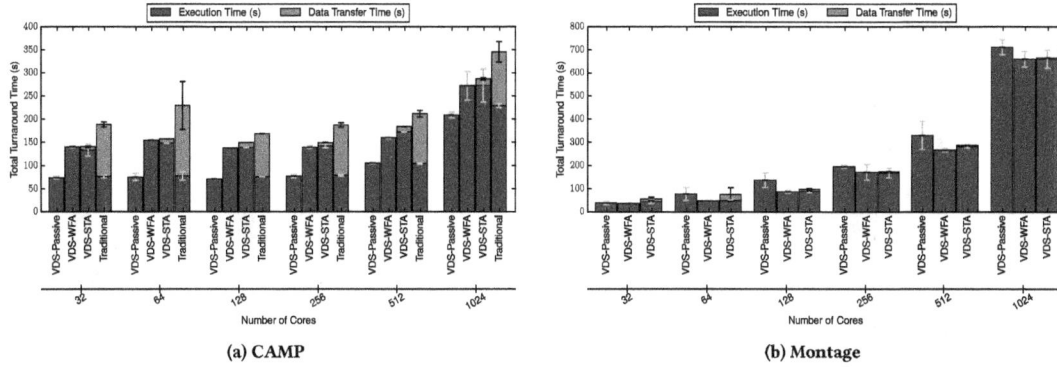

(a) CAMP
(b) Montage

Figure 7: Weak scaling results for CAMP and Montage: All the MaDaTS strategies scale uniformly with increasing data size and number of compute resources. One or more of the MaDaTS strategies scale consistently better than the traditional approach. For Montage, traditional approach shows similar results to VDS-STA. The overall performance starts decreasing at 1024 for MaDaTS strategies due to the limitations of the application, but they always perform better or at par to the traditional approach.

execution (i.e., data is moved only before and after the workflow execution). We show the average over five runs in the plots except for BLAST. BLAST encountered system issues since the BB usage modes are still evolving, We were only able to run BLAST experiments once each. We used one job-script per workflow when using single-job execution mode unless otherwise mentioned.

Workflow Turnaround Time. Figure 6 shows the turnaround time and overlapping data transfer time under different data management strategies (Table 2) for different synthetic (sequence and split) and science workflows (Montage, BLAST, CAMP). Workflow turnaround time is calculated from start of the first workflow task (including the data movement) to end of the workflow execution. For each workflow, we compare the results of storage-aware (VDS-STA), workflow-aware (VDS-WFA) and user-driven (VDS-Passive) data management strategies to the traditional approach. While using VDS-Passive, we use the Lustre parallel file system to store workflow data and avoid moving data to the Burst Buffer. Figure 6a shows that VDS-WFA always performs better than the traditional approach because it overlaps the movement of data and the execution of tasks, whenever possible (Figure 6b). In addition to the overlapping data movement, VDS-WFA is opportunistic and also moves the data selectively based on the workflow structure. Hence, it always performs better than the traditional approach. VDS-STA moves all the data larger than a threshold (> 1 MB in this case) to the Burst Buffer. Since all the workflows process large amounts of data, VDS-STA moves almost all the data to the Burst Buffer, but overlapping any computation, whenever possible. Its worst case matches the traditional approach when all the data needs to be moved but when data movement does not overlap with the compute stages.

Figure 6 also shows that VDS-Passive results in lower turnaround times than the traditional approach for all workflows except Montage and BLAST. These two workflows have very small data transfer overheads and have I/O patterns that can benefit from the Burst Buffer. VDS-Passive performs better overall by not moving the data, when compared to the traditional approach. VDS-Passive also performs better than VDS-WFA for CAMP because CAMP is dominated by data transfers, and not the the execution time of the

Workflow	Space Saved (GB)	% Space Saved
sequence	400.0	57.06
split	200.0	66.44
camp	1.0	18.18
blast	0.49	4.55

Table 4: Amount of space saved with VDS-WFA as compared to using the traditional approach of executing workflows.

tasks. Overall, we see that the different data management strategies in MaDaTS provide significant benefits for all the workflows and allow users to select the appropriate strategy based on the workflow requirements. Typically, workflows that benefit from caching the data to fast storage like the Burst Buffer, benefit from using VDS-STA. Workflows that need to stage the data during workflow execution benefit from using VDS-WFA (e.g., sequence workflow). Finally, workflows that are dominated by data transfers (e.g., CAMP) benefit by using custom data rules for moving data.

Storage Requirements. The Burst Buffer provides additional performance. However, it also comes at an additional usage cost that is calculated differently by different sites. Thus, it is important that it is used optimally. Table 4 shows the amount of space saved for each workflow when using VDS-WFA relative to the traditional approach. The storage requirements for each strategy is calculated based on the total space used on the Burst Buffer. The amount of space saved is the difference between the storage used by the MaDaTS strategies and the traditional approach. VDS-WFA uses 4% - 66% less space as compared to the traditional approach.

VDS-WFA strategy allows MaDaTS to selectively move the data between the different storage layers, thereby reducing the total space used on Burst Buffer while executing the workflows. The storage space savings for BLAST are smaller because large part of the total data (i.e., the BLAST database > 6 GB) gets copied to the Burst Buffer in both approaches. Only the inputs and the outputs (which are only a few MBs) are used directly from the final storage (scratch Lustre file system). The output data in CAMP, which is large part of the total data, gets generated directly at the target storage layer, saving 18% of the Burst Buffer space. For split and

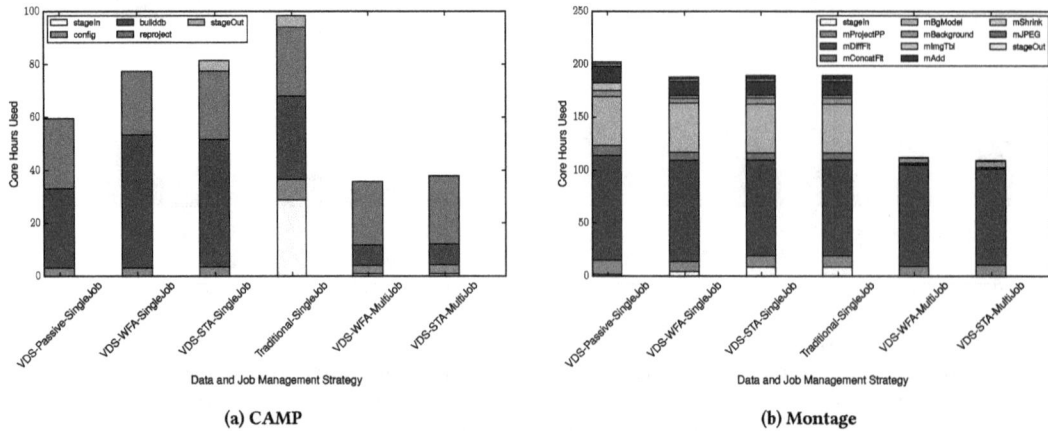

(a) CAMP   (b) Montage

Figure 8: Total CPU time (in core hours) for CAMP and Montage under different MaDaTS strategies: Multi-job execution mode with VDS-WFA uses the least amount of CPU time, implying maximum usage and minimum wastage of compute resources during workflow execution.

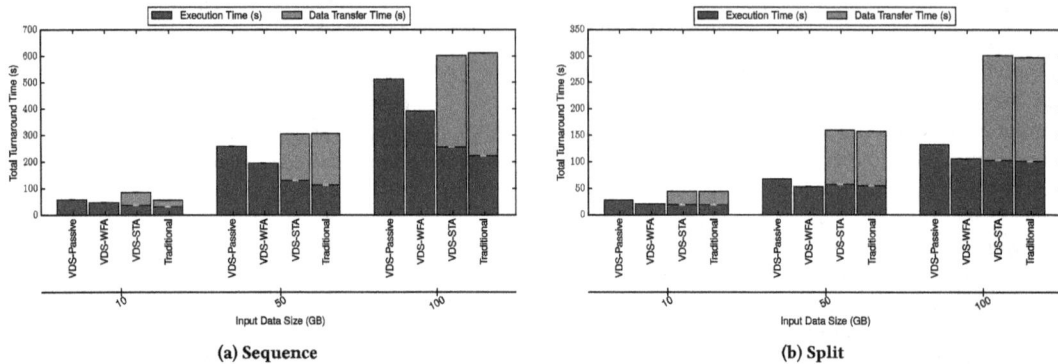

(a) Sequence   (b) Split

Figure 9: Effect of increasing data-size on sequence and split workflows: Both sequence and split workflows benefit from overlapping and selective data movement of VDS-WFA. It minimizes the overheads of data movement, whereas the overheads continue to increase with increasing data sizes for the traditional approach.

sequence workflows, only the intermediate data sets are generated and used from the Burst Buffer, whereas the large input and output data sets are stored on the target storage system. Thus, this leads to a saved storage space of to up to 66%. This shows that the storage savings from MaDaTS's strategies will be higher for workflows with larger input and output data.

Scalability. Figure 7 compares the performance of different data management strategies with weak scaling (from 32 to 1024 cores) for CAMP and Montage. In weak scaling, we increase the number of tasks with increasing cores and increasing data sizes. All three MaDaTS data management strategies scale better than the traditional approach for the two workflows. However, at 1024 cores the performance deteriorates due to application limitations (i.e., load on the metadata server [6]).

Montage requires its data to be present in a single working directory, and much of the performance gain is due to the intermediate files being written on to the fast storage. Figure 7b shows that with increasing data size and number of tasks, VDS-WFA and VDS-STA tend to perform better as compared to VDS-Passive since cost of data movement is low and the I/O performance improves

significantly when the data is on Burst Buffer. For Montage, the traditional approach shows similar results to VDS-STA while scaling up, because the data movement stages are similar for both.

Total CPU Time. In this section, we evaluate the two job execution modes (single-job and multi-job) in MaDaTS along with the data management strategies for CAMP and Montage. We compare the core hours used under both execution modes for different data management strategies (Figure 8). X-axis of the graph shows the data management strategies with the job execution mode. Y-axis shows core hours for each strategy. The maximum number of nodes requested for the parallel tasks in both workflows was set to 32 (= 1024 cores). Hence, the single-job execution mode requested 1024 cores for the entire execution of the workflow job-script, whereas the multi-job execution requested as many cores as are required by each stage of the workflow, up to a maximum of 1024 cores.

Figure 8a shows that the traditional approach for CAMP consumes large core hours for data transfers. It uses a single allocation of resources for the entire workflow execution. MaDaTS' multi-job strategy uses less core hours as each task of the workflow consumes only as many resources as required by the task. Figure 8b shows

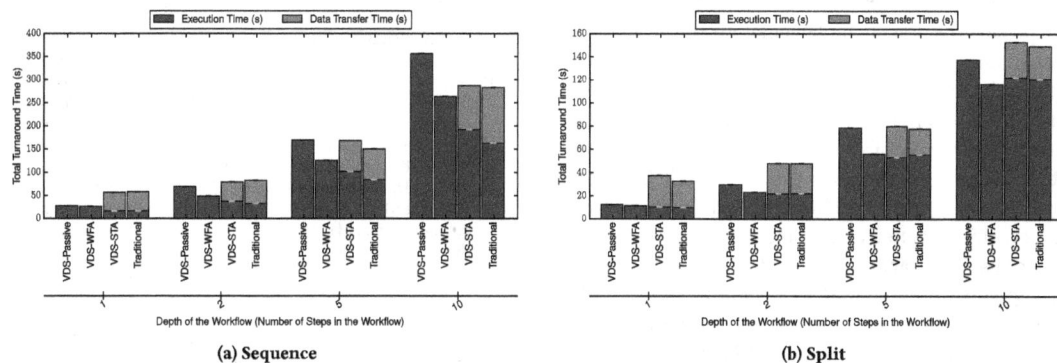

(a) Sequence   (b) Split

Figure 10: Effect of the depth of workflow on sequence and split workflows: Both the workflows benefit from VDS-WFA due to overlapping and selective data movement. However, with the increasing depth of the workflow, the initial cost of moving the data for VDS-STA and the traditional approach is overshadowed by the performance gains of caching the intermediate data.

significant differences in core hours used between the single-job and multi-job strategies. The large number of sequence stages in Montage have resources allocated but not used in a single-job mode.

4.4 Factors Affecting Data Management Strategies

In this section, we study the impact of the data management strategies in MaDaTS. Specifically, we evaluate three workflows characteristics – a) size of data, b) depth of workflow, and c) width of workflow. We use synthetic sequence and split workflows.

Effect of Workflow Data Size. Figure 9 shows the effect of increasing data size on workflow turnaround time. X-axis shows the aggregate input size for each workflow. Each workflow has two dependent stages and there are ten parallel tasks in each stage of the split workflow. As can be seen from the figure, for both sequence and split workflows VDS-WFA performs better with increasing data sizes by minimizing the data movements between the storage layers. The difference in turnaround times between VDS-WFA and the other data management strategies increase as we increase the input data sizes because larger data sets are moved between the storage layers when using the other strategies.

Effect of Workflow Depth. Figure 10 shows the effect of different data management strategies on turnaround time with increasing depth of the workflows. The depth of the workflow refers to the number of stages in the workflow. X-axis shows the number of stages in the workflow. The input data size is 10 GB per task and the split workflow has ten tasks per stage. As shown in the figure, VDS-WFA performs better for both the workflows with increasing data sizes. VDS-STA and the traditional approach have significantly lower execution times because of the improved I/O performance through Burst Buffer. However, due to large data transfer times both the strategies suffer a slowdown in turnaround time. VDS-Passive I/O performance degrades when not using Burst Buffer due to increasing data sizes that affects the overall performance of the workflow.

Effect of Workflow Width. Figure 11 shows the effect of increasing width of the split workflow on turnaround time. The X-axis of the graph shows the number of parallel tasks (from 2 to 10) for each stage in the workflow. The total input data size is 100 GB

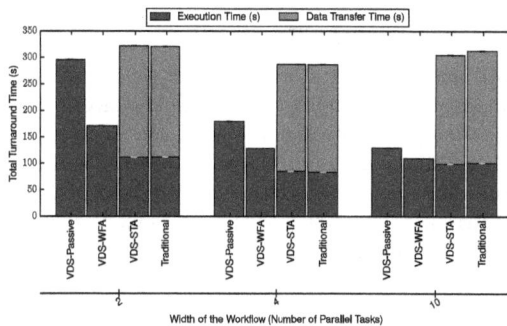

Figure 11: Effect of the workflow width on the split workflow: VDS-WFA and VDS-Passive continue to perform better by avoiding unnecessary data movements. With increasing number of parallel tasks, the I/o performance of VDS-WFA and VDS-Passive continue to improve, whereas for the traditional approach the performance remains the same due to staging overheads.

that is split between the tasks equally and the workflow has two stages (i.e., depth=2). The results show that with increasing number of parallel tasks, MaDaTS strategies perform significantly better or at par to the traditional approach. Again, due to selective and overlapping data movement, VDS-WFA performs much better with increasing number of parallel I/O tasks in the workflow.

4.5 Summary

MaDaTS improves the performance of scientific workflows by providing different data management strategies for different requirements. Workflows with significant I/O and that can benefit from caching data (e.g., Montage) benefit by using VDS-STA. Sequence and split workflows that need to manage data as part of the workflow execution benefit from VDS-WFA. Workflow with dominant data transfer stages (e.g., CAMP) benefits from VDS-Passive. VDS-WFA used up to 66% less storage space as compared to the traditional approach, when using multiple storage layers. Our weak scaling experiments up to 1024 cores showed that MaDaTS as well as the underlying software systems scale to run multi-job workflows on HPC resources and is only limited by application characteristics.

5 CONCLUSIONS AND FUTURE WORK

In this paper, we present the design, implementation and evaluation of MaDaTS, that enables management of workflow data on multi-tiered storage hierarchy on HPC systems. MaDaTS uses virtual data space to map user-level requirements to system-level abstractions. We demonstrate through the use of science and synthetic workflows that our infrastructure provides the users flexibility while transparently managing data. Our evaluation shows that MaDaTS enables workflow tools to achieve better turnaround time and resource usage through various data management strategies.

Our current implementation of MaDaTS is built to work with current software stack in HPC systems. However, our design is extensible and enables other workflow engines and batch schedulers to be used with MaDaTS. Additionally, the deeper memory-storage hierarchy is spearheading advancements in file systems and programming models that MaDaTS will be able to leverage in the future.

ACKNOWLEDGMENTS

This work and the resources at NERSC are supported by the U.S. Department of Energy, Office of Science and Office of Advanced Scientific Computing Research (ASCR) under Contract No. DE-AC02-05CH11231, program manager Lucy Nowell. The authors would also like to thank Christopher Daley from NERSC, Harinarayan Krishnan from LBL, and Sudharshan S. Vazhkudai from ORNL for their valuable suggestions and feedback.

REFERENCES

[1] Asif Akram, J Kewley, and Rob Allan. 2006. A Data centric approach for Workflows. In *2006 10th IEEE International Enterprise Distributed Object Computing Conference Workshops (EDOCW'06)*.

[2] William Allcock, John Bresnahan, Rajkumar Kettimuthu, Michael Link, Catalin Dumitrescu, Ioan Raicu, and Ian Foster. 2005. The Globus Striped GridFTP Framework and Server. In *Proceedings of the 2005 ACM/IEEE Conference on Supercomputing (SC '05)*. IEEE Computer Society, Washington, DC, USA, 54–.

[3] Javier Rojas Balderrama, Matthieu Simonin, and Cédric Tedeschi. 2015. *GinFlow: A Decentralised Adaptive Workflow Execution Manager*. Ph.D. Dissertation. Inria.

[4] Chao Chen, Michael Lang, Latchesar Ionkov, and Yong Chen. 2016. Active Burst-Buffer: In-Transit Processing Integrated into Hierarchical Storage. In *Networking, Architecture and Storage (NAS), 2016 IEEE International Conference on*.

[5] Ann L. Chervenak, Robert Schuler, Matei Ripeanu, Muhammad Ali Amer, Shishir Bharathi, Ian Foster, Adriana Iamnitchi, and Carl Kesselman. 2009. The Globus Replica Location Service: Design and Experience. *IEEE Trans. Parallel Distrib. Syst.* 20, 9 (Sept. 2009).

[6] Christopher Daley, Devarshi Ghoshal, Glenn Lockwood, Sudip Dosanjh, Lavanya Ramakrishnan, and Nicholas Wright. 2016. Performance Characterization of Scientific Workflows for the Optimal Use of Burst Buffers. In *11th Workshop on Workflows in Support of Large-Scale Science (WORKS'16)*.

[7] E. Deelman and A. Chervenak. 2008. Data Management Challenges of Data-Intensive Scientific Workflows. In *Cluster Computing and the Grid, 2008. CCGRID '08. 8th IEEE International Symposium on*.

[8] Ewa Deelman, Gurmeet Singh, Mei-Hui Su, James Blythe, Yolanda Gil, Carl Kesselman, Gaurang Mehta, Karan Vahi, G Bruce Berriman, John Good, and others. 2005. Pegasus: A framework for mapping complex scientific workflows onto distributed systems. *Scientific Programming* 13, 3 (2005), 219–237.

[9] Ciprian Docan, Manish Parashar, and Scott Klasky. 2012. DataSpaces: an interaction and coordination framework for coupled simulation workflows. *Cluster Computing* 15, 2 (2012).

[10] Ian T. Foster, Jens-S. Vöckler, Michael Wilde, and Yong Zhao. 2002. Chimera: A Virtual Data System for Representing, Querying, and Automating Data Derivation. In *Proceedings of the 14th International Conference on Scientific and Statistical Database Management (SSDBM '02)*. IEEE Computer Society.

[11] Michael Franklin, Alon Halevy, and David Maier. 2005. From databases to dataspaces: a new abstraction for information management. *ACM Sigmod Record* 34, 4 (2005).

[12] Valerie Hendrix, James Fox, Devarshi Ghoshal, and Lavanya Ramakrishnan. 2016. Tigres workflow library: Supporting scientific pipelines on hpc systems. In

[13] D. Henseler, B. Landsteiner, D. Petesch, C. Wright, and N.J. Wright. 2016. Architecture and Design of Cray DataWarp. In *Cray User Group CUG*.

[14] Stephen Herbein et al. 2016. Scalable I/O-Aware Job Scheduling for Burst Buffer Enabled HPC Clusters. In *Proceedings of the 25th ACM International Symposium on High-Performance Parallel and Distributed Computing (HPDC '16)*.

[15] Chen Jin, Scott Klasky, Stephen Hodson, Weikuan Yu, Jay Lofstead, Hasan Abbasi, Karsten Schwan, Matthew Wolf, W Liao, Alok Choudhary, and others. 2008. Adaptive io system (adios). *Cray User's Group* (2008).

[16] Youngjae Kim, Aayush Gupta, Bhuvan Urgaonkar, Piotr Berman, and Anand Sivasubramaniam. 2011. HybridStore: A Cost-Efficient, High-Performance Storage System Combining SSDs and HDDs. In *Proceedings of the 2011 IEEE 19th Annual International Symposium on Modelling, Analysis, and Simulation of Computer and Telecommunication Systems (MASCOTS '11)*. Washington, DC, USA.

[17] David T. Liu and Michael J. Franklin. 2004. GridDB: A Data-centric Overlay for Scientific Grids. In *the 30th International Conference on Very Large Data Bases*.

[18] N. Liu, J. Cope, P. Carns, C. Carothers, R. Ross, G. Grider, A. Crume, and C. Maltzahn. 2012. On the role of burst buffers in leadership-class storage systems. In *IEEE 28th Symposium on Mass Storage Systems and Technologies (MSST)*.

[19] A. Luckow, L. Lacinski, and S. Jha. 2010. SAGA BigJob: An Extensible and Interoperable Pilot-Job Abstraction for Distributed Applications and Systems. In *2010 10th IEEE/ACM International Conference on Cluster, Cloud and Grid Computing*.

[20] Henry M. Monti, Ali R. Butt, and Sudharshan S. Vazhkudai. 2013. On Timely Staging of HPC Job Input Data. *IEEE Transactions on Parallel and Distributed Systems* 24, 9 (2013).

[21] Bill Nitzberg and Virginia Lo. 1991. Distributed Shared Memory: A Survey of Issues and Algorithms. *Computer* 24, 8 (Aug. 1991).

[22] Ramya Prabhakar, Sudharshan S Vazhkudai, Youngjae Kim, Ali R Butt, Min Li, and Mahmut Kandemir. 2011. Provisioning a multi-tiered data staging area for extreme-scale machines. In *2011 31st International Conference on Distributed Computing Systems (ICDCS)*.

[23] Arcot Rajasekar, Reagan Moore, Chien-yi Hou, Christopher A Lee, Richard Marciano, Antoine de Torcy, Michael Wan, Wayne Schroeder, Sheau-Yen Chen, Lucas Gilbert, and others. 2010. iRODS Primer: integrated rule-oriented data system. *Synthesis Lectures on Information Concepts, Retrieval, and Services* 2, 1 (2010), 1–143.

[24] Lavanya Ramakrishnan and Beth Plale. 2010. A Multi-dimensional Classification Model for Scientific Workflow Characteristics. In *the 1st International Workshop on Workflow Approaches to New Data-centric Science (Wands '10)*. ACM.

[25] Melissa Romanus, Fan Zhang, Tong Jin, Qian Sun, Hoang Bui, Manish Parashar, Jong Choi, Saloman Janhunen, Robert Hager, Scott Klasky, Choong-Seock Chang, and Ivan Rodero. 2016. Persistent Data Staging Services for Data Intensive In-situ Scientific Workflows. In *Proceedings of the ACM International Workshop on Data-Intensive Distributed Computing (DIDC '16)*. ACM, New York, NY, USA, 8.

[26] Masahiro Tanaka and Osamu Tatebe. 2010. Pwrake: A Parallel and Distributed Flexible Workflow Management Tool for Wide-area Data Intensive Computing. In *the 19th ACM International Symposium on High Performance Distributed Computing (HPDC '10)*. ACM, New York, NY, USA.

[27] Ian J Taylor, Ewa Deelman, Dennis B Gannon, and Matthew Shields. 2014. *Workflows for e-Science: scientific workflows for grids*. Springer Publishing Company.

[28] Teng Wang, Sarp Oral, Michael Pritchard, Kevin Vasko, and Weikuan Yu. 2015. Development of a Burst Buffer System for Data-Intensive Applications. *CoRR* (2015).

[29] Michael Wilde, Mihael Hategan, Justin M Wozniak, Ben Clifford, Daniel S Katz, and Ian Foster. 2011. Swift: A language for distributed parallel scripting. *Parallel Comput.* 37, 9 (2011).

[30] Matei Zaharia, Mosharaf Chowdhury, Tathagata Das, Ankur Dave, Justin Ma, Murphy McCauley, Michael J. Franklin, Scott Shenker, and Ion Stoica. 2012. Resilient Distributed Datasets: A Fault-tolerant Abstraction for In-memory Cluster Computing. In *Proceedings of the 9th USENIX Conference on Networked Systems Design and Implementation (NSDI'12)*. USENIX Association, Berkeley, CA, USA, 15–28.

[31] F. Zhang, C. Docan, M. Parashar, S. Klasky, N. Podhorszki, and H. Abbasi. 2012. Enabling In-situ Execution of Coupled Scientific Workflow on Multi-core Platform. In *26th International Parallel Distributed Processing Symposium (IPDPS)*.

[32] G. Zhang, L. Chiu, C. Dickey, L. Liu, P. Muench, and S. Seshadri. 2010. Automated lookahead data migration in SSD-enabled multi-tiered storage systems. In *2010 IEEE 26th Symposium on Mass Storage Systems and Technologies (MSST)*.

[33] Zhe Zhang, Chao Wang, Sudharshan S. Vazhkudai, Xiaosong Ma, Gregory G. Pike, John W. Cobb, and Frank Mueller. 2007. Optimizing Center Performance Through Coordinated Data Staging, Scheduling and Recovery. In *the 2007 ACM/IEEE Conference on Supercomputing (SC '07)*. ACM, New York, NY, USA.

[34] Fang Zheng, Hasan Abbasi, Ciprian Docan, Jay Lofstead, Qing Liu, Scott Klasky, Manish Parashar, Norbert Podhorszki, Karsten Schwan, and Matthew Wolf. 2010. PreDatA–preparatory data analytics on peta-scale machines. In *Parallel & Distributed Processing (IPDPS), 2010 IEEE International Symposium on*. IEEE.

ArrayUDF: User-Defined Scientific Data Analysis on Arrays

Bin Dong[†], Kesheng Wu[†], Surendra Byna[†], Jialin Liu[†], Weijie Zhao[‡], Florin Rusu[†‡]

[†]Lawrence Berkeley National Laboratory, 1 Cyclotron Rd, Berkeley, CA 94720
[‡]University of California, Merced, 5200 Lake Rd, Merced, CA 95343
{DBin,KWu,SByna,Jalnliu}@lbl.gov,{wzhao23,frusu}@ucmerced.edu

ABSTRACT

User-Defined Functions (UDF) allow application programmers to specify analysis operations on data, while leaving the data management tasks to the system. This general approach enables numerous custom analysis functions and is at the heart of the modern Big Data systems. Even though the UDF mechanism can theoretically support arbitrary operations, a wide variety of common operations – such as computing the moving average of a time series, the vorticity of a fluid flow, etc., – are hard to express and slow to execute. Since these operations are traditionally performed on multi-dimensional arrays, we propose to extend the expressiveness of structural locality for supporting UDF operations on arrays. We further propose an *in situ* UDF mechanism, called ArrayUDF, to implement the structural locality. ArrayUDF allows users to define computations on adjacent array cells without the use of join operations and executes the UDF directly on arrays stored in data files without requiring to load their content into a data management system. Additionally, we present a thorough theoretical analysis of the data access cost to exploit the structural locality, which enables ArrayUDF to automatically select the best array partitioning strategy for a given UDF operation. In a series of performance evaluations on large scientific datasets, we have observed that – using the generic UDF interface – ArrayUDF consistently outperforms Spark, SciDB, and RasDaMan.

KEYWORDS

ArrayUDF; User-Defined Data Analysis; Array Structural Locality; SciDB; MapReduce; Spark

1 INTRODUCTION

As technology advancements in large-scale scientific experiments, observations, and simulations are generating unprecedented amounts of data, scientists are in need of novel techniques to process the data. Scientific datasets typically contain multi-dimensional arrays and are stored as files in shared disk-based storage systems [36]. Analysis of these large datasets has to be conducted directly on the

ACM acknowledges that this contribution was authored or co-authored by an employee, or contractor of the national government. As such, the Government retains a nonexclusive, royalty-free right to publish or reproduce this article, or to allow others to do so, for Government purposes only. Permission to make digital or hard copies for personal or classroom use is granted. Copies must bear this notice and the full citation on the first page. Copyrights for components of this work owned by others than ACM must be honored. To copy otherwise, distribute, republish, or post, requires prior specific permission and/or a fee. Request permissions from permissions@acm.org.

HPDC '17, June 26-30, 2017, Washington, DC, USA

© 2017 ACM. 978-1-4503-4699-3/17/06...$15.00

DOI: http://dx.doi.org/10.1145/3078597.3078599

raw data files, in an *in situ* manner [1], because loading the data into database systems that typically assume shared-nothing architecture is a very expensive and cumbersome operation. Furthermore, analysis operations on datasets are different from one run to another. Therefore, it is necessary to allow application programmers to customize their analysis operations through the User-Defined Function (UDF) mechanism. To provide such an extensible analysis capability, we propose a novel UDF abstraction for multi-dimensional arrays and present an *in situ* system that executes UDF operations over large datasets dramatically faster than the state-of-the-art data management systems.

UDFs have been explored extensively in data management literature [4, 33] and are widely implemented in database servers [13, 30, 33, 44], recent parallel data processing systems [15, 18, 26, 28], as well as specialized scientific data processing systems [5, 6, 9, 17]. The assumption behind UDFs is that most data analysis operations and their input data have a relatively simple relationship. Typically, the relationship is that a single operation is applied to each element of a dataset, e.g., a tuple of a relational table or a cell of an array. In these cases, a user only needs to specify the operation on a single data element, while the underlying system automatically executes the operation over all the elements. To the user, the operation on a single data element is the application logic, while the task to manage the dataset is a support function. However, this support function is often much more complex, especially for large datasets that tend to be processed in parallel. The UDF mechanism allows users to concentrate on the application logic and leave the data management task to the system, which significantly improves productivity of the users.

A critical limitation of most existing UDF implementations is that they typically allow users to define an operation only on a single element. However, most real-world data analysis tasks, such as computing the moving average of a time series or the vorticity of a flow field [14] (see detailed examples in Section §2), require the values of not just a single element, but also many of its neighbors. This dependency on adjacent elements is referred as *structural locality* in the literature [27]. To alleviate this limitation and to support a flexible UDF mechanism, some DBMS systems allow UDFs on an entire data table [30, 42, 44], while MapReduce systems [18] allow users to define an operation on a set of related elements in the *reduce* stage. However, this flexibility comes at the expense of tedious aggregation that is required to build the input of UDF properly. Moreover, since a data element is required by multiple neighbors in real applications, the data management system often replicates each element multiple times during execution, which

---

[1]The ability to process data directly in their native file formats has been referred to as "*in situ* processing" in data management literature [3, 8].

degrades the performance significantly. Furthermore, the reduction operations are performed uniformly on all neighboring elements involved, while real applications typically need to perform different operations on different neighboring elements. In short, there are many real-world operations that are not well-supported by the existing UDF mechanisms, i.e., these operations are hard to express and slow to execute.

In this paper, we present the design and implementation of ArrayUDF, a novel *in situ* UDF abstraction optimized for multi-dimensional arrays. ArrayUDF supports generalized *structural locality* by allowing users to define operations not only on the local value of an array cell, but also on the values of its neighbors. Meanwhile, using ArrayUDF to define an operation for a given cell, users can define a specific operation for each neighbor of this cell in the UDF. ArrayUDF automatically identifies the optimal array chunking strategy that guarantees the efficient execution of each operation. In summary, the contributions of this paper include:

- Introduction of ArrayUDF, the first UDF mechanism for multi-dimensional arrays with a generalized structural locality support. By providing a novel operator to express the relative position of a neighbor, ArrayUDF allows users to define complex analysis operations directly on arrays. Compared with the computing model of MapReduce, ArrayUDF uses a single step to complete the task for both Map and Reduce operations.

- Implementation of ArrayUDF and its processing system using the SDS framework [19], a database-like system for high-performance computing (HPC). ArrayUDF executes in an *in situ* manner [3, 8] for efficiency. ArrayUDF works directly on raw scientific file formats, e.g., HDF5 [39], where the files are stored in parallel file systems.

- Algorithms to dynamically identify the optimal chunking strategy and build a "ghost zone" for a given UDF based on the data access cost. Compared with the chunking strategies for shared-nothing array databases, these unique features of ArrayUDF enable it to work efficiently on dynamically-scheduled resources in an HPC environment as well as on the large scientific datasets stored on shared-storage systems as files.

- An analytical performance model for providing theoretical support to justify the chunking strategies of ArrayUDF and also for tuning ArrayUDF to different array organizations on disk.

- Evaluation of ArrayUDF using both synthetic and real scientific datasets on a Cray XC30 supercomputer and also a commodity Linux server. We have compared ArrayUDF with SciDB [9] and RasDaMan [6] – specialized systems for multi-dimensional array processing – and Spark, the state-of-the-art MapReduce system that supports generic UDFs. Our evaluations show that ArrayUDF is considerably faster than existing alternatives. For instance, using the generic UDF interface, ArrayUDF is up to 2070 times faster than Spark to complete a real-world data analysis.

In Section §2, we present several motivating examples from real scientific applications. In Section §3, we introduce ArrayUDF and its design and implementation. We present performance evaluation of ArrayUDF in Section §4. In Section §5, we discuss related research efforts. We conclude the paper in Section §6.

2 BACKGROUND AND MOTIVATION

Here we introduce several real-word applications that motivate this research. Our work can be the building blocks for advanced data mining algorithms [32] and systems, e.g., TensorFlow[2].

2.1 Motivating examples

Example 1: Moving average based smoothing for time series. A variety of applications produce 1D time series data. Examples include collection of temperature periodically on a flux tower in climate observations and daily stock prices in finance industry. These time series datasets usually contain two parts: a meaningful pattern (e.g, seasonal trend) and a superimposed noise with limited scientific meaning. Moving average based smoothing is widely used to extract the meaningful patterns. Specifically, at a time t, moving average based smoothing has to determine the average of observed values that are close to this particular time, as shown in the following equation:

$$V'_t = \frac{w_{t-k}V_{t-k}+...+w_{t-1}V_{t-1}+w_tV_t+...+w_{t+m}V_{t+m}}{k+m+1}, \qquad (1)$$

where V_t is the observed value, w_t the weight and V'_t the smoothed value. k and m are the steps before and after t.

Example 2: Vorticity computation. S3D is a high-fidelity direct numerical simulation (DNS) designed to capture key turbulence-chemistry interactions in a combustion engine [14]. A key variable related to the turbulent motion is vorticity. It defines the local spinning motion around a given location. To simplify the description, we give the z component of the vorticity at a point (i, j):

$$\zeta_{i,j} = \frac{\partial u}{\partial x} + \frac{\partial v}{\partial y} \approx \frac{u_{i,j+1}-u_{i,j-1}}{2\triangle x} + \frac{v_{i+1,j}-v_{i-1,j}}{2\triangle y}, \qquad (2)$$

where u and v are the flow velocity (i.e., 2D arrays) on the x and y axes, respectively, and $\triangle x$ and $\triangle y$ are the constant differences. Note four neighbors per cell are required in this computation.

Example 3: Peak detection. Mass-spectrometry imaging (MSI) is an essential technology required by biological sciences to understand metabolism [34]. In MSI, the mass-to-charge ratio (m/z) is a variable of interest which is usually a 3D array for a single object (e.g., brain tissue sample). A key data analysis task in MSI is to find peaks of m/z via calculating the gradient of each point, typically through the Laplacian operator [31]. The Laplacian for a given point (i, j, k) is defined as:

$$\begin{aligned} g_{i,j,k} = 6 \times v_{i,j,k} - (v_{i,j,k+1} + v_{i,j,k-1} + v_{i,j+1,k} \\ + v_{i,j-1,k} + v_{i+1,j,k} + v_{i-1,j,k}), \end{aligned} \qquad (3)$$

where v is the m/z value and g denotes the gradient value. Note that seven values of v are needed for each value of g.

Example 4: Trilinear interpolation. Plasma physics simulations, such as VPIC, are used to study magnetic reconnection [11]. During a simulation, magnetic field values are computed at mesh points. However, data analysis requires to find the magnetic field at the location of each particle. Generally, the magnetic field at the location of a particle is interpolated from the nearest *eight* mesh points in a 3D mesh. For a particle at (x, y, z), its magnetic value $v_{x,y,z}$ can be computed with the trilinear interpolation equation:

$$\begin{aligned} v_{x,y,z} = v_{i,j,k}N_0 + v_{i,j,k+1}N_1 + v_{i,j+1,k}N_2 + v_{i,j+1,k+1}N_3 + \\ v_{i+1,j,k}N_4 + v_{i+1,j,k+1}N_5 + v_{i+1,j+1,k}N_6 + v_{i+1,j+1,k+1}N_7 \end{aligned} \qquad (4)$$

where N_i ($i \in \{0, \ldots, 7\}$) are the distances to each corner. Thus, we can see that the trilinear interpolation for a single particle requires access to eight adjacent magnetic values.

Key observations from the examples above: .

- The computation follows a stencil [7, 29] pattern. In general, a new array B is computed from an existing array A, where the value of B at location (i, j, k) is determined not only by $A(i, j, k)$, but also by its neighbors. This is called *structural locality* in a previous work [27].
- The neighbors of $A(i, j, k)$ do not go through the same operation. Previous work – such as MapReduce [18] and GLADE [15] – generally assume that a uniform reduction or aggregation operation is sufficient.
- There is a variety of analysis operations for different applications. The best option for implementing all of them is to follow the UDF approach to support the common data management operations, while allowing users to define custom operations on data.

2.2 Research challenges

SciDB, RasDaMan, and AML [27] implement the "window" operator, which supports some form of structural locality. However, the operations on the values within a window are generally a reduction operation, while the above examples show a variety of operations. Furthermore, the "window" typically has to be a rectangular subdomain, e.g., a 2×2 square, while the above examples contain more complex definitions of neighborhood. Additional flexibility is needed in specifying both the operations and the neighborhood. While UDFs provide a general framework to express custom analysis operations, they have to address the following challenges in order to be applicable to structural operations defined over arrays:

- How to define neighborhood cells involved in a UDF operation? These definitions have to be compact, easy to construct, and – at the same time – efficient to evaluate.
- How to develop UDFs that support *in situ* array data analysis? As most scientific datasets are stored in file formats such as HDF5 and netCDF [36], a new UDF mechanism has to work directly on these files without loading the data into a separate DBMS.
- How to effectively partition the data and computation on parallel computing systems? As each array cell is needed at different computation steps, the data partition may require overlapping. Maintaining load-balance and reducing overlap is critical to achieve good overall performance.

3 ArrayUDF APPROACH

To address the identified challenges, we propose a UDF system named ArrayUDF. With ArrayUDF, we extend the expressiveness of structural locality to allow users to easily define operations on adjacent cells of an array and to perform data management tasks efficiently for supporting these user-defined operations. ArrayUDF is also capable of identifying the minimum portion of an array accessed on each process (e.g., CPU core) and operate on that portion of the array data stored in files, without loading the entire array into the system. This optimization is possible because the array syntax used by ArrayUDF to describe the operations provide a clear mechanism to identify the relevant cells and the optimal data partition can be determined analytically.

ArrayUDF computational model. For comparison, we first introduce the computational models of relational databases and MapReduce systems. We use f to denote a user-defined function. For relational tables T and T', the generic UDF model is:

$$t' \leftarrow f(t) \tag{5}$$

where f is applied to each tuple $t \in T$ and t' represents the tuple in the output table T'. There is a one-to-one mapping between input and output tuples. Aggregate UDFs allow for more input tuples to determine an output tuple. However, it is done by grouping on the values of some attributes, i.e., the SQL GROUP-BY operator.

In the MapReduce paradigm, the input of a UDF is a ($key, value$) pair, or (k, v) for short. MapReduce has two components – *Map* and *Reduce* – which can be formally expressed as:

$$Map : \left\{ (k_i, v_i) \mid i \in [1, m] \right\} \leftarrow f_1 \Big((k, v) \Big)$$

$$Reduce : \left\{ (k_i', v_i') \mid i \in [1, p] \right\} \leftarrow f_2 \Big(\left\{ (k', v_i) \mid i \in [1, n] \right\} \Big) \tag{6}$$

where $m, n, p \in \mathbb{N}$, $\mathbb{N}$ is the natural number set, f_1 is an enhanced UDF that implements a one-to-many mapping from the input pair to an intermediate set of key-value pairs and f_2 is a SQL GROUP-BY AGGREGATE identical to the relational aggregate UDF. Key k' is the grouping parameter in f_2. Value v' is generated by f_2 through uniformly applying a single operator – such as SUM – to each v_i.

The computational model of the ArrayUDF is defined on two d-dimensional arrays, A and A' ($d \in \mathbb{N}$). The cell c' at coordinate $(i_1, i_2, \ldots, i_d)$ in A' is computed by a stencil S of the cell c at the same coordinate in A. Theoretically, the stencil S is a set of array cells which have structural locality. Specifically, for the cell c at coordinate $(i_1, i_2, \ldots, i_d)$, $S = \{c_{i_1 + \delta_1, i_2 + \delta_2, \ldots, i_d + \delta_d} | \forall j \in [1, d], \delta_j \in [L_j, R_j]\}$, where $L_j \in [-i_j, 0]$, $R_j \in [0, N_j - i_j]$, and the N_j is the size of the jth dimension. Obviously, the $\delta_1, \delta_2, \ldots, \delta_d$ are relative distances from the cell c. For simplicity, each cell in S is expressed as $s_{\delta_1, \delta_2, \ldots, \delta_d}$, which is $c_{i_1 + \delta_1, i_2 + \delta_2, \ldots, i_d + \delta_d}$. With these notations, the formal computational model of ArrayUDF is:

$$c'_{i_1, \ldots, i_d} \leftarrow f \Big(\left\{ s_{\delta_1, \ldots, \delta_d} \mid \forall j \in [1, d], \delta_j \in [L_j, R_j] \right\} \Big). \tag{7}$$

Distinct from the UDF models of relational databases and of MapReduce, in the model of ArrayUDF, the function f has a stencil S as input. A stencil S allows ArrayUDF to express any neighborhood shape implicitly via relative distance. This is also different from AML [27], where a shape parameter is required to express neighbor cells. Meanwhile, users can specify different operators on different cells of S within the UDF. This distinguishes ArrayUDF from most existing aggregate UDFs [15], where a single aggregate operator is applied onto all values. In the relational model, this functionality requires a chain of self-joins having cardinality equal to the number of cells in the stencil. In MapReduce, the self-joins are substituted by the one-to-many replications in the *Map* stage. In general, when the size of S is equal to one, ArrayUDF is identical to the relational and *Map* UDFs. Otherwise, ArrayUDF is similar to relational aggregates and the *Reduce* function. In summary, ArrayUDF eliminates the shape operators for computing a stencil (S) and allows a more concise definition of UDFs for arrays.

System overview. Towards implementing the computational model of ArrayUDF, we introduce its key software components:

- **Array** is a data structure that encapsulates the multi-dimensional array stored in files. This is the primary object a user interacts with. **Array** implements the function *Apply* to execute the UDF defined by the user. On a parallel computing system, each process creates its own instance of the **Array** object with the same arguments, and invokes the same UDF with the function *Apply*. Moreover, **Array** has functions to partition the multi-dimensional array automatically, to build the necessary overlapping regions (known as ghost zones), and to divide the computation among the processes. This partitioning method is guided by a theoretical analysis to be discussed in § 3.3. More details on **Array** are reported in Section § 3.2.

- The data structure **Stencil** represents an array cell and its neighborhood cells in relative coordinates. As defined earlier, **Stencil** is a relative coordinate-based notation that allows users to describe the operations to be performed on each neighbor separately. Previously used notations for "shape" and "window" demand all neighbors to be described in a collective form, which limits aggregation operations used in scientific data analysis. In contrast, our relative coordinate-based notation is more flexible. Users define their UDFs with these **Stencils**. In C++ syntax, this relative coordinate is expressed using the parenthesis operator of the **Stencil** object. More details about **Stencil** are in § 3.1.

ArrayUDF is currently implemented as part of the Scientific Data Services (SDS) framework [19], which provides the basic I/O drivers for reading and writing the data from parallel file systems. We implement **Array** and **Stencil** as C++ classes. We show an example of using ArrayUDF in Fig. 1, where "MyAvg" is a UDF to compute the average value using four adjacent cells. "MyAvg" is executed by calling the *Apply* function of an **Array** instance within the main function. The template feature is used to support different data types, e.g., float and double.

3.1 Stencil design considerations

The **Stencil** data structure represents an array cell and its neighbors needed for a single invocation of the UDF. **Stencil** plays a role similar to a tuple in a database or a key-value pair concept, working as the input to the UDF. It is more flexible than existing concepts such as "window" and "shape" in two ways. A **Stencil** can be used to define more complex neighborhoods than "window" and "shape" and it allows the user to specify a different operation on each of the neighboring cells. This flexibility allows a much wider variety of analysis operations to be defined.

Since modern CPUs can carry out many arithmetic operations quickly, we anticipate that the complexity in arithmetic operations is less dominant in the overall performance of a UDF than the cost of data accesses. As with "window" and "shape," we expect operations defined on our relatively compact stencils to access a small number of neighbors and, therefore, can be carried out efficiently, while operations involving a large number of neighbors, no matter in the form of a "window", a "shape", or a "stencil", require more data accesses and take a longer time to complete. In short, we expect the flexibility to address individual neighboring cells in a UDF not to impose a significant cost on its own.

```
//A UDF on a stencil containing four neighborhood cells
float MyAvg(Stencil<float> &s){
  return (s(1,0)+s(-1,0)+s(0,-1)+s(0,1))/4;
}
int main(){
  vector<int> cs(2)={2,2};//Chunk size
  vector<int> gs(2)={1,1};//Ghost zone size
  Array<float> A("d2d.h5",cs,gs);
  Array<float> B("d2davg.h5");
  //Run UDF code using Apply function
  //Store the result in B
  A->Apply(MyAvg, B);
  ...   //Other operations on B or A
}
```

Figure 1: An example using ArrayUDF to compute user-defined average, i.e., "MyAvg", on a 2D array A, stored in a HDF5 file, named "d2d.h5". The results are stored in array B, which has the same dimensions as that of A and is stored in file "d2davg.h5". Given different UDF operators, B can have different dimensions from A. The user-specified chunk size (cs) and ghost zone size (os) are used to support parallel processing. Both cs and os are optional and can be determined by ArrayUDF automatically.

To understand the relative coordinates used in the definition of a **Stencil**, it is useful to visualize the coordinates of a multi-dimensional array to be a set of mesh points in space and each array to be an attribute of a mesh point. For example, one set of attributes might be their location in space, (e.g., x, y, and z dimensions), and another set might be temperature, pressure, and concentrations of some chemical species. The analysis examples given in earlier sections follow this basic schema and a typical analysis function computes $B(i, j, ...)$ from $A(i, j, ...)$ and its neighbors. Furthermore, the neighbors are of a fixed combination of offsets around $A(i, j, ...)$. In applied math, the pattern formed by these offsets (positions relative to a center $(i, j, ...)$) is known as a "stencil". ArrayUDF uses a syntax implemented as the parenthesis operator of C++ to allow each cell in the stencil to be explicitly named. For example, in a 2D case, $S(0, 0)$ refers to the "center" of the stencil $A(i, j)$, and $S(1, 0)$ refers to the neighbor $A(i + 1, j)$.

The use of relative coordinates in the UDF allows the users to define the operations without mentioning the coordinates $(i, j, ...)$. When the function is actually evaluated, we need to convert these relative coordinates back to the absolute coordinates in order to access the specific cells. In this context, the use of the relative coordinates also allows each execution thread to work on its own portion of the global mesh as illustrated in § 3.2 and Fig. 6.

3.2 Array design considerations

The **Array** class is a high-level abstraction and representation for multi-dimensional arrays that contains a group of functions for run-time tasks. Users employ **Array** to represent an array stored either in memory as std::array or on disk as an HDF5 dataset. For this work, the key function of **Array** is *Apply*, which executes a UDF. Behind this function, we are able to implement a number of data management techniques for parallelizing the execution of the UDF automatically through partitioning the global mesh into suitable sub-domains and overlapping the sub-domains through ghost zones.

3.2.1 Parallel processing with dynamic chunking. A typical approach for parallel processing of a large problem is to divide the problem into smaller *partitions* or *chunks*. Following this general practice of data management systems, we also divide the evaluation of the UDF by partitioning data. We observe that an invocation of UDF requires access to values near $(i, j, ...)$. Therefore, it is essential for us to keep the neighbors close to each other as much as possible. This basic requirement is similar to many parallel computing applications [25], which allows us to borrow a number of techniques for designing an efficient data partitioning algorithm. Our overall approach can be viewed as partitioning (chunking) the mesh defined by the multi-dimensional coordinates into chunks, and then map each chunk to a parallel processing element (PE). We assume that each chunk is small enough to fit into the available memory on a PE. A processing element is responsible for producing the output array belonging to the chunk. To complete this task, it not only needs to access the corresponding chunk of the input data array, but also some extra portion of the array, which we call *ghost zone* (as illustrated in Fig. 2). Since ArrayUDF is designed to process data directly on raw data files, there is no data pre-processing step (e.g., loading data into the system) for it to figure out an efficient chunking strategy in advance. We need to perform all the chunking related decisions (e.g., chunk size) dynamically. Moreover, for a given chunk, it is necessary to consider its logical view (i.e., shape) and its physical view (i.e., data layout on storage) as they affect the performance of reading the data.

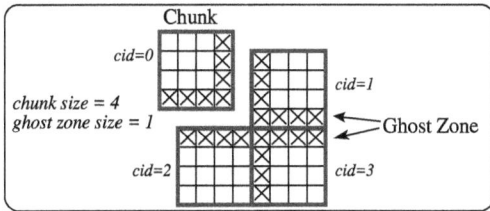

Figure 2: Example of chunks and ghost zones in a 2D array.

Chunk management overview. In order to maintain load balance among processing elements, ArrayUDF attempts to keep the size and the shape of chunks similar. An example of chunking in ArrayUDF is shown in Fig. 2, where four chunks are created. Each chunk has a dynamically assigned ID (i.e., *cid* in the example). The ID is calculated using the row-major ordering from the coordinates of chunks, which allows ArrayUDF to identify a chunk quickly.

FUNCTION *ArrayUDFChunk*$(M, P, (N_0, ..., N_d))$
  M: the available memory size per process;
  P: the total number of processes;
  $(N_0, ..., N_d)$: the size of an array for d dimension
  0. $S = \min (M, (\prod_{i=1}^{d} N_i)/P)$
  1. **if** general chunking **then**
  2.   Find an integer w that minimizes $|S - w^d|$
  3. $c_1 = w, c_2 = w, ..., c_d = w$
  4. **if** layout-aware chunking **then**
  5.   **for** $i \in (d, d-1, ..., 2)$ **do**
  6. $c_i = S \% N_i; S = S/N_i$
  7. $c_1 = S$
  8. return $(c_1, c_2, ..., c_d)$

Figure 3: The method for selecting chunking parameters.

Optimal chunking strategy selection. A key challenge to support dynamic chunking is to decide the optimal chunking parameters, including chunk size, chunk shape, and chunk layout. The chunk size is the number of cells within a chunk, the shape is its logical view, and the layout is its physical data layout on disk. To address this challenge, ArrayUDF provides two chunking strategies: **a general chunking** and **a layout-aware chunking**, as shown in the pseudocode in Fig. 3. We describe the theoretical reasoning for these strategies in § 3.3. In the following, we describe the high-level idea and concrete applications.

- To find **an optimal and general chunking**, we assume that each array cell is accessed separately. Such an assumption guarantees that the chunk layout has no impact on the performance of accessing a chunk. In other words, we consider it as an average case for different chunk layouts. Users can choose this chunking strategy when the layout of the array on disk is unknown. As shown in line 0 in Fig. 3, the chunk size in this strategy is set to be as large as possible to fit in the memory of each processing element to reduce the startup overhead of I/O as well as to assign at least one chunk to each process to maximize parallelism. In terms of the chunk shape, ArrayUDF chooses a square shape (lines 2 and 3 in Fig. 3) to minimize the number of ghost cells for each chunk. A formal analysis of this strategy is given in § 3.3 and is illustrated in Fig. 4, where the square chunk reads 12 ghost cells but the non-square one reads 20 ghost cells.

- To identify **an optimal and layout-aware chunking**, we take the row-major layout as an example because it is popular in most array data formats. A storage system typically organizes the elements of a multi-dimensional array in a linear order based on their coordinates. With the row-major layouts, the 1st dimension is the slowest varying dimension and the last dimension is the fastest varying dimension. In this case, ArrayUDF chooses the chunk whose layout on disk is as contiguous as possible by maximizing the fast-varying (or higher) dimensions for a chunk. In other words, ArrayUDF chooses the chunk size based on the linearized organization of an array in row-major order (lines 5 to 7 in Fig. 3). We also consider the memory limit and the parallelism (line 0 in Fig. 3). The impact of reading extra ghost cells is not considered here because the cells from the chunk and the ghost zones often form a single or few contiguous reads as illustrated in Fig. 5. More detailed analysis is given in § 3.3.

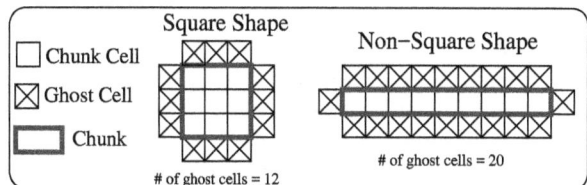

Figure 4: An example showing the number of ghost cells for different chunk shapes.

3.2.2 Dynamic ghost zone building using a trial run. In most use cases, the programmer who develops the UDF can determine the thickness of the ghost zone and therefore can provide the information to the **ARRAY** object to help with dynamic data chunking. However, it is possible that the size of ghost zones are unknown

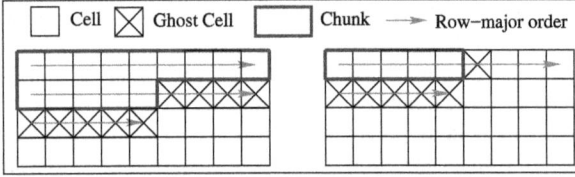

Figure 5: An example showing the layout-aware chunking for a 4×9 array. On the left, a chunk occupies more than one row. On the right, a chunk occupies a partial row.

a priori, for example when the UDF source code is not accessible to the user. In such cases, ArrayUDF provides a mechanism based on a "trial run" to determine the ghost zone size. During the trial run, ArrayUDF gathers all the relative coordinates used in the UDF. We assume the relative coordinates do not depend on the values of the input array, and, therefore, only perform the trial run on a small number of cells. At this time, we only perform this trial run on the first data point on each PE. After the trial run, ArrayUDF chooses the maximum absolute value among the gathered relative coordinates for a dimension as the number of ghost cells of this dimension. Therefore, different dimensions can have a different number of ghost cells. For a certain dimension, the current ArrayUDF implementation requires that both directions have the same number of ghost cells. This reduces the number of input parameters needed by ArrayUDF, but it also causes reading unnecessary ghost cells. However, as observed in most example applications, they require the same number of cells in both directions of a given dimension. We can easily extend ArrayUDF to set the sizes of a ghost zone for different directions of a dimension. Sometimes, it is impossible to determine the ghost zone size using the trial run. In this situation, ArrayUDF uses the default ghost zone size. Moreover, users can specify a default ghost zone size when initializing **Array** object, as shown in Fig. 1.

*3.2.3 Putting it all together: the **Apply** algorithm.* The **Apply** function of **Array** is the entry point to execute a UDF and it also contains a skeleton of our runtime system. The pseudocode of **Apply** is outlined in Fig. 6. Overall, the pseudocode shows that the UDF P_{udf} processes array A and stores the results in array B. As shown in Fig. 1, users can provide their own chunk size (*cs*) and ghost zone size (*gs*), both of which are therefore considered as the input. To support parallel processing, each process (PE) initializes an **Array** instance by itself and follows the same algorithm without any communication. During the initialization, each process obtains the total number of processes P and the rank R of itself among all processes using certain library calls such as MPI. In the following, we describe how **Apply** works on a single process.

From line 0 to line 1, the **Apply** algorithm determines the chunk size and ghost zone size, if a user does not provide them. The methods for determining these two parameters are discussed in § 3.2.1 and § 3.2.2. Then, the algorithm starts to read a chunk into memory for processing (lines 2 and 3). The ID of the first chunk to be read by a process is equal to the rank of the process, which permits each process to have different chunks to process concurrently. Reading the chunk is performed by the *LoadNextChunk* function, which first converts the chunk id to the coordinates of the top-left corner and bottom-right corner of a chunk. Then, it extends the coordinates of

the chunk to include the ghost zone. Finally, the *LoadNextChunk* function reads the chunk into memory if the coordinates are valid.

Once the **Apply** algorithm receives the chunk data from *LoadNextChunk*, it starts to apply the UDF (i.e., P_{udf}) on each cell of the chunk (lines 4 – 6). Specifically, a new instance of **Stencil** is initialized. Then, P_{udf} is called with the new **Stencil** instance. The returned result of the UDF is stored in B. After a PE processes a chunk, it reads the next chunk to process. The ID of the next chunk is the current id plus the total number of processes (line 7). The data stored in B can be flushed to persistent storage, depending on the available memory space.

3.3 Analytical model for ArrayUDF

In this section, we present an analytical model to characterize the performance of ArrayUDF, with the primary goal of deriving a chunking strategy. We first build a generic model without considering array layout and then adapt the model for specific array layouts. The notations used in the model are shown in Table 1.

Table 1: Notations used in the chunking strategy model

c_i	Chunk size in the ith dimension, $i \in (1, \ldots, d)$
c	Number of cells in a chunk, $c \equiv \prod_{i=1}^{d} c_i$
C	Number of chunks $C \equiv \prod_{i=1}^{d} \lceil N_i / c_i \rceil$
δ	Size of a ghost zone
e	Number of elements in a chunk plus its ghost zones
G	Number of elements in all ghost zones
d	Rank of an array (number of dimensions)
M	Memory size of a single process
N_i	Size of the ith dimension, $i \in (1, \ldots, d)$
N	Number of array elements, $N \equiv \prod_{i=1}^{d} N_i$
P	Number of parallel processes

Execution of a computation function typically contain three overheads: computation time, communication time, and I/O time. In the following analysis, we will ignore the computation and communication costs. By design, each process in ArrayUDF can evaluate the UDF in parallel without inter-process communication. We will, therefore, assume that there is no communication overhead. The computation time for each element of the output array can be reasonably represented as a constant, independent of the logical array layout and the physical chunk layout; therefore, as long as there are enough array cells to be divided evenly among processes, the computation cost can be divided evenly and will not depend on how we partition the chunks. Similarly, selection of the layout of the chunks does not affect the computation time. To further simplify the analysis, we also assume the ghost zones are of the same width in each direction and every dimension.

Overall, ArrayUDF divides the evaluation into chunks whose shape and size is determined analytically. On each process, the evaluation proceeds independently. From Fig. 6, we see that the key I/O cost is to read a chunk of the input array and the ghost zones. Let c and e denote the number of elements in a chunk and the extended region including the chunk and its surrounding ghost zones, as shown in Table 1. Given the size of a chunk ($c_1 \times c_2 \times \ldots \times c_d$), the total volume of data in the chunks is $c = \prod_{i=1}^{d} c_i$. To evaluate the size of e, we need to know how many ghost zones are present. For simplicity, if a part of the ghost zone is available, we will count it as

```
FUNCTION A→Apply(P_udf, B)
    P_udf : pointer to user-defined function. A : an array to Apply P_udf. B : result array.
    A→cs : chunk size. A→gs : ghost zone size. A→P : the total number of processes.   A→R : the rank of current process.
    0. if(A→cs == NULL) then Determine the chunk size A→cs, as discussed in § 3.2.1        //No user-defined chunk size
    1. if(A→gs == NULL) then Issue a trial-run to get A→gs, as discussed in § 3.2.2        //No user-defined ghost zone size
    2. cid = A→R;       // the ID for the first chunk is equal to the rank of current process
    3. while ((cbuf=LoadNextChunk(cid, A→gs, A→cs) ) != NULL) do
    4.       for each cell c within the chunk cbuf do
    5.           cell_udf = STENCIL(c, A→gs, A→cs, cbuf)        //Initialize a Stencil to represent the real cell c
    6.           B = P_udf (cell_udf)       //Run the UDF function on the Stencil
    7.       cid = cid + A→P        //Next chunk in round-robin manner
    8.       flush B to disk if necessary
FUNCTION LoadNextChunk(cid, A→gs, A→cs)
    0. Obtain the top-left corner coordinate c_tl and the below-right corner coordinate c_br from cid        //See section § 3.2.1
    1. c_tl = c_tl − A→gs; c_br = c_br + A→gs       //expand chunk with ghost cells
    2. if checking array boundary fails then
    3.       return NULL
    4. Read all cells from c_tl to c_br within A into buffer cbuf
    5. read cbuf
```

Figure 6: *Apply* **algorithm in ArrayUDF. We use "→" symbol to denote the components of** *A*. **For example,** $A \rightarrow Apply$ **is the** *Apply* **method of** *A* **and** $A \rightarrow cs$ **is the chunk size metadata of** *A*.

present. As shown in Figure 4, it is possible for a chunk to have two ghost zones along each dimension i. However, those ghost zones might not be present if the expected ghost zones are outside of the extent of the array[2], as shown in Fig. 2. For dimension i with chunk size c_i, the N_i points are divided into $\lceil N_i/c_i \rceil$ chunks, which creates need for $2(\lceil N_i/c_i \rceil - 1)$ ghost zones along this dimension. Given the surface area perpendicular to this dimension to be $\prod_{j \neq i} N_j$, the total volume of ghost zones along dimension i is $2\delta(\lceil N_i/c_i \rceil - 1)\prod_{j \neq i} N_j$, and the total volume of data in ghost zones over all dimensions is:

$$G = 2\delta \sum_{i=1}^{d} \left((\lceil N_i/c_i \rceil - 1) \prod_{j \neq i} N_j \right) \qquad (8)$$

The average number of elements for processing a chunk is:

$$e = c + G/C \qquad (9)$$

3.3.1 Generic performance model. In this performance model, we assume the layout of the array dimensions is unknown or the time to read an arbitrarily shaped subarray is strictly a linear function of the number of elements in the subarray. Thus, the time to read a chunk plus its surrounding ghost zones is given by:

$$t_{io} = \alpha_0 e + \beta_0 \qquad (10)$$

For C chunks and P processes, each process has at most $\lceil C/P \rceil$ chunks and the maximum read time is:

$$T_{io}^{ge} = (\alpha_0 e + \beta_0) \lceil C/P \rceil \qquad (11)$$

The selection of the optimal chunk size can be formulated as an optimization problem:

$$\min_{c_1, c_2, \ldots, c_d} T_{io}^{ge}(c_1, c_2, \ldots, c_d) \quad \text{s.t.}$$

$$(1)\ c_i \leq N_i, 1 \leq i \leq d; \quad (2) \prod_{i=1}^{d} c_i \leq M; \quad (3)\ C \geq P \qquad (12)$$

Constraint (2) guarantees that each chunk fits within the available memory while constraint (3) enforces that each process has at

least one chunk to work on. Given a large array – the case we are interested in – constraint (3) is easily satisfied and constraint (2) can be turned into:

$$\prod_{i=1}^{d} c_i = M \qquad (13)$$

To generate an analytical solution for the above optimization problem, we further assume the ceiling operator can be removed from all the above expressions, which leads to:

$$T_{io}^{ge} \sim \left(\alpha_0 \left[\prod_{i=1}^{d} c_i + \frac{2\delta \sum_{i=1}^{d}((N_i/c_i - 1)\prod_{j \neq i} N_j)}{\prod_{i=1}^{d} N_i/c_i} \right] + \beta_0 \right) \frac{\prod_{i=1}^{d} N_i/c_i}{P}$$

$$= \frac{\alpha_0 N}{P} + \frac{2\alpha_0 \delta N}{P} \sum_{i=1}^{d}(\frac{1}{c_i} - \frac{1}{N_i}) + \frac{\beta_0 N}{PM} \qquad (14)$$

In the above expression for T_{io}^{ge}, the only term that is affected by the choices of c_i is the expression $\sum 1/c_i$ (multiplied by a positive constant). Given the constraint in Eq. 13, the minimal value of T_{io}^{ge} is obtained with $c_1 = c_2 = \ldots = \sqrt[d]{M}$, which minimizes the total number of ghost cells G. In short, when there are no preferred dimensions, the chunks should be as large as they can fit in the available memory and have each side of the same size.

3.3.2 Layout-aware performance model. When the layout of an array in a file is known, typically there are preferred dimensions for partitioning the array into chunks. The key reason for this is that the sequential read operations are significantly more efficient than random reads. In many cases, a multi-dimensional array is organized in row-major ordering. Hence, there are significant advantages to partition along the slowest varying dimension:

- Under the row-major ordering, when partitions are based on the slowest varying dimension, each partition can be read with a single sequential scan operation.
- When a dimension is fully contained in a chunk ($c_i = N_i$), there is no ghost zone for the dimension, which reduces the number of read operations needed for ghost cells.

---

[2]It is possible to have a periodic boundary condition, which has a different requirement on ghost zones.

- When the partition is only along the slowest varying dimension, the ghost cells follow the chunk in the file, which allows the ghost cells to be read with the chunk in a single sequential scan. Therefore, partitioning along the first dimension (i.e., the slowest varying dimension) is highly desirable as long as the array can be evenly divided onto the P processes. In this case, Eq. 8 turns into:

$$G = 2\delta(\lceil N_1/c_1 \rceil - 1) \prod_{j=2}^{d} N_j \sim 2\delta N(1/c_1 - 1/N_1)$$

This leads to the following expression for the read time:

$$T_{io}^1 \sim \frac{\alpha_1 N}{P} + \frac{2\alpha_1 \delta N}{P} \left(\frac{1}{c_1} - \frac{1}{N_1} \right) + \frac{\beta_1 N}{PM} \tag{15}$$

As c_1 approaches 1, the value of G approaches $2N$, which means each process reads more ghost cells than in the generic case considered above. However, since the read operations in this case are large sequential scans, the value of α_1 is considerably smaller than α_0 in the generic case. Thus, dividing chunks along the slowest varying dimension still reduces the overall execution time.

In practice, we find that dividing the array according to the linearization order gives the same advantage as sequential scans, while maintaining better load balance among the processes. This chunking approach may produce ghost zones of irregular shape as illustrated in Fig. 5, however, the ghost zones can still be read with the array elements in the chunk in a single sequential scan operation. Lines 5 and 6 in Fig. 3 implement this approach.

4 PERFORMANCE EVALUATION

We have evaluated ArrayUDF extensively to demonstrate its effectiveness. We explored the design considerations of ArrayUDF and the assumptions used by its performance model with synthetic datasets. We have also performed several tests to compare ArrayUDF with RasDaMan [6], SciDB [9], and EXTASCID [16, 17], where we used the latest versions of these systems available online. Finally, we compared ArrayUDF with Spark – the system with the state-of-the-art generic UDFs – using four real-world scientific datasets and analysis operations.

Experimental setup. We ran our tests on Edison, a Cray XC30 supercomputer at the National Energy Research Scientific Computing Center (NERSC). Edison is equipped with 5576 computing nodes. Each computing node has two 12-core 2.4 GHz Intel "Ivy Bridge" processors and 64 GB DDR3 memory. All tested datasets are stored as HDF5 files in a Lustre parallel file system. The ArrayUDF implementation is compiled with the Intel C/C++ Compiler version 16.0. The Spark installation used as the main comparison is state of the art on HPC [12]. Since Spark does not have native support for HDF5 files, we have use H5Spark [26] to read HDF5 data directly into its RDDs, and therefore reduce the potential impact of the file system and have a fair comparison between ArrayUDF and Spark on the same storage model.

4.1 Synthetic data and Poisson equation solver

To explore the impact of chunking parameters, to verify the analytical model, and to compare with the performance of SciDB, RasDaMan, EXTACID, and Spark, we have used synthetic two datasets. We have created these datasets that contain two multi-dimensional arrays, $S1$ and $S2$, containing floating point data. $S1$ is a 2D array

with ranges (100000, 100000) for (x, y) dimensions, giving 38 GB in file size. $S2$ is a 3D array with ranges (10000, 1000, 1000) for x, y, and z, respectively, resulting in 38 GB in file size. We have used the Poisson equation solver, which is widely used in financial mathematics, Riemannian geometry, and, thus, topology. Using the stencil operator of ArrayUDF, we can express the 2D Poisson equation solver as $4S(0, 0) - S(-1, 0) - S(0, 1) - S(1, 0) - S(-1, 0)$. Similarly, the 3D Poisson equation solver can be expressed as $6S(0, 0, 0) - S(-1, 0, 0) - S(0, 1, 0) - S(1, 0, 0) - S(-1, 0, 0) - S(0, 0, -1) - S(0, 0, 1)$. For the tests describing SciDB in this subsection, we used at most 11 compute nodes. These 11-node tests were dedicated to match the SciDB installation at NERSC supercomputing center, where 10 nodes are used for the data instances of SciDB and 1 node for the metadata instance of SciDB.

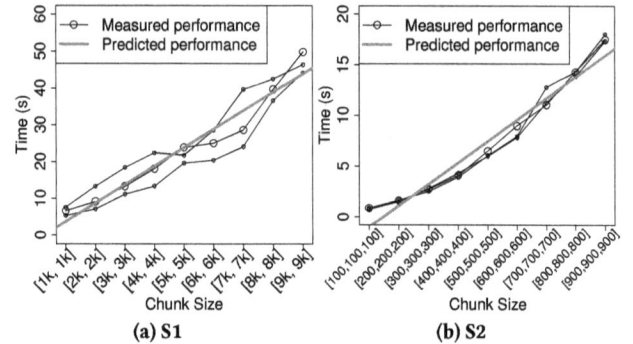

Figure 7: Linear relationship between the chunk size and the cost of reading a chunk.

Linear relationship between the chunk size and the time of reading it. In our performance model, we assume that the cost of reading a chunk is proportional to its size. To evaluate this assumption, we ran tests on $S1$ and $S2$ multiple times for a certain configuration and then to build a theoretical model. We show the I/O cost with different chunk sizes for $S1$ and $S2$ in Fig. 7. It is obvious that as the chunk size increases, the time to read the chunk increases linearly as well. The residual standard deviations of this fitting are 3.53 and 1.30 for $S1$ and $S2$, respectively. Thus, we can conclude that the linear relationship exists between the size of a chunk and its read time.

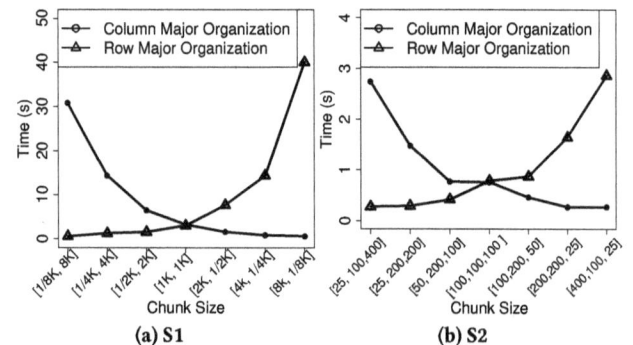

Figure 8: Cost of reading ghost cells for different chunk shapes and for different layouts.

Impact of chunk shape on the cost of reading ghost cells. Using the general performance model (i.e., Eq. 12), we predict that the chunk shape has a significant impact on data read performance. Specifically, for a fixed size chunk, the square shape guarantees that the number of ghost cells is minimum and, therefore, it has minimum I/O cost. Since we develop the general performance model without relying on any specific data organization, it can characterize the average performance of different organizations. To justify this result, we consider two data organizations, including row-major and column-major, in this test. We compare the performance of reading a chunk with the same shape from these two organizations. As the HDF5 format uses row-major organization to store data, we use the transpose-based data reorganization service of SDS framework [19, 38] to turn the row-major organization into the column-major one. We report the results in Fig. 8. As the chunk shape changes from the left (row-major) to the right (column-major), the time for reading the chunk from column-major organization decreases but the time for row-major organization increases. The square shaped chunk in the middle has the smallest overhead when we consider both organizations together. In other worlds, without considering the organization, the square-shaped chunk has minimum overhead. Taking only the row-major data organization as an example, we can observe that the squared chunk is not always the optimal shape, although it needs minimum amount of ghost cells. Actually, at this time, the chunk layout on disk is the dominant factor for the I/O performance. Our analysis in Section 3.3.2 takes this into account. In summary, these test results confirm our model formed based on a theoretical analysis.

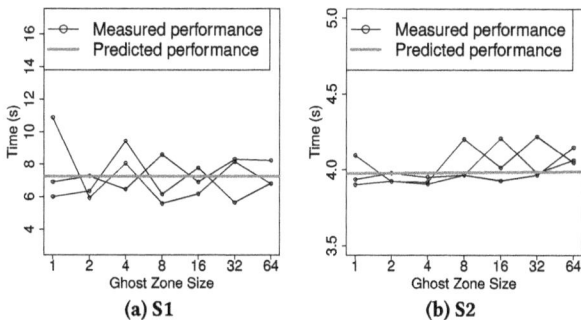

Figure 9: Performance of reading ghost zone in row-major layout.

Overhead of reading ghost cells with layout-aware chunking. In the layout-aware performance model, we assume that the overhead of reading ghost zone can be ignored. To justify this assumption, we have designed a test to measure the time for reading ghost zone sizes, from 1 to 64. In Fig. 9, we show the performance of reading ghost cells from $S1$ and $S2$ datasets. From the figure, we conclude that by increasing the ghost zone from 1 to 64, the time spent to read a single chunk remains flat. Linear regression of multiple measured times show a flat line to represent constant time. With the layout-aware chunking, the ghost cells tend to be contiguously organized with other cells on disk, resulting in the same read performance. Therefore, reading a small amount of ghost zone cells has negligible impact on the performance of reading a chunk. We conclude that during the layout-aware chunking, the assumption we used in the model is reasonable.

Overhead of a "trial run" to detect the size of the ghost zone. ArrayUDF uses a "trial-run" approach to decide the size of

Table 2: Overhead of the trial run (microsecond).

Data sets	The number of cells used by UDF						
	4	8	16	32	64	128	256
S1	0.37	0.38	0.46	0.48	0.54	0.59	0.80
S2	0.48	0.52	0.65	0.75	0.79	0.84	1.04

the ghost zone for a given UDF. In this test, we have measured the overhead of a "trial run" with respective to different numbers of array cells used by UDF. These numbers range from 4 to 256. When the number of the tested cells is larger than the number of cells required by the Poisson equation solver, we append random array cells at the end. In Table 2, we show the overhead of a "trial run". Overall, we observe that the overhead of trial run is less that *one* microsecond. Compared with the other components of ArrayUDF presented above, this overhead is negligible.

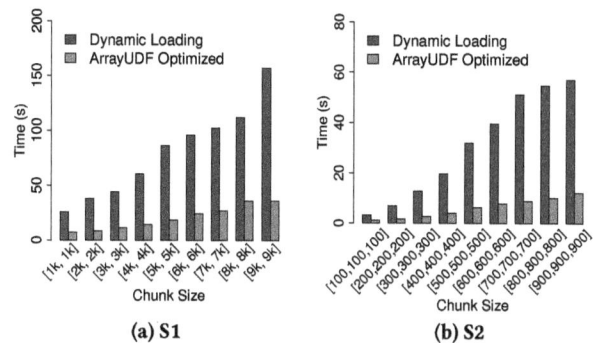

Figure 10: Comparing two methods to handle ghost zone.

Comparing different methods to handle ghost zone. Array data management systems, such as ArrayStore [37], used a dynamic loading method to access ghost cells. In this method, when a chunk needs to access ghost cells from its neighborhood chunk, this method reads the neighborhood chunk from disk into memory. Based on the fact that a UDF has a well-determined access pattern for ghost cells, ArrayUDF optimizes the accessing of ghost cells via statically extending each chunk by a ghost zone when the chunk is first read from disk. As a result, separate disk accesses are not needed for ghost cells in ArrayUDF. We use the low-overhead "trial run" approach to obtain accurate size estimates for a ghost zone. In this test, we compare these two methods by implementing the dynamic chunk loading in ArrayUDF. As shown in Fig. 10, in reading ghost zones from $S1$ and $S2$ datasets, the optimized method in ArrayUDF is on average *four* times faster than the dynamic chunk loading method. Thus, ArrayUDF has an efficient way in handling access to ghost zones.

Comparing ArrayUDF with SciDB, RasDaMan, EXTASCID, and Spark in executing the standard "window" operator. As we discussed in the previous sections, the Poisson equation solver cannot be expressed directly using the "window" operators of SciDB and RasDaMan. To compare the performance and versatility of ArrayUDF, we compare the performance of the "window" operator these systems provide, where the operation is to compute the average for a 2×2 window on 2D data and a $2\times2\times2$ window on 3D data. We also include EXTASCID and Spark for a complete comparison. For fairness of the evaluation platform for all these systems, we have installed them on a single Linux desktop. The desktop has two

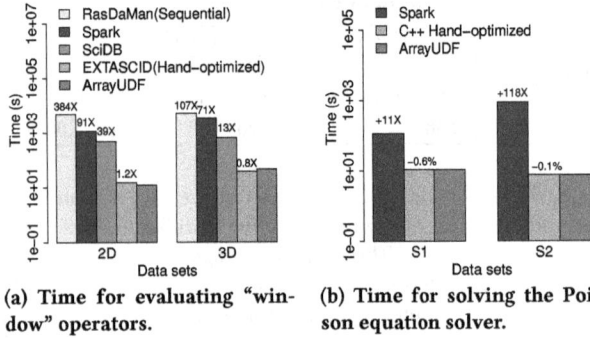

(a) Time for evaluating "window" operators.

(b) Time for solving the Poisson equation solver.

Figure 11: Comparison of ArrayUDF with the state-of-the-art data processing systems.

CPU cores (Intel i7-5557U CPU with 3.10 GHz), two threads per core, and a local disk (Seagate ST1000LM014-1EJ1) with the EXT4 file system. We show these test results in Fig. 11a. The original datasets $S1$ and $S2$ are too large for the processing on a single node. Thus, we used smaller size datasets for tests. The tested 2D dataset has an array with a size of $(10000, 30000)$ and the 3D dataset has a size of $(1000, 1000, 400)$. The chunk size for all the systems is set to be $(5000, 15000)$ for 2D and $(1000, 1000, 100)$ for 3D which give 4 chunks per array—equivalent the number of threads in the system.

RasDaMan has the highest execution time because the version that is publicly available only supports "inter-query parallelization" and, thus, it can only use one core to perform the calculation. Spark can use its Map and Reduce interface to implement the window-based average, however, it needs to duplicate the data for different windows. As a result, it has the second highest execution time. In terms of SciDB, it handles each window independently and inefficiently [23], thus SciDB is also much slower than ArrayUDF. We also scale the SciDB tests to 11 nodes on the Edison system for $S1$ and $S2$ datasets. In these tests, we observe similar results. EXTASCID provides a robust array data storage model, but it has no portable window-like operator yet. For comparison, we have implemented the window function manually as a generalized linear aggregate (GLA) function, which is the abstract interface in EXTASCID. Basically, the window functions are written in C++ and they use the EXTASCID I/O driver to access the arrays. Even with this hand-optimized code, the execution times of EXTASCID are similar to those of ArrayUDF. In other words, the performance of ArrayUDF is very close to the C++ hand-optimized code. Thus, we conclude that ArrayUDF provides more flexibility to define operations, and it is as efficient as highly-optimized code in performing "window" based analysis tasks.

Comparing ArrayUDF with Spark on solving the Poisson equation on datasets $S1$ and $S2$. In this test, we compare the performance of using ArrayUDF and Spark to solve the Poisson equation with 64 computing nodes. By using ArrayUDF, we can directly define and execute the Poisson equation solver on arrays stored in datasets $S1$ and $S2$, as shown at the beginning of this section. To use Spark for expressing these operations, we apply the "flatmap" and "reducebykey" functions. The general idea is that all the adjacent stencil cells required by a cell are viewed as a group and all cells within the group are aggregated onto a single reducer to perform the computation. Since each cell belongs to

multiple groups (of its neighbors), we use "flatmap" to transform each cell into multiple (key, value) pairs, where the key is the group ID and the value is the actual data. After "flatmap" finishes, we use "reducebykey" to consolidate all the cells with the same group ID together. Basically, each reducer is responsible for computing a cell in the result array. One may argue that users can write a specific Map function without a Reduce funtion to solve the Poisson equation. However, as discussed in previous sections, both ArrayUDF and Spark aim at providing a generic UDF mechanism for users to express high-level operations without burdening users to write custom programs for performing different operations.

We compare the performance of ArrayUDF and Spark in executing the Poisson equation solver in Fig. 11b. For datasets $S1$ and $S2$, ArrayUDF is 11 and 118 times faster than Spark, respectively. Since the Poisson equation solver on 3D data needs to access more adjacent cells than on 2D data, ArrayUDF achieves a higher performance improvement for processing $S2$. Basically, the more neighbor cells are required, the more times the entire array is replicated in Spark. As the size of the data to be replicated increases, Spark spends more time on communication and shuffling for "flatmap" and "reducebykey" functions. Compared with Spark, ArrayUDF allows users to define and execute the Poisson equation solver directly on an array. Thus, there is no data replication during the runtime. Moreover, as ArrayUDF can automatically build the ghost zone using a trial-run, the expensive communication is avoided.

4.2 ArrayUDF for real scientific data analysis

We have evaluated ArrayUDF to perform several real-world analysis tasks on four scientific data sets: S3D, VPIC, MSI, and CoRTAD. We summarize the properties of these datasets and the analysis operations performed in this study in Table 3. A brief background is presented in § 2. To compare performance, we use Spark to implement the same analysis tasks on these datasets. The method to implement these analysis operations is the same as the one we use for the Poisson solver on the $S1$ and $S2$ datasets. We test each task with different numbers of CPU cores, scaling from 384 (i.e., 16 compute nodes) to 1536 (i.e., 64 nodes). As shown in Fig. 12, for S3D, VPIC, and MSI analysis, ArrayUDF outperforms Spark by up to 26×, 220×, and 2070×, respectively. For CoRTAD, Spark crashes due to out-of-memory (OOM) errors. We discuss the performance of each of these analysis tasks in the following.

Table 3: Real-world scientific datasets and operations

dataset	Rank	Size (GB)	Operation
S3D	3D	301	Vorticity computation
MSI	3D	21	Laplacian calculator
VPIC	3D	36	Trilinear interpolation
CoRTAD	3D	225	Simple moving average

S3D. For the S3D dataset, we compute the vorticity, which is defined in Eq. 2. For a single point in S3D, the vorticity computation needs the values of four neighbors in total and two neighbors per direction. In this test, we use the dataset in the x direction. This data has $1100 \times 1080 \times 1408$ dimensions, resulting in a file size of 22 GB. We show the execution time for vorticity computation using ArrayUDF and Spark in Fig. 12a. On average, ArrayUDF is 18 times faster than Spark. We observe similar performance speedup in the y and z dimensions. In summary, we observe that ArrayUDF is more efficient than Spark in computing vorticity over the S3D dataset.

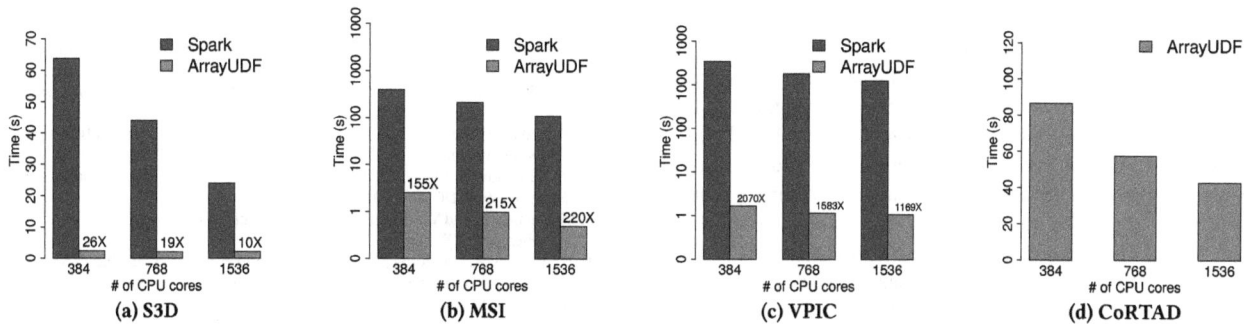

Figure 12: Evaluation with analyzing real-world scientific datasets. ArrayUDF is up to 2070X faster than Spark. For the CoRTAD dataset, where we show the performance only for ArrayUDF, Spark crashes due to out-of-memory (OOM) error.

MSI. The MSI data [34] used in our test contains a $123 \times 463 \times 188960$ 3D array which has 21 GB in file size. This array contains images of a potato eye. The operation of interest on this dataset is the Laplacian calculator, as presented in Eq. 3. In our tests, we observe that ArrayUDF is 196 times faster than Spark. Since the Laplacian calculator needs five neighbor cells, but vorticity on S3D only needs *two*, ArrayUDF achieves a higher speedup in this test. As discussed before, the more adjacent cells are needed in UDF, the higher speedup ArrayUDF can achieve.

VPIC. In the space weather simulation using VPIC, the total size for the magnetic field data is 36 GB and the data has x, y and z dimensions [11]. The dimensions of the dataset are $2000 \times 2000 \times 800$. We use both ArrayUDF and Spark to implement the trilinear interpolation shown in Eq. 4. For simplicity, we assume that there is a particle in a cell. But, our ArrayUDF can be extended to support more flexible interpolation. We report the results for the x dimension in Fig.12c—we obtain similar results for dimensions. On average, ArrayUDF is 1607X faster than Spark in this test.

CoRTAD. CoRTAD is a collection of sea surface temperatures (SST) [1]. It contains the weekly temperature for 1617×4320 sites from 1981 to 2010. Thus, it is a 3D array with size $1617 \times 4320 \times 8640$, where the third dimension is the number of weeks (i.e., 8640 weeks). We compute a moving average based smoothing on this data. Basically, for each site, we smoothen its temperature based on the month, i.e., compute the average of four neighbor array cells. In Fig. 12d, we depict only the performance of ArrayUDF. For the tests with the same number of CPU cores, Spark crashes with out-of-memory errors. The reason for the OOM errors is the need for Spark to replicate the entire dataset 4 times in oder to compute the moving average. Moreover, since we also need to use the (key, value) pair structure and the Scala object type to store the data, the total data size increases by more than 8 times, which contributes to the OOM errors. Meanwhile, ArrayUDF successfully completes the moving average computation for this large dataset without any memory footprint pressure.

5 RELATED WORK

UDFs are widely supported by relational database management systems, such as SQL Server [13], IBM DB2 [44], MySQL [42], and PostgreSQL [30]. MonetDB [33] has an extension to support vector-based UDFs that take advantage of the columnar data representation. The UDFs within these systems are based on the relational set semantics and permit users to define operations at tuple or table level—known as User-Defined Aggregates (UDA) [15]. The

key difference between ArrayUDF and these types of UDFs is that ArrayUDF is developed for multi-dimensional arrays and allows more general structural locality based operations.

In MapReduce [18], UDFs consist of two steps—Map and Reduce. Map applies the UDF on a single key-value pair and produces one or more key-value pairs as output. Reduce consolidates key-value pairs having the same key and then applies another UDF. Reduce requires expensive data shuffling to repartition data across nodes. Among all extensions to MapReduce [4, 10, 21, 22, 40], Spark provides a much richer set of UDFs for iterative in-memory analysis. Compared to MapReduce and its extensions, ArrayUDF requires a single step to express UDFs on a set of related array cells, thus avoiding the expensive shuffle stage.

Array database systems such as RasDaMan[6], AML[27], SciDB[9], SciQL[24] and EXTASCID[17], have UDF support. Rusu et al. [35] provides a complete survey on this topic. Typically, these array UDFs follow a similar idea to relational database systems, where users define an operation on a single element, i.e., array cell. If the UDF requires multiple adjacent cells, these have to be mapped into tuples and then apply the UDF. ArrayUDF is a novel UDF type for arrays that allows users to define operations directly on adjacent array cells, without any mapping. Moreover, to support efficient data access in a shared-disk system, ArrayUDF performs dynamic chunking and ghost zone building. In contrast, array database management systems have a shared-nothing architecture and rely on data ingestion to handle chunking and ghost zones. A specific type of array UDF is the window-based *Apply* operator [27]. SciDB provides this function via a highly optimized *window* operator. RasDaMan has a similar operator named *condense*. While similar to ArrayUDF, these operators support only fixed-size windows and the operations on a window are limited. ArrayUDF generalizes the window shape and the operations for the cells within a window. *Join* operators are found to be expensive to support these operations because of data replication [20, 43]. SAGA [41] explores aggregate operations on scientific arrays stored in native data formats.

The domain-specific languages (DSL) [7, 29] share similarity with our ArrayUDF in leveraging stencil behaviors to improve performance of array based data analytics. These DSLs are mostly developed as programming language and compiler extensions with the goal of increasing the efficiency of calculation and memory data access. But, in ArrayUDF, we developed a flexible computing model towards large-scale data analytics, i.e., to derive knowledge from the multidimensional arrays in data files directly. The ArrayUDF generalizes the *MapReduce − like* systems to realize a wider range of operations on arrays, including the stencil operator supported by these DSLs. Beyond that, ArrayUDF has the capability to express other types of operations, such as aggregation, filtering, etc. Moreover, ArrayUDF provides optimizations (e.g., *trial run* based ghost zone determination, disk layout aware/unaware partitions for multidimensional array) for efficiently processing out-of-core data sets, which are too large to be quickly loaded into memory, even with multiple nodes. Our analytical performance model for ArrayUDF can also be used as the foundation to optimize these existing stencil DSL systems in handling large-scale scientific datasets on disk.

6 CONCLUSIONS AND FUTURE WORK

Customized data analysis, especially for data stored as multidimensional arrays in large files, is a common method to extract insights from data and the UDF mechanism is a general strategy to support this analysis. However, the current UDF implementations are not able to effectively express the structural locality present in most array based data analysis operations, such as computing the vorticity for a 3D flow field, the moving average for a time series, etc. These operations have to be expressed as expensive *join* or *reduction* operations. We design ArrayUDF to easily capture the generalized structural locality and implement an *in situ* processing system optimized for multi-dimensional arrays. The generalized structural locality mechanism of ArrayUDF allows users to define a different operation on each neighbor separately and, therefore, express more complex customized data analysis. The *in situ* processing system automatically partitions data stored in raw data files and creates ghost zones for the arrays stored in files without an expensive data ingestion phase. Our automatic data partitioning minimizes the execution time based on a an analytical model of the expected performance. It is also able to take advantage of the layout of arrays in input data files. Our evaluation using a number of different scientific datasets show that ArrayUDF is up to three orders of magnitude faster than Apache Spark. In future, we plan to enhance ArrayUDF with a filter feature to reduce loading of unnecessary array cells in the result arrays. We will also explore the use of ArrayUDF to process stream and real-time data.

Acknowledgment. This effort was supported by the U.S. Department of Energy (DOE), Office of Science, Office of Advanced Scientific Computing Research under contract number DE-AC02-05CH11231 and by a DOE Career award (program manager Dr. Lucy Nowell). This research used resources of the National Energy Research Scientific Computing Center (NERSC), a DOE Office of Science User Facility.

REFERENCES

[1] The Coral Reef Temperature Anomaly Database (CoRTAD) Version 4 - Global, 4 km Sea Surface Temperature and Related Thermal Stress Metrics for 1981-10-31 to 2010-12-31 (NODC Accession 0087989), 2012.
[2] M. Abadi, A. Agarwal, et al. Tensorflow: Large-scale machine learning on heterogeneous distributed systems, 2015.
[3] I. Alagiannis, R. Borovica, M. Branco, S. Idreos, and A. Ailamaki. Nodb: Efficient query execution on raw data files. In *SIGMOD '12*, 2012.
[4] L. Antova, A. El-Helw, M. A. Soliman, Z. Gu, M. Petropoulos, and F. Waas. Optimizing Queries over Partitioned Tables in MPP Systems. In *SIGMOD*, 2014.
[5] P. Baumann. Management of Multidimensional Discrete Data. *VLDB J.*, 1994.
[6] P. Baumann, A. Dehmel, P. Furtado, R. Ritsch, and N. Widmann. The Multidimensional Database System RasDaMan. *SIGMOD Rec.*, 27(2):575–577, 1998.
[7] M. Bianco and B. Cumming. A generic strategy for multi-stage stencils. In *Euro-Par'14*, pages 584–595, 2014.
[8] S. Blanas, K. Wu, S. Byna, B. Dong, and A. Shoshani. Parallel Data Analysis Directly on Scientific File Formats. In *SIGMOD'2014*.

[9] P. G. Brown. Overview of SciDB: Large Scale Array Storage, Processing and Analysis. In *SIGMOD*, 2010.
[10] J. B. Buck, N. Watkins, and et al. SciHadoop: Array-based Query Processing in Hadoop. In *Supercomputing Conference (SC)*, 2011.
[11] S. Byna, J. Chou, O. Rübel, H. Karimabadi, et al. Parallel I/O, Analysis, and Visualization of a Trillion Particle Simulation. In *SC*, 2012.
[12] N. Chaimov, A. Malony, S. Canon, C. Iancu, and et al. Scaling Spark on HPC Systems. In *HPDC 2016*, 2016.
[13] S. Chaudhuri and V. R. Narasayya. An Efficient Cost-Driven Index Selection Tool for Microsoft SQL Server. In *VLDB '97*, 1997.
[14] J. H. Chen, A. Choudhary, B. de Supinski, and et al. Terascale Direct Numerical Simulations of Turbulent Combustion Using S3D. *Computational Science & Discovery*, 2(1):015001, 2009.
[15] Y. Cheng, C. Qin, and F. Rusu. GLADE: Big Data Analytics Made Easy. In *SIGMOD 2012*.
[16] Y. Cheng and F. Rusu. Astronomical Data Processing in EXTASCID. In *SSDBM 2013*.
[17] Y. Cheng and F. Rusu. Formal Representation of the SS-DB Benchmark and Experimental Evaluation in EXTASCID. *Distributed and Parallel Databases*, 33(3):277–317, 2015.
[18] J. Dean and S. Ghemawat. MapReduce: Simplified Data Processing on Large Clusters. *Commun. ACM*, 51(1):107–113, Jan. 2008.
[19] B. Dong, S. Byna, and K. Wu. SDS: A Framework for Scientific Data Services. In *Proceedings of the 8th Parallel Data Storage Workshop*, PDSW '13, pages 27–32, New York, NY, USA, 2013. ACM.
[20] B. Dong, S. Byna, and K. Wu. Spatially Clustered Join on Heterogeneous Scientific Data Sets. In *2015 IEEE Big Data*, pages 371–380, Oct 2015.
[21] E. Friedman, P. Pawlowski, and J. Cieslewicz. SQL/MapReduce: A Practical Approach to Self-describing, Polymorphic, and Parallelizable User-defined Functions. *Proc. VLDB Endow.*, 2(2):1402–1413, Aug. 2009.
[22] Y. Huai, A. Chauhan, A. Gates, G. Hagleitner, E. N. Hanson, O. O'Malley, J. Pandey, Y. Yuan, R. Lee, and X. Zhang. Major Technical Advancements in Apache Hive. In *SIGMOD '14*, 2014.
[23] L. Jiang, H. Kawashima, and O. Tatebe. Efficient Window Aggregate Method on Array Database System. *Journal of Information Processing*, 24(6):867–877, 2016.
[24] M. Kersten, Y. Zhang, M. Ivanova, and N. Nes. Sciql, a query language for science applications. In *AD '11*, 2011.
[25] D. E. Keyes, Y. Saad, and D. G. Truhlar, editors. *Doman-Based Parallelism and Problem Decomposition Methods in Computational Science and Engineering*. SIAM, Philadelphia, PA, 1995.
[26] J. Liu, E. Racah, Q. Koziol, and et al. H5Spark: Bridging the I/O Gap between Spark and Scientific Data Formats on HPC Systems. In *Cray User Group*, 2016.
[27] A. P. Marathe and K. Salem. A Language for Manipulating Arrays. In *VLDB '97*.
[28] V. Markl. Breaking the Chains: On Declarative Data Analysis and Data Independence in the Big Data Era. *Proc. VLDB Endow.*, 7(13):1730–1733, Aug. 2014.
[29] N. Maruyama, T. Nomura, K. Sato, and S. Matsuoka. Physis: an implicitly parallel programming model for stencil computations on large-scale gpu-accelerated supercomputers. In *SC '11*, pages 11:1–11:12, New York, NY, USA, 2011. ACM.
[30] B. Momjian. *PostgreSQL: Introduction and Concepts*. Addison-Wesley Longman Publishing Co., Inc., Boston, MA, USA, 2001.
[31] M. A. Onabid. Solving Three-Dimensional (3D) Laplace Equations by Successive Over-Relaxation Method. *AJMCSR*, 5(13), 2012.
[32] Y. Peng et al. The design of the variable sampling interval generalized likelihood ratio chart for monitoring the process mean. *Qual. Reliab. Engng. Int*, 31(2), 2015.
[33] M. Raasveldt. Vectorized UDFs in Column-Stores (Master Thesis), 2015.
[34] O. Rübel, A. Greiner, and et al. OpenMSI: A High-Performance Web-Based Platform for Mass Spectrometry Imaging. *Analytical Chemistry*, 2013.
[35] F. Rusu and Y. Cheng. A Survey on Array Storage, Query Languages, and Systems. *CoRR*, abs/1302.0103, 2013.
[36] A. Shoshani and D. Rotem, editors. *Scientific Data Management: Challenges, Technology, and Deployment*. Chapman & Hall/CRC Press, 2010.
[37] E. Soroush, M. Balazinska, and D. Wang. ArrayStore: A Storage Manager for Complex Parallel Array Processing. In *SIGMOD'2011*, 2011.
[38] H. Tang, S. Byna, S. Harenberg, et al. Usage pattern-driven dynamic data layout reorganization. In *CCGrid'2016*, pages 356–365, May 2016.
[39] The HDF Group. HDF5 User Guide, 2010.
[40] Y. Wang, W. Jiang, and G. Agrawal. SciMATE: A Novel MapReduce-Like Framework for Multiple Scientific Data Formats. In *CCGrid'2012*, pages 443–450, 2012.
[41] Y. Wang, A. Nandi, and G. Agrawal. SAGA: Array Storage As a DB with Support for Structural Aggregations. In *SSDBM '14*, New York, NY, USA, 2014. ACM.
[42] M. Widenius and D. Axmark. *MySQL Reference Manual*. O'Reilly & Associates, Inc., Sebastopol, CA, USA, 2002.
[43] W. Zhao, F. Rusu, B. Dong, and K. Wu. Similarity Join over Array Data. In *SIGMOD 2016*.
[44] P. C. Zikopoulos and R. B. Melnyk. *DB2: The Complete Reference*. McGraw-Hill, Inc., New York, NY, USA, 2001.

Deep Learning in Cancer and Infectious Disease: Novel Driver Problems for Future HPC Architecture

Rick Stevens

Argonne National Laboratory

The University of Chicago

stevens@cs.uchicago.edu

ABSTRACT

The adoption of machine learning is proving to be an amazingly successful strategy in improving predictive models for cancer and infectious disease. In this talk I will discuss two projects my group is working on to advance biomedical research through the use of machine learning and HPC. In cancer, machine learning and in deep learning in particular, is used to advance our ability to diagnosis and classify tumors. Recently demonstrated automated systems are routinely out performing human expertise. Deep learning is also being used to predict patient response to cancer treatments and to screen for new anti-cancer compounds. In basic cancer research its being used to supervise large-scale multi-resolution molecular dynamics simulations used to explore cancer gene signaling pathways. In public health, it's being used to interpret millions of medical records to identify optimal treatment strategies. In infectious disease research machine learning methods are being used to predict antibiotic resistance and to identify novel antibiotic resistance mechanisms that might be present. More generally machine learning is emerging as a general tool to augment and extend mechanistic models in biology and many other fields. It's becoming an important component of scientific workloads. From a computational architecture standpoint, deep neural network (DNN) based scientific applications have some unique requirements.

They require high compute density to support matrix-matrix and matrix-vector operations, but they rarely require 64bit or even 32bits of precision, thus architects are creating new instructions and new design points to accelerate training.

Most current DNNs rely on dense fully connected networks and convolutional networks and thus are reasonably matched to current HPC accelerators. However future DNNs may rely less on dense communication patterns. Like simulation codes, power efficient DNNs require high-bandwidth memory be physically close to arithmetic units to reduce costs of data motion and a high-bandwidth communication fabric between (perhaps modest scale) groups of processors to support network model parallelism. DNNs in general do not have good strong scaling behavior, so to fully exploit large-scale parallelism they rely on a combination of model, data and search parallelism. Deep learning problems also require large-quantities of training data to be made available or generated at each node, thus providing opportunities for NVRAM.

Discovering optimal deep learning models often involves a large-scale search of hyper parameters. It's not uncommon to search a space of tens of thousands of model configurations. Naïve searches are outperformed by various intelligent searching strategies, including new approaches that use generative neural networks to manage the search space. HPC architectures that can support these large-scale intelligent search methods as well as efficient model training are needed.

BIOGRAPHY

I am interested in the development of innovative tools and techniques that enable computational scientists to solve large-scale problems more effectively on the most advanced high-performance computers. Specifically, my research focuses on three principal areas: collaborative visualization environments, high-performance computer architectures, and performance modeling.

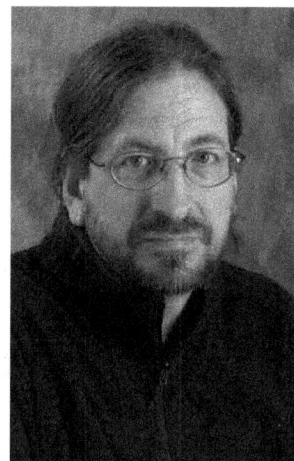

In the area of collaborative visualization, I am exploring the use of virtual reality in the visualization of scientific data and processes. My efforts include improving displays, recording, and playback of virtual reality experiences; developing new methods for tracking and control and close coupling with parallel supercomputers; and devising new ways of collaborating in virtual environments. Of particular interest to me is tele immersion - strategies for synthesizing networking and multimedia technologies to enhance the development of wide-area collaborative computational science.

In the area of high-performance computers, I am studying approaches to computing at the Petaflops Scale, focusing on analysis, modeling, and simulation tools for these ultra-high-performance computers. I am also particularly interested in algorithm and software for multithreaded computer architectures and for hierarchical processor and memory architectures.

In a related area, I am investigating analytic performance models that will help researchers understand the performance relationship between high-performance computer systems and scientific applications. My goal is to enable scientific simulations to achieve the very high-performance potential of next-generation computer architectures with deep memory hierarchies.

HPDC'17, June 26–30, 2017, Washington, DC, USA.

ACM ISBN 978-1-4503-4699-3/17/06.

DOI: http://dx.doi.org/10.1145/3078597.3091526

knor: A NUMA-Optimized In-Memory, Distributed and Semi-External-Memory k-means Library

Disa Mhembere
Dept. of Computer Science,
Johns Hopkins University
Baltimore, Maryland

Da Zheng
Dept. of Computer Science,
Johns Hopkins University
Baltimore, Maryland

Carey E. Priebe
Dept. of Applied Math and Statistics,
Johns Hopkins University
Baltimore, Maryland

Joshua T. Vogelstein
Institute for Computational Medicine,
Dept. of Biomedical Engineering,
Johns Hopkins University
Baltimore, Maryland

Randal Burns
Dept. of Computer Science,
Johns Hopkins University
Baltimore, Maryland

ABSTRACT

k-means is one of the most influential and utilized machine learning algorithms. Its computation limits the performance and scalability of many statistical analysis and machine learning tasks. We rethink and optimize k-means in terms of modern NUMA architectures to develop a novel parallelization scheme that delays and minimizes synchronization barriers. The *k-means NUMA Optimized Routine* (knor) library has (i) in-memory (knori), (ii) distributed memory (knord), and (ii) semi-external memory (knors) modules that radically improve the performance of k-means for varying memory and hardware budgets. knori boosts performance for single machine datasets by an order of magnitude or more. knors improves the scalability of k-means on a memory budget using SSDs. knors scales to billions of points on a single machine, using a fraction of the resources that distributed in-memory systems require. knord retains knori's performance characteristics, while scaling in-memory through distributed computation in the cloud. knor modifies Elkan's triangle inequality pruning algorithm such that we utilize it on billion-point datasets without the significant memory overhead of the original algorithm. We demonstrate knor outperforms distributed commercial products like H_2O, Turi (formerly Dato, GraphLab) and Spark's MLlib by more than an order of magnitude for datasets of 10^7 to 10^9 points.

KEYWORDS

NUMA, k-means, semi-external memory, cloud, clustering, parallel

ACM Reference format:
Disa Mhembere, Da Zheng, Carey E. Priebe, Joshua T. Vogelstein, and Randal Burns. 2017. knor: A NUMA-Optimized In-Memory, Distributed and Semi-External-Memory k-means Library. In *Proceedings of HPDC '17, Washington , DC, USA, June 26-30, 2017,* 12 pages.
DOI: http://dx.doi.org/10.1145/3078597.3078607

1 INTRODUCTION

Clustering data to maximize within-cluster similarity and cross-cluster variance is highly desirable for the analysis of big data. K-means is an intuitive and highly popular method of clustering n points in d-dimensions into k clusters. A very popular synchronous variant of k-means is Lloyd's algorithm [22]. Similar to Expectation Maximization [8], Lloyd's algorithm proceeds in two phases. In phase one, we compute the distance from each data point to each centroid (cluster mean). In phase two, we update the centroids to be the mean of their membership. This proceeds until the centroids no longer change from one iteration to the next. The algorithm locally minimizes within-cluster *distance*, for some distance metric that often is Euclidean distance (Section 4). Despite k-means' popularity, state-of-the-art machine learning libraries [16, 23, 28] experience many challenges scaling performance well with respect to growing data sets. Furthermore, these libraries place an emphasis on scaling-out computation to the distributed setting, neglecting to fully utilize the resources within each machine.

The decomposition of extremely large datasets into clusters of data points that are similar is a topic of great interest in industry and academia. For example, clustering is the backbone upon which popular user recommendation systems at Netflix [3] are built. Furthermore, partitioning multi-billion data points is essential to targeted ad-driven organizations such as Google [6] and Facebook [38]. In addition, clustering is highly applicable to neuroscience and genetics research. Connectomics [4, 24, 25], uses clustering to group anatomical regions by structural, physiological, and functional similarity, for the purposes of inference. Behavioromics [39] uses clustering to map neurons to distinct motor patterns. In genetics, clustering is used to infer relationships between genetically similar species [20, 30].

The greatest challenges facing tool builders are *(i)* reducing the cost of the synchronization barrier between the first and second phase of k-means, *(ii)* mitigating the latency of data movement through the memory hierarchy, and *(iii)* scaling to arbitrarily large datasets, while maintaining performance. In addition, fully asynchronous computation for Lloyd's algorithm is infeasible because each iteration updates global state, membership and centroids. The resulting global barriers pose a major challenge to the performance and scalability of parallel and distributed implementations; this is especially true for data that require large numbers of iterations to converge.

Popular frameworks [23, 28, 29] have converged on scale-out, distributed processing in which data are partitioned among cluster nodes, often randomly, and global updates are transmitted at the speed of the interconnect. These frameworks are negatively affected by inefficient data allocation, management, and task scheduling protocols with regards to k-means. This design incurs heavy network traffic owing to data shuffling and centralized master-worker designs. Furthermore, such frameworks struggle to capitalize on potential gains from the use of computation pruning techniques, such as Elkan's triangle inequality algorithm (TI) [11]. Pruning introduces skew in which few workers have the bulk of the computation. Skew degrades parallelism. While skew can be dealt with through dynamic scheduling, this incurs data movement and message passing overheads.

In contrast, our k-means prefers scale-up computation on shared-memory multicore machines in order to eliminate network traffic and perform fine-grained synchronization. A current trend for hardware design scales up a single machine, rather than scaling out to many networked machines, integrating large memories and using solid-state storage devices (SSDs) to extend memory capacity. This conforms to the node design for supercomputers [2]. Recent findings, from Frank McSherry [27, 35] and our prior work [45], show that the largest graph analytics tasks can be done on a small fraction of the hardware, at less cost, as fast, and using less energy on a single shared-memory node, rather than a distributed compute engine. Our findings reveal that clustering has the same structure. We perform k-means on a single or few machines to minimize network bottlenecks and find that even our single node performance (with SSDs) outperforms our competitor's distributed performance on many instances.

Our approach advances Lloyd's algorithm for modern, multicore NUMA architectures to achieve a high degree of parallelism by significantly merging the two phases in Lloyd's. We present knori, a fast in-memory, module that performs several orders of magnitude faster than other state-of-the-art systems for datasets that fit into main memory. We implement a practical modification to TI, that we call the minimal triangle inequality (MTI). TI incurs a memory increment of $O(nd)$, limiting its scalability. MTI requires an increase of only $O(n)$ memory, drastically improving its utility for large-scale datasets. In practice, MTI outperforms TI because it requires significantly less data structure maintenance, while still pruning computation comparably. knor clusters data an order of magnitude faster than competitors.

The knord distributed module builds directly on knori and runs across multiple machines using a decentralized driver. It runs on larger datasets that fit in the aggregate memory of multiple nodes.

knors is a semi-external memory implementation that scales the computation of a single node beyond memory bounds. Semi-external memory (SEM) k-means holds $O(n)$ data in memory while streaming $O(nd)$ data from disk for a dataset, $\vec{V} \in \mathbb{R}^{n \times d}$. This notion of SEM is analogous to the definition of SEM for graph algorithms [1, 31] in which vertex state is kept in memory and edge lists on disk. We build knors on a modified FlashGraph [45] framework to access asynchronous I/O and overlap I/O and computation. knors uses a

fraction of the memory of popular frameworks and outperforms them by large factors using less hardware.

This work demonstrates that k-means on extremely large datasets can be run on increasingly smaller/fewer machines than possible before; creating reductions in monetary expense and power consumption. Furthermore, our routines are highly portable. We simply require the C++11 standard library be available, with thread-level parallelism is implemented using the POSIX thread (p-threads) library. Distributed routines rely on the Message Passing Library, MPI [12]. The I/O components for SEM routines are implemented using low-level Linux interfaces.

2 RELATED WORK

Zhao et al [43] developed a parallel k-means routine on Hadoop!, an open source implementation of MapReduce [7]. Their implementation has much in common with Mahout [29], a machine learning library for: Hadoop!. The Map-Reduce paradigm consists of a Map phase, a synchronization barrier in which data are shuffled to *reducers*, then a Reduce phase. For k-means one would perform distance computations in the Map phase and build centroids to be used in the following iteration in Reduce phase. The model allows for effortless scalability and parallelism, but little flexibility in how to achieve either. As such, the implementation is subject to skew within the reduce phase as data points assigned to the same centroid end up at a single *reducer*.

MLlib is a machine learning library for Spark [42]. Spark imposes a functional paradigm to parallelism allowing for delayed computation through the use of transformations that form a lineage. The lineage is then evaluated and automatically parallelized. MLlib's performance is highly coupled with Spark's ability to efficiently parallelize computation using the generic data abstraction of resilient distributed datasets [41].

Other works focus on developing fast k-means approximations. Sophia-ML uses a mini-batch algorithm that uses sampling to reduce the cost of Lloyd's algorithm (also referred to as batched k-means) and stochastic gradient descent k-means [36]. Sophia-ML's target application is online, real-time applications, which differs from our goal of exact k-means on large scale data. Shindler et al [37] developed a fast approximation that addresses scalability by streaming data from disk sequentially, limiting the amount of memory necessary to iterate. This shares some similarity with knors, but is designed for a single processor, passing over the data just once and operating on medium-sized data. We avoid approximations; they see little widespread use owing to questions of cluster quality.

Elkan proposed the use of the triangle inequality (TI) with bounds [11], to reduce the number of distance computations to fewer than $O(kn)$ per iteration. TI determines when the distance of data point, v_i, that is assigned to a cluster, c_i, is far enough from any other cluster, $c_x, x \in \{1..k\} - i$, so that no distance computation is required between v_i and c_x. This method is extremely effective in pruning computation in real-world data, i.e. data with multiple natural clusters. The method relies on a sparse lower bound matrix of size $O(nk)$. Yinyang k-means [9] develop a competitor pruning technique to TI that maintains a lower-bound matrix of size $O(nt)$, where t is a parameter and $t = k/10$ is generally optimal. Yingyang k-means outperforms TI by reducing the cost of maintenance of their lower-bound matrix. Both Yinyang k-means and TI suffer from scalability limitations because the lower-bound matrix increases in-memory state asymptotically. We propose MTI for computation pruning. MTI costs a constant $O(n)$ more memory making it practical for use with big-data.

FlashGraph [45] is a SEM graph computation framework that places edge data on SSDs and allows user-defined vertex state to be held in memory. FlashGraph partitions a graph then exposes a vertex-centric programming interface that permits users to define functions written from the perspective of a single vertex, known as *vertex programs*. Parallelization is obtained from running multiple vertex programs concurrently. FlashGraph overlaps I/O with computation to mask latency in data movement through the memory hierarchy. FlashGraph is also tolerant to in-memory failures, allowing recovery in SEM routines through lightweight checkpointing.

FlashGraph is built on top of a userspace filesystem called SAFS [44]. SAFS provides a framework to perform high speed I/O from an array of SSDs. To facilitate this, both SAFS and FlashGraph work to merge I/O requests for multiple requests when requests are made for data located near one another on disk. This I/O merging amortizes the cost of accesses to SSDs. SAFS creates and manages a *page cache* that pins frequently touched pages in memory. The page cache reduces the number of actual I/O requests made to disk. Section 6.1 discusses the modifications we make to FlashGraph to build knors on top of FlashGraph.

3 NOMENCLATURE

We define notation that we use throughout the manuscript. Let $\mathbb{N}$ be the set of all natural numbers. Let $\mathbb{R}$ be the set of all real numbers. Let $\vec{v}$ be a d-dimension vector in the dataset $\vec{V}$ with cardinality, $|\vec{V}| = n$. Let j be the number of iterations of Lloyd's algorithm we perform in a single run of k-means. Let $t \in \{0...j\}$ be the current iteration within a run of k-means. Let $\vec{c}^t$ be a d-dimension vector representing the mean of a cluster (i.e., a centroid), at iteration t. Let $\vec{C}^t$ be the set of the k centroids at iteration t, with cardinality $|\vec{C}^t| = k$. In a given iteration, t, we can cluster any point, $\vec{v}$ into a cluster $\vec{c}^t$. We use Euclidean distance, denoted as $\mathbf{d}$, as the dissimilarity metric between any $\vec{v}$ and $\vec{c}^t$, such that $\mathbf{d}(\vec{v}, \vec{c}^t) = \sqrt{(\vec{v}_1 - \vec{c}_1^t)^2 + (\vec{v}_2 - \vec{c}_2^t)^2 + ... + (\vec{v}_{d-1} - \vec{c}_{d-1}^t)^2 + (\vec{v}_d - \vec{c}_d^t)^2}$.

Let $f(\vec{c}^t | t > 0) = \mathbf{d}(\vec{c}^t, \vec{c}^{t-1})$. Finally, let T be the number of threads of concurrent execution, P be the number of processing elements available (e.g. the number of cores in the machine), and N be the number of NUMA nodes.

4 PARALLEL LLOYD'S ALGORITHM

Underlying further optimizations is our parallel version of Lloyd's algorithm (||Lloyd's) that boosts the performance of knor and reduces factors limiting parallelism in a naïve parallel Lloyd's algorithm. Traditionally Lloyd's operates in two-phases each separated by a global barrier as follows:

(1) Phase I: Compute the nearest centroid, $c\_nearest^t$ to each data point, $\vec{v}$, at iteration t.
(2) Global barrier.
(3) Phase II: Update each centroid, for the next iteration, $\vec{c}^{t+1}$ to be the mean value of all points nearest to it in Phase I.

(4) Global barrier.
(5) Repeat until converged.

Naïve Lloyd's uses two major data structures; A read-only global centroids structure, $\vec{c}^t$, and a shared global centroids for the next iteration, $\vec{c}^{t+1}$. Parallelism in Phase II is limited to k threads because $\vec{c}^{t+1}$ is shared. As such, Phase II is plagued with substantial locking overhead because of the high likelihood of data points concurrently attempting to update the the same nearest centroid. Consequently, as n gets larger with respect to k this interference worsens, further degrading performance.

||Lloyd's retains the read-only global centroid structure $\vec{c}^t$, but provides each thread with its own local copy of the next iteration's centroids. Thus we create T copies of $\vec{c}^{t+1}$. Doing so means ||Lloyd's merges Phase I and II into a super-phase and eliminates the barrier (Step 3 above). The super-phase concurrently computes the nearest centroid to each point and updates a local version of the centroids to be used in the following iteration. These local centroids can then be merged in parallel through a reduction operation at the end of the iteration. ||Lloyd's trades-off increased parallelism for a slightly higher memory consumption by a factor of $O(T)$ over Lloyd's. This algorithm design naturally leads to lock-free routines that require fewer synchronization barriers as we show in Algorithm 1.

Algorithm 1 || Lloyd's algorithm

1: **procedure** ||MEANS($\vec{V}, \vec{C}^t, k$)
2:     $pt\vec{C}^t$ ▷ Per-thread centroids
3:     $clusterAssignment^t$ ▷ Shared, no conflict
4:     tid   ▷ Current thread ID
5:     **parfor** $\vec{v} \in \vec{V}$ **do**
6:         $dist = \infty$
7:         $c\_nearest^t$ = INVALID
8:         **for** $\vec{c}^t \in \vec{C}^t$ **do**
9:             **if** $\mathbf{d}(\vec{v}, \vec{c}^t) < dist$ **then**
10:                 $dist = \mathbf{d}(\vec{v}, \vec{c}^t)$
11:                 $c\_nearest^t = \vec{c}^t$
12:            **end if**
13:        **end for**
14:        $pt\vec{C}^t[tid][c\_nearest^t] \mathrel{+}= \vec{v}$
15:    **end parfor**
16:    clusterMeans = MERGEPTSTRUCTS($pt\vec{C}^t$)
17: **end procedure**

18: **procedure** MERGEPTSTRUCTS($\vec{vectors}$)
19:    **while** $|\vec{vectors}| > 1$ **do**
20:        PAR_MERGE($\vec{vectors}$)   ▷ $O(T log n)$
21:    **end while**
22:    **return** vectors[0]
23: **end procedure**

Minimal Triangle Inequality (MTI) Pruning

We simplify Elkan's Algorithm for triangle inequality pruning (TI) [11] by removing the the necessity for the lower bound matrix of size $O(nd)$. Omitting the lower bound matrix means we forego the opportunity to prune certain computations; we accept this tradeoff in order to limit main memory consumption and prioritize usability. Due to space limitations, we omit experiments exhibiting that in practice pruning benefits of maintaining a lower bound matrix are minimal. With $O(n)$, memory we implement three of the four [11] pruning clauses invoked for each data point in an iteration of a knor module with pruning *enabled*. Let $u^t = \mathbf{d}(\vec{v}, c\_nearest^t) + f(c\_nearest^t)$, be the upper bound of the distance of a sample, $\vec{v}$, in iteration t from its assigned cluster $c\_nearest^t$. Finally, we define U to be an update function such that $U(u^t)$ fully tightens the upper bound of u^t.

Clause 1: if $u^t \leq \min \mathbf{d}(c\_nearest^t, \vec{c}^t \ \forall \ \vec{c}^t \in \vec{C}^t)$, then $\vec{v}$ remains in the same cluster for the current iteration. For knors, this is extremely significant because no I/O request is made for data.

Clause 2: if $u^t \leq \mathbf{d}(c\_nearest^t, \vec{c}^t \ \forall \ \vec{c}^t \in \vec{C}^t)$, then the distance computation between data point $\vec{v}$ and centroid $\vec{c}^t$ is pruned.

Clause 3: if $U(u^t) \leq \mathbf{d}(c\_nearest^t, \vec{c}^t \ \forall \ \vec{c}^t \in \vec{C}^t)$, then the distance computation between data point $\vec{v}$ and centroid $\vec{c}^t$ is pruned.

5 IN-MEMORY DESIGN

We prioritize practical performance when we implement knori optimizations. We make design tradeoffs to balance the opposing forces of minimizing memory usage and maximizing CPU cycles spent on parallel computing. Section 5 chronicles the memory bounds that we achieve and optimizations that we apply.

5.1 Asymptotic Memory Consumption

knori with MTI *disabled*, which we call knori-, retains the computation complexity of a serial routine, i.e., $O(ndk)$, but has a memory bound of $O(nd + Tkd)$ as compared to the original $O(nd + kd)$. The factor of T arises from the per-thread centroids we maintain. knori (MTI *enabled*) uses additional memory $O(k^2 + n)$, which does not increase the asymptotic bound. The $O(k^2)$ comes from maintaining an upper/lower triangular centroid-to-centroid distance matrix and $O(n)$ comes from maintaining the upper bound of each data point's distance to any centroids. The $O(n)$ in practice adds between 6-10 Bytes per data point or $\leq 1GB$ when $n = 100$ million and d is unrestricted. We justify the tradeoff of slightly higher memory consumption for an improvement in performance in Section 8. A complete summary of knor routine memory bounds is shown in Table 1.

5.2 In-memory optimizations

The following design principles and optimizations improve the performance of Algorithm 1.

Prioritize data locality for NUMA: Non-uniform memory access (NUMA) architectures are characterized by groups of processors that have affinity to a local memory bank via a shared local bus. Other non-local memory banks must be accessed through a globally shared interconnect. The effect is low latency accesses with high throughput to local memory banks, and conversely higher latency and lower throughput for remote memory accesses to non-local memory.

To minimize remote memory accesses, we bind every thread to a single NUMA node, equally partition the dataset across NUMA nodes, and sequentially allocate data structures to the local NUMA

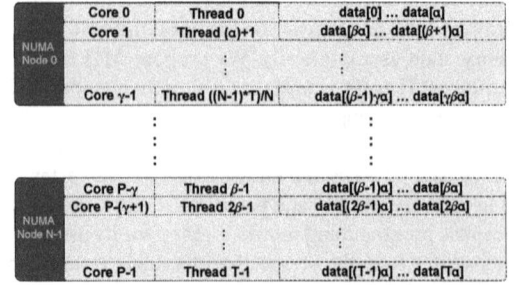

Figure 1: The memory allocation and thread assignment scheme we utilize for knori and knord on each machine. $\alpha = n/T$ is the amount of data per thread, $\beta = T/N$ is the number of threads per NUMA node, and $\gamma = P/N$ is the number of physical processors per NUMA node. Distributing memory across NUMA nodes maximizes memory throughput while binding threads to NUMA nodes reduces remote memory accesses.

node's memory. Every thread works independently. Threads only communicate or share data to aggregate per-thread results. Figure 1 shows the data allocation and access scheme we employ. We bind threads to NUMA nodes rather than specific CPU cores because the latter is too restrictive to the OS scheduler. CPU thread-binding may cause performance degradation if the number of worker threads exceeds the number of physical cores.

Dynamic Scheduling and Work Stealing: To achieve optimal performance when MTI pruning is *disabled*, statically scheduling thread tasks to locally allocated data partitions is sufficient. When MTI is *enabled*, we see worker skew at the thread level. In response, we develop a NUMA-aware partitioned priority task queue, (Figure 2), to feed worker threads, prioritizing tasks that maximize local memory access and thus limit remote memory accesses.

The task queue enables idle threads to *steal* work from threads bound to the same NUMA node first, minimizing remote memory accesses. The queue is partitioned into T parts, each with a lock required for access. We allow a thread to cycle through the task queue once looking for high priority tasks before settling on another, possibly lower priority task. This tradeoff avoids starvation and ensures threads are idle for negligible periods of time. The result is good load balancing when pruning in addition to optimized memory access patterns.

Avoid interference and delay the synchronization barrier: We employ per-thread local centroids and write-conflict free shared data structures to eliminate interference. Local centroids are unfinalized running totals of global centroids used in the following iteration for distance computations. Local centroids are concurrently updated. Finally, we require only a single global barrier prior to merging local clusters in a parallel funnelsort-like [14] reduction routine for use in the following iteration.

Effective data layout for CPU cache exploitation: Both per-thread and global data structures are contiguously allocated chunks of memory. Contiguous data organization and sequential access patterns when computing cluster-to-centroid distances maximizes both prefetching and CPU caching opportunities.

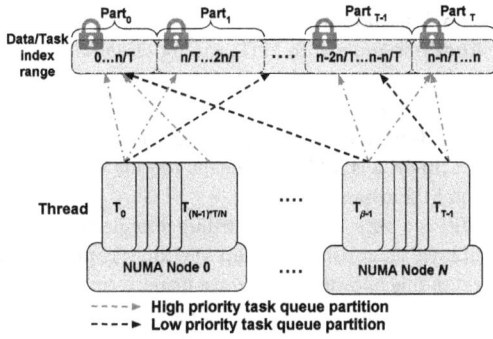

Figure 2: The NUMA-aware partitioned task scheduler we utilize for knori and knord on each machine. The scheduler minimizes task queue lock contention and remote memory accesses by prioritizing tasks with data in the local NUMA memory bank.

6 SEMI-EXTERNAL MEMORY DESIGN

We design a highly optimized semi-external memory module, knors, that targets the stand-alone server environment and when data are too large to reside fully in main memory. knors extends its in-memory counterpart from the perspective of scalability by placing data on SSDs and requesting data as necessary. Data requests are performed asynchronously allowing the overlap of I/O and computation. The SEM model allows us to reduce the asymptotic memory bounds so as to scale to larger datasets. A SEM routine uses $O(n)$ memory for a dataset, $\vec{V} \in \mathbb{R}^{n \times d}$ that when processed completely in memory would require $O(nd)$ memory. For completeness, we summarize all knor memory asymptotic bounds in Table 1.

6.1 FlashGraph modifications

We modify FlashGraph to support matrix-like computations. Flash-Graph's primitive data type is the page_vertex that is interpreted as a vertex with an index to the edge list of the page_vertex on SSDs. We define a *row* of data to be equivalent to a d-dimension data point, $\vec{v}_i$. Each row is composed of a unique identifier, *row-ID*, and d-dimension data vector, *row-data*. We add a page_row data type to FlashGraph and modify FlashGraph's I/O layer to support reading floating point row-data from SSD rather than the numeric data type associated with edge lists. The page_row type computes it row-ID and row-data location on disk meaning only user-defined state is stored in-memory. The page_row reduces the memory necessary to use FlashGraph by $O(n)$ because it does not store a row-data index to data on SSDs unlike a page_vertex. This allows knors to scale to larger datasets than possible before on a single machine.

6.2 Semi-external Memory Asymptotic Analysis

SEM implementations do not alter the computation bounds, whereas they do lower the memory bounds for k-means to $O(n + Tkd)$. This improves on the $O(nd + Tkd)$ bound of knori and the $O(nd + kd)$ bound of Lloyd's original algorithm. In practice, the disk I/O bound of knors is much lower than the worst case of $O(nd)$ obtained when MTI pruning is *disabled* (knors-), especially for data with natural clusters.

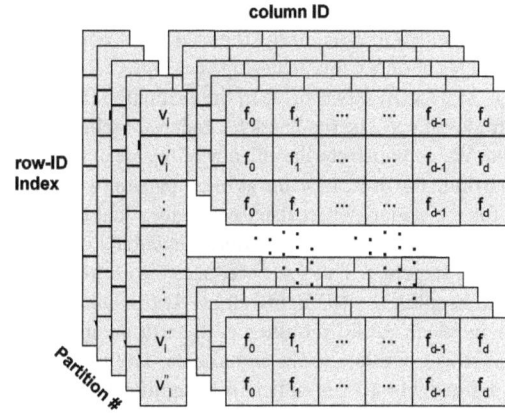

Figure 3: The structure of the row cache we utilize for knors. Partitioning the row cache eliminates the need for locking during cache population.

6.2.1 I/O minimization. I/O bounds the performance of k-means in the SEM model. Accordingly, we reduce the number of data-rows that need to be brought into memory each iteration. Only Clause 1 of MTI (Section 4) facilitates the skipping of all distance computations for a data point. In this case we do not issue an I/O request for the data point's row-data. This results in a reduction in I/O, but because data are pruned in a near-random fashion, we retrieve significantly more data than necessary from SSDs due to fragmentation. Reducing the filesystem *page size*, i.e. minimum read size from SSDs alleviates this to an extent, but a small page size can lead to higher amounts of I/O requests, offsetting any gains achieved by the reduction in fragmentation. We utilize a minimum read size of $4KB$; even with this relatively small value we still receive significantly more data from disk than we request (Figure 6b). To address this, we develop a lazily-updated partitioned *row cache* described in Section 6.2.2, that drastically reduces the amount of data brought into memory as shown in Figure 6a.

6.2.2 Partitioned Row Cache (RC). We add a layer to the memory hierarchy for SEM applications by designing a lazily-updated row cache (Figure 3). The row cache improves performance by reducing I/O and minimizing I/O request merging and page caching overhead in FlashGraph. A row is *active* when it performs an I/O request in the current iteration for its row-data. The row cache pins active rows to memory at the granularity of a row, rather than a page, improving its effectiveness in reducing I/O compared to a page cache.

The row cache lazily updates at certain iterations of the k-means algorithm based on a user defined *cache update interval* (I_{cache}). The cache updates/refreshes at iteration I_{cache} then the update frequency increases exponentially such that the next RC update is performed after $2I_{cache}$ iterations and so forth. This means that row-data in the RC remains static for several iterations before the RC is flushed then repopulated. We justify lazy updates by observing that k-means, especially on real-world data, follows predictable row activation patterns. In early iterations the cache's utility is of minimal benefit as the row activation pattern is near-random. As the algorithm progresses, data points that are active tend to stay active for many iterations as they are near more than one established centroid. This means the cache can remain static for longer periods of time while achieving very high cache hit rates. We set I_{cache} to 5 for all experiments in the evaluation (Section 8). The design trade-off is cache freshness for reduced cache maintenance overhead. We demonstrate the efficacy of this design in Figure 7.

We partition the row cache into as many partitions as FlashGraph creates for the underlying matrix, generally equal to the number of threads of execution. Each partition is updated locally in a lock-free caching structure. This vastly reduces the cache maintenance overhead, keeping the RC lightweight. At the completion of an iteration in which the RC refreshes, each partition updates a global map that stores pointers to the actual data. The size of the cache is user-defined, but $1GB$ is sufficient to significantly improve the performance of billion-point datasets.

7 DISTRIBUTED DESIGN

knord scales to distributed clusters through the Message Passing Interface (MPI). We employ modular design principles and build our distributed routines as a layer above our parallel in-memory routines. The implication is that each machine maintains a decentralized *driver* (MPI) process that launches *worker* (pthread) threads that retain the NUMA performance optimizations we develop for knori in Section 5.

We do not address load balancing between machines in the cluster. We recognize that in some cases it may be beneficial to dynamically dispatch tasks, but we argue that this would negatively affect the performance enhancing NUMA polices we implement. We further argue that the gains in performance of our data partitioning scheme (shown in Figure 1) outweigh the effects of skew in this setting. We validate these assertions empirically in Section 8.9.

8 EXPERIMENTAL EVALUATION

We evaluate knor by benchmarking optimizations in addition to comparing its performance against other state-of-the-art frameworks. In Section 8.3 we evaluate the performance of our baseline single threaded implementation to ensure all speedup experiments are relative to a state-of-the-art baseline performance. Sections 8.4 and 8.5 evaluate the effect of specific optimizations on our in-memory and semi-external memory tools respectively. Section 8.7 evaluates the performance of knori and knors relative to other popular frameworks from the perspective of time and resource consumption. Section 8.9 specifically performs comparison between knord and MLlib in a cluster.

We evaluate knor optimizations on the Friendster top-8 and top-32 eigenvector datasets, because the Friendster dataset represents real-world machine learning data. The Friendster dataset is derived from a graph that follows a power law distribution of edges. As such, the resulting eigenvectors contain natural clusters with well defined centroids, which makes MTI pruning effective, because many data points fall into strongly rooted clusters and do not change membership. These trends hold true for other large scale datasets, albeit to a lesser extent on uniformly random generated data (Section 8.7). The datasets we use for performance and scalability evaluation are shown in Table 2.

We use the following notation throughout the evaluation:

- **knori-** is knori with MTI pruning *disabled*.
- **knors-** is knors with MTI pruning *disabled*.
- **knors--** is knors with both MTI pruning and the row cache (RC) *disabled*.
- **knord-** is knord with MTI pruning *disabled*.
- **MLlib-EC2** is MLlib's k-means routine running on Amazon EC2 instances [18].
- **MPI** is a pure MPI [12] distributed implementation of our ||Lloyd's algorithm (Section 4) with MTI pruning. We develop this in order to compare its performance to knord.
- **MPI-** is a pure MPI distributed implementation of our ||Lloyd's algorithm with MTI pruning *disabled*.

Table 1: Asymptotic memory complexity of knor routines.

Module / Routine	Memory complexity
Naïve Lloyd's	$O(nd + kd)$
knors-, knors--	$O(n + Tkd)$
knors	$O(2n + Tkd + k^2)$
knori-, knord-	$O(nd + Tkd)$
knori, knord	$O(nd + Tkd + n + k^2)$

Table 2: The datasets under evaluation in this study.

Data Matrix	n	d	Size
Friendster-8 [13] eigenvectors	66M	8	4GB
Friendster-32 [13] eigenvectors	66M	32	16GB
Rand-Multivariate (RM_{856M})	856M	16	103GB
Rand-Multivariate (RM_{1B})	1.1B	32	251GB
Rand-Univariate (RU_{2B})	2.1B	64	1.1TB

For completeness we note versions of all frameworks and libraries we use for comparison in this study; Spark v2.0.1 for MLlib, H_2O v3.7, Turi v2.1, R v3.3.1, MATLAB R2016b, BLAS v3.7.0, Scikit-learn v0.18, MLpack v2.1.0.

8.1 Single Node Evaluation Hardware

We perform single node experiments relating to knori, knors on a NUMA server with four Intel Xeon E7-4860 processors clocked at 2.6 GHz and 1TB of DDR3-1600 memory. Each processor has 12 cores. The machine has three LSI SAS 9300-8e host bus adapters (HBA) connected to a SuperMicro storage chassis, in which 24 OCZ Intrepid 3000 SSDs are installed. The machine runs Linux kernel v3.13.0. The C++ code is compiled using mpicxx.mpich2 version 4.8.4 with the -O3 flag.

8.2 Cluster Evaluation Hardware

We perform distributed memory experiments relating to knord on Amazon EC2 compute optimized instances of type c4.8xlarge with 60GB of DDR3-1600 memory, running Linux kernel v3.13.0-91. Each machine has 36 vCPUS, corresponding to 18 physical Intel Xeon E5-2666 v3 processors, clocking 2.9 GHz, sitting on 2 independent sockets. We allow no more that 18 independent MPI processes or equivalently 18 Spark workers to exist on any single machine. We constrain the cluster to a single availability zone, subnet and placement group, maximizing cluster-wide data locality and minimizing network latency on the 10 Gigabit interconnect. We measure all experiments from the point when all data is in

RAM on all machines. For MLlib we ensure that the Spark engine is configured to use the maximum available memory and does not perform any checkpointing or I/O during computation.

8.3 Baseline Single-thread Performance

knori, even with MTI pruning *disabled*, performs on par with state-of-the-art implementations of Lloyd's algorithm. This is true for implementations that utilize generalized matrix multiplication (GEMM) techniques and vectorized operations, such as MATLAB [26] and BLAS [21]. We find the same to be true of popular statistics packages and frameworks such as MLpack [5], Scikit-learn [32] and R [33] all of which use highly optimized C/C++ code, although some use scripting language wrappers. Table 3 shows performance at 1 thread. Table 3 provides credence to our speedup results since our baseline single threaded performance tops other state-of-the-art serial routines.

Table 3: Serial performance of popular, optimized k-means routines, all using Lloyd's algorithm, on the Friendster-8 dataset. For fairness all implementations perform all distance computations. The Language column refers to the underlying language of implementation and not any user-facing higher level wrapper.

Implementation	Type	Language	Time/iter (sec)
knori	Iterative	C++	7.49
MATLAB	GEMM	C++	20.68
BLAS	GEMM	C++	20.7
R	Iterative	C	8.63
Scikit-learn	Iterative	Cython	12.84
MLpack	Iterative	C++	13.09

8.4 In-memory Optimization Evaluation

We show NUMA-node thread binding, maintaining NUMA memory locality, and NUMA-aware task scheduling for knori is highly effective in improving performance. We achieve near-linear speedup (Figure 4). Because the machine has 48 physical cores, speedup degrades slightly at 64 cores; additional speedup beyond 48 cores comes from simultaneous multithreading (hyperthreading). The NUMA-aware implementation is nearly 6x faster at 64 threads compared to a routine containing no NUMA optimizations, henceforth referred to as *NUMA-oblivious*. The NUMA-oblivious routine relies on the OS to determine memory allocation, thread scheduling, and load balancing policies.

We further show that although both the NUMA-oblivious and NUMA-aware implementation speedup linearly, the NUMA-oblivious routine has a lower linear constant when compared with a NUMA-aware implementation (Figure 4).

Increased parallelism amplifies the performance degradation of the NUMA-oblivious implementation. We identify the following as the greatest contributors:

- the NUMA-oblivious allocation policies of traditional memory allocators, such as `malloc`, place data in a contiguous chunk within a single NUMA memory bank whenever possible. This leads to a large number of threads performing remote memory accesses as T increases;

- a dynamic NUMA-oblivious task scheduler may give tasks to threads that cause worker threads to perform many more remote memory accesses than necessary when thread-binding and static scheduling are employed.

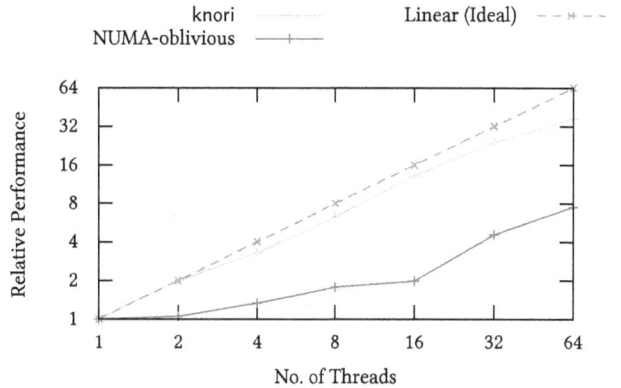

Figure 4: Speedup of knori (which is NUMA-aware) vs. a NUMA-oblivious routine for on the Friendster top-8 eigenvector dataset, with $k = 10$.

We demonstrate the effectiveness of a NUMA-aware partitioned task scheduler for pruned computations via knori (Figure 5). We define a *task* as a block of data points in contiguous memory given to a thread for computation. We set a minimum *task size*, i.e. the number of data points in the block, to 8192. We empirically determine that this task size is small enough to not artificially introduce skew in billion-point datasets. We compare against a static and a first in, first out (FIFO) task scheduler. The static scheduler preassigns n/T rows to each worker thread. The FIFO scheduler first assigns threads to tasks that are local to the thread's partition of data, then allows threads to steal tasks from straggler threads whose data resides on any NUMA node.

We observe that as k increases, so does the potential for skew. When $k = 10$, the NUMA-aware scheduler performs negligibly worse than both FIFO and static static scheduling, but as k, increases the NUMA-aware scheduler improves performance—by more than 40% when $k = 100$. We observe similar trends in other datasets; we omit these results for space reasons and to avoid redundancy.

8.5 Semi-external Memory Evaluation

We evaluate knors optimizations, performance and scalability. knors utilizes a 4KB FlashGraph *page cache* size, minimizing the amount of superfluous data read from disk due to data fragmentation. Additionally, we disable checkpoint failure recovery during performance evaluation for both our routines and those of our competitors.

We drastically reduce the amount of data read from SSDs by utilizing the row cache. Figure 6a shows that as the number of iterations increase, the row cache's ability to reduce I/O and improve speed also increases because most rows that are active are pinned in memory. Figure 6b contrasts the total amount of data that an implementation requests from SSDs with the amount of data SAFS actually reads and transports into memory. When knors *disables* both MTI pruning and the row cache (i.e., knors--, every request

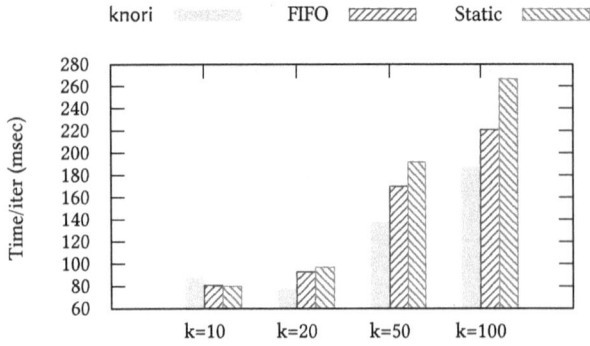

Figure 5: Performance of the partitioned NUMA-aware scheduler (default for knori) vs. FIFO and static scheduling for knori on the Friendster-8 dataset.

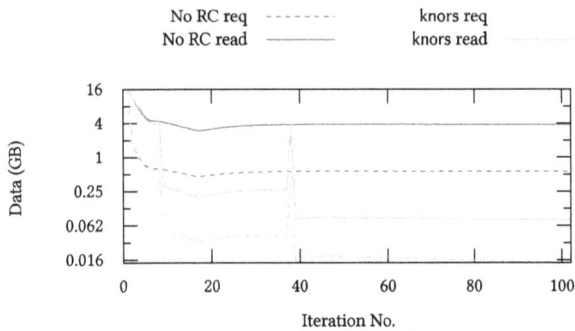

(a) knors data requested (req) from SSDs vs. data read (read) from SSDs each iteration when the row cache (RC) was _enabled_ or _disabled_. Because of MTI pruning, algorithms may request only a few points from any block, but the entire block must still be read from SSD.

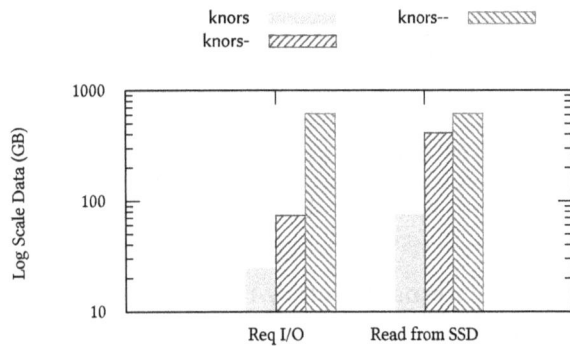

(b) Total data requested (req) vs. data read from SSDs when (i) both MTI and RC are _disabled_ (knors--), (ii) Only MTI is _enabled_ (knors-), (iii) both MTI and RC are _enabled_ (knors). Without pruning, all data are requested and read.

Figure 6: The effect of the row cache and MTI on I/O for the Friendster top-32 eigenvectors dataset. Row cache size = 512MB, page cache size = 1GB, $k = 10$.

issued to FlashGraph for row-data is either served by FlashGraph's page cache or read from SSDs. When knors _enables_ MTI pruning, but _disables_ the row cache (i.e., knors-, we read an order of magnitude more data from SSDs than when we _enable_ the row cache. Figure 6 demonstrates that a page cache is **not** sufficient for k-means and that caching at the granularity of row-data is necessary to achieve significant reductions in I/O and improvements in performance for real-world datasets.

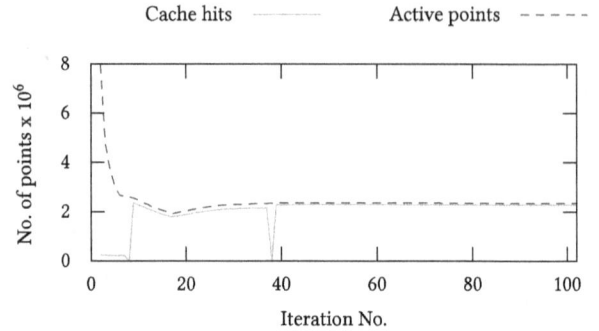

Figure 7: Row cache hits per iteration contrasted with the maximum achievable number of hits on the Friendster top-32 eigenvectors dataset.

Lazy row cache updates reduce I/O significantly. Figure 7 justifies our design decision for a lazily updated row cache. As the algorithm progresses, we obtain nearly a 100% cache hit rate, meaning that knors operates at in-memory speeds for the vast majority of iterations.

8.6 MTI Evaluation

Figures 8a and 8b highlight the performance improvement of knor modules with MTI _enabled_ over MTI _disabled_ counterparts. We show that MTI provides a few factors of improvement in time even without some of the pruning ability Elkan's TI [11] provides. Figure 8c highlights that MTI increases the memory load by negligible amounts compared to non-pruning modules. We conclude that MTI (unlike TI) is a viable optimization for large-scale datasets.

8.7 Comparison with Other Frameworks

We evaluate the performance of our routines in comparison with other frameworks on the datasets in Table 2. We show that knori achieves greater than an order of magnitude improvement over other state-of-the-art frameworks. Finally, we demonstrate knors outperforms other state-of-the-art frameworks by several factors.

Both our in-memory and semi-external memory modules incur little memory overhead when compared with other frameworks. Figure 9c shows memory consumption. We note that MLlib requires the placement of temporary Spark block manager files. Because the block manager cannot be disabled, we provide an in-memory RAM-disk so as to not influence MLlib's performance negatively. We configure MLlib, H$_2$O and Turi to use the minimum amount of memory necessary to achieve their highest performance. We acknowledge that a reduction in memory for these frameworks is possible, but would degrade computation time and lead to unfair

(a) The Friendster graph top-8 eigenvector dataset.

(b) The Friendster graph top-32 eigenvector dataset.

(c) Memory comparison of fully optimized knor routines (knori, knors) compared to more vanilla knor routines (knori-, knors--)

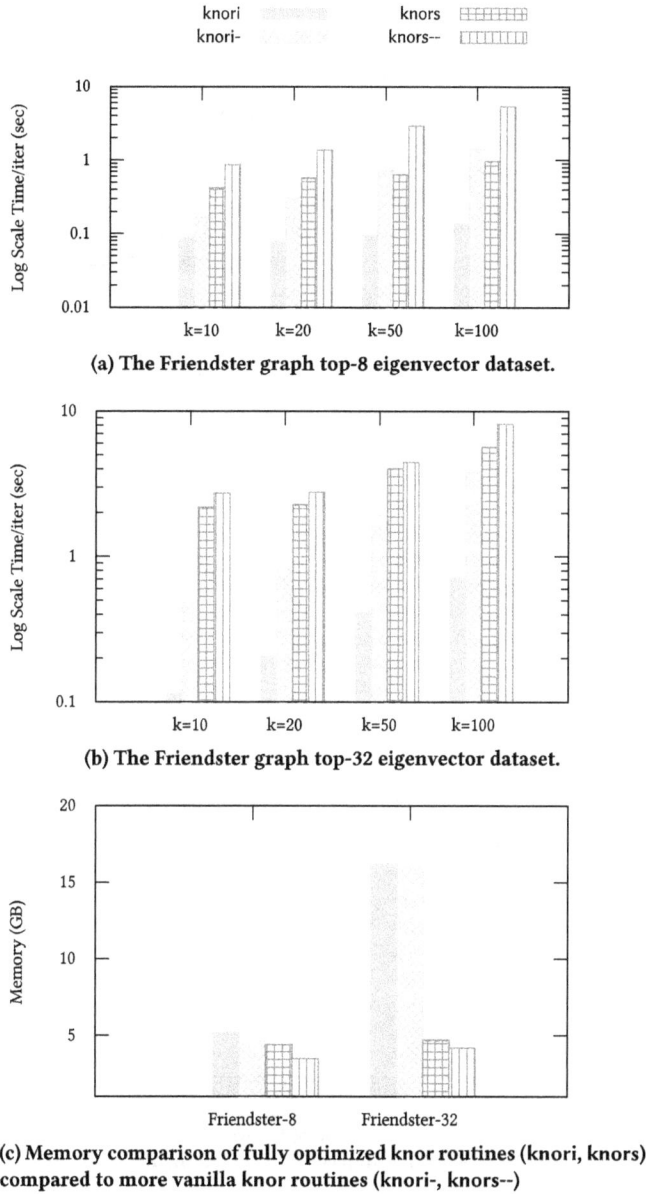

Figure 8: Performance and memory usage comparison of knor modules on matrices from the Friendster graph top-8 and top-32 eigenvectors.

(a) The Friendster graph top-8 eigenvector dataset.

(b) The Friendster graph top-32 eigenvector dataset.

(c) Peak memory consumption on the Friendster eigenvectors dataset, with $k = 10$. Row cache size = 512MB, page cache size = 1GB.

Figure 9: Performance comparison on matrices from the Friendster [13] graph top-8 and top-32 eigenvectors.

comparisons. All measurements are an average of 10 runs; we drop all caches between runs.

We demonstrate that knori is no less than an order of magnitude faster than all competitor frameworks (Figure 9). knori is often hundreds of times faster than Turi. Furthermore, knors is consistently twice as fast as competitor in-memory frameworks. We further demonstrate performance improvements over competitor frameworks on algorithmically identical implementations by *disabling* MTI. knori- is nearly 10x faster than competitor solutions, whereas knors- is comparable and often faster than competitor in-memory solutions. We attribute our performance gains over other frameworks when MTI is *disabled* to our parallelization scheme for

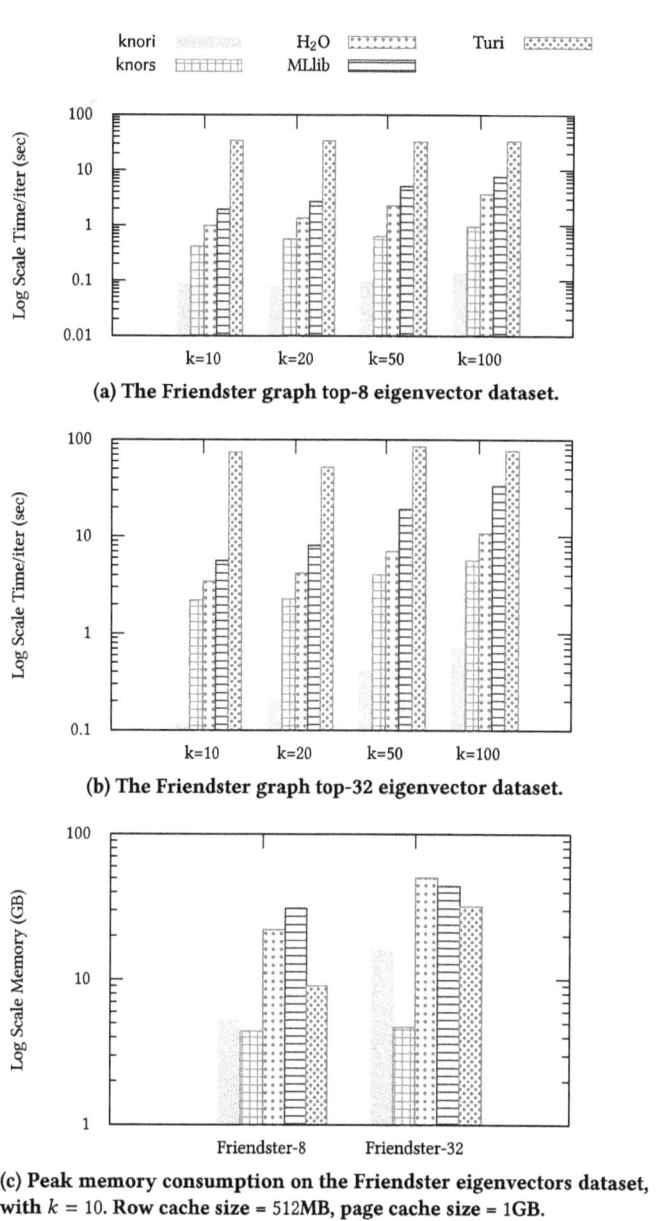

Lloyd's (Algorithm 1). Lastly, Figure 8 demonstrates a consistent 30% improvement in knors when we utilize the row cache. This is evidence that the design of our lazily updated row cache provides a performance boost.

Finally, comparing knori- and knors-- to MLlib, H_2O and Turi (Figures 8 and 9) reveals knor to be several times faster and to use significantly less memory. This is relevant because knori- and knors-- are algorithmically identical to k-means within MLlib, Turi and H_2O.

8.8 Single-node Scalability Evaluation

To demonstrate scalability, we compare performance on synthetic datasets drawn from random distributions that contain hundreds of millions to billions of data points. Uniformly random data are typically the worst case scenario for the convergence of k-means, because many data points tend to be near several centroids.

Both in-memory and SEM modules outperform popular frameworks on 100GB+ datasets. We achieve 7-20x improvement when in-memory and 3-6x improvement in SEM when compared to MLlib, H_2O and Turi. As data increases in size, the performance difference between knori and knors narrows since there is now enough data to mask I/O latency and to turn knors from an being I/O bound to being computation bound. We observe knors is only 3-4x slower than its in-memory counterpart in such cases.

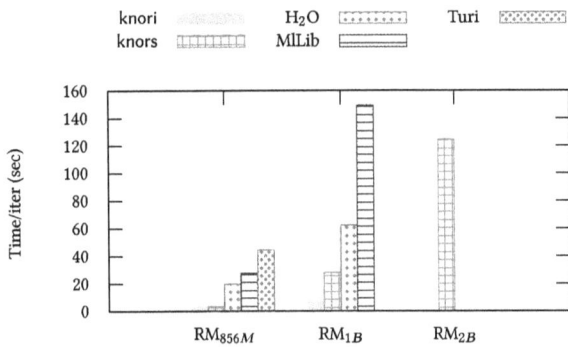

(a) Per iteration time elapsed of each routine.

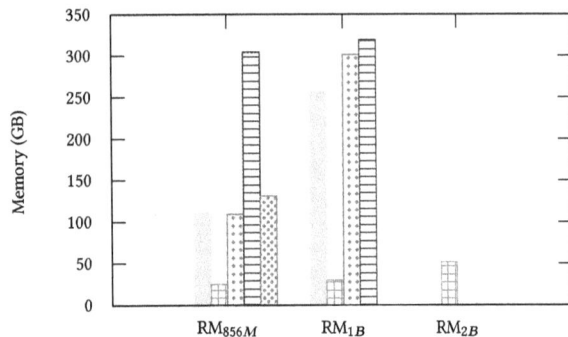

(b) Memory consumption of each routine.

Figure 10: Performance comparison on RM_{856M} and RM_{1B} datasets. Turi is unable to run on RM_{1B} on our machine and only SEM routines are able to run on RU_{2B} on our machine. Page cache size = 4GB, Row cache size = 2GB.

Memory capacity limits the scalability of k-means and semi-external memory allows algorithms to scale well beyond the limits of physical memory. The 1B point matrix (RM_{1B}) is the largest that fits in 1TB of memory on our machine. At 2B points (RU_{2B}), semi-external memory algorithms continue to execute proportionally and all other algorithms fail.

8.9 Distributed Comparison vs. Other Frameworks

We analyze performance of knord and knord- on Amazon's EC2 cloud in comparison to that of (i) MLlib (**MLlib-EC2**), (ii) a pure MPI implementation of our ||Lloyd's algorithm with MTI pruning (**MPI**), and (iii) a pure MPI implementation of ||Lloyd's algorithm with pruning *disabled* (**MPI-**). Note that H_2O has no distributed memory implementation and Turi discontinued their distributed memory interface prior to our experiments.

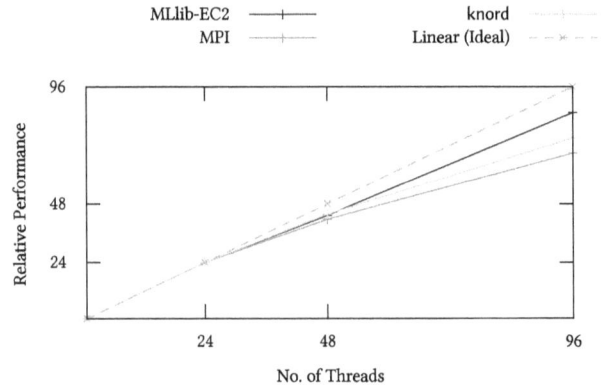

(a) Distributed speedup comparison on the Friendster-32 dataset.

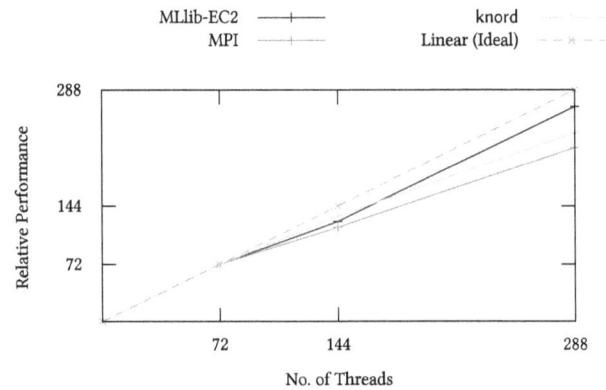

(b) Distributed speedup comparison on the RM_{1B} dataset.

Figure 11: Speedup experiments are normalized to each implementation's serial performance. Each machine has 18 physical cores with 1 thread per core.

Figures 11 and 12 reveal several fundamental and important results. Figure 11 shows that knord scales well to very large numbers of machines, performing within a constant factor of linear performance. This is a necessity today as many organization push big-data computation to the cloud. Figure 12 shows that in a cluster, knord, even with TI *disabled*, outperforms MLlib by a factor of 5 or more. This means we can often use fractions of the hardware required by MLlib to perform equivalent tasks. Figure 12 demonstrates that knord also benefits from our in-memory NUMA optimizations as we outperform a NUMA-oblivious MPI routine by 20-50%, depending on the dataset. Finally, Figure 12 shows that MTI remains a low-overhead, effective method to reduce computation even in the distributed setting.

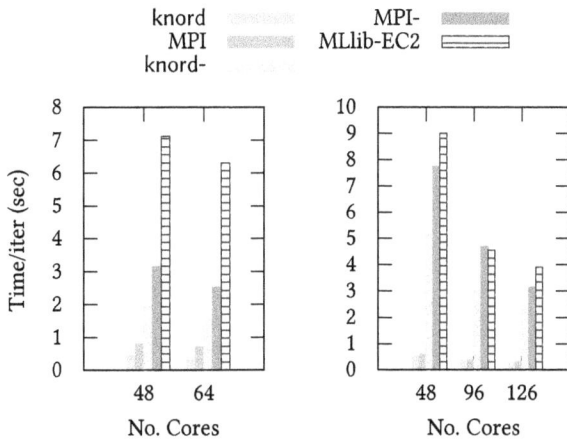

(a) Friendster8 (left) and Friendster32 (right) datasets computation time per iteration for $k = 100$.

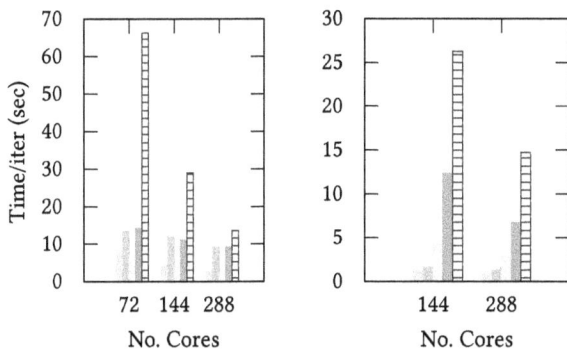

(b) RM_{856M} (left) and RM_{1B} (right) datasets computation time per iteration for $k = 10$.

Figure 12: Distributed performance comparison of knord, MPI and MLlib on Amazon's EC2 cloud. Each machine has 18 physical cores with 1 thread per core.

8.9.1 Semi-External Memory in the Cloud. We conclude our experiments by measuring the performance of knors on a single 32 core i3.16xlarge machine with 8 SSDs on Amazon EC2 compared to knord, MLlib and an optimized MPI routine running in a cluster. We run knors with 48 threads, with extra parallelism coming from symmetric multiprocessing. We run all other implementations with the same number of processes/threads as physical cores.

Figure 13 highlights that knors often outperforms MLlib even when MLLib runs in a cluster that contains more physical CPU cores. knors has comparable performance to both MPI and knord, leading to our assertion that the SEM scale-up model should be considered prior to moving to the distributed setting.

9 FUTURE WORK AND DISCUSSION

We intend to expand the distributed aspects of knor into a generalized programming framework for distributed machine learning on NUMA machines. We observe that NUMA architectures are

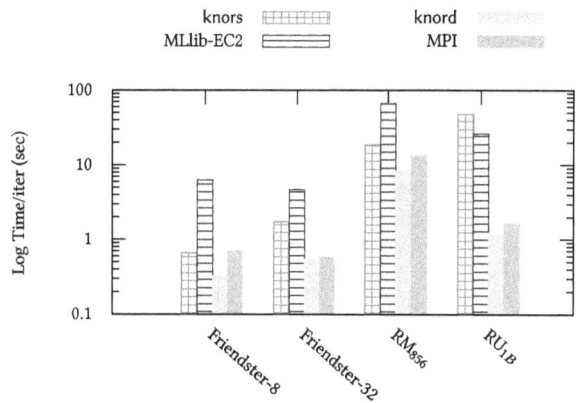

Figure 13: Performance comparison of knors to distributed packages. knors uses one i3.16xlarge machine with 32 physical cores. knord, MLlib-EC2 and MPI use 3 c4.8xlarge with a total of 48 physical cores for all datasets other than RU_{1B} where they use 8 c4.8xlarge with a total of 128 physical cores.

prevalent today in cloud computing. A large contingency of machines available through Unix-based cloud service providers such as Amazon EC2, IBM Cloud [46] and Google Cloud Platform [19] are indeed NUMA systems.

We aim to build a suite of machine learning algorithms on top of the generalized derivative framework. We aim to demonstrate that the NUMA optimizations we deploy for knor are applicable to a variety of compute-intensive applications. The initial phase will target other variants of k-means like spherical k-means [17], semi-supervised k-means++ [40] etc. Later phases will target machine learning algorithms like GMM [15], agglomerative clustering [34] and k-nearest neighbors [10]. Finally, we aim to provide a C++ interface upon which users may implement custom algorithms and benefit from our NUMA and external memory optimizations.

We are an open source project available at https://github.com/flashxio/knor

10 CONCLUSION

We accelerate k-means by over an order of magnitude by rethinking Lloyd's algorithm for modern multiprocessor NUMA architectures through the minimization of critical regions. We demonstrate that our modifications to Lloyd's are relevant to both in-memory (knori), distributed memory (knord) and semi-external memory (knors) applications as we outperform state-of-the-art frameworks running the exact same algorithms.

We formulate a minimal triangle inequality pruning technique (MTI) that further boosts the performance of k-means on real-world billion point datasets by over 100x when compared to some popular frameworks. MTI does so without significantly increasing memory consumption.

The addition of a row caching layer yields performance improvements over vanilla SEM implementations. We demonstrate that k-means in SEM performs only a small constant factor slower than in-memory algorithms for large scale datasets and scales beyond the limits of memory at which point in-memory algorithms fail.

Finally, we demonstrate that there are large performance benefits associated with NUMA-targeted optimizations. We show that data locality optimizations such as NUMA-node thread binding, NUMA-aware task scheduling, and NUMA-aware memory allocation schemes provide several times speedup for k-means on NUMA hardware.

11 ACKNOWLEDGMENTS

This work is partially supported by DARPA GRAPHS N66001-14-1-4028 and DARPA SIMPLEX program through SPAWAR contract N66001-15-C-4041.

REFERENCES

[1] J. Abello, A. L. Buchsbaum, and J. R. Westbrook. A functional approach to external graph algorithms. In *Algorithmica*, pages 332–343. Springer-Verlag, 1998.

[2] J. Ang, R. F. Barrett, R. Benner, D. Burke, C. Chan, J. Cook, D. Donofrio, S. D. Hammond, K. S. Hemmert, S. Kelly, et al. Abstract machine models and proxy architectures for exascale computing. In *Hardware-Software Co-Design for High Performance Computing (Co-HPC), 2014*, pages 25–32. IEEE, 2014.

[3] J. Bennett and S. Lanning. The netflix prize. In *Proceedings of KDD cup and workshop*, volume 2007, page 35, 2007.

[4] N. Binkiewicz, J. T. Vogelstein, and K. Rohe. Covariate assisted spectral clustering. *arXiv preprint arXiv:1411.2158*, 2014.

[5] R. R. Curtin, J. R. Cline, N. P. Slagle, W. B. March, P. Ram, N. A. Mehta, and A. G. Gray. Mlpack: A scalable c++ machine learning library. *Journal of Machine Learning Research*, 14(Mar):801–805, 2013.

[6] A. S. Das, M. Datar, A. Garg, and S. Rajaram. Google news personalization: scalable online collaborative filtering. In *Proceedings of the 16th international conference on World Wide Web*, pages 271–280. ACM, 2007.

[7] J. Dean and S. Ghemawat. MapReduce: Simplified data processing on large clusters. In *Proceedings of the 6th Conference on Symposium on Opearting Systems Design & Implementation - Volume 6*, 2004.

[8] A. P. Dempster, N. M. Laird, and D. B. Rubin. Maximum likelihood from incomplete data via the em algorithm. *Journal of the royal statistical society. Series B (methodological)*, pages 1–38, 1977.

[9] Y. Ding, Y. Zhao, X. Shen, M. Musuvathi, and T. Mytkowicz. Yinyang k-means: A drop-in replacement of the classic k-means with consistent speedup. In *Proceedings of the 32nd International Conference on Machine Learning (ICML-15)*, pages 579–587, 2015.

[10] R. O. Duda, P. E. Hart, et al. *Pattern classification and scene analysis*, volume 3. Wiley New York, 1973.

[11] C. Elkan. Using the triangle inequality to accelerate k-means. In *ICML*, volume 3, pages 147–153, 2003.

[12] M. P. Forum. Mpi: A message-passing interface standard. Technical report, Knoxville, TN, USA, 1994.

[13] Friendster graph. https://archive.org/download/friendster-dataset-201107, Accessed 4/18/2014.

[14] M. Frigo, C. E. Leiserson, H. Prokop, and S. Ramachandran. Cache-oblivious algorithms. In *Foundations of Computer Science, 1999. 40th Annual Symposium on*, pages 285–297. IEEE, 1999.

[15] C. F. Gauss. *Theory of the motion of the heavenly bodies moving about the sun in conic sections: a translation of Carl Frdr. Gauss" Theoria motus": With an appendix. By Ch. H. Davis*. Little, Brown and Comp., 1857.

[16] h2o. h2o. http://h2o.ai/, 2005–2015.

[17] K. Hornik, I. Feinerer, M. Kober, and C. Buchta. Spherical k-means clustering. *Journal of Statistical Software*, 50(10):1–22, 2012.

[18] A. Inc. Amazon web services.

[19] G. Inc. Google cloud platform.

[20] L. B. Jorde and S. P. Wooding. Genetic variation, classification and'race'. *Nature genetics*, 36:S28–S33, 2004.

[21] C. L. Lawson, R. J. Hanson, D. R. Kincaid, and F. T. Krogh. Basic linear algebra subprograms for fortran usage. *ACM Transactions on Mathematical Software (TOMS)*, 5(3):308–323, 1979.

[22] S. P. Lloyd. Least squares quantization in pcm. *Information Theory, IEEE Transactions on*, 28(2):129–137, 1982.

[23] Y. Low, J. E. Gonzalez, A. Kyrola, D. Bickson, C. E. Guestrin, and J. Hellerstein. Graphlab: A new framework for parallel machine learning. *arXiv preprint arXiv:1408.2041*, 2014.

[24] V. Lyzinski, D. L. Sussman, D. E. Fishkind, H. Pao, L. Chen, J. T. Vogelstein, Y. Park, and C. E. Priebe. Spectral clustering for divide-and-conquer graph matching. *Parallel Computing*, 2015.

[25] V. Lyzinski, M. Tang, A. Athreya, Y. Park, and C. E. Priebe. Community detection and classification in hierarchical stochastic blockmodels. *arXiv preprint arXiv:1503.02115*, 2015.

[26] MATLAB. *version 7.10.0 (R2010a)*. The MathWorks Inc., Natick, Massachusetts, 2010.

[27] F. McSherry, M. Isard, and D. G. Murray. Scalability! but at what cost? In *15th Workshop on Hot Topics in Operating Systems (HotOS XV)*, 2015.

[28] X. Meng, J. Bradley, B. Yavuz, E. Sparks, S. Venkataraman, D. Liu, J. Freeman, D. Tsai, M. Amde, S. Owen, et al. Mllib: Machine learning in apache spark. *arXiv preprint arXiv:1505.06807*, 2015.

[29] S. Owen, R. Anil, T. Dunning, and E. Friedman. *Mahout in action*. Manning Shelter Island, 2011.

[30] N. Patterson, A. L. Price, and D. Reich. Population structure and eigenanalysis. 2006.

[31] R. Pearce, M. Gokhale, and N. M. Amato. Multithreaded asynchronous graph traversal for in-memory and semi-external memory. In *Proceedings of the 2010 ACM/IEEE International Conference for High Performance Computing, Networking, Storage and Analysis*, 2010.

[32] F. Pedregosa, G. Varoquaux, A. Gramfort, V. Michel, B. Thirion, O. Grisel, M. Blondel, P. Prettenhofer, R. Weiss, V. Dubourg, J. Vanderplas, A. Passos, D. Cournapeau, M. Brucher, M. Perrot, and E. Duchesnay. Scikit-learn: Machine learning in Python. *Journal of Machine Learning Research*, 12:2825–2830, 2011.

[33] R Core Team. *R: A Language and Environment for Statistical Computing*. R Foundation for Statistical Computing, Vienna, Austria, 2015.

[34] L. Rokach and O. Maimon. Clustering methods. In *Data mining and knowledge discovery handbook*, pages 321–352. Springer, 2005.

[35] Scalability! but at what cost? http://www.frankmcsherry.org/graph/scalability/cost/2015/01/15/COST.html, Accessed 9/3/2016.

[36] D. Sculley. Web-scale k-means clustering. In *ACM Digital library*, pages 1177–1178, 2010.

[37] M. Shindler, A. Wong, and A. W. Meyerson. Fast and accurate k-means for large datasets. In *Advances in neural information processing systems*, pages 2375–2383, 2011.

[38] J. Ugander, B. Karrer, L. Backstrom, and C. Marlow. The anatomy of the facebook social graph. *arXiv preprint arXiv:1111.4503*, 2011.

[39] J. T. Vogelstein, Y. Park, T. Ohyama, R. A. Kerr, J. W. Truman, C. E. Priebe, and M. Zlatic. Discovery of brainwide neural-behavioral maps via multiscale unsupervised structure learning. *Science*, 344(6182):386–392, 2014.

[40] J. Yoder and C. E. Priebe. Semi-supervised k-means++. *arXiv preprint arXiv:1602.00360*, 2016.

[41] M. Zaharia, M. Chowdhury, T. Das, A. Dave, J. Ma, M. McCauley, M. J. Franklin, S. Shenker, and I. Stoica. Resilient distributed datasets: A fault-tolerant abstraction for in-memory cluster computing. In *Proceedings of the 9th USENIX conference on Networked Systems Design and Implementation*, pages 2–2. USENIX Association, 2012.

[42] M. Zaharia, M. Chowdhury, M. J. Franklin, S. Shenker, and I. Stoica. Spark: Cluster computing with working sets. *HotCloud*, 10:10–10, 2010.

[43] W. Zhao, H. Ma, and Q. He. Parallel k-means clustering based on mapreduce. In *Cloud Computing*, pages 674–679. Springer, 2009.

[44] D. Zheng, R. Burns, and A. S. Szalay. Toward millions of file system IOPS on low-cost, commodity hardware. In *Proceedings of the International Conference on High Performance Computing, Networking, Storage and Analysis*, 2013.

[45] D. Zheng, D. Mhembere, R. Burns, J. Vogelstein, C. E. Priebe, and A. S. Szalay. FlashGraph: Processing billion-node graphs on an array of commodity SSDs. In *13th USENIX Conference on File and Storage Technologies (FAST 15)*, 2015.

[46] J. Zhu, X. Fang, Z. Guo, M. H. Niu, F. Cao, S. Yue, and Q. Y. Liu. Ibm cloud computing powering a smarter planet. In *IEEE International Conference on Cloud Computing*, pages 621–625. Springer, 2009.

CuMF_SGD: Parallelized Stochastic Gradient Descent for Matrix Factorization on GPUs

Xiaolong Xie*
Center for Energy-efficient Computing and Applications,
EECS, Peking University, Beijing, China
xiexl_pku@pku.edu.cn

Wei Tan
IBM Thomas J. Watson Research Center
Yorktown Heights, NY, USA
wtan@us.ibm.com

Liana L. Fong
IBM Thomas J. Watson Research Center
Yorktown Heights, NY, USA
llfong@us.ibm.com

Yun Liang
Center for Energy-efficient Computing and Applications,
EECS, Peking University , Beijing, China
ericlyun@pku.edu.cn

ABSTRACT

Stochastic gradient descent (SGD) is widely used by many machine learning algorithms. It is efficient for big data applications due to its low algorithmic complexity. SGD is inherently serial and its parallelization is not trivial. How to parallelize SGD on many-core architectures (e.g. GPUs) for high efficiency is a big challenge.

In this paper, we present **cuMF_SGD**, a parallelized SGD solution for matrix factorization on GPUs. We first design high-performance GPU computation kernels that accelerate individual SGD updates by exploiting **model parallelism**. We then design efficient schemes that parallelize SGD updates by exploiting **data parallelism**. Finally, we scale cuMF_SGD to large data sets that cannot fit into one GPU's memory. Evaluations on three public data sets show that cuMF_SGD outperforms existing solutions, including a 64-node CPU system, by a large margin using only one GPU card.

CCS CONCEPTS

• **Computing methodologies** → **Factor analysis**;
• **Computer systems organization** → **Heterogeneous (hybrid) systems**;
• **Theory of computation** → *Massively parallel algorithms*;

KEYWORDS

Matrix Factorization, GPGPU, Parallel Computing.

ACM Reference format:
Xiaolong Xie, Wei Tan, Liana L. Fong, and Yun Liang. 2017. CuMF_SGD: Parallelized Stochastic Gradient Descent for Matrix Factorization on GPUs. In *Proceedings of ACM Symposium on High-Performance Parallel and Distributed Computing, Washington , DC, USA, June 26-30, 2017 (HPDC '17)*, 14 pages.
https://doi.org/http://dx.doi.org/10.1145/3078597.3078602

*Work done while the author was with IBM as an summer research intern.

1 INTRODUCTION

Matrix Factorization (MF) is a popular algorithm that is widely used in modern machine learning applications, including collaborative filtering [12, 34], topic modeling [62], word embedding [43], and tensor decomposition [33]. It also has a natural connection with the embedding layers in deep neural network [43]. Without loss of generality, we use collaborative filtering as the example. Figure 1 shows a $m \times n$ rating matrix R which is sparse and with $N = 9$ observed samples. The goal of matrix factorization is to obtain two lower-rank feature matrices P ($m \times k$) and Q ($k \times n$) such that $R \approx P \times Q$. The feature vector dimension k is typically much smaller than m and n. Feature matrices P and Q can be used to predict the unknown samples in R, or as the features of the corresponding entities in subsequent machine learning tasks.

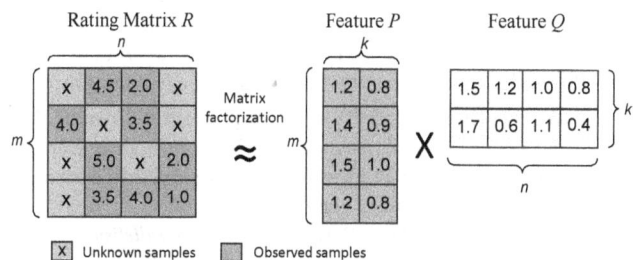

Figure 1: Matrix factorization, m=4, n=4, k=2.

Due to its algorithmic simplicity, Stochastic Gradient Descent (SGD) is often used in modern machine learning applications [17, 44]. Instead of calculating the gradient on the whole training set, SGD randomly picks up one sample from the training set and updates using the gradient on that particular sample. Such a simple approach has been demonstrated efficient in e.g., deep learning and matrix factorization [8, 65]. However, as SGD is inherently serial, how to parallelize it to exploit parallel processors becomes a major challenge [17]. Besides SGD, Coordinate Gradient Descent (CGD) [60] and Alternate Least Square (ALS) [34] are also used to solve MF problems. Previous works have demonstrated that CGD is prone to reach local optima [15]. ALS is inherently parallel and converges faster than SGD [51]. However, ALS is not efficient when processing large data sets due to its high algorithmic complexity. In this paper, we use SGD as the algorithm to solve MF and compare with ALS-based solutions.

CPU-based SGD solutions for MF, including both shared memory-based [16] and distributed system-based [63] have been studied. In contrast, we propose to use GPUs to accelerate SGD-based MF. Our insight is, **SGD-based MF is memory bound**. Previous works [15, 63] spend effort to improve the cache efficiency of CPUs. However, due to the limited cache capacity, shared memory-based solutions face serious performance degradation when processing large data sets. Distributed systems partition the data sets to fit into CPU caches, however, they are limited by the slow network. Therefore, we propose to use GPU to accelerate SGD-based MF as it provides large amount of computational resources [32], extreme high off-chip memory bandwidth [28, 30], and energy efficiency [49, 50].

Recent effort has been spent to use GPUs to accelerate the SGD-based MF. Kaleem et al. [31] evaluated different workload scheduling policies that parallelize SGD on GPUs. Jin et al. [27] propose an MF solution based on matrix blocking. Canny et al. [11] release BID-Mach, a machine learning library that supports matrix factorization. However, to the best of our knowledge, none of them outperforms state-of-the-art CPU solutions. The main reason is, they simply port CPU-based algorithms to GPUs and do not fully exploit GPU architecture [59]. Unlike these efforts, our study is to fully explore and exploit the power of GPUs.

We develop **CuMF_SGD**[1], an SGD-based MF solution on GPUs, with the goal to scale to large data sets and to achieve near-linear scalability when increasing the level of parallelism. We first design high-performance GPU kernels to fully utilize the memory bandwidth on GPUs for individual SGD updates. We then evaluate the existing SGD parallelization policies, and design lightweight scheduling policies specifically for GPUs to minimize the scheduling overhead. Finally, we design workload partition schemes to accommodate large data sets and minimize the CPU-GPU communication overhead. We contribute to the state-of-the-art of machine learning and high-performance computing in the following aspects:

- We characterize the SGD-based MF problem and identify that it is bound by memory bandwidth. We propose an accelerated solution, cuMF_SGD, by exploiting GPUs and their extremely high off-chip memory bandwidth.
- We show how cuMF_SGD exploits *model parallelism* through high-performance GPU kernels, and *data parallelism* through lightweight scheduling schemes. In this way, cuMF_SGD is able to scale to large data sets that cannot fit into the device memory.
- We evaluate cuMF_SGD on two modern GPU generations with benchmark data sets. Evaluations illustrate that cuMF_SGD achieves good performance on all data sets on both platforms. Compared with previous works [16], cuMF_SGD achieves 3.1X to 28.1X performance improvements. Moreover, cuMF_SGD outperforms a 64-node CPU cluster with only one GPU card. CuMF_SGD is also able to scale to multiple GPUs and different generations of GPUs.

We organize the remainder of the paper as follows. Section 2 present the baseline SGD algorithm, GPU architectural details, and workload characterization. Section 3 shows the overview of cuMF_SGD. Section 4 presents the GPU kernel design, Section 5 shows the SGD scheduling algorithms, and Section 6 shows how

cuMF_SGD scales to large data sets. Section 7 presents the experiment results and analysis, Section 8 discusses the related work and Section 9 concludes this paper.

2 BACKGROUND

We first present the basics of SGD-based matrix factorization in Section 2.1. Then Section 2.2 presents the details of experimental setup and Section 2.3 characterizes the workload.

2.1 SGD-based Matrix Factorization

Given a sparse $m \times n$ matrix R, the goal of matrix factorization is to train a $m \times k$ dense feature matrix P and a $k \times n$ dense feature matrix Q such that:

$$\mathbf{R} \approx \mathbf{P} \times \mathbf{Q} \tag{1}$$

We use $r_{u,v}$ to refer to the sample at the u_{th} row and the v_{th} column of R. We use p_u to represent the u_{th} row of P and q_v to represent the v_{th} column of Q. In a recommender system, $r_{u,v}$ indicates the preference or rating of u_{th} user on v_{th} item, p_u is used to represent the preference of the u_{th} user and q_v is used to represent the feature of the v_{th} item. The training process of matrix factorization is to minimize the root mean square error (RMSE) between the original matrix and trained model:

$$\sum_{r_{u,v} \in R}^{N} (r_{u,v} - \mathbf{p}_u\mathbf{q}_v)^2 + \lambda_p \parallel \mathbf{p}_u \parallel^2 + \lambda_q \parallel \mathbf{q}_v \parallel^2 \tag{2}$$

where λ_p and λ_q are regularization parameters to avoid overfitting and N is the number of non-zero samples in matrix R. Such a simple model and its variants are now widely used in recommender systems [34], topic modeling [62], word embeddings [43], and others.

To solve Eq.2, it is necessary to go through $R_{m \times n}$. Consider $R_{m \times n}$ may contain up to billions of samples, the process is time-consuming. To address the problem, *stochastic gradient descent* (SGD), is often employed in modern machine learning applications [17]. Instead of going through rating matrix $R_{m \times n}$, SGD only randomly picks one sample at each step and Eq.2 is reduced to:

$$(r_{u,v} - \mathbf{p}_u\mathbf{q}_v)^2 + \lambda_p \parallel \mathbf{p}_u \parallel^2 + \lambda_q \parallel \mathbf{q}_v \parallel^2 \tag{3}$$

Algorithm 1 shows a typical SGD-based matrix factorization algorithm. The input of the algorithm includes the rating matrix $R_{m \times n}$, the feature dimension k (typically ranges from $O(10)$ to $O(100)$), the learning rate γ, and the regularization parameter λ. In this paper, we use the same λ for both P and Q. The output is the trained model (i.e., feature matrices P and Q). Lines 1-3 show the data pre-processing, lines 5-12 show the SGD training process, and lines 14-16 show the data post-processing. The SGD training process is the most time-consuming part and not different with previous work, and we focus on optimizing this part. The training process is composed of two loops. Each iteration (also known as an *epoch*) of the outer loop represent a full pass of the rating matrix. The number of iterations of the outer loop is set by users. In each step of the inner loop, one sample is randomly picked to decrease Eq.3 (details shown in Line 5-12). The SGD training is finished when the given number of iterations (*Ite*) is reached or the model converges.

---

[1]http://github.com/cumf/cumf_sgd/

The optimization work on matrix factorization contains two streams: *algorithm* and *system*. The algorithmic stream tries to optimize update schemes such as learning rate (γ) in gradient descent, in order to **reduce the number of epochs (iterations)** needed to converge [16]. The system stream tries to accelerate the computation, in order to **run each epoch faster** [15, 51, 61, 63]. We focus on the system stream and the proposed techniques can be combined with other algorithmic optimizations.

Algorithm 1 A Typical SGD-based Matrix Factorization Algorithm.

Input: $R_{m \times n}$ (N samples), k (feature dimension), γ (learning rate), λ (regularization parameter);
1: ▷ Data pre-processing.
2: $random\_shuffle(\mathbf{R}_{m \times n})$;
3: $\mathbf{P}_{m \times k}, \mathbf{Q}_{k \times n} \leftarrow random(0, sqrt(1/(k * scale\_factor)))$;
4:
5: ▷ SGD training
6: **for** $iteration \leftarrow 1$ to Ite **do**
7:    **for** Randomly select $r_{u,v}$ from $\mathbf{R}_{m \times n}$ **do**
8:       $error \leftarrow r_{u,v} - \mathbf{p}_u \times \mathbf{q}_v$;
9:       $\mathbf{p}_u \leftarrow \mathbf{p}_u + \gamma(error * \mathbf{q}_v^T - \lambda * \mathbf{p}_u)$
10:      $\mathbf{q}_v \leftarrow \mathbf{q}_v + \gamma(error * \mathbf{p}_u^T - \lambda * \mathbf{q}_v)$
11:    **end for**
12: **end for**
13:
14: ▷ Data post-processing.
15: $model\_shuffle(\mathbf{P}, \mathbf{Q})$;
16: $model\_save(\mathbf{P}, \mathbf{Q})$;
Output: $\leftarrow$ P,Q

As we see in Algorithm 1, the SGD training process is serial. One SGD update contains a dot product (Line 8) and a few vector operations (Line 9, 10) at length k. How to efficiently execute individual SGD updates, i.e., exploit the *model parallelism*, becomes one major design factor of matrix factorization. As one SGD update can not saturate the resources on modern processors, how to parallelize the SGD updates is also a challenge (*data parallelism*). Our proposed cuMF_SGD exploits both model parallelism and data parallelism.

2.2 Experimental Setup

Platform. Table 1 shows the configurations of the platforms used in this paper. The Maxwell platform is with Intel Xeon CPUs and NVIDIA TITAN X GPUs. The TITAN X GPU is Maxwell architecture [3] with CPUs and GPUs connected via PCIe 3.0. The Pascal platform is equipped with IBM PowerNV8 CPUs and NVIDIA Pascal P100 GPUs. The P100 GPU is Pascal architecture [5], newer than Maxwell architecture. The CPUs and GPUs are connected by NVLink that is much faster than PCIe. Overall, the Pascal platform is more powerful than the Maxwell platform in terms of both computational power and interconnection bandwidth.

Data sets. We use three public data sets: *Netflix, Yahoo!Music,* and *Hugewiki*. Details of them are shown in Table 2. They are also used in other matrix factorization systems [16, 38]. *Netflix* and *Yahoo!Music* comes with a test set but *Hugewiki* does not. For *Hugewiki*, we randomly sample and extract out 1% of the data as the test set.

Table 1: Configuration of the Maxwell [3] and Pascal [5] Platform.

	Maxwell Platform
CPU	12-core Intel Xeon CPU E5-2670*2 (up to 48 threads), 512 GB memory.
GPU	TITAN X GPU*4, per GPU: 24 SMs, 12 GB device memory, 360GB/s memory bandwidth, per SM: 128 CUDA cores, 2K threads.
Interconnection	PCIe 3.0, up to 16 GB/s.
	Pascal Platform
CPU	2*10 PowerNV 8 processors with SMT 8 and NVLink, 512 GB memory.
GPU	Pascal P100 GPU*4, per GPU: 56 SMs, 16 GB device memory, 780GB/s memory bandwidth, per SM: 64 CUDA cores, 2K threads.
Interconnection	NVLink, up to 80 GB/s.

Table 2: Details of workload data sets.

Dataset	Netflix	Yahoo!Music	Hugewiki
m	480,190	1,000,990	50,082,604
n	17,771	624,961	39,781
k	128	128	128
Train Set	99,072,112	252,800,275	3,069,817,980
Test Set	1,408,395	4,003,960	31,327,899

2.3 Workload Characterization

Before optimizing the SGD-based MF, we first characterize the workload features. We start with analyzing the computation to memory ratio. We adopt a metric, *Flops/Byte*, which is defined as the ratio of floating point operations to memory access density (byte) (Eq. 4). When *Flops/Byte* is extremely high (e.g. in matrix multiplication), the application is *compute bound*, otherwise, the application is *memory bound*.

$$Flops/Byte = \frac{\#FloatingPointOps}{\#MemoryOps(Byte)} \quad (4)$$

Eq. 5 shows how to compute the *Flops/Byte* metric for SGD-based MF. Consider that, for $k = 128$ and $sizeof(r_{u,v}) = 12$ (2 integers and 1 float in COO format), the *Flops/Byte* is 0.43 ops/byte. Given the fact that a modern CPU processor provides ~600 GFLOPS computational horsepower and ~60 GB/s off-chip memory bandwidth (600/60=10), SGD-based MF has low *Flops/Byte* ratio and is bound by memory.

$$Flops/Byte = \frac{6k + \sum_{i=1}^{logk} \frac{k}{2^i}}{sizeof(r_{u,v}) + 4k * sizeof(float)} \quad (5)$$

For shared memory based solutions, to address the memory problem, cache efficiency has to be carefully optimized. Chin et al. release LIBMF [15, 16], a CPU-based high-performance SGD solution to MF. As reported in the original paper, they optimize the cache efficiency at the expense of sacrificing randomness. We evaluate LIBMF on our Maxwell platform and show the effective memory bandwidth in Figure 2(a). On the smallest *Netflix* data set, LIBMF achieves 194GB/s effective memory bandwidth. The bandwidth is much higher than the theoretical memory bandwidth due to cache effect. However, on the largest *HugeWiki* data set, the effective memory bandwidth drops by 45%, to 106GB/s. The main reason is that increased data size leads to decreased cache efficiency, and thus degrades the performance. Hence, single-node CPU solution is not scalable to large data sets.

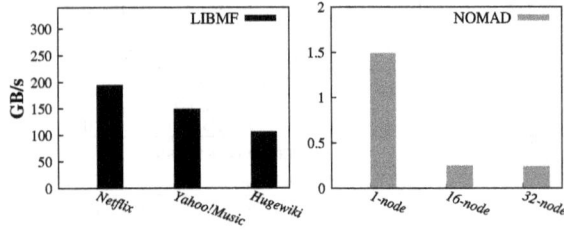

Figure 2: (a) The effective memory bandwidth of LIBMF drops when solving large data sets. (b) NOMAD achieves lower memory efficiency when scaling to multiple nodes.

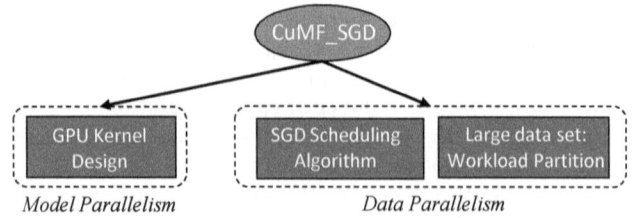

Figure 3: Overview of cuMF_SGD.

One solution to the cache performance degradation is to distribute the workload to multiple nodes. Yun et al. develop *NOMAD*, a distributed SGD-based MF solution [63]. By distributing the data to multiple nodes, the working set can fit into to L3 cache of CPUs. Hence, the cache efficiency is improved. However, the overall performance is bound by the slow network speed [47]. On the *Netflix* data set, NOMAD only achieves ~5.6X speedup when scaling from 1 node to 32, which is far from perfect scaling. Figure 2 (b) shows the achieved memory efficiency of NOMAD on *Netflix* data with different number of nodes. The memory efficiency is the ratio of effective memory bandwidth to total memory bandwidth of all nodes. We observe that the efficiency of distributed solution is extremely low.

In this paper, we propose to accelerate SGD-based MF on GPUs. One main aspect is to maximize the usage of GPUs' high off-chip memory bandwidth. Compared with CPUs, GPUs do not rely on the cache and are scalable to process large data sets. For example, NVIDIA Maxwell architecture GPU TITAN X is equipped with up to 360GB/s memory bandwidth, which is multiple times higher than CPUs (<100 GB/s). New generation NVIDIA P100 GPUs provide even higher bandwidth (780 GB/s). Moreover, NVIDIA GPUs introduce NVLink as new generation interconnect network between CPUs and GPUs. NVLink provides up to 80 GB/s memory bandwidth. For data sets that can not fit into GPU's memory, the high-speed CPU to GPU bandwidth makes GPUs more efficient than distributed systems.

3 OVERVIEW

In this section, we present the overview of cuMF_SGD, as shown in Figure 3. Parallelizing SGD on GPUs is a not a trivial task. SGD is inherently serial, which does not fit the flavor of GPUs [17]. Many machine learning solutions [37] employs batch SGD on GPUs to exploit model parallelism. They process a batch of, say, 16 to 256, samples to saturate GPUs. Given that the each individual SGD update in MF is lightweight, thousands of SGD updates are required to saturate GPUs. However, increasing the size of each batch may hurt convergence and in the end prolong the training time. Hence, we carefully design cuMF_SGD to fully utilize the resources on GPUs.

The design of cuMF_SGD is composed of two streams. The first stream is to exploit the *model parallelism*. We design high-performance GPU kernels to optimize the execution of each individual SGD update. In this paper, we term a group of threads that

work coordinately to perform one SGD update as a *parallel worker*. On CPUs, a parallel worker is usually composed of one thread. On GPUs, we set a parallel worker as one thread block to exploit the SIMD features. We optimize the kernel using various GPU optimization techniques, including warp shuffle, memory coalescing, and on-chip caching. Details are shown in Section 4. The other stream is to exploit the *data parallelism*. There are hundreds of parallel workers (thread blocks) running on one GPU, SGD updates are scheduled and executed in parallel. How to design efficient scheduling algorithm that incurs minimal scheduling overhead becomes a key design factor. We design lightweight SGD scheduling algorithms that are effective in terms of both system throughput and convergence, with details discussed in Section 5. The GPU memory capacity is limited (~10GB per GPU). When processing large data sets, the data set has to be partitioned to fit into the GPU's memory. The memory transfer between CPU and GPU happens frequently to migrate the data. We design workload partitioning algorithm and optimize the CPU-GPU memory transfer to maximize the system performance. The algorithm is presented in Section 6.

4 GPU KERNEL DESIGN

In this section, we present how to design the GPU kernel of cuMF_SGD. When designing the kernel, we assume that the SGD workloads have been assigned to parallel workers. Hence, we only focus on how to efficiently execute the SGD updates within each parallel worker.

In MF, one SGD update consists of four steps: 1) read one sample $(r_{u,v})$ from the rating matrix, 2) read two feature vectors (p_u, q_v), 3) compute prediction error($r_{u,v} - p_u q_v$), and 4) update the features. Except for the first step, other three steps are all vector operations at length k. k is the feature dimension and typically ranges from $O(10)$ to $O(100)$. On a CPU, a parallel worker can be one or more threads of a process, where vector instructions such as SSE and AVX can be used to accelerate the computation. GPUs are SIMD architectures [48], where a thread block is a vector group. Hence, in cuMF_SGD, we use a thread block as a parallel worker. Figure 4 shows a code snippet of the computational part of cuMF_SGD, where we use $k = 64$ as an example. We highlight the major optimization techniques in Figure 4 and explain them in the following.

Warp shuffle. Warp shuffle instructions [19] are used to compute the dot product $p_u \times q_v$ and broadcast the result. Compared with traditional shared memory system-based approaches, this warp shuffle-based approach performs better because: (1) warp shuffle instructions have extra hardware support, (2) register is faster than shared memory, and (3) no thread synchronization is

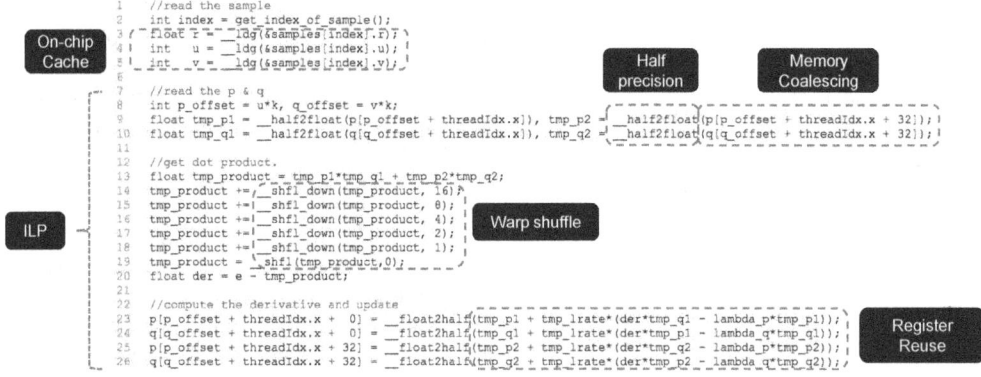

Figure 4: The exemplify kernel code of cuMF_SGD, where $k = 64$. The used optimization techniques are highlighted.

involved. To exploit the warp shuffle feature, we fix the thread blocks size as warp size(32).

On-chip cache. Since Fermi architecture, NVIDIA GPUs feature on-chip L1 cache and allow programmers to control the cache behavior of each memory instruction (cache or bypass). While many GPU applications do not benefit from the cache due to cache contention [36, 56, 57], some memory instructions may benefit from the cache as the accessed data may be frequently reused in the near future (temporal reuse) or by other threads (spatial reuse). Following the model provided by [56], we observe that the memory load of the rating matrix benefits from cache and use the intrinsic instruction __ldg [2] to enable cache-assisted read.

Memory coalescing. On GPUs, when threads within one warp access the data within one cache line, the access is coalesced to minimize the bandwidth consumption [29, 59]. This is called memory coalescing. In cuMF_SGD, the read/write of P and Q are carefully coalesced to ensure that consecutive threads access consecutive memory addresses.

ILP. Modern GPUs support compiler-aided super scalar to exploit the instruction-level parallelism (ILP). In cuMF_SGD, when $k > 32$, a thread is responsible for processing $k/32$ independent scalars. Hence, with awareness of the low-level architecture information, we reorder the instructions to maximize the benefit of ILP.

Register usage. The register file is an important resource on GPUs. As the total number of registers on GPUs is fixed, if each thread uses too many registers, the register consumption may become the limitation to concurrency. In our case, the CUDA compiler reports that allocating 33 registers for each thread is enough to fit all active variables. The concurrency is only limited by the number of thread blocks of GPUs [2, 55]. Hence, we allocate as many as possible registers to each thread such that every reusable variable is kept in the fastest register file.

Half-precision. As addressed before, SGD is memory bound. Most of the memory bandwidth is spent on the read/write to the feature matrices. Recently, GPU architectures support the storage of half-precision (2 bytes vs. 4 bytes of single-precision) and fast transformation between floating point and half-precision. In practice, after parameter scaling, half-precision is precise enough to store the feature matrices and does not incur accuracy loss. CuMF_SGD uses

half-precision to store feature matrices, which halves the memory bandwidth need when accessing feature matrices.

5 WORKLOAD SCHEDULING ALGORITHM

The original SGD algorithm is serial, with samples in the rating matrix picked up randomly and updated in sequence. To exploit the data parallelism and execute SGD updates in parallel, a workload scheduling algorithm that assigns tasks to parallel workers becomes necessary. The parallelization of SGD updates for MF is based on the observation that in Algorithm 1, one SGD update on sample $r_{u,v}$ only updates the uth row of $P(P_u)$ and v^{th} row of $Q(Q_u)$. Consider two samples, $r_{u1,v1}$ and $r_{u2,v2}$, they can be updated simultaneously if

$$u1 \neq u2 \ \&\& \ v1 \neq v2 \tag{6}$$

We term them as *independent* updates. We term simultaneous dependent updates as *conflicts*. To evaluate the efficiency of workload scheduling algorithm, we define a metric, *updates per second* as the performance indicator:

$$\#Updates/s = \frac{\#Iterations \times N}{Elapsed\ Time} \tag{7}$$

where *#Iterations*, N, *Elapsed Time* are the number of iterations, the number of non-zero samples in the input matrix R, and the elapsed time in seconds, respectively. As we discussed before, the SGD-based MF is memory bound. According to the roofline model [54], the application is limited by the memory bandwidth. Hence, the design goal of workload scheduling algorithm is to minimize the scheduling overhead and exhaust the memory bandwidth on GPUs.

We start our scheduling algorithm design from examining existing solutions. We analyze and evaluate the workload scheduling algorithm proposed in CPU-based LIBMF [15], as it is publicly available. Figure 5(a) shows the basics of scheduling algorithm used in LIBMF. It evenly divides the rating matrix into $a \times a$ blocks and uses s threads ($s < a$). It also uses a table to manage the matrix blocks to comply to Eq. 6. When a thread is idle, it accesses the table and finds an independent block. Then, the thread executes the SGD updates in the block in serial. Overall, it requires atomic operations to manage the table and $O(a^2)$ time complexity to search the table.

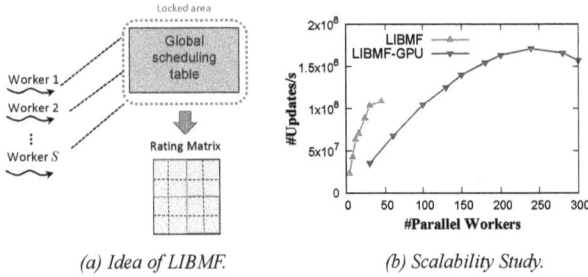

(a) Idea of LIBMF.   *(b) Scalability Study.*

Figure 5: (a) LIBMF uses a centralized table to manage parallel workers. (b) LIBMF scales to only 30 CPU threads and 240 GPU thread blocks.

We evaluate LIBMF on the Maxwell platform using the *Netflix* data set. Figure 5(b) shows the evaluation results that the performance of LIBMF saturates around 30 concurrent workers (CPU threads), which is consistent with the previous study [41].

As GPUs are more sensitive to synchronization overhead than CPUs [9], we optimize the scheduling algorithm by reducing its time complexity. In each scheduling step, we first search all a columns and a rows to find the independent rows or columns. Then we randomly choose one independent block that is in the independent rows and columns. By doing so, the time complexity of the scheduling algorithm is reduced to $O(a)$. We combine the optimized scheduling algorithm with our designed GPU kernel(Section 4). However, as shown in Figure 5(b) (labled as LIBMF-GPU), it can only scale to 240 thread blocks, much lower than the hardware limit (768 thread blocks on Maxwell).

The reason why LIBMF cannot scale to many parallel workers is that it uses a global scheduling table to manage all parallel workers. At each time, only one parallel worker can access the table and it is also time-consuming to find a free block to process. Therefore, when the number of workers increases, the waiting time also increases. As the number of workers grows, the waiting time becomes dominating. This shows that cuMF_SGD can not simply re-use existing scheduling policies. To overcome the scheduling overhead, we propose two GPU-specific scheduling schemes, *batch-Hogwild!* and *Wavefront-update*. Batch-Hogwild! avoids matrix blocking-based scheduling and improves the cache efficiency by process samples in batch. Wavefront-update is still blocking-based, but only requires a local look-up instead of the expensive global lookup as in LIBMF.

5.1 Batch-Hogwild!

We propose batch-Hogwild!, a variant of Hogwild! [44] with improved cache efficiency. Hogwild! is efficient as its lock-free scheme incurs negligible scheduling overhead. It is not efficient, however, in terms of data locality [15]. In Hogwild!, each parallel worker randomly selects one sample from the rating matrix at each step. After each update, Hogwild! may not access the consecutive samples in the rating matrix and corresponding rows and columns in the feature matrices for a long time interval, leading to low cache efficiency. As shown in Section 4, we carefully align the memory access of the feature matrices to achieve perfect memory coalescing and the high memory bandwidth on GPUs, such that eliminating

accessing feature matrices as a performance bottleneck. To accelerate the access to rating matrix, we exploit the spatial data locality using L1 data cache. We let each parallel worker, instead of fetching one sample randomly at a time, fetch f consecutive samples and update them serially. The data locality is fully exploited when the following constraint is met,

$$f \gg \lceil \frac{CacheLineSize}{sizeof(r_{u,v})} \rceil \qquad (8)$$

Note that these samples are consecutive in their memory storage; because we shuffle samples, they are still random in terms of their coordinates in R. By doing so, the data locality is fully exploited. Consider the L1 cache line size is 128 bytes and the size of each sample is 12 bytes (one floating point and two integers), $f \gg \lceil 128/12 \rceil$ is enough to exploit the locality. We evaluate different values of f and find that they yield similar benefit. Therefore we choose $f = 256$ without loss of generality.

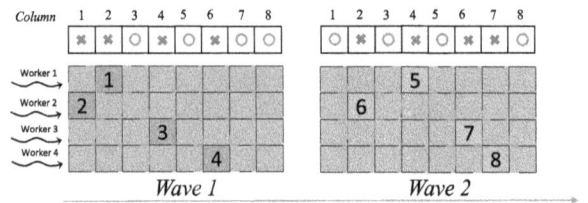

Figure 6: Wavefront-update. Each parallel worker is assigned to a row and a randomized column update sequence. For example, when Worker 3 completes Block 3 in Wave 1, it releases Column 4 such that Worker 1 can start Block 5 in Wave 2.

5.2 Wavefront-update

As previously discussed, existing scheduling schemes [15, 23] impose a global synchronization, where all workers look up a global table to **find both row and column coordinates** to update. This is expensive and has been shown not scalable to the hundreds of workers on GPUs. To overcome this, we propose wavefront-update, a lightweight scheme that **locks and looks up columns only**.

In the exemplary Figure 6, we use four parallel workers to process an R which is partitioned into 4×8 blocks. Each worker is assigned to a row in this 4×8 grid, and each generates a permutation of $\{1, 2, 3, ..., 7, 8\}$ as its column update sequence. By this, an epoch is conducted in eight waves given this sequence. In each wave, one worker update one block, and workers do not update blocks in the same column. Assume *Worker 1* has the sequence defined as $\{2, 4, ...\}$ and *Worker 3* has sequence $\{4, 6, ...\}$. With this sequence, *Worker 1* updates *Block 1* in wave 1 and *Block 5* in wave 2. To avoid conflicts, we propose a lightweight synchronization scheme between waves using the column lock array. As shown in the figure, we use an array to indicate the status of each column. Before a worker moves to next wave, it checks the status of the next column defined in its sequence. For example, after *Worker 1* finishes *Block 1*, it needs to check the status of column 4 and does not need to care about the status of other columns. When *Worker 3* finishes *Block 3* and releases column 4, *Worker 1* is allowed to move to wave

2. There are two main benefits by doing so: firstly to reduce the two-dimension look-up table in [15, 23] to a one-dimension array; secondly to minimize the workload imbalance problem, as a worker can start the next block earlier without waiting for all other workers to finish.

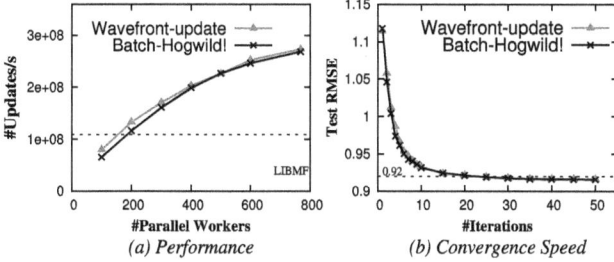

(a) Performance   *(b) Convergence Speed*

Figure 7: Performance Comparison of *batch-Hogwild!* and *wavefront-update* on *Netflix* data set. Both schemes scale much better than LIBMF.

5.3 Evaluation of scheduling schemes

We evaluate both scheduling schemes in terms of performance and convergence speed using the *Netflix* data set on the Maxwell platform. We use metric *#Updates/s* to quantify the performance. Figure 7(a) shows the scalability of *batch-Hogwild!* and *wavefront-update* with a different number of parallel workers (i.e., thread blocks). When increasing the number of parallel workers, both schemes achieve near-linear scalability. When the number of parallel workers hits the hardware limit of 768 on the Maxwell GPU, both techniques achieve ~0.27 billion updates per second, the rate which is 2.5 times faster than LIBMF. Therefore, we conclude that our proposed schemes can perfectly solve the scalability problem of the scheduling policy and fully exploit the equipped hardware resources on GPUs. We also evaluate the convergence speed of both schemes. We use the *root mean square root* error on the standard test data set (*Test RMSE*) as the indication of convergence. Figure 7(b) shows the decrease of *Test RMSE* as the number of iterations increases. Overall, batch-Hogwild! converges a little bit faster than wavefront-update. The reason is that batch-Hogwild! enforces more randomness in update sequence, as compared with the block-based wavefront-update. Based on this observation, we use batch-Hogwild! as the default scheme on one GPU experiments.

6 WORKLOAD PARTITION

In the previous discussions, we assume that the rating matrix and feature matrices fully reside in GPU's memory. However, the limited GPU memory capacity [45] prevents cuMF_SGD from solving large-scale problems. For example, NVIDIA TITAN X GPU has 12 GB device memory that can only store 1 billion samples (one sample needs one float and two integers). Nowadays, real-world problems may have 10^{11} samples [51]. Techniques such as *Unified Virtual Memory* [2] allow GPU to access CPU's memory but with high overhead. Consider these factors, to solve large-scale MF problems that can not fit into one GPU's memory, we need to partition the data sets and stage the partitions to GPUs in batches. Moreover, we should overlap the data transfer with computation to alleviate the

delay caused by slow CPU-GPU memory transfer. Please note that the partitions can be processed by one or multiple GPUs.

6.1 Workload Partitioning

Figure 8 shows our proposed multi-GPU solution for large data sets. The main idea is to partition the rating matrix R into multiple blocks; each block is small enough to fit into one GPU's memory such that independent blocks can be updated concurrently on different GPUs. The multi-GPU solution works as follows,

(1) Divide the rating matrix R into $i \times j$ blocks. Meanwhile, divide feature matrix p into i segments and feature matrix q into j segments accordingly.
(2) When a GPU is idle, randomly select one matrix block from those independent blocks and dispatch it to the GPU.
(3) Transfer the matrix block and corresponding feature sub-matrices p and q to the GPU. Then update the matrix block using the single GPU implementation discussed in Section 5. After the update, transfer p and q back to CPU.
(4) Iterate from 2 until convergence or the given number of iterations is reached.

We further explain the proposed scheme using the example shown in Figure 8(a). In Step 1, we divide R into 4×4 blocks and use two GPUs. In Step 2, we send block $R2$ to GPU 0 and $R11$ to GPU 1. Again, consider the nature of MF, updating $R2$ only touches sub-matrices $p1$ & $q2$ while updating $R11$ only touches $p3$ & $q3$. Hence, GPU 0 only needs to store $R2$, $p1$, and $q2$ in its device memory while GPU 1 only needs to store $R11$, $p3$, and $q3$. By doing so, the problem is divided and conquered by multiple GPUs. After deciding the block scheduling order, cuMF_SGD transfers $p1$, $q2$, $R2$ to GPU 0 and $p3$, $q3$, $R11$ to GPU 1. Then cuMF_SGD performs the computation on two GPUs in parallel. The GPU-side computation follows the rules we discussed in Section 5. After finishing the computation, the updated $p1$, $q2$, $p3$, and $q3$ are transferred back to CPU memory. Note that we don't have to transfer $R2$ or $R11$ back to CPU memory as they are read-only.

Scalability problem. We mentioned that LIBMF faces serious scalability issue, as the scheduling overhead increases quickly with the number of workers [41]. Our multiple-GPU scheduling scheme has similar complexity with that of LIBMF. However, it does not face the same scalability issue as we only need to schedule to a few GPUs instead of hundreds of workers.

6.2 Optimizing Data Transfer

GPUs' memory bandwidth are much higher than the CPU-GPU memory transfer bandwidth. For example, NVIDIA TITAN X GPU provides 360 GB/s device memory bandwidth while the CPU-GPU memory bandwidth is only ~16 GB/s (PCIe v3.0 16x). In the single-GPU implementation, CPU-GPU memory transfer only happens at the start and end of MF, and therefore not dominant. However, when the data set can not fit into the GPU memory, memory transfer happens frequently and has a significant impact on the overall performance.

Given the memory transfer overhead, we overlap the memory transfer and computation when solving large problems, as shown in Figure 8(b). Due to space limitation, we only plot one GPU. The

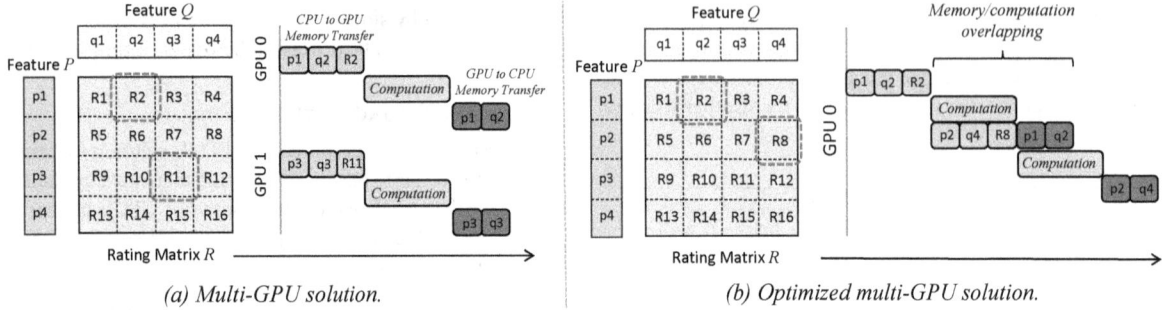

(a) Multi-GPU solution.   *(b) Optimized multi-GPU solution.*

Figure 8: (a) Multi-GPU solution of cuMF_SGD, where the rating matrix is partitioned and each partition can fit into a GPU's device memory. (b) Optimizing the multi-GPU solution by overlapping memory transfer with computation.

key idea is, at the block scheduling time, instead of randomly selecting one independent block for the GPU, the optimized technique randomly **selects multiple blocks at a time**. Those blocks are pipelined to overlap the memory transfer and computation. In that case, we schedule two blocks to GPU 0, and overlap the memory transfer of the second block (*R8*) with the computation of the first block (*R2*). Note that the two blocks scheduled to one GPU do not need to be independent as they are updated in serial; meanwhile, blocks scheduled to different GPUs have to be independent of each other to avoid conflicts. By doing so, we can minimize the overhead of slow CPU-GPU memory transfer and improve the overall performance.

Discussion. Allocating more blocks to one GPU would yield more performance benefit as more memory/computation overlapping can be achieved. However, the number of available blocks is limited by how we divide the rating matrix *R*. Consider we divide *R* to $i \times i$ and we have two GPUs running in parallel, the number of blocks per GPU cannot be more than $i/2$. In practice, i is determined by the size of the rating matrix *R* and the available hardware resources on the GPU. We will discuss it in Section 7.6.

6.3 Implementation Details

Multiple GPUs management. We implement it using multiple CPU threads within one process. Within the process, there is one *host thread* and multiple *worker threads*, where each GPU is bound to one worker thread. The host thread manages the workload scheduling and informs worker threads of the scheduling decision. Each worker thread then starts the data transfer and launches compute kernels on a GPU.

Overlapping. Each worker thread will overlap the computation and CPU-GPU memory transfers. We use CUDA *streams* to achieve this. A *stream* contains a list of GPU commands that are executed in serial, and commands in different streams are executed in parallel if hardware resources permit. Each worker thread uses three streams that manage CPU-GPU memory transfer, GPU-CPU memory transfer, and GPU kernel launch, respectively.

7 EXPERIMENTS

We implement cuMF_SGD using CUDA C (source code available at http://github.com/cumf/cumf_sgd/), evaluate its performance on public data sets, and demonstrate its advantage in performance

and cost. The following experiments are designed to answer the following questions:

- Compared with state-of-the-art SGD-based MF solutions [11, 16, 63], is cuMF_SGD better and why? (Section 7.2)
- What is the implication of using different generations of GPUs? (Section 7.3)
- Compared with the ALS-based GPU library **cuMF_ALS** that we published earlier [51], what is the advantage of cuMF_SGD? (Section 7.4)
- Parallelizing SGD is always tricky and may lead to converge problems, how does cuMF_SGD perform with different parallelization parameters? (Section 7.5)
- Is there any limitation that may incur convergence problems with matrix blocking-based algorithms? (Section 7.6)
- When scaling up to multiple GPUs, is cuMF_SGD still efficient? (Section 7.7)

7.1 Machine Learning Parameters

As mentioned in the introduction and background, this paper focuses on system-level optimization, not algorithmic-level optimization. Therefore, we do not spend much effort on machine learning parameter tuning. Instead, we use the parameters adopted by earlier works [15, 16, 51, 63]. For the learning rate, we adopt the learning rate scheduling technique used by Yun et al. [63], where the learning rate γ_t at epoch t is monotonically reduced in the following routine:

$$\gamma_t = \frac{\alpha}{1 + \beta \cdot t^{1.5}} \quad (9)$$

α is the given initial learning rate and β is another given parameter. The parameters used by cuMF_SGD are listed in Table 3.

Table 3: Machine learning parameters used for all three data sets.

Dataset	λ	α	β
Netflix	0.05	0.08	0.3
Yahoo!Music	1.0	0.08	0.2
Hugewiki	0.03	0.08	0.3

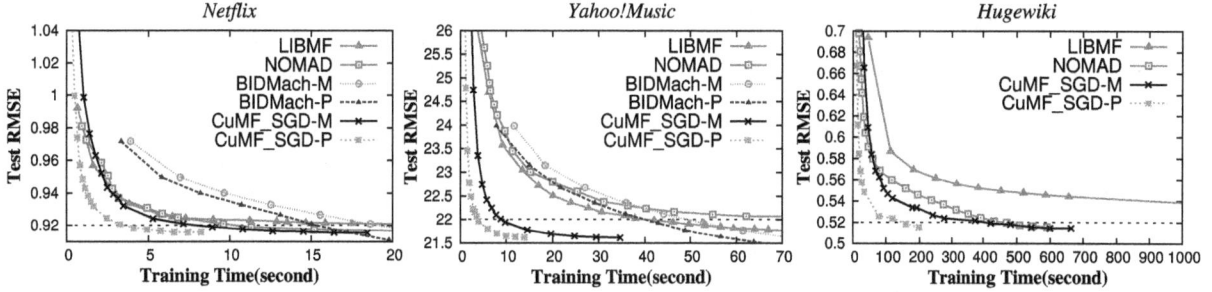

Figure 9: Test RMSE over training time on three data sets. CuMF_SGD converges faster than all other approaches with only one GPU card.

7.2 Comparison of SGD-based approaches

We only compare with MF-specific solutions as they represent the performance upper bound of MF solutions. Machine learning frameworks, such as TensorFlow [6], MXNet [14], also support matrix factorization. Their goal is to provide a unified interface for all machine learning applications. Hence, they are not neccessarily efficient in terms of performance. We compare cuMF_SGD with the following state-of-the-art approaches.

- **LIBMF** [15]. LIBMF is a representative matrix blocking-based solution on shared-memory systems. Its main design purpose is to balance the workload across CPU threads and accelerate the memory access using caches. It also leverages SSE instructions and a novel learning rate schedule to speed up the convergence [16]. The Maxwell platform supports up to 48 concurrent physical threads. We exhaustively evaluate all possible numbers of threads (1~48) on the Maxwell platform and we choose to use 40 CPU threads as it yields fastest convergence. LIBMF divides the rating matrix into $a \times a$ blocks. We evaluate different values for a(40~160) and select the optimal value(100). We set its initial learning rate as 0.1 as suggested in the original paper.
- **NOMAD** [63]. NOMAD is a representative distributed matrix factorization solution. It uses a 64-node HPC cluster to solve MF. It proposes a decentralized scheduling policy to reduce the synchronization overhead and discusses how to reduce the inter-node communication overhead. We cite the best results presented in the original paper, i.e., using 32 nodes for *Netflix* and *Yahoo!Music* data sets and using all 64 nodes for *Hugewiki* data set on the HPC cluster. Each node employs 4 CPU cores. That is, NOMAD launches 128 parallel workers for *Netflix* and *Yahoo!Music*, 256 parallel workers for *Hugewiki*.
- **BIDMach**. BIDMach [11] is a machine learning acceleration library that supports SGD-based MF on GPU. We evaluate BIDMach on both Maxwell and Pascal platforms using the default GPU configurations. We name the results on Maxwell as *BIDMach-M* and those on Pascal as *BIDMach-P*. We are not able to successfully run BIDMach for *Hugewiki* due to memory allocation error. *Hugewiki* has over 3B non-zero samples. BIDMach requires ~62GB memory space, exceeding single GPU's memory(12 GB on Maxwell, 16GB on Pascal).

- **CuMF_SGD**. We evaluate cuMF_SGD on both Maxwell and Pascal platforms, with all three data sets. We name the results on Maxwell as *cuMF_SGD-M* and those on Pascal as *cuMF_SGD-P*. We use one GPU in this subsection. The number of parallel workers (thread blocks) is set as the maximum of the corresponding GPU architecture (768 on Maxwell platform and 1792 on Pascal platform). We use half precision to store feature matrices, however, *Hugewiki* still requires ~49GB memory space, exceeding the GPU's memory. We divide it into 64×1 blocks and at each scheduling time, we schedule 8 blocks to overlap memory transfer and computation. Each block only occupies 0.77GB memory space. CuMF_SGD needs to keep two blocks in the memory to overlap computation and memory transfer. Overall, cuMF_SGD only occupies 1.54GB memory space in GPU's memory.

Figure 9 shows the test RMSE w.r.t. the training time. Table 4 summarizes the training time required to converge to a reasonable RMSE (0.92, 22.0, and 0.52 for *Netflix*, *Yahoo!Music*, and *Hugewki*, respectively). Results show that **with only one GPU, cuMF_SGD-P and cuMF_SGD-M perform much better (3.1X to 28.2X) on all data sets compared than all existing works**, including NO-MAD on a 64-node HPC cluster. In the following, we analyze the reasons.

Table 4: Training time speedup normalized to LIBMF.

Data set	*Netflix*	*Yahoo!Music*	*Hugewiki*
LIBMF	23.0s	37.9s	3020.7s
NOMAD	9.6s(2.4X)	108.7s(0.35X)	459.1s(6.6X)
BIDMach-M	18.6s(1.24X)	48.6s(0.78X)	-
BIDMach-P	15.0s(1.53X)	39.5s(0.96X)	-
CuMF_SGD-M	7.5s(3.1X)	8.8s(4.3X)	442.3s(6.8X)
CuMF_SGD-P	3.3s(7.0X)	3.8s(10.0X)	107.0s(28.2X)

Compared with LIBMF. As shown in Figure 9 and Table 4, cuMF_SGD outperforms LIBMF on all data sets, on both Maxwell and Pascal. More precisely, cuMF_SGD-M is 3.1X - 6.8X as fast as LIBMF and cuMF_SGD-P is 7.0X - 28.2X as fast. CuMF_SGD outperforms LIBMF because it can do more updates per second, as shown in Figure 10(a). We have already mentioned that matrix factorization is memory bound, LIBMF is also aware of that and strives to keep all frequently used data in the CPU cache. However, the limited cache capacity on a single CPU makes LIMBF suboptimal in large data sets. As shown in Figure 10(b), LIBMF achieves an effective memory bandwidth of 194 GB/s[2] on the *Netflix* data set (with 99M samples) – close to cuMF_SGD-M. However its achieved bandwidth drops almost by half, to 106 GB/s on the larger *Hugewiki* data set (with 3.1B samples) – while cuMF_SGD achieves similar bandwidth in all data sets.

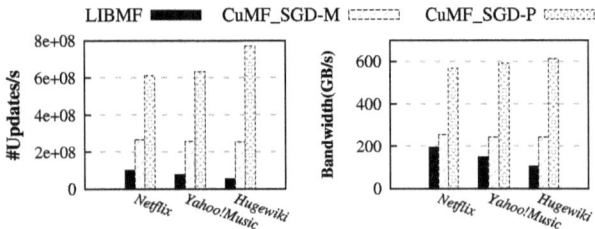

Figure 10: Achieved #*Updates/s* and memory bandwidth of LIBMF, cuMF_SGD-M, and cuMF_SGD-P. The achieved memory bandwidth explains the advantage of cuMF_SGD.

Simply porting LIBMF to GPUs leads to resource under-utilization due to the scalability problem of it scheduling policy (recall Figure 5). In contrast, the workload scheduling policy and memory/computation pattern of cuMF_SGD are delicately designed to fully exploit the computation and memory resources on GPUs. Hence, as shown in Figure 10 (b), cuMF_SGD achieves much higher bandwidth than LIBMF. Moreover, cuMF_SGD uses half-precision (2 bytes for a float number) to store feature matrices. As a result, it can perform twice updates as LIBMF with the same bandwidth consumption.

Compared with NOMAD. As presented in [63], NOMAD uses 32 nodes for *Netflix* and *Yahoo!Music* and 64 HPC nodes for *Hugewiki*. Despite the tremendous hardware resources, NOMAD is still outperformed by cuMF_SGD on all data sets. As observed in Section 2, MF is a memory bound application and data communication happens frequently between parallel workers. When NOMAD distributes parallel workers to different nodes, the network bandwidth, which is much lower than intra-node communication bandwidth, becomes the bottleneck. Consequently, NOMAD achieves suboptimal scalability when scaling from single node to multiple nodes, especially for small data sets. For example, on *Yahoo!Music*, NOMAD performs even worse than LIBMF that uses only one node.

NOMAD (on a 64-node HPC cluster) has similar performance with cuMF_SGD-M on *Hugewiki*, while it is much slower than cuMF_SGD-P. Obviously, cuMF_SGD is not only faster, using a single GPU card, it is also more cost-efficient.

Table 5: Achieved #*Updates/s* of BIDMach and cuMF_SGD.

Data set	Netflix	Yahoo!Music	Hugewiki
BIDMach-M	25.2M	21.6M	-
BIDMach-P	29.6M	32.3M	-
CuMF_SGD-M	267M	258M	256M
CuMF_SGD-P	613M	634M	710M

---

[2]The achieved memory bandwidth measures the data processed by the compute units per second, and can be higher than the theoretical off-chip memory bandwidth thanks to the cache effect.

Compared with BIDMach. BIDMach implements SGD-based MF on GPUs. Different from cuMF_SGD, BIDMach employs the ADAGRAD [20] algorithm to fine tune the learning rate for faster convergence. However, as shown in Figure 9 and Table 4, BIDMach is still outperformed by cuMF_SGD. CuMF_SGD is designed to execute the SGD updates efficiently (Section 4) with low scheduling overhead (Section 5) and minimize the CPU-GPU transfer overhead (Section 6). CuMF_SGD is able to fully exploit the hardware resources on GPUs and achieves higher throughputs (Table 5) than BIDMach. Besides, cuMF_SGD yields better cross-architecture scalability than BIDMach as cuMF_SGD achieves more speedup when porting from Maxwell to Pascal GPUs. In addition, cuMF_SGD can also use ADAGRAD or other learning rate schedulers, for faster convergence. We leave it as future work.

7.3 Implication of GPU Architectures

We have evaluated cuMF_SGD on the two current generations of GPUs, Maxwell and Pascal. As we presented, cuMF_SGD performs consistently well on both platforms. We believe that cuMF_SGD is able to scale to future GPU architectures with minor tuning effort. In this section, we explain the performance gap between Maxwell and Pascal in three aspects: computation resources, off-chip memory bandwidth, and CPU-GPU memory bandwidth.

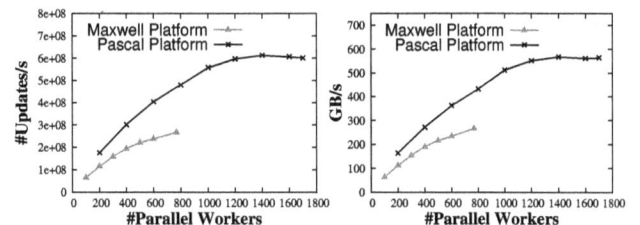

Figure 11: #*Updates/s* and achieved memory bandwidth cuMF_SGD on Maxwell and Pascal platforms, using the *Netflix* data set. CuMF_SGD performs better on the more recent Pascal platform.

Computation resources. We show the #*Updates/s* metric of two platforms with different numbers of parallel workers using *Netflix* in Figure 11(a). Results show that Pascal platform scales to more parallel workers and achieves much higher #*Updates/s* than Maxwell. This is because the Maxwell platform has 24 streaming multiprocessors (SMs) within each GPU, with each SM allowing up to 32 parallel workers (thread blocks). Hence, one Maxwell GPU allows up to 768 parallel workers. Meanwhile, the Pascal GPU used has 56 SMs and allows 32 thread blocks on each SM. Hence, a Pascal GPU allows up to 1792 parallel workers, which is 2.3 times of that of Maxwell GPU. Overall, a Pascal GPU is more powerful than a Maxwell GPU in term of the amount of computation resources.

Off-chip memory bandwidth. As we discussed before, SGD is memory bound. Optimized for throughput, GPUs are able to overlap memory access and computation by fast context switch among concurrent threads [2]. When there are enough threads concurrently running on GPUs, long memory latencies can be hidden, which is exactly what happens with cuMF_SGD. In this scenario, memory bandwidth, instead of memory latency, becomes the limitation of

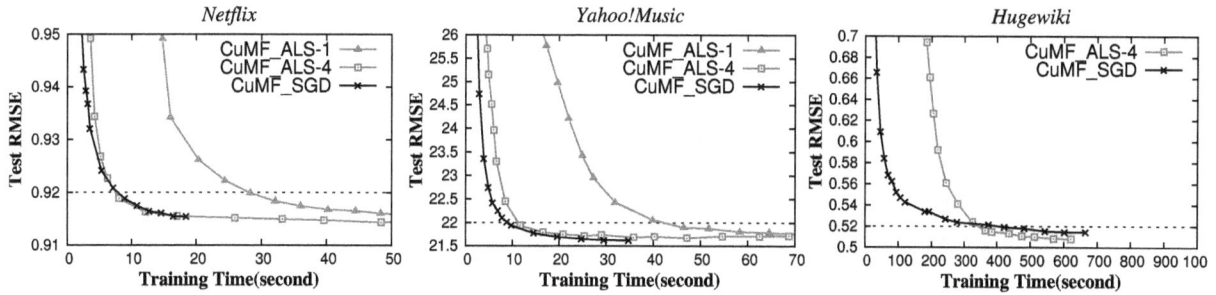

Figure 12: CuMF_SGD vs. CuMF_ALS. With one GPU, cuMF_SGD converges ~4X faster than cuMF_ALS-1 (one GPU) and similar to cuMF_ALS-4 (four GPUs).

the performance. Pascal platforms provide twice as much theoretical peak off-chip memory bandwidth (780 GB/s per GPU) as Maxwell platforms(360 GB/s per GPU). Figure 11(b) shows the achieved memory bandwidth on two platforms with different number of parallel workers. On Maxwell and Pascal, cuMF_SGD achieves up to 266 GB/s and 567 GB/s memory bandwidth, respectively.

CPU-GPU memory bandwidth. *Netflix* and *Yahoo!Music* data sets are small enough to fit into the GPU device memory. For *Hugewiki*, memory transfer occurs multiple times as the data cannot fit into GPU device memory and the overhead is non-negligible. In Section 6.2, we propose to overlap data transfer with computation. Despite of this optimization, the CPU-GPU memory bandwidth still has a noticeable impact on the overall performance as the perfect overlapping cannot be achieved. On the Maxwell platform, the memory transfer between CPU and GPU is via PCIe v3.0 16x with 16 GB/s bandwidth (we observe that on average, the achieved bandwidth is 5.5 GB/s). The very recent Pascal platform is with NVLink [4] that can provide 80 GB/s in theory (we observe an average 29.1 GB/s CPU-GPU memory transfer bandwidth, which is 5.3X as that on Maxwell). This also explains why cuMF_SGD achieves much more speedup on *Hugewiki* using Pascal platform (28.2X) than that on Maxwell platform (6.8X).

7.4 Comparison with cuMF_ALS

Our earlier work **CuMF_ALS** [51] represents the state-of-art ALS-based matrix factorization solution on GPUs. We use one GPU for cuMF_SGD, and one and four GPUs for cuMF_ALS. Figure 12 compares their performance on three data sets on Maxwell. We observe that cuMF_SGD, with one GPU, is faster than cuMF_ALS-1 and achieves similar performance with cuMF_ALS-4.

It is expected that cuMF_SGD is faster than cuMF_ALS, for the following reason. Each epoch of SGD needs memory access of $O(N * k)$ and computation of $O(N * k)$. Each epoch of ALS needs memory access of $O(N*k)$ and computation of $O(N*k^2+(m+n)*k^3)$. Thus, ALS's epochs run slower due to its much more intensive computation. Although ALS needs fewer epochs to coverage, as a whole it converges slower.

Despite the fact that cuMF_ALS is slower than cuMF_SGD, both solutions are maintained at https://github.com/cuMF/ because they serve different purposes: SGD converges faster and is easy to do incremental update, while ALS is easy to parallelize and is able to deal with non-sparse rating matrices [34].

7.5 Convergence analysis of cuMF_SGD

The original SGD algorithm is serial. To speed it up, we discuss how to parallelize it on one GPU in Section 5 and on multiple GPUs in Section 6.1. It is well-known that SGD parallelization may have subtle implications on convergence [15, 63]. In this Section, we provide convergence analysis of cuMF_SGD.

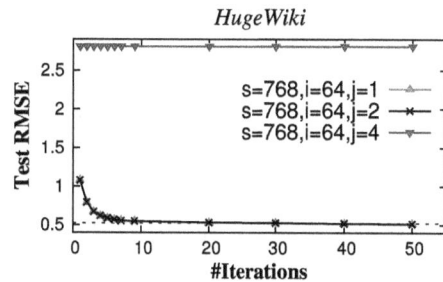

Figure 13: Convergence speed of cuMF_SGD on *Hugewiki* with different parallelization parameters.

Section 5.1 proposes the batch-Hogwild! scheme to schedule the workload and cuMF_SGD adopts it to exploit the data parallelism. As a vectorized version of Hogwild!, batch-Hogwild! inherits the limitation of Hogwild!. Given a rating matrix of $m \times n$ and s parallel workers, convergence is ensured only when the following condition is satisfied [44]:

$$s \ll min(m, n)$$

For multiple GPUs, Section 6 proposes to first divide the rating matrix R into $i \times j$ blocks and process one block on one GPU in parallel if possible. In this case, the above condition needs to change to:

$$s \ll min(\lfloor m/i \rfloor, \lfloor n/j \rfloor)$$

To evaluate the convergence speed of cuMF_SGD and find out the potential convergence problem with it, we conduct the following experiments.

We first fix i and j for all three datasets and vary s. *Netflix* and *Yahoo!Music* data sets are small enough to fit into one GPU's memory, we fix $i = 1$ and $j = 1$. We fix $i = 64$ and $j = 1$ for *Hugewiki*. On both Maxwell and Pascal platforms, we enumerate all possible values of s([1, 768] on Maxwell, [1, 1792] on Pascal) and collect the performance metrics. We observe that the #*Updates*/s varies with s as we discussed in Section 7.3. As a result, *Test RMSE* w.r.t. training time varies with s. At the mean-time, we observe that *Test RMSE* w.r.t. *#Iterations* does not change. Therefore, for the used data sets, the convergence speed of cuMF_SGD does not decrease with parallelism increasing within one GPU.

We conduct another experiment to find out the convergence limitation in cuMF_SGD. Among the three data sets, *Hugewiki* is the largest one and intuitively, cuMF_SGD should gain more speedup through employing multiple GPUs. However, the n of *Hugewiki* is only 40 thousand, preventing cuMF_SGD from further increasing the parallelism beyond one GPU. When we try to partition the *Hugewiki* data set into more blocks (increase i and j), convergence is not ensured. We show an empirical study on *Hugewiki* in Figure 13. *Hugewiki* has $min(m, n) = 40k$ and we fix $s = 768$; convergence is achieved when $j \leq 2$ ($40k/20/768 \approx 2$), and fails when $j = 4$. The result shows that, to ensure the converge, we can not infinitely increase the parallelism and the following regulation has to be complied,

$$s < 1/20 * min(\lfloor m/i \rfloor, \lfloor n/j \rfloor)$$

We believe this is a limitation for all Hogwild!-style solutions.

7.6 Convergence analysis of matrix blocking

Matrix blocking is used to parallelize SGD-based MF by many applications, e.g., LIBMF. CuMF_SGD uses matrix blocking to tackle with workload partitioning. The purpose of matrix blocking is to avoid conflicts between parallel workers. However, we observe that matrix blocking can have a negative impact on convergence. We use LIBMF as a case study. Figure 14 illustrates the convergence speed of LIBMF on *Netflix* data set with different parameters. In this study, we fix the number of parallel workers $s = 40$; without loss of generality, we divide R into $a \times a$ blocks and vary the value of a. Figure 14 shows that when a is less than or close to s, convergence speed is much slower or even cannot be achieved. We have similar observations on other data sets and using cuMF_SGD. We briefly explain the reason with a simple example shown in Figure 15.

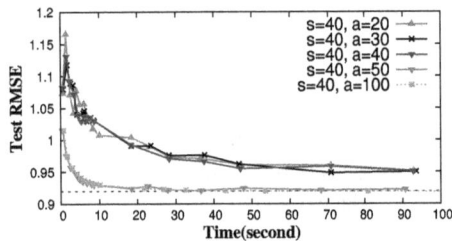

Figure 14: Convergence speed of LIBMF on *Netflix*. We fix #parallel-workers $s = 40$ and vary value a to partition to $a \times a$ blocks.

In Figure 15, we divide the rating matrix into 2×2 blocks and use 2 parallel workers. In theory, 4 blocks can have $4 \times 3 \times 2 \times 1 = 24$ possible update orders. We also show all update orders in Figure 15. However, only orders 1~8 out of the total 24 orders are feasible so as to avoid update conflicts. For example, when *Block 1* is issued to one worker, only *Block 4* can be issued to another worker. Hence, *Blocks*

2 and 3 cannot be updated between 1 and 4, which precludes order 9~12. This demonstrated that when $s \geq a$, all independent blocks have to be updated concurrently to make all workers busy, which enforces certain update order constraints and hurts the randomness. As a consequence, convergence speed can deteriorate. In practice, when cuMF_SGD uses two GPUs, R should at least be divided into 4×4 blocks.

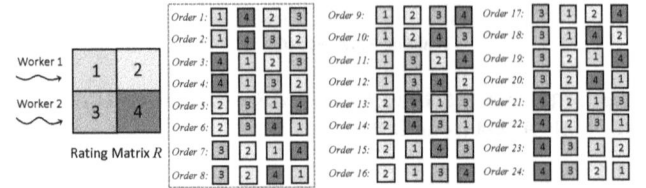

Figure 15: A simple example to demonstrate the limitation of matrix blocking. The rating matrix is divided into 2×2 blocks and updated using two parallel workers.

7.7 Scale up to multiple GPUs

System wise, cuMF_SGD is designed to scale to multiple GPUs. However, algorithmic wise, the scaling is restricted by factors such as problem dimension and number of parallel workers, as discussed earlier in Section 7.5 and Section 7.6. Among the three data sets used in this paper, *Netflix* and *Hugewiki* have very small $n(20k$ and $40k$, receptively), preventing cuMF_SGD from solving them on multiple GPUs. In comparison, *Yahoo!Music* can be solved on multiple GPUs as the dimension of it R is $1M \times 625k$. We divide its R into 8×8 blocks and run it with two Pascal GPUs. Figure 16 shows the convergence speed. With 2 Pascal GPUs, cuMF_SGD takes 2.5s to converge to RMSE 22, which is 1.5X as fast as 1 Pascal GPU (3.8s). The reason behind this sub-linear scalability is that the multi-GPU cuMF_SGD needs to spend time on CPU-GPU memory transfer so as to synchronize two GPUs.

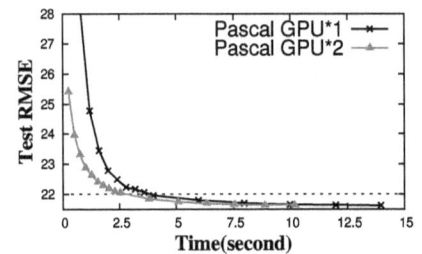

Figure 16: Convergence of cuMF_SGD on *Yahoo!Music*: two Pascal GPUs is 1.5X as fast as one.

8 RELATED WORK

Algorithms. SGD has been widely used to solve matrix factorization [34]. Serial SGD can be parallelized to improve performance [8, 67]. ALS is naturally easy to parallelize and it can also be used in dense matrix factorization [33]. Coordinate descent is another algorithm to solve matrix factorization [26, 61]. It updates the feature matrix along one coordinate direction in each step. Our earlier work [51] focuses on ALS algorithm.

Parallel SGD solutions have been discussed in multi-core [15, 16, 42], multi-node [52, 63], MapReduce [23, 35] and parameter-servers [46] settings. Existing works are mostly inspired by Hogwild! [44] that allows lock-free update, use matrix-blocking partitioning to avoid conflicts, or use a combination of them. LIBMF [15, 16] is a representative shared-memory system-based solution. Evaluations have shown that it outperforms all previous single-node approaches. Although it has been optimized for cache efficiency, it is still not efficient at processing large-scale data sets. Moreover, the high complexity of its scheduling policy makes it infeasible to scale to many cores. NOMAD [63] partitions the data on HPC clusters to improve the cache performance. At the meantime, it proposes to minimize the communication overhead. Compared with LIBMF, it has similar performance on one machine and is able to scale to 64 nodes. However, none of the above solutions use GPU as accelerators.

Parallelization is also used in coordinate descent [61]. Compared with SGD, coordinate descent has lower overhead and runs faster at the first few epochs of training. However, due to the algorithmic limitation, coordinate descent is prone to reach local optima [15] in the later epochs of training. Compared with CGD and SGD, ALS is inherently easy to parallel, ALS-based parallel solutions are widely discussed [1, 22, 39, 40, 66]. Our earlier work, cuMF_ALS [51] focuses on optimizing ALS to matrix factorization on GPUs. As ALS algorithm has more compute intensive epochs, it runs slower than cuMF_SGD.

GPU solutions. The emerging of CUDA and OpenCL programming models makes GPUs popular as accelerators [21, 24]. Applications, including storage system [7], graph processing [25], hash table [53], neural network [18, 58], linear algebra [13], have enjoyed the tremendous computational horsepower equipped on GPUs. Prior to our work, [10] applies Restricted Boltzmann Machines on GPUs to solve MF. [64] implements both SGD and ALS on GPU to solve MF. [27] proposes matrix blocking-based MF solution on GPUs and [31] evaluates the workload scheduling overhead for SGD on GPUs. BIDMach [11] supports SGD-based MF and uses GPUs as accelerators. To the best of our knowledge, cuMF_SGD outperforms all existing solutions because we optimize both memory access and workload scheduling.

9 CONCLUSION

Matrix factorization is widely used in recommender systems and other applications. SGD-based MF is limited by memory bandwidth that single and multi-CPU systems cannot effectively provision. We propose a GPU-based solution, by observing that GPUs offer abundant memory bandwidth and fast intra-node connection. We design workload partitioning and scheduling schemes to dispatch tasks inside a GPU and across GPUs, without impacting the randomness required by SGD. We also develop highly-optimized GPU kernels for individual SGD updates. With only one Maxwell or Pascal GPU, cuMF_SGD runs **3.1X-28.2X** as fast compared with state-of-art CPU solutions on 1-64 CPU nodes. Evaluations also show that cuMF_SGD scales well on multiple GPUs for large data

sets. In future, we plan to extend cuMF_SGD to multiple nodes and investigate how to deal with incremental training.

REFERENCES

[1] Recommending items to more than a billion people, 2015. https://code.facebook.com/posts/861999383875667/recommending-items-to-more-than-a-billion-people/.
[2] NVIDIA CUDA programming guide., 2016. http://docs.nvidia.com/cuda/cuda-c-programming-guide.
[3] NVIDIA Maxwell Architecture . https://developer.nvidia.com/maxwell-compute-architecture, 2016.
[4] NVIDIA NVLink, 2016. http://www.nvidia.com/object/nvlink.html.
[5] NVIDIA Pascal Architecture, 2016. http://www.geforce.com/hardware/10series/architecture.
[6] M. Abadi, P. Barham, J. Chen, Z. Chen, A. Davis, J. Dean, M. Devin, S. Ghemawat, G. Irving, M. Isard, et al. Tensorflow: A system for large-scale machine learning. In *Proceedings of the 12th USENIX Symposium on Operating Systems Design and Implementation (OSDI). Savannah, Georgia, USA*, 2016.
[7] S. Al-Kiswany, A. Gharaibeh, and M. Ripeanu. GPUs as storage system accelerators. *IEEE Transactions on Parallel and Distributed Systems*, 24(8):1556–1566, 2013.
[8] L. Bottou. Large-scale machine learning with stochastic gradient descent. In *Proceedings of COMPSTAT'2010*, pages 177–186. Springer, 2010.
[9] M. Butler, K. Sajjapongse, and M. Becchi. Improving application concurrency on GPUs by managing implicit and explicit synchronizations. In *Parallel and Distributed Systems (ICPADS), 2015 IEEE 21st International Conference on*, pages 535–544. IEEE, 2015.
[10] X. Cai, Z. Xu, G. Lai, C. Wu, and X. Lin. GPU-accelerated restricted boltzmann machine for collaborative filtering. In *International Conference on Algorithms and Architectures for Parallel Processing*. Springer, 2012.
[11] J. Canny and H. Zhao. Bidmach: Large-scale learning with zero memory allocation. In *BigLearning, NIPS Workshop*, 2013.
[12] S. Chang, Y. Zhang, J. Tang, D. Yin, Y. Chang, M. A. Hasegawa-Johnson, and T. S. Huang. Streaming recommender systems. In *Proceedings of the 26th International Conference on World Wide Web, WWW '17*, 2017.
[13] J. Chen, L. Tan, P. Wu, D. Tao, H. Li, X. Liang, S. Li, R. Ge, L. Bhuyan, and Z. Chen. GreenLA: green linear algebra software for GPU-accelerated heterogeneous computing. In *Proceedings of the International Conference for High Performance Computing, Networking, Storage and Analysis*, page 57. IEEE Press, 2016.
[14] T. Chen, M. Li, Y. Li, M. Lin, N. Wang, M. Wang, T. Xiao, B. Xu, C. Zhang, and Z. Zhang. Mxnet: A flexible and efficient machine learning library for heterogeneous distributed systems. *arXiv preprint arXiv:1512.01274*, 2015.
[15] W.-S. Chin, Y. Zhuang, Y.-C. Juan, and C.-J. Lin. A fast parallel stochastic gradient method for matrix factorization in shared memory systems. *ACM Transactions on Intelligent Systems and Technology (TIST)*, 2015.
[16] W.-S. Chin, Y. Zhuang, Y.-C. Juan, and C.-J. Lin. A learning-rate schedule for stochastic gradient methods to matrix factorization. In *Pacific-Asia Conference on Knowledge Discovery and Data Mining*. Springer, 2015.
[17] J. Dean, G. Corrado, R. Monga, K. Chen, M. Devin, M. Mao, A. Senior, P. Tucker, K. Yang, Q. V. Le, et al. Large scale distributed deep networks. In *Advances in neural information processing systems*, pages 1223–1231, 2012.
[18] B. Del Monte and R. Prodan. A scalable GPU-enabled framework for training deep neural networks. In *Green High Performance Computing (ICGHPC), 2016 2nd International Conference on*, pages 1–8. IEEE, 2016.
[19] C. del Mundo and W.-c. Feng. Enabling efficient intra-warp communication for Fourier transforms in a many-core architecture. In *Supercomputing, 2013. Proceedings of the 2013 ACM/IEEE International Conference on*, 2013.
[20] J. Duchi, E. Hazan, and Y. Singer. Adaptive subgradient methods for online learning and stochastic optimization. *Journal of Machine Learning Research*, 12(Jul):2121–2159, 2011.
[21] J. Fang, A. L. Varbanescu, and H. Sips. A comprehensive performance comparison of CUDA and OpenCL. In *2011 International Conference on Parallel Processing*, pages 216–225. IEEE, 2011.
[22] M. Gates, H. Anzt, J. Kurzak, and J. Dongarra. Accelerating collaborative filtering using concepts from high performance computing. In *Big Data, 2015 IEEE International Conference on*, 2015.
[23] R. Gemulla, E. Nijkamp, P. J. Haas, and Y. Sismanis. Large-scale matrix factorization with distributed stochastic gradient descent. In *Proceedings of the 17th ACM SIGKDD international conference on Knowledge discovery and data mining*. ACM, 2011.
[24] A. Goswami, J. Young, K. Schwan, N. Farooqui, A. Gavrilovska, M. Wolf, and G. Eisenhauer. GPUShare: Fair-sharing middleware for GPU clouds. In *Parallel and Distributed Processing Symposium Workshops, 2016 IEEE International*, pages 1769–1776. IEEE, 2016.

[25] S. Heldens, A. L. Varbanescu, and A. Iosup. Dynamic load balancing for high-performance graph processing on hybrid CPU-GPU platforms. In *Proceedings of the Sixth Workshop on Irregular Applications: Architectures and Algorithms*, pages 62–65. IEEE Press, 2016.

[26] C.-J. Hsieh and I. S. Dhillon. Fast coordinate descent methods with variable selection for non-negative matrix factorization. In *Proceedings of the 17th ACM SIGKDD international conference on Knowledge discovery and data mining*. ACM, 2011.

[27] J. Jin, S. Lai, S. Hu, J. Lin, and X. Lin. GPUSGD: A GPU-accelerated stochastic gradient descent algorithm for matrix factorization. *Concurrency and Computation: Practice and Experience*, 2015.

[28] A. Jog, O. Kayiran, N. Chidambaram Nachiappan, A. K. Mishra, M. T. Kandemir, O. Mutlu, R. Iyer, and C. R. Das. OWL: cooperative thread array aware scheduling techniques for improving GPGPU performance. In *ACM SIGPLAN Notices*, volume 48, pages 395–406. ACM, 2013.

[29] A. Jog, O. Kayiran, T. Kesten, A. Pattnaik, E. Bolotin, N. Chatterjee, S. W. Keckler, M. T. Kandemir, and C. R. Das. Anatomy of GPU memory system for multi-application execution. In *Proceedings of the 2015 International Symposium on Memory Systems*, pages 223–234. ACM, 2015.

[30] A. Jog, O. Kayiran, A. K. Mishra, M. T. Kandemir, O. Mutlu, R. Iyer, and C. R. Das. Orchestrated scheduling and prefetching for GPGPUs. In *ACM SIGARCH Computer Architecture News*, volume 41, pages 332–343. ACM, 2013.

[31] R. Kaleem, S. Pai, and K. Pingali. Stochastic gradient descent on GPUs. In *Proceedings of the 8th Workshop on General Purpose Processing using GPUs*, pages 81–89. ACM, 2015.

[32] D. B. Kirk and W. H. Wen-mei. *Programming massively parallel processors: a hands-on approach*. Newnes, 2012.

[33] T. G. Kolda and B. W. Bader. Tensor decompositions and applications. *SIAM review*, 51(3):455–500, 2009.

[34] Y. Koren, R. Bell, and C. Volinsky. Matrix factorization techniques for recommender systems. *Computer*, 2009.

[35] B. Li, S. Tata, and Y. Sismanis. Sparkler: supporting large-scale matrix factorization. In *Proceedings of the 16th International Conference on Extending Database Technology*. ACM, 2013.

[36] C. Li, S. L. Song, H. Dai, A. Sidelnik, S. K. S. Hari, and H. Zhou. Locality-driven dynamic GPU cache bypassing. In *Proceedings of the 29th ACM on International Conference on Supercomputing*, pages 67–77. ACM, 2015.

[37] M. Li, T. Zhang, Y. Chen, and A. J. Smola. Efficient mini-batch training for stochastic optimization. In *SIGKDD*, pages 661–670. ACM, 2014.

[38] Z. Liu, Y.-X. Wang, and A. Smola. Fast differentially private matrix factorization. In *Proceedings of the 9th ACM Conference on Recommender Systems*, RecSys'15, 2015.

[39] Y. Low, D. Bickson, J. Gonzalez, C. Guestrin, A. Kyrola, and J. M. Hellerstein. Distributed GraphLab: a framework for machine learning and data mining in the cloud. *Proceedings of the VLDB Endowment*, 2012.

[40] X. Meng, J. Bradley, B. Yuvaz, E. Sparks, S. Venkataraman, D. Liu, J. Freeman, D. Tsai, M. Amde, S. Owen, et al. Mllib: Machine learning in apache spark. *JMLR*, 2016.

[41] Y. Nishioka and K. Taura. Scalable task-parallel SGD on matrix factorization in multicore architectures. In *Proceedings of the 2015 IEEE International Parallel and Distributed Processing Symposium Workshop*, IPDPSW '15, pages 1178–1184, Washington, DC, USA, 2015. IEEE Computer Society.

[42] J. Oh, W.-S. Han, H. Yu, and X. Jiang. Fast and robust parallel SGD matrix factorization. In *Proceedings of the 21st ACM SIGKDD International Conference on Knowledge Discovery and Data Mining*. ACM, 2015.

[43] J. Pennington, R. Socher, and C. D. Manning. Glove: Global vectors for word representation. In *EMNLP*, 2014.

[44] B. Recht, C. Re, S. Wright, and F. Niu. Hogwild: A lock-free approach to parallelizing stochastic gradient descent. In *Advances in Neural Information Processing Systems*, pages 693–701, 2011.

[45] S. Ryoo, C. I. Rodrigues, S. S. Baghsorkhi, S. S. Stone, D. B. Kirk, and W.-m. W. Hwu. Optimization principles and application performance evaluation of a multithreaded GPU using CUDA. In *Proceedings of the 13th ACM SIGPLAN Symposium on Principles and Practice of Parallel Programming*, PPoPP '08, 2008.

[46] S. Schelter, V. Satuluri, and R. Zadeh. Factorbird-a parameter server approach to distributed matrix factorization. *arXiv preprint arXiv:1411.0602*, 2014.

[47] G. M. Shipman, T. S. Woodall, R. L. Graham, A. B. Maccabe, and P. G. Bridges. Infiniband scalability in Open MPI. In *Proceedings 20th IEEE International Parallel and Distributed Processing Symposium*, pages 10–pp. IEEE, 2006.

[48] D. Song and S. Chen. Exploiting SIMD for complex numerical predicates. In *2016 IEEE 32nd International Conference on Data Engineering Workshops (ICDEW)*, 2016.

[49] S. Song and K. W. Cameron. System-level power-performance efficiency modeling for emergent GPU architectures. In *PACT*, pages 473–474, 2012.

[50] J. Tan, S. L. Song, K. Yan, X. Fu, A. Marquez, and D. Kerbyson. Combating the reliability challenge of GPU register file at low supply voltage. In *Parallel Architecture and Compilation Techniques (PACT), 2016 International Conference on*, pages 3–15. IEEE, 2016.

[51] W. Tan, L. Cao, and L. Fong. Faster and Cheaper: Parallelizing large-scale matrix factorization on GPUs. In *Proceedings of the 25th ACM International Symposium on High-Performance Parallel and Distributed Computing*, HPDC '16, 2016.

[52] C. Teflioudi, F. Makari, and R. Gemulla. Distributed matrix completion. In *IEEE 12th International Conference on Data Mining*. IEEE, 2012.

[53] A. Todd, H. Truong, J. Deters, J. Long, G. Conant, and M. Becchi. Parallel gene upstream comparison via multi-level hash tables on GPU. In *22nd IEEE International Conference on Parallel and Distributed Systems (ICPADS)*, 2016.

[54] S. Williams, A. Waterman, and D. Patterson. Roofline: an insightful visual performance model for multicore architectures. *Communications of the ACM*, 52(4):65–76, 2009.

[55] X. Xie, Y. Liang, X. Li, Y. Wu, G. Sun, T. Wang, and D. Fan. Enabling coordinated register allocation and thread-level parallelism optimization for GPUs. In *Proceedings of the 48th International Symposium on Microarchitecture*, MICRO-48.

[56] X. Xie, Y. Liang, G. Sun, and D. Chen. An efficient compiler framework for cache bypassing on GPUs. In *IEEE/ACM International Conference on Computer-Aided Design*, 2013.

[57] X. Xie, Y. Liang, Y. Wang, G. Sun, and T. Wang. Coordinated static and dynamic cache bypassing for GPUs. In *International Symposium on High Performance Computer Architecture*, HPCA'15, pages 76–88, 2015.

[58] F. Yan, O. Ruwase, Y. He, and E. Smirni. SERF: efficient scheduling for fast deep neural network serving via judicious parallelism. In *Proceedings of the International Conference for High Performance Computing, Networking, Storage and Analysis*, page 26. IEEE Press, 2016.

[59] Y. Yang, P. Xiang, J. Kong, and H. Zhou. A GPGPU compiler for memory optimization and parallelism management. In *2010 ACM SIGPLAN Conference on Programming Language Design and Implementation*, PLDI '10, pages 86–97, 2010.

[60] H.-F. Yu, C.-J. Hsieh, S. Si, and I. Dhillon. Scalable coordinate descent approaches to parallel matrix factorization for recommender systems. In *2012 IEEE 12th International Conference on Data Mining*. IEEE, 2012.

[61] H.-F. Yu, C.-J. Hsieh, S. Si, and I. Dhillon. Scalable coordinate descent approaches to parallel matrix factorization for recommender systems. In *2012 IEEE 12th International Conference on Data Mining*. IEEE, 2012.

[62] H.-F. Yu, C.-J. Hsieh, H. Yun, S. Vishwanathan, and I. S. Dhillon. A scalable asynchronous distributed algorithm for topic modeling. In *Proceedings of the 24th International Conference on WWW*, pages 1340–1350. ACM, 2015.

[63] H. Yun, H.-F. Yu, C.-J. Hsieh, S. V. N. Vishwanathan, and I. Dhillon. NOMAD: Nonlocking, stochastic multi-machine algorithm for asynchronous and decentralized matrix completion. *Proc. VLDB Endow.*, 2014.

[64] D. Zastrau and S. Edelkamp. Stochastic gradient descent with GPGPU. In *Annual Conference on Artificial Intelligence*. Springer, 2012.

[65] T. Zhang. Solving large scale linear prediction problems using stochastic gradient descent algorithms. In *Proceedings of the twenty-first international conference on Machine learning*, page 116. ACM, 2004.

[66] Y. Zhou, D. Wilkinson, R. Schreiber, and R. Pan. Large-scale parallel collaborative filtering for the Netflix prize. In *International Conference on Algorithmic Applications in Management*. Springer, 2008.

[67] M. Zinkevich, M. Weimer, L. Li, and A. J. Smola. Parallelized stochastic gradient descent. In *NIPS*, 2010.

To Push or To Pull: On Reducing Communication and Synchronization in Graph Computations

Maciej Besta[1], Michał Podstawski[2][3], Linus Groner[1], Edgar Solomonik[4], Torsten Hoefler[1]

[1] Department of Computer Science, ETH Zurich; [2] Perform Group Katowice,; [3] Katowice Institute of Information Technologies;
[4] Department of Computer Science, University of Illinois at Urbana-Champaign

maciej.besta@inf.ethz.ch, michal.podstawski@performgroup.com, gronerl@student.ethz.ch, solomon2@illinois.edu, htor@inf.ethz.ch

ABSTRACT

We reduce the cost of communication and synchronization in graph processing by analyzing the fastest way to process graphs: pushing the updates to a shared state or pulling the updates to a private state. We investigate the applicability of this push-pull dichotomy to various algorithms and its impact on complexity, performance, and the amount of used locks, atomics, and reads/writes. We consider 11 graph algorithms, 3 programming models, 2 graph abstractions, and various families of graphs. The conducted analysis illustrates surprising differences between push and pull variants of different algorithms in performance, speed of convergence, and code complexity; the insights are backed up by performance data from hardware counters. We use these findings to illustrate which variant is faster for each algorithm and to develop generic strategies that enable even higher speedups. Our insights can be used to accelerate graph processing engines or libraries on both massively-parallel shared-memory machines as well as distributed-memory systems.
Site: https://spcl.inf.ethz.ch/Research/Parallel_Programming/PushPull

1 INTRODUCTION

Graph processing underlies many computational problems in social network analysis, machine learning, computational science, and others [33]. Designing efficient parallel graph algorithms is challenging due to several properties of graph computations such as irregular communication patterns or little locality. These properties lead to expensive synchronization and movements of large data amounts on shared- and distributed-memory (SM, DM) systems.

Direction optimization in breadth-first search (BFS) [4] is one of the mechanisms that are used to alleviate these issues. It combines the traditional *top-down* BFS (where vertices in the active frontier iterate over all unvisited neighbors) with a *bottom-up* scheme (where unvisited vertices search for a neighboring vertex in the active frontier [48]). Combining these two approaches accelerates BFS by ≈2.4x on real-world graphs such as citation networks [4].

We first illustrate that distinguishing between bottom-up and top-down BFS can be generalized to many other graph algorithms, where updates can be either *pushed* by a thread to the shared state (as in the top-down BFS), or *pulled* to a thread's private state (as in the bottom-up BFS). As another example, consider a PageRank (PR) computation and assume a thread X is responsible for a vertex v. X

can either push v's rank to update v's neighbors, or it can pull the ranks of v's neighbors to update v [52]. Despite many differences between PR and BFS (e.g., PR is not a traversal), PR can similarly be viewed in the push-pull dichotomy.

This notion sparks various questions. Can pushing and pulling be applied to *any* graph algorithm? How to design push and pull variants of various algorithms? Is pushing or pulling faster? When and why? Does it depend on the utilized programming model and abstraction? When and how can pushing or pulling be accelerated?

We seek to answer these and other questions and provide the first extensive analysis on the push-pull dichotomy in graph processing. Now, this dichotomy was identified for some algorithms [4, 52] and was used in several graph processing frameworks, such as Ligra [46] and Gemini [57]. Yet, none of these works analyzes the differences in formulations, complexity, and performance between the two approaches for various algorithms, environments, or models.

As a motivation, consider Figure 1 with the results of our push/pull variants of graph coloring [6]. They unveil consistent advantages of pushing. The figure also shows the speedup from a strategy GrS ("Greedy-Switch") that (1) reduces the number of memory access with a traversal-based graph coloring, and (2) switches between push- or pull-based scheme and an optimized greedy variant.

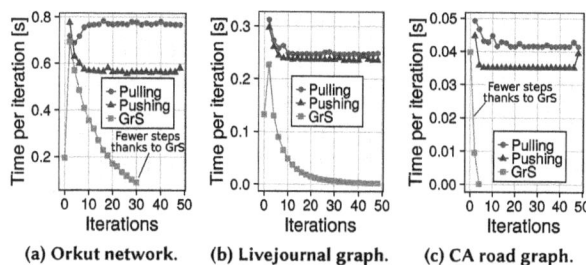

(a) Orkut network. (b) Livejournal graph. (c) CA road graph.

Figure 1: (§ 6.1) Boman graph coloring [6] results and (§ 6.2) the analysis of the strategy Greedy-Switch (GrS); single node of a Cray XC30, 16 threads.

We provide the following contributions:

- We apply the push-pull dichotomy to various classes of graph algorithms and obtain detailed formulations of centrality schemes, traversals, calculating minimum spanning trees, graph coloring, and triangle counting. We also show that several existing graph processing schemes are included in the push-pull dichotomy.
- We analyze pushing and pulling with PRAM and derive the differences in the amount of synchronization and communication in both variants of the considered algorithms.
- We analyze performance of push- and pull-based algorithms for both SM and DM systems that represent fat-memory nodes and supercomputers. Various programming models are incorporated, including threading, Message Passing (MP), and Remote Memory Access (RMA) [20] for various classes of graphs. For detailed insights, we gather performance data (e.g., cache misses or issues braches and atomic instructions) using PAPI counters.

HPDC '17,, June 26–30, 2017, Washington, DC, USA

© 2017 Copyright held by the owner/author(s). Publication rights licensed to Association for Computing Machinery.
ACM ISBN 978-1-4503-4699-3/17/06...$15.00.
https://doi.org/http://dx.doi.org/10.1145/3078597.3078616

- We incorporate strategies to reduce the amount of synchronization in pushing and memory accesses in pulling and illustrate that they accelerate various algorithms.
- We provide performance insights that can be used to enhance graph processing engines or libraries.
- Finally, we discuss whether the push-pull dichotomy is applicable in the algebraic formulation of graph algorithms.

2 MODELS, NOTATION, CONCEPTS

We first describe the necessary concepts.

2.1 Machine Model and Simulations

Parallel Random Access Machine (PRAM) [17] is a well-known model of a parallel computer. There are P processors that exchange data by accessing cells of a shared memory of size M cells. They proceed in tightly-synchronized steps: no processor executes an instruction $i + 1$ before all processors complete an instruction i. An instruction can be a local computation or a read/write from/to the memory. We use S and W to denote *time* and *work*: the longest execution path and the total instruction count. There are three PRAM variants with different rules for concurrent memory accesses to the same cell. EREW prevents any concurrent accesses. CREW allows for concurrent reads but only one write at a time. CRCW enables any concurrent combination of reads/writes and it comes with multiple flavors that differently treat concurrent writes. We use the Combining CRCW (CRCW-CB) [25]: the value stored is an associative and commutative combination of the written values.

Now, a simulation of one PRAM machine on another is a scheme that enables any instruction from the former to be executed on the latter. Simulation schemes are useful when one wants to port an algorithm developed for a stronger model that is more convenient for designing algorithms (e.g., CRCW) to a weaker one that models hardware more realistically (e.g., CREW). The used simulations are:

Simulating CRCW/CREW on CREW/EREW Any CRCW with M cells can be simulated on an MP-cell CREW/EREW with a slow-down of $\Theta(\log n)$ and memory MP (similarly to simulating a CREW on an EREW) [25].

Limiting P (LP) A problem solvable on a P-processor PRAM in S time can be solved on a P'-processor PRAM ($P' < P$) in time $S' = \left\lceil \frac{SP}{P'} \right\rceil$ for a fixed memory size M.

2.2 Graph Model, Layout, and Notation

A tuple (V, E) models an undirected graph G; V is a set of vertices and $E \subseteq V \times V$ is a set of edges; $|V| = n$ and $|E| = m$. $d(v)$ and $N(v)$ are the degree and the neighbors of a vertex v. The (non-negative) weight of an edge (v, w) is $\mathcal{W}_{(v,w)}$. We denote the maximum degrees for a given G as $\hat{d}$, $\hat{d}_{in}$ (in-degree), and $\hat{d}_{out}$ (out-degree). The average degree is denoted with a bar ($\bar{d}$). G's diameter is D.

The neighbors of each v form an array. The arrays of all the vertices form a contiguous array accessed by all the threads; we also store offsets into the array that determine the beginning of the array of each vertex. The whole representation takes $n + 2m$ cells.

We partition G by vertices (1D decomposition) [11]. We denote the number of used threads/processes as P. We name a thread (process) that owns a given vertex v as $t[v]$. We focus on *label-setting* algorithms. In some of the considered schemes (e.g., PageRank) the number of iterations L is a user-specified parameter.

2.3 Atomic Operations

Atomic operations (atomics) appear to the system as if they occur instantaneously. They are used in lock-free graph computations to perform fine-grained updates [24, 39]. Here, we use CPU atomics that operate on integers. We now present the relevant operations:

Fetch-and-Add(*target, arg) (FAA): it increases *target by arg and also returns *target's previous value.

Compare-and-Swap(*target, compare, value, *result) (CAS): if *target == compare then *target = value and *result = true are set, otherwise *target is not changed and *result = false.

2.4 Communication & Synchronization

Unless stated otherwise, we associate *communication* with: intra- or inter-node reads and writes, messages, and collective operations other than barriers. *Synchronization* will indicate: any atomic operations, locks, and any form of barrier synchronization.

3 PUSH-PULL: APPLICABILITY

We first analyze what algorithms can be expressed in the push-pull (PP) dichotomy; we revisit existing schemes and discuss new cases.

3.1 PageRank (PR)

PR [10] is an iterative centrality algorithm that obtains the *rank* of each vertex v: $r(v) = (1 - f)/|V| + \sum_{w \in N(v)} (f \cdot r(w)/d(w))$; f is the *damp factor* [10]. PR is used to rank websites.

Pushing and Pulling? PR can be expressed in both [52]. In the former, $t[v]$ updates all v's neighbors with a value $r(v)/d(v)$ (it pushes the value from v to $N(v)$). In the latter, $t[v]$ updates v with values $r(u)/d(u)$, $u \in N(v)$ (it pulls the updates from $N(v)$ to v).

3.2 Triangle Counting (TC)

In TC, one counts the number of triangles that each vertex $v \in V$ is a part of; a triangle occurs if there exist edges $\{v, w\}, \{w, u\}, \{v, u\}$, where $u, w \in V$ and $u, w \neq v, u \neq w$. TC is used in various statistics and machine learning schemes [43] and libraries such as igraph [14].

Pushing and Pulling? This algorithm is also expressible in both schemes. Consider a thread $t[v]$ that counts the number of triangles associated with a vertex v ($tc(v)$). It iterates over $N(v)$ and, for each $u \in N(v)$, it iterates over $N(u)$ and checks if $\exists w \in V, v \neq w \neq u$ such that $w \in N(u) \cap N(v)$; the final sums are divided by 2 at the end. If yes, then, in the push variant, it increments either one of $tc(u)$ and $tc(w)$ while in the pull scheme it increments $tc(v)$.

3.3 Breadth-First Search (BFS)

The goal of BFS [13] is to visit each vertex in G. The algorithm starts with a specified *root* vertex r and visits all its neighbors $N(r)$. Then, it visits all the unvisited neighbors of the root's neighbors, and continues to process each level of neighbors in one step. BFS represents graph traversals and is used the HPC benchmark Graph500 [39].

Pushing and Pulling? There exist both variants. The former is the traditional *top-down* BFS where $t[v]$ (if v is in a frontier) checks each unvisited $u \in N(v)$ and adds it to the next frontier F (it pushes the updates from v to $N(v)$). The latter is the *bottom-up* approach [4, 48]: in each iteration every unvisited vertex u is tested if it has a parent in F (the updates are pulled from $N(u)$ to u).

3.4 Single Source Shortest Path (SSSP)

SSSP outputs the distance from a selected source vertex s to all other vertices. We consider Δ-Stepping (SSSP-Δ) [37] that combines the well-known Dijkstra's and Bellman-Ford algorithms by trading work-optimality for more parallelism. It groups vertices into *buckets* and only vertices in one bucket can be processed in parallel. SSSP has applications in, e.g., operations research.

Pushing and Pulling? Both are applicable when relaxing edges of each vertex v from the current bucket. In the former, v pushes relaxation requests to its neighbors in the buckets with unsettled vertices. In the latter, vertices in unsettled buckets look for their neighbors in the current bucket and perform (pull) relaxations. A similar scheme was used in the DM implementation of SSSP-Δ [12].

3.5 Betweenness Centrality (BC)

BC measures the importance of a vertex v based on the number of shortest paths that lead through v. Let σ_{st} be the number of shortest paths between two vertices s, t, and let $\sigma_{st}(v)$ be the number of such paths that lead through v. BC of v equals $bc(v) = \sum_{s \neq v \neq t \in V} \frac{\sigma_{st}(v)}{\sigma_{st}}$. Here, we consider Brandes' algorithm [9, 41]. Define the dependency of a source vertex s on v as: $\delta_s(v) = \sum_{t \in V} \frac{\sigma_{st}(v)}{\sigma_{st}}$. Then, we have $bc(v) = \sum_{s \neq v \in V} \delta_s(v)$ where $\delta_s(v)$ satisfies the following recurrence: $\delta_s(v) = \sum_{w:v \in pred(s,w)} \frac{\sigma_{sv}}{\sigma_{sw}}(1 + \delta_s(w))$; $pred(s, w)$ is a list of immediate *predecessors* of w in the shortest paths from s to w. Brandes' scheme uses this recurrence to compute $bc(v)$ in two phases. First, BFS or SSSP traversals compute $pred(s, v)$ and σ_{sv}, $\forall_{s,v \in V}$, obtaining a tree $\mathcal{T}$ over G. Next, $\mathcal{T}$ is traversed backwards (from the highest to the lowest distance) to compute $\delta_s(v)$ and $bc(v)$ based on the equations above. BC is a complex centrality scheme used in biology, transportation, and terrorism prevention [3].

Pushing and Pulling? Both parts of Brandes BC can be expressed using push and pull. The first phase can compute shortest path information using either top-down or bottom-up BFS or push-and pull-based versions of SSSP. The second phase (backward accumulation) may also be cast as BFS from a starting frontier. In particular, one can either push partial centrality scores to predecessors or pull them from lists of *successors* [34].

3.6 Graph Coloring (GC)

GC assigns colors to vertices so that no two incident vertices share the same color and the number of colors is minimized. We consider Boman graph coloring (BGC) [6]. Here, each iteration has two phases. In phase 1, colors are assigned to vertices owned by each thread (i.e., to each partition $\mathcal{P} \in \mathscr{P}$) separately without considering other partitions ($\mathscr{P}$ denotes a set of all partitions). The maximum number of available colors can be specified as a parameter C. In phase 2, *border* vertices (i.e., vertices with at least one edge leading to another partition; they form a set $\mathcal{B}$) are verified for conflicts. If there are any, the colors are reassigned. This may cause conflicts within partitions, which are resolved during the next iteration. More iterations L may improve a solution (fewer colors used). GC has multiple applications in scheduling and pattern matching.

Pushing and Pulling? Both can be used in phase 2. For every border vertex v, each $u \in N(v)$ $(t[u] \neq t[v])$ is analyzed. If v and u share the assigned color, then either u's or v's color is scheduled for a change (the update is pushed to or pulled from $N(v)$).

3.7 Minimum Spanning Tree (MST)

The goal of MST is to derive a spanning tree of G with the lowest sum of the included edge weights. The classical sequential algorithms: Prim [13] and Kruskal [13] lack parallelism. Therefore, we

focus on the Boruvka [8] algorithm (more details on pushing and pulling in Prim and Kruskal are still provided in the technical report). In Boruvka, each vertex is first associated with its own supervertex. In each iteration, two incident supervertices are merged into one along an edge e_m of a minimum weight. The algorithm proceeds until there is only one supervertex left. The selected minimum edges form the MST. MST algorithms are utilized in problems such as the design of broadcast trees [13].

Pushing and Pulling in Boruvka? First, selecting e_m adjacent to a given supervertex can be done by pushing (each supervertex overrides adjacent supervertices and their tentative minimal edges if it has a less expensive one) or by pulling (each supervertex picks its own e_m). Next, merging adjacent supervertices can also be done with pushing or pulling. Assume that each thread owns a number of supervertices. Now, it can either push the changes to the supervertices owned by other threads, or pull the information on the adjacent supervertices and only modify its owned ones.

3.8 Push-Pull Insights

First, we present a generic difference between pushing and pulling. Recall that $t[v]$ indicates the thread that owns v. Define $t \rightsquigarrow v$ to be true if t modifies v during the execution of a given algorithm ($t \rightsquigarrow v \Leftrightarrow t$ modifies v). Then

$$\text{(Algorithm uses pushing)} \Leftrightarrow \left(\exists_{t \in \{1..T\}, v \in V} \; t \rightsquigarrow v \wedge t \neq t[v] \right)$$

$$\text{(Algorithm uses pulling)} \Leftrightarrow \left(\forall_{t \in \{1..T\}, v \in V} \; t \rightsquigarrow v \Rightarrow t = t[v] \right)$$

In pushing, any thread t may access and modify any vertex $v \in V$ so that we may have $t \neq t[v]$. In pulling, t can only modify its assigned vertices: $t[v] = t$ for any v modified by t. In § 4, we show that this property determines that pulling requires less synchronization compared to pushing. However, pushing can often be done with less work, when only a subset of vertices needs to update its neighbors.

Second, our analysis shows that the push-pull dichotomy can be used in two algorithm classes: *iterative* schemes (PR, TC, GC, Boruvka MST) that derive some vertex properties and perhaps proceed in iterations until some convergence condition is met, and *traversals* (BFS, SSSP-Δ, BC).

4 THEORETICAL ANALYSIS

We now derive detailed specifications of push and pull algorithm variants and use them to investigate the differences between pushing and pulling. We (1) identify *read and write conflicts*, (2) conduct complexity analyses, and (3) investigate the amount of required atomics or locks. We focus on the CRCW-CB and CREW models. There exist past works on the parallel complexity of the considered algorithms [2, 6, 21, 30, 34, 37, 41]. Yet, we are the first to investigate the differences between pushing and pulling variants.

Algorithm Listings Our schemes have multiple variants as many nested loops can be parallel; we indicate them with [in par]. Unless specified otherwise, we only consider the loops without square brackets in complexity analyses. We mark the read/write conflicts in the parts of the code related to pushing or pulling with ®/Ⓦ, respectively. We indicate the data type in the modified memory cell to be either integer (∎) or float (∎). Finally, we use grey backgrounds to indicate pushing/pulling variants.

Cost Derivations We consider up to one processor per vertex, $P \leq n$ (and $P > \hat{d}$). Thus, pulling avoids write-conflicts, as each thread accumulates updates for a given vertex. Still, pushing can update the same vertices multiple times at every iteration.

We formulate cost analyses of all algorithms via the primitives k-RELAXATION and k-FILTER. k-RELAXATION corresponds to simultaneously propagating updates from/to k vertices to/from one of their neighbors for pushing/pulling. k-FILTER is used to extract the vertices updated in one or more k-RELAXATIONS, and is non-trivial only when pushing updates. We let $\bar{k} = \max(1, k/P)$ and quantify the cost of these primitives. When pulling, k-RELAXATION takes $O(\bar{k})$ time and $O(k)$ work. A k-FILTER invocation requires $O(\log(P) + \bar{k})$ time and $O(\min(k, n))$ work via a prefix sum.

When pushing, the cost of k-RELAXATION depends on the PRAM model. In the CRCW-CB model, k-RELAXATION takes $O(\bar{k})$ time and $O(k)$ work. In the CREW model, k-RELAXATION can be processed in $O(\bar{k}\log(\hat{d}))$ time via binary-tree reductions. To update each vertex of degree d in the CREW model, we use a binary merge-tree with d leaves. Over all trees, at most k of m leaves contain actual updates. We can avoid work for all nodes that are the roots of subtrees that do not contain updates, effectively computing a forest of incomplete binary trees with a total of k leaves and maximum height $O(\log(\hat{d}))$. Each of P processors propagates k/P updates up the complete binary merge-tree associated with its vertices (requiring no setup time) in $O(\bar{k}\log(\hat{d}))$ time with a total of $O(k\log(\hat{d}))$ work.

4.1 PageRank

PR (Algorithm 1) performs $O(L)$ steps of power iteration. For each step of power iteration, k_i-RELAXATION is called for $i \in \{1, \ldots, \hat{d}\}$ with $\sum_{i=1}^{\hat{d}} = m$. Thus the PRAM complexities of PR are (1) $O(L(m/P + \hat{d}))$ time and $O(Lm)$ work using pulling, (2) $O(L(m/P + \hat{d}))$ time and $O(Lm)$ work in pushing in CRCW-CB, and (3) $O(L\log(\hat{d})(m/P + \hat{d}))$ time and $O(Lm\log(\hat{d}))$ work using pushing in CREW.

Conflicts Pushing/pulling entail $O(Lm)$ write/read conflicts.

Atomics/Locks Pulling does not require any such operations. Contrarily, pushing comes with write conflicts to floats. To the best of our knowledge, no CPUs offer atomics operating on such values. Thus, $O(Lm)$ locks are issued.

4.2 Triangle Counting

TC is shown in Algorithm 2; this is a simple parallelization of the well-known NodeIterator scheme [44]. It employs k_i-RELAXATION for $i \in \{1, \ldots, \hat{d}^2\}$ with $\sum_{i=1}^{\hat{d}} = O(m\hat{d})$. Thus the PRAM complexities of TC are (1) $O(\hat{d}(m/P + \hat{d}))$ time and $O(m\hat{d})$ work using pulling, (2) $O(\hat{d}(m/P + \hat{d}))$ time and $O(m\hat{d})$ work using pushing in CRCW-CB, and (3) $O(\hat{d}\log(\hat{d})(m/P + \hat{d}))$ time and $O(m\hat{d}\log(\hat{d}))$ work using pushing in CREW. One can leverage more than n processors to lower the PRAM time-complexity of TC [47].

Conflicts Both variants generate $O(m\hat{d})$ read conflicts; pushing also has $O(m\hat{d})$ write conflicts.

Atomics/Locks We use FAA atomics to resolve write conflicts.

4.3 Breadth-First Search

BFS is shown in Algorithm 3. We define a generalized version of BFS, where vertices enter the frontier only after a given number of neighbors have been in the frontier. The standard BFS is obtained by setting this number to 1, but to use BFS from within BC, we will employ a counter specific to each vertex. The BFS pseudo-code also employs a given accumulation operator to compute values for each

```
1  /* Input: a graph G, a number of steps L, the damp parameter f
2     Output: An array of ranks pr[1..n] */
3
4  function PR(G,L,f) {
5    pr[1..v] = [f..f]; //Initialize PR values.
6    for(l = 1; l < L; ++l) {
7      new_pr[1..n] = [0..0];
8      for v ∈ V do in par {
9        update_pr(); new_pr[v] += (1-f)/n; pr[v] = new_pr[v];
10 } } }
11
12 function update_pr() {
13   for u ∈ N(v) do [in par] {
14     {new_pr[u] += (f·pr[v])/d(v) Ⓦ 🅵;}        PUSHING
15
16     {new_pr[v] += (f·pr[u])/d(u) Ⓡ;}           PULLING
17 } }
```

Algorithm 1: (§ 4.1) Push- and pull-based PageRank.

```
1  /* Input: a graph G. Output: An array of triangle counts
2   * tc[1..n] that each vertex belongs to. */
3
4  function TC(G) {tc[1..n] = [0..0]
5    for v ∈ V do in par
6      for w1 ∈ N(v) do [in par]
7        for w2 ∈ N(v) do [in par]
8          if adj(w1,w2) Ⓡ update_tc();
9    tc[1..n] = [tc[1]/2 .. tc[n]/2]; }
10 function update_tc() {
11   {++tc[w1]; /* or ++tc[w2]. */} Ⓦ 🅸          PUSHING
12
13   {++tc[v];}                                    PULLING
14 }
```

Algorithm 2: (§ 4.2) Push- and pull-based Triangle Counting.

```
1  /* Input: a graph G, a set of ready counters and initial values
             R0 for each node, and an accumulation operator ⇐.
2   * Output: R[1..n] where R[F[i]]=R0[i] and other otherwise
             contains accumulation of all R values of predecessors. */
3
4  function BFS(G,ready,R0,⇐) {
5    my_F[1..P] = [0..0]; R = R0; F⊂V, such that for each v ∈F,
       ready[v]=0;
6    while (F ≠ ∅)
7      explore_my_F(); {
8        F = my_F[1] ∪ my_F[2] ∪ .. ∪ my_F[P];  } }
9
10 function explore_my_F() {
11   for v ∈ F do in par                          PUSHING
12     for w ∈ N(v) do [in par]
13       if ready[w] > 0 Ⓡ
14         R[w] ⇐ R[v] Ⓦ;
15       for w ∈ N(v) do [in par] {
16         ready[w]--;
17         if ready[w]==0 { my_F[pID] = my_F[pID] ∪ {w}; } }
18
19   for v ∈ V do in par {                         PULLING
20     if ready[v] > 0 {
21       for w ∈ N(v) do [in par] {
22         if w ∈ F Ⓡ {
23           R[v] ⇐ R[w];
24           ready[v]--;
25           if ready[v] == 0 { my_F[pID] = my_F[pID] ∪ {v}; }
26 } } } }
```

Algorithm 3: (§ 4.3) Push- and pull-based Breadth-First Search.

vertex as a function of values of its predecessors in the BFS tree. Our analysis assumes this operator is commutative and associative. The frontier F is represented as a single array while my_F is private for each process and contains vertices explored at each iteration. All my_Fs are repeatedly merged into the next F (Line 8). We let f_i be the size of F in the ith iteration of the while loop.

The call to explore_my_F in pulling requires checking all edges, so it takes $O(m/P + \hat{d})$ time and $O(m)$ work. The call to explore_my_F in pushing needs $O(\hat{d})$ consecutive f_i-RELAXATIONS, so it takes $O(\bar{f}_i\hat{d})$ time where $\bar{f}_i = \max(1, f_i/P)$ and work $O(f_i\hat{d})$ in CRCW-CB (and $O(\log(\hat{d}))$ more in CREW). Second, the merge of frontiers can be done via a $\hat{d}f_i$-RELAXATION and, in pushing, a $\hat{d}f_i$-FILTER. The $\hat{d}f_i$-FILTER is not required in pulling, since we check whether each vertex is in the frontier anyway. In pushing, the merge requires $O(\log(P) + \hat{d}f_i/P)$ time and $O(\min(\hat{d}f_i, n))$ work.

Thus, for a graph of diameter D (with D while-loop iterations) we derive the total cost using the fact that $\sum_{i=1}^{D} f_i = n$, obtaining: (1) $O(D(m/P + \hat{d}))$ time and $O(Dm)$ work in pulling, (2) $O(m/P + D(\hat{d} + \log(P)))$ time and $O(m)$ work in pushing in CRCW, and (3) a factor of $O(\log(\hat{d}))$ more time and work in the CREW model. It is possible to achieve a lower time-complexity for BFS, especially if willing to sacrifice work-efficiency [18].

Conflicts There are $O(m)$ write conflicts in pushing; pulling involves $O(Dm)$ read conflicts.

Atomics/Locks Pushing requires $O(m)$ CAS atomics.

4.4 Δ-Stepping SSSP

```
1  /* Input: a graph G, a vertex r, the Δ parameter.
2     Output: An array of distances d */
3
4  function Δ-Stepping(G, r, Δ){
5    bckt=[∞..∞]; d=[∞..∞]; active=[false..false];
6    bckt_set={0}; bckt[r]=0; d[r]=0; active[r]=true; itr=0;
7
8    for b ∈ bckt_set do { //For every bucket do...
9      do {bckt_empty = false; //Process b until it is empty.
10     process_buckets();} while(!bckt_empty); } }
11
12 function process_buckets() {
13   for v ∈ bckt_set[b] do in par                        PUSHING
14     if(bckt[v]==b && (itr == 0 or active[v])) {
15       active[v] = false; //Now, expand v's neighbors.
16       for w ∈ N(v) {weight = d[v] + W_(v,w);
17         if(weight < d[w]) { ® //Proceed to relax w.
18           new_b = weight/Δ; bckt[w] = new_b;
19           bckt_set[new_b] = bckt_set[new_b] ∪ {w};}
20           d[w] = weight; ® ▊;
21           if(bckt[w]==b)® {active[w]=true; bckt_empty=true;}}} ®
22   for v ∈ V do in par                                   PULLING
23     if(d[v] > b) {for w ∈ N(v) do {
24       if(bckt[w] == b && (active[w] or itr == 0)) {®
25         weight = d[w] + W_(w,v) ®;
26         if(weight < d[v]) {d[v]=weight; new_b=weight/Δ;
27           if(bckt[v] > new_b) {
28             bckt[v] = new_b; bckt_set = bckt_set ∪ {new_b};}
29             if(new_b == b) {active[v]=true; bckt_empty=true;}}}}}
30 }
```

Algorithm 4: (§ 4.4) Push- and pull-based Δ-Stepping SSSP.

The algorithm works in epochs. In each epoch, a bucket b is initialized with vertices whose tentative distances are $[(b-1)\Delta, b\Delta)$, and relaxations are computed until all vertices within distance $b\Delta$ are found. This means that in epoch b, edges are relaxed only from vertices whose final distances are within $[(b-1)\Delta, b\Delta)$.

Let L be the maximum weighted distance between any pair of vertices in the graph, and let l_Δ be the number of iterations done in any epoch. If n_i vertices fall into the ith bucket, at the ith epoch $O(l_\Delta \hat{d})$ executions of n_i-RELAXATION will relax edges of vertices in the current bucket and up to l_Δ executions of n_i-FILTER will be used to update the set of vertices in the current bucket. So each edge will be relaxed $O(l_\Delta)$ times. There are a total of L/Δ epochs, so the complexity of Δ-stepping is (1) $O((L/\Delta)l_\Delta(m/P + \hat{d}))$ time and $O((L/\Delta)ml_\Delta)$ work using pulling, (2) $O(ml_\Delta/P + (L/\Delta)l_\Delta\hat{d})$ time and $O(ml_\Delta)$ work using pushing in CRCW-CB, (3) $O(\log(\hat{d}))$ more than (2) using pushing in CREW. Pushing achieves a smaller cost, since we relax the edges leaving each node in only one of L/Δ epochs. These results may be extrapolated to specific types of graphs considered in the original analysis [37].

Conflicts In pushing, there is a write conflict for each of $O(ml_\Delta)$ edge relaxations. In pulling, there is a read conflict for each of $O((L/\Delta)ml_\Delta)$ edge relaxations.

Atomics/Locks In pushing, each edge relaxation can be performed via a CAS atomic (in total $O(ml_\Delta)$ of these).

4.5 Betweenness Centrality

BC is illustrated in Algorithm 5. For each source vertex, we first compute a BFS to count the multiplicities of each shortest path and store all predecessors that are on some shortest path for each destination vertex. The list of predecessors is then used to define a shortest path tree. To calculate the partial centrality scores, this tree is traversed via BFS starting from the tree leaves. We use the ready array to ensure tree-nodes enter the frontier only once the partial centrality updates of all of their children are accumulated.

This algorithm (parallel Brandes) was described in detail [9, 34]. The approach is dominated by $2n$ BFS invocations, the cost of which is analyzed in § 4.3. For directed graphs, SSSP (e.g., Δ-stepping) must be used to compute each shortest-path tree. Given the shortest-path tree the partial centrality scores can be computed via BFS in the same way as for undirected graphs. Computationally, the most significant difference of BC from SSSP and BFS, is the presence of additional parallelism. Many source vertices can be processed independently, so up to $O(n^2)$ processors can be used by running n independent instances of BFS or SSSP.

Conflicts and Atomics/Locks The number of conflicts as well as atomics or locks matches that of BFS or SSSP and can vary by the factor of up to $O(n)$ (depending on the amount of additional parallelism). Yet, since the accumulation operator for the second BFS uses floating point numbers, locks are required instead of atomics. This can be alleviated by maintaining sets of successors instead of predecessors as proposed by Bader et al. [3], which we identify as another opportunity for using either pushing or pulling. We elaborate on it in the technical report.

```
1  /* Input: a graph G. Output: centrality scores bc[1..n]. */
2
3  function BC(G) { bc[1..n] = [0..0]
4    Define Π so that any Π ∋ u = (index_u, pred_u, mult_u, part_u);
5    Define u ⇐_pred v with u, v ∈ Π so that u becomes
                      u = (index_u, pred_u ∪ index_v, mult_u + mult_v);
6    Define u ⇐_part v with u, v ∈ Π so that u becomes
                      u = (index_u, pred_u, mult_u, part_u + (mult_u/mult_v)(1 + part_v));
7
8    for s ∈ V do [in par] {
9      ready = [1, ..., 1]; ready[s] = 0;
10     R = BFS(G, ready, [(1, ∅, 0, 0)..(s, ∅, 1, 0)..(n, ∅, 0, 0)], ⇐_pred)];
11     Define graph G' = (V, E') where (u, v) ∈ E' iff index_v ∈ pred_u;
12     Let ready[u] be the in-degree of u ∈ V in G';
13     R = BFS(G', ready, R, ⇐_part);
14     for (index_u, pred_u, mult_u, part_u) ∈ R do [in par]
15       bc[u] += part_u; }
```

Algorithm 5: (§ 4.5) Push- and pull-based Betweenness Centrality.

4.6 Boman Graph Coloring

We present BGC in Algorithm 6. The algorithm proceeds for L iterations, a quantity that is sensitive to both the schedule of threads and the graph structure. To limit the memory consumption, we bound the maximum count of colors to C. We use an opaque function init that partitions G and thus initializes the set of border vertices $\mathcal{B}$ and all the partitions $\mathcal{P} = \{\mathcal{P}_1...\mathcal{P}_s\}$. The algorithm alternates between doing sequential graph coloring (seq_color_partition) and adjusting colors of bordering vertices. The adjustment of colors of bordering vertices corresponds to an invocation of $|\mathcal{B}|$-RELAXATION, in the worst case $|\mathcal{B}| = \Theta(n)$. Therefore, the complexity of BGC is (1) $O(L(m/P + \hat{d}))$ time and $O(Lm)$ work using pulling, (2) $O(L(m/P + \hat{d}))$ time and $O(Lm)$ work using pushing in CRCW-CB, (3) $O(\log(\hat{d}))$ more than (2) using pushing in CREW.

Conflicts Pushing/pulling require $O(Lm)$ write/read conflicts.

Atomics/Locks In pushing and pulling the write conflicts can be resolved via CASes (a total of $O(Lm)$ of these).

```
1 // Input: a graph G. Output: An array of vertex colors c[1..n].
2 // In the code, the details of functions seq_color_partition and
3 // init are omitted due to space constrains.
4
5 function Boman-GC(G) {
6   done = false; c[1..n] = [0..0]; //No vertex is colored yet
7   //avail[i][j]=1 means that color j can be used for vertex i.
8   avail[1..n][1..C] = [1..1][1..1]; init(B, P);
9   while (!done) {
10    for P ∈ P do in par {seq_color_partition(P);}
11    fix_conflicts(); } }
12
13 function fix_conflicts() {
14   for v ∈ B in par do {for u ∈ N(v) do
15     if (c[u] == c[v]) {
16       {avail[u][c[v]] = 0 W i;}                          PUSHING
17
18       {avail[v][c[v]] = 0 R i;}                          PULLING
19   }}
```

Algorithm 6: (§ 4.6) Push- and pull-based Boman Graph Coloring.

4.7 Boruvka Minimum Spanning Tree

Push- and pull-based Boruvka is shown in Algorithm 7. Due to space constraints, it only displays pushing/pulling when selecting the minimum edge adjacent to each supervertex. The algorithm starts with n supervertices and reduces their number by two at every iteration. The supervertex connectivity graph can densify throughout the process with supervertices having degree $\Theta(n)$. However, the supervertices will always contain no more than m edges overall. Determining the minimum-weight edge for all supervertices requires $O(n^2/P)$ time and $O(m)$ work assuming each supervertex is processed sequentially. Merging the vertices requires $O(\log(n))$ time and $O(n)$ work via a tree contraction [19] (our implementation uses a more simplistic approach). Merging the edges connected to each vertex can be done via $O(n)$ invocations of a k-RELAXATION, where $k = O(n)$ at the first iteration and then the bound decreases geometrically. Over all $\log(n)$ steps, the complexity of Boruvka is (1) $O(n^2/P)$ time and $O(n^2)$ work using pulling, (2) $O(n^2/P)$ time and $O(n^2)$ work using pushing in CRCW-CB, (3) $O(\log(n))$ more than (2) using pushing in CREW.

Theoretically, known PRAM algorithms for finding connectivity and minimal spanning forests [1] are much faster in time complexity. Still, our simple scheme is fairly efficient in practice as supervertex degree generally grows much slower than in the worst case.

Conflicts Pushing/pulling require $O(n^2)$ write/read conflicts.

Atomics/Locks The write conflicts in pushing can be handled via CAS atomics (in total $O(n^2)$ of them).

4.8 Further Analytical Considerations

We discuss some further extensions to our cost analyses. Please note that due to space constrains, several additional analyses can be found in the technical report.

More Parallelism Our analysis considered parallelism with $P \le O(n)$. However, our pseudocodes specify additional potential sources of parallelism in many of the algorithms. Up to m processors can be used in many cases (and even more for TC), but in this scenario, the distinction between pushing and pulling disappears.

Directed Graphs Pushing and pulling differ interestingly for directed graphs. Pushing entails iterating over all outgoing edges

```
1 function MST_Boruvka(G) {
2   sv_flag=[1..v]; sv=[{1}..{v}]; MST=[0..0];
3   avail_svs={1..n}; max_e_wgt=max_{v,w∈V}(W_{(v,w)}+1);
4
5   while avail_svs.size() > 0 do {avail_svs_new = ∅;
6     for flag ∈ avail_svs do in par {min_e_wgt[flag] = max_e_wgt;}
7     for flag ∈ avail_svs do in par {
8       for v ∈ sv[flag] do {
9         for w ∈ N(v) do [in par] {
10          if (sv_flag[w] ≠ flag) ∧                             PUSHING
11             (W_{(v,w)} < min_e_wgt[sv_flag[w]]) R {
12             min_e_wgt[sv_flag[w]] = W_{(v,w)} W i;
13             min_e_v[sv_flag[w]] = w; min_e_w[sv_flag[w]] = v W i;
14             new_flag[sv_flag[w]] = flag W i; }
15          if (sv_flag[w] ≠ flag) ∧ (W_{(v,w)} < min_e_wgt[flag]) R {
16             min_e_wgt[flag] = W_{(v,w)}; min_e_v[flag] = v;    PULLING
17             min_e_w[flag] = w; new_flag[flag] = sv_flag[w]; }R
18   } } }
19   while flag = merge_order.pop() do {
20     neigh_flag = sv_flag[min_e_w[flag]];
21     for v ∈ sv[flag] do sv_flag[flag] = sv_flag[neigh_flag];
22     sv[neigh_flag] = sv[flag] ∪ sv[neigh_flag];
23     MST[neigh_flag] = MST[flag] ∪ MST[neigh_flag]
24              ∪ { (min_e_v[flag], min_e_w[flag]) }; } }
```

Algorithm 7: (§ 4.7) Push- and pull-based Boruvka MST.

of a subset of the vertices, while pulling entails iterating over all incoming edges of all (or most) of the vertices. Thus, instead of $\hat{d}$ some cost bounds would depend on $\hat{d}_{out}$ and $\hat{d}_{in}$ for pushing and pulling, respectively; more details are in the technical report.

4.9 Discussion & Insights

We finally summarize the most important insights.

Write/Read Conflicts Pushing entails more write conflicts that must be resolved with locks or atomics (read conflicts must be resolved only under the EREW model). An exception is BC where the difference lies in the type of the data that causes conflicts (floats for pushing and integers for pulling as was remarked in the past work [34]). Moreover, traversals (BFS, BC (Part 2), SSSP) entail more read conflicts with pulling (e.g., $O(Dn\hat{d})$ in the BFS based on pulling and none in the push-based BFS).

Atomics/Locks We now summarize how conflicts translate into used atomics or locks. In many algorithms, pulling removes atomics or locks completely (TC, PR, BFS, Δ-Stepping, MST). In others (BC), it changes the type of conflicts from f to i, enabling the utilization of atomics and removing the need for locks [26].

Communication/Synchronization The above analyses show that pulling reduces synchronization compared to pushing (e.g., fewer atomics in TC). In contrast, pushing limits communication (e.g., the number of memory reads in BFS).

Complexity Pulling in traversals (BFS, BC, SSSP-Δ) entails more time and work (e.g., see BFS). On the other hand, in schemes such as PR that update all vertices at every iteration, pulling avoid write conflicts. As a result, for PR and TC, pulling is faster than pushing in the PRAM CREW model by a logarithmic factor.

5 ACCELERATING PUSHING & PULLING

Our analysis in § 4 shows that most push- and pull-based algorithms entail excessive counts of atomics/locks and reads/writes, respectively. We now describe strategies to reduce both.

Partition-Awareness (PA, in Pushing) We first decrease the number of atomics by *transforming the graph representation to limit memory conflicts*. For this, we partition the adjacency array of each v into two parts: *local* and *remote*. The former contains the neighbors $u \in N(v)$ that are owned by $t[v]$ and the latter groups the ones owned by other threads. All local and remote arrays form two contiguous arrays; offsets for each array are stored separately. This increases the representation size from $n + 2m$ to $2n + 2m$ but also enables detecting if a given vertex v is owned by the executing thread (to be updated with a non-atomic) or if it is owned by a different thread (to be updated with an atomic). This strategy can be applied to PR, TC, and BGC. Consider PR as an example. Each iteration has two phases. First, each thread updates its own vertices with non-atomics. Second, threads use atomics to update vertices owned by other threads. Here, the exact number of atomics depends on the graph distribution and structure, and is bounded by 0 (if $\forall_{v \in V} \forall_{w \in N(v)} t[v] \neq t[w]$) and $2m$ (if $\forall_{v \in V} \forall_{w \in N(v)} t[v] = t[w]$). The former occurs if $G = (V, E)$ is bipartite (i.e., $V = U \cup W, U \cap W = \emptyset$) and each thread only owns vertices from either U or W. The latter occurs if each thread owns all vertices in some G's connected component. The number of non-atomics stays similar. We show this example in Algorithm 8. The overhead from a barrier (line 10) is outweighed by fewer write conflicts (none in line 8).

```
1 //The code below corresponds to lines 19-10 in Algorithm 1.
2 //V_L is a set of vertices owned by a local executing tread.
3 //V_G is a set of vertices owned by a tread different from the
4 //local one. V_L ∪ V_G = V; V_L ∩ V_G = ∅.
5
6 for v ∈ V_L do in par                    PART 1: LOCAL UPDATES
7   for u ∈ N(v) do [in par]
8     new_pr[u] += (f·pr[v])/d(v)
9
10 barrier(); //A lightweight barrier to synchronize all threads.
11
12 for v ∈ V_G do in par                    PART 2: REMOTE UPDATES
13   for u ∈ N(v) do [in par]
14     new_pr[u] += (f·pr[v])/d(v)  Ⓦ Ⓘ
```

Algorithm 8: (§ 5) Using Partition-Awareness for push-based PageRank.

Frontier-Exploit (FE, in Pushing/Pulling) The number of excessive reads/writes can be reduced by accessing only a fraction of vertices in each iteration (the *Frontier-Exploit* strategy), similarly to BFS. For example, consider BGC. In each iteration, every vertex is verified for potential conflicts, entailing many memory reads, regardless of whether pushing or pulling is used. To reduce the number of such reads, a set of vertices $F \subseteq V$ that form a stable set (i.e., are not neighbors) is selected at first and is marked with a specified color c_0 (we denote different colors with $c_i, i \in \mathbb{N}$). Then, the algorithm enters the main loop. In each iteration $i \geq 1$, all neighbors of vertices in F that have not yet been colored are assigned a color c_i; at the end of each iteration, F is set to $\emptyset$ and the newly marked neighbors become the elements of F. While iterating, for each vertex $v \in F$, if any of its neighbors $u \in N(v)$ has the same color (c_i), then a conflict occurs and either v or u (depending on the selected strategy) is assigned a color c_{i+1} that was not used before. This scheme resembles a BFS traversal with multiple sources selected at the beginning and marked with a color c_0, and a frontier constituted by vertices in F. In pushing, the vertices in F look for their uncolored neighbors and mark them with c_i. In pulling, uncolored vertices look for colored neighbors that are in F.

Generic-Switch (GS, in Pushing/Pulling) Next, we use the idea of switching between pushing and pulling; we want to not only reduce communication, but also *limit the iteration count*. We refer to the strategy as *Generic-Switch*. As an example, consider the above-described BGC enhanced with Frontier-Exploit. Pushing itself results in the excessive number of iterations. This is because, when the number of vertices to be colored is low (our experiments indicate $< 0.1n$), threads often conflict with each other, requiring

more iterations. Switching to pulling may prevent new iterations as no conflicts are generated. Yet, using pulling too early would entail excessive memory accesses (few vertices are colored). Thus, one must carefully select a switching moment or strategy, for example switch if the ratio of the number of the colored vertices to the generated conflicts (in a given iteration) exceeds a certain threshold.

Greedy-Switch (GrS, in Pushing/Pulling) Generic-Switch not always brings the desired speedups. For example, BGC with Frontier-Exploit may still need many iterations to color a small fraction of the remaining vertices due to many conflicts between threads that share vertices. In such cases, it is more advantageous to completely switch from a parallel variant (regardless of whether it does pushing or pulling) to an optimized greedy scheme.

Conflict-Removal (CR, Pushing/Pulling) The final strategy (see Algorithm 9) completely removes conflicts in both pushing and pulling. Consider BGC as an example. Instead of solving conflicts over border vertices (the set $\mathcal{B}$) in each iteration, one can first use an optimized scheme (e.g., greedy sequential) to color them without any conflicts (thus, this scheme is advantageous if $|\mathcal{B}|$ is small compared to $|V|$). The remaining vertices can then be colored in parallel; no conflicts occur either as every $v \in \mathcal{B}$ is already colored.

```
1 //The code below corresponds to lines 9-11 in Algorithm 6.
2 seq_color_partition(B)
3 for P ∈ 𝒫 do in par {seq_color_partition(P);}
```

Algorithm 9: (§ 5) Example of Conflict-Removal with BGC.

6 PERFORMANCE ANALYSIS

Finally, we investigate the performance of push/pull variants and the described acceleration strategies. Due to a large amount of data we present and discuss in detail a small representative subset; the remainder is in the report (see the link on page 1).

Selected Benchmarks & Parameters We consider the push- and pull-based variants, strategies from § 5, strong- and weak-scaling, Hyper-Threading (HT), and static/dynamic OpenMP scheduling. Two types of synthetic graphs are used: power-law Kronecker [31] and Erdős-Rényi [16] graphs with $n \in \{2^{20}, ..., 2^{28}\}$ and $\bar{d} \in \{2^1, ..., 2^{10}\}$. We also use real-world graphs (Table 2) of various sparsities: low $\bar{d}$ and large D (road networks), low $\bar{d}$ and D (purchase graphs), and large $\bar{d}$ with low D (communities). The graphs have up to 268M vertices and 4.28B edges.

Used Programming Models We use threading to harness SM systems. For DM machines, we use Message Passing (MP, also denoted as Msg-Passing) and Remote Memory Access (RMA) [20]. In MP, processes communicate explicitly and synchronize implicitly with messages. In RMA, processes communicate and synchronize explicitly by accessing remote memories with puts, gets, or atomics, and ensuring consistency with flushes [20].

Counted Events We incorporate the total of nine performance counters for detailed analyses of: cache misses (L1, L2, L3), reads and writes, conditional/unconditional branches, and data/instruction TLB misses. We also manually count issued atomics and acquired locks. Memory operations and cache/TLB misses are important as many graph algorithms are memory-bound [5]. Branches were also shown to impact performance in graph processing [23]. Finally, in distributed settings we count sent/received messages, issued collective operations, and remote reads/writes/atomics.

Experimental Setup and Architectures We use the following systems to cover various types of machines:

Event	orc (PR) Push	Push+PA	Pull	rca (PR) Push	Push+PA	Pull	ljn (TC) Push	Pull	rca (TC) Push	Pull	orc (BGC) Push	Pull	rca (BGC) Push	Pull	pok (SSSP-Δ) Push	Pull	rca (SSSP-Δ) Push	Pull
L1 misses	335M	382M	572M	2,062M	10,560M	2,857M	10,815B	10,684B	4,290M	4,150M	3,599B	4,555B	76,117M	75,401M	54,57M	469M	11,01k	76,19M
L2 misses	234M	289M	446M	640k	7,037M	1,508M	700M	645M	2,303M	2,215M	3,656B	4,418B	74,48M	73,92M	50,74M	472M	9,46k	75,56M
L3 misses	64,75M	53,49M	181M	348M	537k	866k	439M	404M	1,075M	1,030M	36,94M	186M	229k	226k	8,52M	11,43M	308	279k
TLB misses (data)	130M	142M	129M	12,21k	274k	21628	66,44M	56,05M	37,45k	18,37k	229M	411M	4,046M	3,801M	3,763M	26,17M	403	513k
TLB misses (inst)	1188	336	1161	218	250	218	1090	660	214	233	141k	507k	510	577	1,984k	11,22k	71	370
atomics	234M	219M	0	5,533M	5,374M	0	1,066B	0	724k	0	0	0	0	0	0	0	0	0
locks	0	0	0	0	0	0	0	0	0	0	219M	219M	5,358M	5,358M	902k	44.60M	370	5.523M
reads	1,196B	1,183B	1,187B	43,39M	62,59M	37,49M	3,169T	3,158T	158M	135M	17,90B	23,04B	419M	404M	2.435B	2.339B	42,32k	454M
writes	474M	460M	237M	14.99M	14,86M	7,499M	10,71B	1,066B	18,97M	725k	3,866B	4,201B	97,44M	96,95M	718M	663M	9,545k	100M
branches (uncond)	234M	222M	1971	5,533M	7,340M	533	8,585B	616k	19,48M	631	2,714B	2,902B	67,58M	67,40M	441M	421M	5,171k	64.3M
branches (cond)	474M	466M	240M	15M	18,79M	9.467M	3,173T	3,173T	156M	156M	23,62B	32,46B	524M	495M	2.27B	2,192B	35,03k	518M

Table 1: (§ 6.1) PAPI events for PR, BGC (average per iteration), and TC, SSSP-Δ (total count) for the SM setting (Daint, XC30, $T = 16$).

Type	ID	n	m	$\bar{d}$	$\bar{D}$
R-MAT graphs	rmat	33M-268M	66M-4.28B	2-16	19-33
Social networks	orc	3.07M	117M	39	9
	pok	1.63M	22.3M	18.75	11
Ground-truth [53] community	ljn	3.99M	34.6M	8.67	17
Purchase network	am	262k	900k	3.43	32
Road network	rca	1.96M	2.76M	1.4	849

Table 2: (§ 6) The analyzed graphs with skewed degree distributions.

G	PageRank [ms] orc	pok	ljn	am	rca	Triangle Counting [s] orc	pok	ljn	am	rca
Pushing	572	129	264	4.62	6.68	11.78k	139.9	803.5	0.092	0.014
Pulling	557	103	240	2.46	5.42	11.37k	135.3	769.9	0.083	0.014

Table 3: (§ 6.1) Time per iteration for PageRank [ms] and the total time to compute for Triangle Counting [s] (SM setting, Daint, XC30, $T = 16$).

- **Cray XC nodes** from the CSCS supercomputing systems. We use XC50 and XC40 nodes from the Piz Daint machine. An XC50 node contains a 12-core Intel Xeon E5-2690 CPU with 64 GiB RAM. Each XC40 node contains an 18-core Intel Xeon E5-2695 CPU with 64 GiB RAM. We also show results for XC30 nodes (with an 8-core Intel E5-2670 Sandy Bridge CPU and 32 GiB RAM) from a past Daint version. Finally, we also provide results for XC40 nodes from a past Piz Dora system (referred to as XC40*); they contained 12-core Intel Haswells E5-2690 and 64 GiB RAM. All nodes are HT-enabled. The interconnection in all the cases is based on Cray's Aries and it implements the Dragonfly topology [28]. This machines represents massively parallel HPC systems.
- **Trivium V70.05** is a server with Intel Core i7-4770 (with four 3.4 GHz Haswell 2-way multi-threaded cores). Each core has 32 KB of L1 and 256 KB of L2 cache. The CPU has 8 MB of shared L3 cache and 8 GB of RAM. This option represents commodity machines.

Infrastructure and Implementation Details We use the PAPI library (v5.4.1.1) to access performance counters. We spawn one MPI process per core (or per one HT resource if applicable). We use Cray-mpich (v.7.2.2) for MP and the foMPI library (v0.2.1) [20] for RMA. We also use OpenMP 4.0 and TBB from the Intel Programming Environment 6.0.3. We compile the code (with the -O3 flag) with g++ v4.9.2 (on Trivium) and Cray GNU 5.2.40 g++ (on CSCS systems). The information refers to the current Daint system; others are covered in the technical report.

6.1 Shared-Memory Analysis

We first analyze the differences in the SM setting. The representative PAPI data for selected schemes is in Table 1. For each scheme, we discuss in more detail the results for graphs with: large $\bar{d}$ and low D, and low $\bar{d}$ and large D.

PageRank PR results can be found in Table 3. In graphs with both high $\bar{d}$ (orc, ljn, poc) and low $\bar{d}$ (rca, am), pulling outperforms pushing by ≈3% and ≈19%, respectively. The former requires no atomics, but its speedup is moderate as it also generates more cache misses and branches as it accesses various neighbors, requiring more random memory reads.

Triangle Counting We now proceed to TC (Table 3). Large amounts of time are due to the high computational complexity (§ 4.2); this is especially visible in graphs with high $\bar{d}$. Here, pulling always outperforms pushing (by ≈4% for orc and ≈2% for rca). This is due to atomics but also more cache misses caused by atomics.

Graph Coloring The BGC results are presented in Figure 1. Pushing is always faster than pulling (by ≈10% for orc and ≈9% for rca for iteration 1). More detailed measurements indicate that the number of locks acquired is the same in both variants, but pushing always entails fewer cache/TLB misses and issued reads and writes.

Δ-Stepping The outcomes for orc and am can be found in Figure 2). Both push and pull variants use locks. Yet, a higher number of memory accesses issued in most iterations in the pull-based scheme limits performance. As expected, the difference decreases after several iterations because the frontier grows (with pushing), requiring more memory accesses. This is especially visible in graphs with high $\bar{d}$ where pulling outperforms pushing (e.g., iteration 6 for orc). Moreover, illustrate in Figure 2c that the larger Δ is, the smaller the difference between pushing and pulling becomes.

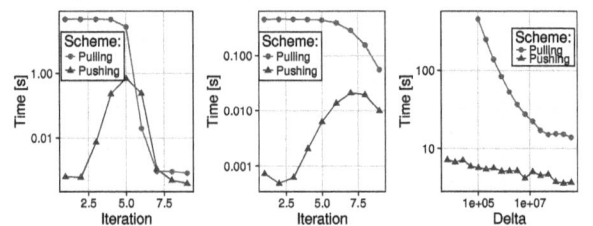

(a) The orc graph. (b) The am graph. (c) Varying Δ (orc).

Figure 2: (§ 6.1) SSSP-Δ SM analysis (XC30, $T = 16$).

Breadth-First Search The results are similar to SSSP-Δ; pushing outperforms pulling in most cases. This is most visible for rca (high D, low $\bar{d}$) due to many memory accesses.

Minimum Spanning Trees We illustrate the MST results in Figure 4. We analyze time to complete each of the three most time-consuming phases of each iteration: Find Minimum (FM; looking for minimum-weight edges), Build Merge Tree (BMT; preparing metadata for merging), and Merge (M; merging of subtrees). Now, pushing is faster than pulling in BMT and comparable in M. Yet, it is slower in the most computationally expensive FM. In summary,

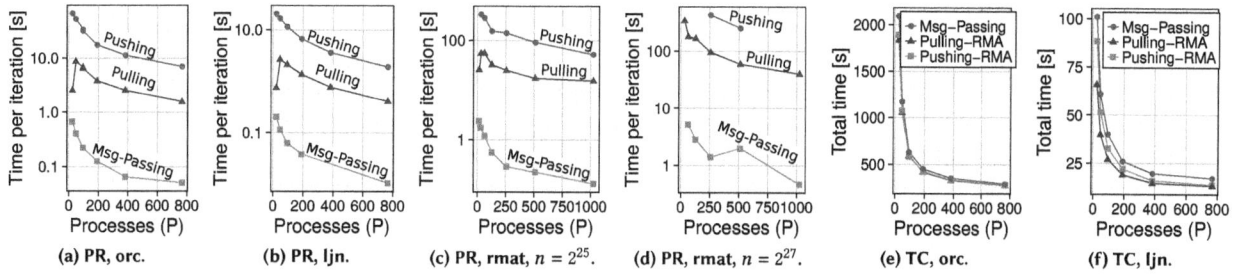

Figure 3: (§ 6.3) The results of the scalability analysis in the DM setting, strong scaling (rmat graphs: XC40, $T = 24$; real-world graphs: XC40*, $T = 24$).

performance trends are similar to those of TC: pushing is consistently slower ($\approx$20 for $T = 4$) than pulling. This is because the latter entails no expensive write conflicts.

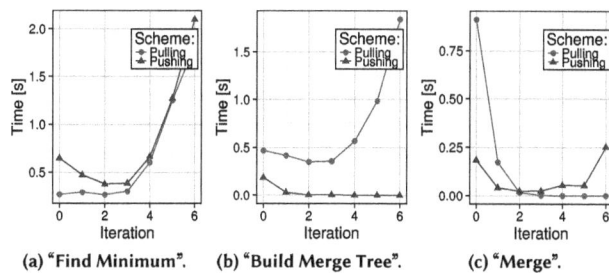

Figure 4: (§ 6.1) Illustration of the MST analysis, each subplot relates to a different phase (XC40, HT enabled, the orc graph, $T = 16$).

Betweenness Centrality The results for BC can be found in Figure 5. We present the running times of both BFS traversals and the total BC runtime. In each case, pushing is slower than pulling because of the higher amount of expensive write conflicts that entail more synchronization in both BC parts.

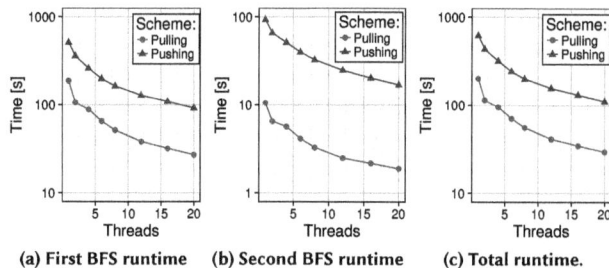

Figure 5: (§ 6.1) Illustration of the BC analysis (scalability, XC40, HT enabled, the orc graph, $T = 16$).

6.2 Acceleration Strategies

We now evaluate the acceleration strategies (§ 5).

Partition-Awareness (PA) We start with adding PA to PR (Table 6a). In graphs with higher $\bar{d}$ (orc, ljn, poc), pushing+PA outperforms pulling (by $\approx$24%). This is because PA decreases atomics (by 7%) and comes with fewer cache misses ($\approx$30% for L1, $\approx$34% for L2, and $\approx$69% for L3) than pulling. In sparser graphs (rca, am), surprisingly pushing+PA is the slowest ($\approx$205% than pushing). This is because fewer atomics issued in pushing+PA ($\approx$4%) are still dominated by more branches ($\approx$23%), reads ($\approx$44%), and cache misses ($\approx$53% for L3). We conjecture that in graphs with high $\bar{d}$, PA enhances pushing as the latter entails more atomics that dominate the performance. This is visible as both variants reduce the number

of cache misses if adjacency lists are long and use better cache prefetchers. Then, for low $\bar{d}$, adjacency lists are short on average, giving more cache misses in pushing+PA and pushing, making pulling the fastest. The worst performance of pushing+PA is due to the synchronization overheads (it splits each iteration into two phases separated by a barrier) that are no longer compensated with more effective cache utilization.

Frontier-Exploit (FE), Generic/Greedy-Switch (GS/GrS) We now apply these strategies to BGC, ensuring the same number of colors for each coloring. All three strategies entail very similar ($<$ 1% of difference) times to compute each iteration. Here, we select GrS and compare it to simple pushing/pulling; see Figure 1. Faster iterations are due to fewer memory accesses as predicted in § 5. Next, we show that the strategies differ in the number of iterations, see Table 6b. The largest iteration count (especially visible foe orc/ljn) is due to FE. As predicted, this is because of conflicts. Both switching strategies reduce the iteration count.

G	Push	+PA		G	Push	+FE	+GS	+GrS
orc	557.985	425.928		orc	49	173	49	49
pok	103.907	87.577		pok	49	48	49	47
ljn	240.943	145.475		ljn	49	334	49	49
am	2.467	5.193		am	49	10	10	9
rca	5.422	13.705		rca	49	5	5	5

Figure 6: (§ 6.2) Acceleration strategy analysis (SM, Daint, XC30, $T = 16$). Time per iteration (ms) for PageRank (the left table). Number of iterations to finish for BGC (the right table).

6.3 Distributed-Memory Analysis

We also conduct a distributed-memory analysis.

6.3.1 PageRank. First, we use RMA for push- and pull-based PR. The former uses remote atomics (MPI_Accumulate) to modify ranks. The latter read the ranks with remote gets (MPI_Get). Next, we design PR with MP. Here, we use the collective MPI_Alltoallv [38] to exchange the information on the rank updates among processes. This variant is unusual as it *combines pushing and pulling*: each process contributes to the collective by both providing a vector of rank updates (it pushes) and receiving updates (it pulls).

Performance The performance outcomes (strong scaling) can be found in Figure 3. MP consistently outperforms RMA (by >10x); pushing is the slowest. This may sound surprising as MP comes with overheads due to buffer preparation. Contrarily to RMA, the communicated updates must first be placed in designated send buffers. Yet, the used MPI_Accumulate is implemented with costly underlying locking protocol. Next, pulling suffers from communication overheads as it fetches both the degree and the rank of each neighbor of each vertex.

Memory Consumption RMA variants only use $O(1)$ storage (per process) in addition to the adjacency list. Contrarily, PR with MP may require up to $O((n\hat{d})/P)$ storage (per process) for send and receive buffers.

6.3.2 Triangle Counting. Similarly to PR, we develop push- and pull-based TC with RMA and with MP. In pushing, we increase remote counters with an FAA. The MP-based TC uses messages to instruct which counters are augmented. To reduce communication costs, updates are buffered until a given size is reached.

Performance The results are in Figure 3. RMA variants always outperform MP; pulling is always faster than pushing (<1% for orc and ≈25% for ljn for $P = 48$). This is different from PR as the counters in TC are *integer* and the utilized RMA library offers fast path codes of remote atomic FAAs that access 64-bit integers. The MP variant is the slowest because of the communication and buffering overheads.

Memory Consumption Both RMA schemes fetch $N(v)$ of each analyzed vertex v to check for potential triangles. This is done with multiple MPI_Gets, with two extremes: a single get that fetches all the neighbors, or one get per neighbor. The former requires the largest amount of additional memory ($O(\hat{d})$ storage per process) but least communication overheads. The latter is the opposite.

6.4 Further Analyses

We now show that the relative differences between pushing and pulling do not change significantly when varying the used machine. We verify that PR comes with the most relevant difference; see Table 4. Results vary most in denser graphs (orc, pok, ljn); for example pushing outperforms pulling on Trivium while the opposite is true on Dora. Contrarily, the results are similar for rca and am. Thus, the overheads from branches, reads, and cache misses (that are the highest in graphs with lowest $\bar{d}$) dominate performance.

Trivium:	orc	pok	ljn	am	rca
Push	1426.966	191.340	373.134	6.199	16.818
Pull	1583.094	279.261	421.396	2.819	12.504
Push+PA	1289.123	190.541	400.634	8.549	52.068
Daint (XC40):					
Push	499.463	123.784	248.602	5.744	7.753
Pull	456.532	86.812	206.604	2.828	5.810
Push+PA	378.548	78.883	128.255	6.157	14.102

Table 4: (§ 6.4) **Time to compute one iteration in PR [ms] (SM setting with full parallelism (HT enabled); Trivium, $T = 8$; Daint, XC40, $T = 24$).**

6.5 Push-Pull Insights

We finally summarize the most important insights on the push-pull performance for the considered systems.

Shared-Memory Settings First, some algorithms are the fastest with pushing (SSSP-Δ, BFS, and PR for dense graphs) except for some data points (e.g., iteration 6 for orc in SSSP-Δ). This contradicts the intuition that pulling comes with less overheads from atomics. Yet, they either entail more reads that dominate performance (e.g., SSSP-Δ) or use cache prefetchers less effectively by not accessing contiguous structures (e.g., PR). The results for PR+PA illustrate that atomics do not always dominate performance; this can happen if effects such as cache misses become less dominant.

Second, SSSP-Δ on SM systems is surprisingly different from the variant for the DM machines presented in the literature, where pulling is faster [12]. This is because intra-node atomics are less costly than messages. Next, HT accelerates each considered scheme, maintaining the relative differences between pushing and pulling. Finally, several pulling schemes (in BGC and MST) are faster than their push counterparts.

Distributed-Memory Settings The choice of PR and TC illustrates that two algorithms with push and pull variants having similar algorithm designs may come with substantially different performance patterns. Intuitively, RMA should ensure highest performance in both PR and TC as both require the same MPI_Accumulate remote atomic function. Yet, the different operand type results in different underlying implementations and thus results. With the setting considered in this work, RMA and MP ensured best performance for TC and PR, respectively.

7 DISCUSSION

We now discuss various aspects of push and pull variants.

7.1 Push-Pull: Linear Algebra

Various graph algorithms can be expressed with linear algebra (LA) operations such as matrix-vector (MV) multiplication. It enables a concise specification by abstracting from details such as scheduling vertices for processing in the next iteration [27]. We now illustrate that it is possible to frame LA-based graph algorithms in push and pull variants.

Brief Recap A crucial notion is the adjacency matrix of G (denoted as $\mathbf{A}$) that encodes G's structure. The element in row i and column j of $\mathbf{A}$ equals 1 iff there is an edge from vertex j to vertex i, and equals 0 otherwise. For simplicity, we focus on unweighted graphs, but our conclusions apply to the weighted case.

The graph algorithms that we consider can be cast as matrix-vector multiplications (MVs) $\mathbf{A} \otimes \mathbf{x}^{(k)}$, where $\mathbf{x}^{(k)}$ is the algorithm state in iteration k and $\otimes$ is matrix-vector multiplication operator over an appropriate semiring. The adjacency matrix $\mathbf{A}$ is generally sparse, while $\mathbf{x}^{(k)}$ may or may not be sparse depending on the computation. For example, in PR, each $\mathbf{x}^{(k)}$ is dense, while in BFS, the sparsity of $\mathbf{x}^{(k)}$ depends on the number of vertices in the kth frontier. We refer to the case when the vector is dense as SpMV, and when the vector is sparse, SpMSpV. The dichotomy between push and pull algorithm variants is mirrored by the dichotomy between the Compressed Sparse Column (CSC) and Compressed Sparse Row (CSR) representations of $\mathbf{A}$.

A CSR representation stores each row of $\mathbf{A}$ contiguously. The ith row of $\mathbf{A}$ contains all vertices with an edge to vertex i. Consequently, performing an SpMV in the CSR layout involves iterating over each row and multiplying each nonzero element in the row by appropriate entries of the vector. Thus, each entry of the output can be computed independently by a thread. This scheme is equivalent to pulling updates for each vertex. For SpMV, CSR (pulling) works extremely well, but for SpMSpV, it is not clear how to efficiently exploit the sparsity of the vector $\mathbf{x}^{(k)}$.

A CSC representation stores each column of $\mathbf{A}$ contiguously. The ith row of $\mathbf{A}$ contains all vertices with an edge from vertex i. Consequently, performing an SpMV in the CSC layout involves iterating over each column and multiplying each nonzero element in the column by the same entry of the vector, while accumulating to different elements of the output vector. Here, atomics or a reduction tree are necessary to combine updates to each output vector element. This scheme is equivalent to pushing updates from each vertex, as each thread is naturally assigned a different column of $\mathbf{A}$ and nonzero entry of $\mathbf{x}^{(k)}$. For SpMSpV, CSC (pushing) facilitates exploiting the sparsity of the vector by simply ignoring columns of $\mathbf{A}$ that match up to zeros in $\mathbf{x}^{(k)}$.

7.2 Push-Pull: Programming Models

Push/pull differences depend on the programming model:

Threading/RMA The difference lies in the used atomics. An example is TC: no atomics (pulling) and FAA (pushing).

MP (Point-to-Point Messages) In iterative algorithms with fixed communication patterns (e.g., TC) pushing gives more speedup as pulling increases the message count. In traversals, pushing-pulling switching offers highest performance [4, 12].

MP (Collectives) In collectives such as MPI_Alltoallv, all processes both push and pull the data, eliminating the distinction between these two.

7.3 Push-Pull: Code Complexity

Push and pull variants considered in this work come with similar code complexity. Still, pull schemes can be more challenging in achieving high performance. Consider the inner loop in PR where a thread iterates over $N(v)$ of a given v. In pushing, updates are conducted simply with atomics. Contrarily, in pulling, one must also fetch the degrees of neighbors. This is similar for other pull variants and poses more challenges in making the code fast.

7.4 Push-Pull: Gather-Apply-Scatter

Finally, we discuss the relationship between the push-pull dichotomy and the well-know Gather-Apply-Scatter (GAS) abstraction [22]. In GAS, one develops a graph algorithm by specifying the gather, apply, and scatter functions. They run in parallel for each vertex v and respectively: bring some data from v's neighbors, use it to modify v's value, and write the result to a data structure. We now describe two algorithms designed with GAS (SSSP and GC) [22] and show how to develop them with pushing or pulling.

SSSP Here, each vertex v is processed in parallel by selecting v's incident edge e that offers a path to the selected root s with the lowest distance. If it is lower than the current distance from v to s, the value is updated accordingly and $N(s)$ are scheduled for processing in the next iteration. Now, push or pull can be applied when v updates its distance to s. In the former, a neighboring vertex that performed a relaxation in the previous iteration updates its neighbors (pushes the changes) with new distances. In the latter, each vertex scheduled for updates iterates over its neighbors (pulls the updates) to perform a relaxation by itself.

GC Every vertex v collects the set of colors on $N(v)$ to compute a new unique color. Next, the new colors are scattered among $N(v)$. Any conflicting vertices are then scheduled for the color recomputation in the next iteration. This algorithm is a special case of BGC: each vertex constitutes a separate partition (i.e., $\forall_{v \in V} \forall_{u \in N(v)} t[v] \neq t[u]$). Thus, the same approach can be incorporated.

8 RELATED WORK

Push and Pull Algorithm Variants Several graph algorithms that approach the pushing and pulling distinction have been proposed. The bottom-up (pull) BFS was described by Suzumura et al. [48] while Beamer et al. [4] introduced a direction-optimizing BFS that switches between top-down (push) and bottom-up (pull) variants. Madduri et al. [34] proposed several improvements to BC, one of which inverts the direction of modifications in the backward traversal to eliminate critical sections. Whang et al. [52] described pulling and pushing in PR. Finally, Chakaravarthy et al. [12] inverts the direction of message exchanges in the distributed Δ-Stepping algorithm. All these schemes are solutions to single problems. We embrace and generalize them in the push-pull analysis.

Pushing/Pulling in Graph Frameworks Various graph processing frameworks were introduced, for example PBGL [24], Pregel [35], GraphBLAS [36], Galois [29], HAMA [45], PowerGraph [22], GraphLab [32], and Spark [54]. Some use pushing and pulling in certain ways, by: sending and receiving messages (Pregel), using the GAS abstraction (PowerGraph), switching between sparse and dense graph structures (Ligra [46]), switching the direction of updates in a distributed environment (Gemini [57]), using pushing and pulling in 3D task-partitioning [55], or pushing and pulling to/from disk [51]. Yet, none of them comes with an analysis on the push-pull dichotomy, focusing on the framework design. Finally, Doekemeijer et al. [15] list graph processing frameworks that have push- or pull-based communication. Our theoretical analysis and performance observations can serve to help better understand and improve graph processing frameworks.

Accelerating Strategies The Grace framework [40] partitions the graph similarly to Partition-Awareness, but its goal is to reduce caching overheads instead of atomics in pushing. Ligra uses a scheme similar to Generic-Switch as it switches between sparse and dense graph representations [46]. Finally, Salihoglu et al. [42] enhance Pregel-based systems with various schemes. Among others, similarly to Greedy-Switch, they propose to switch from a Pregel-based distributed scheme to a sequential algorithm variant.

Pushing/Pulling outside Graph Processing Borokhovich et al. [7] analyzed gossip algorithms in network coding for information spreading using push, pull, and exchange communication schemes. Swamy et al. [49] designed an asymptotically optimal push-pull method for multicasting over a random network. Intel TBB uses a push-pull protocol in its flow graphs, biasing communication to prevent polling and to reduce unnecessary retries [50]. An analysis of push and pull in software engineering has also been conducted [56]. None of these works addresses graph processing.

9 CONCLUSION

Graph processing has become an important part of various CS research and industry fields, including HPC, systems, networking, and architecture. Its challenges, described by Lumsdaine et al. almost 10 years ago [33], have still not been resolved and accelerating graph computations remains an important goal that must be attained for the ability to process the enormous amounts of data produced today.

In this work, we accelerate graph algorithms by deriving the most advantageous direction of graph updates out of the two options: *pushing* the updates from the private to the shared state, or *pulling* the updates in the opposite direction. We illustrate in a detailed analysis that the *Push-Pull (PP) dichotomy*, namely using either pushing or pulling, can be applied to various algorithms such as triangle counting, minimum spanning tree computations, or graph coloring. We provide detailed specifications, complexity analyses, and performance data from hardware counters on which variant serves best each algorithm and why pushing and pulling differ. These insights can be used to improve various graph processing engines.

Furthermore, we identify that pushing usually suffers from excessive amounts of atomics/locks while pulling entails more memory reads/writes. We use generic strategies to limit the amount of both, accelerating the processing of road networks, citation graphs, social networks, and others.

Our analysis illustrates that the decision on using either pushing or pulling is not limited to merely applying updates in PageRank or sending messages in BFS, but is related to a wide class of algorithms, strategies, graph abstractions, and programming models. Our PP dichotomy can easily be generalized to other concepts related to graph processing, for example vectorization.

Acknowledgments. We thank Hussein Harake, Colin McMurtrie, and the whole CSCS team granting access to the Greina, Piz Dora, and Daint machines, and for their excellent technical support. Maciej Besta is supported by Google European Doctoral Fellowship.

REFERENCES

[1] B. Awerbuch and Y. Shiloach. New connectivity and MSF algorithms for shuffle-exchange network and PRAM. *IEEE Trans. on Comp.*, 36(10):1258–1263, 1987.

[2] D. A. Bader and G. Cong. Fast shared-memory algorithms for computing the minimum spanning forest of sparse graphs. In *Par. and Dist. Proc. Symp. (IPDPS)*, page 39. IEEE, 2004.

[3] D. A. Bader et al. Approximating betweenness centrality. In *Algorithms and Models for the Web-Graph*, pages 124–137. Springer, 2007.

[4] S. Beamer, K. Asanović, and D. Patterson. Direction-optimizing breadth-first search. *Scientific Programming*, 21(3-4):137–148, 2013.

[5] S. Beamer, K. Asanović, and D. Patterson. GAIL: the graph algorithm iron law. In *Workshop on Ir. App.: Arch. and Alg.*, page 13, 2015.

[6] E. G. Boman et al. A scalable parallel graph coloring algorithm for distributed memory computers. In *Euro-Par*, pages 241–251. 2005.

[7] M. Borokhovich et al. Tight bounds for algebraic gossip on graphs. In *Inf. Theory Proc. (ISIT), IEEE Intl. Symp. on*, pages 1758–1762, 2010.

[8] O. Boruvka. O jistém problému minimálním. 1926.

[9] U. Brandes. A faster algorithm for betweenness centrality. *J. of Math. Sociology*, 25(2):163–177, 2001.

[10] S. Brin and L. Page. The anatomy of a large-scale hypertextual Web search engine. In *Proc. of Intl. Conf. on World Wide Web*, WWW7, pages 107–117, 1998.

[11] U. Catalyurek and C. Aykanat. A Fine-Grain Hypergraph Model for 2D Decomposition of Sparse Matrices. In *Proc. of the Intl. Par. &Amp; Dist. Proc. Symp.*, IPDPS '01, pages 118–, 2001.

[12] V. T. Chakaravarthy et al. Scalable single source shortest path algorithms for massively parallel systems. In *Par. and Dist. Proc. Symp., IEEE Intl.*, pages 889–901, 2014.

[13] T. H. Cormen, C. Stein, R. L. Rivest, and C. E. Leiserson. *Introduction to Algorithms.* McGraw-Hill Higher Education, 2nd edition, 2001.

[14] G. Csardi and T. Nepusz. The igraph software package for complex network research. *InterJournal, Complex Systems*, 1695(5):1–9, 2006.

[15] N. Doekemeijer and A. L. Varbanescu. A survey of parallel graph processing frameworks. *Delft University of Technology*, 2014.

[16] P. Erdős and A. Rényi. On the evolution of random graphs. *Selected Papers of Alfréd Rényi*, 2:482–525, 1976.

[17] S. Fortune and J. Wyllie. Parallelism in random access machines. In *Proc. of ACM Symp. on Theory of Comp.*, pages 114–118, 1978.

[18] H. Gazit et al. An improved parallel algorithm that computes the BFS numbering of a directed graph. *Inf. Proc. Let.*, 28(2):61–65, 1988.

[19] H. Gazit et al. Optimal tree contraction in the EREW model. In *Concurrent Computations*, pages 139–156. Springer, 1988.

[20] R. Gerstenberger, M. Besta, and T. Hoefler. Enabling Highly-scalable Remote Memory Access Programming with MPI-3 One Sided. In *Proc. of the ACM/IEEE Supercomputing*, SC '13, pages 53:1–53:12, 2013.

[21] A. Goel and K. Munagala. Complexity measures for map-reduce, and comparison to parallel computing. *arXiv preprint arXiv:1211.6526*, 2012.

[22] J. E. Gonzalez et al. PowerGraph: Distributed Graph-Parallel Computation on Natural Graphs. In *OSDI*, volume 12, page 2, 2012.

[23] O. Green et al. Branch-Avoiding Graph Algorithms. *arXiv:1411.1460*, 2014.

[24] D. Gregor and A. Lumsdaine. The parallel BGL: A generic library for distributed graph computations. *Par. Obj.-Or. Scientific Comp. (POOSC)*, page 2, 2005.

[25] T. J. Harris. A survey of PRAM simulation techniques. *ACM Comp. Surv. (CSUR)*, 26(2):187–206, 1994.

[26] Intel, Inc. 64 and IA-32 Architectures Software Developer's Manual, 2015.

[27] J. Kepner and J. Gilbert. *Graph algorithms in the language of linear algebra*, volume 22. SIAM, 2011.

[28] J. Kim et al. Technology-Driven, Highly-Scalable Dragonfly Topology. In *Ann. Intl. Symp. on Comp. Arch.*, ISCA '08, pages 77–88, 2008.

[29] M. Kulkarni et al. Optimistic parallelism requires abstractions. In *ACM SIGPLAN Conf. on Prog. Lang. Des. and Impl.*, PLDI '07, pages 211–222, 2007.

[30] C. E. Leiserson and T. B. Schardl. A work-efficient parallel breadth-first search algorithm (or how to cope with the nondeterminism of reducers). In *Proc. of ACM Symp. on Par. in Alg. and Arch.*, pages 303–314, 2010.

[31] J. Leskovec et al. Kronecker graphs: An approach to modeling networks. *J. of Machine Learning Research*, 11(Feb):985–1042, 2010.

[32] Y. Low et al. Graphlab: A new framework for parallel machine learning. *preprint arXiv:1006.4990*, 2010.

[33] A. Lumsdaine, D. Gregor, B. Hendrickson, and J. W. Berry. Challenges in Parallel Graph Processing. *Par. Proc. Let.*, 17(1):5–20, 2007.

[34] K. Madduri et al. A faster parallel algorithm and efficient multithreaded implementations for evaluating betweenness centrality on massive datasets. In *Par. & Dist. Proc. (IPDPS), IEEE Intl. Symp. on*, pages 1–8, 2009.

[35] G. Malewicz et al. Pregel: a system for large-scale graph processing. In *ACM SIGMOD Intl. Conf. on Manag. of Data*, SIGMOD '10, pages 135–146, 2010.

[36] T. Mattson et al. Standards for graph algorithm primitives. *arXiv preprint arXiv:1408.0393*, 2014.

[37] U. Meyer and P. Sanders. Δ-stepping: a parallelizable shortest path algorithm. *Journal of Algorithms*, 49(1):114–152, 2003.

[38] MPI Forum. MPI: A Message-Passing Interface Standard. Version 3, 2012.

[39] R. C. Murphy et al. Introducing the graph 500. *Cray User's Group (CUG)*, 2010.

[40] V. Prabhakaran et al. Managing large graphs on multi-cores with graph awareness. In *USENIX Annual Technical Conference*, volume 12, 2012.

[41] D. Prountzos and K. Pingali. Betweenness centrality: algorithms and implementations. In *ACM SIGPLAN Notices*, volume 48, pages 35–46. ACM, 2013.

[42] S. Salihoglu and J. Widom. Optimizing graph algorithms on Pregel-like systems. *Proceedings of the VLDB Endowment*, 7(7):577–588, 2014.

[43] N. Satish et al. Navigating the maze of graph analytics frameworks using massive graph datasets. In *ACM SIGMOD Intl. Conf. on Man. Data*, pages 979–990, 2014.

[44] T. Schank. *Algorithmic aspects of triangle-based network analysis.* PhD thesis, University Karlsruhe, 2007.

[45] S. Seo et al. HAMA: An Efficient Matrix Computation with the MapReduce Framework. In *Intl. Conf. on Cloud Comp. Tech. and Science*, CLOUDCOM'10, pages 721–726, 2010.

[46] J. Shun and G. E. Blelloch. Ligra: a lightweight graph processing framework for shared memory. In *ACM SIGPLAN Notices*, volume 48, pages 135–146, 2013.

[47] J. Shun and K. Tangwongsan. Multicore triangle computations without tuning. In *2015 IEEE 31st Intl. Conf. on Data Engineering*, pages 149–160, April 2015.

[48] T. Suzumura et al. Performance characteristics of Graph500 on large-scale distributed environment. In *Workload Char. (IISWC), IEEE Intl. Symp. on*, pages 149–158, 2011.

[49] V. N. Swamy et al. An Asymptotically Optimal Push–Pull Method for Multicasting Over a Random Network. *Inf. Theory, IEEE Tran. on*, 59(8):5075–5087, 2013.

[50] M. Voss. Understanding the internals of tbb::graph : Balancing Push and Pull.

[51] Z. Wang et al. Hybrid Pulling/Pushing for I/O-Efficient Distributed and Iterative Graph Computing. In *ACM Intl. Conf. on Man. of Data*, pages 479–494, 2016.

[52] J. J. Whang et al. Scalable Data-Driven PageRank: Algorithms, System Issues, and Lessons Learned. In *Euro-Par: Par. Proc.*, pages 438–450. 2015.

[53] J. Yang and J. Leskovec. Defining and evaluating network communities based on ground-truth. *Knowledge and Information Systems*, 42(1):181–213, 2015.

[54] M. Zaharia et al. Resilient Distributed Datasets: A Fault-tolerant Abstraction for In-memory Cluster Computing. In *Proc. of the USENIX Conf. on Net. Sys. Design and Impl.*, NSDI'12, pages 2–2, 2012.

[55] M. Zhang et al. Exploring the hidden dimension in graph processing. In *USENIX Symp. on Op. Sys. Des. and Impl. (OSDI 16)*, 2016.

[56] Y. Zhao. *A model of computation with push and pull processing.* PhD thesis, Citeseer, 2003.

[57] X. Zhu et al. Gemini: A computation-centric distributed graph processing system. In *USENIX Symp. on Op. Sys. Des. and Impl. (OSDI 16)*, 2016.

Better Safe than Sorry: Grappling with Failures of In-Memory Data Analytics Frameworks

Bogdan Ghiţ
Delft University of Technology, the Netherlands
b.i.ghit@tudelft.nl

Dick Epema
Delft University of Technology, the Netherlands
d.h.j.epema@tudelft.nl

ABSTRACT

Providing fault-tolerance is of major importance for data analytics frameworks such as Hadoop and Spark, which are typically deployed in large clusters that are known to experience high failures rates. Unexpected events such as compute node failures are in particular an important challenge for in-memory data analytics frameworks, as the widely adopted approach to deal with them is to recompute work already done. Recomputing lost work, however, requires allocation of extra resource to re-execute tasks, thus increasing the job runtimes. To address this problem, we design a checkpointing system called PANDA that is tailored to the intrinsic characteristics of data analytics frameworks. In particular, PANDA employs fine-grained checkpointing at the level of task outputs and dynamically identifies tasks that are worthwhile to be checkpointed rather than be recomputed. As has been abundantly shown, tasks of data analytics jobs may have very variable runtimes and output sizes. These properties form the basis of three checkpointing policies which we incorporate into PANDA.

We first empirically evaluate PANDA on a multicluster system with single data analytics applications under space-correlated failures, and find that PANDA is close to the performance of a fail-free execution in unmodified Spark for a large range of concurrent failures. Then we perform simulations of complete workloads, mimicking the size and operation of a Google cluster, and show that PANDA provides significant improvements in the average job runtime for wide ranges of the failure rate and system load.

CCS CONCEPTS

• **Computer systems organization** → **Distributed architectures**; • **Software and its engineering** → **Software performance**; **Checkpoint / restart**;

1 INTRODUCTION

The performance of large-scale data analytics frameworks such as Hadoop and Spark has received major interest [15, 22] from both academia and industry over the past decade. Surprisingly, this research assumes an ideal execution environment, which is in sharp contrast with the resilience-oriented design goals of these systems.

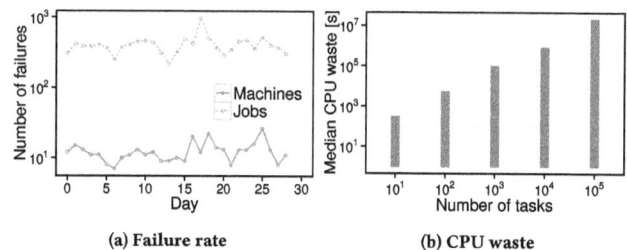

(a) Failure rate   (b) CPU waste

Figure 1: The average number of job and machine failures per hour (a) and the median CPU waste per job size range (b) in the Google trace. The vertical axes are in log-scale.

In turn, these goals are motivated by the high rates of failures experienced by large-scale systems operating in clusters [12, 17] and datacenters [16, 20]. A key feature influencing the adoption of data analytics frameworks is their *fault-tolerant* execution model, in which a master node keeps track of the tasks that were running on machines that failed and restarts them from scratch on other machines. However, we face a fundamental limitation when the amount of work lost due to failure and re-execution is excessive because we need to allocate extra resources for recomputing work which was previously done. Frameworks such as Spark provide an API for checkpointing, but leave the decision of which data to checkpoint to the user. In this work, we design PANDA, a cluster scheduler that performs automatic checkpointing and so improves the resilience of in-memory data analytics frameworks.

Failures in large-scale clusters are inevitable. The likelihood of having hardware crashes during the first year of a typical 10,000-machine cluster is very high according to several reports from the Google infrastructure team [5]. In particular, the system administrators expect about 1,000 individual machine failures and thousands of disk failures. In order to put into perspective the impact of failures on production workloads, we analyze failure reports from a Google cluster of 12,000 machines running half billion jobs over a month [16]. In Figure 1a we show the rate of machine and job failures in this Google cluster. Despite the relatively small number of machine failures (13 machines every hour), we observe a huge number of jobs (400 jobs every hour) that either fail, get killed by the system, or are simply abandoned by users. We expect this large number of failures to result into large amounts of wasted work. In Figure 1b we show the median job waste, that is the amount of work completed but lost due to failures for the complete range of job sizes (number of tasks). Indeed, the amount of wasted work increases linearly with the job size. The Google infrastructure is only one of a long series of multicluster systems experiencing problems in their infancy and in the long term. For example, the grid computing community has uncovered high failure rates [8], and in particular the flagship project CERN LCG had high failure rates years after going into production, with more than 25% unsuccessful jobs across all sites [3].

As today's clusters have large amounts of free memory [13], frameworks such as Spark advocate in-memory data processing, as opposed to previous on-disk approaches such as Hadoop. Unfortunately, as has been abundantly reported by the community, manipulating large datasets with Spark is challenging, and we have identified three causes of frequent failures in Spark that necessitate jobs to be restarted from scratch. First, the job runtime is very sensitive to the way the framework allocates the available memory during its execution. As a result, it may have variable performance across different applications depending on how much memory they are allowed to use for storage and for job execution [22]. A second cause is that several built-in operators (e.g., groupBy, join) require that all values for one key fit in the memory. This constraint is in sharp contrast with the design of the framework which only supports coarse-grained memory allocation (per worker). Finally, memory-hungry tasks that produce a large number of persistent objects that stay in memory during the task runtime result in expensive garbage collection [13].

Using checkpointing to improve fault tolerance has a long history in computer systems [25]. In particular, the most commonly used method for checkpointing high-performance computing applications is coordinated checkpointing, where an application *periodically* stops execution and writes its current state to an external stable storage system. As setting the optimal checkpointing interval has been acknowledged as a challenging problem [9], existing solutions require the failure rates and the checkpointing cost to be known upfront, and to be constant over time. These assumptions are unrealistic for data analytics frameworks, which typically run computations in multiple inter-dependent stages each of which generates an *intermediate dataset* that is used as input by other stages. According to several reports from production clusters [4], the sizes of the intermediate datasets may vary significantly across stages of a single job, and as a result they cannot be anticipated.

Checkpointing a task has resource implications which are important to consider. While a task may be quickly recovered from a checkpoint, occupying an extra slot to perform the checkpoint may increase the job runtime due to the high cost of reliably saving the task's output. To remedy this, we propose PANDA, a checkpointing system that carefully balances the opportunity cost of persisting a task's output to an external storage system and the time required to recompute when the task is lost. This opportunity cost is driven by the evidence of *unpredictable intermediate data sizes* and *outlier tasks* of jobs in production traces from Google and Facebook [4, 16], which form the basis of our checkpointing policies. Firstly, we propose the *greedy* policy that greedily selects tasks for checkpointing until a predefined budget is exceeded. Secondly, our *size-based* policy considers the longest tasks of a job because those tasks are more likely to delay the job completion if they are lost. Finally, we design the *resource-aware* policy that checkpoints tasks only if their recomputation cost is likely to exceed the cost of checkpointing it.

In this paper we make the following contributions:

(1) We design PANDA, a fine-grained checkpointing system that checkpoints tasks at stage boundaries by persisting

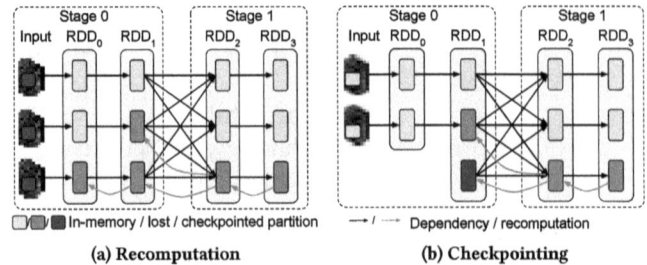

(a) Recomputation   (b) Checkpointing

Figure 2: An example of a lineage graph with data dependencies between RDD partitions. The recomputation tree of a missing partition in unmodified Spark (a) and in Spark with checkpointing (b). All lost partitions are located on a single machine and the input dataset is replicated in stable storage.

their output data to stable storage (Section 3). We reduce the checkpointing problem to a task selection problem and we incorporate into PANDA three policies designed from first principle analysis of traces from production clusters. These policies take into account the size of task output data, the distribution of task runtimes, or both (Section 4).

(2) With a set of experiments in a multicluster system, we analyze and compare the performance of our policies with single, failing applications under space-correlated failures (Section 5). With a set of large-scale simulations, mimicking the size and the operation of a Google cluster, we analyze the effectiveness of PANDA in reducing the average job runtime of a complete workload (Section 6).

2 SYSTEM MODEL

In this section we present the main abstractions used by Spark to perform both efficient and fault-tolerant in-memory data processing (Section 2.1). Furthermore, we describe the scheduling mechanism employed by Spark to execute parallel jobs on a cluster with many machines (Section 2.2).

2.1 Lineage Graphs

We explain the RDD data abstraction used by Spark to persist large datasets in the memory of multiple cluster machines and we discuss the notion of *lineage graph*, a fault-tolerant data structure that guards the framework against data loss when machine failures are expected.

Data analytics frameworks such as Spark [26] leverage the distributed memory of the cluster machines with a new abstraction called *resilient distributed datasets* (RDDs), which provides efficient data processing across a broad range of applications (SQL queries, graph processing, machine learning, and streaming). An RDD is a collection of *data partitions* distributed across a set of cluster machines. Users have access to a rich set of transformations (e.g., map, filter, join) to create RDDs from either data in stable storage (e.g., HDFS, S3) or other RDDs. Typically, such transformations are *coarse-grained* because they apply the same operation in parallel to each partition of the RDD.

RDDs may not be materialized in-memory at all times. Instead, Spark maintains the sequence of transformations needed to compute each RDD in a data structure called the *lineage graph*. In other words, the lineage graph is a directed acyclic graph (DAG) where a vertex represents an RDD partition and an incoming edge represents the transformation used to compute the RDD. Furthermore, Spark distinguishes two main types of data dependencies between RDDs: (1) the *narrow* dependency, in which each partition of the parent RDD is used by at most one partition of the child RDD (e.g., map, filter), and (2) the *wide* dependency, in which multiple child partitions may depend on the same parent partition (e.g., join, groupBy).

As RDDs are typically persisted in volatile memory without replicas, a machine failure causes the loss of all partitions that are located on it. Spark automatically recovers a missing partition by identifying in the lineage graph its *recomputation tree*, which is the minimum set of missing ancestor partitions and the dependencies among them needed to recover the partition. Thus, the *critical recomputation path* of a given partition is the sequence of partitions in its recomputation tree that determine the minimum time needed to recover the partition. In the worst case, the critical recomputation path may go back as far as the origin of the input data. Then, Spark applies for each missing partition the sequence of transformations in its recomputation tree according to the precedence constraints among them. As different partitions of the same RDD may have different recomputation trees, the recovery of a complete RDD typically results in recomputing a sub-DAG of the initial lineage graph.

To avoid long critical recomputation paths, Spark allows its users to *cut-off* the lineage graph through a *checkpointing* operation that reliably saves a complete RDD to stable storage. Checkpointing an RDD in Spark is similar to how Hadoop spills shuffle data to disk, thus trading off execution latency with fast recovery from failures. Figure 2 shows an example of a lineage graph for a simple Spark computation, with both narrow and wide dependencies between RDDs. The figure depicts the recovery of a missing partition by recomputing all its ancestors (a) and by reading an existing checkpoint (b).

Spark exposes a basic interface for checkpointing complete RDDs, but it is the user's decision to select which RDDs to checkpoint. As the intermediate RDD sizes are not known upfront, selecting RDDs statically, prior to the execution of an application, is difficult. Spark checkpoints a given RDD by creating a parallel job with tasks that save the RDD partitions from memory to stable storage. However, when the memory is fully utilized, Spark evicts RDD partitions using a *least-recently-used* (LRU) policy. This way of checkpointing RDDs is inefficient because it may trigger recomputations if some RDD partitions are evicted from memory.

2.2 DAG Scheduler

We present an overview of the scheduling architecture used by Spark to (re-)allocate compute slots to jobs that consist of multiple sets of tasks with precedence constraints among them.

To compute an RDD, Spark's scheduler creates a job by translating the RDD dependencies in the lineage graph into a DAG of *processing stages*. Each stage consists of a set of *parallel tasks* that apply the same operation (transformation) to compute independently each RDD partition. In this DAG, tasks pipeline as many transformations with narrow dependencies as possible, and so we identify *stage*

boundaries by transformations with wide dependencies. Such transformations typically require a *shuffle* operation, as illustrated in Figure 2. A shuffle operation splits the output partitions of each task in the *parent* stage into multiple shuffle files, one for each task in the *child* stage. Tasks in the child stage may only run once they have obtained all their shuffle files from the parent stage.

In order to compute an RDD, the scheduler executes tasks in successive stages on *worker* machines based on their precedence constraints (data dependencies), data locality preferences (run tasks closer to input data), or fairness considerations (per job quotas). Similarly to Dryad and MapReduce, Spark jobs are *elastic* (or *malleable*) and can run simultaneously, taking any resources (compute slots) they can get when it is their turn. The DAG scheduler in Spark schedules the tasks of a stage only after all its parent stages have generated their output RDDs. Scheduling tasks based on a strict queueing order such as *first-in-first-out* (FIFO) compromises locality, because the next task to schedule may not have its input data on the machines that are currently free. Spark achieves task locality through delay scheduling, in which a task waits for a limited amount of time for a free slot on a machine that has data for it.

Next, we present the main mechanisms that Spark uses to detect and to recover from worker failures. Similarly to other fault-tolerant cluster frameworks, Spark relies on timeouts and connection errors to infer worker failures. The scheduler expects heartbeats from its healthy *workers* every 10 seconds, and marks as lost a worker that has not sent any heartbeat for at least 1 minute. A dead worker not only leads to the failure of its running tasks, but also makes all previously computed work on that worker unavailable. As a consequence, tasks that fail to transfer data from a lost worker trigger fetch errors that may also serve as an early indication of a failure. Spark re-executes failed tasks as long as their stage's parents are still available. Otherwise, the scheduler resubmits tasks recursively in parent stages to compute the missing partitions.

3 DESIGN CONSIDERATIONS

In this section we identify three techniques for checkpointing in-memory data analytics jobs (Section 3.1). Moreover, we investigate the main properties of workloads from Facebook and Google that we use as first principles in the design of our checkpointing policies (Section 3.2). Finally, we propose a scheduling and checkpointing structure for automatic checkpointing of data analytics jobs (Section 3.3).

3.1 Checkpointing Tasks

The basic fault-tolerance mechanism used by data analytics frameworks to mitigate the impact of machine failures is to recompute lost data by repeating tasks based on their precedence constraints in the lineage graph. Obviously, this approach may be time-consuming for applications with large lineage graphs. Checkpointing the running tasks of a job to stable storage allows the job to only partially recompute data generated since the last checkpoint. However, checkpointing introduces an overhead proportional to the size of the data persisted to stable storage.

We identify different ways of checkpointing data analytics jobs. One way of doing so is to employ traditional checkpointing mechanisms available in operating systems that suspend the execution of running tasks and store their states for later resumption. In this

Table 1: The workload traces from two large production clusters at Facebook [4] and Google [16].

Trace	Facebook	Google
Dates	October 2010	May 2011
Duration (days)	45	29
Framework	Hadoop	Borg
Cluster size (machines)	600	12,000
Number of jobs	25,000	668,048
Task runtimes	No	**Yes**
Data sizes	**Yes**	No
Failed machines per hour	Unknown	7 to 25

method, checkpointing jobs is performed *at any point*, as opposed to the later two approaches. However, this process may degrade performance considerably and may trigger frequent machine reboots [11]. Tasks of in-memory data analytics jobs are allocated large heap sizes of multiple GBs, and so checkpointing their states is relatively slow. In addition, recovery from a checkpoint stored on another machine triggers additional network traffic, which may hurt the performance of other jobs in the cluster.

Another approach is to checkpoint tasks at *safe points* from where the remaining work can be executed without requiring any context from the current execution. At a higher level, tasks in data analytics jobs pipeline a sequence of narrow transformations between successive RDD partitions. Tasks split each RDD partition they process into a sequence of *non-overlapping subsets* each of which may have multiple records that share the same *key*. Thus, a natural way to checkpoint tasks for many transformations (e.g., map, reduce, join) is at key boundaries, when all the processing for a key is complete. This approach has been previously proposed in Amoeba [1], a system that aims at achieving true elasticity by trimming the durations of long task through checkpointing. However, because tracking such safe points in data analytics frameworks is notoriously difficult, as they typically require a global view of intermediate data, Amoeba originally supported only a small number of transformations in MapReduce frameworks and has not evolved since.

Finally, we can checkpoint tasks at *stage boundaries* by persisting their *output data* to stable storage. A stage boundary for a task is the point from where the output data is split into multiple shuffle files each of which aggregates input data for a single reducer. Shuffle files are written to the buffer cache, thus allowing the operating system to flush them to disk when the buffer capacity is exceeded. Because checkpointing shuffle files requires complex synchronization between multiple tasks that write sequentially to the same shuffle file, we perform checkpointing on the output data before splitting it into shuffle files. We choose this way of checkpointing because it integrates well with the lineage-based mechanism adopted by current frameworks. We need to recompute a task when either the machine on which it runs fails, or when (part of) the output it produced was located on a machine that fails and is still needed. Checkpointing tasks at stage boundaries helps only in the latter case. After checkpointing the output of a task completely, we no longer need to know how to compute or recover its input, and so we can cut-off its lineage graph.

3.2   Task Properties

Although there is a rich body of work that studies the characteristics of datacenter workloads [4, 16], not many public traces exist. The largest traces available are from the Hadoop production cluster

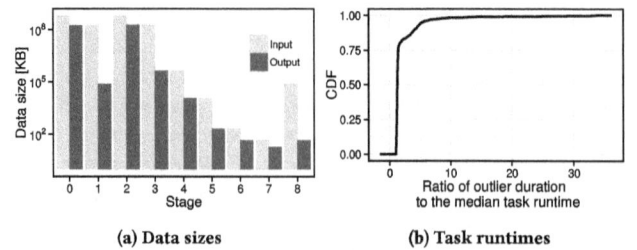

(a) Data sizes   (b) Task runtimes

Figure 3: The variability of the intermediate data sizes (a, vertical axis in log scale) and the prevalence of outliers (b) in the BTWORLD application.

at Facebook [4] and from Google's Borg resource manager [16]. Table 1 shows the relevant details of these traces. An investigation of these traces reveals that datacenter workloads are largely dominated by the presence of outlier tasks, and that the sizes of the intermediate data of jobs may be very variable. Although both traces are relatively old, it is unlikely that these task properties have changed since their collection. In this section we check their validity by analyzing the BTWORLD application [10], which we use to process *monitoring data* from the BitTorrent global network; this application is later described in Section 5.

Unlike a job's input size, which is known upfront, intermediate data sizes cannot be anticipated. Complex applications such as BTWORLD consist of many processing stages, out of which only a few require the complete input, while the others run on intermediate data. Figure 3a shows that there is no strong correlation between the input and output data sizes, and that the output sizes range from a few KB to hundreds of GB. We compute the stage selectivity, defined as the ratio of the output size and the input size, for each job in the Facebook trace. We find that the stage selectivities may span several orders of magnitude: a small fraction of the stages perform data transformations (selectivity of 1), while the large majority are either data compressions (selectivity less than 1) or data expansions (selectivity higher than 1).

In data analytics workloads, tasks may have inflated runtimes due to poor placement decisions (resource contention) or imbalance in the task workload (input data skew). Indeed, Figure 3b shows that 70% of the task outliers in the BTWORLD application have a uniform probability of being delayed between 1.5x and 3x the median task runtime. The distribution is heavy-tailed, with top 5% of the outliers running 10x longer than the median. Similarly, the tasks in the Google cluster are also very variable and fit well a heavy-tailed distribution (Pareto with shape parameter 1.3).

We use the large variability of the intermediate data sizes in the design of a *greedy* checkpointing policy, which employs a specified budget to avoid excessive checkpointing. Similarly, the prevalence of outliers forms the basis of a *size-based* checkpointing policy, which seeks to checkpoint the long running tasks in a job. Finally, we use both properties in a *resource-aware* checkpointing policy, which checkpoints tasks only when the cumulative cost of recomputing them is larger than the cost of checkpointing. In Section 4 we present the design of our policies starting from first principles, with all the features needed to perform well in a datacenter.

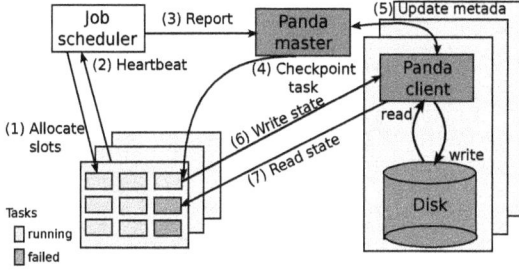

Figure 4: The system architecture for the PANDA checkpointing mechanism in data analytics frameworks.

3.3 Checkpointing Architecture

We present the main design elements and the operation of PANDA, an adaptive checkpointing system for in-memory data analytics jobs which integrates well with the architecture of current framework schedulers.

Figure 4 shows the architecture of a typical data analytics framework, with a cluster-wide *job scheduler* and a fault-tolerant *distributed filesystem* which coordinate the execution of tasks on a set of cluster machines with co-located processors and storage volumes (illustrated for simplicity as separate entities). The job scheduler handles the allocation of compute slots to numerous parallel tasks of a data analytics job with user-defined constraints (step 1) and waits for periodic heartbeats to keep track of the state of the running tasks (step 2). The distributed filesystem (e.g., HDFS in our deployment) employs a three-way replication policy for fault-tolerance and allows our system to *reliably persist* a data analytics job by saving its input, intermediate, or output datasets.

PANDA's architecture consists of a *checkpoint master* and a set of *clients* located at each cluster machine. The PANDA master is periodically updated by the job scheduler with progress reports of the running tasks (step 3). A progress report incorporates for each task the following properties: the amount of input/output data size read/written so far and the current task runtimes. The master's main role is to decide *when* to checkpoint running tasks and *which* among the running tasks of a job to checkpoint (step 4). To do so, PANDA employs one of the policies presented in Section 4.

The checkpoint master receives updates from clients with the location of each checkpoint in the reliable storage system and maintains a global mapping between every checkpointed partition and the dataset it belongs to (step 5). The PANDA clients access the distributed filesystem for saving and/or fetching partitions on behalf of the job (steps 6 and 7). Thus, before a task starts running, it first uses the PANDA client to retrieve from the checkpoint master the location of its checkpoint. The PANDA client fetches the checkpoint from the distributed filesystem so that the task gracefully resumes its execution from that point onwards. If the task was not previously checkpointed, it executes its work completely.

4 CHECKPOINTING POLICIES

We will now address the question of which subsets of tasks to checkpoint in order to improve the job performance under failures while keeping the overhead of checkpointing low. The policies we propose for this purpose may use the size of the task output data (GREEDY), the distribution of the task runtimes (SIZE), or both

Table 2: PANDA's policy framework for checkpointing in-memory data analytics jobs in datacenters.

Policy	Data size	Task runtime	Description
GREEDY	yes	no	fraction of the input data
SIZE	no	yes	longest tasks in the job
AWARE	yes	yes	checkpoint vs. recompute
PERIODIC	yes	no	every τ seconds

(AWARE). Furthermore, we use an adaptation of the widely known periodic checkpointing approach (PERIODIC) to data analytics frameworks that periodically checkpoints all completing tasks. In Table 2 we state the main differences between our policies.

Greedy checkpointing. Our GREEDY policy seeks to limit the checkpointing cost in every stage of a job in terms of the amount of data persisted to disk to a specified *budget*. Intuitively, we want to reduce the number of recomputations after a failure in a *best-effort* way by selecting in each stage as many tasks for checkpointing as the budget allows. The GREEDY policy sets the checkpointing budget of a stage to some fraction of the size of the total input data transferred to it from the tasks of its parent stages. This fraction may depend on the selectivities of the tasks of the stage—if the latter are low, the fraction can be small. For example, for the BTWORLD workflow with a median task selectivity of 0.1, it can be set to 10%.

The GREEDY policy is invoked for every stage of a job once all its parent stages have generated their output RDDs. It will then start checkpointing *any* completing task as long as it does not exceed the stage's budget. Tasks that are in the process of checkpointing when the budget is exceeded are allowed to complete their checkpoints.

Size-based checkpointing. Our SIZE policy aims to reduce the amount of work lost after a failure by checkpointing *straggler* tasks that run (much) slower than other tasks of the job. The main intuition behind the SIZE policy is to avoid recomputing time-consuming tasks that prevent pending tasks of the job from starting.

Straggler tasks in data analytics frameworks may be due to large variations in the *code* executed and the *size of the data* processed by tasks. Across all stages of the BTWORLD workflow, the coefficient of variation in task runtimes is 3.4. Although the code is the same for all tasks in each stage, it differs significantly across stages (e.g., map and reduce). Furthermore, the amount of data processed by tasks in the same stage may vary significantly due to limitations in partitioning the data evenly.

The SIZE policy now works in the following way. In order to differentiate straggler tasks, SIZE builds up from scratch for every running job a history with the durations of its finished tasks. Thus, at any point in time during the execution of a job, SIZE has an estimation of its median task runtime, which becomes more accurate as the job completes a larger fraction of its tasks. SIZE checkpoints only those tasks it considers stragglers, that is, tasks whose durations are at least some number of times (called the *task multiplier*) as high as the current estimation of the median task runtime.

Resource-aware checkpointing. The AWARE policy aims to checkpoint a task only if the estimated benefit of doing so outweighs the cost of checkpointing it. We explain below how the AWARE policy estimates both the recomputation and the checkpointing cost of a task, which is done after it has completed.

Prior to the execution of a job, AWARE sets the probability of failure by dividing the number of machines that experienced failures during a predefined time interval (e.g., a day) by the cluster size.

AWARE derives these data from the operation logs of the cluster that contain all machine failing events.

A machine failure may cause data loss, which may require recomputing a task if there are pending stages that need its output in order to run their tasks. However, the recomputation of a task may cascade into its parent stages if its inputs are no longer available and need to be recomputed in turn. We define the DAG level of a task as the length of the longest path in the lineage graph that needs to be recomputed to recover the task from a failure.

AWARE estimates the recomputation cost of a task as the product of the probability that the machine on which it ran fails and its *recovery time*, which is the actual cost of recomputing it, including the recursive recomputations if its recomputation cascades into its parent stages. When the input files of a lost task are still available, either in the memory of other machines or as checkpoints in stable storage, the recovery time is equal to the task runtime. If multiple input files of a task to be recomputed are lost, we assume that they can be recomputed in parallel, and we add the maximum recomputation cost among the lost tasks in its parent stages to its recovery time. We do this recursively as also input files of tasks in parent stages may be lost in turn.

The checkpointing cost of a task is a function of the amount of data that needs to be persisted, the write throughput achieved by the local disks the task is replicated on, and the contention on the stable storage caused by other tasks that are checkpointed at the same time. While the former two may be anticipated, the latter is highly variable and difficult to model accurately. In particular, checkpointing a task along with other tasks that require replicating large amounts of data to stable storage may inflate the checkpointing cost. In order to solve this problem, we propose the following method to approximate the checkpointing cost of a task in a given stage. When a stage starts, we artificially set the cost of checkpointing its tasks 0, thus making AWARE checkpoint the first few waves of tasks in order to build up a partial distribution of task checkpointing times. Then we let AWARE set the checkpointing cost of a task to the 95th percentile of this distribution, which is all the time adapted with the checkpointing times of the checkpointed tasks in the stage.

The AWARE policy now works in the following way. It is invoked whenever a stage becomes eligible for scheduling its tasks, and then, using the job's lineage graph, it estimates the recomputation costs of its tasks. We amortize the checkpointing cost of a task by its DAG level, so that tasks with long recomputation paths are more likely to be checkpointed. AWARE checkpoints only those tasks whose potential resource savings are strictly positive, that is, tasks whose recomputation costs exceed the amortized checkpointing cost.

5 EXPERIMENTAL SETUP

We evaluate the checkpointing policies described in Section 4 through experiments on the DAS multicluster system. In this section we present the cluster configuration and the data analytics benchmarks that we use to assess the performance of PANDA.

5.1 Cluster Setup

We have implemented PANDA in Spark and we evaluate our checkpointing policies on the fifth generation of the Dutch wide-area computer system DAS [7]. In our experiments we use DAS machines that have dual 8-core compute nodes, 64 GB memory, and two

Table 3: The cluster configurations for our applications.

Application	Benchmark	Nodes	Dataset	Input [GB]	Runtime [s]
BTWORLD	real-world	20	BitTorrent	600	1587
PPPQ	standard	20	TPC-H	600	1461
NMSQ	standard	20	TPC-H	600	656
PageRank	real-world	5	Random	1	128
KMeans	real-world	5	Random	10	103

4 TB disks, connected within the cluster through 64 Gbit/s FDR InfiniBand network. We perform experiments with two cluster configurations for long and short jobs with allocations of 20 and 5 machines, respectively.

We co-locate PANDA with an HDFS instance that we use to store the input datasets and the checkpoints performed by our policies. We setup the HDFS instance with a standard three-way replication scheme and a fixed data block size of 128 MB. We assume the HDFS instance runs without failures so that both the input datasets and the checkpoints are always available for PANDA.

We want to analyze the performance of typical data analytics applications under different patterns of *compute node failures*. Therefore, we consider Spark *worker failures*, which may cause loss of work already done that is stored in the local memory of the workers. We assume that new worker machines may be provisioned immediately to replace the lost workers, so that the size of our cluster remains constant during the execution of the application.

We clear the operating system buffer cache on all machines before each experiment, so that the input data is loaded from disk. To emulate a production environment with long-running processes, we warm up the JVM in all our experiments by running a full trial of the complete benchmark. For the experiments we show in Section 6, we report the mean over three executions.

5.2 Applications

In our evaluation we use a diverse set of applications ranging from real-world workflows to standard benchmarks that are representative for data analytics frameworks. Table 3 presents the configuration we use in our experiments for each job. We analyze the performance of PANDA with both long-running jobs that have durations in the order of tens of minutes (e.g., BTWORLD, PPPQ, and NMSQ) and short interactive jobs that take minutes to complete (e.g., PageRank and KMeans). We describe these jobs in turn.

BTWorld. The BTWORLD [21] application has observed since 2009 the evolution of the global-scale peer-to-peer system BitTorrent, where files are broken into hashed pieces and individually shared by users, whether they have completely downloaded the file or not. To help users connect to each other, BitTorrent uses trackers, which are centralized servers that give upon request lists of peers sharing a particular file. BTWORLD sends queries to public trackers of the BitTorrent system and so it collects statistics about the aggregated status of users. These statistics include for each *swarm* in the tracker (users who share the same torrent file) the number of *leechers* (users who own some but not all pieces of the file), the number of *seeders* (users who own all pieces of the file), and the total number of *downloads* since the creation of the torrent.

We have designed a MapReduce-based workflow [10] to answer several questions of interest to peer-to-peer analysts in order to understand the evolution over time of the BitTorrent system. The complete BTWORLD workflow seeks to understand the evolution of

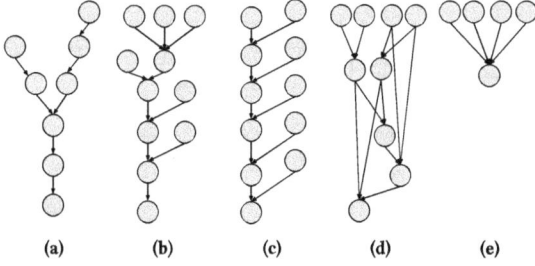

Figure 5: The data flow of BTWORLD **(a),** PPPQ **(b),** NMSQ **(c),** PageRank **(d), and KMeans (e) as a** DAG **of stages: the nodes and the edges represent the stages and the wide dependencies among them.**

each individual tracker we monitor, to determine the most popular trackers (over fixed time intervals and over the entire monitoring period), and to identify the number of new swarms created over time. In our experiments with PANDA, BTWORLD takes an input dataset of 600 GB. As we show in Figure 5a, the lineage graph of BTWORLD consists of a long chain of stages and a single join.

TPC-H. The TPC-H benchmark [2] consists of a suite of business oriented ad-hoc queries and concurrent data modifications. The queries and the dataset have been chosen to have broad industry-wide relevance while maintaining a sufficient degree of ease of implementation. This benchmark illustrates decision support systems that analyze large volumes of data, execute queries with high degrees of complexity, and give answers to critical business questions. The benchmark randomly generates eight relational tables with a schema that represents a typical data warehouse dealing with sales, customers, and suppliers. For a detailed description of the benchmark we refer to its standard specification [2].

We use two queries from this benchmark: the Potential Part Promotion Query (PPPQ) and the National Market Share Query (NMSQ). PPPQ seeks candidates for a promotional offer by selecting suppliers in a particular nation that have an excess of a given product – more than 50% of the products shipped in a given year for a given nation. NMSQ determines how the market share of a given nation within a given region has changed over two years for a given product. In our experiments we execute both queries with an input dataset of 600 GB. Figures 5b and 5c show the lineage graphs of both TPC-H queries that combine in almost every stage results from two or three parent stages.

PageRank. PageRank is the original graph-processing application used by the Google search engine to rank documents. PageRank runs multiple iterations over the same dataset and updates the rank of a document by adding the contributions of documents that link to it. On each iteration, a document sends its contribution of r_i/n_i to its neighbors, where r_i and n_i denote its rank and number of neighbors, respectively. Let c_{ij} denote the contribution received by a document i from its neighbor j. After receiving the contributions from its neighbors, a document i updates its rank to $r_i = (\alpha/N) + (1 - \alpha) \sum c_{ij}$, where N is the total number of documents and α a tuning parameter.

We use the optimized PageRank implementation from the graphx library of Spark with a 1 GB input dataset. We generate a random input graph with 50,000 vertices that has a log-normal out-degree distribution with parameters μ and σ set to 4 and 1.3, respectively.

Table 4: An overview of the experiments performed to evaluate PANDA.

Experiment	Jobs	Policies	Baselines	Failure pattern	Sec.
Parameters	BTWORLD PPPQ	all	none	none	6.1
Overhead	all	all	Spark	none	6.2
Machine failures	BTWORLD PPPQ NMSQ	all	Spark	space-correlated	6.3
Lineage length	PageRank KMeans	AWARE	Spark	single failure	6.4
Simulations	BTWORLD PPPQ PageRank	AWARE	Spark	space-correlated	6.5

In Figure 5d we show the lineage graph for a single iteration of PageRank. An interesting property of this application is that its lineage becomes longer with the number of iterations.

KMeans. Clustering aims at grouping subsets of entities with one another based on some notion of similarity. KMeans is one of the most commonly used clustering algorithms that clusters multidimensional data points into a predefined number of clusters. KMeans uses an iterative algorithm that alternates between two main steps. Given an initial set of means, each data point is assigned to the cluster whose mean yields the least *within-cluster sum of squares* (WCSS). In the update step, the new means that become the *centroids* of the data points in the new clusters are computed.

We use the optimized implementation from the mllib library of Spark with a 10 GB dataset that consists of 10 millions data points sampled from a 50-dimensional Gaussian distribution. Figure 5e shows that KMeans with four iterations has a relatively simple lineage graph, with a single shuffle operation that combines results from multiple stages that have narrow dependencies to the input dataset.

6 EXPERIMENTAL EVALUATION

In this section we present the results of five sets of experiments that each address a separate aspect of the performance of PANDA. Table 4 presents an overview of these experiments. We investigate the setting of the parameters in GREEDY, SIZE, and AWARE (Section 6.1). We measure the checkpointing overhead to determine how far we are from the default Spark implementation without checkpointing (Section 6.2). Thereafter, we evaluate the performance of our policies under various patterns of space-correlated failures (Section 6.3). Moreover, we assess the impact of the length of the lineage graph on the performance of PANDA when failures are expected (Section 6.4). Finally, we perform simulations to evaluate the benefit of checkpointing at larger scale (Section 6.5).

6.1 Setting the Parameters

All our policies have parameters needed in order to operate in a real environment. In particular, GREEDY and SIZE use the checkpointing budget and the task multiplier, respectively. In contrast with these policies that both set workload-specific parameters, AWARE sets the probability of failure that quantifies the reliability of the machines, and so it is independent of the workload properties. In this section we seek to find good values of these parameters.

One way of setting the parameters for GREEDY and SIZE is to evaluate the performance of each policy for a range of parameter values with various failure patterns. However, this method is

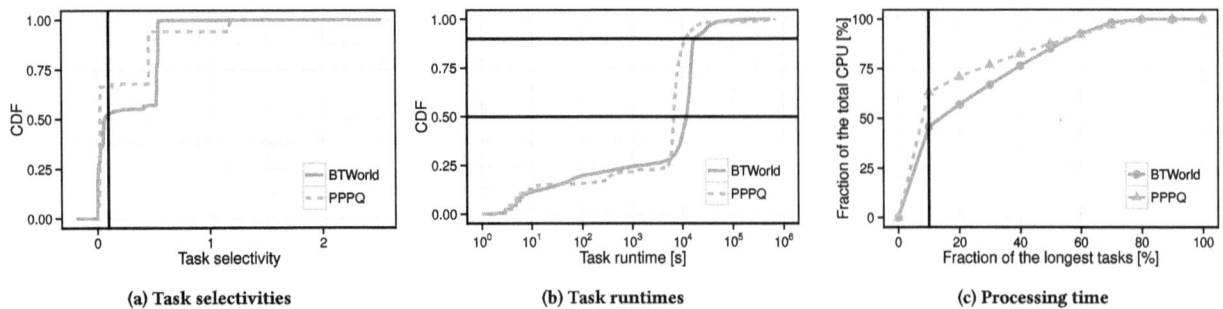

(a) Task selectivities   **(b) Task runtimes**   **(c) Processing time**

Figure 6: The distributions of the task selectivity (a) and the task runtime (b) for BTWORLD and PPPQ, and the fraction of the total CPU time versus the fraction of the longest tasks in BTWORLD and PPPQ (c). The vertical lines represent the task selectivity of 0.1 (a) and the longest 10% tasks (c), and the horizontal lines represent the median and the 90th percentile of the task runtimes (b).

time-consuming, and may in practice have to be repeated often. To remove the burden of performing sensitivity analysis for each policy, we propose two simple rules of thumb based on the history of job executions in production clusters and in our DAS multicluster system. We show in Sections 6.2 through 6.5 that our policies perform well with these rules.

The GREEDY *policy sets the checkpointing budget to the median selectivity of the tasks across all jobs that we use in our experiments.* The checkpointing budget limits the amount of data that is replicated to HDFS in each stage. We expect GREEDY to have a large overhead when setting the checkpointing budget to a large value. In Section 3.2 we have shown that in the Facebook production cluster, a large majority of tasks have relatively low selectivities. Figure 6a shows the distributions of the task selectivity in BTWORLD and PPPQ. Because the median task selectivity is below 0.1 for both jobs, we set the checkpointing budget in our experiments with GREEDY to 10%.

The SIZE *policy sets the task multiplier to the ratio of the 90th percentile and the median of the runtimes of the tasks across all jobs that we use in our experiments.* The task multiplier aims at identifying the longest tasks in a job, and so setting a small value may result in checkpointing a large fraction of tasks. As we have shown in Section 3.2, this is unlikely to happen for data analytics jobs because they typically run tasks that have heavy-tailed durations. Figure 6c shows that only 10% of tasks in BTWORLD and PPPQ account for roughly 50% of the total processing time of the job. As Figure 6b shows, the ratio of the 90th percentile and the median of the distribution of task runtimes for both BTWORLD and PPPQ is 1.5. Thus, we set the task multiplier in our experiments with SIZE to 1.5.

Unlike the previous two policies, which both require an analysis of task properties, the AWARE policy only needs as parameter the likelihood of being hit by a failure. We want AWARE to checkpoint more tasks as it operates on less reliable machines and vice versa. In order to highlight the checkpointing overhead and the performance of AWARE in unfavorable conditions, we assume that all machines allocated to execute our jobs experienced failures. Thus, we set the probability of failure in our experiments with AWARE to 1.

Finally, in order to show the improvements provided by our policies relative to the traditional way of checkpointing, in our experiments with the PERIODIC policy we set the optimal checkpointing interval based on Young's approximation for each application. To

do so, our version of the PERIODIC policy requires an estimation of the checkpointing cost and the mean time to failure. Thus, we assume that we know prior to the execution of each job both its checkpointing cost and the failure time.

6.2 The Impact of the Checkpointing Overhead

Spark has been widely adopted because it leverages memory-locality, and so it achieves significant speedup relative to Hadoop. Because checkpointing typically trades-off performance for reliability, we want to evaluate how far the performance of PANDA is from the performance of unmodified Spark when it runs on reliable machines. In this section we evaluate the overhead due to checkpointing tasks in PANDA relative to the performance of unmodified Spark without failures and without checkpointing.

Unlike previous approaches to checkpointing that typically save periodically the intermediate state of an application, PANDA reduces the checkpointing problem to a task selection problem. Therefore, we first want to assess how selective our policies are in picking their checkpointing tasks. To this end, in Figure 7a we show the number of tasks that are checkpointed by each policy for all applications. We find that GREEDY is rather aggressive in checkpointing tasks, while SIZE is the most conservative policy. In particular, we observe that with the GREEDY policy, PANDA checkpoints between 26-51% of the running tasks in our applications. Further, because the SIZE policy targets only the outliers, it checkpoints at most 10% of the running tasks for all applications. Similarly to SIZE, our adaptation of the PERIODIC policy checkpoints relatively small fractions of tasks for all applications.

Because AWARE balances the recomputation and the checkpointing costs for each task, the number of checkpointing tasks is variable across different jobs. We observe that for jobs that have relatively small intermediate datasets such as NMSQ and PageRank, AWARE checkpoints roughly 40% of the tasks. However, for BTWORLD and PPPQ, which both generate large amounts of intermediate data, AWARE is more conservative in checkpointing and so it selects roughly 20% of the tasks.

PANDA assumes the presence of an HDFS instance to persist its checkpoints that is permanently available. Running many large applications in a cluster may lead to significant amount of storage space used by PANDA. In Figure 7b we show the amount of data

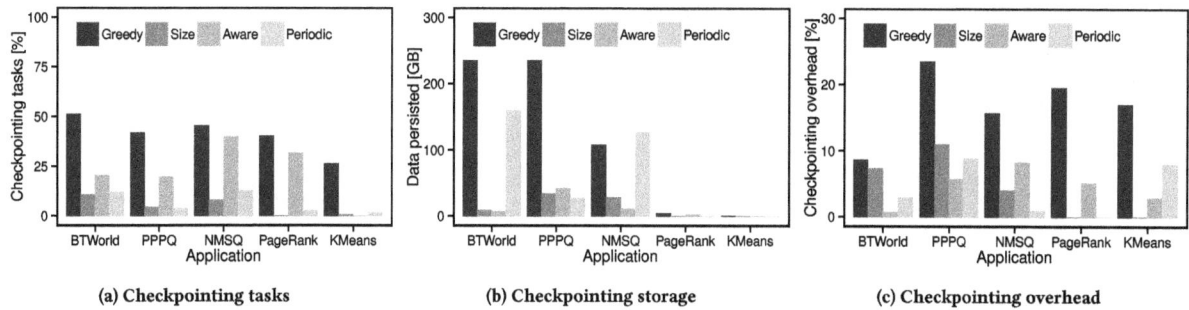

(a) Checkpointing tasks   (b) Checkpointing storage   (c) Checkpointing overhead

Figure 7: The fraction of checkpointing tasks (a), the amount of data persisted to HDFS (b), and the checkpointing overhead (c) with all our policies. The baseline is unmodified Spark.

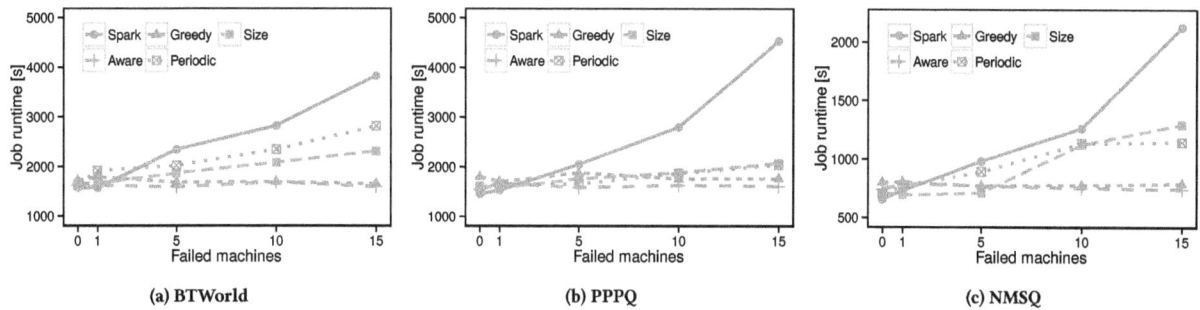

(a) BTWorld   (b) PPPQ   (c) NMSQ

Figure 8: The job runtime versus the number of failures with all our policies for BTWORLD, PPPQ, and NMSQ. The baseline is Spark with its default lineage-based recomputation.

persisted by our policies in each application. We find that GREEDY checkpoints significantly more data than both SIZE and AWARE for all applications. In particular, GREEDY replicates 30 times as much data as SIZE and AWARE with BTWORLD. To perform the checkpoints of all four applications, GREEDY requires a storage space of 1.8 TB (including replicas), whereas SIZE and AWARE require 212 GB and 190 GB, respectively. We also find that despite being rather conservative in selecting its checkpointing tasks, the PERIODIC policy requires a storage space of 1 TB.

Finally, we assess the checkpointing overhead of our policies as a percentage increase in the job runtime relatively to a vanilla version of Apache Spark (see Table 4). Figure 7c shows the checkpointing overhead for all four applications. GREEDY suffers significant performance degradation and its checkpointing overhead may be as high as 20%. However, both SIZE and AWARE incur less than 10% overhead, and so they are very close to the performance of Spark without checkpointing. This result can be explained by what is the main difference between our policies. Whereas GREEDY checkpoints tasks in a best-effort way, both SIZE and AWARE employ more conservative ways of selecting checkpointing tasks based on outliers or cost-benefit analysis. Further, because PERIODIC performs its checkpoints at fixed intervals during the application runtime, the contention on the HDFS is relatively low at all times. As a consequence, although PERIODIC checkpoints significantly more data than both SIZE and AWARE, they all have similar overheads.

We conclude that both SIZE and AWARE deliver very good performance and they are close to the performance of Spark without checkpointing. These policies are very selective when picking

checkpointing tasks, they use relatively small storage space to persist the output data of tasks, and they incur a checkpointing overhead that is usually below 10%.

6.3 The Impact of the Machine Failures

Space-correlated failures, defined as groups of machine failures that occur at the same time across the datacenter, have been frequently reported in large-scale systems such as grids and clusters [17], and more recently in datacenters [16]. Therefore, in this section, we evaluate the performance of PANDA under space-correlated failures. To this end, we report in Figure 8 the job runtime with and without our checkpointing policies for a range of concurrent failures that occur in the last processing stage of our BTWORLD, PPPQ, and NMSQ applications. As a hint of reading this figure, the values at 0 machine failures represent the job runtimes with our policies and with Spark when the job completes without experiencing failures.

Without checkpointing, the recomputation time due to failures causes a significant performance degradation for the entire range of concurrent failures. We observe that the job runtime in unmodified Spark increases linearly with the number of concurrent failures for all applications. For example, when only 25% of the cluster size is lost due to failures, the job runtime increases by 48% for BTWORLD, and by 40% for the two TPC-H queries. For the stress test we consider with 15 out of 20 machines that fail, Spark delivers very poor performance with all applications completing between 2.5 and 3 times as slow as when no failures occur.

Figure 8 also shows that all our checkpointing policies deliver very good performance for the complete range of failures. Both

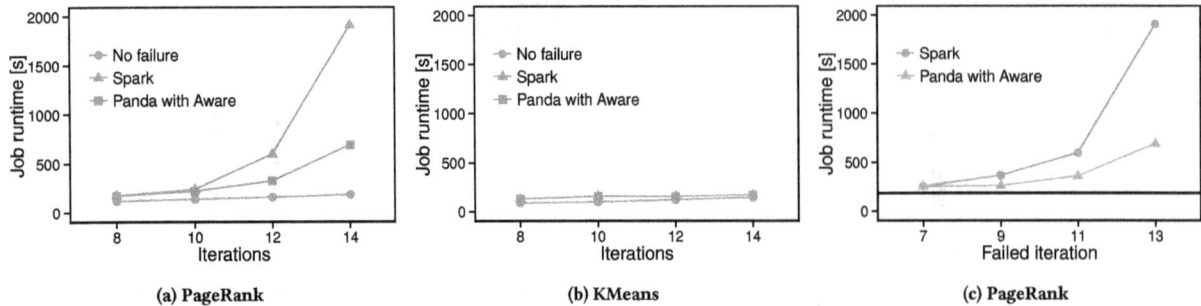

Figure 9: The job runtime when a single machine fails before the job completes for PageRank and KMeans with different numbers of iterations (a), (b), and the job runtime when a single machine fails in a given iteration for PageRank with 14 iterations (the horizontal line represents the job runtime without failures in unmodified Spark c).

GREEDY and AWARE provide constant runtimes irrespective of the number of failures for all applications. The reason for this result is that they cut-off the lineage graph at key stages, thus avoiding recomputing previously completed work. We also observe that AWARE performs slightly better than GREEDY because it introduces a lower checkpointing overhead, as we have shown in Figure 7. SIZE also reduces the impact of failures, but the job runtime still increases linearly with the number of failures. However, SIZE performs at its best and gets very close to the performance of GREEDY and AWARE for jobs such as PPPQ that have outlier tasks with very long durations. In particular, we have shown in Figure 6c that in PPPQ only 10% of the tasks account for more than 60% of the total processing time. Further, we find that PERIODIC has poor performance for BTWORLD, but its performance is very close to the performance of SIZE for the two TPC-H queries.

We conclude that our policies outperform unmodified Spark for any number of space-correlated failures. While both GREEDY and AWARE provide constant job runtimes for the complete range of machine failures, AWARE is our best policy because it introduces a much lower overhead than GREEDY.

6.4 The Impact of the Lineage Length

Although Spark may use the job lineage graph to recover lost RDD partitions after a failure, such recovery may be time-consuming for jobs such as PageRank that have relatively long lineage chains with many wide dependencies (see its DAG in Figure 5d). Conversely, applications such as KMeans, in which narrow dependencies prevail, may be recovered relatively fast from data in stable storage (see its DAG in Figure 5e). In this section we seek to highlight the impact of the lineage graph structure on the job runtime with and without checkpointing in the presence of a single machine failure that occurs at different moments during the job execution.

Figures 9a and 9b show the differences in performance of PANDA with the AWARE policy on the job runtime when a single machine fails before the job completes for different numbers of iterations of PageRank and KMeans. We observe that PageRank completes relatively fast for Spark without failures for the complete range of iterations from 8 to 14. However, the performance of PageRank degrades significantly even when a single failure perturbs the last iteration of the job. In particular, the job runtime is 11 times as large

as the fail free execution in Spark for PageRank with 14 iterations. Because PageRank requires many shuffle operations, a machine failure may result in the loss of some fraction of data from each parent RDD, thus requiring a long chain of recomputations. Figure 9a also shows that PANDA with the AWARE policy performs very well and bounds the recomputation time for any number of iterations. Not only does PANDA complete the job four times as fast as the recomputation-based approach in Spark, its performance is also very close to the performance of Spark without failures.

Unlike PageRank, which suffers significantly from failures, we show in Figure 9b that KMeans is rather insensitive to faulty machines and that Spark is less than 5% off the fail-free execution for any number of iterations. The reason for this result can be explained by what is the main difference between the lineage graphs of PageRank and KMeans. As we have shown in Section 5.2, the length of the PageRank lineage graph is proportional to the number of iterations of the job, and so the amount of recomputations triggered by a single failure grows significantly for jobs with many iterations. In contrast with PageRank, KMeans has a much simpler lineage graph, with many narrow dependencies followed by a shuffle, and so its length remains constant irrespective of the number of iterations. As a consequence, checkpointing KMeans is not worthwhile, because these narrow dependencies may be quickly recovered from stable storage. However, because our AWARE policy avoids checkpointing stages that are one hop away from the input dataset, we observe that its operation falls back to default Spark in the case of KMeans.

Finally, Figure 9c shows the results of experiments in which a single machine fails at different moments during the job execution for PageRank with 14 iterations. In general, we observe that Spark performs well when the failure occurs in the early stages of the job. However, it delivers poor performance when the time of failure is closer to the job completion time. We find that PANDA is effective in reducing the recovery time and outperforms Spark irrespective of the time of failure.

We conclude that applications such as PageRank that have many wide dependencies are good candidates for checkpointing, while machine learning applications such as KMeans may be recovered with relatively small recomputation cost. Furthermore, we have shown that PANDA performs very well for lineage graphs in which the recomputation cost is excessive irrespective of the time of failure.

Table 5: The distribution of job types in our simulated workload.

Application	Total nodes	Failed nodes	Scale	Runtime [s]	Jobs [%]
BTWORLD	20	5	1.0	1587	16
	20	5	5.0	7935	5
	20	5	10.0	15870	5
PPPQ	20	5	1.0	1461	16
	20	5	5.0	7305	5
	20	5	10.0	14610	5
PageRank (14 iterations)	5	1	1.0	185	16
	5	1	5.0	925	16
	5	1	10.0	1850	16

6.5 The Impact of the Failure Pattern

So far, we have evaluated different aspects of the operation of PANDA with single applications that experience space-correlated failures at a certain time during their execution. We have shown that our policies deliver very good performance with relatively small checkpointing overhead. However, it is not clear whether the improvements hold for a long-running system when multiple jobs receive service in the cluster only a fraction of which experience failures. Thus, we want to evaluate the improvement in the average job runtime achieved by AWARE for a complete workload relative to unmodified Spark.

We have built our own simulator in order to evaluate the impact of the frequency of failures on the overall improvement of PANDA with the AWARE policy. We simulate the execution of a 3-day workload on a 10,000-machine cluster (similar to the size of the Google cluster discussed in Section 1). We perform simulations at a higher-level than the earlier single-application experiments, and so we use the overall job durations (with or without failures) from experiments rather than simulating the execution of separate tasks.

In our event-based simulator, jobs are submitted according to a Poisson process and they are serviced by a FIFO scheduler. The scheduler allocates to each job a fixed number of machines which are released only after the job completes. Although the Google trace consists of mostly short jobs in the order of minutes, the longest jobs may take hours or even days to complete. To generate a similar realistic workload, we scale up the durations of our jobs by different scaling factors as shown in Table 5. Table 5 also shows the distribution of the job types in our workload. In particular, 80% of the jobs complete within 30 minutes (short jobs), whereas the durations of the remaining jobs exceed 2 h (long jobs).

In order to reuse the results from the experiments, we create the following failure pattern. We assume that failures occur according to a Poisson process that may hit every job at most once. Each failure in our simulation is a space-correlated failure event that triggers the failure of 5 machines. Table 5 shows for every job in our workload the number of failed machines when it is hit by a failure event. In particular, a failure event may hit a single BTWORLD query, a single PPPQ query, or 5 different PageRank jobs. To simulate the execution of a job that is hit by a failure we replace the job runtime given in Table 5 by the job runtime shown in Figure 8 or 9 multiplied by the job's scaling factor. Our assumption here is that both the checkpointing overheads and the improvements in the job runtime achieved by AWARE hold irrespective of the scaling factor of the job. Similarly to the experiments we performed on the DAS, we report averages over three simulations.

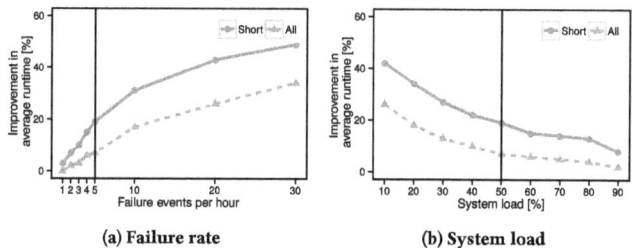

(a) Failure rate　　　　　(b) System load

Figure 10: The improvement achieved by PANDA with the AWARE policy for short jobs and for the complete workload under a system load of 50% versus the failure rate (a), and for a failure rate of 5 versus the system load (b).

Figure 10a shows the results of the simulations for different values of the failure rate under a system load of 50%, which is the average utilization of the Google cluster. PANDA provides significant gains when machines are more likely to fail but may not be worthwhile when failures occur rarely. Intuitively, jobs are more likely to be hit by failures when the failure rate is high. In particular, the fraction of failed jobs increases from 0.7% to 24% when the failure rate increases from 1 to 30 failure events per hour. We find that PANDA with AWARE reduces the average job runtime with 34% relative to the execution in unmodified Spark when the failure rate is 30 per hour. However, PANDA stops being beneficial when the cluster experiences less than one failure event per hour. Furthermore, Figure 10a shows that the improvement for short jobs is significantly higher than the overall improvement for our workload. For example, for a failure rate of 5, which is equivalent to the maximum failure rate in the Google cluster (see Table 1), short jobs improve by 19% on average, whereas the overall improvement is only 7%.

Finally, in Figure 10b we show the results of the simulations for different values of the system load when 5 failure events are expected every hour. We find that PANDA provides significant improvements over the complete range of system loads, but becomes less beneficial under high loads. The intuition of this result is that failed jobs account for larger fractions of the total number of jobs when the system load is low. In particular, the fraction of failed jobs decreases from 18% to 2.5% when the system load increases from 10% to 90%.

7 RELATED WORK

Checkpointing has traditionally been very important in high-performance computing (HPC) systems, but has lately also received quite some attention for data analytics frameworks.

BlobCR [14] seeks to efficiently capture and roll-back the state of scientific HPC applications in public clouds. Recent work [9] analyzed practical methods for optimizing the checkpointing interval using real-world failure logs. Multi-level checkpointing [6] aims at reducing the overhead of checkpointing in large-scale platforms by setting different levels of checkpoints each of which has its own overhead and recovery capability. An adaptive checkpointing scheme with work migration [24] has been developed to minimize the cost of running applications on resources from spot markets. Similar techniques that aim to reduce the checkpointing overhead of the naive periodic checkpointing policy exploit the temporal locality in failures [19].

Closest to our work, TR-Spark [23] and Flint [18] propose checkpointing policies for data analytics applications that run on transient resources which are typically instable, but not necessarily due to faults. In particular, TR-Spark employs cycle-scavenging to leverage such transient resources which are kept idle as a resource buffer by cloud providers and may be revoked due to load spikes. TR-Spark takes a statistical approach to prioritize tasks that have a high probability of being completed before the resources where they run are revoked and to checkpoint data blocks that are likely to be lost before they are processed by the next processing stages. To do so, TR-Spark requires both the distribution of the task runtimes and the distribution of the inter-arrival failure time for each resource allocated to the framework. Similarly, Flint provisions instances available on the spot market which have relatively low prices and may be revoked due to price spikes. Flint supports RDD-level checkpointing using an adaptation of the periodic checkpointing policy to data analytics applications. In contrast, PANDA targets a datacenter environment where applications may suffer from outright node failures and proposes a more comprehensive set of task-level checkpointing policies that take into account not only the lineage structure of the applications, but also workload properties such as the task runtimes and the intermediate data sizes.

8 CONCLUSIONS

The wide adoption of in-memory data analytics frameworks is motivated by their ability to process large datasets efficiently while sharing data across computations at memory speed. However, failures in datacenters may cause long recomputations that degrade the performance of jobs executed by such frameworks. In this paper we have presented PANDA, a checkpointing system for improving the resilience of in-memory data analytics frameworks that reduces the checkpointing problem to a task selection problem. We have designed three checkpointing policies starting from first principles, using the size of the task output data (GREEDY), the distribution of the task runtimes (SIZE), or both (AWARE). The GREEDY policy employs a best-effort strategy by selecting as many tasks for checkpointing as a predefined budget allows. The SIZE policy checkpoints only straggler tasks that run much slower than other tasks of the job. The AWARE policy checkpoints a task only if the cost of recomputing it exceeds the time needed to persist its output to stable storage.

With a set of experiments on a multicluster system, we have analyzed and compared these policies when applied to single failing applications. We have found that our policies outperform both unmodified Spark and the standard periodic checkpointing approach. We have also analyzed the performance of PANDA with the AWARE policy by means of simulations using a complete workload and the failure rates from a production cluster at Google. We have found that PANDA is beneficial for a long-running system and can significantly reduce the average job runtime relative to unmodified Spark. In particular, the SIZE policy delivers good performance when the failure rate (fraction of failed machines per day) is relatively low (less than 6%). Although both GREEDY and AWARE turn out to provide significant improvements for a large range of failure rates (more than 6%), AWARE is our best policy because it introduces a

much lower overhead than GREEDY. However, when the datacenter is prone to failures of complete racks, the rather aggressive checkpointing strategy of the GREEDY policy may be worthwhile.

9 ACKNOWLEDGMENT

This research was supported by the Dutch national program COMMIT.

REFERENCES

[1] Ganesh Ananthanarayanan, Christopher Douglas, Raghu Ramakrishnan, Sriram Rao, and Ion Stoica. 2012. True Elasticity in Multi-tenant Data-intensive Compute Clusters. ACM SoCC (2012).
[2] TPC Benchmarks. 2016. http://www.tpc.org. (2016).
[3] CERN. 2016. http://wlcg-public.web.cern.ch/. (2016).
[4] Yanpei Chen, Archana Ganapathi, Rean Griffith, and Randy Katz. 2011. The Case for Evaluating MapReduce Performance using Workload Suites. IEEE Mascots (2011).
[5] Jeff Dean. 2009. Designs, Lessons and Advice from Building Large Distributed Systems. Keynote from LADIS (2009).
[6] Sheng Di, Yves Robert, Frédéric Vivien, and Franck Cappello. 2017. Toward an Optimal Online Checkpoint Solution under a Two-Level HPC Checkpoint Model. IEEE TPDS 28, 1 (2017).
[7] Distributed ASCI Supercomputer. 2015. http://www.cs.vu.nl/das5. (2015).
[8] Catalin L Dumitrescu, Ioan Raicu, and Ian Foster. 2005. Experiences in Running Workloads over Grid3. Grid and Cooperative Computing (2005).
[9] Nosayba El-Sayed and Bianca Schroeder. 2014. Checkpoint/Restart in Practice: When Simple is Better. IEEE Cluster (2014).
[10] Tim Hegeman, Bogdan Ghit, Mihai Capota, Jan Hidders, Dick Epema, and Alexandru Iosup. 2013. The BTWorld Use Case for Big Data Analytics: Description, MapReduce Logical Workflow, and Empirical Evaluation. IEEE Big Data (2013).
[11] Michael Isard. 2007. Autopilot: Automatic Data Center Management. ACM SIGOPS Operating Systems Review 41, 2 (2007).
[12] Bahman Javadi, Derrick Kondo, Alexandru Iosup, and Dick Epema. 2013. The Failure Trace Archive: Enabling the Comparison of Failure Measurements and Models of Distributed Systems. Elsevier JPDC 73, 8 (2013).
[13] Zhaolei Liu and TS Eugene Ng. 2017. Leaky Buffer: A Novel Abstraction for Relieving Memory Pressure from Cluster Data Processing Frameworks. IEEE TPDS 28, 1 (2017).
[14] Bogdan Nicolae and Franck Cappello. 2011. BlobCR: Efficient Checkpoint-Restart for HPC Applications on IaaS Clouds using Virtual Disk Image Snapshots. ACM Supercomputing (2011).
[15] Kay Ousterhout, Ryan Rasti, Sylvia Ratnasamy, Scott Shenker, Byung-Gon Chun, and VMware ICSI. 2015. Making Sense of Performance in Data Analytics Frameworks. USENIX NSDI (2015).
[16] Charles Reiss, Alexey Tumanov, Gregory R Ganger, Randy H Katz, and Michael A Kozuch. 2012. Heterogeneity and dynamicity of clouds at scale: Google trace analysis. ACM SoCC (2012).
[17] Bianca Schroeder and Garth Gibson. 2010. A Large-Scale Study of Failures in High-Performance Computing Systems. IEEE TDSC 7, 4 (2010).
[18] Prateek Sharma, Tian Guo, Xin He, David Irwin, and Prashant Shenoy. 2016. Flint: Batch-Interactive Data-Intensive Processing on Transient Servers. ACM EuroSys (2016).
[19] Devesh Tiwari, Saurabh Gupta, and Sudharshan S Vazhkudai. 2014. Lazy Checkpointing: Exploiting Temporal Locality in Failures to Mitigate Checkpointing Overheads on Extreme-Scale Systems. IEEE/IFIP DSN (2014).
[20] Kashi Venkatesh Vishwanath and Nachiappan Nagappan. 2010. Characterizing Cloud Computing Hardware Reliability. ACM SoCC (2010).
[21] Maciej Wojciechowski, Mihai Capotă, Johan Pouwelse, and Alexandru Iosup. 2010. BTWorld: Towards Observing the Global BitTorrent File-Sharing Network. ACM HPDC (2010).
[22] Luna Xu, Min Li, Li Zhang, Ali R Butt, Yandong Wang, and Zane Zhenhua Hu. 2016. MEMTUNE: Dynamic Memory Management for In-memory Data Analytic Platforms. IEEE IPDPS (2016).
[23] Ying Yan, Yanjie Gao, Yang Chen, Zhongxin Guo, Bole Chen, and Thomas Moscibroda. 2016. TR-Spark: Transient Computing for Big Data Analytics. ACM SoCC (2016).
[24] Sangho Yi, Artur Andrzejak, and Derrick Kondo. 2012. Monetary Cost-Aware Checkpointing and Migration on Amazon Cloud Spot Instances. IEEE TSC 5, 4 (2012).
[25] John W Young. 1974. A First Order Approximation to the Optimum Checkpoint Interval. Comm. of the ACM 17, 9 (1974).
[26] Matei Zaharia, Reynold S Xin, Patrick Wendell, Tathagata Das, Michael Armbrust, Ankur Dave, Xiangrui Meng, Josh Rosen, Shivaram Venkataraman, Michael J Franklin, and others. 2016. Apache Spark: A Unified Engine for Big Data Processing. Comm. of the ACM 59, 11 (2016).

LetGo: A Lightweight Continuous Framework for HPC Applications Under Failures

Bo Fang
Electrical and Computer Engineering
University of British Columbia
bof@ece.ubc.ca

Qiang Guan
Ultrascale System Research Center
Los Alamos National Laboratory
qguan@lanl.gov

Nathan Debardeleben
Ultrascale System Research Center
Los Alamos National Laboratory
ndebard@lanl.gov

Karthik Pattabiraman
Electrical and Computer Engineering
University of British Columbia
karthikp@ece.ubc.ca

Matei Ripeanu
Electrical and Computer Engineering
University of British Columbia
matei@ece.ubc.ca

ABSTRACT

Requirements for reliability, low power consumption, and performance place complex and conflicting demands on the design of high-performance computing (HPC) systems. Fault-tolerance techniques such as checkpoint/restart (C/R) protect HPC applications against hardware faults. These techniques, however, have non negligible overheads particularly when the fault rate exposed by the hardware is high: it is estimated that in future HPC systems, up to 60% of the computational cycles/power will be used for fault tolerance.

To mitigate the overall overhead of fault-tolerance techniques, we propose *LetGo*, an approach that attempts to continue the execution of a HPC application when crashes would otherwise occur. Our hypothesis is that a class of HPC applications have good enough intrinsic fault tolerance so that its possible to re-purpose the default mechanism that terminates an application once a crash-causing error is signalled, and instead attempt to repair the corrupted application state, and continue the application execution. This paper explores this hypothesis, and quantifies the impact of using this observation in the context of checkpoint/restart (C/R) mechanisms.

Our fault-injection experiments using a suite of five HPC applications show that, on average, LetGo is able to elide 62% of the crashes encountered by applications, of which 80% result in correct output, while incurring a negligible performance overhead. As a result, when LetGo is used in conjunction with a C/R scheme, it enables significantly higher efficiency thereby leading to faster time to solution.

ACM acknowledges that this contribution was authored or co-authored by an employee, or contractor of the national government. As such, the Government retains a nonexclusive, royalty-free right to publish or reproduce this article, or to allow others to do so, for Government purposes only. Permission to make digital or hard copies for personal or classroom use is granted. Copies must bear this notice and the full citation on the first page. Copyrights for components of this work owned by others than ACM must be honored. To copy otherwise, distribute, republish, or post, requires prior specific permission and/or a fee. Request permissions from permissions@acm.org.
HPDC '17, June 26-30, 2017, Washington, DC, USA
© 2017 ACM. 978-1-4503-4699-3/17/06...$15.00
DOI: http://dx.doi.org/10.1145/3078597.3078609

1 INTRODUCTION

Transient hardware faults, caused by particle strikes and cosmic rays, have become one of the major concerns for current high-performance computing (HPC) systems [51]. Today's large HPC systems have a mean-time between failure (MTBF) of tens of hours [30], even with hardware- and software-based protection techniques employed together. As the hardware feature sizes shrink and the complexity of the HPC systems increase, the failure rate is expected to further increase, which mandates that a larger portion of computation cycles are used for fault tolerance [15].

Transient hardware faults (i.e., bit flips) often result in application crashes, due to the runtime system detecting the error and terminating the application, thereby losing the application's work. Checkpoint/restart (C/R) is one of the most popular methods to recover from such faults [19, 54, 55] by loading a previously saved intermediate state of the application (i.e., a checkpoint), and restarting the execution. While useful, checkpoint/restart techniques incur high overheads in terms of performance, energy and memory, which will be exacerbated as the failure rate increases [13, 58].

This paper proposes LetGo, which upon detecting an impending crash, attempts to repair the application state to enable it to continue its execution (instead of recovering from a checkpoint). LetGo is based on three observations. First, a large class of HPC applications are, intrinsically, resilient to localized numerical perturbations as they require computation results to converge over time. As a result, they are able to mask some data corruptions. For example, Casas et al. [7] show that the algebraic multi-grid (AMG) solver, which is based on iterative methods, has high intrinsic resiliency. Second, many HPC applications have application-specific acceptance checks (e.g., based on energy conservation laws). These checks can be used to filter out obvious deviations in the application's output, and reduce the probability of producing incorrect results. For example, High Performance Linpack (HPL) solves a linear system using LU decomposition [46] and tests the correctness of the result by checking the residual of the linear system as a norm-wise backward error [29, 41]. Third, most crash-causing errors lead to program crashes within a small number of dynamic instructions, and are hence unlikely to propagate to a large part of the application state [36, 48]. Therefore, the impact of crash-causing faults is likely to be confined to a small portion of the application's state, thus allowing recovery.

Taken together, these observations offer an optimistic hypothesis that it may be possible to re-purpose the default mechanism that terminates an application once a crash-causing error is signalled, and attempt to repair the corrupted application state and continue the application execution. This paper explores this hypothesis, proposes heuristics to repair the application state, and quantifies the impact of using this observation in the context of C/R mechanisms.

To enable this exploration we design and implement *LetGo*. LetGo works by monitoring the application at runtime; when a crash-causing error occurs, LetGo intercepts the hardware exception (e.g., segmentation fault), and does not pass the exception on to the application. Instead, it advances the program counter of the application to the next instruction, bypassing the crash-causing instruction. Further, LetGo employs various heuristics to adjust the state of the application's register file to hide the effects of the ignored instruction and ensure, to the extent possible, that the application state is not corrupted.

Figure 1 illustrates how LetGo can be used in the context of a checkpoint/restart (C/R) scheme. As shown in Figure 1a and 1b, the default action of a C/R scheme on fail-stop failures is to rewind to the last checkpoint. LetGo allows the HPC run-time to continue the execution of an application once a crash-causing error occurs (Figure 1c) and later use application-level correctness test to detect possible state corruption. If the application passes these checks, LetGo assumes that intermediate/final states of an application are correct, and hence no recovery is needed. This reduces checkpoint overheads in two ways: first, LetGo avoids the overhead of restarting from a previous checkpoint upon the occurrence of a crash-causing error; second, since crashes are less frequent, checkpoints can be taken less frequently as well (or not at all if the developer is prepared to accept the risk of unrecoverable failures). The potential cost of LetGo is an increased rate of Silent Data Corruption (SDC) leading to incorrect results. We argue that this may be acceptable for two reasons: first, our experiments indicate that this increase is low (the resulting SDC rate is in the same range as the SDC rate of the original application), and, second, since the possibility of undetected incorrect results exists even with the original application (i.e., without using LetGo), application users independently need to develop efficient techniques to increase confidence in the application results. By leveraging these application checks, LetGo reduces the chances of an error causing a SDC. *To the best of our knowledge, LetGo is the first system that applies the idea of tolerating errors by repairing application state in the context of C/R in HPC applications.*

This paper makes the following contributions:

- We propose a methodology to reduce the overhead of C/R techniques for HPC applications by resuming the execution of an application upon the occurrence of a crash-causing error without going back to the last checkpoint.
- We design LetGo, a light-weight run-time system that consists of two main components: a *monitor* that intercepts and handles operating system signals generated when a crash-causing error occurs, and a *modifier* that employs heuristics to adjust program state to increase the probability of successful application continuation (Section 4.1). Importantly, LetGo requires neither modifications to the

application, nor the availability of the application's source code for analysis (Section 4.3 and Section 4.2). therefore, it is practical to deploy in today's HPC context.

- We evaluate LetGo through fault-injection experiments using five DoE mini-applications. We find that LetGo is able to continue the application's execution in about 62% of the cases when it encounters a crash-causing error (for the remaining 38%, it gives up and the application can be restarted from a checkpoint as before). The increase in the SDC rate (undetected incorrect output) is low: 0.913% arithmetic mean. (Section 6.1).
- Finally, we evaluate the end-to-end impact of LetGo in the context of a C/R scheme and its sensitivity to a wide range of parameters. We find that LetGo offers significant efficiency gains (1.01x to 1.20x) in the ratio between the time spent for useful work and the total time cost, compared to the standard C/R scheme, across a wide range of parameters.

Our evaluation shows that, on average, LetGo is able to continue to completion 62% of the crashes while increasing the overall application SDC rates from 0.75% to 1.6%. This highlights a key contribution of LetGo: it creates the opportunity to trade off confidence in results for efficiency (time to solution). Certainly, for some applications - or for some operational situations - confidence in results is the user's primary concern, and LetGo will not be used. We believe, however, that there are many situations that make LetGo attractive: Firstly, since Silent Data Corruptions (SCD) can occur anyways (due to bit-flips even when LetGo is not used), users of HPC applications are already taking the risk of getting incorrect results, and have developed techniques to validate their results. Application-specific checks to diminish this risk are an active area of research [21, 22, 28, 39] and LetGo will benefit from all these efforts. Secondly, for some applications LetGo performs extremely well (e.g., for CLAMR and SANP all faults that would lead to crashes can be elided by LetGo, without resulting in any additional SDCs). In these cases, LetGo certainly represents an appealing solution. Finally, note that it is trivial to collect information on whether a run has benefited from LetGo repair heuristics and thus offers users additional information base on which to reason about confidence.

2 RELATED WORK

There have been many efforts to provide comprehensive solutions for HPC system to recover from failures. Recovery strategies can be grouped along two dimensions: first, on whether they are application-aware or application-agnostic, and, second on whether they roll-back to previously correct state or use heuristics to attempt to repair state and roll-forward. An example of application-agnostic approach is that of Chien et al. [18] who propose a global view resilience (GVR) framework that allows applications to store and compute an approximation from the current and versioned application data for a forward recovery. Aupy et al. [1] discuss how to combine the silent error detection and checkpointing, and schedule the checkpointing and verification in an optimal-balanced way with a rollback recovery. Other approaches rely on a detailed understanding of the application: Gamel et al. [23] design and implement a local recovery scheme specialized for stencil-based applications for a fast

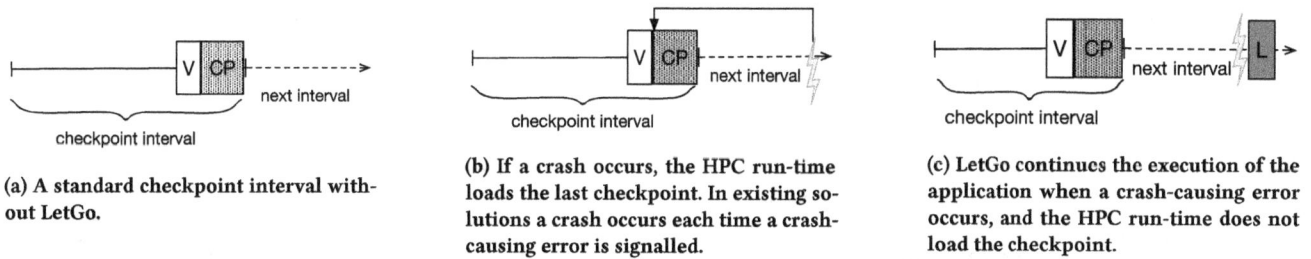

(a) A standard checkpoint interval without LetGo.

(b) If a crash occurs, the HPC run-time loads the last checkpoint. In existing solutions a crash occurs each time a crash-causing error is signalled.

(c) LetGo continues the execution of the application when a crash-causing error occurs, and the HPC run-time does not load the checkpoint.

Figure 1: Illustration of how LetGo changes the behavior of an HPC application that uses checkpointing by continuing the execution when a crash-causing error occurs. Axes indicate time. The labels used for time intervals: CP - checkpoint; V - application acceptance check/verification; L - LetGo framework, lightning bolt: crash-causing error

rollback in the minimum scale, while algorithm-based fault tolerance (ABFT) techniques such as [14, 56] compute checksums for the intermediate states of the LU factorization problems and enable forward recovery. LetGo aims to provide an application-agnostic and forward recovery solution, in the same vein as GVR [18] however it is more general and efficient (as there is no need to store previous program states, and no need of any data structure or interface support).

LetGo is inspired by two key areas: *failure-oblivious computing*, which focuses on recovering from failures caused by software bugs [49, 50]; and *approximate computing* which makes the assumption that ignoring some errors during application execution, will still lead to producing acceptable results. We discuss below how LetGo relates to these areas and highlight the differences.

Failure oblivious computing: Rinard et al. [49, 50] propose failure oblivious computing, an approach that continues application execution when memory-related errors occur during execution. To this end it relies on a technique called boundless memory block: when there is a out-of-bound write, the written value is stored in a hash table indexed by the its memory location, then for out-of-bound reads it retrieves the value from the hash table if the same memory address is used (or uses a default value if the hash table has not been initialized for that value). This is enabled by compile-time instrumentation and checks for all memory accesses at runtime. Our approach differs from theirs majorly in two ways: (1) LetGo focuses on all types of crashes whereas the technique above focuses on out-of-bound memory accesses, a subset of sources of crashes in HPC systems, and (2) we focus on HPC applications where we believe such techniques are likely to have a high impact.

Recently, Long et al. [38] proposed a run-time repair and containment in the same style at the original failure-oblivious computing work. They expand the solution used to drop assumptions on application structure and impose no instrumentation on program during execution. This technique works for errors including divide-by-zero and null pointer de-referencing. Both Rinard et al. [49] and Long et al. [38] find that that the one of the biggest reasons to the success of their techniques is the common computational pattern that occurs in all of their benchmark applications, that the input of the applications can be divided into units and no interaction between computations on different input units. This is not a typical computation model for HPC applications.

Approximate computing [27, 42] starts with the observation that, in many scenarios, an approximate result is sufficient for the purpose of the task, hence energy and performance gains may be achieved when relaxing the precision constraints. The philosophy of approximate computing is applied to different system levels including circuit design [26, 57], architectural design [24, 47] and application characterization and kernel design [9]. This concept, along with related body of research such as probabilistic computing [8, 44], offer potential platforms for applications that can tolerate imprecision in the final answer. However, LetGo does not aim to aggressively relax the accuracy of the computation, which is a different philosophy from Approximate computing or Probabilistic computing.

Failure escaping: Carbin et al. [6] design Jolt, a system that detects when an application has entered an infinite loop and allows the program to escape from the loop and continue. Jolt has a similar philosophy as LetGo: adjusting the program state when a program appears to be traped in a failing state. However, Jolt and LetGo target different failure types: Jolt is only designed to help programs escape from a infinite loop (a hang), a relatively infrequent failure scenario as our fault-injection experiments indicate.

3 BACKGROUND

Context: The effectiveness of LetGo is influenced by two factors: (1) the application-level acceptance checks that detect whether the application state is corrupted before delivering results to users, (2) the resilience characteristics of the HPC application making it able to withstand minor numerical perturbations. This section argues that a large class of HPC applications present these characteristics, and offers an example that illustrate how these two factors affect application fault-tolerance.

Factor 1: Application acceptance checks. Since the rate of hardware faults is expected to increase and applications become increasingly complex (and, as a result, the design and implementation process is error-prone), there is an increased awareness for the need of result acceptance tests, to boost the confidence in the results offered by HPC applications. Result acceptance checks are usually written by application developers to ensure that computation results do not violate application-specific properties, such as energy conservation or numeric tolerance for result approximation. These acceptance checks are typically placed at the end of the computation (i.e. the residual check performed in HPL application [46]), but they can be also placed during application execution to detect earlier possible state corruption such as [43].

Factor 2: Fault masking in HPC applications. A large class of HPC applications are based on iterative processes (For example, stencil computations iteratively compute physical properties at time T+1 based on values at time T; iterative solvers work by improving the accuracy of the solution at each step. For an iterative method that is convergent, numerical errors introduced by a hardware fault can be eliminated during this convergence process (although it may take longer). Prior studies such as [7] show that the algebraic multi-grid solver always masks errors if it is not terminated by a crash.

Terminology. We use standard trminology for the fault-tolerance domain: fault/error/failure [2]. Hardware *faults* are defects in the system that may be caused by cosmic rays or particle strikes. We are concerned with the faults that are not masked by the hardware and are thus visible at the application level. *Errors* are the manifestation of faults visible in the application state. *Failures* are the final outcomes of errors, and include crashes, application hangs, and SDCs.

4 SYSTEM DESIGN

Our goal is to demonstrate the feasibility and evaluate the potential impact of a run-time framework that allows the program to avoid termination and correct its state after a crash-causing error occurs. The four main requirements of LetGo are:

a) *Transparency:* LetGo should be able to transparently track the system behavior, monitor for crash-causing errors, and modify the application state to enable application continuation once a crash-causing error occurs, all without modifying the application's code (R1).

b) *Convenience:* As HPC applications tend to be conservative and sensitive to the computation environment, LetGo should not make any assumption about the application's compilation level or require changes the application's compilation process (R2).

c) *Low overhead:* To be attractive for deployment in production systems, LetGo should incur minimum overheads in terms of performance, energy and memory footprint (R3).

d) *A low rate of newly introduced failures:* LetGo inherently trades the ability to continue application execution for the risk of introducing new failures. For LetGo to be practical, the increase in the rate of undetected incorrect results should be low (R4).

The rest of this section describes LetGo design in detail and, shows how LetGo satisfies the above requirements.

4.1 Overall Design

LetGo is activated when a crash-causing error occurs. LetGo detects the exceptions raised by the OS, intercepts the OS signals, and modifies the default behavior of the application for these signals. Then it diagnoses which states of the program have been corrupted, and modifies the application state to ensure, to the extent possible, application continuation. Figures 2 and 3 show this process.

LetGo contains two components: the *monitor* and the *modifier*.

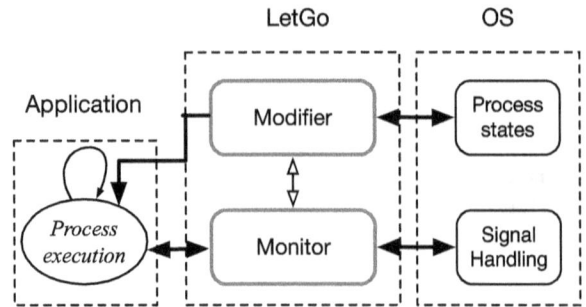

Figure 2: LetGo architecture overview.

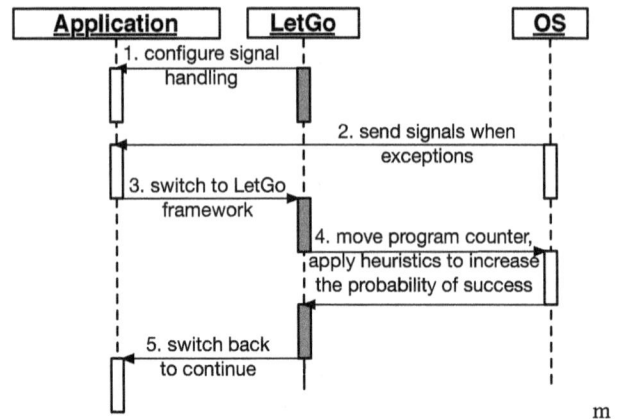

Figure 3: A sequence diagram highlighting LetGo use: the step 1-5 describe the interactions between LetGo, the application, and the operating system: LetGo starts by installing the monitor - i.e., configuring the the signal handling, and launches the application in a debugger (step 1). If the application encounters a signal, LetGo detects it (step 2) and takes the control of the application (step 3). To avoid the failure, LetGo increments the program counter (i.e., instruction pointer) of the application and adjusts the necessary program states (step 4). After the modification, LetGo lets the application continue without any further interference (step 5).

The monitor is attached to the application at startup. It changes the default behavior of the application from termination to pausing when operating system signals such as SIGSEGV and SIGBUS are received. The monitor intercepts these signals and hands the control over to the modifier.

The modifier kicks in when executing the current application instruction would lead to an application termination (crash). The modifier attempts to avoid the crash: it advances the program counter (i.e., instruction pointer) to the next instruction, and inspects and modifies application state (e.g., the stack pointer) to increase the probability of a successful continued execution. The details of the modifier are discussed in Section 4.2. Note that the application might still not be able to finish successfully and it may crash again - if so, LetGo does not intervene and allows the application to terminate.

4.2 Heuristics

We describe the modifications that the LetGo mmodifier makes to the application state (in Step 4 of Figure 3). These modifications have two goals: first, increase the likelihood that, once the application continues execution, it does not crash again; and, second, reduce the chance that data corruption propagates further.

There are two issues to deal with: first, advancing the program counter may bypass memory loads or stores, and hence the destination register that is supposed to hold the value from the memory load (or the memory location used for store) may contain an incorrect value , which may cause subsequent errors in case this register is later used; and, second, if the fault has corrupted the stack pointer register sp (i.e., rsp in X86-64) or the base pointer register bp (i.e., rbp in X86-64), and the application continues due to LetGo, the likelihood of receiving another system exception due to a memory-related violation high because sp and bp are repeatedly used. To mitigate these challenges, LetGo employs two heuristics (to satisfy R4).

Heuristic I - This heuristic deals with memory load/store instructions. If the program crashes due to the error in a memory-load instruction, LetGo feeds the to-be-written register(s) (which holds the data loaded from the memory) with a "fake" value(s). In practice, 0 is chosen as the value to feed to the register. We choose 0 by default because the memory often contains a lot of 0s as initialization data [12]. For the case where the program stops at a memory-store instruction, the value in that memory location remains the same because the memory-store operation is not successful. In this case, we do nothing - our empirical experience suggests that this is a more practical decision than assigning a random value. In the future, this heuristic can be combined with run-time analysis for more realistic and application-dependent behaviour.

Heuristic II - As discussed above, if a fault affects the values in the stack pointer register or the base pointer register, the corrupted registers may cause consecutive memory access violations. Since LetGo avoids performing run-time tracking, determining the correctness of the values in sp and bp statically becomes challenging. To overcome this challenge, LetGo implements the following heuristic that include a detection and a correction phase:

(1) *Detection*: for each function, the difference between the values in sp and bp can be approximately bound in a range via static analysis, hence this range can be calculated with minimum effort and can be used to indicate the corruption in sp or bp at run-time.

(2) *Correction*:: since sp and bp usually hold the same value at the beginning of each function, one can be used to correct the error in the other one if necessary.

We explain the intuition behind this heuristic with two observations based on the code in Listing 1. First, bp is normally pointed to the top of the stack (line 2), hence sp and bp usually carry the same value at the beginning of every function call. Second, based on the size of the memory allocated on the stack (line 3), the range of bp can be inferred as $sp < bp < sp + 0x290$ (bp is always greater than sp because the stack grows downwards. Therefore, when the program receives an exception and stops at an instruction that involves stack operation, LetGo runs the following steps: First, it gets the size of the allocated memory by searching for the beginning of the function that the instruction belongs to and then locating the instruction that shows how much memory the function needs on the stack (by analyzing the assembly code). Second, it calculates

Signal	Stop	Pass to program	Description
SIGSEGV	Yes	No	Segfault
SIGBUS	Yes	No	Bus error
SIGABRT	Yes	No	Aborted

Table 1: *gdb* signal handling information redefined by LetGo. 'Stop' means the program will stop upon a signal, and 'Pass to program' means this signal will not be passed to the program

the valid range based on the size and checks if the bp is in it, and, finally, if the range constraint is invalid, LetGo copies the value of the sp to the bp (or vice versa depending on which one is used in the instruction causing the crash).

Listing 1: Example of a common sequence of X86 instructions at the beginning of a function

```
1  push \%rbp
2  mov  \%rsp,\%rbp
3  sub  \$0x290, \%rsp
```

For the rest of this paper, we refer to the version of LetGo that applies these heuristics as **LetGo-E**(nhanced) and the version without heuristics as **LetGo-B**(asic). We evaluate the effectiveness of LetGo-B and LetGo-E in Section 6.

4.3 Implementation

We implement the LetGo prototype with three production-level tools that are widely adopted and readily available on HPC systems: gdb, PIN [45] and pexpect [52].

gdb: LetGo relies on *gdb* to control the application's execution. *gdb* provides the interfaces to handle operating system signals and to change the values in the program registers. We describe these two aspects in turn. LetGo uses *gdb* to redefine the behaviour of an application against OS signals as described in Table 1. Since most of application crashes are due to memory-related errors such as segmentation faults or bus errors [21, 25], LetGo currently supports three signals related to memory errors: SIGSEGV, SIGBUS and SIGABRT, and can be easily extended for more signals if needed (e.g., exceptions generated by ECC or chipkill). (Satisfying R1).

Note that the LetGo use of *gdb* does not require any source-code level analysis (or changes to the application). Applications therefore do not need to run in the debug mode, which inhibits code optimization and often results in significant performance degradation (satisfying R2 and R3). Applications can run with LetGo for any optimization/compilation requirement levels they need. We evaluate the generated overhead in Section 5.

b) PIN: It is a tool that supports dynamic instrumentation of programs. *PIN* can insert arbitrary code at arbitrary locations of an executable during its execution. LetGo uses *PIN* to conduct instruction-level analysis, such as obtaining the next PC, parsing an instruction and finding the size of allocated memory on the stack. Since LetGo only needs the static information of a program, there is no need for LetGo to keep track of dynamic program states and only dissembler inside PIN is needed. Therefore, LetGo incurs minimum performance overhead (Satisfying R3). It is possible to use other lightweight tools for parsing instructions instead of PIN.

c) pexpect: expect [37] is a tool that automates interactive applications (e.g. telnet, ftp, etc.) and it is widely for testing. LetGo uses *pexpect*, the Python extension of *expect* to automate all interactions between LetGo and the application: e.g., configuring signal handlers and updating register values. Since these are relatively rarely executed operations, the overall performance impact is small.

All the interactions between a *gdb* process and the target application are automated via *pexpect*, and confined to a limited number of *gdb* commands such as "print" or "set". When heuristics need to be applied, LetGo relies on *PIN* to analyze the program and feed the result to *gdb*. As a prototype, the current implementation of LetGo is used to support the experimentation, to demonstrate the ability of automation, and to investigate the overheads incurred - for a production version, one can directly and efficiently implement the functionality offered by each of these tools, so the overhead estimates we offer are conservative.

5 EVALUATION METHODOLOGY

This section focuses on evaluating the ability of LetGo to transform crashes into successful application runs To this end, this section first describes the fault model and the fault injection methodology we use, then explains how the various failure outcome categories are impacted by LetGo, and proposes metrics to quantitatively evaluate LetGo effectiveness. Using this information, the next section evaluates LetGo impact on reducing C/R overheads.

5.1 Fault Model

Soft errors are one of the main sources of hardware errors in processors [4], and are the focus of this work. We consider faults occurring in the computational units of processors, such as the ALUs, pipeline latches and register files. Our methodology is agnostic to whether a fault arises in the register file or is propagated to the registers from elsewhere. We do not consider faults in caches or main memory because we assume that they are protected by ECC or chipkill in HPC systems. We use the single-bit-flip model as it is the most common transient fault model in today's systems [53]. We also assume that at most one fault occurs in an application run leading to a crash-causing error, as soft errors are relatively rare compared to typical application execution times.

5.2 Categories of Fault Outcomes

The traditional outcomes of a fault affecting an application can be categorized as crashes, detected by the application acceptance check, hangs, SDCs, and benign outcomes. When applying LetGo, (some of the) crash outcomes are transferred to other categories, thus, to evaluate LetGo we further categorize the outcomes that correspond to a crash in a non-LetGo context in multiple new classes as presented in Figure 4.

At the top level of our taxonomy (Figure 4), a fault either causes a program to crash, or not. In Figure 4 we label these two classes - *Finished* and *Crash*.

(1) A *finished* run can result further in two outcomes: the program contains errors in the output that are detected by the application's acceptance checks (labeled as *Detected*), or the output of the program passes those checks (labeled as *Pass check*). If the output passes the check, it may differ

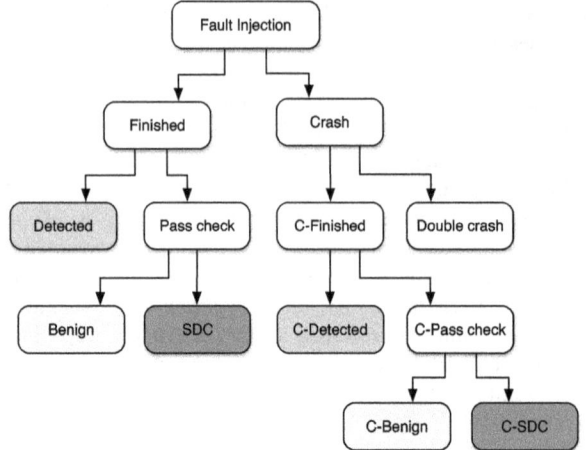

Figure 4: Classification of the fault injection outcomes. LetGo has impact only on the right side of the tree above as it attempts to avoid a crash outcome.

from the golden run, in which case we consider it an *SDC*[1]; or the output matches the golden run, labeled as *Benign*.

(2) A *Crash* run is where LetGo has impact. When LetGo is deployed, it may fail to continue the application and lead to a second crash (labeled as *DoubleCrash*) or make the application to finish successfully labeled *C-Finished*. In this case, the program may have similar outcomes as in the *Finished* case (when no crash occurs) - we label these as *C-Benign* (no observable outcome of the fault), *C-Detected* (incorrect output detected by application acceptance checks), and *C-SDC* (incorrect output not detected by those checks, but different from the golden run). Compared to a situation when LetGo is not used, LetGo is able to transfer some of the crash outcomes to C-Benign, C-SDC, or C-Detected outcome.

5.3 Metrics of Effectiveness

The effectiveness of LetGo can be estimated by answering questions like "How many crashes can be converted to continued execution?", "what is the likelihood of producing correct results after continuation?", "How often the application check can catch the errors after continuation?" and "How many incorrect results will be produced after continuation?". To this end, we define four metrics to quantitatively evaluate LetGo effectiveness:

Continuability is the likelihood that LetGo is able to convert a crashing program into the program that would finish (regardless of the correctness of the output).

$$Continuability = \frac{C\text{-}Pass\ check + C\text{-}Detected}{Crash} \quad (1)$$

Continued_detected is the likelihood that the application acceptance check catches errors in the application (if any) after continuation.

---

[1]This is a conservative assumption as we do not know how the results of the application are used. The application output also includes the application data that is compared between such data from the golden run, as defined in Table 2

Application	Domian	# dynamic instructions (billions)	Application data used to check for SDCs	Criteria used in application acceptance check
LULESH	Hydrodynamics	1.0	Mesh	Number of iterations: exactly the same Final origin energy: correct to at least 6 digits Measures of symmetry: smaller than 10^{-8}
CLAMR	Adaptive mesh refinement	2.8	Mesh	Threshold for the mass change per iteration
HPL	Dense linear solver	1.2	Solution vector	Residual check on the solution vector
COMD	Classical molecular dynamics	5.1	Each atom's property	Energy conservation
SNAP	Discrete ordinates transport	1.6	Flux solution	The flux solution output should be symmetric
PENNANT	Unstructured mesh physics	1.7	Mesh	Energy conservation

Table 2: Benchmark description. The last two columns present which data is used for bit-wise comparison to determine SDCs (undetected incorrect results), and, respectively describe the result acceptance check used by each application. All benchmarks are compiled with g++ 4.93 using O3 except for SNAP, which is a FORTRAN program.

$$Continued\_detected = \frac{C\text{-}Detected}{Crash} \qquad (2)$$

Continued_correct is the likelihood that the programs result in the correct output after continuation.

$$Continued\_correct = \frac{C\text{-}Benign}{Crash} \qquad (3)$$

Continued_SDC indicates the likelihood that application finished but results in SDCs - undetected incorrect results.

$$Continued\_SDC = \frac{C\text{-}SDC}{Crash} \qquad (4)$$

Note that the Continuability is the sum of Continued_detected, Continued_correct and Continued_SDC metrics. All four values range from 0 to 1.

For an application to benefit from LetGo, it needs to satisfy the following properties: first, there is a low probability that the key program states are not affected by the failure (indicated by high Continuability), and second, there is a high probability that the program states adjusted by LetGo converge to the original path (indicated by the high Continued_correct and low Continued_SDC).

5.4 Fault Injection Methodology

To evaluate LetGo, we implement a software-based fault injection tool based on *gdb* and *PIN* [2]. Our injector does not require the application's source code, nor does it need the application to be compiled using special compilers or compilation flags.

The fault injection experiments for an application consists of two phases: we first perform *a one-time profiling phase* to count the number of dynamic instructions using the PIN tool. As we assume all dynamic instructions have equal likelihood of being affected by a fault, we use the number of total instructions to randomly choose an instruction to inject a fault for each fault injection run. During this phase, we also profile the number of times each static instruction in the program is executed during the profiling phase so at to be able to inject a fault at the appropriate dynamic instruction. For example, if we choose to inject into the 5th dynamic instance

of an instruction, we need to skip the first 4 instances when the breakpoint is reached (using the *continue* command of *gdb*).

During the *fault injection phase*, we then use *gdb* to set a breakpoint at the randomly-chosen dynamic instruction and inject a fault at the instruction by flipping a single bit in its destination register (after the instruction completes). This emulates the effect of a fault in the computational units involved in the instruction.

The profiling phase is run once per application and is relatively slow. The injection phase, on the other hand, is executed tens of thousands of times, and is much faster as it does not involve running the application inside a virtual machine as PIN does. *We perform a total of* 20,000 *fault injections per application, one per run, to obtain tight error bounds of 0.1% to 0.2% at the 95% confidence interval.*

5.5 Benchmarks

We use six HPC mini-applications namely LULESH [20], CLAMR [43], HPL [46], SNAP [35], PENNANT [33] and COMD [10] (details in Table 2). Note that these benchmarks meet the assumption that application-level acceptance checks are well defined/implemented. All benchmarks exhibit convergence-based iterative computation patterns except for HPL, which is implemented with a direct method[3] [16]. Therefore, we separate the results of HPL from others and discuss them in Section 8.

Table 2 briefly describes the acceptance checks for each benchmark. For *CLAMR, HPL, PENNANT*, we use the built-in acceptance checks (written by the developers), while for *LULESH, COMD and SNAP*, we wrote the checks ourselves based on their verification specifications: Section 6.2 in [31] for *LULESH*, "Verification correctness" section in [11] for *COMD* and "Verification of Results" section in [34] for *SNAP*.

6 EXPERIMENTAL RESULTS

This section presents experiments that aim to understand whether LetGo is indeed able to continue application execution when a crash-causing error occurs with minimal impact on application correctness and efficiency. The next section evaluates the impact of LetGo in the context of an C/R mechanism.

---

[2]The tool is publicly available at https://github.com/flyree/pb_interceptor

[3]A direct method computes the exact answers after a finite number of steps (in the absence of roundoff)

Benchmark	Finished			Crash			
	Detected	Pass check		Double crash	C-Detected	C-Pass check	
		Benign	SDC			C-Benign	C-SDC
LULESH	0.90%	22.00%	0.13%	25.00%	2.30%	49.50%	0.17%
CLAMR	0.50%	33.30%	0.50%	25.00%	1.10%	39.60%	0.00%
SNAP	0.02%	43.94%	0.01%	20.77%	0.06%	35.20%	0.00%
COMD	1.00%	55.00%	1.10%	18.32%	0.85%	22.13%	1.60%
PENNANT	1.00%	50.00%	2.00%	19.00%	2.50%	22.70%	2.80%
AVERAGE	**0.68%**	**40.85%**	**0.75%**	**21.62%**	**1.36%**	**34.02%**	**0.91%**

Table 3: Fault injection results for five iterative benchmarks when using LetGo-E. The value for each outcome category is normalized using the total number of fault injection runs for the application. Error bars range from 0.1% to 0.2% at the 95% confidence level.

6.1 Effectiveness of LetGo

We run the fault injection experiments for both LetGo-B (the basic version that uses minimal repair heuristics) and LetGo-E (the version that uses the advanced heuristics described in Section 4). Table 3 shows the fault injection result for the five benchmarks that use iterative, convergence-based solutions when using LetGo-E. We discuss HPL, a direct method, separately in the discussion section.

We note the following: First, the the average crash rate over all applications is 56%, showing that more than half of the time when a fault occurs the application will crash (i.e., in the table this shows as the sum of values in the four columns under the "Crash" category). Second, with LetGo-E, on average, 62% of these crashes can be transformed to continue running the application to termination (only 38% are double crashes). We first discuss the results for LetGo-E, and then compare these results with those for LetGo-B to understand the effectiveness of the heuristics introduced by LetGo-E. We observe the following:

(1) **The ability of LetGo-E to enable continued execution when facing a crash-causing error**: The mean *continuability* for the benchmark set is 62%, which indicates that 62% of the time when the benchmark program receives a crashing signal, LetGo-E resumes the execution and the application completes successfully without crashing again.

(2) **LetGo-E is able to convert more than half of the crashes to produce correct results** (and thus possibly offer a solution to lower checkpoint overheads for a long-running applications).

(3) **Low rate of undetected incorrect results.** The rate of *Continued_SDC* cases for all benchmarks is on average in the same range as the SDC rate of the unmodified application. For *CLAMR* and *SNAP*, we do not observe new SDCs after applying LetGo-E. Overall, LetGo-E maintains the low SDC rate of the original application (yet it doubles it only 1.6% of the cases did the program produce incorrect results after continuing it with LetGo-E, compared with 0.75% when not using LetGo). We further discuss the impact of the increased SDC rates, and techniques to mitigate it, in Section 8.

(4) **Continued_detected of the application-level acceptance checks.** The Continued_detected of LetGo-E across the five benchmarks is 2.4%: for our benchmarks, after LetGo-E continues the execution, the application acceptance checks would detect the errors 2.4% of the time - this is slightly higher than the case without LetGo-E.

Thus, we find that LetGo-E has a high likelihood to convert crashes into either benign or detected states, while only marginally increasing the SDCs produced.

Figure 5 compares LetGo-B and LetGo-E over the four metrics. Figure 5a shows that LetGo-E achieves an improvement in Continuability for CLAMR by 32% and for PENNANT by 5% over LetGo-B , but not much for the other benchmarks (considering the error bars). Overall, LetGo-E achieves 14% on average higher Continuability than LetGo-B. Figure 5b shows that the Continued_detected declines by 1% from LetGo-B to LetGo-E on average and with only 0.8% increase in *CLAMR*. Therefore, the efficacy of the acceptance checks is not much affected by the heuristics employed by LetGo-E. Figure 5c shows that LetGo-E has higher Continued_correct over LetGo-B by 4% on average across all benchmarks. This shows that it allows more crashes to be converted into correct results than LetGo-B. In Figure 5d, we find that Continued_SDC ratio for LetGo-E remains the same as that of LetGo-B on average. In Figure 5d, we can observe that LetGo-E totally eliminate the SDCs for *CLAMR* and *SNAP*, and has almost the marginally different values of the Continued_SDC metric for all benchmarks - the worst case is 2% higher Continued_SDC faults for PENNANT. Thus, the heuristics used by LetGo-E does not add much to the incorrect executions.

Overall, the heuristics introduced by LetGo-E lead to better continuablility (by about 14%) over LetGo-B for continuing the programs, and producing 5% more correct results than LetGo-B.

6.2 Performance Overhead

To estimate performance overhead, we experimentally measure the performance LetGo for a single application run outside the context of a C/R scheme. In Section 7, we will evaluate the end-to-end impact of LetGo when used in the context of an C/R scheme, that is in the presence of failures and considering C/R overheads.

There are two source of overhead in LetGo: a). Running the program with *gdb*. b). Adjusting program states after a crash happens. We report the time overhead for each part below. Since LetGo-E is a superset of the operations performed by LetGo-B, we report only the LetGo-E overheads to get the worst-case time overhead.

We first measure the execution time of LULESH with LetGo, under three input sizes. We find that for the three different input sizes, the number of dynamic instructions range from 1 billion

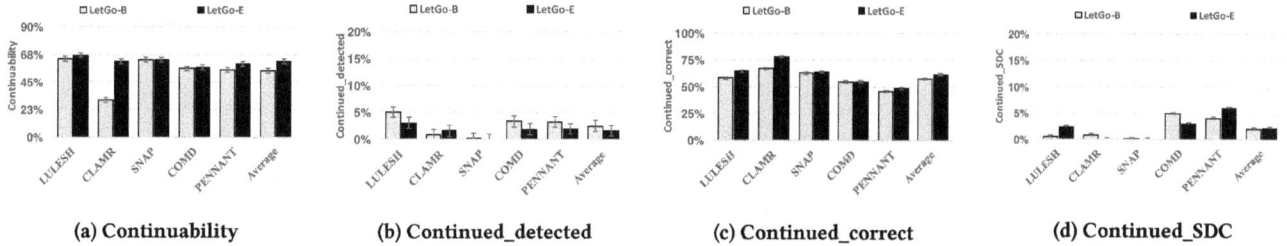

(a) Continuability   (b) Continued_detected   (c) Continued_correct   (d) Continued_SDC

Figure 5: Comparison of Continuability, Continued_detected, Continued_correct and Continued_SDC between the LetGo-B and LetGo-E. LetGo-E has a higher likelihood of converting crashes into correctly executions for our benchmarks than LetGo-B but no increase in Continued_SDC cases.

to 180 billion, and LULESH with *gdb* exhibits consistently low overhead (i.e., less than 1% compared to running it without *gdb* for each case). We have observed a similar trend for the rest of the benchmarks as well. As explained in Section 4, this is because LetGo neither changes the applications' compilation levels nor does it set breakpoints on the application.

We also measured the time overhead of adjusting program states after a crash by measuring how much time is spent in LetGo-E for each benchmark (i.e., the time spent in step 4 of the Figure 3). We find that across all of our benchmarks, the wall-clock time spent in LetGo is roughly around 2-5 seconds, and, as expected, it stays constant when we increase the input size. This time is trivial compared to the overall execution time of most HPC programs. Recall that LetGo takes two actions to adjust the program states: 1). finding the next PC, 2) applying the two heuristics if necessary. As explained in Section 4.2 and Section 4.3, both actions only need a disassembler to acquire the static instruction-level information of a program - we use PIN. With a more efficient disassembler, the time overhead can be even further reduced. *Thus, LetGo incurs insignificant performance overheads in most cases, and this overhead does not increase with increase in applications' input sizes.*

7 LETGO IN A C/R CONTEXT

The previous section demonstrated that LetGo is indeed able to often continue application execution with minimal impact on application correctness and efficiency. This section aims to evaluate the end-to-end impact of LetGo in the context of a long-running parallel application using a C/R mechanism. The main challenge in this evaluation is that there are multiple configuration scenarios that need to be considered, and hence direct measurement is prohibitively expensive. To address this issue, we model a typical HPC system using C/R as a state machine and have built a continuous-time event simulation of the system. This simulation framework enables us to compare resource usage efficiency with and without LetGo. We predict the overall performance gains using LetGo, based on the effectiveness of LetGo estimated with fault injections on an application-specific basis in the previous section. We focus on LetGo-E as we found that it achieves higher Continuability and Continued_correct compared to LetGo-B. In the rest of this section, when we say LetGo, we mean LetGo-E.

Model assumptions. We make a number of assumptions that are standard for most of the checkpointing literature [5, 13, 17, 58]. Our models assume that all crashes are due to transient hardware

faults, and hence restarting the application from a checkpoint will be sufficient to recover from the crash. In a similar vein, we assume that the checkpointing process itself is not corrupted by a fault. We further assume that the application does not have any other fault-tolerance mechanism than C/R (and LetGo), and that it does not modify its behaviour based on the faults encountered. Finally, when modelling a multi-node platform, we assume the HPC system uses synchronous coordinated checkpointing, which implies that checkpoints are taken at the same time across different nodes via synchronization; and that, when one node crashes, all nodes in the system have to fall back to the last checkpoint and re-execute together.

Parameter description We categorize the model parameters into three classes, summarized in Table 4:

(1) Configured: The time to write a checkpoint (*T_chk*), and the mean time between faults (*MTBFaults*) are configured by the model users based on the characteristics of the platform and the application;

(2) Estimated: The probability of a crash after a fault occurs (*P_crash*), the probability that an application passes an application-defined acceptance check (*P_v*, the probability that an application passes an an application-defined acceptance check after LetGo has been used to repair state (*P_v'*), and LetGo Continuability (*P_letgo*) are obtained from the fault injection experiments on a per application basis.

(3) Derived: The checkpoint interval T is determined to be a value that maximizes efficiency for the current configuration based on Young's formula [58] (when not explicitly mentioned otherwise in the experiment description). The recovery time (*T_r*) is, conservatively, chosen to be equal to the checkpoint overhead *T_c* as we assume the equal write and read speed access to the stable storage (also used in prior work [5]), and neglect the additional coordination overhead. We assume that the time spent for an acceptance check (*T_v*) is proportional to the checkpoint overhead because the size of the data to check is the same. We use: *T_v* = *0.01 * T_c*. The overhead for synchronizing multiple nodes (*T_sync*) to take a coordinated checkpoint is (optimistically, as we do not consider system scaling effects) a constant fraction of the per/node checkpointing time (*T_chk*). We use two values for the synchronization overhead as 10% and 50% of the checkpointing overhead.

Parameter	Description	Value
T	Checkpoint interval (useful work)	$\sqrt{2} * T\_chk * MTBF^{\dagger}$
T_r	Time spent for recovery from a previous checkpoint	T_chk
T_chk	Time spent writing a checkpoint	System-dependent
T_sync	Time spent in synchronization across nodes	50%*T_chk and 10%*T_chk
T_v	Time spent in application acceptance check	1%*T_chk
T_letgo	Time spent in LetGo	5s
P_crash	The probability that a application crashes when a fault occurs	Application-dependent
P_v	The probability that an application passes the verification check	Application-dependent
P_v'	The probability that an application passes the verification check with LetGo	Application-dependent
P_letgo	The Continuability of LetGo	Application-dependent
MTBF	Mean time between failure	System-dependent
MTBF_letgo	Mean time between failure with LetGo	MTBF/(1-62%)
MTBFaults	Mean time between faults	System-dependent

$\dagger$ EI-Sayed et al. [17] show that checkpointing under Young's formula achieves almost identical performance as more sophisticated schemes, based on exhaustive observations on the production systems.

Table 4: The description of parameters of the models

Finally we can derive mean time between failures (*MTBF*) based on the experiments in the previous section. As we observe from the fault injection experiments in the previous section, on average 56% of faults lead to crashes. Thus for simplicity, we use *MTBFaults* = 2**MTBF*. The C/R scheme with LetGo helps the application avoid crashes, which results in a longer MTBF. We refer to this new MTBF of the system after LetGo is applied as MTBF_letgo, and since the Continuability of LetGo is about 62% on average, we set *MTBF_letgo* equal to *MTBF*/(1-62%).

Model description. The state machine modelling a system that does not use LetGo is depicted in Figure 6a and has three states: **COMP**utation, **Check**point, and **VERIF**-ication. In the beginning, the application enters the COMP state for normal computation. A transition is made from the state COMP to VERIF if no crash happens (①), and the acceptance check is applied on the application data/output. If this check passes, a transition is made from the state VERIF to CHK (⑤) and a checkpoint is taken immediately. If the application does not pass the check, it transits from the state VERIF to COMP (②). A transition from the state COMP back to itself occurs when a failure is detected (④), or faults occur when the application is in the COMP state but none of them cause crashes, so that the application stays in the COMP state and the number of faults will be increased (③). When faults are accumulated in the system, the probability that the application passes the verification check is modeled as $(P\_v)^{faults}$, given the assumption that hardware transient faults occur as independent events.

Figure 6b illustrates the model for the C/R scheme when using LetGo. The state machine contains two more states: "LETGO" and "CONT"inue. Due to space limitations, we emphasize here only the transitions related to the new states. When there is a failure (i.e., crash) occurring during the computation (i.e., the application stays in the COMP state), a transition is made to the LETGO state (③). The application moves from the LetGo state to CONT if LetGo continues the execution of the application (④), otherwise, the application transits back to the COMP state (①). While the application stays in

the CONT state, the occurring fault can either cause another crash and make the application transit to the COMP state (⑥), or not cause a crash and make the application proceed to the state VERIF. The "isLetGo" flag is set for choosing the different base probabilities (P_v or P_v') that the application passes the verification check (⑤). The base probability is used in the conditions of the state transitions ② and ⑨. The actual probability is then calculated using $(P\_v)^{faults}$ or $(P\_v')^{faults}$ in ⑧ and ⑦.

Evaluation metric. The goal of the simulation is to understand the impact of LetGo on resource usage efficiency in the context of a long running application using a C/R scheme in the presence of faults. We define resource usage efficiency as the ratio between the accumulated useful time and the total time spent (i.e., u/cost). To evaluate the efficiency of both setups (with and without LetGo), we perform simulations for configuration parameters corresponding to different benchmarks and different platforms.

Choice of parameters. We justify the chocies for the checkpointing overhead, and the MTBF. We first discuss the checkpointing overhead: the time spent to write a checkpoint to the persistent storage depends on the characteristics of the hardware. For more advanced hardware, the checkpointing overhead becomes less significant. However, on one side, advanced hardware support such as burst buffers represent additional costs. To the degree these are added to reduce checkpointing overheads, a checkpointing scheme with lower overhead would enable provisioning systems for lower overall cost. On the other side, even in the presence of burst-buffers, checkpointing is still a major bottleneck on deployed systems as our simulations show. We use two criteria for choosing the checkpoint overheads. Here are two data points that justify our choice of parameters to seed our simulations:

- *Back-of-the-envelope calculation*: For each checkpointing overhead value we pick for our simulations we assume that the system-level checkpointing writes some portion of the main memory to the persistent storage. A modern HPC node normally features 32 to 128GB memory. For a

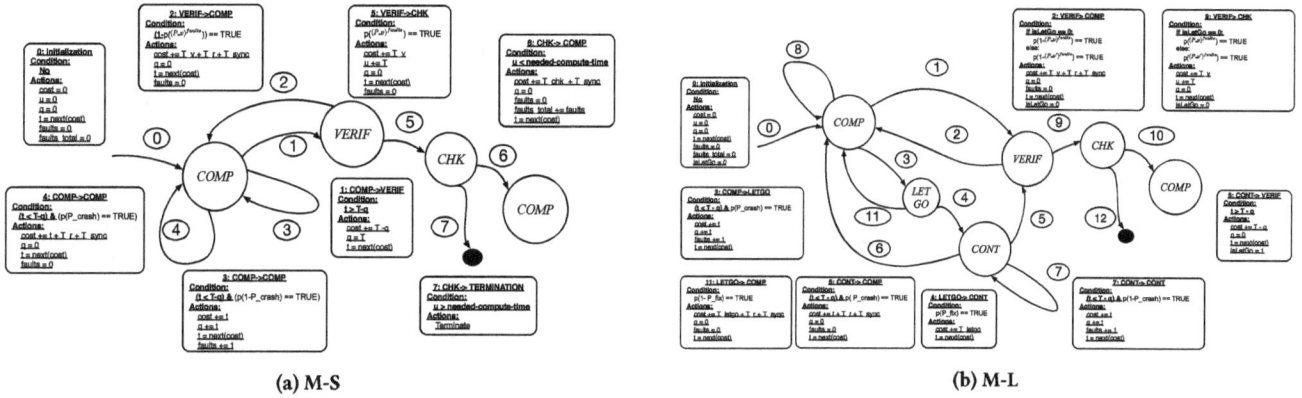

(a) M-S   (b) M-L

Figure 6: The state machines for the standard C/R scheme (a) and the C/R scheme with LetGo (b). The black circle represents the termination state of the model. We use u/cost to represent the efficiency of the model. *t: time interval till the next fault; cost: accumulated runtime; u: accumulated useful work; q: accumulated useful work within the current checkpoint interval; faults: number of faults that did not lead to crashes since the last checkpoint; faults_total: total number of faults that did not lead to crashes; isLetGo: a flag that indicates that if the P_v' is chosen or not*

burst buffer implemented with SSD, the average I/O bandwidth for write is around 1GiB/s, and the peak value is 6GiB/s [3]. For spinning disks, the I/O bandwidth is usually around 50MiB/s to 500MiB/s. As a result, our choices for the checkpoint overhead of (12s, 120s or 1200s) respectively represent, (i) a well provisioned system using burst buffers, (ii) and averagely provisioned system (e.g., using burst buffers, or compression and spinning disks); and (iii) a naive, under-provisioned system. We note that a similar set of values is also used in prior work [5, 17].

- *Future system requirements*: The Alliance for application Performance at EXtreme scale (APEX) 2020 document [32] requires that the systems delivered in 2020 have a single job mean time to interrupt of more than 24 hours, and for a delta-checkpoint scheme (i.e., the time to checkpoint 80% of aggregate memory of the system to persistent storage), the time for writing the checkpoint to be less than 7.2 minutes (432s). This suggests that our parameters are in the same ballpark as those of the current and future systems.

Along similar lines, we derive *MTBFaults* for existing systems from previously reported studies: we start with the system presented by [5] as a baseline. This system contains about 10, 000 nodes, and usually experiences around 2 failures per day [40] (*MTBF* of 12 hours). Based on this data, we scale *MTBF* for larger systems, and also consider systems with lower node-level reliability.

Running the Simulation. We assume that the hardware transient faults hitting the system are governed by a Poisson process and we generate a random time sequence for the occurrences of the hardware faults. Then, we seed the models with various sets of parameters and run the simulation over the generated sequence for a long simulation time (10 years), to determine the asymptotic efficiency value for each benchmark.

Experimental Results. We first show the efficiency for the C/R system with and without LetGo under different checkpoint overheads. We take the system that has a MTBFaults of 21600 seconds (i.e., *MTBF* = 12*hours*) and a synchronization overhead of 10% of the checkpoint interval as an example.

The efficiency improvement enabled by LetGo is between 1% to 11% across our benchmarks (absolute values, the relative values are much higher (nearly 20%)). As the checkpoint overhead scales up (from 12s to 1200s), the efficiency gain increases for all applications, while, at the same time, the absolute efficiency per application decreases. Figure 7 shows the applications that have the highest and lowest efficiency gains respectively, *LULESH* and *SNAP*, when the checkpoint overhead is 1200 seconds. This trend is consistent across all applications, and across different synchronization overheads. Our results thus show that LetGo offers significant efficiency gains.

We then scale the system from 100, 000 nodes to 200, 000 and 400, 000 nodes. Scaling results in lower MTBF for the whole system: 6 and 3 hours. Again, we use two benchmarks namely *CLAMR* and *PENNANT* as examples, shown in Figure 8. As the scale of the system increases, the efficiency of the system both with and without LetGo decreases, as expected. Importantly, the rate of decrease of efficiency is lower for the system with LetGo than without. This trend is consistent with all our benchmarks, suggesting that LetGo offers better efficiency as the system scale increases.

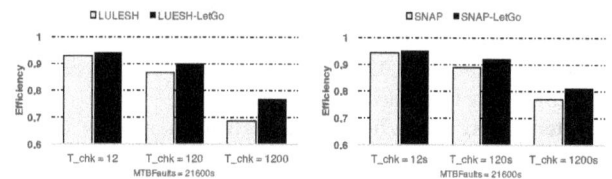

(a) Efficiency of LULESH with and without LetGo
(b) Efficiency of SNAP with and without LetGo

Figure 7: Efficiency with and without LetGo under different checkpoint overheads for LULESH and SNAP.

8 DISCUSSION

We address a number of interrelated issues.

What is LetGo effectiveness when used for applications that do not use convergent methods? We have evaluated LetGo on five benchmarks that use convergent methods. We have also

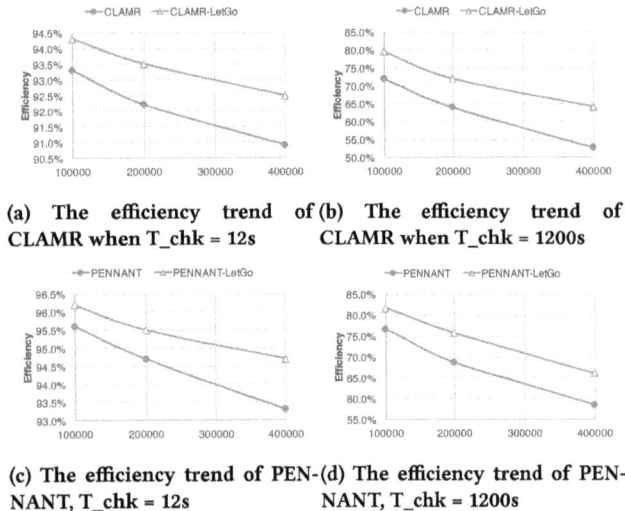

(a) The efficiency trend of CLAMR when T_chk = 12s

(b) The efficiency trend of CLAMR when T_chk = 1200s

(c) The efficiency trend of PEN-NANT, T_chk = 12s

(d) The efficiency trend of PEN-NANT, T_chk = 1200s

Figure 8: The trend of the efficiency for the C/R scheme with and without LetGo when the system scales from 100,000 nodes to 200,000 nodes and 400,000 nodes

evaluated LetGo on *HPL*, which is a linear algebra solver that uses a direct method. Our fault injection experiments show that, without the presence of LetGo, 34% of faults lead to crashes, 38% lead to incorrect output detected by the HPL residual check, about 1% lead to SDCs, and 27% lead to correct output. We find that the application-level acceptance checks are much more selective than for the applications in our initial set, and this would make HPL a good candidate for use with LetGo. However, while the crash rate is still high (34%), it is lower than that of the other applications, where it was around 60% - this would potentially reduce the impact of LetGo. When using LetGo with HPL, we obtain around 70% Continuability and 2x increases in SDC rate (from 1% to 3%). To understand the overall performance, we run the simulation of a C/R scheme with the potential results from applying LetGo-E to HPL. Our simulation results show that the efficiency of the standard C/R scheme applied to *HPL* is around 40%, and LetGo-E only marginally improves efficiency. Thus, LetGo by itself is not a good fit for applications like HPL - other error correcting mechanisms (e.g. ABFT) may be needed for such programs.

Determining when/how to use LetGo An operator will decide whether to use LetGo depending on a mix of factors: i) how frequently the system experience hardware faults that crashes the application, ii) what is the likelihood of the application to experience additional SDCs given the use of LetGo, iii) what is the checkpoint overhead for a specific C/R scheme for that application and deployment, iv) what is the acceptable increase in the SDC rate. It is reasonable to assume that the operator has (an approximation for) some of the information above as she needs to configure the checkpoint interval when LetGo is not used. Additionally, the operator needs information to estimate the increase in SDC rate due to LetGo. A large characterization study with applications from multiple categories that extends the preliminary data provided in this paper is necessary to provide these estimates.

Towards large-scale application The current implementation of LetGo focuses on the single-threaded scenario. As an initial effort, we considered this work to be the "proof of concept" for the continuous execution upon failures, and bridges the system level continuation with the correctness of application behaviors. Thus, it is in the early stage of being practical in large-scale production systems. However, the main design and implementation foundations hold no obstacles to be extended for concurrent/multi-threaded applications. Meanwhile, we would like to understand the possibility of integrating LetGo with parallel programming systems such as MPI.

Hardware Fault Models Precise data on the bit-flip rates observed in practice is notoriously hard to obtain. However, we maintain that bit-flips leading to application application crashes are still a frequent root cause for failure. For example, Martino et al. [40] show that in Blue Waters, hardware related issues are the single largest cause of failures (42%) - bugs and configuration errors are only 23%. Of these, 67% of hardware errors are memory errors, and 30% of memory errors manifested as multiple bit flips that cannot be corrected via ECC. While LetGo does not support ECC errors today, there is no fundamental obstacle in adding support for such errors. Moreover, since LetGo allows applications to continue with errors, it may be possible to use it for application-specific (re)configuration of the hardware fault tolerance mechanisms to enable energy savings.

9 CONCLUSION

This paper demonstrates that it is possible to continue HPC application execution rather than terminate it when facing crash-causing errors due to hardware transient faults. We have implemented the above idea in a system called LetGo, which monitors the execution of an application and modifies its default behavior when a termination-causing OS signal is generated. When used in the context of a C/R scheme, LetGo enables sizable resource usage efficiency gains. More specifically, for a set of HPC benchmarks, LetGo offers over 50% chance that the application can continue and produce correct results without performing a roll-back/recovery. We evaluate the impact of LetGo for long-running applications that use C/R, and find that LetGo enables sizable efficiency gains. The efficiency gains increase with both the system scale and checkpointing overheads, thus suggesting that LetGo will likely be even more important for future large-scale HPC applications and systems.

ACKNOWLEDGMENT

The authors would like to thank Panruo Wu, Sijia Gao and Bader Alahmad for their feedback on the project. This work was supported in part by the Natural Sciences and Engineering Research Council of Canada (NSERC), and the Canada Foundation for Innovation (CFI). This work was supported in part by the U.S. Department of Energy contract AC52-06NA25396. The publication has been assigned the LANL identifier LA-UR-17-20241.

REFERENCES

[1] Guillaume Aupy, Anne Benoit, Thomas Hérault, Yves Robert, Frédéric Vivien, and Dounia Zaidouni. 2013. On the Combination of Silent Error Detection and Checkpointing. In *Proceedings of the 2013 IEEE 19th Pacific Rim Interna-*

tional Symposium on Dependable Computing (PRDC '13). IEEE Computer Society, Washington, DC, USA, 11–20. DOI:https://doi.org/10.1109/PRDC.2013.10

[2] A. Avizienis, J. C. Laprie, B. Randell, and C. Landwehr. 2004. Basic concepts and taxonomy of dependable and secure computing. IEEE Transactions on Dependable and Secure Computing (2004). DOI:https://doi.org/10.1109/TDSC.2004.2

[3] Wahid Bhimji, Debbie Bard, Melissa Romanus, David Paul, Andrey Ovsyannikov, Brian Friesen, Matt Bryson, Joaquin Correa, Glenn K Lockwood, Vakho Tsulaia, and others. 2016. Accelerating science with the nersc burst buffer early user program. Proceedings of Cray Users Group.[Online]. Available: https://cug.org/proceedings/cug2016 proceedings/includes/files/pap162. pdf (2016).

[4] Shekhar Borkar. 2005. Designing Reliable Systems from Unreliable Components: The Challenges of Transistor Variability and Degradation. IEEE Micro 25, 6 (Nov. 2005), 10–16.

[5] George et al. Bosilca. 2013. Unified Model for Assessing Checkpointing Protocols at Extreme-scale. Concurr. Comput. : Pract. Exper. (2013), 2772–2791.

[6] Michael Carbin, Sasa Misailovic, Michael Kling, and Martin C. Rinard. 2011. Detecting and Escaping Infinite Loops with Jolt. In Proceedings of the 25th European Conference on Object-oriented Programming (ECOOP'11).

[7] Marc Casas, Bronis R. de Supinski, Greg Bronevetsky, and Martin Schulz. Fault Resilience of the Algebraic Multi-grid Solver. In Proceedings of the 26th ACM International Conference on Supercomputing (ICS '12). 91–100.

[8] Suresh Cheemalavagu, Pinar Korkmaz, Krishna V. Palem, Bilge E. S. Akgul, and Lakshmi N. Chakrapani. 2005. A probabilistic CMOS switch and its realization by exploiting noise. In the Proceedings of the IFIP international.

[9] V. K. Chippa, S. T. Chakradhar, K. Roy, and A. Raghunathan. Analysis and characterization of inherent application resilience for approximate computing. In Design Automation Conference (DAC), 2013.

[10] P. Cicotti, S. M. Mniszewski, and L. Carrington. An Evaluation of Threaded Models for a Classical MD Proxy Application. In Hardware-Software Co-Design for High Performance Computing (Co-HPC), 2014.

[11] P. Cicotti, S. M. Mniszewski, and L. Carrington. 2013. CoMD: A Classical Molecular Dynamics Mini-app. (2013). http://exmatex.github.io/CoMD/doxygen-mpi/index.html

[12] J. J. Cook and C. Zilles. A characterization of instruction-level error derating and its implications for error detection. In 2008 DSN. DOI:https://doi.org/10.1109/DSN.2008.4630119

[13] J. T. Daly. 2006. A Higher Order Estimate of the Optimum Checkpoint Interval for Restart Dumps. Future Gener. Comput. Syst. 22, 3 (Feb. 2006), 303–312. DOI: https://doi.org/10.1016/j.future.2004.11.016

[14] Teresa Davies and Zizhong Chen. 2013. Correcting Soft Errors Online in LU Factorization. In Proceedings of the 22Nd International Symposium on High-performance Parallel and Distributed Computing (HPDC '13). ACM, New York, NY, USA, 167–178. DOI:https://doi.org/10.1145/2462902.2462920

[15] N DeBardeleben, J Laros, JT Daly, SL Scott, C Engelmann, and B Harrod. 2009. High-end computing resilience: Analysis of issues facing the HEC community and path-forward for research and development. Whitepaper, Dec (2009).

[16] James W. Demmel. 1997. Applied Numerical Linear Algebra. Society for Industrial and Applied Mathematics, Philadelphia, PA, USA.

[17] Nosayba El-Sayed and Bianca Schroeder. 2014. Checkpoint/restart in practice: When âĂŸsimple is betterâĂŹ. In 2014 IEEE International Conference on Cluster Computing (CLUSTER). IEEE, 84–92.

[18] A. Chien et al. 2015. Versioned Distributed Arrays for Resilience in Scientific Applications: Global View Resilience. Procedia Computer Science 51 (2015), 29 – 38. DOI:https://doi.org/10.1016/j.procs.2015.05.187

[19] G. Bosilca et al. MPICH-V: Toward a Scalable Fault Tolerant MPI for Volatile Nodes. In Supercomputing, ACM/IEEE 2002 Conference.

[20] Ian Karlin et al. 2012. LULESH Programming Model and Performance Ports Overview. Technical Report LLNL-TR-608824. 1–17 pages.

[21] Bo Fang, Qining Lu, Karthik Pattabiraman, Matei Ripeanu, and Sudhanva Gurumurthi. 2016. ePVF: An Enhanced Program Vulnerability Factor Methodology for Cross-layer Resilience Analysis. In DSN.

[22] Shuguang Feng, Shantanu Gupta, Amin Ansari, and Scott Mahlke. 2010. Shoestring: Probabilistic Soft Error Reliability on the Cheap. SIGPLAN Not. 45, 3 (March 2010), 385–396. DOI:https://doi.org/10.1145/1735971.1736063

[23] Marc Gamell, Keita Teranishi, Michael A. Heroux, Jackson Mayo, Hemanth Kolla, Jacqueline Chen, and Manish Parashar. 2015. Local Recovery and Failure Masking for Stencil-based Applications at Extreme Scales. In Proceedings of the International Conference for High Performance Computing, Networking, Storage and Analysis (SC '15). ACM, New York, NY, USA, Article 70, 12 pages. DOI: https://doi.org/10.1145/2807591.2807672

[24] B. Grigorian and G. Reinman. Accelerating divergent applications on SIMD architectures using neural networks. In 2014 IEEE 32nd International Conference on Computer Design (ICCD).

[25] Weining Gu, Z. Kalbarczyk, and R. K. Iyer. Error sensitivity of the Linux kernel executing on PowerPC G4 and Pentium 4 processors. In Dependable Systems and Networks, 2004 International Conference on.

[26] V. Gupta, D. Mohapatra, A. Raghunathan, and K. Roy. 2013. Low-Power Digital Signal Processing Using Approximate Adders. IEEE Transactions on Computer-Aided Design of Integrated Circuits and Systems 32, 1 (Jan 2013), 124–137.

[27] J. Han and M. Orshansky. Approximate computing: An emerging paradigm for energy-efficient design. In 2013 18th IEEE European Test Symposium (ETS).

[28] Siva Kumar Sastry Hari, Sarita V. Adve, Helia Naeimi, and Pradeep Ramachandran. 2012. Relyzer: Exploiting Application-level Fault Equivalence to Analyze Application Resiliency to Transient Faults. SIGPLAN Not. 47, 4 (March 2012), 123–134. DOI:https://doi.org/10.1145/2248487.2150990

[29] Nicholas J. Higham. Accuracy and Stability of Numerical Algorithms (second ed.). Society for Industrial and Applied Mathematics, Philadelphia, PA, USA. xxx+680 pages.

[30] Chung hsing Hsu and Wu chun Feng. 2005. A Power-Aware Run-Time System for High-Performance Computing. In Supercomputing, 2005. Proceedings of the ACM/IEEE SC 2005 Conference. 1–1. DOI:https://doi.org/10.1109/SC.2005.3

[31] I.Karlin. 2012. LULESH Programming Model and Performance Ports Overview. (2012). https://codesign.llnl.gov/pdfs/lulesh_Ports.pdf

[32] Los Alamos National Laboratory. 2016. APEX 2020. (2016). http://www.lanl.gov/projects/apex/_assets/docs/2.4-RFP-Technical-Requirements-Document.doc

[33] Los Alamos National Laboratory. 2016. The PENNANT Mini-App v0.9. (2016). https://github.com/losalamos/PENNANT

[34] Los Alamos National Laboratory. 2016. SNAP - SN Application Proxy Summary. (2016). https://asc.llnl.gov/CORAL-benchmarks/Summaries/SNAP_Summary_v1.3.pdf

[35] Los Alamos National Laboratory. 2016. SNAP: SN (Discrete Ordinates) Application Proxy v107. (2016). https://github.com/losalamos/SNAP

[36] G. Li, Q. Lu, and K. Pattabiraman. 2015. Fine-Grained Characterization of Faults Causing Long Latency Crashes in Programs. In DSN. 450–461. DOI:https://doi.org/10.1109/DSN.2015.36

[37] Don Libes. 1990. expect: Curing Those Uncontrollable Fits of Interaction. In PROCEEDINGS OF THE SUMMER 1990 USENIX CONFERENCE. 183–192.

[38] Fan Long, Stelios Sidiroglou-Douskos, and Martin Rinard. 2014. Automatic Runtime Error Repair and Containment via Recovery Shepherding. SIGPLAN Not. (2014).

[39] Qining Lu, Karthik Pattabiraman, Meeta S. Gupta, and Jude A. Rivers. 2014. SDCTune: A Model for Predicting the SDC Proneness of an Application for Configurable Protection. In Proceedings of the 2014 International Conference on Compilers, Architecture and Synthesis for Embedded Systems (CASES '14). ACM, New York, NY, USA, Article 23, 10 pages. DOI:https://doi.org/10.1145/2656106.2656127

[40] C. D. Martino, Z. Kalbarczyk, R. K. Iyer, F. Baccanico, J. Fullop, and W. Kramer. 2014. Lessons Learned from the Analysis of System Failures at Petascale: The Case of Blue Waters. In 2014 44th Annual IEEE/IFIP International Conference on Dependable Systems and Networks. 610–621. DOI:https://doi.org/10.1109/DSN.2014.62

[41] Sarah E. Michalak, William N. Rust, John T. Daly, Andrew J. DuBois, and David H. DuBois. 2014. Correctness Field Testing of Production and Decommissioned High Performance Computing Platforms at Los Alamos National Laboratory (SC '14). Piscataway, NJ, USA, 609–619.

[42] Sparsh Mittal. 2016. A Survey of Techniques for Approximate Computing. ACM Comput. Surv. (2016). DOI:https://doi.org/10.1145/2893356

[43] D. Nicholaeff, N. Davis, D. Trujillo, and R. W. Robey. 2012. Cell-Based Adaptive Mesh Refinement Implemented with General Purpose Graphics Processing Units. (2012).

[44] K. Palem and A. Lingamneni. What to do about the end of Moore's law, probably!. In Design Automation Conference (DAC), 2012. DOI:https://doi.org/10.1145/2228360.2228525

[45] H. et al. Patil. Pinpointing Representative Portions of Large Intel Itanium Programs with Dynamic Instrumentation. In MICRO-37.

[46] A. Petitet, R. C. Whaley, J. Dongarra, and A. Cleary. 2008. HPL - a portable implementation of the high-performance linpack benchmark for distributed-memory computers. (2008). http://www.netlib.org/benchmark/hpl

[47] A. Rahimi, L. Benini, and R. K. Gupta. 2013. Spatial Memorization: Concurrent Instruction Reuse to Correct Timing Errors in SIMD Architectures. IEEE Transactions on Circuits and Systems II: Express Briefs (Dec 2013).

[48] L. Rashid, K. Pattabiraman, and S. Gopalakrishnan. 2015. Characterizing the Impact of Intermittent Hardware Faults on Programs. IEEE Transactions on Reliability 64, 1 (March 2015), 297–310. DOI:https://doi.org/10.1109/TR.2014.2363152

[49] Martin Rinard, Cristian Cadar, Daniel Dumitran, Daniel M Roy, and Tudor Leu. 2004. A dynamic technique for eliminating buffer overflow vulnerabilities (and other memory errors). In Computer Security Applications Conference, 2004. 20th Annual. IEEE, 82–90.

[50] Martin Rinard, Cristian Cadar, Daniel Dumitran, Daniel M. Roy, Tudor Leu, and William S. Beebee, Jr. Enhancing Server Availability and Security Through Failure-oblivious Computing (OSDI'04). USENIX Association. http://dl.acm.org/citation.cfm?id=1251254.1251275

[51] Marc et al. Snir. 2014. Addressing failures in exascale computing. *International Journal of High Performance Computing Applications* (2014).

[52] Noah Spurrier and contributors. 2013. Pexpect is a Pure Python Expect-like module. (2013). https://pexpect.readthedocs.io/en/stable/index.html

[53] V. Sridharan, N. DeBardeleben, and K. Ferreira S. Blanchard, J. Stearley, J. Shalf, and S. Gurumurthi. 2015. Memory Errors in Modern Systems: The Good, The Bad, and the Ugly. In *Proceedings of International Conference on Architectural Support for Programming Languages and Operating Systems*.

[54] C. Wang, F. Mueller, C. Engelmann, and S. L. Scott. 2010. Hybrid Checkpointing for MPI Jobs in HPC Environments. In *Parallel and Distributed Systems (ICPADS), 2010 IEEE 16th International Conference on*. 524–533. DOI:https://doi.org/10.1109/ICPADS.2010.48

[55] L. Wang, Z. Kalbarczyk, R. K. Iyer, and A. Iyengar. 2015. VM-ÎijCheckpoint: Design, Modeling, and Assessment of Lightweight In-Memory VM Checkpointing. *IEEE Transactions on Dependable and Secure Computing* (March 2015).

[56] Panruo Wu, Qiang Guan, Nathan DeBardeleben, Sean Blanchard, Dingwen Tao, Xin Liang, Jieyang Chen, and Zizhong Chen. 2016. Towards Practical Algorithm Based Fault Tolerance in Dense Linear Algebra. In *Proceedings of the 25th ACM International Symposium on High-Performance Parallel and Distributed Computing (HPDC '16)*. ACM, New York, NY, USA, 31–42. DOI:https://doi.org/10.1145/2907294.2907315

[57] Z. Yang, A. Jain, J. Liang, J. Han, and F. Lombardi. 2013. Approximate XOR/XNOR-based adders for inexact computing. In *Nanotechnology (IEEE-NANO)*. DOI:https://doi.org/10.1109/NANO.2013.6720793

[58] John W. Young. 1974. A First Order Approximation to the Optimum Checkpoint Interval. *Commun. ACM* 17, 9 (Sept. 1974), 530–531. DOI:https://doi.org/10.1145/361147.361115

Towards a More Complete Understanding of SDC Propagation

Jon Calhoun
University of Illinois at Urbana-Champaign
201 N. Goodwin Ave.
Urbana, Illinois 61801
jccalho2@illinois.edu

Marc Snir
University of Illinois at Urbana-Champaign
201 N. Goodwin Ave.
Urbana, Illinois 61801
snir@illinois.edu

Luke N. Olson
University of Illinois at Urbana-Champaign
201 N. Goodwin Ave.
Urbana, Illinois 61801
lukeo@illinois.edu

William D. Gropp
University of Illinois at Urbana-Champaign
201 N. Goodwin Ave.
Urbana, Illinois 61801
wgropp@illinois.edu

ABSTRACT

With the rate of errors that can silently effect an application's state/output expected to increase on future HPC machines, numerous application-level detection and recovery schemes have been proposed. Recovery is more efficient when errors are contained and affect only part of the computation's state. Containment is usually achieved by verifying all information leaking out of a statically defined containment domain, which is an expensive procedure. Alternatively, error propagation can be analyzed to bound the domain that is affected by a detected error. This paper investigates how silent data corruption (SDC) due to soft errors propagates through three HPC applications: HPCCG, Jacobi, and CoMD. To allow for more detailed view of error propagation, the paper tracks propagation at the instruction and application variable level. The impact of detection latency on error propagation is shown along with an application's ability to recover. Finally, the impact of compiler optimizations are explored along with the impact of local problem size on error propagation.

KEYWORDS

Silent Data Corruption; Error Propagation; Reliability; Error Detection; Error Recovery

ACM Reference format:
Jon Calhoun, Marc Snir, Luke N. Olson, and William D. Gropp. 2017. Towards a More Complete Understanding of SDC Propagation. In *Proceedings of HPDC '17, Washington, DC, USA, June 26–30, 2017,* 12 pages.
https://doi.org/http://dx.doi.org/10.1145/3078597.3078617

1 INTRODUCTION

Machine errors both hard and soft are expected to increase [42] as the number of components in processors increases and as chip technologies, such as smaller feature sizes [9] or near-threshold-voltage [26], are introduced to reduce power consumption. This places increased demands on both fabrication quality and on the underlying system and numerical software stacks.

Energetic particles from cosmic radiation can invert the state of transistors [3, 34]. Manufacturing defects can lead to the same effect. One consequence is that these faults produce soft errors that can cause a silent data corruption (SDC) — i.e., an erroneous deviation in system/application state. Corrupted state can be masked by the application causing no change in the output, or in extreme cases, can lead to corruption in the output. Modern hardware supports redundancy and techniques such as error correcting codes (ECC) to detect soft errors and to prevent them from affecting the computation state. As soft error rates increase, hardware may not provide adequate protection [43], allowing for corrupted state to impact application state. To combat this, software based SDC detection schemes have been developed, with many leveraging application properties and heuristics [10, 12, 25]. Others have taken application agnostic approaches [5, 6, 8] or leverage various forms of redundancy [19, 28, 37].

Global checkpoint-restart is the *de-facto* fault tolerance protocol used by HPC applications to recover from fail-stop failures. The limited bandwidth of persistent storage is the main performance bottleneck of checkpointing methods. Current versions mitigate storage bandwidth issues by leveraging the memory hierarchy [7, 35] and use compression techniques [40].

Another way to limit the impact of storage bandwidth is to avoid the need for global checkpointing and global restart. Checkpoint-restart schemes often coordinate checkpointing and global restart: at checkpoint time, all processors are synchronized and the application state is saved, while at restart time, the entire application state is restored. This results in bursts of I/O that slow down checkpoint and recovery. Various schemes have been proposed to support uncoordinated checkpointing and localized restarts [21, 22, 47]. Similarly, application specific recovery reconstructs lost data from the remaining correct data [1].

Most recovery schemes assume that a corruption is limited to a subset of values — e.g., values in the memory of one compute node. This condition is easy to satisfy with fail-stop failures, but may not be valid in the case of SDC detection with high latency. One solution is to verify all state outside of a corrupted subset [14]. However, such checks are expensive. An alternative is to determine the propagation of corruption when a detection occurs and to restrict recovery to the potentially impacted state. In this case, some corruption can be ignored as it is attenuated by the algorithm; in other scenarios, corrupted values may permanently influence the solution.

Prior work has explored how deviations from bit-flips in floating-point computation impact on convergence properties [16, 17]. Other work has used corruption propagation in the development of low-level instruction based detection schemes that check invariants or create SDC detectors inside the compiler [23, 38] or utilize code replication to detect corruption in instructions that are likely lead to and propagate corrupted state [18, 27, 28], and understanding long latency crashes [30, 45]. This paper combines the latency of programmatic systems of corruption — e.g., segfaults, detection, control flow divergence, with corruption propagation in state variables to discuss the impact of detection latency on recovery options. In the context of tracking corruption propagation inside applications, [2] looks at state corruption propagation in MPI codes by tracking number of incorrect memory addresses, but does not relate corruption back to application level data structure nor explore compiler optimizations and the impact of local problem size on corruption propagation. [31] quantifies corruption in different GPU and host memories in GPGPU programs. This papers focus on MPI applications and tracks corruption in state variables and across MPI processes.

A detailed view of corruption propagation offers a measure of an application's ability to withstand soft errors. Moreover, it also helps application developers identify where to place detectors and to identify locations for data recovery. This paper makes the following contributions:

- the impact of detection latency on recovery options;
- the data structures critical to corruption and the risk of obtaining invalid results;
- the influence of compiler optimizations on state corruption propagation; and
- the analysis of problem size and inter-node corruption propagation.

The remainder of this paper is structured as follows. Section 2 discusses corruption propagation for sparse matrix-vector multiplication and motivates the need to investigate state corruption propagation in application codes. Section 3 details the design and overview of the corruption propagation tool and how it tracks propagation at a micro and macro-level. Error propagation results are presented in Section 4 along with a discussion on detection and recovery options. Related work is discussed in Section 5.

2 MOTIVATION

2.1 Sparse Matrix-Vector Multiplication

Sparse matrix-vector multiplication (SpMV) is the core compute kernel in many HPC applications. To understand corruption propagation, it is helpful to view a SpMV as of series of inner-products between the rows of the matrix and the input vector or more simply as an unstructured series of multiplications and additions.

In Figure 1, one element of the input vector is corrupted (red square). The corrupted value spreads through three inner products (rows), resulting in the corruption (red squares) in the output vector.

If this SpMV is used as part of an iterative method or solver, then the corrupted values propagate further as the output vector is used in other parts of the method and with repeated application of the SpMV. Consequently, corruption in element i of the input vector influences element j of the output vector if row j in column i is non-zero. Thus, the propagation of corrupted values with dense matrices is more rapid than with sparse matrices [13].

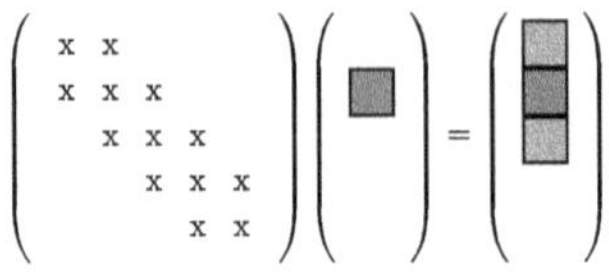

Figure 1: Propagation of corrupted state via a sparse matrix-vector multiplication.

One important caveat of corruption propagation for a SpMV is that corruption is modeled through the algorithm and not by the code as executed on a computer. A complete analysis of corruption propagation for the SpMV requires investigating the effect of corruptions of loads, stores, address calculations, branching, looping, etc. This is often complex as deep inspection of the code is needed in order consider all paths of execution. The corruption propagation tool presented in this paper allows for tracking the propagation of corruption at the level of application variables and with load/store granularity.

3 TRACKING PROPAGATION

Figure 2 details the flow of a fault occurring in a system that transitions to a failure. Once a fault is activated, error is present in the system. In this paper, error resulting from an activated fault is referred to as state corruption or corruption to avoid confusion with numerical errors in HPC applications. The location of the initial corrupted value is critical to identifying corruption propagation. During the execution the remaining program instructions, the corruption can be masked due to programmatic or algorithmic properties, can lead to a system detectable event such as a segmentation fault, or can propagate to corrupt more of the program state and become a silent data corruption (SDC). SDC detection schemes rely on a portion of the application state being corrupted, or a large magnitude in the deviation to detect simulation divergence.

Two levels of corruption propagation are considered:

macro tracks deviations in the state variables through the simulation; and

micro tracks deviations in the loads, stores, and other low-level operations.

In order to track corruption propagation at both the micro and macro level, an LLVM-based [29] instrumentation tool is developed to emulate lock-step execution of a correctly executed *gold*

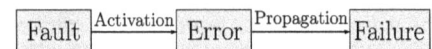

Figure 2: Logical flow of error propagation from initial fault to subsequent failure.

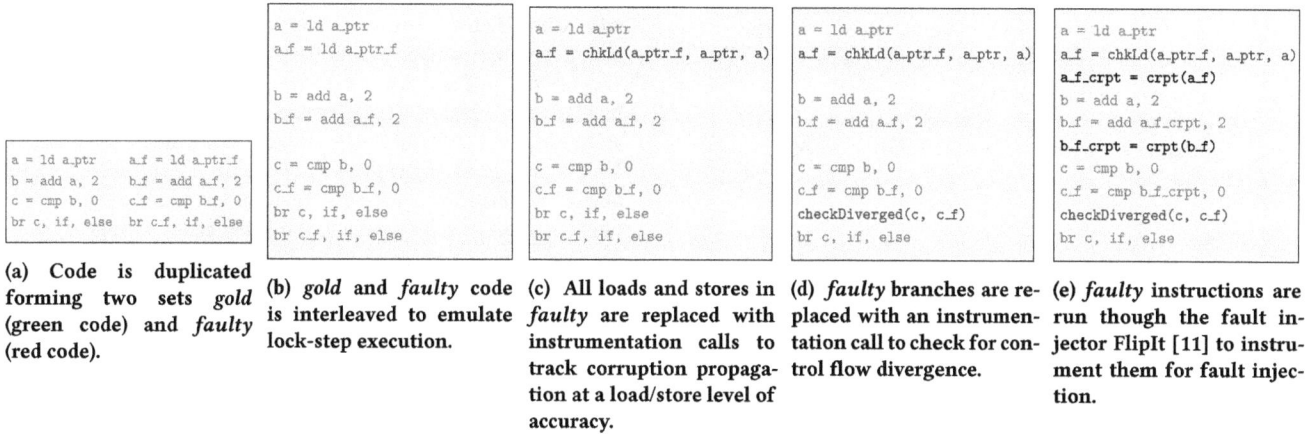

(a) Code is duplicated forming two sets *gold* (green code) and *faulty* (red code).

(b) *gold* and *faulty* code is interleaved to emulate lock-step execution.

(c) All loads and stores in *faulty* are replaced with instrumentation calls to track corruption propagation at a load/store level of accuracy.

(d) *faulty* branches are replaced with an instrumentation call to check for control flow divergence.

(e) *faulty* instructions are run though the fault injector FlipIt [11] to instrument them for fault injection.

Figure 4: Overview of the code transformation for micro-level propagation tracking.

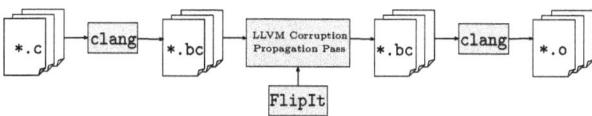

Figure 3: Overview of the instrumentation process that transforms source code to be able to track propagation and inject faults.

along with a faulty execution *faulty*. Optimized LLVM IR code is run though a compiler pass to instrument it to track corruption propagation and to inject faults before being compiled to object code — see Figure 3. Figure 4 illustrates the instrumentation process performed in the compiler pass. Source code is instrumented (Section 3.1) after compiler optimizations are performed to mitigate the impact of instrumentation on the object code generated. An API call at natural points in the application — e.g., end of an iteration — tracks propagation of application level memory allocations at the macro-level. At the micro-level, the LLVM compiler pass adds instrumentation to track propagation at a load/store granularity and relates loads/stores to application level memory allocations.

After replication, there exists two distinct sets of instructions: one for the *gold* application (green) and one for the *faulty* application (red). Instructions for the *gold* application forms a reference set of loads, stores, and correct program behavior that the *faulty* application instructions are compared against. Replicating all instructions creates separate memory images for both the *gold* and *faulty* applications. Thus, these two sets of instructions do not share the same data.

3.1 Micro-level Propagation Tracking

At the micro-level, loads and stores are monitored for deviations since these operations directly impact the state variables. Stores *commit* erroneous values to state variables, while loads allow for reuse and propagation of corrupted data. Examining corruption propagation at the micro-level allows a fine grain view of how corruption propagates inside the application. This is useful to assess

the bound on a pointer reference leading to a segmentation fault, to determine the number of loads and stores that are perturbed, to quantify the deviation when a corruption is masked by the application, and to examine the impact of compiler optimizations at a fine-grain level.

Because instructions from *gold* and *faulty* are interleaved, corresponding operations — i.e. loads and stores — are next to each other allowing for straightforward comparison of both the values and the addresses. To simplify the comparison, all loads and stores in *faulty* are replaced with an instrumentation call, see Figure 4c. In addition to determining if a loaded or stored value deviates from the expected *gold* value, the deviation can be calculated (with additional computational cost) along with information on the associated allocation. The latter requires the base address and size of all memory allocations to be logged by instrumenting memory allocation calls and by inserting the base address and size into a table. Information that relates the *gold* and *faulty* allocations is also logged since it is used to assess macro-level propagation.

Algorithms 1 and 2 detail the logic of the instrumentation calls for loads and stores, respectively. The function call to checkInMemory determines whether an address is contained in a logged memory allocation of the *faulty* application. The information collected inside the function logDeviation of Algorithm 3 accumulates information into the same variables for both loads and stores; however, in practice a vector of statistics exists for loads and stores. If a store is outside an allocated memory region of the *faulty* application, then the address and value are added into an outside store hash table to allow subsequent loads to read the incorrectly written value and to prevent overwriting of data used by the *gold* application. Conversely, if a load from *faulty* occurs outside an allocated memory region, the load proceeds only if the address does not exist in the outside store hash table. If the address is found in the outside store hash table, the *faulty* address is de-referenced in an effort to generate a segmentation fault, but execution proceeds with the value from the store hash table.

Once a fault is injected, it propagates to registers and memory locations based on data-dependencies. Periodically, these data-dependencies flow to a comparison used in a branch. Control flow

---

Algorithm 1: Logic for load instrumentation function call.

```
1  Function chkLd(fptr, gptr, gvalue)
2      inMemory ← checkInMemory(fptr)
3      if !inMemory then
4          inStoreTable ← checkInStoreTable(fptr)
5      if inStoreTable then
6          fvalue ← readStoreTable(fptr)
7      else
8          fvalue ← *fptr
9      logDeviation(fptr, gptr, fvalue, gvalue, inMemory)
10     return fvalue
```

Algorithm 2: Logic for store instrumentation function call.

```
1  Function chkSt(fptr, fvalue, gptr, gvalue)
2      inMemory ← checkInMemory(fptr)
3      logDeviation(fptr, gptr, fvalue, gvalue, inMemory)
4      if !inMemory then
5          writeStoreTable(fptr, fvalue)
6      else
7          fptr ← *fvalue
8      return
```

Algorithm 3: Logic for logging information on deviation of load or store at the micro-level.

```
1  Function logDeviation(fptr, gptr, fvalue, gvalue, inMemory)
2      dev ← abs(fvalue - gvalue)
3      if dev != 0 then
4          if !inMemory then
5              numAccessOut ← numAccessOut + 1
6          maxDeviation ← max(maxDeviation, dev)
7          numDevAccess ← numDevAccess + 1
8      return
```

in the lock-step execution relies on the values from the *gold* application — see Figure 4d. Comparisons in *faulty* remain, but the branching instruction is replaced with an instrumentation call to log information about this branching deviation. Due to lock-step style execution, micro-level propagation tracking is unable to accurately resolve control flow divergence. Resolving this requires a coarser view of propagation tracking: macro-propagation tracking.

To resolve control flow divergence and to handle regions of code not open to instrumentation — e.g., MPI_Send, MPI_Recv — function calls are duplicated. For functions that modify global state and yield a different result when called by both the *gold* and *faulty* code — e.g., rand(), MPI_Init() — the return value is duplicated allowing both the *gold* and *faulty* codes to proceed with the intended value/action.

For functions open to instrumentation, the LLVM pass creates a new version of that function with an extended interface. The function's argument list is duplicated providing arguments for the *gold* and *faulty* code. In addition, the return type is modified to return a structure containing two elements: the return value for both the *gold* and the *faulty* code. Code contained inside the original function is duplicated and combined as shown in Figure 4. *faulty*

code depends on and consumes the *faulty* arguments, and the *gold* code depends on and consumes the *gold* arguments.

After the *gold* and *faulty* code has been merged and all instrumentation is complete, *faulty* instructions are passed to FlipIt [11], an LLVM based fault injector, to instrument the faulty instructions for fault injection — see Figure 4e. For instructions that have been replaced with instrumentation calls, FlipIt is instructed to only inject faults in arguments belonging to the *faulty* code. Arguments coming from *gold* will never suffer fault injection in instrumentation calls.

3.2 Macro-level Propagation Tracking

Macro-level propagation tracking targets the deviation of high-level state variables, data structures, and propagation across process boundaries. To facilitate tracking propagation of corruption in state variables, the base address of all memory allocations along with the allocation's length are stored in a table. During compilation, the LLVM corruption propagation pass inserts an instrumentation call after the memory allocation in the *gold* and *faulty* code that logs both allocations into the table. Furthermore, this instrumentation call creates a relationship between the two allocations allowing for comparison of indices when computing propagation statistics. Algorithm 4 details the logic used when comparing two memory allocations. By default, only the percent of elements corrupted, ℓ_2-norm, and max-norm between the *gold* and *faulty* memory allocations is logged for post run analysis.

Algorithm 4: Logic for comparing two memory allocations and generating propagation statistics.

```
1  for i ← 0 to num_Allocs do
2      gbase ← goldAllocAddr[i]
3      fbase ← faultyAllocAddr[i]
4      gsize ← goldAllocSize[i]
5      fsize ← faultyAllocSize[i]
6      numElem ← calcNumDiffElem(gbase, fbase, gsize, fsize, tol)
7      norm2 ← calc2norm(gbase, fbase, gsize, fsize)
8      maxNorm ← calcMaxNorm(gbase, fbase, gsize, fsize)
9      saveResults(fbase, numElem, norm2, maxNorm)
```

Comparing the state of all allocated variables is expensive; therefore, comparison points are placed at natural termination points — e.g., end of an iteration. These locations correspond to locations where SDC checks are often placed and checkpointing occurs. Initially, corruption is confined to the process in which the fault occurred. As the application progresses, inter-process communication allows corruption to propagate beyond the process suffering the fault. Understanding how fast this occurs and which processes are likely to have corrupted data allows for only a subset of processes to recover by checkpoint-restart or a more tailored algorithmic solution.

Unlike micro-level propagation tracking, macro-level propagation tracking is able to resolve divergence in control flow graph by executing functions to completion once for the *gold* arguments and lastly for the *faulty* arguments. Control flow may diverge inside the function, but at the point the function call returns both the *gold* and *faulty* applications are at the same point in the control flow graph. Thus, comparing the states of the *gold* and *faulty* memory allocations is safe and meaningful.

4 EXPERIMENTAL RESULTS

4.1 Testing Methodology

4.1.1 System. Results are collected on Blue Waters, a Cray supercomputer managed by the National Center for Supercomputing Applications and supported by the National Science Foundation and the University of Illinois. Each compute node has 2 AMD 6276 Interlagos CPUs and 64 GB of RAM. Clang and LLVM version 3.5.2 compile and instrument the source code.

4.1.2 Fault Injection. The fault model used in this paper assumes that transient faults arise in processor logic during execution. That is, the fault manifests as a single bit-flip in the result register of the instruction. In addition, it is assumed that register files and memories such as SRAM and DRAM are sufficiently protected by error correcting codes (ECC) or more advance features such as Chipkill [15], and that faults are not injected in these locations. The LLVM corruption propagation pass uses the open-source LLVM based fault injector FlipIt [11] to instrument instruction from the *faulty* application, allowing for faults to be injected dynamically at runtime.

This paper does not inject faults into the initialization of the applications. Instead, faults are injected during the main computation. The selected applications use MPI, and in the tests, MPI process rank 3 is selected to experience a single bit-flip error during the execution of a unique, random dynamic LLVM instruction. Instructions selected for fault injection are classified into the following categories based on its use in code: floating-point arithmetic (*Arith-FP*), fixed-point integer arithmetic (*Arith-Fix*), pointer and address calculation (*Pointer*), and branching, comparisons, and control flow (*Control*). Latency, in number of instructions, counts dynamically executed LLVM instructions.

Although a single MPI process suffers a fault, all MPI processes still track propagation via the methods outlined in Section 3 in order to determine if propagation occurs between nodes.

Each application is run 1500 times with a different random fault each time. The kernels WAXPY and SpMV are run 1500 times per optimization level each with a different random fault.

4.1.3 Applications. **Jacobi:** This defines Jacobi relaxation on a unit square with fixed boundaries using a 5-point stencil and 1-D row partitioning of parallel processes. This test uses 4 MPI processes with 4096 grid points per process. Instrumentation yields a $102\times$ slowdown. Jacobi relaxation does not guarantee a reduction in the residual, however unexpected large jumps often indicate the presence of state corruption. This paper flags any increase in the residual by an order of magnitude as SDC. The stopping tolerance use for Jacobi is $1e-3$, and the floating-point comparison tolerance when tracking propagation is set to $1e-5$. Finally, macro-level propagation results are logged at the end of each iteration.

CoMD: CoMD[1] is a molecular dynamics mini-app created and maintained by the Exascale Co-Design Center for Materials in Extreme Environments (ExMatEx). CoMD is parallelized with MPI

and uses a link-cell structure to determine the interaction regions for the atoms. This test uses 16 MPI processes to simulate the motion and interaction of 32000 atoms over 500 time-steps, where forces between atoms are computed using the Embedded-Atom Method (EAM). Instrumentation results in a $33\times$ slowdown and SDC is detected by ensuring that the total energy is within five standard deviations of the ensemble mean. Macro-level propagation results are logged at the end of each iteration. Deviations smaller than $1e-10$ are considered insignificant to accuracy of CoMD.

HPCCG: HPCCG[2] is a conjugate gradient (CG) benchmark from the Mantevo Suite that simulates a 3D chimney domain using a 27-point finite difference matrix. This test is run with 16 MPI processes and a local block size of $nx = ny = nz = 13$ and instrumentation results in a $460\times$ slowdown. As with Jacobi, the CG algorithm does not guarantee a reduction in the residual. Here, any increase in the residual by an order of magnitude is flagged as SDC. Macro-level propagation results are logged at the end of each iteration. The convergence tolerance used for HPCCG is $1e-7$ — when tracking corruption propagation, deviations smaller than $1e-10$ are ignored.

4.2 Micro-level Propagation

4.2.1 Latency of Detection. Each injected fault starts as a single-bit error in the result register of an instruction. As the program executes, the single-bit error propagates to other registers and memory locations. Depending on the type of instruction the fault is injected into, the latency to detection often varies. The analysis in this paper looks at three triggers to failure: segmentation fault, detection, and control flow divergence. Table 1 shows the breakdown of each symptom based on instruction type across the tests in Section 4.1.3.

Segmentation faults account for 30–35% of all injected faults in each application. From Table 1, the majority (over 50%) of segmentation faults are triggered by *Pointer* instructions. Figure 5 shows the segmentation fault latency for each application in number of LLVM instructions executed after an injection. A significant number (90%) of segmentation faults occur within 4 LLVM instructions. Of the runs with a segmentation fault within 4 LLVM instructions, 61% percent are classified as *Pointer*, 32% percent are classified as *Arith-Fix*, 0% percent are classified as *Arith-FP*, and 13% percent are classified as *Control*. Looking at the remaining segmentation faults, 16% percent are classified as *Pointer*, 8% percent are classified as *Arith-Fix*, 0% percent are classified as *Arith-FP*, and 76% percent are classified as *Control*. Short latencies are attributed to corruption of address calculation — e.g., corrupting an address or offset, before a load or a store. Longer latencies are the result of corruption in the loop induction variables. The instructions used to check a loop conditional increases the segmentation fault latency slightly before the induction variable is used as part of a load/store during the subsequent iteration. Segmentation fault latencies for these applications are consistent with those reported for the Linux kernel [20] and other benchmarks [30].

Figure 6 shows the bit locations that generated a segmentation fault. The results highlight that most segmentation faults occur due to a bit-flip near the most-significant bit (MSB). Bit-flips in bits near the least-significant bit (LSB) lead to incorrect indexing and using

[1]https://github.com/exmatex/CoMD

[2]https://mantevo.org/packages.php

Table 1: Breakdown of failure symptom by instruction type.

Instruction Type	Failure Symptom		
	Segmentation Fault	Detection	Control Flow Divergence
Arith-FP	0%	49%	20%
Arith-Fix	24%	24%	26%
Pointer	56%	27%	16%
Control	20%	0%	38%

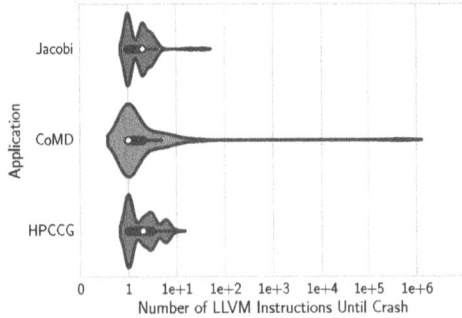

Figure 5: Latency (number of LLVM instructions) until a segmentation fault.

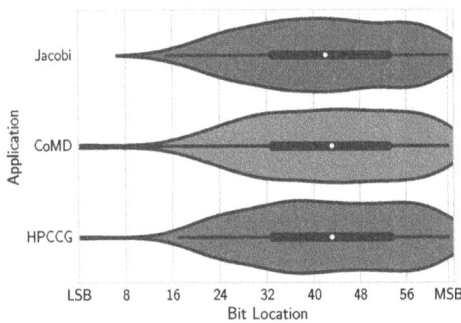

Figure 6: Bit positions where injected fault resulted in a segmentation fault.

incorrect data. Flipping bits 0–2 result in unaligned data access for double precision arrays and can cause significant deviation in the load/store, but rarely generates a segmentation fault. As the local problem size grows, the amount of allocated memory also increases. As a result, the number of segmentation faults decreases for low order bits by replacing them with load/store on incorrect addresses.

Segmentation faults are an excellent detector that allow little corruption propagation in most cases. Since segmentation faults occur in only 30–35% of the tests most faults allow for propagation and SDC. Typical HPC SDC detectors check for errors at a coarse granularity (thousands or millions of instructions) by looking for

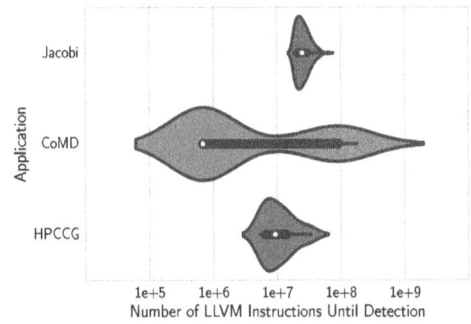

Figure 7: Latency (number of LLVM instructions) until SDC detection.

latent errors that have corrupted the state of application level variables to cause a noticeable deviation. Overall the lightweight SDC detectors added to tests (Section 4.1.3) detect data corruption in 11% of Jacobi runs, 1% of HPCCG runs, and 2% of CoMD runs. Breaking down which faults are detected by instruction type, Table 1, shows most detected faults occur in *Arith-FP* instructions. Figure 7 shows the latency in number of LLVM instructions executed before the detection occurs. Compared to detection via segmentation faults, detection latency of specially designed detectors is much larger.

Each test checks for SDC at the end of each iteration. Converting detection latency from LLVM instructions executed to iterations executed shows all runs with detection for CoMD and HPCCG are within 2 iterations of injection. Detected SDC in Jacobi has a longer maximal latency at 492 iterations. Faults that cause an order of magnitude differences in floating-point values are detected during the following iteration. Without SDC detectors 100% of HPCCG runs and 56% of Jacobi would require extra iterations to converge to the correct solution. All CoMD runs with detection appear as outliers when forming an ensemble distribution at the final time-step if no SDC detectors are present.

If checkpoint-restart routines are used to recover from the detected SDC, then for runs with a high latency of detection, a domino effect of needing to roll back older and older checkpoints is possible if recovery proceeds from frequently taken in-memory checkpoints; this is common for multi-level checkpointing schemes [7, 35]. At the time of detection, if the extent of corruption is known in terms of state variables and processes, then forward-recovery schemes offer the best solution to avoid the domino effect of checkpoint-restart (backward-recovery).

4.2.2 Abnormal Behavior. HPC applications commonly iterate over and compute on vectors of data. Faults in *Pointer* and *Arith-Fix* instructions often lead to corruption in pointers used in load/store operations, and can lead to segmentation faults. However, corruption of loop control variables can lead to divergence in the control flow graph. Control flow divergence in loops (see Figure 8) results in an early loop exit; consequently, elements of a vector may not be updated or computed. Control flow divergence occurs in 3% of Jacobi runs, 6% of HPCCG runs, and 20% of CoMD runs. Unlike HPCCG and Jacobi where data distribution is static, CoMD has atoms that migrate between processes that dynamically modify the

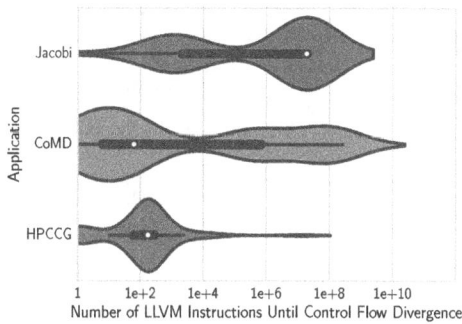

Figure 8: Latency (number of LLVM instructions) until control flow diverges.

Table 2: Dynamic LLVM instruction type percentage

Instruction Type	Application		
	HPCCG	Jacobi	CoMD
Arith-FP	35%	41%	35%
Arith-Fix	22%	28%	16%
Pointer	22%	21%	34%
Control	21%	10%	15%

data distribution. The extreme latencies for control flow divergence in CoMD are due to corruption of the atom positions that modifies the control flow of the atom exchange routine as atoms migrate incorrectly (inter-process corruption propagation). In the remaining cases, most control flow diverges within the injected loop structure, leaving some vector entries unmodified. To ensure correct execution of these loops, instruction duplication techniques such as IPAS [28] and FlipBack [36] or low-cost invariant checks [23], offer the ability to ensure correct control flow with minor overheads.

An optimization to lower the overhead of algorithmic based SDC detection schemes is to assume static data — e.g., the matrix in a linear solver is sufficiently protected that it does not need explicit checks for consistency and leaving SDC checks to inspect dynamic data. With a fault model that only allows for corruption in *Arith-FP* values, this is a valid assumption, however once corruption occur in *Arith-Fix* and *Pointer* type instructions, static data can be written by errant store instructions. Although very rare (less than 0.1% of runs) it does have the ability to make a convergent algorithm non-convergent or converge to a different solution. To mitigate corruption of static data, checksums can be employed to ensure consistency or pages containing static data can be marked *read-only* after initialization to ensure no errant stores corrupt the data.

4.2.3 Effect of Compiler Optimizations. The ratios of the different instruction types impact the probability of different failure symptoms. Table 2 shows the percentage of dynamic LLVM instructions for each application classified as a given instruction type. Across all applications, instructions classified as *Arith-FP* comprises the majority dynamic instructions followed by instruction types *Pointer* and *Arith-Fix* that are used to compute addresses. Finally, *Control* flow makes up the smallest classification percentage.

Instruction mix depends on the data structures, compiler, and optimization level. Two key operations in the HPCCG mini-app and other linear solvers are the sparse matrix-vector multiply (SpMV) and scaled vector addition (WAXPBY). The impact of compiler optimizations on these small kernels helps identify the impact on the full mini-app and production application.

WAXPY: A WAXPY operation, Algorithm 5 scales two input vectors **x** and **y** when performing the vector addition operation. Compiling without any optimizations (-O0) produces verbose and explicit code as every load and store references memory. Register allocating variables i and N along with hoisting loads outside the loop with -O1 reduces address calculation and loads/stores that often lead to segmentation faults, see Section 4.2. Furthermore, optimization levels -O2 and -O3 unroll and vectorize the loop, further reducing the need for control flow instructions. For this kernel, -O2 and -O3 produces identical code. To support higher level optimizations such as loop unrolling and vectorization, extra instructions are added to ensure correctness for all sizes of N. Table 4 summarizes the impact of compiler optimizations. Vectorization increases the number of integer operations which causes an increase in runs that experience a segmentation fault. Loop unrolling removes branching instructions and instructions that update the loop induction variable which removes locations where corruption of loop induction variables are possible lowering control flow divergence.

Algorithm 5: Scaled Vector Addition (WAXPBY).

```
1  for i ← 0 to N do
2  │   w[i] ← a * x[i] + b * y[i]
```

Table 3: Dynamic LLVM instruction percentage for WAXPBY kernel.

Optimizations	Arith-Fix	Pointer	Control	Arith-FP
O0	31%	23%	15%	31%
O1	8%	23%	23%	46%
O2/O3	17%	40%	3%	40%

SpMV: The SpMV kernel, Algorithm 6, is more complicated than that of WAXPBY both mathematically and in machine code. Because the SpMV uses a sparse matrix representation (compressed sparse row in Algorithm 6), the level of indirection needed to access entries of the matrix increases. Each increase in indirection involves a pointer dereference; therefore, with more address manipulations and loads/stores, the number of dynamic instructions of *Arith-Fix* and *Pointer* are higher than with WAXPBY, as shown in Table 5. This

Table 4: WAXPBY kernel failure symptom percentage.

Symptom	Optimizations		
	O0	O1	O2/O3
Segmentation Fault	29%	27%	40%
Control Flow Divergence	10%	4%	2%
No Symptom	61%	69%	58%

also implies that common symptoms of these types of operations will be more prevalent.

Algorithm 6: Sparse Matrix-Vector Multiplication.

```
1  for i ← 0 to num_row do
2      tmp ← 0
3      for jj ← A_i[i] to A_i[i+1] do
4          tmp ← tmp + A_data[jj] * x_data[A_j[jj]]
5      y_data[i] ← tmp
```

With the baseline optimization level -O0, the code is explicit and verbose. Higher levels of optimizations retain the base addresses of the arrays A_i, A_j, A_data in register temporaries along with loop induction variables and hoists loads with -O1. Optimization levels -O2 and -O3 do not vectorize this kernel. Instead, the inner most loop is unrolled removing comparisons and branching instructions along with hoisting the load of num_row to outside the loops.

Table 6 shows that without vectorization, the rate of segmentation faults remains around 30% of executions, which is consistent with WAXPBY and the applications. Loop unrolling fails to reduce divergence in control flow compared to WAXPBY. Control flow for the inner most loop is more complex than with WAXPBY resulting in more locations in which a fault can occur that influences control flow.

4.3 Macro-level Propagation

After a fault occurs, an erroneous value is present in the application state. Over time, as this value is used/reused, the corruption propagates to infect larger portions of the application state. Most HPC SDC detectors ensure correctness of application level variables. Knowing which application variables are corrupted and the extent of corruption can assist in placement of detection and recovery schemes.

4.3.1 Jacobi. Each iteration of Jacobi refines a solution u to improve the solution accuracy resulting in an updated solution in a separate vector u_{new}. These two vectors represent the two key data structures and is the focus when measuring corruption

Table 5: Dynamic LLVM instruction classification percentage for SpMV kernel.

Optimizations	Arith-Fix	Pointer	Control	Arith-FP
O0	38%	40%	6%	16%
O1	22%	24%	21%	33%
O2/O3	24%	23%	19%	34%

Table 6: SpMV kernel failure symptom percentage.

	Optimizations		
Symptom	O0	O1	O2/O3
Segmentation Fault	25%	32%	29%
Control Flow Divergence	12%	13%	14%
No Symptom	63%	55%	57%

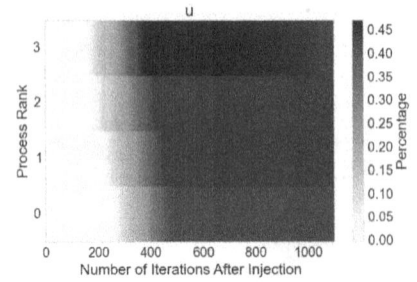

Figure 9: Average percentage of corrupted elements of iterative solution u for Jacobi.

propagation. Figure 9 shows the average percentage of elements that are corrupted due to an injected fault (intensity of color) across all MPI processes (y-axis) in the iterations following the injection iteration (x-axis) for the solution variable u. The variable u_{new} is not shown as it is qualitatively similar to u. All runs are aggregated to align the iteration where injection occurs. This allows corruption percentages in all remaining iterations to be averaged over all runs. All faults are injected on rank 3, and as time evolves corruption propagation occurs inside this process indicated by the increase in the intensity of color on the horizontal row for rank 3. Overtime, corruption propagates inside rank 3 and reaches the region of the array that is communicated via a halo-exchange corrupting process 2. This process continues until all processes are corrupted or the corruption is attenuated. Because Jacobi converges to a solution, over time the corruption in the variables is removed. When tracking propagation in u, comparisons are made between the memory of u from the *gold* and *faulty* applications. As Jacobi continues to iterate, error does not appear to reduce because as error due to the fault is removed from the *faulty* u it is being compared to an ever more accurate u from the *gold* application. Only with extra iterations on *faulty* (beyond what is run for *gold*) do the two solution vectors converge.

After a fault, corruption appears immediately on rank 3. As corruption propagates inside rank 3, it corrupts values set to process 2 in a halo exchange the speed of this corruption depends on the stencil size. This problem uses a 5-point stencil, and the average worst case propagation latency occurs when an element interior to a local domain is corrupted. This requires $n/2$ iterations were n is the local block size. SDC detected in Jacobi is within 492 iterations of injection. For any reasonable local block size, once SDC is detected it can be confined to a process and its immediate neighbors; allowing a customized local recovery scheme to be applied.

4.3.2 HPCCG. Conjugate Gradient (CG) — see Algorithm 7 — is a popular solver for systems of linear equations. This algorithm relies on four key variables: the iterative solution x^k, search directions p^k that are used to update x^k, residual vector r^k, and the matrix-vector product $A * p$.

As with Jacobi, propagation results for HPCCG are aggregated to align the iteration in which injection occurs. Figure 11 shows corruption propagation in the form of the average percentage of

---

Algorithm 7: Conjugate Gradient Method.

1   $\mathbf{r}_0 = \mathbf{b} - \mathbf{A}\mathbf{x}_0$

2   $\mathbf{p}_0 = \mathbf{r}_0$

3   $k = 0$

4   **while** $\| r_k \|_2 < tol$ **do**

5      $\alpha_k = \dfrac{\mathbf{r}_k^T \mathbf{r}_k}{\mathbf{p}_k^T \mathbf{A}\mathbf{p}_k}$

6      $\mathbf{x}_{k+1} = \mathbf{x}_k + \alpha_k \mathbf{p}_k$

7      $\mathbf{r}_{k+1} = \mathbf{r}_k - \alpha_k \mathbf{A}\mathbf{p}_k$

8      $\beta_k = \dfrac{\mathbf{r}_{k+1}^T \mathbf{r}_{k+1}}{\mathbf{r}_k^T \mathbf{r}_k}$

9      $\mathbf{p}_{k+1} = \mathbf{r}_{k+1} + \beta_k \mathbf{p}_k$

10      $k = k + 1$

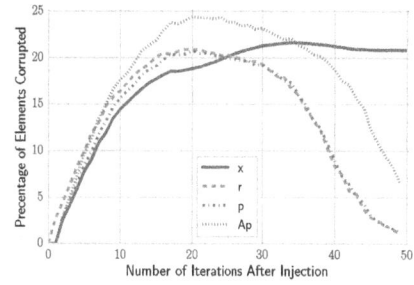

Figure 10: Average corruption in selected variables on rank 3 for HPCCG.

elements corrupted (color) per variable across all MPI processes (y-axis) for subsequent iterations after injection (x-axis). As corruption propagates locally inside each variable, the horizontal color for that row grows darker. As corruption is removed, the color lightens. Propagation between processes can be seen by looking at the color progression of columns at each iteration.

Initially, the average percentage of elements corrupted in each vector is small. However, as HPCCG continues to iterate, corruption begins to propagate both internally and externally of the corrupted process, rank 3. The most severe corruption is confined to rank 3 and the neighboring processes across the majority of the iterations. Dependencies between the four variables in Figure 11 are due a corruption in the variables r, p, or Ap, which leads to corruption in the solution vector x. Furthermore, the SpMV propagates corruption as shown in the corresponding corruption in p and Ap on every processes of each iteration. Data dependencies in updating other vectors further propagates corruption in Ap to all other variables. Ensuring the correctness of p limits corruption propagation from the SpMV in Ap and subsequently corruption propagating to r and x.

To see corruption propagation between variables more closely, Figure 10 shows the average percentage of elements from each variable corrupted on rank 3. As with Jacobi, the iterative solution x increases in error initially, but over time does not appear to remove error due to soft error corruption. This error is reduced at each iteration, however the iteration does not converge back to *gold x*. Errors in r closely follow those in p as both are used in updating the other through a WAXPBY. As corruption in p grows and subsides, Ap reflects and propagates the corruption accordingly.

The search direction p is central to corruption propagation as it is used in updating the other variables. Ensuring that p is computed correctly helps ensure that the other variables are computed correctly. Because CG uses inner-products, if masking does not occur, then corruption in input vectors propagates to all processes in one iteration. Therefore, some form of corruption is resident in all variables within 3 iterations for runs that did not produce a segmentation fault. Local recovery is still possible, though it is complicated by the presence of corruption on multiple processes.

4.3.3 CoMD. Molecular dynamics codes such as CoMD do not converge to the same solution with each execution of the program as with HPCCG and Jacobi. Instead, a single run is combined with

many other runs to form a statistical ensemble to analyze the distribution of key properties such as energy. This implies that small deviations can be masked if they do not modify the distribution. The key variables in CoMD for propagation analysis are: atom positions, atom momenta, atom forces, and atom energy. CoMD also differs from the other applications in how it stores its data. Because atoms migrate between processes, arrays are over allocated leaving space for other atoms from remote processes. This slack space is not contiguous within the arrays because it is allocated per local cell and not collectively for the entire local domain. The unused regions of the atoms complicate tracking propagation. Without modifying the data layout of CoMD this paper factors out the unused atom storage by using the number of atoms per process instead of the memory allocation size when computing corruption statistics.

Figure 12 shows the average percentage of corruption in the key variables of CoMD. For simplicity, only the force variable is shown. The remaining variables have a similar propagation pattern in terms of percentage of elements and ranks corrupted. Unlike HPCCG, where the SpMV rapidly propagates corruption between processes, the propagation in CoMD resembles Jacobi with corruption slowly propagating to neighboring domain regions. Although slow, the corruption propagation increases monotonically as time evolves which leads to an increased likelihood of the run becoming an outlier for large numbers of iterations. Over the iterations after an injection, 1% of the runs are classified as outliers when looking at the energy distribution at the final iteration. All of these outliers are caught by the SDC check.

The communication pattern in CoMD consists of point-to-point messages as atoms migrate from process to process. A single atom contributes to the force calculation of neighboring atoms. This region of influence is small and needs many iterations for the corruption to spread beyond the initially corrupted region of influence. This accounts for slow rate of propagation inside CoMD. Although corruption can propagate to neighbor processes, it requires tens to hundreds of iterations before corruption of an atom propagates to all processes. Corruption that impacts the simulation's energy distribution are detected within two iterations which allows for little inter-process propagation. Containment domains can be established around the process triggering the SDC detector and nearest neighbors to allow for partial recovery.

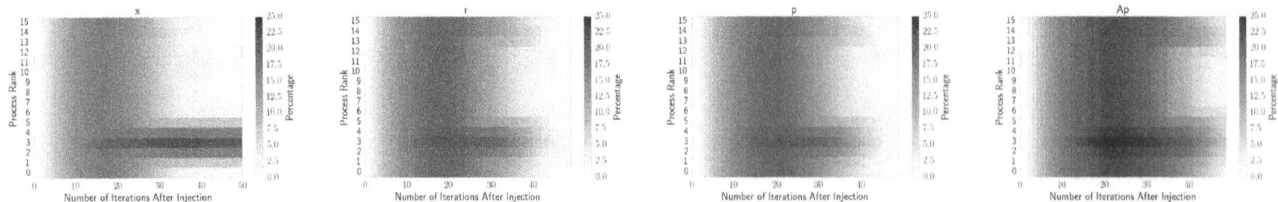

(a) Average percentage of corrupted vector elements for iterative solution x.

(b) Average percentage of corrupted vector elements for residual r.

(c) Average percentage of corrupted vector elements for search directions p.

(d) Average percentage of corrupted vector elements for result of the SpMV of A*p.

Figure 11: Average percentage of corrupted vector elements for variables in the mini-app HPCCG in iterations after injection.

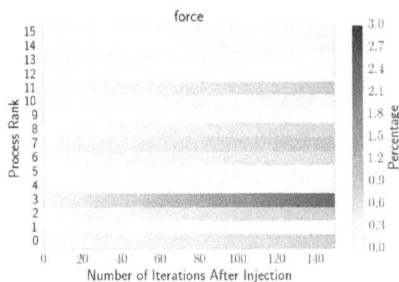

Figure 12: Average percentage of corrupted vector elements in the atom force array in the iterations following an injection for CoMD.

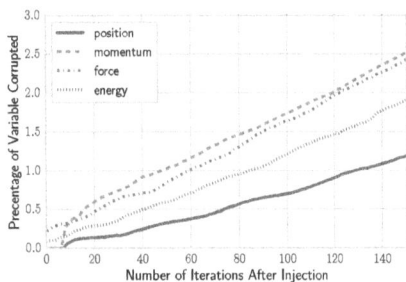

Figure 13: Average corruption in selected variables on rank 3 for CoMD.

4.3.4 Impact of Local Problem Size. To explore how problem size impacts corruption propagation. The preceding application experiments are re-run with the same number of MPI processes, but with more local work per process. Jacobi sees a 2.25× increase in the number of grid points per process at 36864. The HPCCG local problem is $nx = ny = nz = 16$, a 1.9× increase. Whereas CoMD is run with 62500 atoms, resulting in a 1.9× increase in problem size.

For Jacobi increasing the local problem size causes an increase in the average number of iterations to corrupt other processes by roughly 2×. Corruption propagation patterns and failure symptoms resemble that shown previously. Increasing the local problem size

for HPCCG sees no decrease in the speed of propagation to other ranks or a discernible change in failure symptoms. Due to the increased number of atoms in CoMD, more atoms fit into the same sized domain. When the force computation includes more atoms in the cutoff region, a single corrupted atom is now in more cut-off regions, thus propagating the corruption faster than previously observed. Beyond an increase in the propagation speed, failure symptoms for CoMD are comparable with previous results.

5 RELATED WORK

Redundancy: Redundancy is a common tool in detection schemes. Triple modular redundancy (TMR) [33] ensures correctness by computing values through triplicate and majority voting. Redundant threads or processes have been used to detect transient and permanent errors in hardware and software [19, 37]. Redundancy at these levels often yield high overheads, but also high protection from soft errors. The GangES error simulator [41] seeks to limit the time required for fault injection experiments on applications running on micro-architectural simulators by checking for similarities in application state to prior fault injection runs. GangES does not consider parallel applications.

Tools: Corruption propagation modeling in static analysis combined with fault injection experiments is used extensively in compiler based protection schemes to identify the protection of key instructions. IPAS [28] leverages machine learning on fault injection experiments to learn which instructions are good candidates for replication to prevent program output corruption. However, this approach can be limited by a training dependence. Compiler analysis with profiling [27] can be used to improve the effectiveness of an instruction replication scheme; however the long term impact of corruption is not considered, such as between processes. SDCTune [32] uses static analysis, heuristics, and fault injection data to construct a probability model for corruption to decide what instructions are likely to generate SDC. Extensions of the Program Vulnerability Factor [18] metric have been used to distinguish between crashes and SDC allowing for more accurate estimates of SDC and crash rates. The modeling of corruption propagation is again limited to sequential programs. CrashFinder [30] explores the effectiveness of combining compiler analysis and fault injection results to identify instructions that generate long latency crashes due to pointer, loop, and state corruption; the propagation of corruption is not investigated. SymPLFIED [39] uses symbolic execution to abstract the state of corrupted values in the program to find hard-to-detect fault injection locations that random fault-injection may reveal; this is limited to sequential integer programs.

Characterization: A study of the numerical impact of a single bit-flip on matrix-vector computations and GMRES is presented in [16, 17], respectively. An analysis of long latency crashes [45], shows corruptions in memory have long fault activation times leading to long latencies for crashes compared to corruption in registers, but does not investigate the extent of corruption propagation at the time of detection and the ability to recover locally. The impact of soft errors on the Linux kernel is determined [20], but does not quantify the corruption of system state variables to determine how to prevent propagation for long latency crashes. Y-branches [44] explores how control flow divergence impacts applications correctness and performance. Control flow re-converges if the architectural state exactly matches a golden copy; however, for applications that can remove/mask corruption over-time, this may underestimate the number Y-branches.

Characterizations of corruption in floating-point computation inside HPC applications is presented in [2]. Corruption is tracked based on terms of number of incorrect memory accesses and does not relate this to application level variables. A similar study [31], quantifies corruption in GPU and host memories for GPU benchmarks, but does not look at how corruption propagation in a distributed memory environment.

Recovery: Establishing a bound on the subset of total program state that is corrupted allows for localized recovery. Containment domains [14] surround code regions, using verification to ensure correctness. Identifying the location of code containment remains open. Similarly, transactional semantics [24] can be used for MPI, but not on application variables that may be corrupted. Esoftcheck [46], uses compiler analysis to remove redundant SDC detectors to maintain high reliability, but does not consider the latency of detection and how it effects propagation. An analytic version of this problem which investigates optimal placement of detectors of different capabilities to verify a checkpoint is corruption free is presented in [4], but considers a fixed recovery time that does not change based on how much state is corrupted.

6 CONCLUSION

As HPC systems trend toward larger numbers of smaller components at lower voltages, the rate of errors due to hardware faults is expected to increase. To mitigate these issues in HPC applications, many SDC detection and recovery schemes have been proposed. This paper explores how state corruption due to a soft error propagates at a micro (instruction level) and macro (application variable) level for three applications: Jacobi, HPCCG, and CoMD.

At a micro-level, latency of segmentation faults, divergence of control flow and detection are investigated. In addition, the impact of compiler optimizations is explored on two kernels: WAXPBY and SpMV. Results show that the majority of segmentation faults occur shortly after a fault occurs allowing for little propagation. Deviations in control flow predominantly occur as premature loop termination in loops where the fault occurs.

Macro-level results highlight the speed and intensity of corruption on the processes where the failure occurs and between other

processes. Corruption results for critical data structures are discussed along with the ability to define regions of containment for local recovery. Finally, increasing the local problem size increases the latency of inter-process corruption propagation in Jacobi, while decreases the latency in CoMD (and does not influence the latency for HPCCG).

Latencies are useful in determining the effectiveness of a detection scheme — i.e., short latencies limit corruption propagation and can lower recovery costs. However, low cost recovery in a parallel application requires knowing the corrupted processes and data structures. Tracking propagation at the macro-level enables discovery of the variables that are most susceptible to corruption, it identifies the speed of corruption between processes, and indicated whether operations reduce or amplify corruption. The probability of corruption is valuable in developing more precise SDC detectors.

ACKNOWLEDGMENT

We would like to our reviewers and shepherd for their helpful and insightful comments on improving the quality of this paper.

This work was sponsored by the Air Force Office of Scientific Research under grant FA9550-12-1-0478. This work was supported in part by the Office of Advanced Scientific Computing Research, Office of Science, U.S. Department of Energy award DE-FG02-13ER26138/DE-SC0010049. This material is based upon work supported by the National Science Foundation under Grant No. SHF-1617488. This research is part of the Blue Waters sustained-petascale computing project, which is supported by the National Science Foundation (awards OCI–0725070 and ACI–1238993) and the state of Illinois. Blue Waters is a joint effort of the University of Illinois at Urbana-Champaign and its National Center for Supercomputing Applications.

REFERENCES

[1] E. Agullo, L. Giraud, A. Guermouche, J. Roman, and M. Zounon. Towards resilient parallel linear krylov solvers: recover-restart strategies. Rapport de recherche RR-8324, INRIA, July 2013.

[2] R. A. Ashraf, R. Gioiosa, G. Kestor, R. F. DeMara, C.-Y. Cher, and P. Bose. Understanding the propagation of transient errors in HPC applications. In *Proceedings of the International Conference for High Performance Computing, Networking, Storage and Analysis*, SC '15, pages 72:1–72:12, New York, NY, USA, 2015. ACM.

[3] R. C. Baumann. Radiation-induced soft errors in advanced semiconductor technologies. *Device and Materials Reliability, IEEE Transactions on*, 5(3):305–316, Sept. 2005.

[4] L. Bautista-Gomez, A. Benoit, A. Cavelan, S. K. Raina, Y. Robert, and H. Sun. Which verification for soft error detection? In *HiPC*, pages 2–11. IEEE Computer Society, 2015.

[5] L. Bautista-Gomez and F. Cappello. Detecting silent data corruption for extreme-scale MPI applications. In *Proceedings of the 22Nd European MPI Users' Group Meeting*, EuroMPI '15, pages 12:1–12:10, New York, NY, USA, 2015. ACM.

[6] L. Bautista-Gomez and F. Cappello. Exploiting spatial smoothness in HPC applications to detect silent data corruption. In *Proceedings of the 2015 IEEE 17th International Conference on High Performance Computing and Communications, 2015 IEEE 7th International Symposium on Cyberspace Safety and Security, and 2015 IEEE 12th International Conf on Embedded Software and Systems*, HPCC-CSS-ICESS '15, pages 128–133, Washington, DC, USA, 2015. IEEE Computer Society.

[7] L. Bautista-Gomez, S. Tsuboi, D. Komatitsch, F. Cappello, N. Maruyama, and S. Matsuoka. FTI: high performance fault tolerance interface for hybrid systems. In *Proceedings of 2011 International Conference for High Performance Computing, Networking, Storage and Analysis*, SC '11, pages 32:1–32:32, New York, NY, USA, 2011. ACM.

[8] E. Berrocal, L. Bautista-Gomez, S. Di, Z. Lan, and F. Cappello. Lightweight silent data corruption detection based on runtime data analysis for HPC applications. In *Proceedings of the 24th International Symposium on High-Performance Parallel*

and Distributed Computing, HPDC '15, pages 275–278, New York, NY, USA, 2015. ACM.

[9] S. Borkar. Designing reliable systems from unreliable components: The challenges of transistor variability and degradation. *IEEE Micro*, 25(6):10–16, Nov. 2005.

[10] P. G. Bridges, K. B. Ferreira, M. A. Heroux, and M. Hoemmen. Fault-tolerant linear solvers via selective reliability. *CoRR*, abs/1206.1390, 2012.

[11] J. Calhoun, L. Olson, and M. Snir. FlipIt: An LLVM based fault injector for HPC. In *Proceedings of the 20th International Euro-Par Conference on Parallel Processing (Euro-Par '14)*, 2014.

[12] J. Calhoun, L. Olson, M. Snir, and W. D. Gropp. Towards a more fault resilient multigrid solver. In *Proceedings of the Symposium on High Performance Computing*, HPC '15, pages 1–8, San Diego, CA, USA, 2015. Society for Computer Simulation International.

[13] J. Calhoun, M. Snir, L. Olson, and M. Garzaran. Understanding the propagation of error due to a silent data corruption in a sparse matrix vector multiply. In *Proceedings of the 2015 IEEE International Conference on Cluster Computing*, CLUSTER '15, pages 541–542, Washington, DC, USA, 2015. IEEE Computer Society.

[14] J. Chung, I. Lee, M. Sullivan, J. H. Ryoo, D. W. Kim, D. H. Yoon, L. Kaplan, and M. Erez. Containment domains: A scalable, efficient, and flexible resilience scheme for exascale systems. In *Proceedings of the International Conference on High Performance Computing, Networking, Storage and Analysis*, SC '12, pages 58:1–58:11, Los Alamitos, CA, USA, 2012. IEEE Computer Society Press.

[15] T. J. Dell. A white paper on the benefits of chipkillcorrect ECC for PC server main memory. Technical report, IBM Microelectronics Division, 1997.

[16] J. Elliott, M. Hoemmen, and F. Mueller. Evaluating the impact of SDC on the GMRES iterative solver. In *Proceedings of the 2014 IEEE 28th International Parallel and Distributed Processing Symposium*, IPDPS '14, pages 1193–1202, Washington, DC, USA, 2014. IEEE Computer Society.

[17] J. Elliott, F. Mueller, M. Stoyanov, and C. Webster. Quantifying the impact of single bit flips on floating point arithmetic. Technical report, Oak Ridge National Laboratory, August 2013.

[18] B. Fang, Q. Lu, K. Pattabiraman, M. Ripeanu, and S. Gurumurthi. ePVF: an enhanced program vulnerability factor methodology for cross-layer resilience analysis. *2016 46th Annual IEEE/IFIP International Conference on Dependable Systems and Networks (DSN)*, 00:168–179, 2016.

[19] D. Fiala, F. Mueller, C. Engelmann, R. Riesen, K. Ferreira, and R. Brightwell. Detection and correction of silent data corruption for large-scale high-performance computing. In *Proceedings of the International Conference on High Performance Computing, Networking, Storage and Analysis*, SC '12, pages 78:1–78:12, Los Alamitos, CA, USA, 2012. IEEE Computer Society Press.

[20] W. Gu, Z. Kalbarczyk, R. K. Iyer, and Z.-Y. Yang. Characterization of linux kernel behavior under errors. In *DSN*, pages 459–468. IEEE Computer Society, 2003.

[21] A. Guermouche, T. Ropars, E. Brunet, M. Snir, and F. Cappello. Uncoordinated checkpointing without domino effect for send-deterministic MPI applications. In *Parallel & Distributed Processing Symposium (IPDPS), 2011 IEEE International*, pages 989–1000. IEEE, 2011.

[22] A. Guermouche, T. Ropars, M. Snir, and F. Cappello. Hydee: Failure containment without event logging for large scale send-deterministic MPI applications. In *Parallel & Distributed Processing Symposium (IPDPS), 2012 IEEE 26th International*, pages 1216–1227. IEEE, 2012.

[23] S. K. S. Hari, S. V. Adve, and H. Naeimi. Low-cost program-level detectors for reducing silent data corruptions. In *Proceedings of the 2012 42Nd Annual IEEE/IFIP International Conference on Dependable Systems and Networks (DSN)*, DSN '12, pages 1–12, Washington, DC, USA, 2012. IEEE Computer Society.

[24] A. Hassani, A. Skjellum, P. V. Bangalore, and R. Brightwell. Practical resilient cases for fa-mpi, a transactional fault-tolerant mpi. In *Proceedings of the 3rd Workshop on Exascale MPI*, ExaMPI '15, pages 1:1–1:10, New York, NY, USA, 2015. ACM.

[25] L. Jaulmes, M. Casas, M. Moretó, E. Ayguadé, J. Labarta, and M. Valero. Exploiting asynchrony from exact forward recovery for DUE in iterative solvers. In *Proceedings of the International Conference for High Performance Computing, Networking, Storage and Analysis*, SC '15, pages 53:1–53:12, New York, NY, USA, 2015. ACM.

[26] H. Kaul, M. Anders, S. Hsu, A. Agarwal, R. Krishnamurthy, and S. Borkar. Near-threshold voltage (NTV) design: Opportunities and challenges. In *Proceedings of the 49th Annual Design Automation Conference*, DAC '12, pages 1153–1158, New York, NY, USA, 2012. ACM.

[27] D. S. Khudia, G. Wright, and S. Mahlke. Efficient soft error protection for commodity embedded microprocessors using profile information. In *Proceedings of the 13th ACM SIGPLAN/SIGBED International Conference on Languages, Compilers, Tools and Theory for Embedded Systems*, LCTES '12, pages 99–108, New York, NY, USA, 2012. ACM.

[28] I. Laguna, M. Schulz, D. F. Richards, J. Calhoun, and L. Olson. IPAS: intelligent protection against silent output corruption in scientific applications. In *Proceedings of the 2016 International Symposium on Code Generation and Optimization*, CGO 2016, pages 227–238, New York, NY, USA, 2016. ACM.

[29] C. Lattner and V. Adve. LLVM: a compilation framework for lifelong program analysis & transformation. In *Proceedings of the 2004 International Symposium on Code Generation and Optimization (CGO'04)*, Palo Alto, California, Mar 2004.

[30] G. Li, Q. Lu, and K. Pattabiraman. Fine-grained characterization of faults causing long latency crashes in programs. In *DSN*, pages 450–461. IEEE Computer Society, 2015.

[31] G. Li, K. Pattabiraman, C.-Y. Cher, and P. Bose. Understanding error propagation in GPGPU applications. In *Proceedings of the International Conference for High Performance Computing, Networking, Storage and Analysis*, SC '16, pages 21:1–21:12, Piscataway, NJ, USA, 2016. IEEE Press.

[32] Q. Lu, K. Pattabiraman, M. S. Gupta, and J. A. Rivers. SDCTune: a model for predicting the sdc proneness of an application for configurable protection. In *Proceedings of the 2014 International Conference on Compilers, Architecture and Synthesis for Embedded Systems*, CASES '14, pages 23:1–23:10, New York, NY, USA, 2014. ACM.

[33] R. E. Lyons and W. Vanderkulk. The use of triple-modular redundancy to improve computer reliability. *IBM J. Res. Dev.*, 6(2):200–209, Apr. 1962.

[34] T. C. May and M. H. Woods. Alpha-particle-induced soft errors in dynamic memories. *Electron Devices, IEEE Transactions on*, 26(1):2–9, Jan. 1979.

[35] A. Moody, G. Bronevetsky, K. Mohror, and B. R. d. Supinski. Design, modeling, and evaluation of a scalable multi-level checkpointing system. In *Proceedings of the 2010 ACM/IEEE International Conference for High Performance Computing, Networking, Storage and Analysis*, SC '10, pages 1–11, Washington, DC, USA, 2010. IEEE Computer Society.

[36] X. Ni and L. V. Kale. FlipBack: automatic targeted protection against silent data corruption. In *Proceedings of the International Conference for High Performance Computing, Networking, Storage and Analysis*, SC '16, pages 29:1–29:12, Piscataway, NJ, USA, 2016. IEEE Press.

[37] X. Ni, E. Meneses, N. Jain, and L. V. Kale. ACR: automatic checkpoint/restart for soft and hard error protection. In *ACM/IEEE International Conference for High Performance Computing, Networking, Storage and Analysis*, SC '13. IEEE Computer Society, Nov. 2013.

[38] K. Pattabiraman, R. K. Iyer, and Z. T. Kalbarczyk. Automated derivation of application-aware error detectors using static analysis: The trusted illiac approach. *IEEE Transactions on Dependable and Secure Computing*, 8:44–57, 2009.

[39] K. Pattabiraman, N. M. Nakka, Z. T. Kalbarczyk, and R. K. Iyer. SymPLFIED: symbolic program-level fault injection and error detection framework. *IEEE Transactions on Computers*, 62(11):2292–2307, 2013.

[40] N. Sasaki, K. Sato, T. Endo, and S. Matsuoka. Exploration of lossy compression for application-level checkpoint/restart. In *Proceedings of the 2015 IEEE International Parallel and Distributed Processing Symposium*, IPDPS '15, pages 914–922, Washington, DC, USA, 2015. IEEE Computer Society.

[41] S. K. Sastry Hari, R. Venkatagiri, S. V. Adve, and H. Naeimi. GangES: gang error simulation for hardware resiliency evaluation. In *Proceeding of the 41st Annual International Symposium on Computer Architecuture*, ISCA '14, pages 61–72, Piscataway, NJ, USA, 2014. IEEE Press.

[42] M. Snir, R. W. Wisniewski, J. A. Abraham, S. V. Adve, S. Bagchi, P. Balaji, J. Belak, P. Bose, F. Cappello, B. Carlson, A. A. Chien, P. Coteus, N. A. DeBardeleben, P. C. Diniz, C. Engelmann, M. Erez, S. Fazzari, A. Geist, R. Gupta, F. Johnson, S. Krishnamoorthy, S. Leyffer, D. Liberty, S. Mitra, T. Munson, R. Schreiber, J. Stearley, and E. V. Hensbergen. Addressing failures in exascale computing. *International Journal of High Performance Computing Applications*, 28(2):127 – 171, May 2014.

[43] V. Sridharan, N. DeBardeleben, S. Blanchard, K. B. Ferreira, J. Stearley, J. Shalf, and S. Gurumurthi. Memory errors in modern systems: The good, the bad, and the ugly. In *Proceedings of the Twentieth International Conference on Architectural Support for Programming Languages and Operating Systems*, ASPLOS '15, pages 297–310, New York, NY, USA, 2015. ACM.

[44] N. Wang, M. Fertig, and S. Patel. Y-branches: When you come to a fork in the road, take it. In *Proceedings of the 12th International Conference on Parallel Architectures and Compilation Techniques*, PACT '03, pages 56–, Washington, DC, USA, 2003. IEEE Computer Society.

[45] K. S. Yim, Z. T. Kalbarczyk, and R. K. Iyer. Quantitative analysis of long-latency failures in system software. In *Proceedings of the 2009 15th IEEE Pacific Rim International Symposium on Dependable Computing*, PRDC '09, pages 23–30, Washington, DC, USA, 2009. IEEE Computer Society.

[46] J. Yu, M. J. Garzaran, and M. Snir. ESoftCheck: removal of non-vital checks for fault tolerance. In *Proceedings of the 7th Annual IEEE/ACM International Symposium on Code Generation and Optimization*, CGO '09, pages 35–46, Washington, DC, USA, 2009. IEEE Computer Society.

[47] G. Zheng, L. Shi, and L. V. Kalé. FTC-Charm++: an in-memory checkpoint-based fault tolerant runtime for Charm++ and MPI. In *Cluster Computing, 2004 IEEE International Conference on*, pages 93–103. IEEE, 2004.

Diagnosing Machine Learning Pipelines with Fine-grained Lineage

Zhao Zhang
Texas Advanced Computing Center,
The University of Texas at Austin
zzhang@tacc.utexas.edu

Evan R. Sparks
Computer Science Division,
University of California, Berkeley
sparks@cs.berkeley.edu

Michael J. Franklin
Department of Computer Science,
University of Chicago
mjfranklin@uchicago.edu

ABSTRACT

We present the Hippo system to enable the diagnosis of distributed machine learning (ML) pipelines by leveraging fine-grained data lineage. Hippo exposes a concise yet powerful API, derived from *primitive lineage types*, to capture fine-grained data lineage for each data transformation. It records the input datasets, the output datasets and the cell-level mapping between them. It also collects sufficient information that is needed to reproduce the computation. Hippo efficiently enables common ML diagnosis operations such as code debugging, result analysis, data anomaly removal, and computation replay. By exploiting the metadata separation and high-order function encoding strategies, we observe an $O(10^3)$x total improvement in lineage storage efficiency vs. the baseline of cell-wise mapping recording while maintaining the lineage integrity. Hippo can answer the real use case lineage queries within a few seconds, which is low enough to enable interactive diagnosis of ML pipelines.

KEYWORDS

machine learning; diagnostics; fine-grained lineage

ACM Reference format:
Zhao Zhang, Evan R. Sparks, and Michael J. Franklin. 2017. Diagnosing Machine Learning Pipelines with Fine-grained Lineage. In *Proceedings of HPDC '17, Washington , DC, USA, June 26-30, 2017,* 11 pages.
DOI: http://dx.doi.org/10.1145/3078597.3078603

1 INTRODUCTION

Machine learning frameworks are increasingly popular as practitioners and researchers can quickly build applications (referred to as ML pipelines or pipelines in the rest of this paper) with a high-level programming language to pipeline data preparation, feature extraction, model training, and prediction. Among these systems, Scikit-learn [32] is a single-computer-based framework while TensorFlow [17], MLlib [25], SystemML [16], and KeystoneML [37] focus on a distributed environment.

In practice, to obtain and deploy a working model, users often need to try a number of different datasets, featurization techniques, training parameters, and model families. When experimenting with these options, users frequently analyze results together with the corresponding input data, locate code segments responsible for unexpected outcomes, or rerun the computation with the removal of suspicious data anomalies.

As a concrete example, consider the task of light source extraction in astronomy: this pipeline reads telescope images and produces a list of potential celestial objects with their positions, luminous flux, estimated error, and other information. One routine quality check involves tracing those abnormally bright objects in the result to the contributing pixels in the original input images. Then with further mathematical analysis or human intervention, this user must be able to validate if these abnormally bright objects are caused by a bad charge-coupled device (CCD) pixel. Once an erroneous pixel is confirmed, the user may then want to find out how this erroneous data item propagates to the rest of the results. Such an inspection involves two types of operations: *forward queries* that trace the resulting output cells given an input cell and *backward queries* that trace the contributing input cells given an output cell. These two query types are made possible by the cell-level consumption-production dependency mapping. This cell-wise dependency is also referred to as fine-grained data lineage.

Given that such diagnosis is a commonly repeated work pattern, it is natural to add system support to capture and work with fine-grained data lineage directly in an ML framework. In this paper, we describe the design of a distributed ML pipeline diagnostic system that leverages fine-grained data lineage. Compared to coarse-grained lineage at file or relational table metadata level, fine-grained lineage is at the data structure cell level, e.g., elements in a matrix or attributes in a record. We assume an ML framework with a programming model that abstracts a pipeline as a chain of data transformations, such as KeystoneML, TensorFlow, and SystemML. In particular, KeystoneML builds on top of Apache Spark [44] and uses two building blocks: **transformers** and **estimators**. A **transformer** applies a unary function to data items and produce new ones. An **estimator** takes a collection of data items, feeds them to a training procedure, and produces a **transformer**. We choose this model because it is widely adopted and allows users to declare and instrument lineage capturing directly in the transformer. Our diagnostic system provides:

- A concise and flexible interface for users to declare and instrument lineage capturing
- Low overhead for capturing and storing lineage
- Interactive lineage query for pipeline diagnosis

Lineage tracking has been investigated in many contexts. Scientific workflow systems such as Chimera [13], Taverna [28], ESSW [15], Kepler [2], and Karma2 [36] can collect coarse-grained lineage at the level of files and computations. The Taverna 2 workflow system [38] proposes a fine-grained lineage model on the collection

Table 1: Performance Penalty Reported by Existing Lineage Systems

Project	Underlying System	Perf Penalty
RAMP [19]	Hadoop [4]	16-76%
Newt [22]	Hadoop [4]	20-50%
SubZero [42]	SciDB [7]	50%-150%
Titian [20]	Spark [44]	10%-29%

element level. And the later work by Missier *et al.* [26] presents two mapping types between input and output as data collection cross-product and index-projection. In the context of distributed processing, RAMP [19, 31] and Newt [22] present solutions for MapReduce systems. Titian [20] captures Apache Spark's lineage at collection element level. Fine-grained lineage is also investigated in the filed of database and data warehouse by works [9, 10, 40, 42].

Unfortunately, these existing lineage tracking systems are not suitable for distributed ML frameworks for three reasons. First, coarse-grained lineage information collected by scientific workflow systems (e.g., Chimera) lacks the necessary detail of cell-level mapping. Even Titian only captures Spark lineage at collection element level, e.g., a matrix in a list, whereas ML pipeline diagnosis requires mapping at one level deeper on the matrix cells. Second, the two mapping types presented in the work of Missier *et al.* [26] partially address the input and output mapping in workflow computations. But they are not sufficient to cover the data transformation in ML pipelines. Third, the lineage capturing interface in other related systems is often designed with the underlying system operators (e.g., SQL operators for RDBMS, mappers and reducers in MapReduce systems, and input-stage-aggregation operators for Apache Spark.). In contrast, ML frameworks do not have such a set of well-defined low level operators, which makes it difficult to design a general lineage capturing interface. Other challenges of building an ML framework diagnostic system include the cost introduced by lineage capturing and the low latency requirement for lineage queries to enable interactive diagnosis. Table 1 shows the performance penalty incurred by lineage capturing in recent work.

Because ML pipeline builders have deep understanding of data transformations, we present a lineage capturing interface that lets users decide what data to capture and how to capture it. The lineage capturing interface is designed by formulating the cell level mapping of an ML pipeline as a sequence of multi-dimensional space transformations. This interface contains seven primitive mapping types: namely, **collapse**, **flatten**, **identity**, **all**, **linear combination**, **geometry**, and **join**. These seven primitive mappings cover 87% (39 of 45), 89% (130 of 146), and 89% (72 of 81) of the pre-defined data transformations in KeystoneML, TensorFlow, and SystemML, respectively. For transformations that are not covered, the lineage capturing interface allows users to specify customized mapping functions. A formal definition of the mapping types is in Section 4.

In this paper, we present Hippo[1], a fine-grained lineage capturing and serving system for distributed ML pipelines. Hippo exposes the lineage capturing interface by exploiting the seven primitive mapping types. It also provides the cell-level tracing functionality with a query interface so that users are able to find the contributing and resulting cells given a cell of interest. Hippo is also flexible so

that users can collect optional data inside a data transformation. These optional data include the input/output dataset, the transformation itself, the model, and the state parameter (e.g., a random seed). Hippo optimizes lineage data storage efficiency with techniques of data structure metadata(e.g., the size of each dimension of a space) separation and high-level function encoding. To speedup the query, Hippo employs the techniques of spatial index and a rule-based mapping and query reduction strategy.

To showcase the effectiveness of Hippo's design and optimization, we integrated Hippo with the open source KeystoneML distributed machine learning framework. We demonstrate the utility of Hippo by studying three distinct use cases enabled by fine-grained lineage. These use cases are: code validation, results inspection, and data cleaning. A detailed discussion of these three use cases is presented in Section 2.3. All these use cases are enabled by either fine-grained lineage query or by intermediate data reuse. Hippo's lineage capturing and serving functionalities alleviate users from repeatedly modifying the source code and executing the pipeline to obtain the necessary diagnosis information. Compared to the naive solution of materializing cell-wise mapping, Hippo's techniques (spatial index and high-order function) enable 2x-31x speedups at lineage query time. This new capability comes at the cost of modest performance overheads during pipeline training/execution. The overhead is measured in wall clock time, memory consumption, and storage space. For the three use cases, the wall clock time overhead for lineage capturing is 41%-61%, which is comparable to other distributed lineage systems summarized in Table 1. Hippo increases memory usage by 31%-79%, and the storage space for lineage information varies case by case from ~100 MB to ~1 TB.

In summary, we make the following contributions:

- We design a concise and powerful lineage capturing interface by formulating the cell-wise mapping in ML pipelines as multi-dimensional space transformations.
- We map many common ML operations such as featurization and labeling to the lineage capturing interface.
- We introduce a high-order function approach for describing geometry to reduce storage overhead. Meanwhile, we use spatial indices to speed up queries and evaluate a set of spatial indexing strategies.
- We define two sets of optimization rules to accelerate pipeline lineage queries.
- We present and analyze three real use cases of using fine-grained data lineage for code validation, results inspection, and data cleaning, respectively.

The rest of the paper is organized as following: We briefly review the KeystoneML framework, the semantics of fine-grained lineage query, and present three diagnostic use cases in Section 2. Section 3 presents the data model in Hippo. Section 4 defines the primitive mapping types between input and output datasets. Section 5 and Section 6 describe the design and implementation of Hippo, respectively. We present performance measurements in Section 7 and conceptually compare Hippo with existing lineage system in Section 8. Finally, we conclude and envision future work in Section 9.

---

[1]https://github.com/zhaozhang/keystone/tree/lineage-v4

2 BACKGROUND

In this section, we first review KeystoneML to help understand the technical background of this work. Then we discuss the basic lineage query functions in the context of ML pipelines. To motivate Hippo, we present three representative use cases of using fine-grained lineage for ML pipeline diagnostics.

2.1 KeystoneML

In principle, Hippo is general for distributed ML frameworks whose programming interface can be abstracted as transformers and estimators. We integrate Hippo with KeystoneML to show the effectiveness of the design. KeystoneML is an application framework designed for the implementation of robust large-scale machine learning pipelines. Built on the principles of declarative programming and modular design, KeystoneML provides a light-weight and elegant API that allows users to describe these pipelines as the composition of two types of operator–transformers, which perform data transformation, and estimators, which "learn" transformers based on training data. KeystoneML pipelines are fit and executed in parallel using Apache Spark. These pipelines are compiled into an application directed acyclic graph (DAG) and optimized before execution. Current optimizations include online decisions about intermediate state materialization, standard optimizations such as common subexpression elimination, as well as machine-learning specific optimizations such as cost-based physical operator selection for solvers and other logical operators. KeystoneML includes a library of standard feature extractors in domains including computer vision, audio, and text processing, as well as standard statistical procedures and Estimators for several types of machine learning model.

Listing 1 shows a simplified image classification pipeline with KeystoneML. In the example, PixelScaler, GrayScaler, FeatureExtractor, and MatrixVectorizer are transformers while LeastSquareEstimator is an estimator. Applying this pipeline to the training dataset generates a new pipeline that consists of the first four transformers and an additional transformer with the linear model trained by LeastSquareEstimator. Line 8 shows how the trained pipeline is used for predictions with the test dataset.

Listing 1: A Simplified Image Classification Pipeline

```
1 val pipeline = PixelScaler andThen GrayScaler
2   andThen FeatureExtractor
3   andThen MatrixVectorizer
4   andThen (LeastSquareEstimator, trainData, trainLabel)
5
6 val predictor = pipeline.fit()
7
8 val predictions = predictor(testData)
```

To define a transformer, users need to supply data transformation via the apply() interface. Listing 2 shows the PixelScaler example, where the transformation is to rescale an input image by dividing each pixel by 255.0.

Listing 2: PixelScaler Definition

```
1 object PixelScaler extends Transformer{
2   def apply[in: Dataset[Image]]: Dataset[Image] = {
3     in.map(image => image.map(_/255.0))
4   }
5 }
```

PixelScaler		GrayScaler		FeatureExtractor	
Input Coor	Output Coor	Input Coor	Output Coor	Input Coor	Output Coor
(0,0,0)	(0,0,0)	(0,0,0)	(0,0)	(0,0)	(0,0), (1,0),...., (127,0)
(0,0,1)	(0,0,1)	(0,0,1)	(0,0)	(0,1)	(0,0), (1,0),...., (127,0)
(0,0,2)	(0,0,2)	(0,0,2)	(0,0)	(0,2)	(0,1), (1,1),...., (127,1)
(0,1,0)	(0,1,0)	(0,1,0)	(0,1)	(0,3)	(0,1), (1,1),...., (127,1)
...	...	...	...	...	...

Figure 1: Cell Level Mapping in PixelScaler, GrayScaler, and FeatureExtractor.

2.2 Fine-grained Lineage Query

Conceptually, the fine-grained lineage of the pipeline shown in Listing 1 records the input and output cell mapping in a table for each transformer. Figure 1 shows the mapping tables of PixelScaler, GrayScaler, and FeatureExtractor. PixelScaler first scales the pixels of the 3-channel images with a factor of 255.0. Then GrayScaler converts the scaled images to single channel gray images. FeatureExtractor extracts visual features from the gray images then for each feature, it outputs a 128-dimension vector. For a single transformer such as PixelScaler, to trace the resulting output cells of an input cell, it filters the mapping table to find out records whose "Input Coor" fields are equal to the input cell. With multiple transformers in a chain, the fine-grained lineage is derived by joining a sequence of mapping tables on the "Output Coor" field of the current table and the "Input Coor" field of the next table. Then tracing the resulting output cells can be done in a similar way as in a single transformer.

Two typical tracing functions that a fine-grained lineage system provides are **forward query** and **backward query**. **Forward query** takes input coordinates as keys and returns the resulting output cells. **Backward query** takes output coordinates as keys and returns the contributing input cells. In the context of this paper, these queries return cell coordinates, and the actual cell value can be retrieved by accessing the data structure with the coordinates.

2.3 Use Cases

We now present three use cases which come from real ML pipelines of image classification and astronomy image processing. These three cases are representative of code validation, results inspection, and data cleaning, respectively, and demonstrate the utility of a fine-grained lineage system in the context of real world ML pipeline development.

2.3.1 Code Validation. In this case we use lineage for the debugging process as pipelines change and are augmented. Typical ML pipelines are constructed via an iterative process of refinement with a machine learning developer or data scientist in the loop. These users are constantly engineering new features, adding new datasources, and trying out new machine learning methods at all stages of the pipeline. Lineage offers a natural way for these users to hone in on the areas where two similar pipelines diverge in terms of their intermediate data, and presents a new avenue for investigation of model performance by allowing users to pinpoint the point at which their data diverged from a known good pipeline and to inspect *what* changed during the data processing procedure.

As a concrete example, consider the SIFTFisher pipeline, shown as Figure 2. It has been shown that augmenting traditional SIFT [23] (Scale-invariant feature transform) descriptors with their locations in the input image can improve classification performance. However, when we first developed such a pipeline, our results conflicted with published work indicating that these features provided a statistically significant improvement in classification accuracy. By employing lineage based debugging, we could isolate exactly where in the pipeline our calculations diverged from the original features, and diagnose impacts seen downstream like an under-fit GMM (Gaussian Mixture Model), and trace the ultimate lack of classification improvement to a bug in the underlying C library which we called into. Practically, this is done by first comparing the lineages of two executions to locate the intermediate result divergence in the SIFTExtractor transformer. Then by tracing the input of GMM backward to the output of SIFTExtractor, we could see that the new features added to our SIFT descriptors did not correspond to positions in the image. Rather they contained values outside of a suitable range for these features, which turned out to be randomly allocated memory. The SIFT feature investigation involves a backward query on the DimensionReducer and ColumnSampler transformer that applies Principal Component Analysis (PCA) and random sampling on the available vectors, respectively.

2.3.2 Results Inspection. Fine-grained data lineage of ML pipelines enables results interpretation, potential data anomaly detection, and retrospection of supporting input data.

One such use case is results inspection in the SourceExtractor pipeline, shown in Figure 3, that processes telescope images and produces astronomical object catalogs. The astronomical object catalog includes the position, shape, and other statistical properties of the object. In this case, astronomers find the abnormally bright objects over a threshold and validate that these objects are indeed astronomical objects rather than errors caused by malfunctioning CCD pixels. With the lineage information, astronomers can first filter the results to find the objects whose brightness is above the threshold. Then using backward query, they can find corresponding pixels for these bright objects. Either through mathematical analysis or human intervention, they are able to validate the correctness of the bright objects. Then the astronomer can use forward query to figure out how a bad pixel propagates to the catalogs. The backward query for this use case first joins with output data to find out the coordinates of the values that are over the threshold. Then the backward query is executed on the complete pipeline lineage to find the contributing pixels. If an erroneous pixel is confirmed, the forward query takes the erroneous pixel coordinate as the key and traces the complete pipeline lineage then return all results that are polluted by this erroneous pixel.

2.3.3 Data Cleaning. Another use of the lineage information is for users to apply a subset of the prepared dataset to fit the model. The ML expert who is building a SIFTFisher pipeline, shown in Figure 2, identifies bad training data items (e.g., the images that

have both dogs and cats) due to measurement error. A natural investigation is then to remove these images, and test if that improves prediction accuracy.

With Hippo, the user can intercept the pipeline by loading the output of RowNormalizer (the last transformer before training process) directly into KeystoneML, filter out the data items that are derived from the images with both dogs and cats, and apply the filtered dataset directly to the linear solver. In this way, the rerunning process can bypass the expensive data preparation procedure (from PixelScaler to RowNormalizer) resulting in shorter turnaround time. Without lineage information, the user has to remove the according images from the training set and rerun the data preparation part (from PixelScaler to RowNormalizer), then feed the dataset to linear solver to train the model again.

3 DATA MODEL

Before discussing how ML pipeline cell-level dependency is recorded, we first introduce Hippo's data model and explain how to use this hierarchical model to represent the datasets in pipelines.

A dataset is often in the form of a nested data collection, e.g., `Collection[Matrix]`. Hippo uses a 3-tier model to describe this nested data structure, as shown in Figure 4. On the top of the hierarchy is the "space" abstraction, which is defined by a number of dimensions. Each dimension corresponds to one layer of the nested collection. The cell positions inside the dataset are represented by the "coordinate" abstraction. In the middle of the model is the "shape" abstraction. The

| Space |
| Shape |
| Coordinate |

Figure 4: Hippo's Hierarchical Data Model

"shape" abstraction is a high-order representation of the underlying coordinates. Hippo describes a single coordinate as a point shape and a set of coordinates as a geometry shape, such as, a circle, a rectangle, or an ellipse. A space is then in the form of the union of a set of shapes. The "shape" abstraction is particularly space-efficient when storing lineage information in **geometry** mapping, which is discussed in details in Section 4.2

Taking an example dataset in the type of `Collection[Matrix]`, Hippo analyzes the nested collection from outer to inner layer. In this case, the dataset is a 3D space where the first dimension corresponds to the outer collection, while the second and third dimension refer to the row and column of the matrix, respectively. The size of each dimension can be determined by the actual data structure. Please note that the `Collection` type in the model can be either a single-node collection such as a list or a distributed collection such as Resilient Distributed Dataset (RDD) in Apache Spark.

More formally, given a dataset in a nested collection, we refer to its outermost layer as Dimension 0, and its second outermost layer as Dimension 1, and so on.

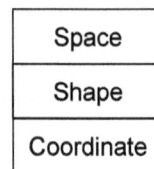

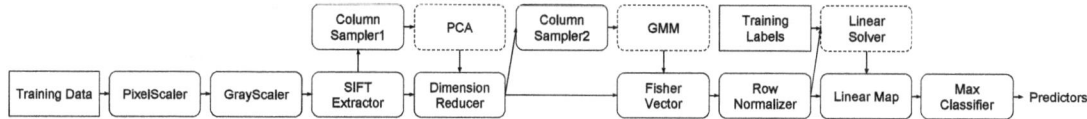

Figure 2: The SIFTFisher pipeline, boxes are dataset, rounded-corner boxes are transformers, dashed rounded-corner boxes are estimators.

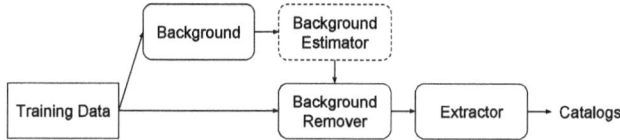

Figure 3: The SourceExtractor pipeline, boxes are dataset, rounded-corner boxes are transformers, dashed rounded-corner boxes are estimators.

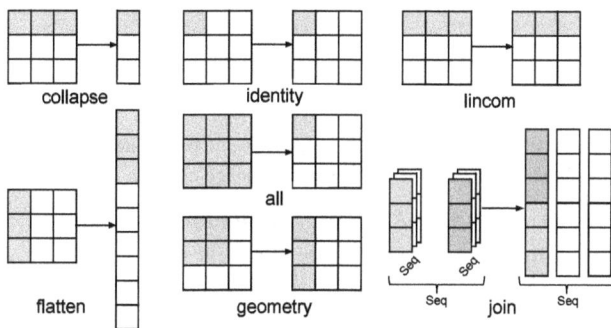

Figure 5: Primitive Mapping Types

4 MAPPING TYPES

At the core of Hippo is the cell-level dependency mappings between input and output datasets. In Section 3, we explain how to represent a dataset with a multi-dimensional space. In this section, we introduce the seven primitive mapping types to record the cell-level dependency between datasets.

4.1 Overview

We identify seven frequently occurring mapping types by analyzing the pre-defined data transformations of the KeystoneML, TensorFlow, and SystemML frameworks, From a higher dimension space to a lower dimension space, the mapping can be **collapse** or **flatten**. Between the equal dimension spaces, the mapping can be **identity**, **all**, **geometry**, **lincom**, and **join**. Figure 5 visualizes the seven primitive mapping types, with the involved cells highlighted.

4.2 Geometry Mapping

Geometry mapping records a many to many relation between input and output cells. Such data transformations take a group of cells from the input dataset and outputs another group of cells. These cell groups may be fit to higher order functions (geometries) such as circles, ellipses, and rectangles in a 2D space. Recording

the mappings between higher order functions can significantly reduce the space consumption compared to the cell-wise mapping. In practice, a SIFT feature (a vector) can be recorded as a rectangle in a 2D space and its contributing pixels can be recorded as a circle of cells. Similarly for SourceExtractor, the light source pixels are in the shape of an ellipse and the output cells form a rectangle (a row) in a matrix. We also use the **Geometry** mapping for the column sampling operations, where a subset of input vectors is selected as output. The mapping is in the form of a pair of rectangles.

4.3 Join Mapping

Join Mapping is a fundamental mapping type that occurs any place two datasets are merged into one. We explore two common scenarios in machine learning processing pipelines. The first scenario is feature vector concatenation, where features of the same entity are extracted from different data sources. For example, a feature vector for an astronomical object in SourceExtractor may contain the image pixel values, the weather condition, and the camera condition. Data from these sources are processed separately and joined to a single vector with the object identity as the key. The other scenario is "labeling" in supervised learning, where users join the feature vectors with labels then feed them to the training process to obtain a model.

4.4 Other Mappings

Collapse mapping describes a space collapsing into a lower space along dimensions which need to be specified by the user. Examples include gray scaling a multi-channel image. **Flatten** mapping is where a space flattens to a one-dimension lower space, e.g., flattening a matrix to a vector with column major. For data transformations with a reverse direction as **flatten** mapping, e.g., reorganizing a vector into a matrix, users can still declare such mapping as **flatten**. Hippo can infer the mapping direction based on the input and output space.

In **identity** mapping, each output cell only depends on the cell with the identical coordinate in the input data structure, e.g., type conversion. We also extend the **identity** mapping to address the transpose operation with a user option to specify the two transposing dimensions. In **all** mapping, each output cell depends on all input cells. **Lincom** mapping describes the linear dependency in a data structure, e.g., vector normalization and linear model prediction.

4.5 Mapping Coverage

To verify the generality of these seven primitive mapping types, we analyze the data transformation operators in three distributed ML frameworks. These ML frameworks are KeystoneML v0.2.0,

TensorFlow v0.7, and SystemML v0.9. They have 45, 146, and 81 predefined operators, respectively. Table 2 shows the operator coverage in these frameworks by each of the primitive mapping types.

Table 2: Hippo's Primitive Mapping Coverage in Existing Systems

	Coll	Flat	Iden	All	Lincom	Join	Geo	Total
KeystoneML	4%	4%	24%	24%	9%	2%	18%	87%
TensorFlow	14%	3%	27%	17%	10%	0%	18%	89%
SystemML	1%	4%	28%	26%	26%	0%	4%	89%

In general, Hippo's primitive mapping types cover ∼ 90% of each framework. The reason for the low presence of **join** mapping in TensorFlow and SystemML is that these two frameworks do not explicitly expose the combination of labels and feature vectors as a single operator. However, the **join** mapping occurs in every training process in supervised learning. For the rest of the mapping types that Hippo does not cover, we supply an additional CustomMapping() type, so users can use arbitrary data structure to record the cell-level dependency.

5 DESIGN

In Section 3 and 4, we present the underlying data model of Hippo and the primitive mapping types that record the cell-level dependency between the input and output datasets in a data transformation. In this section, we introduce the design of Hippo. We begin the discussion with the functional requirements of an ML pipeline diagnostic tool. Then we discuss how Hippo exposes its lineage declaration, instrumentation, and query interface to meet these requirements.

5.1 Functional Requirements

Hippo, as an ML pipeline diagnostic tool, has two basic functions: lineage capturing and serving. Lineage capturing requires a user-friendly, flexible, and powerful interface for lineage declaration and instrumentation. Lineage serving should be able to answer cell-level queries to enable diagnostics.

5.2 Overview

To study the applicability, we integrate Hippo with KeystoneML. Figure 6 shows the overview of Hippo and its interactions with other components. Rounded-corner rectangles are components around and inside KeystoneML. The two-sided arrows indicate interactions between components. Users compose machine learning pipelines with KeystoneML and submit the compiled DAG to Spark. All computation and I/O are done through the Spark Resilient Distributed Dataset (RDD) abstraction. With Hippo, users can declare and instrument lineage at the transformer level, so that the compiled DAG also contains lineage capturing and instrumentation operations. Lineage in Hippo is stored to HDFS [34] via Spark's RDD abstraction. Hippo can load the stored lineage in HDFS to Spark interactive command line interface. By interacting with the query interface, users can query cells of interest, replay transformation, or analyze the lineage for other purposes.

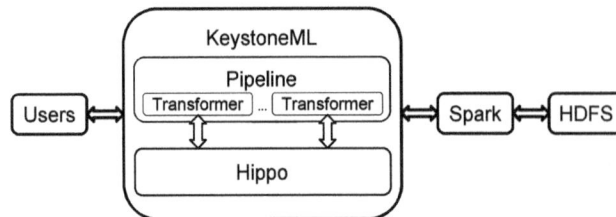

Figure 6: Overview of Hippo and its surrounding components.

5.3 Lineage Interface

Hippo exposes the lineage capturing interface by naming the lineage type with its mapping types between input and output datasets. All the type specific class inherits an abstract class of Lineage, which define common methods shared among the type specific classes:

```
1 abstract class Lineage(inSpace: Space, outSpace: Space){
2   def qForward(keys: List[Coor]): List[Coor]
3   def qBackward(keys: List[Coor]): List[Coor]
4   def saveMapping()
5   def saveInput()
6   def saveOutput()
7 }
```

Listing 3 summarizes the lineage types and parameters. All these lineage classes inherent the abstract Lineage class.

Listing 3: Hippo's Lineage Declaration Interface

```
1 class CollapseLineage(in, out, transformer, dimension)
2 class FlattenLineage(in, out, transformer, dimension)
3 class IdentityLineage(in, out, transformer)
4 class AllLineage(in, out, transformer)
5 class GeoLineage(in, out, transformer, mapping)
6 class LinComLineage(in, out, transformer, model)
7 class JoinLineage(in, out, transformer, dimension)
8 class CustomLineage(in, out, transformer, model, state)
```

In general, Hippo collects six types of data: the input dataset (in), the output dataset (out), the transformer (transformer), the customized mapping (mapping), the optional model (model), and one state parameter which captures the internal state of the transformer, e.g., a random seed in a column sampler.

Hippo's lineage declaration interface can determine the space, the dimension count, and the size of each dimension of the datasets by examining the nested data structure and the parameters specified by users.

Listing 4: PixelScaler with Lineage Definition

```
1 object PixelScaler extends Transformer{
2   def apply[in: Dataset[Image]]: Dataset[Image] = {
3     in.map(image => image.map(_/255.0))
4   }
5   def applyWithLineage(in: Dataset[Image]):
6   Dataset[Image] = {
7     val out = apply(in)
8     val lineage = IdentityLineage(in, out, this)
9     return out
10   }
11 }
```

For example, Listing 4 rewrites the PixelScaler transformer in Listing 2 with lineage declaration. Line 8 in the listing instantiates the spaces with the input and output datasets, and specify the mapping type as **Identity**.

6 IMPLEMENTATION

There are three performance requirements for an ML pipeline diagnostic tool. First, the lineage capturing should add a modest wall clock time overhead to the original pipeline. Second, the storage space of the lineage should be within a manageable size. Third, the lineage serving function should be with a low latency for interactive diagnostics. As documented in the report [27] in human computer interaction, 1 second latency is the boundary to keep users' thought flow while 10 seconds is the boundary to loose users' attention.

In this section, we present system implementation details to address the three performance requirements.

6.1 Metadata Separation

Hippo separates the metadata of a data structure (e.g., the coordinates of cells in a matrix) from the actual data and leaves it as an option for users to decide whether or not to collect the actual data.

Under the constraint of complete pipeline lineage integrity, a minimal lineage to be captured is all the metadata mapping of the transformers. All the intermediate and result datasets can always be reproduced with the KeystoneML transformer given the its deterministic replay property. A profile on the SIFTFisher and SourceExtractor pipeline shows that this metadata separation can reduce storage space by a factor of 13.7x (from 725.6 GB to 109.9 GB) and 2480.9x (from 507.1G to 204.4M), respectively.

6.2 Lineage Storage

Hippo uses the RDD abstraction for lineage information storage. At a high level, Hippo creates a unique directory on the underlying file system with a naming pattern of concatenating the transformer name and the initial input dataset identifier of the pipeline. In this way, Hippo can tell between the training path and testing path based on the input dataset identifier, if the training and testing are run in a single program with distinct datasets.

In the current implementation, Hippo stores lineage information as serialized objects in HDFS. However, this lineage information could just as easily be stored virtually on any distributed storage system, including an in-memory system such as Alluxio [21].

6.3 Geometry Mapping Indexing

Among the primitive mapping types, **geometry** mapping consumes the most space due to its lack of a regular mapping pattern. In a **geometry** mapping, the geometries can be randomly spread in a space and the pairing between input and output geometries can also be random. Using high-order functions (the shape abstraction in the data model) can reduce the storage space, but querying the cells in the high-order functions can be slow due to the encoding. In this section, we present four indexing strategy to address the slow querying problem. The four indexing strategies are referred to as **NoIndex**, **Direct**, **RTree**, and **KMeans**, respectively. An empirical performance study is presented in Section 7.1. For simplicity, only forward query is discussed in this section. The backward query works in a similar way by reverting the geometry pair.

Figure 7 shows the mapping example in the following discussion. Table 3 shows the 2D geometry mapping.

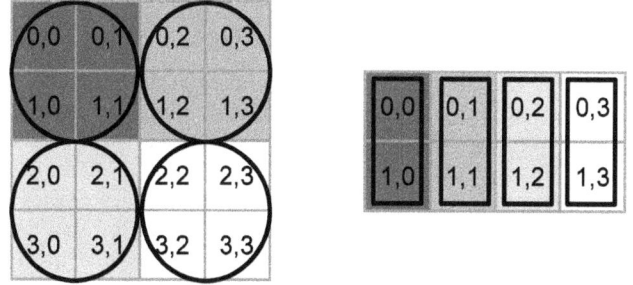

Figure 7: A geometry mapping example, the left matrix is input and the right matrix is output. The mapping between the geometries are shown using gray shades.

Table 3: Cell-wise and geometry mapping of the example in Figure 7

Input	Geometry	Output	Geometry
(0,0),...,(1,1)	Circle_0	(0,0),(1,0)	Rect_0
(0,2),...,(1,3)	Circle_1	(0,1),(1,1)	Rect_1
(2,0),...,(3,1)	Circle_2	(0,2),(1,2)	Rect_2
(2,2),...,(3,3)	Circle_3	(0,3),(1,3)	Rect_3

6.3.1 No Index. Using the example in Table 3, with **NoIndex** strategy, a query for a cell needs to traverse all circles (input geometries). If the cell is in a circle, the query returns all output cells expanded from the mapping rectangle.

6.3.2 Direct Index. To build the **Direct** index, Hippo uses each input cell as key and the associated geometry as the value, as shown in Figure 8. Hippo relies on the underlying runtime system for the optimization of storing repeated geometries with a single copy. A query on a cell directly returns the cells in the corresponding rectangle.

Key	Value
(0,0)	Rect_0
(0,1)	Rect_0
(0,2)	Rect_1
(0,3)	Rect_1
...	...

Figure 8: Direct Index

6.3.3 RTree Index. R-tree [18] indices are widely used to index multidimensional information. Variants of R-tree, such as R+-tree [33] and R*-tree [5], seek to improve the worst case query by minimizing the overlapped geometry at leaf nodes by paying the index building cost. In our use cases, it is rare that a single cell occurs in all geometries. Thus R-tree is sufficient to validate the idea of using spatial indexing for geometry mapping. Hippo uses the Archery [30] package to build the **RTree** index.

6.3.4 KMeans Index. Since the geometries are spread in a space, it is reasonable to first cluster these geometries then build a hierarchical spatial index on the clusters. We design a two-layer tree index with its leaf nodes as a cluster of geometries and its non-leaf nodes as the bounding box of the cluster. The geometries are distributed to each cluster using the KMeans [24] algorithm.

6.4 Key Count and Mapping Sequence Reduction

With Hippo, the lineage of an ML pipeline is in the form of a sequence of mappings, with each mapping recording the cell-level dependency for each transformer. Querying one cell in the very beginning mapping can return all resulting output cells of the last transformer. In this process, Hippo recursively query the mappings in the sequence with the previous results as keys. However, the number of intermediate keys can explode depending on the transformer. For example, FisherVector transforms a matrix of 80 rows and 60,000 columns to a matrix of 80 rows and 512 columns in an **all** mapping type. A backward query of any output cell will result in 4.8 million intermediate keys, which will be used to query the remaining mappings. In a naive sense, if the next mapping is also an **all** mapping, then there is an opportunity to reduce the 4.8 million queries to a single query as all these queries return the same result.

Based on this intuition, we define two types of optimizations to reduce key count. The first set of rules is to check the keys' totality in the input space. If the keys include every cell in the input space, then the query returns all cells in the output space. The only exception is **geometry** mapping, where it returns all cells in all output geometries. The second set of rules exploits the structure of **collapse** and **lincom** mapping. For example in **collapse** mapping along column direction, forward queries with cells in the same row will return identical results. Thus, Hippo will query only once with one of these cells.

One additional optimization is to reduce the number of mappings in a pipeline. For example, a forward query on an **identity mapping** followed by a **collapse** mapping has the exact same results as querying solely on the **collapse** mapping. Thus we can reduce the two mappings to a single one. The complete list of reduction rules is:

```
1  Identity + Any = Any
2  Any + Identity= Any
3  All + Any/Geo² = All
4  Any/Geo + All = All
5  Lincom + Lincom = Lincom
```

If a pair of mappings can not be reduced, Hippo simply records them as a sequence of mappings.

7 EVALUATION

In this section, we evaluate a number of aspects of Hippo's performance. For geometry mapping indexing strategies, we measure the build time, query performance, memory usage and storage consumption. Then we present Hippo's lineage capturing wall clock time overhead with two real ML pipelines on varying cluster sizes. We also measure the performance of the three use cases presented in Section 2.3.

All experiments are run on Amazon EC2 using r3.8xlarge instances. Each machine has 16 physical cores, 244 GB memory, and two 320GB SSDs. Hippo is integrated with KeystoneML 0.3 which in turn runs over Spark 1.3.1 and HDFS from the CDH4 distribution of Hadoop.

The two pipelines we are using are SIFTFisher and SourceExtractor. The datasets are VOC2007 [12] and a subset of Sloan Digital

---

[2]Geo Mapping is not included in Rule 3 and Rule 4

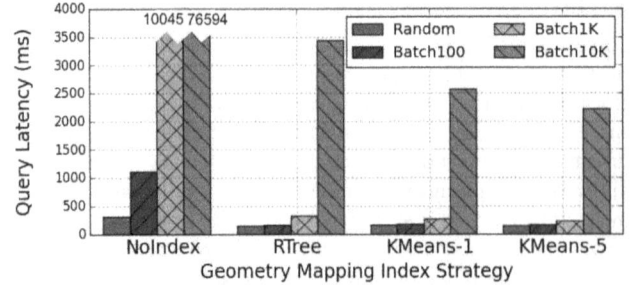

Figure 9: Query performance profile of the geometry mapping with four indexing strategies

Table 4: Summary of Build Time and Additional Memory Usage (over 0.7 TB) for the Four Indexing Strategies

Index	Build Time	Additional Mem
NoIndex	0s	71.4%
RTree	30.6 ± 1.5 s	85.7%
KMeans-1	66.6 ± 4.2 s	85.7%
KMeans-5	342.3 ± 8 s	114.3%

Sky Survey [43] (SDSS) Data Release 7, respectively. The VOC2007 dataset contains 10,000 images with a total size of 828 MB. The SDSS DR7 dataset contains 11,150 images with a total size of 65 GB.

7.1 Geometry Mapping Index

With this experiment we seek to profile the query latency, index build time, and memory usage of the indexing strategies for geometry mapping discussed in Section 6.3. In particular, KMeans-1 and KMeans-5 builds the index with one and five iterations, respectively. We use a workload derived from the SIFTExtractor transformer in the SIFTFisher pipeline. The mapping has 5,000 pairs of input and output matrix, with each pair producing 60,000 geometry tuples (300 million in total) that are uniformly distributed in a 2D space. The experiment is executed on a 16 machine cluster.

Figure 9 presents the query performance with these indexing strategies. For each strategy, we run queries with {1, 100, 1K, 10K} keys. The Direct strategy crashes due to insufficient memory. NoIndex strategy shows a high query latency which quickly grows over 10,000 ms with 100 keys. The other three strategies show a similar scalability, while KMeans-1 runs 17.9% and 25.1% faster than RTree with 1K and 10K keys, respectively. KMeans-5 runs 31.1% and 35.2% faster than RTree with 1K and 10K keys, respectively.

Table 4 summarizes the index build time and additional memory usage. The size of the geometry mapping is 30.8 GB. To summarize, NoIndex has the highest query latency and it is not practical for real use. KMeans-5 has the best query performance and the longest index building time. RTree has a balanced query performance and building time. Thus Hippo uses the RTree strategy as default, leaving the other strategies as users' options.

7.2 Lineage Capturing Overhead

We evaluate lineage capturing wall clock time overhead with the SIFTFisher (test path) and SourceExtractor pipelines. For each pipeline,

Table 5: Data Size of SIFTFisher and SourceExtractor with the Meta-only and Meta+Data settings

Pipeline	SIFTFisher	SourceExtractor
Meta-only	109.9 GB	204.4 MB
Meta+Data	615.7 GB	506.9 GB

Table 6: Relative Lineage Capturing Wall Clock Time Overhead

Pipeline & Setting	8 nodes	16 nodes	32 nodes
SIFTFisher Meta-only	38.4% ± 2.6%	34.3% ± 0.9%	30.4% ± 0.6%
SIFTFisher Meta+Data	142.7% ± 3.7%	88% ± 1.9%	60.6% ± 0.8%
SE Meta-only	39.3% ± 2.9%	23.4% ± 0.9%	20.7% ± 0.6%
SE Meta+Data	238.5% ± 11.2%	94.4% ± 1.3%	54% ± 0.7%

we measure the wall clock time of lineage capturing with two settings. With the first setting (meta-only), Hippo only captures the metadata mapping, since this is the minimal lineage information to preserve the pipeline lineage integrity. With the second setting (meta+data), Hippo captures both the metadata mapping and the output dataset of each transformer. With the lineage information captured in this way, queries on the output dataset does not require any rerunning of data transformations. This is considered as the minimal sufficient lineage information of a pipeline without rerunning. Table 5 presents the dataset size collected with both settings for both pipelines.

Table 6 summarizes the relative wall clock time overhead of lineage capturing of the SIFTFisher and SourceExtractor pipeline. Across the scales, the meta-only lineage capturing introduces a 30%-40% percent overhead compared to the lineage-free SIFTFisher pipeline. The SourceExtractor pipeline's meta-only capturing overhead is 20%-40%. Though capturing all the intermediate data introduces additional overhead for both pipelines, the overhead decreases near linearly with more machines. This is because the additional intermediate data collection is simply writing more data to HDFS and these writing operations scale with more machines.

A further overhead decomposition of the 16 node measurements reveals that the SIFTExtractor transformer contributes to 85.4% of the lineage capturing overhead. The individual overhead for the rest of the transformers ranges from 1.1% to 1.4%. This is because we use **Geometry** mapping for SIFTExtractor and the **Geometry** mapping is the only mapping type that materializes cell-level dependency at runtime among the primitive types. Similarly, the Extractor transformer in the SourceExtractor pipeline solely contributes 65.2% to the lineage capturing overhead.

7.3 Query Latency and Scalability

In Section 6.4, we stated that in the case of a pipeline lineage query, the intermediate key number can increase dramatically. The query with this large key number on a single mapping can impact the query performance substantially. This performance measurement seeks to profile the query scalability of Hippo on a single mapping with a varying key number.

We run queries with varying key numbers and present the performance in Figure 10. For each lineage type, we use a collection of 5,000 pairs of input and output data structures (vector, matrix,

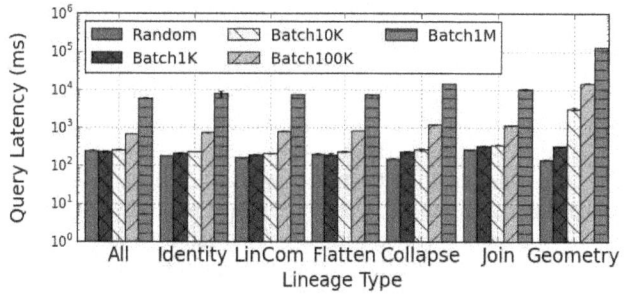

Figure 10: Query latency for the seven lineage types (in log scale).

Table 7: Data Structure Settings

Type	Input Structure	Output Structure
All	Vector(40960)	Vector(40960)
Identity	Matrix(80, 512)	Matrix(80, 512)
LinCom	Vector(40960)	Vector(20)
Flatten	Matrix(80, 512)	Vector(40960)
Collapse	Image(375, 500, 3)	Matrix(375, 500)
Join	Matrix(500, 300), Matrix(500, 300)	Matrix(1000, 300)
Geometry	Matrix(300, 500), 60K geometries	Matrix(128, 60000), 60K geometries

image) and distribute them over 16 machines. Table 7 shows the metadata settings of the input and output data structure in each query.

Given the fact that all mapping, identity mapping, lincom mapping, flatten mapping, collapse mapping, and join mapping only involve trivial computation, queries with 1 to 10K keys show latency under 200 ms. These queries show performance degradation with 100K keys (around 1 second). From 100K keys, the query latency increases proportionally with the key number as shown with the 1M key performance. Geometry Mapping shows a consistent latency under 200 ms from 1 to 1K keys. Beyond that, a query with 10K keys takes 2.41 ± 0.6 seconds and a query with 1M keys take 132.9 ± 0.4 seconds

This query scalability profile shows low latency (~200 ms) for single cell query in a mapping. With the end-to-end pipeline lineage, the query can be slow due to the quickly increasing key number. While in the case of SIFTFisher pipeline, it can take an estimated $O(10^3)$ seconds to finish as the backward query on the SIFTExtractor transformer with a key count of 7.7M. The actual mapping is from a matrix with 128 rows and 60K columns to a matrix with 333 rows and 500 columns. With the optimization rules in Section 6.4, we are able to query the lineage of the complete SIFTFisher pipeline (11 transformers in total) in 75.7 ± 1.7 seconds.

7.4 Use Cases

In the **code validation** case, users instrument the GMM training path of the SIFTFisher pipeline to collect both the metadata mapping and intermediate data. As shown in Figure 2, the GMM training path omits PCA and ColumnSampler1. Upon validation, users load the lineage of DimensionReducer and ColumnSampler2 then apply a backward query on one result vector. With the result coordinates, the users access the actual values of the contributing vector and find out that the new features contain values outside of the suitable range as pixel positions in an image. Such an instrumentation introduces a wall clock time overhead of 60.9% on a 16 machine cluster. The backward query and value retrieval takes 0.44 ± 0.01 seconds.

In the **results inspection** use case, the user of the SourceExtractor pipeline captures the metadata mapping in all transformers along with the output datasets of the Extractor transformer. By joining the metadata mapping with the output dataset, which contains the luminosity information, he first filters out the objects with a threshold brightness. Then the user queries the metadata mapping to find the positions of corresponding pixels in the input images. This instrumentation introduces a wall clock time overhead of 40.8% on a 8 machine cluster. Filtering *luminous flux* $> 300,000$ *lumen* over 1 million objects returns 10,283 objects with the corresponding pixel positions in 1.84 ± 0.14 seconds. A forward query that traces the error propagation given a bad pixel takes 3.3 ± 0.03 seconds to return.

In the **data cleaning** use case, the user of the SIFTFisher pipeline wants to remove the training images that have both dogs and cats. So he instruments the pipeline to capture all metadata mappings and the output datasets for NormalizeRows transformer. Upon removal, he first joins the output dataset of NormalizeRows (a RDD of vectors) with the labels. Then he filters out the corresponding vectors with both cats and dogs in it (eight vectors corresponding to eight images in this case). From here, he can try retrain the model with the cleaned dataset. This particular instrumentation introduces a wall clock time overhead of 46.8%, and the removal takes 25.7 ± 0.27 seconds. Compared to the case of rerunning the data preparation phase of the pipeline, using lineage information speeds up the turnaround time by 16.4x (from 421.3 ± 3.8 seconds to 25.7 ± 0.3 seconds).

8 RELATED WORK

Coarse-grained Lineage: Researchers have extensively studied lineage (in some cases referred as provenance) in different contexts. Scientific workflow systems such as Chimera [13], Taverna [28], ESSW [15], Kepler [2], and Karma2 [36] collect coarse-grained lineage of files and computation. Similar work has been well summarized by surveys [6, 14, 35]. Recent work by Altintas [1] investigates how to integrate workflow lineage in a collaborative environment. Coarse-grained lineage is useful in these systems to trace the data and code dependencies. However, it lacks the cell-level details for ML pipelines diagnosis.

Fine-grained Lineage: Fine-grained lineage has been investigated in the context of data visualization [39, 41], data warehouse [9, 10], RDBMS [40], and user-curated database [8]. Recent works of RAMP [19, 31] and Newt [22] capture fine-grained lineage for the MapReduce systems. The Lipstick [3] system collects fine-grained lineage on declarative querying language Pig Latin [29]. SubZero [42] proposes a lineage system for the array-based SciDB [7]. Titian [20] enables fine-grained lineage capturing and query for Apache Spark. All these systems design lineage capturing interface on the well-defined low level operators. For example, the data warehouse has the aggregate, select, project, join

operators. RDBMS has its SQL operators. MapReduce systems formulates the computation as mappers and reducers. The curated database defines four operators of insert, delete, copy and paste. Though lineage capturing interface designed in these systems is general to support all applications running on top them, they are not suitable for the ML pipeline diagnostics. This is because ML frameworks do not have such a set of well-defined low level operators.

Although Titian solves the lineage problem on Spark, it is insufficient for ML pipelines. This is because Titian tracks lineage at the RDD element level while ML pipeline lineage requires the cell-level mapping inside a RDD element. One of SubZero's contributions is the region lineage that collects fine-grained lineage for UDFs besides the built-in operators in SciDB. However, region lineage is not sufficient for ML pipelines because it only captures many to one relationships between input and output cells, while ML pipelines require many to many relationships as well. Besides, SubZero is implemented on a single computer while Hippo has to work in a distributed environment.

The Taverna 2 workflow system [38] proposes a fine-grained lineage model and the work by Missier *et al.* [26] presents two mapping types as data collection cross-product and index-projection. These mapping types partially address the workflow system computation mapping, however, they are not sufficient to cover the data transformation in ML pipelines.

Other Fine-grained Lineage Capturing Techniques: Researchers also have tried to collect fine-grained lineage with other approaches. Weak inversion and verification methods [41] are proposed to support approximate lineage collection. Dynamic program analysis is employed to capture fine-grained lineage inside non-relational operators [45] with a 7.5~39.8x slowdown compared to the original program. These approaches do not fit the ML pipeline lineage scenario since they either lose the lineage accuracy or introduce excessive performance penalty. The Arnold system [11] can collect fine-grain lineage for operating system processes, however it loses track of the upper level data structures (e.g., vector, matrix, images), which are fundamental to ML pipelines.

9 CONCLUSION AND FUTURE WORK

Hippo enables interactive ML pipeline diagnosis such as code validation, results inspection, and data cleaning by leveraging fine-grained data lineage. Hippo exposes an elegant and powerful interface for users to specify and instrument lineage capturing. This interface has a coverage of ~90% of the transformers in the current KeystoneML, TensorFlow, and SystemML code base. Combining various techniques and optimizations, Hippo is able to reduce the lineage storage space by a factor of $O(10^3)$ compared to the baseline of cell-wise mapping recording and Hippo can answer typical queries within a few seconds to enable interactive ML pipeline diagnosis.

As future work, we are investigating the diagnosability of other model families such as the bayesian network. We will also explore the diagnosability inside the training process. We seek to provide users with fine-grained lineage for queries such as finding supporting training samples for a prediction and the impact of certain feature removal or training data item removal.

10 ACKNOWLEDGMENTS

This research is supported in part by NSF CISE Expeditions Award CCF-1139158, LBNL Award 7076018, and DARPA XData Award FA8750-12-2-0331, and gifts from Amazon Web Services, Google, SAP, The Thomas and Stacey Siebel Foundation, Adatao, Adobe, Apple, Inc., Blue Goji, Bosch, C3Energy, Cisco, Cray, Cloudera, EMC, Ericsson, Facebook, Guavus, Huawei, Intel, Microsoft, NetApp, Pivotal, Samsung, Splunk, Virdata, VMware, and Yahoo!.

REFERENCES

[1] I. Altintas, M. K. Anand, D. Crawl, S. Bowers, A. Belloum, P. Missier, B. Ludäscher, C. A. Goble, and P. M. Sloot. Understanding collaborative studies through interoperable workflow provenance. In *Provenance and Annotation of Data and Processes*, pages 42–58. Springer, 2010.

[2] I. Altintas, O. Barney, and E. Jaeger-Frank. Provenance collection support in the kepler scientific workflow system. In *Provenance and annotation of data*, pages 118–132. Springer, 2006.

[3] Y. Amsterdamer, S. B. Davidson, D. Deutch, T. Milo, J. Stoyanovich, and V. Tannen. Putting lipstick on pig: Enabling database-style workflow provenance. *Proceedings of the VLDB Endowment*, 5(4):346–357, 2011.

[4] Apache. Apache Hadoop. http://hadoop.apache.org/.

[5] N. Beckmann, H.-P. Kriegel, R. Schneider, and B. Seeger. The R*-tree: An efficient and robust access method for points and rectangles. In *Proceedings of the 1990 ACM SIGMOD International Conference on Management of Data*, SIGMOD '90, pages 322–331, New York, NY, USA, 1990. ACM.

[6] R. Bose and J. Frew. Lineage retrieval for scientific data processing: a survey. *ACM Computing Surveys (CSUR)*, 37(1):1–28, 2005.

[7] P. G. Brown. Overview of scidb: large scale array storage, processing and analysis. In *Proceedings of the 2010 ACM SIGMOD International Conference on Management of data*, pages 963–968. ACM, 2010.

[8] P. Buneman, A. Chapman, and J. Cheney. Provenance management in curated databases. In *Proceedings of the 2006 ACM SIGMOD international conference on Management of data*, pages 539–550. ACM, 2006.

[9] Y. Cui and J. Widom. Practical lineage tracing in data warehouses. In *Data Engineering, 2000. Proceedings. 16th International Conference on*, pages 367–378. IEEE, 2000.

[10] Y. Cui and J. Widom. Lineage tracing for general data warehouse transformations. *The VLDB Journal, The International Journal on Very Large Data Bases*, 12(1):41–58, 2003.

[11] D. Devecsery, M. Chow, X. Dou, J. Flinn, and P. M. Chen. Eidetic systems. In *Proceedings of the 11th USENIX Symposium on Operating Systems Design and Implementation (OSDI)*, 2014.

[12] M. Everingham, L. Van Gool, C. K. I. Williams, J. Winn, and A. Zisserman. The PASCAL Visual Object Classes Challenge 2007 (VOC2007) Results. http://www.pascal-network.org/challenges/VOC/voc2007/workshop/index.html.

[13] I. Foster, J. Vöckler, M. Wilde, and Y. Zhao. Chimera: A virtual data system for representing, querying, and automating data derivation. In *Scientific and Statistical Database Management, 2002. Proceedings. 14th International Conference on*, pages 37–46. IEEE, 2002.

[14] J. Freire, D. Koop, E. Santos, and C. T. Silva. Provenance for computational tasks: A survey. *Computing in Science & Engineering*, 10(3):11–21, 2008.

[15] J. Frew and R. Bose. Earth system science workbench: A data management infrastructure for earth science products. In *Scientific and Statistical Database Management, 2001. SSDBM 2001. Proceedings. Thirteenth International Conference on*, pages 180–189. IEEE, 2001.

[16] A. Ghoting, R. Krishnamurthy, E. Pednault, B. Reinwald, V. Sindhwani, S. Tatikonda, Y. Tian, and S. Vaithyanathan. Systemml: Declarative machine learning on mapreduce. In *Data Engineering (ICDE), 2011 IEEE 27th International Conference on*, pages 231–242. IEEE, 2011.

[17] Google. Tensorflow. http://tensorflow.org/.

[18] A. Guttman. R-trees: A dynamic index structure for spatial searching. In *Proceedings of the 1984 ACM SIGMOD International Conference on Management of Data*, SIGMOD '84, pages 47–57, New York, NY, USA, 1984. ACM.

[19] R. Ikeda, H. Park, and J. Widom. Provenance for generalized map and reduce workflows. In *CIDR 2011*. Stanford InfoLab.

[20] M. Interlandi, K. Shah, S. D. Tetali, M. A. Gulzar, S. Yoo, M. Kim, T. Millstein, and T. Condie. Titian: data provenance support in spark. *Proceedings of the VLDB Endowment*, 9(3):216–227, 2015.

[21] H. Li, A. Ghodsi, M. Zaharia, S. Shenker, and I. Stoica. Tachyon: Reliable, memory speed storage for cluster computing frameworks. In *Proceedings of the ACM Symposium on Cloud Computing*, pages 1–15. ACM, 2014.

[22] D. Logothetis, S. De, and K. Yocum. Scalable lineage capture for debugging disc analytics. In *Proceedings of the 4th annual Symposium on Cloud Computing*, page 17. ACM, 2013.

[23] D. G. Lowe. Object recognition from local scale-invariant features. In *Computer vision, 1999. The proceedings of the seventh IEEE international conference on*, volume 2, pages 1150–1157. Ieee, 1999.

[24] J. MacQueen et al. Some methods for classification and analysis of multivariate observations. In *Proceedings of the fifth Berkeley symposium on mathematical statistics and probability*, volume 1, pages 281–297. Oakland, CA, USA., 1967.

[25] X. Meng, J. Bradley, B. Yavuz, E. Sparks, S. Venkataraman, D. Liu, J. Freeman, D. Tsai, M. Amde, S. Owen, et al. Mllib: Machine learning in apache spark. *arXiv preprint arXiv:1505.06807*, 2015.

[26] P. Missier, N. W. Paton, and K. Belhajjame. Fine-grained and efficient lineage querying of collection-based workflow provenance. In *Proceedings of the 13th International Conference on Extending Database Technology*, pages 299–310. ACM, 2010.

[27] J. Nielsen. Powers of 10: Time scales in user experience, 2009. http://www.nngroup.com/articles/powers-of-10-time-scales-in-ux/.

[28] T. Oinn, M. Greenwood, M. J. Addis, M. N. Alpdemir, J. Ferris, K. Glover, C. Goble, A. Goderis, D. Hull, D. Marvin, et al. Taverna: lessons in creating a workflow environment for the life sciences. *Journal of Concurrency and Computation: Practice and experience*, 2002.

[29] C. Olston, B. Reed, U. Srivastava, R. Kumar, and A. Tomkins. Pig latin: a not-so-foreign language for data processing. In *Proceedings of the 2008 ACM SIGMOD international conference on Management of data*, pages 1099–1110. ACM, 2008.

[30] E. Osheim. Archery. https://github.com/meetup/archery.

[31] H. Park, R. Ikeda, and J. Widom. RAMP: A system for capturing and tracing provenance in mapreduce workflows. In *37th International Conference on Very Large Data Bases (VLDB)*. Stanford InfoLab, August 2011.

[32] F. Pedregosa, G. Varoquaux, A. Gramfort, V. Michel, B. Thirion, O. Grisel, M. Blondel, P. Prettenhofer, R. Weiss, V. Dubourg, et al. Scikit-learn: Machine learning in python. *The Journal of Machine Learning Research*, 12:2825–2830, 2011.

[33] T. Sellis, N. Roussopoulos, and C. Faloutsos. The R+-tree: A dynamic index for multi-dimensional objects. 1987.

[34] K. Shvachko, H. Kuang, S. Radia, and R. Chansler. The Hadoop Distributed File System. In *Proceedings of the IEEE Symposium on Mass Storage Systems and Technologies (MSST '10)*, pages 1–10. IEEE, 2010.

[35] Y. L. Simmhan, B. Plale, and D. Gannon. A survey of data provenance in e-science. *ACM Sigmod Record*, 34(3):31–36, 2005.

[36] Y. L. Simmhan, B. Plale, and D. Gannon. Karma2: Provenance management for data-driven workflows. *Web Services Research for Emerging Applications: Discoveries and Trends: Discoveries and Trends*, page 317, 2011.

[37] E. Sparks, S. Venkataraman, T. Kaftan, M. Franklin, and B. Recht. Keystoneml. https://github.com/amplab/keystone.

[38] J. Sroka, J. Hidders, P. Missier, and C. Goble. A formal semantics for the taverna 2 workflow model. *Journal of Computer and System Sciences*, 76(6):490–508, 2010.

[39] M. Stonebraker, J. Chen, N. Nathan, C. Paxson, and J. Wu. Tioga: Providing data management support for scientific visualization applications. In *VLDB*, volume 93, pages 25–38. Citeseer, 1993.

[40] J. Widom. Trio: A system for integrated management of data, accuracy, and lineage. Technical Report 2004-40, Stanford InfoLab, August 2004.

[41] A. Woodruff and M. Stonebraker. Supporting fine-grained data lineage in a database visualization environment. In *Data Engineering, 1997. Proceedings. 13th International Conference on*, pages 91–102. IEEE, 1997.

[42] E. Wu, S. Madden, and M. Stonebraker. SubZero: A fine-grained lineage system for scientific databases. In *Data Engineering (ICDE), 2013 IEEE 29th International Conference on*, pages 865–876. IEEE, 2013.

[43] D. G. York, J. Adelman, J. E. Anderson Jr, S. F. Anderson, J. Annis, N. A. Bahcall, J. Bakken, R. Barkhouser, S. Bastian, E. Berman, et al. The sloan digital sky survey: Technical summary. *The Astronomical Journal*, 120(3):1579, 2000.

[44] M. Zaharia, M. Chowdhury, T. Das, A. Dave, J. Ma, M. McCauley, M. Franklin, S. Shenker, and I. Stoica. Resilient distributed datasets: A fault-tolerant abstraction for in-memory cluster computing. In *Proceedings of the USENIX Conference on Networked Systems Design and Implementation (NSDI '12)*, pages 2–2. USENIX Association, 2012.

[45] M. Zhang, X. Zhang, X. Zhang, and S. Prabhakar. Tracing lineage beyond relational operators. In *Proceedings of the 33rd international conference on Very large data bases*, pages 1116–1127. VLDB Endowment, 2007.

COS: A Parallel Performance Model for Dynamic Variations in Processor Speed, Memory Speed, and Thread Concurrency

Bo Li
Virginia Tech
Blacksburg, Virginia
bxl4074@vt.edu

Edgar A. León
Lawrence Livermore National
Laboratory
Livermore, California
leon@llnl.gov

Kirk W. Cameron
Virginia Tech
Blacksburg, Virginia
cameron@cs.vt.edu

ABSTRACT

Highly-parallel, high-performance scientific applications must maximize performance inside of a power envelope while maintaining scalability. Emergent parallel and distributed systems offer a growing number of operating modes that provide unprecedented control of processor speed, memory latency, and memory bandwidth. Optimizing these systems for performance and power requires an understanding of the combined effects of these modes and thread concurrency on execution time. In this paper, we describe how an analytical performance model that separates pure computation time (C) and pure stall time (S) from computation-memory overlap time (O) can accurately capture these combined effects. We apply the COS model to predict the performance of thread and power mode combinations to within 7% and 17% for parallel applications (e.g. LULESH) on Intel x86 and IBM BG/Q architectures, respectively. The key insight of the COS model is that the combined effects of processor and memory throttling and concurrency on overlap trend differently than the combined effects on pure computation and pure stall time. The COS model is novel in that it enables independent approximation of overlap which leads to capabilities and accuracies that are as good or better than the best available approaches.

ACM Reference format:
Bo Li, Edgar A. León, and Kirk W. Cameron. 2017. COS: A Parallel Performance Model for Dynamic Variations
in Processor Speed, Memory Speed, and Thread Concurrency. In *Proceedings of HPDC '17, Washington , DC, USA, June 26-30, 2017,* 12 pages.
DOI: http://dx.doi.org/10.1145/3078597.3078601

1 INTRODUCTION

Future high-performance, scientific applications will be highly parallel and designed to run in environments of enormous scale but limited power. Efficiency will be key to achieving the promise of exascale. Emergent systems will have large numbers of configurable operating modes that provide unprecedented control of processor speed and memory frequency and bandwidth. Unfortunately, very little is known about the combined effects of these operating modes and thread concurrency on execution time and efficiency.

The performance effects of various operating modes have been studied mostly in isolation. Dynamic voltage and frequency scaling (*DVFS*), the automated adjustment of processor power and speed settings, has been explored extensively [6, 17, 19, 34]. More recently, analogous research on the effects of dynamic memory voltage and frequency throttling (*DMT*), the automated adjustment of DRAM power and speed settings, has surfaced [10, 13, 29]. Other memory power modes such as dynamic bandwidth throttling [1] (*DBT*), where one or more idle clock cycles are inserted between memory accesses to lower peak bandwidth, are emergent. Dynamic concurrency throttling (*DCT*), the automated adjustment of thread concurrency, has also received widespread attention for some time [8].

While some have attempted to study the combined effects of two types of operating modes (e.g., CPU and memory scaling [10, 13], CPU scaling and concurrency throttling [8]), to the best of our knowledge, no one has accurately modeled the combined effects of CPU throttling, memory throttling, and concurrency throttling.

Modeling the combined effects of these three operating modes is incredibly challenging. Capturing the interactive performance effects of a highly configurable problem space could be intractable in highly-parallel, high-performance environments. Furthermore, the interactive effects of these modes are likely to be non-linear, complicating efforts to identify simple but useful analytical models of performance.

In this paper, we present the COS Model of parallel performance for dynamic variations in processor speed, memory speed, and thread concurrency. To the best of our knowledge, this is the first model to accurately capture the simultaneous, combined effects of these three operating modes.

The COS model is based on a simple observation. Past models of operating mode performance tend to combine the overlap of compute and memory performance into either compute time or memory stall time. However, we have observed that the behavior of overlap when these operating modes change is so complex that it must be modeled independently of these other times. This observation leads to the formulation of a Compute-Overlap-Stall (COS) Model where each term can be modeled independently to the others.

In addition to presenting the COS model, we demonstrate how to capture these important (and independent) parameters on both Intel servers and the IBM BG/Q system. We also show how the

---

[1] C.-H. R. Wu, "U.S. patent 7352641: Dynamic memory throttling for power and thermal limitations." Sun Microsystems, Inc., issued 2008.

COS model can be used to classify the best available models. We validate our modeling efforts on 19 HPC kernels and perform extensive sensitivity analyses to identify weaknesses. Our COS Model has more functionality than previously available and the accuracy is as good as or better than best available operating mode models with prediction errors as low as 7% on Intel systems and 17% on the IBM BG/Q system.

2 COMPUTE–OVERLAP–STALL MODEL

2.1 COS Model Parameters

The Compute–Overlap–Stall (COS) model estimates parallel execution time as the sum of pure compute time (T_c), overlap time (T_o), and pure stall time (T_s). More generally,

$$T = T_c + T_o + T_s, \tag{1}$$

where T is total time for a running application.

Figure 1 shows an example execution time profile for a simple, single-threaded application. A single core executes some computation that triggers two separate, non-blocking memory operations. As the code executes, portions of time are spent exclusively on on-chip, in-cache computations; exclusively on off-chip memory operations; and on some form of overlap between computation and memory accesses.

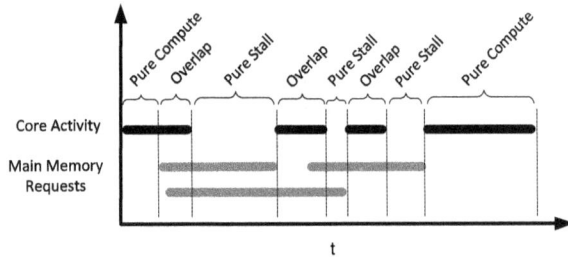

Core Activity

Main Memory Requests

t

Figure 1: An example of a COS Trace for a simple, single-threaded application with hardware support for multiple, simultaneous memory accesses (e.g., multiple loads under misses).

Figure 1 provides context for defining terms of the COS model more precisely. T_c is the sum of the execution times of an application spent exclusively on computation[2] or the ***pure compute time***. In this example, T_c is the sum of the pure compute times identified at the start and end of the application's execution. T_o is the sum of the execution times of an application spent overlapping computation and memory operations or the ***overlap time***. In this example, T_o is the sum of the overlap times, there are three of these stage occurrences over the application's execution. T_s is the sum of the execution times of an application spent exclusively on memory stalls or the ***pure stall time***. In this example, T_s is the sum of

the pure stall times, there are three of these stage occurrences over the application's execution.

2.2 The COS Trace

The ordered summation of the terms of the COS model constitutes a simplified trace of the application. We call this a ***COS Trace***. More precisely, the 8 stage occurrences for the example in Figure 1 are expressed in the following COS Trace:

$$T = T_c(1) + T_o(1) + T_s(1) + T_o(2) + T_s(2) + \\ T_o(3) + T_s(3) + T_c(2) \tag{2}$$

Analogously, we propose a general COS Trace as follows:

$$T = \sum_{i=1}^{cP} T_c(i) + \sum_{j=1}^{oP} T_o(j) + \sum_{k=1}^{sP} T_s(k) \tag{3}$$

where cP, oP, sP are the number of stages corresponding to the three types of time in the COS trace: the pure compute time (T_c), the overlap time (T_o), and the pure stall time (T_s). For Figure 1, $cP = 2$, $oP = 3$, and $sP = 3$. Predicting parallel execution time using the COS model involves estimating the effect of a system or application change on the COS Trace[3].

2.3 COS Model Notations

In succeeding discussions we will use (f_c) and (f_c') to refer to a starting CPU frequency and the changed CPU frequency respectively. Moreover, Δf_c denotes the change from f_c to f_c'. We can define Δf_m and Δt analogously. We use the shorthand (f_c, f_m, t) $\rightarrow$ (f_c', f_m', t') to denote changes to DVFS, DMT/DBT, and thread count respectively. For example, (f_c, f_m, t) $\rightarrow$ (f_c', f_m, t) refers to an isolated change to CPU frequency while (f_c, f_m, t) $\rightarrow$ (f_c, f_m', t') refers to simultaneous memory throttling and changes to thread counts.

2.4 The Importance of Isolating Overlap

Many existing models of parallel performance ignore overlap [3, 16, 22, 31, 33, 36]. When overlap *is* considered, the effects are either captured in the compute time (T_c) or memory stall time (T_s) parameters. If overlap is included in T_c, then the model assumes Δf_c effects apply equally to the overlap portion. If overlap is included in T_s, then the model assumes Δf_m effects apply equally to the overlap portion.

Figure 2 shows the stall time (y-axis) for a code region (R1) of the LULESH OpenMP application kernel [1]. The CPU voltage/frequency increases from left to right (x-axis). The figure shows the measured stall time and the predicted stall time for two best-available performance prediction approaches (stall- and leading-load-based [16, 22, 33]). Notice that both approaches consistently under-predict stall time. Furthermore, in another code region (R2) of the Lulesh OpenMP application (not shown), the same prediction techniques over-predict stall time.

---

[2]We include the performance impact of on-chip caches in pure compute time. This simplification significantly reduces the complexity of the COS model while enabling isolation of the performance effects of power-performance operating modes.

[3]The power-performance operating modes studied include CPU Dynamic Voltage and Frequency Scaling (DVFS) and DRAM Dynamic Memory Frequency Throttling (DMT) on Intel architectures; Dynamic Memory Bandwidth Throttling (DBT) on BG/Q architectures; and Dynamic Concurrency Throttling (DCT) on both architectures.

When stall time dominates, these mis-predictions lead to significant inaccuracies in execution time prediction. The effects are exacerbated by the complex computation and memory overlap scenarios that affect stall and compute time and are more common in mixed operating modes (DVFS, DMT, and DCT).

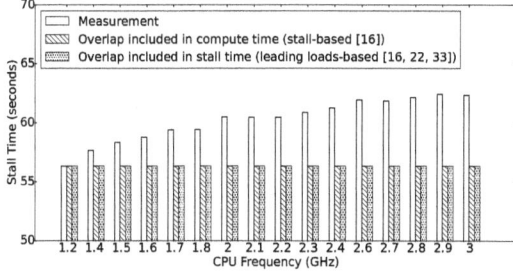

Figure 2: Stall time (y-axis) for varying CPU voltage/frequency settings (x-axis) for the LULESH benchmark on an x86 system. When stall time dominates, these mispredictions lead to significant inaccuracies in execution time prediction. The effects are exacerbated by the complex computation and memory overlap scenarios that affect stall and compute time and are more common in mixed operating modes (DVFS, DMT, and DCT).

2.5 The Challenge of Isolating Overlap

Figure 3 shows a simplified example for three CPU frequencies ($f_{c1} < f_{c2} < f_{c3}$) increasing from left to right. In each subfigure, core activity and memory activity are shown separately as a thread progresses in time (x-axis) from left to right. The COS trace is provided for each subfigure.

In the first subfigure, at the lowest CPU frequency f_{c1}, there are 4 distinct compute and memory overlap phases in the COS trace. This indicates regular memory accesses where the CPU is busy with work during the memory stall time. More precisely, the 9 stage occurrences for f_{c1} in Figure 3 are expressed in the following COS Trace:

$$T = T_c(1) + T_o(1) + T_c(2) + T_o(2) + T_c(3) + T_o(3) + \\ T_c(4) + T_o(4) + T_c(5) \tag{4}$$

The change from $(f_c, f_m, t) \rightarrow (f'_c, f_m, t)$ alters the COS Trace (f_{c2} in Figure 3) as follows:

$$T = T_c(1) + T_o(1) + T_c(2) \tag{5}$$

This reflects a dependency between the resulting COS trace and CPU frequency. In this case, there is a change in the arrival rate of the memory requests due to the CPU frequency changes. In the new configuration, there are no pure compute gaps between memory references leading to a change in the number and length of overlap stages.

Increasing the frequency a second time in this example (f_{c3} in Figure 3) alters the COS trace again, resulting in:

$$T = T_c(1) + T_o(1) + T_s(1) + T_o(2) + T_c(2) \tag{6}$$

This demonstrates the creation of a pure stall stage that did not exist in the previous two COS traces (f_{c1} and f_{c2}) in Figure

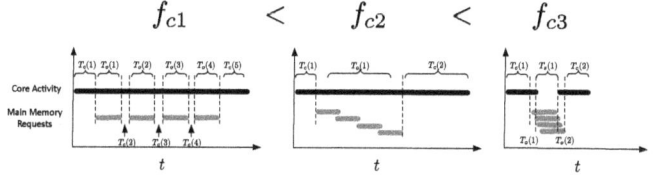

Figure 3: Overlap time and pure stall time are related to computation intensity.

3. We observe similar behaviors for memory throttling changes $((f_c, f_m, t) \rightarrow (f_c, f'_m, t))$ and for thread changes $((f_c, f_m, t) \rightarrow (f_c, f_m, t'))$.

2.6 The Role of Computational Intensity

Estimating the COS terms for simultaneous changes in operating modes such as $(f_c, f_m, t) \rightarrow (f'_c, f'_m, t')$ is even more challenging than the single CPU speed change described in Section 2.5. In theory, each term of the COS trace is affected by all operating mode changes (Δf_c, Δf_m, and Δt). In practice, it depends on the system and application design.

The initial focus of our work is on shared memory systems running multithreaded OpenMP applications where parallel threads are mostly homogeneous and synchronized and the programs use a bulk-synchronous programming model. This focus leads to some simplifying assumptions while still covering a large set of parallel applications of interest to a broad community of scientists [4, 5, 15, 21, 23, 26, 32].

Table 1 shows the application of these assumptions to reduce the set of interactions we need to consider for accurate predictions between system reconfigurations and model parameters. For example, to model T'_c for 7 rows of possible configurations, we need only consider changes to CPU frequency (Δf_c) and thread count (Δt). For T'_o and T'_s, these assumptions simplify all predictions except when all operating modes change simultaneously $(f_c, f_m, t) \rightarrow (f'_c, f'_m, t')$ for any Δf_c, Δf_m, and Δt. This explains why our prediction methods on real systems focus on separating overlap time T'_o from stall time T'_s (see Sections 2.4 and 2.5).

In addition to the system configuration changes (Δf_c, Δf_m, and Δt), Table 1 lists CI as a consideration for both overlap T'_o and pure stall T'_s times. CI here stands for *Computational Intensity*, or the percentage of memory stall time that is overlapped with useful work on the CPU. CI determines how much stall time is affected by CPU speed (Δf_c) and how much is affected by memory throttling (Δf_m).

We conducted statistical analyses to identify a correlation between stall time and measurable hardware counters available on most x86 architectures [2]. Through exhaustive experimentation for all available configurations $(f_c, f_m, t) \rightarrow (f'_c, f'_m, t')$, we found that two widely available counters—last-level cache misses (LLCM) and time-per-instruction (TPI)— effectively captured the stall time effects of Δf_c, Δf_m, and Δt. This finding is key to the COS model's effectiveness since it enables us to use linear approximation methods to separate pure stall time from overlap stall time. For completeness, we studied the effects of CI on compute overlap but

157

Table 1: Effects on COS model parameters of any starting configuration (f_c, f_m, t) to any other operating mode configuration (each row) for changes in processor speed, memory throttling, and number of threads (Δf_c, Δf_m, and Δt). For some configurations, we have additionally identified CI (Computational Intensity) as having significant influence over COS model parameters.

Config	T_c'		T_o'			T_s'		
f_c', f_m, t	Δf_c		Δf_c		CI	Δf_c		CI
f_c, f_m', t				Δf_m	CI		Δf_m	CI
f_c, f_m, t'		Δt		CI	Δt		CI	Δt
f_c', f_m', t	Δf_c		Δf_c	Δf_m	CI	Δf_c	Δf_m	CI
f_c, f_m', t'		Δt		Δf_m CI	Δt		Δf_m CI	Δt
f_c', f_m, t'	Δf_c	Δt	Δf_c	CI	Δt	Δf_c	CI	Δt
f_c', f_m', t'	Δf_c	Δt	Δf_c Δf_m	CI	Δt	Δf_c Δf_m	CI	Δt

we found that compute time was dominated by effects from CPU speed and thread count and not affected significantly by CI.

2.7 Practical Estimation of COS Parameters

We can use the COS trace of Equation 3 to predict the parallel execution time (T') of another system configuration for any combination of Δf_c, Δf_m and Δt. Since the variables may not be directly measurable, the challenge is to collect accurate approximations without requiring system design changes or reverting to simulation. In this section we describe one method for predicting T' using direct measurements readily available on most x86 systems.

Several of the parameters of Equation 3 are directly measurable. Both total time T and the *pure stall time* T_s are directly measurable using the CPU hardware counters available on most modern platforms [2].

We've also observed in our experimental work that overlap consists of a portion affected by CPU speed changes (related to compute time and denoted as T_{oc}) and another portion affected by memory throttling (related to stall time and denoted as T_{os}). The portions vary according to the computational intensity CI of the application (see Section 2.6).

Under these measurements and observations, the operation mode change (f_c, f_m, t) → (f_c', f_m', t') resulting in predicted time T' becomes:

$$T' = [T_c' + T_{oc}'] + [T_{os}' + T_s'] \tag{7}$$

where $[T_c' + T_{oc}']$ can be approximated as $[T - T_s] \times f_c / f_c'$. Multiplying by the ratio of the CPU speed f_c and the new CPU speed f_c' follows the dependencies (Δf_c, Δt) listed in Table 1 for the (f_c, f_m, t) → (f_c', f_m', t') configuration for T_c'. We will discuss how thread changes affect predictions in Section 2.8.

Approximating $[T_{os}' + T_s']$ is more difficult. Table 1 shows that time for the (f_c, f_m, t) → (f_c', f_m', t') configuration for T_s' is affected by a combination of Δf_c, Δf_m, Δt, and IC. Ignoring the impact of multi-threading again for now (see Section 2.8), we propose a linear combination of direct measurements for $LLCM$ and TPI with

direct observations of changes to CPU Speed and memory throttling (f_c' and f_m'). Recall the $LLCM$ and TPI terms capture the Computational Intensity CI effects on the COS trace. This gives the following approximation for the remaining portion of Equation 7:

$$[T_{os}' + T_s'] = \alpha_1 \times LLCM + \alpha_2 \times TPI + \alpha_3 \times f_c' + \alpha_4 \times f_m' \tag{8}$$

Combining our approximations for both sets of terms in Equation 7, our approximation of T' for a operating mode configuration change (f_c, f_m, t) → (f_c', f_m', t') is:

$$T' = [T - T_s] \times \frac{f_c}{f_c'} + \alpha_1 \times LLCM + \alpha_2 \times TPI + \alpha_3 \times f_c' + \alpha_4 \times f_m' \tag{9}$$

In the next section, we describe how we use training sets and linear regression to identify the alpha parameters in this equation to develop a general model for each application in our set of 19.

2.8 Offline Training and Online Prediction

We use a training set measured offline to predict online a larger set of Δf_c, Δf_m, and Δt configurations. Figure 4 illustrates this two step process.

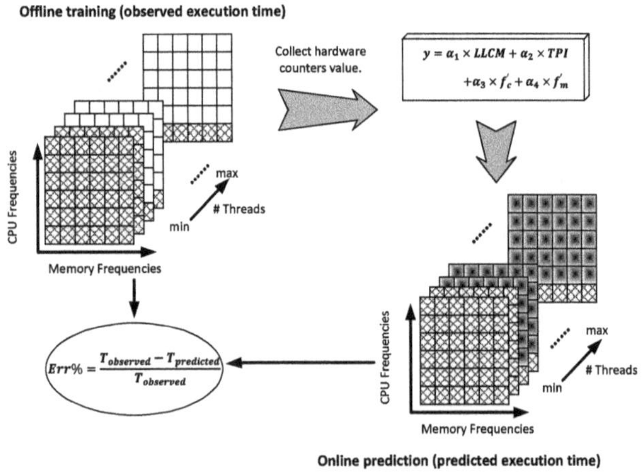

Figure 4: Offline training and online prediction.

The astute reader will notice that Equation 9 contains no term for the number of threads despite our claim to predict for dynamic concurrency changes. The impact of threads is captured in a set of linear approximations for Equation 9 applied to our training sets. What follows is an explanation of the algorithm we use to predict the simultaneous effects of Δf_c, Δf_m, and Δt configurations.

Figure 4 and Algorithm 1 describe our sampling techniques in detail. Basically we gather a set of data for a given application and take samples at various configurations for Δf_c, Δf_m, and Δt. We use this data to conduct linear regression on Equation 9 to determine the values of the four α parameters. For each measurement, we simultaneously gather execution time (T), stall time (T_s), $LLCM$ values, and TPI values.

We designed Algorithm 1 to formally describe the process illustrated by Figure 4. We define f_c^{min}, f_m^{min}, and t^{min} as the minimum speed setting for CPU, minimum throttling setting for memory, and the smallest number of threads respectively for a training set.

Algorithm 1 Train the COS Model for any application

1: **for all** $f_m' \neq f_m^{min}$ **do**
2:   Measure $T, T_s, LLCM, TPI$ for $(f_c^{min}, f_m^{min}, t^{min}) \rightarrow (f_c', f_m', t') \; \forall \; f_c' \neq f_c^{min}$ and $t' = 4, 6$
3:   Measure $T, T_s, LLCM, TPI$ for $(f_c^{min}, f_m^{min}, t^{min}) \rightarrow (f_c^{min}, f_m', t') \; \forall \; t' \neq t^{min}$
4: **end for**
5: Use measured data and linear regression to find α coefficients for Equation 9
6: Use Equation 9 to predict any $(f_c, f_m, t) \rightarrow (f_c', f_m', t') \; \forall \; f_c, f_m, t$ and $\forall \; f_c', f_m', t'$ for this application

---

In Algorithm 1, thread behavior is captured by the training set. Basically, by reapplying Equation 9 to different thread configurations (steps 2 and 3 in Algorithm 1) we are able to capture the effects of threads on the COS model parameters using a combination of direct measurements and linear regression. These effects are incorporated in both $[T - T_s]$ and the $LLCM$ and TPI terms of Equation 9. Thread effects are implicitly captured in the algorithmic application of Equation 9 and thus not explicitly in the formulation.

For a memory modes, b CPU modes, and c thread settings, we require $a \times b \times 2$ measurements for step 2 in Algorithm 1 and $a \times c$ measurements for step 3 in Algorithm 1. These measurements are captured visually by the hashed squares on the left side of Figure 4. This is compared to our ability to predict $a \times b \times c$ combinations using a single training set (see the darker squares on the right side of Figure 4). We have also determined that of the 19 applications studied, only 4-6 models are needed to accurately predict T' for all 19 applications. In future work, we are attempting to reduce the training sets further for online usage. In the remainder of this paper, we compare our predictions with direct measurements and use the resulting COS model for analysis for 19 applications on Intel x86 and IBM BG/Q systems.

3 EMPIRICAL MODEL VALIDATION

In this section, we validate the COS model on a multi-core machine using several application benchmarks with different computational characteristics. We measure the accuracy of the model by comparing the model's prediction versus observed values measured on real hardware.

3.1 Machine Characteristics

We validate the COS model on a cluster comprised of Dell PowerEdge R430 servers. Each node has two Intel Xeon E5-2623 v3 (Haswell) processors and 32 GB of DDR4 memory. Each processor has four cores and each core supports two hardware threads. The Haswell processor supports 16 CPU frequencies ranging from 1.2 to 3.0 GHz. The memory system supports three bus frequencies: 1.333, 1.600, and 1.866 GHz.

3.2 Application Benchmarks

We employ a set of benchmarks and kernels that represent diverse computational characteristics appearing in high-performance, parallel, scientific applications. The application benchmarks include the following codes:

- LULESH (CORAL benchmark suite[4], 5 code regions)
- AMGmk (CORAL benchmark suite, 3 kernels)
- Rodinia benchmark suite (6 applications)
- pF3D from LLNL (5 kernels)

LULESH is an explicit hydrodynamics proxy application that contains data access patterns and computational characteristics of larger hydrodynamics codes at LLNL [1]. We use five code regions within an OpenMP version of LULESH that represent different phases of the application and consume over 90% of the runtime [27]. These five code regions (R1 to R5) were selected in collaboration with domain scientists to isolate the code regions with a diverse set of computational intensity characteristics.

AMGmk includes three compute intensive kernels from AMG, an algebraic multigrid benchmark application derived directly from the BoomerAMG solver in the Hypre linear solvers library [18]. This code is used broadly in a number of applications [26] of interest to the multi-physics community. The default Laplace-type problem is built from an unstructured grid with various jumps and anisotropy in one part. We label these kernels K1 to K3.

Rodinia is a benchmark suite for heterogeneous computing [7]. We use six OpenMP codes from the domains of data mining, graph algorithms, physics simulation, molecular dynamics, and linear algebra: Kmeans, k-Nearest Neighbors (kNN), Breadth-First Search (BFS), HotSpot, LavaMD, and LU Decomposition (LUD). Components of this application suite such as HotSpot are of high interest to domain scientists for use in structured grid applications [4, 5, 21]. There is also high demand for optimized linear algebra solvers [32, 37] such as kNN, Kmeans, and LUD that are used regularly in many high-performance applications and systems.

pF3D is a massively parallel application that simulates laser-plasma interactions at the National Ignition Facility at LLNL [24]. This simulator aids scientists in tuning plasma and laser beam experiments crucial to experimental physics [23]. The pF3D kernels derive from the functions that consume the most time during a typical pF3D run and are written in OpenMP. We use the following kernels: Absorbdt, Acadv K1, Acadv K2, APCPFT, and Advancefi.

In total we used $5 + 3 + 6 + 5 = 19$ code regions and application kernels to evaluate the proposed model. For simplicity, we refer to these as *codes* or *applications* although they are *application benchmarks*.

3.3 Performance Prediction Accuracy

We compare the execution time predicted using modeling with the execution time observed by running the codes. First, for each code, we train its model offline (see Section 2.8) using a sample of Δf_c, Δf_m, and Δt as shown in Table 2. With these configurations we derive the model coefficients. At this point, we can use the model to predict the execution time of any given configuration. Second, we run the code under the configurations not in the training set

---

[4]See https://asc.llnl.gov/CORAL-benchmarks

(a) Average prediction error.

(b) Standard deviation of the prediction error.

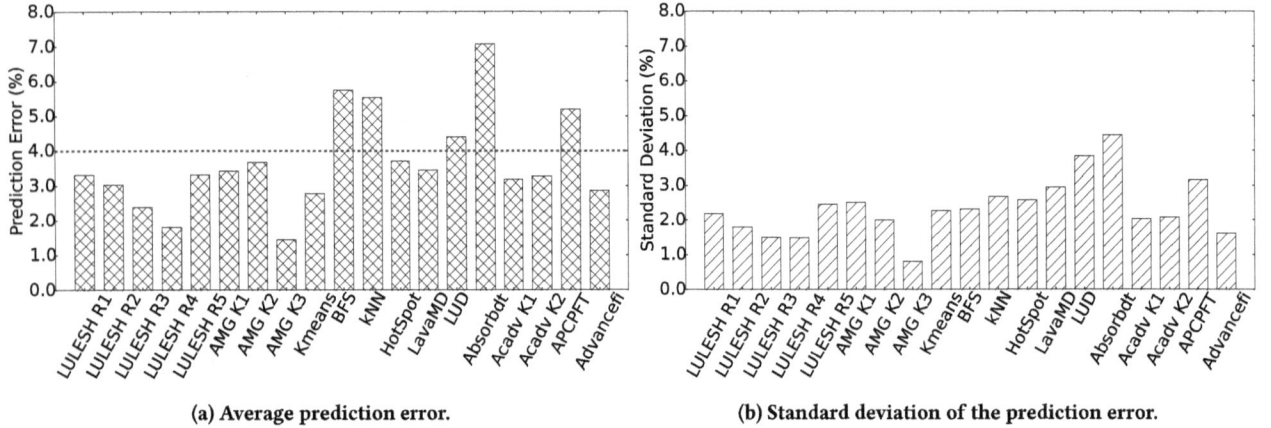

Figure 5: Model prediction accuracy for a wide-range of codes.

for a total of 225 configurations. Each of these is run 20 times to smooth out system noise effects and the average execution time is calculated. Third, we do this for all 19 codes.

Table 2: We use 4- and 6-thread configurations to predict 8, 10, 12, 14, and 16 thread configurations where Δf_c=16 modes, Δf_m=3 modes, Δt=7 thread configurations.

Total	Δf_c (GHz)	Δf_m	Δt (num. threads)
Training configurations			
$16 \times 3 \times 2$	All	All	4, 6
$1 \times 3 \times 5$	1.2	All	8, 10, 12, 14, 16
Configuration space			
$16 \times 3 \times 7$	All	All	4, 6, 8, 10, 12, 14, 16

Figure 5 shows the model prediction accuracy for all of the codes. Figure 5a shows the average prediction error of each code across the entire configuration space not in the training set. The prediction error is calculated as follows (also shown in Figure 4):

$$Err\% = \frac{|T_{measure} - T_{predict}|}{T_{measure}}$$

Figure 5 shows that the average prediction error per code is significantly low: varying from 1.4% to no more than 7%. Most of the codes though have an error lower than 4%. This demonstrates the proposed model is highly accurate for a broad range of applications. We also measure the standard deviation of the prediction error as shown in Figure 5b. The standard deviations for all the codes is within 4.5%. Our proposed model is significantly accurate for the three dimensional configuration space for all 19 applications.

To verify that the tested codes include a wide range of different computational characteristics, we measured the *sensitivity* of a subset of our codes to certain parameters such as processor speed. To capture an application's sensitivity, we focus on *pressure to the memory system* measured as last level cache misses per second. We expect, for example, low memory pressure for compute-intense applications (see Section 2.6) and high pressure for memory bandwidth-intense applications.

Figure 6 shows last-level cache misses (LLCM) per second as a function of different processor and memory speeds and thread concurrency. We employ two processor speeds (1.2 and 3.0 GHz), two memory speeds (1.333 and 1.866 GHz), and two thread counts (4 and 16). Each configuration is represented as a tuple of the following form:

(C: *cpu_frequency*, M: *memory_frequency*, T: *num_threads*)

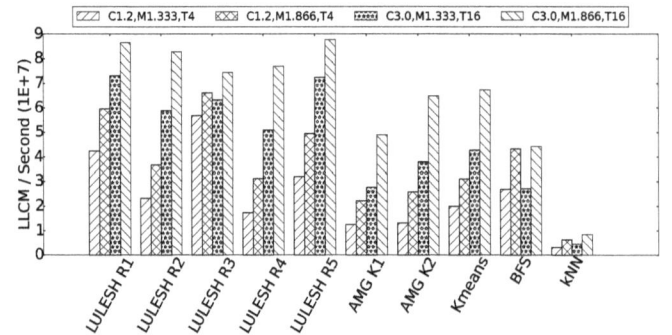

Figure 6: Impact of configuration on memory pressure.

First, we focus on one configuration: (C1.2, M1.333, T4). Codes including kNN, AMG K1 and K2, and LULESH R4 show low memory bandwidth presssure. This matches our expectation since AMG K1 and K2 are compute-intense kernels as is LULESH R4 [28]. While LULESH R1 and R3 are among the ones with the highest usage, Kmeans, BFS, and LULESH R2 exercise higher memory bandwidth utilization. These last two have been shown to be memory bandwidth intensive [27].

Second, we observe that some codes are significantly affected by different parameters such as memory speed and processor speed. LULESH R1 for example shows increased memory pressure with increases in processor speed and also with increases in memory speed. R1 has a high number of instructions per cycle (IPC) that benefit from the increased processor speed shifting the pressure to the memory system. Except for R3, other regions of LULESH show

(a) Average absolute prediction error.

(b) Standard deviation of the absolute prediction error.

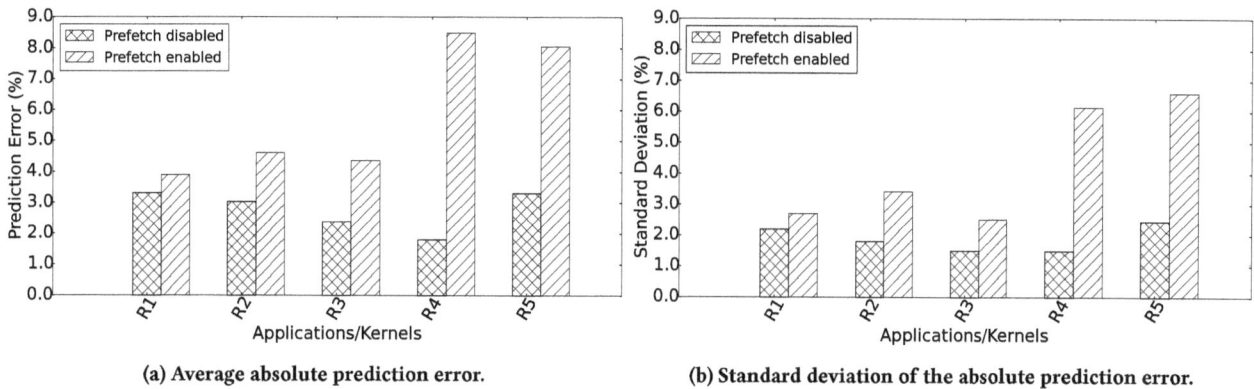

Figure 7: Impact of prefetching on prediction accuracy running LULESH.

a similar pattern but at different scales. Kmeans, AMG K1, and AMG K2 show significant sensitivity to processor speed because of their linear algebra computations.

Third, there are codes that show low sensitivity to different configurations. kNN is a clear example of this. BFS is not affected by increases in processor performance since there is little computation during the graph traversals but does show sensitivity to memory performance as a result of the operations fetching undiscovered graph nodes from memory. LULESH R3 is an interesting case since there are small changes with either processor or memory speed. This is the result of the code being almost exclusively memory bandwidth bound.

Thus, Figure 6 shows that the codes studied in this work capture a diverse set of computational characteristics. Furthermore, the resources in the critical path for some of these codes can change significantly with different configurations. For example, AMG K2 run with a 3.0 GHz processor becomes significantly dependent on the memory system when increasing memory frequency from 1.333 to 1.866 GHz. The low prediction error of the proposed COS model shows that we can capture the effect of these complex interactions accurately.

3.4 COS on Intel Sensitivity Analysis

3.4.1 Memory Prefetching. During development, we noticed the COS model accuracy was sensitive to prefetch settings. The effects of hardware and software prefetching on performance are captured in changes to the COS Trace described by Equation 3. For example, a successful prefetch could increase overlap by preemptively importing data from main memory to cache. An incorrect prefetch however causes cache pollution and could lead to more overlap stages and stall stages.

To better understand these effects, we ran LULESH with hardware prefetching enabled and hardware prefetching disabled and analyzed the results using COS. Figure 7 shows these results using 4 Intel prefetchers: DCU streamer prefetcher (load data to L1 data cache triggered by an ascending access of recently loaded data), DCU IP prefetcher (load data to L1 data cache based on load instruction and its detected regular stride), adjacent line prefetcher (fetch cache line to L2 and last level cache with the pair line), and hardware (streamer) prefetcher (fetch cache lines to L2 and last

level cache based on detection of forward or backward stream of requests from L1).

After enabling all the hardware prefetchers, the accuracy of our predictor worsens as expected. For LULESH R1, the change in average prediction error (Figure 7a) and standard deviation (Figure 7b) are both very minimal. In contrast, LULESH R4 has the largest differential (4x) in accuracy when prefetching is enabled. This is likely due to a large increase in overlap when prefetching is enabled since the R4 region is dominated by compute when overlap is disabled.

When prefetching is disabled, we get excellent accuracy using an extrapolation technique to predict configurations not observed directly in the training set. To improve the accuracy of COS for prefetching, we switched to an interpolation technique using 4- and 16-thread configurations to predict 6-, 8-, 10-, and 12-thread configurations.

The results validate that the COS model based predictor can successfully capture the impact of DVFS, DMT, and DCT simultaneously with prefetching but at the expense of predictor flexibility. The COS approximation techniques implemented in the Intel systems could be extended to better capture the effects of prefetching overlap on performance using approaches similar to those used for power-performance modes.

3.4.2 ROB and MSHR. The sizes of the reorder buffer (ROB) and miss status holding register (MSHR) increase with each generation in CPU design. The ROB reorders instructions to increase instruction-level parallelism and the MSHR increases the number of loads that can be handled under a previous miss. These techniques have the potential to increase overlap and can impact the accuracy of the COS predictor on Intel Systems

We picked nine applications to ascertain the sensitivity of COS to the ROB and MSHR. The Intel hyperthreading design enables us to indirectly control the size of the ROB and MSHR. For a single thread per core, the ROB and MSHR are fixed in size. However, if we overload a core with multiple threads, the ROB and MSHR resources are divided among the threads. We exploit this indirect control in our experiments.

In our experimental setup, we identify two basic configurations: 1) 4-, 6-, and 8-threads where at most one OpenMP thread is mapped to a core, and 2) 10-, 12-, 14-, and 16-threads where at least two

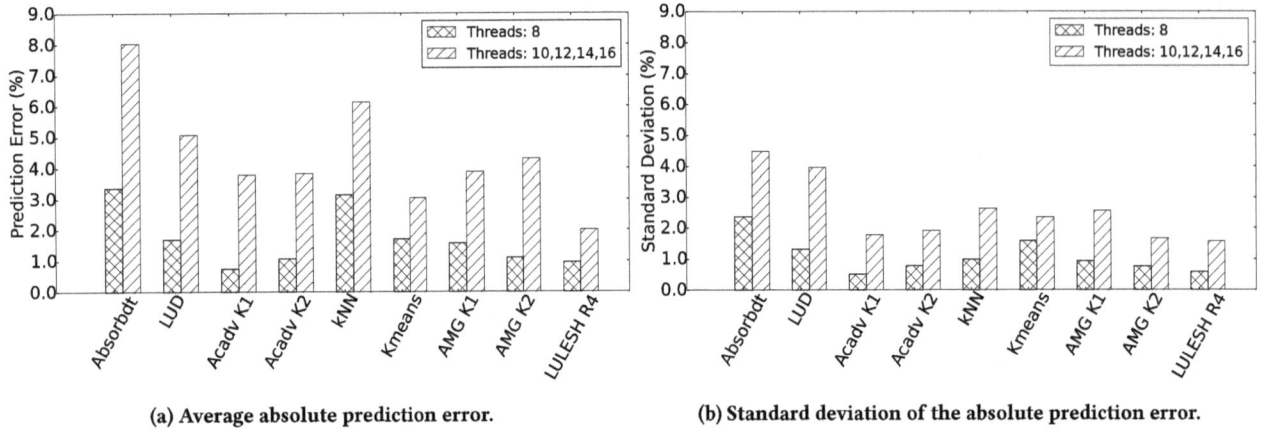

(a) Average absolute prediction error.

(b) Standard deviation of the absolute prediction error.

Figure 8: Impact of ROB and MSHR on prediction accuracy.

cores run two OpenMP threads. As mentioned, these Intel machines have 8 cores each with two hardware threads per core.

For these experiments we disable prefetching and use our extrapolation approach with 4- and 6-threads for training. Figure 8 shows that both average error and the standard deviation for 8 threads are much better than all the other configurations of threads.

There appears to be a correlation between the least accurate of our earlier experiments, ABSORBDT (Figure 5), and the ROB and MSHR results. Though further experimentation is needed, it is likely that ABSORBDT is sensitive to ROB and MSHR sizes and we could consider improvements to our approximations of the COS model that incorporate these characteristics.

4 CROSS-ARCHITECTURE VALIDATION USING IBM'S BLUE GENE/Q

To demonstrate the portability and scalability of our model we validate COS on IBM's Blue Gene/Q (BG/Q) architecture. BG/Q is a scalable, energy efficient, high-performance system. The BG/Q architecture is capable of dynamic memory bandwidth throttling (DBT), where memory bandwidth is dynamically controlled through insertion of a configurable number of memory idle cycles between each DDR memory request.

BG/Q's DBT is different from the dynamic memory frequency throttling (DMT) common to Intel systems. While memory frequency throttling changes the latency of each main memory access, bandwidth throttling reduces the effective bandwidth through inserting idle cycles (or no-ops or bubbles) in the instruction pipeline. The number of memory idle cycles inserted is called the *throttling threshold* and ranges between 0 and 126. Studies have shown this parameter can affect the performance of applications as well as their power consumption [29].

The throttling threshold affects those memory accesses that occur within the threshold window. For instance, if the time between two dependent memory requests at the memory controller is larger than the throttling threshold, the latency of these memory requests is not affected. When the time between two memory requests is smaller than the threshold, the latency of the second memory request would increase by the configurable number of memory idle cycles.

Unlike the Intel system, BG/Q is not capable of CPU frequency scaling and thus we limit our validation of COS to variations in memory bandwidth and thread concurrency. BG/Q has only two levels of cache, L1 and L2, compared to 3 levels of cache on our x86 experimental system.

4.1 Approximating the COS Trace

Assume we change memory speed from f_m to f'_m (Δf_m) using DBT. To illustrate the effect on performance, Figure 9 shows the execution time in cycles (y-axis) for different throttling thresholds represented by number of memory idle cycles (x-axis) for all regions of the LULESH application. For each region (R1, R2, R3, R4, R5) of LULESH, two different phases can be distinguished: 1) a nearly flat or constant segment in the function at low thresholds and 2) a linearly increasing function at a threshold that appears to be different for each region. This forms a hockey stick shaped function for each region with a different inflection point. In a way, this is an example of Amdahl's law applied to an architectural enhancement. A portion of the code (phase 1 in this example) *is not affected* by the enhancement (e.g., insertion of memory idle cycles) while a portion of the code (phase 2 in this example) *is affected* by the enhancement. While this is an oversimplification in some ways, it implies that we can potentially use a piece-wise function to approximate the performance for these codes if we can identify the inflection point (i.e., the number of memory idle cycles) where performance loss begins.

Following a series of experiments, we determined the inflection points correlate to characteristics of a region's memory access behavior. We approximate the COS Trace expressed by Equation 3 using a piecewise function of performance:

$$T = \begin{cases} t_0 & \text{if } f_m \leq a \\ bf_m + t_0 & \text{if } f_m > a \end{cases} \tag{10}$$

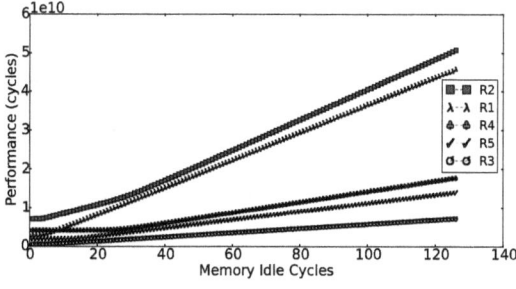

Figure 9: Impact of memory bandwidth throttling on LULESH.

where t_0 is the performance with no memory throttling, a is the threshold of the inflection point, and b is the slope of the linear function.

For the constant function ($T = t_0$), memory throttling has little impact on the COS Trace: performance does not change by inserting memory idle cycles. This can be explained with the following two cases. First, the gap between most of the application memory accesses is larger than the throttling threshold. The number of inserted memory idle cycles is too small to cause delays in memory accesses (T_s is not changing) and thus total execution time. In this case, inserting idle cycles does not change T_c, T_o, and T_s. Second, the gap between memory accesses is smaller than the throttling threshold, but the memory accesses overlap with processor computation. Inserting idle cycles can delay issuing new memory requests but does not change the length of any of the three stages, T_c, T_o, and T_s.

The inflection point a in Equation 10 depends on the memory access patterns of applications. A correlation analysis among some critical compute/memory related hardware events (e.g. floating point operations, L2 cache misses per second, etc.) shows that its value is highly related to memory intensity: *L2 cache misses (L2M) per instruction (INST)*. By applying linear regression, we can approximate the value of a with the following:

$$a = \alpha \times \frac{L2M}{INST} + c_1$$

where α is a coefficient and c_1 is a constant and both will be determined using linear regression.

The impact of memory throttling on the second segment is linear ($T = bf_m + t_0$). This can be explained with the COS Trace as follows. For a sufficiently large number of idle cycles, application memory accesses cannot overlap with computation. In this case, the length of the pure compute stages would not change with memory throttling; the length of the overlap stages would be zero; and the length of the pure stall stages would change linearly with the number of memory idle cycles inserted. Approximating the number of memory accesses with L2 misses, the impact on the COS Trace can be expressed as follows:

$$\Delta T_c = 0$$
$$\Delta T_o = 0$$
$$\Delta T_s = \beta \times L2M \times \Delta f_m$$

where ΔT_c, ΔT_o, and ΔT_s are the resulting change to execution time for each respective phase. Thus, we can approximate the value of b as follows:

$$b = \beta \times L2M + c_2$$

where β is a coefficient and c_2 is a constant and both will be determined using linear regression.

Based on the equations above, we can predict performance using Equation 10 as follows:

$$T = \begin{cases} t_0 & \text{if } f_m \le \alpha \times L2M/INST + c_1 \\ (\beta \times L2M + c_2) \times f_m + t_0 & \text{if } f_m > \alpha \times L2M/INST + c_1 \end{cases} \quad (11)$$

4.2 Offline Training and Online Prediction

We apply linear regression to approximate the model coefficients of Equation 11. The configuration space includes two parameters: the throttling threshold (Δf_m) and the number of threads (Δt). The threshold ranges from 0 to 126 idle cycles and the number of threads from 4 to 64 with an interval of 4. The details of the training configurations and the overall configuration space is given in Table 3. We use the five code regions of LULESH to train the model. Each region has its own trained coefficients.

Table 3: The training configurations and the overall configuration space on BG/Q. The *Total* column shows the number of configurations.

Total	Δf_m	Δt (num. threads)
Training inflection point a		
127×16	0 - 126 cycles	4, 8, 12, ..., 64
Training slope b for Region 1		
27×14	100 - 126 cycles	12, 16, ..., 64
Training slope b for Region 2		
16×10	100 - 115 cycles	28, 32, ..., 64
Training slope b for Region 3		
11×12	35 - 45 cycles	20, 24, ..., 64
Training slope b for Region 4		
16×9	100 - 115 cycles	32, 36, ..., 64
Training slope b for Region 5		
11×11	65 - 75 cycles	24, 28, ..., 64
Configuration space		
127×16	0 - 126 cycles	4, 8, 12, ..., 64

We use the model to predict the performance of the five code regions of LULESH for those configurations in the configuration space that are not in the training set. To measure the accuracy of the model, we compare these predicted values with the performance measured by running the same configurations on the machine.

Figure 10 shows the average error and standard deviation of our model. Four of the five code regions show a reasonable average error, around 10% or less. Region 2, however, shows a large average error of 17%.

There are several factors that affect the model accuracy of the BG/Q implementation of the COS model. First, our experiments

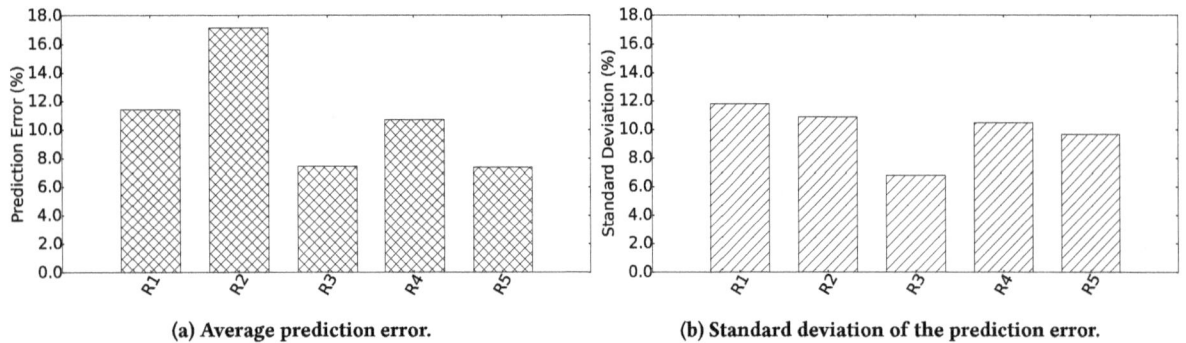

(a) Average prediction error.

(b) Standard deviation of the prediction error.

Figure 10: Multivariate linear regression of LULESH on IBM BG/Q system.

on BG/Q included prefetching, which makes the overlap time T_o more complex as observed on the Intel system. On BG/Q we used L2 cache misses to represent memory pressure similar to the Intel system. We could relax this requirement and use the number of load and store operations on BG/Q for our approximations. This may improve accuracy.

Second, in some cases the value of a may not be strictly constant but a linear function with a small slope value. The number of idle cycles that can be inserted (integers) does not provide fine-enough granularity to estimate a more accurately.

Third, we used a small number of sample configurations for training a because we limited our configuration space to only a subset of the available number of threads. We expect that a larger space using all 64 (from 1 to 64 threads) configurations along the Δt dimension would have resulted in better accuracy.

5 LIMITATIONS AND DISCUSSION

We have demonstrated the use and accuracy of the COS model for predicting the performance of a set of DVFS, DMT/DBT, and DCT configurations. The model can be used in a software or hardware implementation to allocate or deallocate resources to the working threads in a parallel application. This is an advantage to a parallel scheduler or runtime system.

As mentioned the key concept of the COS model is the isolation of overlap. While in an abstract sense this is straight forward, we show in Sections 2.4 – 2.6 that empirically isolating overlap is wrought with challenges. We resolved a number of these challenges using the assumption of regular parallel applications where threads are mostly homogeneous and computation proceeds in a bulk synchronous way with no other dependencies among threads. This leaves a number of limitations to the model that must be addressed to consider irregular parallel codes (e.g., heterogeneous threads, asynchronous, cross-thread dependencies).

Overlap types In our earlier discussions, we simplified the definition of overlap into computation overlap and memory overlap. In general, overlap can also occur between multiple threads on a single core/CPU or across multiple cores/CPUs accessing the same memory. Under our assumptions, these don't affect the COS Trace much, but these must be considered for irregular parallel codes.

Computational intensity Computational intensity (CI) has impact on the overlap as discussed earlier. A key insight gained

from this work is that CI can be used to predict the impact of simultaneous configuration changes in CPU, memory, and threads on overlap. More overlap types, combined with irregular codes, are likely to make accurate prediction more challenging. There could also be non–CI effects that we've not accounted for in parallel irregular applications.

Role of Co-design These challenges could be alleviated somewhat by improvements in our ability to directly measure the overlap of parallel codes. This could be accomplished in software, but would be most effective when co-designed with hardware. Our work indicates that there are meaningful representative hardware counters that give insight to overlap and computational intensity, but they are indirect at best. Furthermore, this data is usually limited to an individual thread with no context for other concurrent threads on the same core or CPU. Mechanisms for tracking this type of information could vastly improve our understanding of overlap as well as our ability to optimize parallel applications and systems.

6 RELATED WORK

To the best of our knowledge, this work is the first to propose an analytical performance model that captures the simultaneous effects of DVFS, DCT, and DMT/DBT on the performance of multithreaded applications on real systems.

Table 4 provides a synopsis of work most closely related to ours. There has been extensive work focused on modeling the effects of CPU DVFS on performance using stall-based approaches [22]; leading loads [16, 22, 33]; CRIT-BW, a leading load derivative [31]; and DEP-BURST, a CRIT-BW derivative [3]. While all of these consider the effects of out-of-order execution and non-blocking caches, only DEP-BURST considers multithreading using a critical path analysis to determine which core to boost.

Table 4 shows how the resulting CPU DVFS performance models capture the characteristics of the COS model: T_c, T_o, T_s from Equation 1. Stall-based approaches assume the CPU DVFS affects overlap time in the same way it affects pure compute time and thus combine T_c and T_o. They also purport that pure stall time (T_s) is constant with changes in CPU frequency – this is in direct contrast to our findings that stall time is affected by CPU frequency (see Figure 2).

Table 4: Summary of existing performance models and the proposed COS model. *OOO Exec* and *NB Cache* refer to processor out-of-order execution and non-blocking cache, respectively.

Model	Predicts	Under			Considering			On	Captures		
		DVFS	DMT	DCT	Multithread	OOO Exec	NB Cache		T_c	T_o	T_s
Stall-based	Runtime	✔				✔	✔	Simulation			
Leading loads	Runtime	✔				✔	✔	Simulation			
CRIT-BW	Runtime	✔				✔	✔	Simulation			
DEP-BURST	Runtime	✔			✔	✔	✔	Simulation			
MemScale	CPI		✔					Simulation			
CoScale	CPI	✔	✔					Simulation			
Joint	# micro-ops	✔	✔		✔	✔		Real system			
COS	Runtime	✔	✔	✔	✔	✔	✔	Real system			

The leading load model and its derivatives combine overlap time (T_o) with pure stall time (T_s) and assume the combined value is constant while T_c is proportional to CPU frequency. This assumption leads to inaccuracies since the impact of CPU frequency on T_o can be quite different from T_c and T_s – as we discussed in Sections 2.4 – 2.7.

Su et. al. [35] is the only work we know of that implements the leading load model on real systems. This is the most accurate model available for a real system but it only models DVFS on AMD architectures. The COS Model implementations in this paper are as accurate or better than this and model the combined effects of DVFS, DMT/DBT, and DCT across multiple architectures. Su et. al. also showed that the leading load approach is less accurate for memory intensive applications and that the accuracy of the leading load model is highly dependent on the level of memory boundedness – these match our findings as well.

Table 4 also shows a comparison with memory power performance modeling tools. Deng et. al. [12, 13] presented a performance model for memory frequency scaling (MemScale and MultiScale) of single threaded applications on in-order processors. They made similar assumptions as those in the CPU DVFS models that the overlap time (T_o) is combined with pure compute time (T_c). Deng et. al. [11] created CoScale to extend MemScale to consider DVFS. The accuracy is very good for single threaded applications on in-order processors. But the limiting combination of T_o and T_c remains.

Sundriyal and Sosonkina [36] proposed the "Joint" performance model that considers the simultaneous effects of CPU DVFS and DMT. However, the model estimates T_o as a constant for all applications on a single system. This contradicts our findings that overlap is affected by CPU frequency (see Figure 2).

Less directly related work relevant to our discussions include: David et al. [10] investigated the impact of memory frequency scaling on power and performance and proposed a model for real systems; Li et al. studied the throttling interface on IBM BG/Q systems and demonstrated its ability to optimize system efficiency [29]; Ercan et. al. [14] presented a heuristic runtime solution for coordinating CPU and memory frequencies to improve energy efficiency; Curtis-Maury et al. created heuristic models that manage DVFS and DCT simultaneously for multi-threaded applications [8, 9, 20, 25, 30].

7 CONCLUSIONS AND FUTURE WORK

In this paper, we propose the COS Model of parallel performance to accurately capture the combine effects of DVFS, DMT/DBT, and thread concurrency on real systems. We applied the COS model to both Intel and IBM architectures within 7% and 17% accuracy for a set of 19 important applications. The key insight to the COS model is the separation of memory and compute overlap from pure compute and pure memory stalls. This separation enables more accurate approximations and a straightforward methodology that is capable of modeling the complexity introduced with concurrency. A key limitation of the model is the focus on structured parallel codes that while representative of many important applications precludes accurate use on irregular parallel codes for now. Despite the limitations, we provide strong evidence that the fundamental focus on overlap in the COS model will be key to steering future high-performance systems and applications to maximize their efficiencies. In future work, we plan to explore extending the COS model to irregular parallel applications in both OpenMP and MPI. We also plan to adapt the techniques described for use in runtime systems.

ACKNOWLEDGMENTS

This material is based upon work supported by the National Science Foundation under Grant No. 1565314 and 1422788. Lawrence Livermore National Laboratory is operated by Lawrence Livermore National Security, LLC, for the U.S. Department of Energy, National Nuclear Security Administration under Contract DE-AC52-07NA27344. LLNL-CONF-728263.

REFERENCES

[1] *Hydrodynamics Challenge Problem, Lawrence Livermore National Laboratory.* Technical Report LLNL-TR-490254. 1–17 pages.
[2] *Intel 64 and IA-32 Architectures Developer's Manual, Intel Corporation.* Technical Report Volume 3B, Part 2.

[3] Shoaib Akram, Jennifer B Sartor, and Lieven Eeckhout. 2016. DVFS Performance Prediction for Managed Multithreaded Applications. In *IEEE International Symposium on Performance Analysis of Systems and Software (ISPASS)*. 12–23.

[4] Sadaf R. Alam and Jeffrey S. Vetter. 2006. An Analysis of System Balance Requirements for Scientific Applications. In *International Conference on Parallel Processing (ICPP'06)*. IEEE, Columbus, OH.

[5] Teresa Bailey, W. Daryl Hawkins, Marvin L. Adams, Peter N. Brown, Adam J. Kunen, Michael P. Adams, Timmie Smith, Nancy Amato, and Lawrence Rauchwerger. 2014. Validation of Full-Domain Massively Parallel Transport Sweep Algorithms. In *American Nuclear Society Winter Meeting and Nuclear Technology Expo*. Anaheim, CA.

[6] Aaron Carroll and Gernot Heiser. 2010. An Analysis of Power Consumption in a Smartphone. In *Proceedings of the 2010 USENIX Conference on USENIX Annual Technical Conference (USENIXATC'10)*. USENIX Association, Berkeley, CA, USA, 21–21. http://dl.acm.org/citation.cfm?id=1855840.1855861

[7] S. Che, M. Boyer, J. Meng, D. Tarjan, J. W. Sheaffer, S. H. Lee, and K. Skadron. 2009. Rodinia: A Benchmark Suite For Heterogeneous Computing. In *Workload Characterization, 2009. IISWC 2009. IEEE International Symposium on*. 44–54. DOI: http://dx.doi.org/10.1109/IISWC.2009.5306797

[8] Matthew Curtis-Maury, James Dzierwa, Christos D. Antonopoulos, and Dimitrios S. Nikolopoulos. 2006. Online Power-performance Adaptation of Multithreaded Programs Using Hardware Event-based Prediction. In *Proceedings of the 20th Annual International Conference on Supercomputing (ICS '06)*. ACM, New York, NY, USA, 157–166. DOI: http://dx.doi.org/10.1145/1183401.1183426

[9] Matthew Curtis-Maury, Ankur Shah, Filip Blagojevic, Dimitrios S. Nikolopoulos, Bronis R. de Supinski, and Martin Schulz. 2008. Prediction Models for Multidimensional Power-performance Optimization on Many Cores. In *Proceedings of the 17th International Conference on Parallel Architectures and Compilation Techniques (PACT '08)*. ACM, New York, NY, USA, 250–259. DOI: http://dx.doi.org/10.1145/1454115.1454151

[10] Howard David, Chris Fallin, Eugene Gorbatov, Ulf R. Hanebutte, and Onur Mutlu. 2011. Memory Power Management via Dynamic Voltage/Frequency Scaling. In *Proceedings of the 8th ACM International Conference on Autonomic Computing (ICAC '11)*. ACM, New York, NY, USA, 31–40. DOI: http://dx.doi.org/10.1145/1998582.1998590

[11] Qingyuan Deng, David Meisner, Abhishek Bhattacharjee, Thomas F. Wenisch, and Ricardo Bianchini. 2012. CoScale: Coordinating CPU and Memory System DVFS in Server Systems. In *Proceedings of the 2012 45th Annual IEEE/ACM International Symposium on Microarchitecture (MICRO-45)*. IEEE Computer Society, Washington, DC, USA, 143–154. DOI: http://dx.doi.org/10.1109/MICRO.2012.22

[12] Qingyuan Deng, David Meisner, Abhishek Bhattacharjee, Thomas F. Wenisch, and Ricardo Bianchini. 2012. MultiScale: Memory System DVFS with Multiple Memory Controllers. In *Proceedings of the 2012 ACM/IEEE International Symposium on Low Power Electronics and Design (ISLPED '12)*. ACM, New York, NY, USA, 297–302. DOI: http://dx.doi.org/10.1145/2333660.2333727

[13] Qingyuan Deng, David Meisner, Luiz Ramos, Thomas F. Wenisch, and Ricardo Bianchini. 2011. MemScale: Active Low-power Modes for Main Memory. In *Proceedings of the Sixteenth International Conference on Architectural Support for Programming Languages and Operating Systems (ASPLOS XVI)*. ACM, New York, NY, USA, 225–238. DOI: http://dx.doi.org/10.1145/1950365.1950392

[14] Furkan Ercan, Neven Abou Gazala, and Howard David. 2012. An Integrated Approach to System-level CPU and Memory Energy Efficiency on Computing Systems. In *Energy Aware Computing, 2012 International Conference on*. 1–6. DOI: http://dx.doi.org/10.1109/ICEAC.2012.6471018

[15] Constantinos Evangelinos, Robert Walkup, Vipin Sachdeva, Kirk E. Jordan, Hormozd Gahvari, I-Hsin Chung, Michael P. Perrone, Ligang Lu, Lurng-Kuo Liu, and Karen A. Magerlein. 2013. Determination of Performance Characteristics of Scientific Applications on IBM Blue Gene/Q. *IBM Journal of Research and Development* 57, 1/2 (2013), 9. DOI: http://dx.doi.org/10.1147/JRD.2012.2229901

[16] S. Eyerman and L. Eeckhout. 2010. A Counter Architecture for Online DVFS Profitability Estimation. *Computers, IEEE Transactions on* 59, 11 (Nov 2010), 1576–1583. DOI: http://dx.doi.org/10.1109/TC.2010.65

[17] R. Ge, X. Feng, W. c. Feng, and K. W. Cameron. 2007. CPU MISER: A Performance-Directed, Run-Time System for Power-Aware Clusters. In *2007 International Conference on Parallel Processing (ICPP 2007)*. 18–18. DOI: http://dx.doi.org/10.1109/ICPP.2007.29

[18] Van Emden Henson and Ulrike Meier Yang. 2000. BoomerAMG: a Parallel Algebraic Multigrid Solver and Preconditioner. *Applied Numerical Mathematics* 41 (2000), 155–177.

[19] Shadi Ibrahim, Tien-Dat Phan, Alexandra Carpen-Amarie, Houssem-Eddine Chihoub, Diana Moise, and Gabriel Antoniu. 2016. Governing Energy Consumption in Hadoop Through CPU Frequency Scaling: An Analysis. *Future Generation Computer Systems* 54 (2016), 219 – 232. DOI: http://dx.doi.org/10.1016/j.future.2015.01.005

[20] Changhee Jung, Daeseob Lim, Jaejin Lee, and SangYong Han. 2005. Adaptive Execution Techniques for SMT Multiprocessor Architectures. In *Proceedings of the Tenth ACM SIGPLAN Symposium on Principles and Practice of Parallel Programming (PPoPP '05)*. ACM, New York, NY, USA, 236–246. DOI: http://dx.doi.org/10.1145/1065944.1065976

[21] Ian Karlin and Mike Collette. 2014. Strong Scaling Bottleneck Identification and Mitigation in Ares. In *Nuclear Explosives Code Development Conference (NECDC'14)*. Los Alamos, NM.

[22] Georgios Keramidas, Vasileios Spiliopoulos, and Stefanos Kaxiras. 2010. Interval-based Models for Run-time DVFS Orchestration in Superscalar Processors. In *Proceedings of the 7th ACM International Conference on Computing Frontiers (CF '10)*. ACM, New York, NY, USA, 287–296. DOI: http://dx.doi.org/10.1145/1787275.1787338

[23] Steven H. Langer, Abhinav Bhatele, and Charles H. Still. 2014. pF3D Simulations of Laser-Plasma Interactions in National Ignition Facility Experiments. *Computing in Science & Engineering* 16, 6 (Nov 2014), 42–50.

[24] Steve H. Langer, A. Bhatele, and C. H. Still. 2014. pF3D Simulations of Laser-Plasma Interactions in National Ignition Facility Experiments. *Computing in Science Engineering* 16, 6 (Nov 2014), 42–50. DOI: http://dx.doi.org/10.1109/MCSE.2014.79

[25] Jaejin Lee, Jung-Ho Park, Honggyu Kim, Changhee Jung, Daeseob Lim, and SangYong Han. 2010. Adaptive execution techniques of parallel programs for multiprocessors. *J. Parallel and Distrib. Comput.* 70, 5 (2010), 467 – 480. DOI: http://dx.doi.org/10.1016/j.jpdc.2009.10.008

[26] Edgar A. Leon, Ian Karlin, Abhinav Bhatele, Steven H. Langer, Chris Chambreau, Louis H. Howell, Trent D'Hooge, and Matthew L. Leininger. 2016. Characterizing Parallel Scientific Applications on Commodity Clusters: An Empirical Study of a Tapered Fat-Tree. In *International Conference for High Performance Computing, Networking, Storage and Analysis (SC'16)*. IEEE/ACM, Salt Lake City, UT.

[27] Edgar A. León, Ian Karlin, and Ryan E. Grant. 2015. Optimizing Explicit Hydrodynamics for Power, Energy, and Performance. In *International Conference on Cluster Computing (Cluster'15)*. IEEE, Chicago, IL.

[28] Edgar A. León, Ian Karlin, Ryan E. Grant, and Matthew Dosanjh. 2016. Program Optimizations: The interplay Between Power, Performance, and Energy. *Parallel Comput.* 58 (Oct. 2016), 56–75. http://dx.doi.org/10.1016/j.parco.2016.05.004

[29] Bo Li and Edgar A. León. 2014. Memory Throttling on BG/Q: A Case Study with Explicit Hydrodynamics. In *6th Workshop on Power-Aware Computing and Systems (HotPower 14)*. USENIX Association, Broomfield, CO. https://www.usenix.org/conference/hotpower14/workshop-program/presentation/li

[30] Dong Li, B.R. de Supinski, M. Schulz, K. Cameron, and D.S. Nikolopoulos. 2010. Hybrid MPI/OpenMP Power-Aware Computing. In *Parallel Distributed Processing (IPDPS), 2010 IEEE International Symposium on*. 1–12. DOI: http://dx.doi.org/10.1109/IPDPS.2010.5470463

[31] R. Miftakhutdinov, E. Ebrahimi, and Y.N. Patt. 2012. Predicting Performance Impact of DVFS for Realistic Memory Systems. In *Microarchitecture (MICRO), 2012 45th Annual IEEE/ACM International Symposium on*. 155–165. DOI: http://dx.doi.org/10.1109/MICRO.2012.23

[32] Pier Giorgio Raponi, Fabrizio Petrini, Robert Walkup, and Fabio Checconi. 2011. Characterization of the Communication Patterns of Scientific Applications on Blue Gene/P. In *International Workshop on System Management Techniques, Processes, and Services (SMTPS'11)*. Anchorage, AK.

[33] B. Rountree, D.K. Lowenthal, M. Schulz, and B.R. de Supinski. 2011. Practical Performance Prediction under Dynamic Voltage Frequency Scaling. In *Green Computing Conference and Workshops (IGCC), 2011 International*. 1–8. DOI: http://dx.doi.org/10.1109/IGCC.2011.6008553

[34] Barry Rountree, David K. Lownenthal, Bronis R. de Supinski, Martin Schulz, Vincent W. Freeh, and Tyler Bletsch. 2009. Adagio: Making DVS Practical for Complex HPC Applications. In *Proceedings of the 23rd International Conference on Supercomputing (ICS '09)*. ACM, New York, NY, USA, 460–469. DOI: http://dx.doi.org/10.1145/1542275.1542340

[35] Bo Su, Joseph L. Greathouse, Junli Gu, Michael Boyer, Li Shen, and Zhiying Wang. 2014. Implementing a Leading Loads Performance Predictor on Commodity Processors. In *2014 USENIX Annual Technical Conference (USENIX ATC 14)*. USENIX Association, Philadelphia, PA. https://www.usenix.org/conference/atc14/technical-sessions/presentation/su

[36] Vaibhav Sundriyal and Masha Sosonkina. 2016. Joint Frequency Scaling of Processor and DRAM. *The Journal of Supercomputing* 72, 4 (2016), 1549–1569. DOI: http://dx.doi.org/10.1007/s11227-016-1680-4

[37] Jeffrey S. Vetter and Frank Mueller. 2002. Communication Characteristics of Large-Scale Scientific Applications for Contemporary Cluster Architectures. In *International Parallel and Distributed Processing Symposium (IPDPS'02)*. IEEE, Fort Lauderdale, FL.

Explaining Wide Area Data Transfer Performance

Zhengchun Liu
Argonne National Laboratory
Lemont, IL, USA
zhengchun.liu@anl.gov

Prasanna Balaprakash
Argonne National Laboratory
Lemont, IL, USA
pbalapra@anl.gov

Rajkumar Kettimuthu
Argonne National Laboratory
Lemont, IL, USA
kettimut@anl.gov

Ian Foster
Argonne National Lab and University of Chicago
Lemont, IL, USA
foster@anl.gov

ABSTRACT

Disk-to-disk wide-area file transfers involve many subsystems and tunable application parameters that pose significant challenges for bottleneck detection, system optimization, and performance prediction. Performance models can be used to address these challenges but have not proved generally usable because of a need for extensive online experiments to characterize subsystems. We show here how to overcome the need for such experiments by applying machine learning methods to historical data to estimate parameters for predictive models. Starting with log data for millions of Globus transfers involving billions of files and hundreds of petabytes, we engineer features for endpoint CPU load, network interface card load, and transfer characteristics; and we use these features in both linear and nonlinear models of transfer performance, We show that the resulting models have high explanatory power. For a representative set of 30,653 transfers over 30 heavily used source-destination pairs ("edges"), totaling 2,053 TB in 46.6 million files, we obtain median absolute percentage prediction errors (MdAPE) of 7.0% and 4.6% when using distinct linear and nonlinear models per edge, respectively; when using a single nonlinear model for all edges, we obtain an MdAPE of 7.8%. Our work broadens understanding of factors that influence file transfer rate by clarifying relationships between achieved transfer rates, transfer characteristics, and competing load. Our predictions can be used for distributed workflow scheduling and optimization, and our features can also be used for optimization and explanation.

1 INTRODUCTION

Many researchers have studied the performance of network architectures, storage systems, protocols, and tools for high-speed file transfer [15, 20, 25, 33, 36, 38]. Using a mix of experiment, modeling, and simulation, often in highly controlled environments, this work has produced a good understanding of how, in principle, to configure hardware and software systems in order to enable extremely high-speed transfers, which can achieve close to line rates on 10 Gbps and even 100 Gbps networks [11, 23].

Yet despite these results, the actual performance achieved by disk-to-disk transfers in practical settings is usually much lower than line rates. For example, a study of more than 3.9 million Globus transfers [8] involving more than 33 billion files and 223 PB over a seven-year period (2010-2016) shows an average transfer speed of only 11.5 MB/s. (On the other hand, 52% of all bytes moved over that period moved at >100 MB/s and 14% moved at >1 GB/s.)

With effort, we can often explain each low-performing transfer, which may result from (mis)configurations and/or interactions among storage devices, file systems, CPUs, operating systems, network interfaces, intermediate network devices, local and wide area networks, file transfer software, network protocols, and competing activities. But we have lacked an approach that could use easily obtainable information sources to explain and improve the performance of arbitrary transfers in arbitrary environments. We believe that lightweight models are required for this purpose and that the construction of such models will require a combination of data-driven analysis of large collections of historical data, the development and testing of expressive analytical models of various aspects of transfer performance, and new data sources. Here we report on steps toward this goal.

This paper makes four contributions. (1) We show how to use machine learning methods to develop data transfer performance models using only historical data. (2) We engineer features for use in these models, including features that characterize competing load at source and destination endpoints. (3) We identify features that have nonlinear impact on transfer performance, in particular those that capture competing load. (4) We demonstrate that model accuracy can be improved even further by using new data sources to obtain more complete knowledge of competing load.

The rest of the paper is organized as follows. In §2 we provide background on the Globus service that manages the transfers considered here. In §3 we introduce a simple three-feature analytical model that provides just an upper bound on performance, and we use this model to identify factors that impact maximum achievable transfer rate. In §4 we analyze additional factors that affect transfer rate, and we define the features that we use in the data-driven models we introduce in §5, where we describe and evaluate both linear and nonlinear regression models. Starting from a different model for each edge, we incorporate endpoint- and edge-specific features to develop one model for all edges. In §6 we review related

Publication rights licensed to ACM. ACM acknowledges that this contribution was authored or co-authored by an employee, contractor or affiliate of the United States government. As such, the Government retains a nonexclusive, royalty-free right to publish or reproduce this article, or to allow others to do so, for Government purposes only.

HPDC '17, June 26-30, 2017, Washington, DC, USA

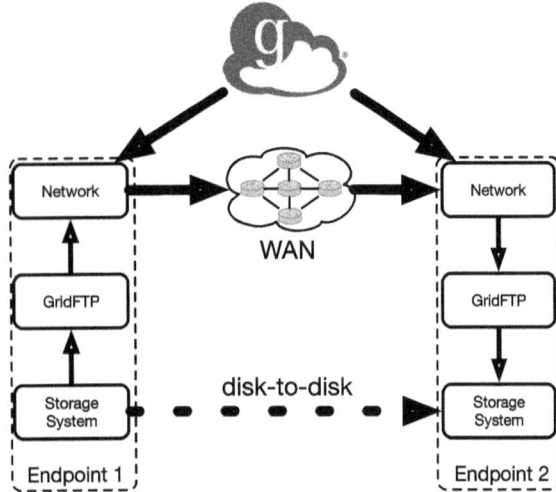

Figure 1: Structure of a Globus end-to-end file transfer from source (left) to destination (right), managed by cloud service.

Figure 2: Globus endpoints, grouped by number of deployments in a single location [8]. (Some endpoints geolocate erroneously to the center of countries.)

work, in §7 discuss the broader applicability of our work, and in §8 summarize our conclusions and briefly discuss future work.

2 BACKGROUND ON THE GLOBUS SERVICE

The Globus transfer service is a cloud-hosted software-as-a-service implementation of the logic required to orchestrate file transfers between pairs of storage systems [2] (see Figure 1). A transfer request specifies, among other things, a source and destination; the files and/or directories to be transferred; and (optionally) whether to perform integrity checking (enabled by default) and/or to encrypt the data (disabled by default). Globus can transfer data with either the GridFTP or HTTP protocol; we focus here on GridFTP transfers, since HTTP support has been added only recently. GridFTP extends FTP with features required for speed, reliability, and security.

Globus has been running since late 2010, providing us with a considerable body of transfer performance data. In the work described here, we consider transfers through the end of 2015. These transfers involved ~26K endpoints, each running Globus Connect software, and 46K unique edges (source–destination endpoint pairs for which at least one transfer has occurred). Figure 2 shows endpoints for which location data are available [8].

These data have limitations: we know relatively little about the endpoints and networks involved in many transfers and little or nothing about competing load. Nevertheless, we can learn some general features about transfer characteristics and performance, as we show in subsequent sections.

3 A SIMPLE ANALYTICAL MODEL

We introduce a simple analytical model for the maximum achievable end-to-end file transfer rate for a given source and destination. We validate this model using both experimental and historical data and draw conclusions about the model's accuracy.

3.1 Maximum achievable transfer rate

As shown in Figure 1, an end-to-end file transfer engages three subsystems: source endpoint, network, and destination endpoint. The maximum achievable transfer rate, R^{max}, cannot be more than the minimum of the maximum rates achievable by each subsystem:

$$R^{max} \leq min(DR^{max}, MM^{max}, DW^{max}), \qquad (1)$$

where DR^{max} is the maximum achievable disk read rate on the source endpoint, MM^{max} is the maximum achievable memory-to-memory transfer rate from source to destination (including the network transfer), and DW^{max} is the maximum achievable disk write rate on the destination endpoint.

To test Equation 1, we conducted data transfer experiments between ESnet testbed nodes to determine R^{max}, DW^{max}, DR^{max}, and MM^{max} separately. The ESnet testbed comprises identical hardware deployed at three DOE labs in the United States (Argonne: ANL; Brookhaven: BNL; and Lawrence Berkeley: LBL) and at CERN in Geneva, Switzerland. Each system features a powerful Linux server configured as a data transfer node (DTN) [11], with an appropriately configured high-speed storage system and 10 Gb/s network link. We use transfers from /dev/zero to disk and from disk to /dev/null on each DTN to measure DW and DR separately; from /dev/zero on source to /dev/null on destination to measure MM; and from disk on source to disk on destination to measure R. We performed at least five repetitions of each experiment and selected the maximum observed values as R^{max}, DW^{max}, DR^{max}, and MM^{max}.

Table 1 gives our results. We see that all edges are consistent with Equation 1.

3.2 Extending the model to other endpoints

Of the 46K unique edges in the Globus log records studied here, 36,599 had been used for only a single transfer, 16,562 for ≥10 transfers, 2,496 for ≥100 transfers, and 182 for ≥1000 transfers. We focus in this work on the 2,496 edges with ≥100 transfers. For most of these endpoints, we cannot get the access that would be required to measure DR^{max}, DW^{max}, and MM^{max}, information that is also not measured by the GridFTP servers. Instead, we estimate these quantities, as we now describe.

Table 1: Experimentally determined R^{max}, DW^{max} (at destination), DR^{max} (at source), and MM^{max}, in Gb/s, on ESnet testbed, with minimum in each row in bold.

From	To	R^{max}	DW^{max}	DR^{max}	MM^{max}
ANL	BNL	**7.843**	**7.843**	9.302	9.412
	CERN	**6.250**	7.080	9.302	8.989
	LBL	**7.547**	7.767	9.302	9.302
BNL	ANL	**7.407**	7.619	9.302	9.524
	CERN	**6.780**	7.080	9.302	9.091
	LBL	**7.339**	7.767	9.302	9.412
CERN	ANL	**7.080**	7.619	8.696	8.989
	BNL	**7.143**	7.843	8.696	9.091
	LBL	**6.349**	7.767	8.696	8.791
LBL	ANL	**7.407**	7.619	9.302	9.412
	BNL	**7.143**	7.843	9.302	9.412
	CERN	**6.557**	7.080	9.302	8.889

We estimate the first two quantities from the historical data. For each endpoint, we set DR^{max} as the maximum rate observed among all transfers with that endpoint as source and DW^{max} as the maximum rate observed among all transfers with it as destination.

We use perfSONAR [16] to estimate MM^{max} for some edges. This network performance-monitoring infrastructure is deployed at thousands of sites worldwide, many of which are available for open testing of network performance. Many sites that run Globus Connect servers also have perfSONAR hosts with network performance measurement tools connected to the same network as the Globus Connect servers.

We grouped the 2,496 edges with 100 or more transfers by location so that nodes at the same site are treated as equivalent. This grouping resulted in 469 edges with ≥100 transfers. We were able to find perfSONAR hosts at the sites associated with 195 of these edges. Some perfSONAR hosts allow anyone on the research and education network to run third-party Iperf3 [17] tests. Of the 195 edges with perfSONAR hosts at both ends, 81 supported third-party tests. We ran third-party tests for a period of several weeks and collected hundreds of network performance measurements.

Four of the 81 edges on which we performed tests show Globus transfer performance significantly greater than MM^{max} as measured by perfSONAR. In two cases, this is because their perfSONAR and data transfer interfaces are different: the site has a single perfSONAR host with a 10 Gbps network interface card (NIC) but either 4 or 8 DTNs, each with a 10 Gbps NIC.

Of the remaining 77 edges, 38 show Globus transfer rates in the interval $[0.8\,R^{max}, 1.2R^{max}]$ when R^{max} is estimated by Equation 1. After accounting for the known load from other simultaneous Globus transfers (i.e., adding $\max(K^{sout}, K^{din})$: see §4.3), the observed rate for seven more edges also falls in this interval. Thus Equation 1 works reasonably well for a total of 45 edges. Of these, the performance of 11 is limited by disk read, 14 by network, and 20 by disk write.

For the remaining 32 edges, we see significantly lower rates than estimated by Equation 1. We thus examine the log data to see how

throughput varies with load from other (competing) Globus transfers. We first calculate the load from competing Globus transfers on a transfer at an endpoint—the *relative endpoint external load*—as follows: We scale the rate of each competing transfer based on the fraction of the time that it overlaps with the transfer with which it competes, sum the scaled rate of all competing transfers (K^{sout} at source and K^{din} at destination), and compute the fraction of competing transfer rate. For example, for a transfer k from endpoint src_k to endpoint dst_k with throughput R_k, we calculate the relative external load of k at src_k and dst_k as $K^{sout}/(R_k + K^{sout})$ and $K^{din}/(R_k + K^{din})$, respectively. We then define the *relative external load* for a transfer as the greater of the relative endpoint external loads for the transfer at the source and destination.

Given this definition, we can then examine how the transfer rate varies with the relative external load. Figure 3 shows one set of results, plotting transfer rate vs. relative external load for each transfer over four edges in the ESnet testbed. As we might expect, the achieved transfer rate declines with the external Globus load, showing that Equation 1 is not sufficient as a model for the end-to-end transfer rate achieved by real transfers. Other features must also be considered.

4 TRANSFER FEATURES

Feature engineering is a general term for methods that combine variables to get around the unreasonably large number of variables that are often available in machine learning, while still describing the data with sufficient accuracy. Such methods are often the key to understanding the complex relationships between independent and dependent variables and to developing successful data-driven models such as those constructed by machine learning algorithms. Feature engineering typically uses domain knowledge to create features that make data-driven models work [14].

Starting with measured data, feature engineering seeks to build derived values that are informative and non-redundant. These *features* can facilitate subsequent learning and generalization, and may also enable better human interpretations. We describe here how we generated various features from Globus transfer logs, and we study the utility of these features through extensive experiments. We use these features in §5 to build a data-driven model of achievable Globus transfer performance.

Our starting point for this work is Globus log data, which provide, for each transfer, start time (Ts), completion time (Te), total bytes transferred, number of files (Nf), number of directories (Nd), values for Globus tunable parameters, source endpoint, and destination endpoint. (The log also tells us the number of faults associated with a transfer, N_{flt}. Since this number is not known in advance, however, we use it for explanation—see Figures 9 and 12—but not prediction.)

We then construct new features by reproducing resource load conditions on endpoints during each transfer. We join these new features with the log data for training and testing, giving us three groups of features: tunable parameters specified by users, transfer characteristics such as number and size of files, and load measurements that quantify competition for transfer resources. For convenience, we list in Table 2 some notation used in this article. The various terms are introduced in the following.

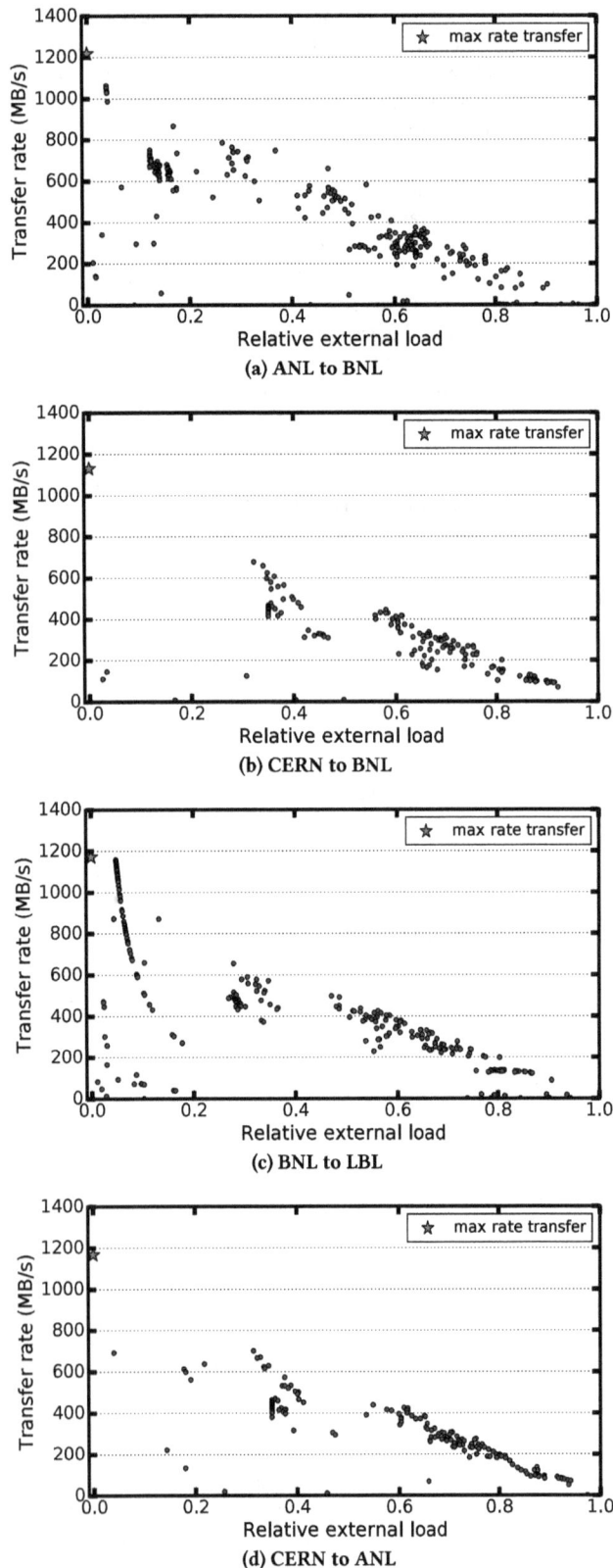

Figure 3: Transfer rate vs. relative external load: ESnet.

4.1 Tunable parameters

The Globus GridFTP implementation includes user-configurable features that can be used to optimize transfer performance [1]. Two that are commonly used are concurrency (C) and parallelism (P). Concurrency involves starting C independent GridFTP processes at the source and destination endpoints. Each of the resulting C process pairs can then work on the transfer of a separate file, thus providing for concurrency at the file system I/O, CPU core, and network levels. In general, concurrency is good for multi-file transfers, since it can drive more filesystem processes, CPU cores, and even endpoint servers, in addition to opening more TCP streams. Parallelism is a network-level optimization, in which data blocks for a single file between a process pair are distributed over P TCP streams. Large files over high-latency links can benefit from higher parallelism, for reasons noted in §6.

While C and P have significant influence on transfer rate, accurately and efficiently tuning these parameters in a dynamically changing network environment is challenging [4]. Furthermore, the performance achieved by a transfer depends also on the concurrency and parallelism associated with other transfers at the same endpoints. For example, as shown in Figure 4, aggregate transfer throughput first increases but eventually declines as total concurrency across all transfers increases.

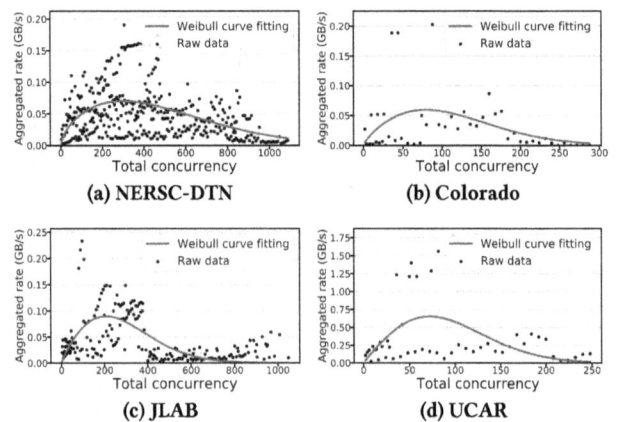

Figure 4: Aggregate incoming transfer rate vs. total concurrency (i.e., instantaneous number of GridFTP server instances) at four endpoints, with Weibull curve [37] fitted.

4.2 Transfer characteristics

The total number of bytes in a transfer and the average file size have a significant impact on the transfer rate. Because of startup costs, a transfer with a relatively small total size achieves a lower rate than does a larger transfer. A transfer with many files incurs more coordination overhead, and a dataset with many directories may incur more overhead because of lock contention on parallel filesystems.

To study these effects, we choose one edge with many transfers, namely, JLAB to NERSC. We first group transfers by total size to form 20 groups. Then we determine the average file size for each transfer, and within each group we create two subgroups

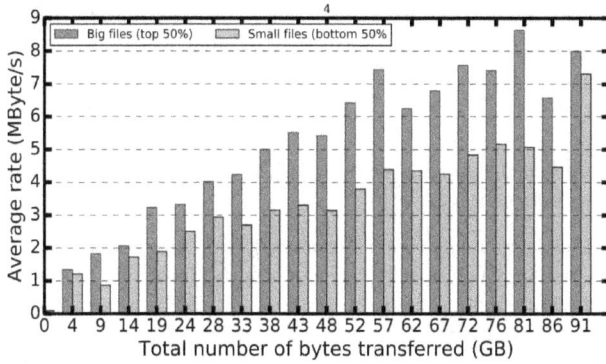

Figure 5: File characteristics versus transfer performance.

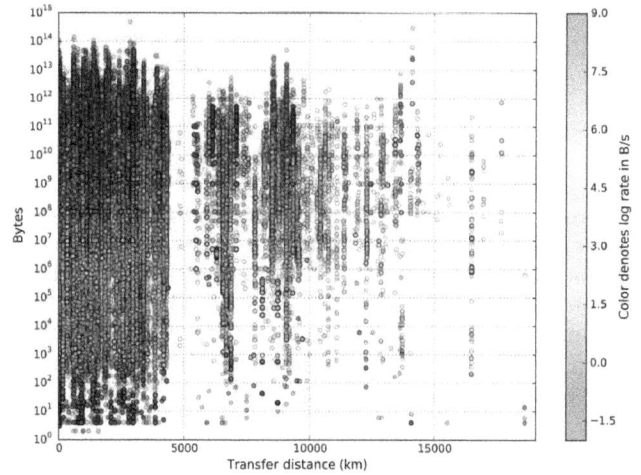

Figure 6: Transfer size vs. estimated transfer distance; color encodes transfer rate.

comprising transfers with average file size below and above the median in each group, respectively.

Figure 5 shows our results. We observe that transfers with smaller total size achieve a lower rate than do transfers with larger total size. Within each total size bucket, transfers with higher average file size achieve a higher rate than do those with lower average file size. Note that the average rates for "small files" and "big files" transfers are not always directly comparable across different size buckets, because a larger total size does not necessarily mean a larger average file size. For example, the average file size of "big files" transfers in the "86 GB total bytes" bucket is less than for the "big files" transfers in the "72 GB total bytes" bucket. Similarly, the reason for the small difference between the average rates for "big files" and "small files" in the "91 GB total bytes" bucket is that the average file sizes in those two groups are similar.

Figure 6 presents a view of overall transfer characteristics across all edges. Each transfer is plotted according to its transfer size and estimated transfer distance (great circle distance between source and destination, a lower bound), with color denoting the transfer rate. We see again evidence of tremendous variety in transfer characteristics, with transfer sizes ranging from 1 byte to close to a petabyte and transfer rates from 0.1 bytes/second to a gigabyte/second. Transfer rate clearly correlates somewhat with transfer size and distance, as we would expect. Note the clear distinction between intracontinental and intercontinental transfers.

4.3 Load measurements

We saw in Figure 3 how transfer rate varies with what we defined in §3.2 as *relative external load*. This dependence reflects the reality that Globus data transfers occur in a shared resource environment. Each transfer may contend with both other Globus transfers and other non-Globus tasks that engage the same source and/or destination endpoint. We have information about the competing Globus transfers from Globus logs; here we integrate domain knowledge of the GridFTP protocol and implementation with Globus log data to define features that we expect to influence transfer rate.

4.3.1 Accounting for competing Globus transfers. The performance of a Globus transfer may be degraded by competing load from other simultaneous Globus transfers that engage the same source and/or destination endpoint. We know a lot about these transfers from Globus logs; the question is how we should translate

Table 2: Notation used in this article. We use the lower 15 terms as features in our models.

src_k	Source endpoint of transfer k.
dst_k	Destination endpoint of transfer k.
Ts_k	Start time of transfer k.
Te_k	End time of transfer k.
R_k	Average transfer rate of transfer k.
N_{flt}	Number of faults a transfer experienced.
K^{sin}	Contending incoming transfer rate on src_k.
K^{sout}	Contending outgoing transfer rate on src_k.
K^{din}	Contending incoming transfer rate on dst_k.
K^{dout}	Contending outgoing transfer rate on dst_k.
C	Concurrency: Number of GridFTP processes.
P	Parallelism: Number of TCP channels per process.
S^{sin}	Number of incoming TCP streams on src_k.
S^{sout}	Number of outgoing TCP streams on src_k.
S^{din}	Number of incoming TCP streams on dst_k.
S^{dout}	Number of outgoing TCP streams on dst_k.
G^{src}	GridFTP instance count on src_k.
G^{dst}	GridFTP instance count on dst_k.
Nf	Number of files transferred.
Nd	Number of directories transferred.
Nb	Total number of bytes transferred.

this information into a small set of features. One obvious feature is the aggregate data transfer rate of the competing transfers. A second feature, given that network performance is often sensitive to interactions among concurrent TCP connections, is the number of TCP connections for the competing transfers. As mentioned

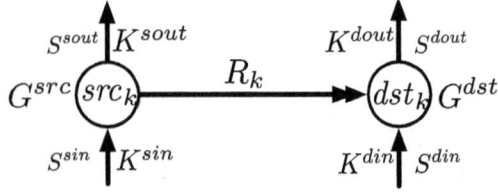

Figure 7: Load experienced by a Globus transfer k from endpoint src_k to endpoint dst_k with rate R_k, from other simultaneous Globus transfers: (a) GridFTP instances at source and destination (G^{src}, G^{dst}); (b) outgoing and incoming TCP streams at source and destination (S^{sout}, S^{sin}, S^{dout}, S^{din}), and (c) contending outgoing and incoming traffic rates at source and destination (K^{sout}, K^{sin}, K^{dout}, K^{din}).

in §4.1, the total number of TCP connections for a transfer is the product of its concurrency (C) and parallelism (P). For example, a GridFTP transfer with C=4, P=4 and a transfer with C=16, P=1 both involve 16 TCP connections. However, these two transfers involve 4 and 16 GridFTP server processes, respectively, and the latter is likely to result in more CPU load than does the former. Thus, we define as a third feature the number of GridFTP server processes associated with competing transfers.

Based on these considerations, we classify the load from such competing Globus transfers in terms of their equivalent contending transfer rate, GridFTP instance count, and parallel TCP streams. Each quantity is an *aggregate*: in each case we sum over all competing transfers. We refer to *equivalent* loads in each case because, as we will see, we scale the load due to a competing transfer by the fraction of the time that it overlaps with the transfer with which it competes. Figure 7 illustrates these different contending features for a transfer k from source src_k to destination dst_k endpoints. As described earlier, we perform a time series analysis to identify the competing Globus transfers.

The Globus **contending transfer rate** for a transfer k at its source (src_k) and destination (dst_k) endpoints (see Figure 7) is

$$K^{x \in \{sout, sin, dout, din\}}(k) = \sum_{i \in A_x} \frac{O(i,k)}{Te_k - Ts_k} R_i, \qquad (2)$$

where A_x is the set of transfers (excluding k) with src_k as source when x=$sout$; src_k as destination when x=sin; dst_k as source when x=$dout$; and dst_k as destination when x=din. $O(i,k)$ is the overlap time for the two transfers:

$$O(i,k) = \max\left(0, \quad \min(Te_i, Te_k) - \max(Ts_i, Ts_k)\right).$$

The **GridFTP instance count** on transfer k's source and destination endpoints (G^{src} and G^{dst}, respectively) due to competing transfers is represented as follows:

$$G^{x \in \{src, dst\}}(k) = \sum_{i \in A_x} \frac{O(i,k)}{Te_k - Ts_k} \min(C_i, F_i),$$

where C_i is the user-specified concurrency and F_i is the number of files transferred in the ith competing transfer, both from the Globus log. The set A_x contains all transfers except k that have src_k as their source or destination. The $\min(C_i, F_i)$ is because a transfer with $F_i < C_i$ can use only F_i GridFTP instances.

The number of simultaneous **parallel TCP streams**, $S(k)$, of the competing transfers in each data flow direction is

$$S^{x \in \{sout, sin, dout, din\}}(k) = \sum_{i \in A_x} \frac{O(i,k)}{Te_k - Ts_k} \min(C_i, F_i) P_i,$$

where P_i is the user-specified parallelism of transfer i. The sets A_x are as in Equation 2.

4.3.2 Accounting for other competing load. Figure 3 illustrates a situation in which transfer rate varies fairly cleanly with external load. We see that the highest transfer rate is always achieved when relative external load (K) is zero, as we expect.

In other settings, things are more complicated. For example, Figure 8 plots transfer rate versus relative external load for each transfer between four edges involving endpoints with high-speed networks and storage systems at the Texas Advanced Computing Center (TACC), Argonne Leadership Computing Facility (ALCF), National Energy Research Scientific Computing Center (NERSC: two different endpoints), San Diego Supercomputer Center (SDSC), and Jefferson Laboratory (JLAB). Here, the relationship between known external load and achieved transfer rate is less clear. In fact, with the exception of the NERSC-DTN to the JLAB edge, the maximum observed transfer rate (marked by a red star) is at a point other than when the load from other Globus transfers is the lowest.

One likely reason for this discrepancy is competition from non-Globus activities, such as file transfers performed with other tools, storage activities performed by other tasks, and other traffic on network link(s) between source and destination. We explore such effects in §5.5.2, but in general we have no information that we can use to quantify this *other competing load*. Thus, we address the limitation of missing information on non-Globus load by considering in our analyses only transfers that achieve a high fraction of peak, under the hypothesis that these transfers are unlikely to have suffered from much other competing load. Specifically, for each edge, E, we first determine the highest transfer rate achieved between the two endpoints, $R^{max}(E)$, and then remove from our dataset transfers that have a rate less than $T.R^{max}(E)$, where T is a load threshold, set to 0.5 except where otherwise specified.

This approach is not ideal. It may also remove transfers that perform badly because of, for example, transfer characteristics (e.g., small files). However, we show in §5.5 that the accuracy of our models improves with load threshold. wide area network conditions.

5 REGRESSION ANALYSIS

We use regression analysis to explain the relationship between the transfer rate and the 15 independent variables in Table 2. In particular, we investigate whether the transfer rate can be modeled as a linear and nonlinear combination of independent variables. To test linear dependence, we use linear regression to fit the data. For the nonlinear testing, there exists a wide range of supervised-machine-learning algorithms of varying complexity. We use gradient boosting [9], a state-of-the-art supervised-machine-learning algorithm that has proven effective on many predictive modeling tasks.

Both methods benefit from preprocessing since the scale of the independent variables is quite different. Therefore, we normalize each input x_i to have zero mean and unit variance, setting $x' =$

(a) TACC to ALCF

(b) TACC to NERSC-Edison

(c) SDSC to TACC

(d) NERSC-DTN to JLAB

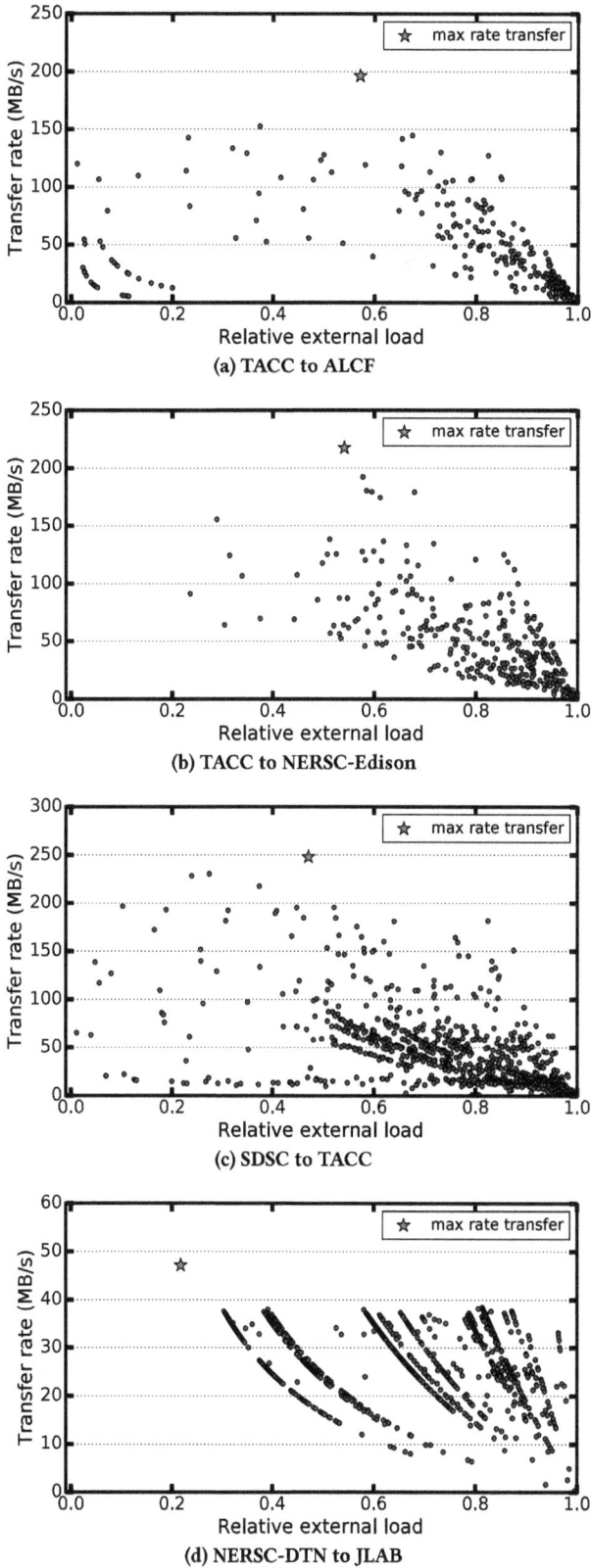

Figure 8: Transfer rate vs. relative external load for four edges, each involving heavily used endpoints.

$(x_i - \overline{x_i})/\sigma_i$, where $\overline{x_i}$ and σ_i are the mean and standard deviation of x_i, respectively.

5.1 Linear regression

Linear regression (LR) assumes that the relationship between the rate R_i for each transfer i and the independent variables is linear:

$$R_i = \beta_0 + \beta_1 x_{i1} + \cdots + \beta_m x_{im}, \qquad (3)$$

where the x_{ij} are the m features for each of the n transfers i and $\beta_0, \cdots, \beta_m$ are coefficients that are estimated by minimizing the residual sum of squares between the observed transfer rates (R_i) and those predicted ($\hat{R_i}$) by the linear approximation. Mathematically, we solve a problem of the form

$$\min_{\beta_0, \cdots, \beta_m} \sum_{i=1}^{n} \left(R_i - \hat{R_i} \right)^2. \qquad (4)$$

We fit this linear regression model separately on each edge. We use edges that have at least 300 transfers with rate greater than 0.5 R^{max}. For each edge, we use these transfers to train and test the model, since these transfers are less likely to have unknown (non-Globus) competing load (detailed in §4.3.2) and thus are more likely to explain the importance of each feature to transfer performance. These transfers account for 46.5% of the raw data over these 30 heavily used edges. For each edge, we randomly select 70% of the log data to train the model and the other 30% to test the model. Both the training and test data, which include the derived and original transfer features, are available online [27]. (The data have been anonymized to protect the privacy of endpoints and users.)

These 30 edges are representative of all edges in the log in important ways. To demonstrate this, we consider three edge characteristics: *edge length*, which we approximate by determining the great circle distance between source and destination and which serves as a proxy for the round-trip time; maximum observed aggregate transfer *rate*; and *edge type*, which is in turn determined by its source and destination endpoint types. Table 3 compares the distribution of great circle length for all edges versus for the 30 edges. For the maximum observed aggregate rate, the 30 edges range from 6.4 MB/s (5th percentile) to 1.2 GB/s (95th percentile), while all edges range from 2.1 MB/s (5th percentile) to 1.2 GB/s (95th percentile). Table 4 compares the distribution of edge types. [There are two endpoint types—server (Globus Connect Server, or GCS) and personal computer (GCP)—and thus four edge types, of which three are represented in the log. (Globus did not support GCP to GCP transfers before 2016.)]

Table 3: Edge length statistics (km) for three percentiles.

Dataset	25th	50th	90th
All edges	235	1,976	3,062
30 edges	247	1,436	3,947

An advantage of the fitted linear regression model is that it reveals the relationship between a single input variable and the transfer rate when all other input variables in the model are kept constant. In particular, the interpretation of β_i is the expected change in R for a one-unit change in x_i when no other input changes at the

Table 4: Edge type statistics (%).

Dataset	$GCS \Rightarrow GCS$	$GCS \Rightarrow GCP$	$GCS \Rightarrow GCP$
All edges	45	34	20
30 edges	51	30	19

same time. This is called the *unique effect* of x_i on R. Figure 9 shows the relative values of the coefficients. (We scaled the coefficients by dividing each coefficient into the maximum value of its edge so that all maximums have the same size). C and P are eliminated for all edges because they do not vary greatly in the log data. Since load on *sout* and *din* represent direct contention, we are not surprised to see that they have considerable influence on transfer rate. Although $S^{\{sin, sout, din, dout\}}$ and $K^{\{sin, sout, din, dout\}}$ all presumably reflect network load, they get different weights in the model. This result tells us that no strong correlation exists between them, which further argues that more TCP streams do not always contribute to higher aggregate transfer rate. G^{src} and G^{dst} are also significant for most edges: more concurrent GridFTP processes mean more contention on CPU, memory, and storage resources.

5.2 Nonlinear model

We conducted an exploratory analysis to check for nonlinear relationships between rate and the independent variables. We computed the Pearson linear correlation and nonlinear maximal information coefficients, as shown in Table 5. Several inputs have a higher nonlinear maximal information coefficient than the Pearson correlation coefficient, indicating nonlinear dependencies between features and rate that cannot be captured by a linear model.

For the nonlinear model, we use a gradient boosting approach, an iterative approach in which at each iteration a new decision tree is added to correct errors made by previous trees. A gradient descent algorithm is used to minimize the error when adding each new tree. Sequentially built trees are combined to produce the final model. An advantage of gradient boosting is that after the trees are constructed, computing the importance scores for each independent variable is straightforward. Intuitively, the more an independent variable is used to make the main splits within the tree, the higher its relative importance. The importance for each independent variable is then averaged across all the decision trees. Note that unlike in the linear model, the importance score does not correspond to the unit increase or decrease in rate.

We use eXtreme Gradient Boosting (XGB) [9], a high-performing gradient boosting implementation that is used widely by data scientists to achieve state-of-the-art results on many machine learning challenges such as Kaggle and KDDCup. The effectiveness of XGB stems from several careful optimizations, both algorithmic (a novel approximate tree learning algorithm and an efficient procedure to handle training point weights in approximate tree learning) and system level (out-of-core computation to process data that is too large to fit in main memory, and cache-aware learning to improve speed and scalability) [9].

For each given edge, we use 70% of the data to train the XGB model and the remaining 30% for testing.

5.3 Prediction results

Now, we compare the LR and XGB prediction errors. We find that nonlinear regression improves over linear regression and that the relationship between input variables and transfer rate is nonlinear. Figures 10 and 11 show the prediction errors for each edge. We see that XGB has lower errors than LR has for most edges, presumably because it captures more information (nonlinear dependencies) about the relationship between features and transfer rate.

Figure 12 shows the importance of features over each edge. Comparing with Figure 9, we see that most features have similar importance across the linear and nonlinear models. Some features (e.g., K^{sout}, S^{sout}, N_b) are important in both. However, the number of faults, N_{flt}, is a far less important feature in the nonlinear case. We know that faults have a significant negative impact on performance, so why are they not important in the nonlinear case? One possible reason is that faults occur when load is high, leading to a correlation between faults and a nonlinear function of load. Thus, the nonlinear model can account for the impact of faults by selecting an appropriate function of load.

5.4 A single model for all edges

The success of our edge-specific regression analyses encourages us to examine the feasibility of capturing endpoint differences in additional features, in order to create a single general model for all edges. Since we lack information about endpoint properties, such as NIC capacity, CPU speed, core count, memory capacity, and storage bandwidth, we use data from Globus logs to construct two new features for each endpoint. Specifically, we define for each endpoint E its maximum outgoing rate, $ROmax_E$, as follows:

(1) Let src_E be all transfers with E as their source.
(2) For each transfer x in src_E, estimate its Globus contending outgoing transfer rate (i.e., from its source endpoint) as $K^{sout}(x)$ from Equation 2.
(3) Determine the maximum outgoing rate for endpoint E:

$$ROmax_E = \max_{x \in Src_E} \left(R_x + K^{sout}(x) \right)$$

Similarly, we determine the endpoint's maximum incoming rate, $RImax_E$, also from Equation 2.

$$RImax_E = \max_{x \in Dst_E} \left(R_x + K^{din}(x) \right)$$

We can then extend Equation 3 to obtain the general model.

$$R_i = \beta_0 + \beta_1 x_{i1} + \cdots + \beta_m x_{im} + \beta_{m+1} ROmax_{s_i} + \beta_{m+2} RImax_{d_i} \tag{5}$$

Here x_{ij} are as in Equation 3; s_i and d_i are the source and destination endpoints for the transfer i; $RImax_{s_i}$ and $ROmax_{d_i}$ are our two new features; and $\beta_0, \cdots, \beta_{m+2}$ are the coefficients. (Intuitively, $\beta_0, \cdots, \beta_m$ capture the behavior of the Globus service and β_{m+1} and β_{m+2} the capabilities of the source and destination endpoints, respectively.) We then estimate $\beta_0, \cdots, \beta_{m+2}$, as we did $\beta_0, \cdots, \beta_m$ in §5.1 except that we perform the minimization over N transfers associated with *all* of our 30 selected edges.

$$\min_{\beta_0, \cdots, \beta_{m+2}} \sum_{i=1}^{N} \left(R_i - \hat{R}_i \right)^2. \tag{6}$$

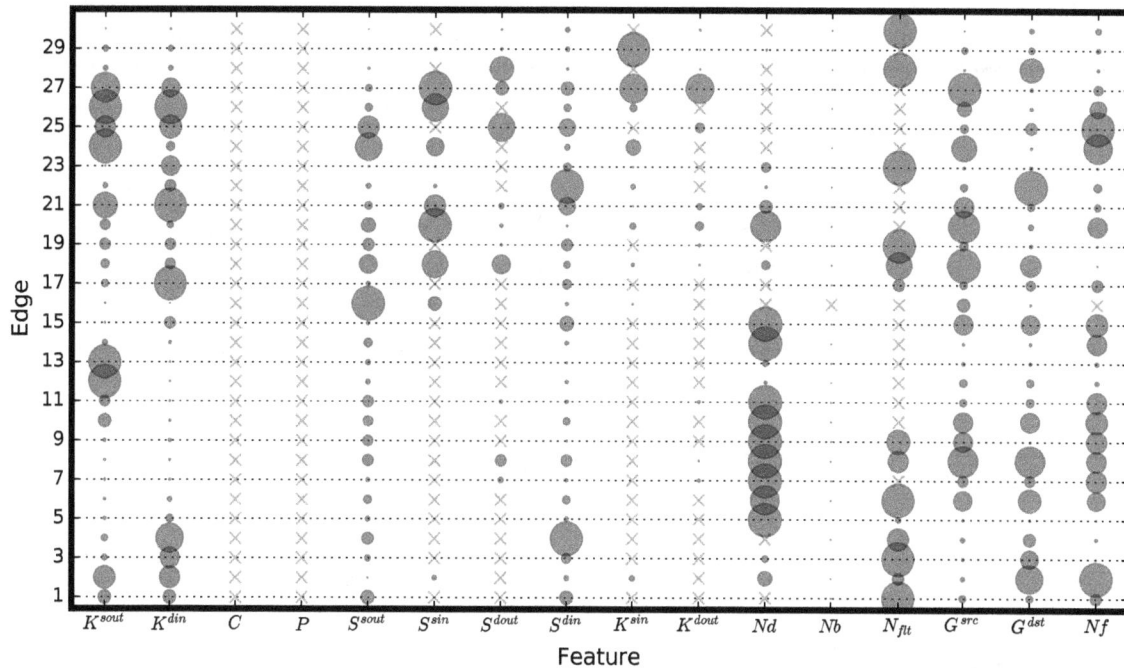

Figure 9: Circle size indicates the relative significance of features in the linear model, for each of 30 edges. A red cross indicates that the corresponding feature is eliminated because of low variance. Features from different samples are not comparable.

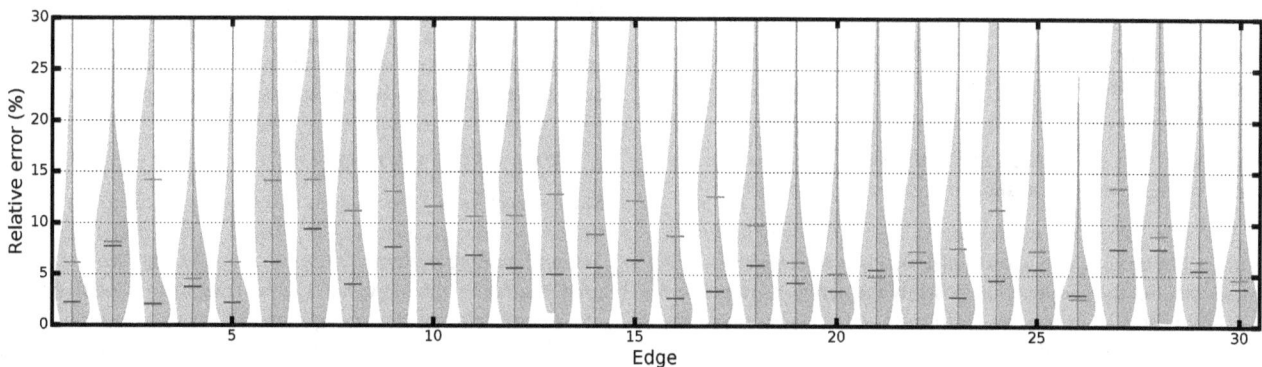

Figure 10: Comparison of linear regression and eXtreme Gradient Boosting models. For each edge, the left Violin plot gives the prediction error of the linear regression model and the right the prediction error of eXtreme Gradient Boosting model.

Specifically, we work with the transfers from the 30 edges with rate greater than $0.5 R^{max}$. We use 70% of these 30,653 transfers to train the linear model and the other 30% for testing. We obtain an MdAPE of 19%: higher than when we train individual models for each edge, but still useful for many purposes. For example, this model can be used to predict transfer rates for an edge that has few or no transfers, if that edge's source and destination endpoints have been involved in transfers to other endpoints. We also train the nonlinear model XGB and obtain an MdAPE of 4.9%. In future work, we will incorporate round-trip times for each edge, which we expect to reduce errors further.

5.5 Reducing or eliminating the unknowns

The unknown aspects that impact the transfer rate contribute to the inaccuracies in the models developed so far. Here we try to reduce or eliminate the unknowns and see how doing so can help improve the accuracy of the models.

5.5.1 Reducing the unknowns. As discussed in §4.3.2, the results reported here are for transfers with rate $\geq 0.5R^{max}$, under the hypothesis that such transfers are less likely to suffer from competing load. To explore whether transfers with higher rates are more likely to have less unknown load, we also applied the eXtreme Gradient Boosting method to datasets obtained by setting the threshold as $0.6R^{max}$, $0.7R^{max}$, and $0.8R^{max}$. Figure 13 shows the prediction errors for all four models for the eight edges that have more than

Table 5: Correlation study between the features of Table 2 and transfer rate. CC is the Pearson correlation coefficient and MIC the maximal information coefficient. Missing data in CC rows (–) mean that the corresponding features have uniform value.

ID	K^{sout}	K^{din}	C	P	S^{sout}	S^{sin}	S^{dout}	S^{din}	K^{sin}	K^{dout}	Nd	Nb	G^{src}	G^{dst}	Nf
CC	0.23	0.41	–	–	0.20	0.16	0.51	0.46	0.16	0.40	0.12	0.12	0.11	0.56	0.13
MIC	0.25	0.66	0.00	0.00	0.30	0.06	0.52	0.63	0.06	0.66	0.17	0.39	0.28	0.66	0.19
CC	0.17	0.10	–	–	0.06	0.11	0.21	0.16	0.09	0.21	0.20	0.32	0.19	0.01	0.20
MIC	0.47	0.33	0.00	0.00	0.48	0.23	0.18	0.45	0.23	0.18	0.13	0.49	0.46	0.49	0.13
CC	0.02	0.03	/	/	0.01	/	0.18	0.03	/	0.11	0.11	0.22	0.11	0.06	0.11
MIC	0.16	0.24	0.00	0.00	0.19	0.00	0.18	0.26	0.00	0.18	0.20	0.41	0.20	0.28	0.20
CC	0.03	0.24	/	/	0.01	0.12	/	0.02	0.14	/	0.03	0.43	0.09	0.02	0.04
MIC	0.26	0.17	0.00	0.00	0.24	0.26	0.00	0.29	0.29	0.00	0.06	0.53	0.26	0.18	0.40

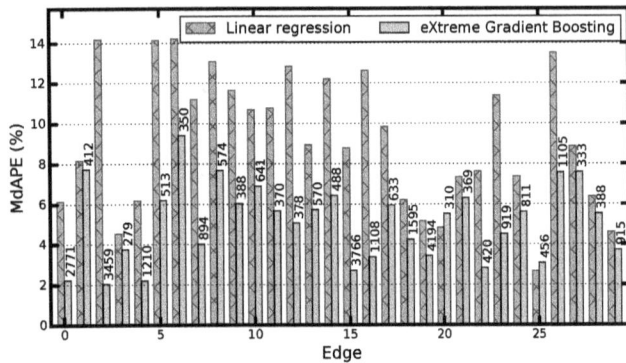

Figure 11: MdAPEs for linear and and eXtreme Gradient Boosting models, and the actual number of samples used.

than that seen in §5.1 and §5.2, which we attribute to the fact that the source and destination are at the same site.

We then introduced four new features to represent storage load: CPU load on source OSS, CPU load on destination OSS, disk read on source OST, and disk write on destination OST. With these new features, a nonlinear model of the type described in §5.2 achieved a 95th percentile error of just 1.26%.

These results suggest that if we can characterize all currently unknown loads, we can build an accurate model for transfer rate. We note, however, that the environment in which we performed this study differs from production environments in important respects. In particular, our transfer characteristics were uniform for all transfers (i.e., N_b, N_f, and N_{dir} are the same across all transfers), and since we transferred data only internally at NERSC, we did not have to deal with the challenging issue of network contention.

300 transfers that satisfy the $0.8R^{max}$ threshold. Prediction errors generally decline as the threshold increases, as we expect.

5.5.2 Eliminating the unknowns. An alternative way to reduce the impact of unknown load on model results is to collect more information about the endpoint and possibly the network. To explore the utility of this approach, we performed test transfers over endpoints for which we could monitor all load (including that external to Globus) on storage. We added this new storage load information to the feature set, used the new feature set to train a data-driven model, and evaluated the prediction accuracy of this new model.

We performed these experiments in an environment comprising two Lustre file systems at NERSC: one shared with the Edison supercomputer and one with a DTN. We used Globus to perform a series of test transfers from one Lustre object storage target (OST) to another, keeping 10 additional simultaneous Globus load transfers running at all times in order to mimic a production environment. Throughout the experiments, we used the Lustre Monitoring Tool (LMT) to collect, every five seconds, both disk I/O load for each Lustre OST and CPU load for each Lustre object storage server (OSS). We performed 666 test transfers in total, of which we randomly picked 70% for training and the rest for testing.

To provide a baseline for evaluation of the utility of the LMT-measured data, we first trained the model described in §5.2 with the same features used in earlier sections, namely, the lower 15 terms in Table 2. The 95th percentile error is 9.29%. This error is lower

6   RELATED WORK

Models have been developed for individual components in the end-to-end file transfer, including TCP based on first principles [13, 31, 34], and storage systems [7, 26, 39, 40]. In other work [19], we used models for the individual system components involved in an end-to-end data transfer and optimized the data transfer using the models. But such modeling is challenging because it requires a lot of information for each individual endpoint.

Parallel TCP streams are extensively used in wide-area data transfers to increase the aggregate TCP window size and provide increased resilience to packet losses [15, 29]. Several researchers have modeled the behavior of parallel TCP streams [3, 10, 15, 24, 29], and some studies [18, 30, 41] have focused on such streams specifically in the context of GridFTP. In our work here, we model the end-to-end performance characteristics of file transfers, where the parallel TCP stream is one of many aspects that impact the performance. In addition to parallel streams, we take into account several other features that impact the transfer rate, including dataset characteristics and load on the transfer hosts, storage, and network.

Other prior work has sought to develop end-to-end file transfer models [4, 21, 22, 28, 35]. Vazhkudai and Schopf [35] and Lu et al. [28] propose models that rely on performance data on individual components such as network, disk, and application. Kim et al. [22] and Arslan et al. [4] rely on real-time probing. Although Kettimuthu et al. [21] consider external load in their model, neither

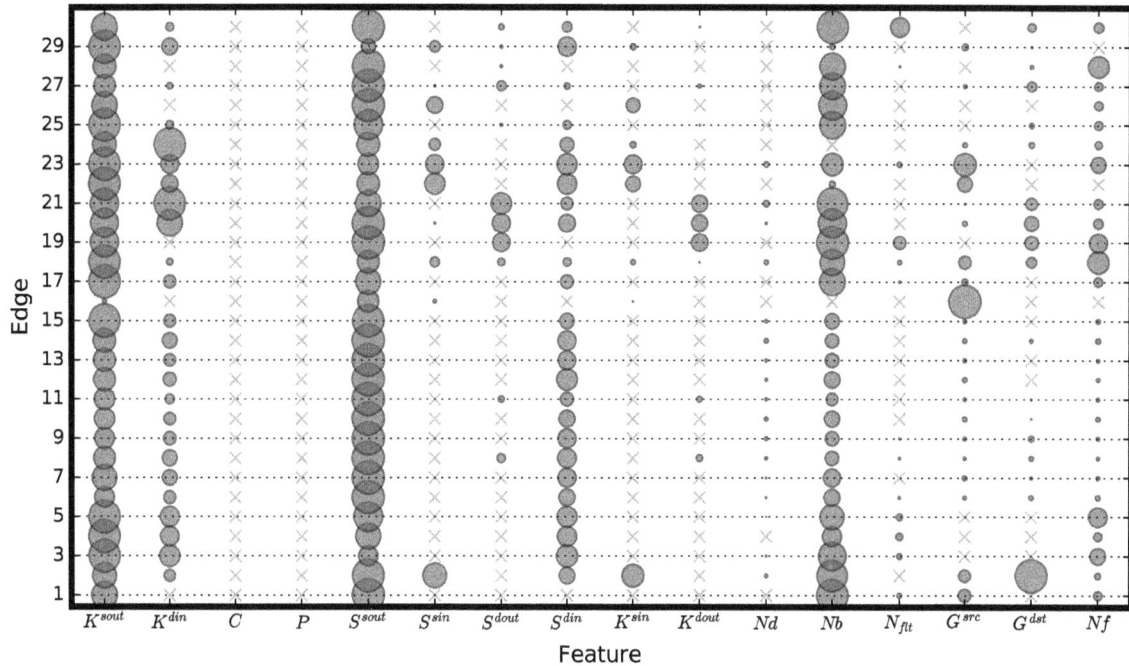

Figure 12: Circle size indicates the relative importance of features in the eXtreme Gradient Boosting model, for each of 30 edges. A red cross indicates a feature that is eliminated due to low variance. Features from different samples are not comparable.

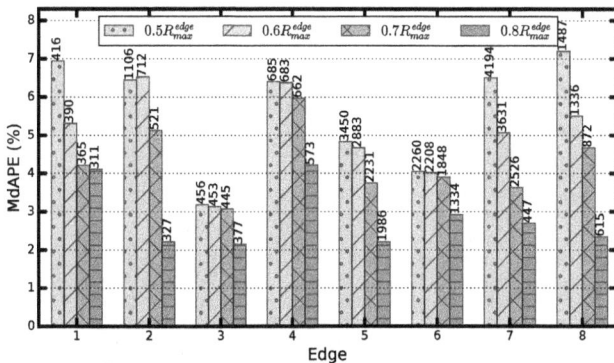

Figure 13: MdAPEs for the linear model on eight edges, when training on sets of transfers with different R^{max} thresholds. We show the number of data points in each case.

they nor other studies examined the impact of the external load as extensively as has been done in this paper.

7 RELEVANCE TO OTHER TOOLS

While we performed this work using Globus data, we believe that our methods and conclusions are applicable to all wide area data transfers. The features that we used (number of TCP connections, number of network and disk I/O threads / processes, size of the data transfer, number of files, competing load) are generic features that impact the performance of any wide area data transfer, irrespective of the tool employed. Features such as number of TCP connections, number of network and disk I/O threads / processes, size of the data

transfer, and number of files can be obtained in a straightforward fashion for other data transfer tools such as FTP, rsync, scp, bbcp [6], FDT [12], and XDD [32]. Given these features, our method can be used to compute competing load for an environment in which one of those other tools dominates. In fact, if the logs for all data transfer tools are available, our method can be used to compute the competing load from all tools, which we can expect to uncover more unknowns and thus improve model accuracy.

8 CONCLUSIONS

We have used a large collection of Globus transfer records to gain insight into the behavior of large science data transfers and the factors that affect their behavior. We generate various features from Globus logs and study the importance of these features in models. For 30,653 transfers over 30 heavily used source-destination pairs ("edges"), totaling 2,053 TB in 46.6 million files, we obtained median absolute percentage prediction errors (MdAPE) of 7.0% and 4.6% when using distinct linear and nonlinear models per edge, respectively. When using a single nonlinear model for all 30 edges, we obtain an MdAPE of 7.8%. We are currently applying these models to other Globus transfers.

Although we have focused on Globus transfers, we expect our approach and proposed features to have broad applicability for wide area file transfers that involve parallel TCP streams. In particular, our feature engineering work provides useful hints and insights for data science practitioners in wide area data transfer. We demonstrate, for example, the importance of creating measures of endpoint load to capture the impact of contention for computer, network interface, and storage system resources. One implication is that contention at endpoints can significantly reduce aggregate performance of even overprovisioned networks. This result suggests that aggregate performance can be improved by scheduling transfers and/or reducing concurrency and parallelism.

We have identified several directions for improved transfer service monitoring that we hope can improve our models by improving knowledge of other loads. Globus currently records information only about its transfers: it collects no information about non-Globus load on endpoints or about network load. A new version with the ability to monitor overall endpoint status is under development. Further research is needed to study the influence of network load. To this end, we plan to incorporate SNMP data from routers to characterize network conditions. Another direction for future work is to see whether more advanced machine learning methods, for example multiobjective modeling with machine learning (AutoMOMML) [5], can yield better models.

ACKNOWLEDGMENTS

This material was supported in part by the U.S. Department of Energy, Office of Science, Advanced Scientific Computing Research, under Contract DE-AC02-06CH11357. We thank Nagi Rao for useful discussions, Brigitte Raumann for help with Globus log analysis, Glenn Lockwood for help with experiments at NERSC described in §5.5, and the Globus team for much good work and advice.

REFERENCES

[1] W. Allcock, J. Bresnahan, R. Kettimuthu, M. Link, C. Dumitrescu, I. Raicu, and I. Foster. The Globus striped GridFTP framework and server. In *SC'05*, pages 54–61, 2005.

[2] B. Allen, J. Bresnahan, L. Childers, I. Foster, G. Kandaswamy, R. Kettimuthu, J. Kordas, M. Link, S. Martin, K. Pickett, and S. Tuecke. Software as a service for data scientists. *Commun. ACM*, 55(2):81–88, Feb. 2012.

[3] E. Altman, D. Barman, B. Tuffin, and M. Vojnovic. Parallel TCP sockets: Simple model, throughput and validation. In *25th IEEE Intl Conf. on Computer Communications*, pages 1–12, April 2006.

[4] E. Arslan, K. Guner, and T. Kosar. HARP: predictive transfer optimization based on historical analysis and real-time probing. In *SC'16*, pages 25:1–25:12, 2016.

[5] P. Balaprakash, A. Tiwari, S. M. Wild, and P. D. Hovland. AutoMOMML: Automatic Multi-objective Modeling with Machine Learning. In *ISC*, pages 219–239, 2016.

[6] BBCP. http://www.slac.stanford.edu/~abh/bbcp/.

[7] P. H. Carns, B. W. Settlemyer, and W. B. Ligon III. Using server-to-server communication in parallel file systems to simplify consistency and improve performance. In *SC'08*, page 6, 2008.

[8] K. Chard, S. Tuecke, and I. Foster. Globus: Recent enhancements and future plans. In *XSEDE'16*, page 27. ACM, 2016.

[9] T. Chen and C. Guestrin. XGBoost: A scalable tree boosting system. *arXiv preprint arXiv:1603.02754*, 2016.

[10] J. Crowcroft and P. Oechslin. Differentiated end-to-end internet services using a weighted proportional fair sharing TCP. *SIGCOMM Comput. Commun. Rev.*, 28(3):53–69, July 1998.

[11] E. Dart, L. Rotman, B. Tierney, M. Hester, and J. Zurawski. The Science DMZ: A network design pattern for data-intensive science. *Scientific Programming*, 22(2):173–185, 2014.

[12] FDT. *FDT - Fast Data Transfer*. http://monalisa.cern.ch/FDT/.

[13] J. Gao and N. S. V. Rao. TCP AIMD dynamics over Internet connections. *IEEE Communications Letters*, 9:4–6, 2005.

[14] I. Guyon and A. Elisseeff. An introduction to variable and feature selection. *J. Mach. Learn. Res.*, 3:1157–1182, Mar. 2003.

[15] T. J. Hacker, B. D. Athey, and B. Noble. The end-to-end performance effects of parallel TCP sockets on a lossy wide-area network. In *16th Intl Parallel and Distributed Processing Symp.*, page 314, 2002.

[16] A. Hanemann, J. W. Boote, E. L. Boyd, J. Durand, L. Kudarimoti, R. Lapacz, D. M. Swany, S. Trocha, and J. Zurawski. PerfSONAR: A service oriented architecture for multi-domain network monitoring. In *3rd Intl Conf. on Service-Oriented Computing*, pages 241–254, Berlin, Heidelberg, 2005. Springer-Verlag.

[17] iperf3. http://software.es.net/iperf/.

[18] T. Ito, H. Ohsaki, and M. Imase. GridFTP-APT: Automatic parallelism tuning mechanism for data transfer protocol GridFTP. In *6th IEEE Intl Symp. on Cluster Computing and the Grid*, pages 454–461, 2006.

[19] E.-S. Jung, R. Kettimuthu, and V. Vishwanath. Toward optimizing disk-to-disk transfer on 100G networks. In *7th IEEE Intl Conf. on Advanced Networks and Telecommunications Systems*, 2013.

[20] T. Kelly. Scalable TCP: Improving performance in highspeed wide area networks. *ACM SIGCOMM Computer Communication Review*, 33(2):83–91, 2003.

[21] R. Kettimuthu, G. Vardoyan, G. Agrawal, and P. Sadayappan. Modeling and optimizing large-scale wide-area data transfers. *14th IEEE/ACM Intl Symp. on Cluster, Cloud and Grid Computing*, 0:196–205, 2014.

[22] J. Kim, E. Yildirim, and T. Kosar. A highly-accurate and low-overhead prediction model for transfer throughput optimization. *Cluster Computing*, 18(1):41–59, 2015.

[23] E. Kissel, M. Swany, B. Tierney, and E. Pouyoul. Efficient wide area data transfer protocols for 100 Gbps networks and beyond. In *3rd Intl Workshop on Network-Aware Data Management*, page 3. ACM, 2013.

[24] G. Kola and M. K. Vernon. Target bandwidth sharing using endhost measures. *Perform. Eval.*, 64(9-12):948–964, Oct. 2007.

[25] T. Kosar, G. Kola, and M. Livny. Data pipelines: Enabling large scale multi-protocol data transfers. In *2nd Workshop on Middleware for Grid Computing*, pages 63–68, 2004.

[26] N. Liu, C. Carothers, J. Cope, P. Carns, R. Ross, A. Crume, and C. Maltzahn. Modeling a leadership-scale storage system. In *Parallel Processing and Applied Mathematics*, pages 10–19. 2012.

[27] Z. Liu, P. Balaprakash, R. Kettimuthu, and I. Foster. Explaining wide area data transfer performance. http://hdl.handle.net/11466/globus_A4N55BB, 2017.

[28] D. Lu, Y. Qiao, P. Dinda, and F. Bustamante. Characterizing and predicting TCP throughput on the wide area network. In *25th IEEE Intl Conf. on Distributed Computing Systems*, pages 414–424, June 2005.

[29] D. Lu, Y. Qiao, P. A. Dinda, and F. E. Bustamante. Modeling and taming parallel TCP on the wide area network. In *19th IEEE Intl Parallel and Distributed Processing Symp.*, page 68b, 2005.

[30] H. Ohsaki and M. Imase. On modeling GridFTP using fluid-flow approximation for high speed Grid networking. In *Symp. on Applications and the Internet-Workshops*, pages 638–, 2004.

[31] J. Padhye, V. Firoiu, D. F. Towsley, and J. F. Kurose. Modeling TCP Reno performance: A simple model and its empirical validation. *IEEE/ACM Trans. Networking*, 8(2):133–145, 2000.

[32] B. W. Settlemyer, J. D. Dobson, S. W. Hodson, J. A. Kuehn, S. W. Poole, and T. M. Ruwart. A technique for moving large data sets over high-performance long distance networks. In *27th Symp. on Mass Storage Systems and Technologies*, pages 1–6, May 2011.

[33] B. Tierney, W. Johnston, B. Crowley, G. Hoo, C. Brooks, and D. Gunter. The NetLogger methodology for high performance distributed systems performance analysis. In *7th Intl Symp. on High Performance Distributed Computing*, pages 260–267, 1998.

[34] G. Vardoyan, N. S. V. Rao, and D. Towsley. Models of TCP in high-BDP environments and their experimental validation. In *24th Intl Conf. on Network Protocols*, pages 1–10, 2016.

[35] S. Vazhkudai and J. Schopf. Using regression techniques to predict large data transfers. *Int. J. High Perf. Comp. Appl.*, 2003.

[36] D. X. Wei, C. Jin, S. H. Low, and S. Hegde. FAST TCP: Motivation, architecture, algorithms, performance. *IEEE/ACM Trans. Networking*, 14(6):1246–1259, 2006.

[37] W. Weibull. A statistical distribution function of wide applicability. *Journal of Applied Mechanics*, pages 293–297, 1951.

[38] R. Wolski. Forecasting network performance to support dynamic scheduling using the Network Weather Service. In *6th IEEE Symp. on High Performance Distributed Computing*, 1997.

[39] J. M. Wozniak, S. W. Son, and R. Ross. Distributed object storage rebuild analysis via simulation with GOBS. In *Intl Conf. on Dependable Systems and Networks Workshops*, pages 23–28, 2010.

[40] Q. M. Wu, K. Xie, M. F. Zhu, L. M. Xiao, and L. Ruan. DMFSsim: A distributed metadata file system simulator. *Applied Mechanics and Materials*, 241:1556–1561, 2013.

[41] E. Yildirim, D. Yin, and T. Kosar. Prediction of optimal parallelism level in wide area data transfers. *IEEE Trans. Parallel Distrib. Syst.*, 22(12):2033–2045, Dec. 2011.

Using Scientific Computing to Advance Wildland Fire Monitoring and Prediction

Janice Coen
National Center for Atmospheric Research
Mesoscale and Microscale Meteorology Laboratory
janicec@ucar.edu

ABSTRACT

New technologies have transformed our understanding of wildland fire behavior, providing a better ability to observe them from a variety of platforms, simulate their growth with computational models, and interpret their frequency and controls in a global context. These tools have shown how wildland fires are among the extremes of weather events and can produce behaviors such as fire whirls, blow-ups, bursts of flame along the surface, and winds ten times stronger than ambient conditions, all of which result from the interactions between a fire and its atmospheric environment.

I will highlight current research in integrated weather – wildland fire computational modeling, fire detection, and observation, and their application to understanding and prediction. Coupled weather-wildland fire models tie numerical weather prediction models to wildland fire behavior modules to simulate the impact of a fire on the atmosphere and the subsequent feedback of these fire-induced winds on fire behavior, i.e. how a fire "creates its own weather". NCAR's CAWFE® modeling system has been used to explain fundamental fire phenomena and reproduce the unfolding of past fire events. Recent work, in which CAWFE has been integrated with satellite-based active fire detection data, addresses the challenges of applying it as an operational forecast tool. This newer generation of tools brought many goals within sight – rapid fire detection, nearly ubiquitous monitoring, and recognition that many of the distinctive characteristics of fire events are reproducible and perhaps predictable in real time. Concurrently, these more complex tools raise new challenges. I conclude with innovative model-data fusion approaches to overcome some of these remaining puzzles.

Author Keywords

Natural hazards; fire remote sensing; computational fluid dynamics

BIOGRAPHY

Dr. Janice Coen is a Project Scientist at the National Center for Atmospheric Research in Boulder, Colorado. She received a B.S. in Engineering Physics from Grove City College and an M.S. and Ph.D. from the Department of Geophysical Sciences at the University of Chicago. She investigates wildland fire behavior and its interaction with weather using computational fluid dynamics models and by analyzing infrared imagery of wildland fires. She has developed two coupled numerical weather prediction – wildland fire behavior models that have become widespread in the research community and transformed how people interpret fire behavior. Her current work applies these models with airborne and satellite fire and fuel remote sensing data to decipher the unfolding of large wildland fire events, improve firefighter safety, understand the impact of fuel accumulation and drought on wildfires, and serve as next-generation model/data assimilation systems to forecast wildfire growth.

She served as Associate Editor for the International Journal of Wildland Fire, on the Editorial Board of Environmental Modelling & Software, and on the Board of Directors of the International Association of Wildland Fire.

http://www2.mmm.ucar.edu/people/coen/

HPDC'17, June 26–30, 2017, Washington, DC, USA.
ACM ISBN 978-1-4503-4699-3/17/06.
DOI: http://dx.doi.org/10.1145/3078597.3091519

Predicting Output Performance of a Petascale Supercomputer

Bing Xie
Duke University
bingxie@cs.duke.edu

Yezhou Huang
Duke University
yhuang@cs.duke.edu

Jeffrey S. Chase
Duke University
chase@cs.duke.edu

Jong Youl Choi
Oak Ridge National Laboratory
choij@ornl.gov

Scott Klasky
Oak Ridge National Laboratory
klasky@ornl.gov

Jay Lofstead
Sandia National Laboratories
gflofst@sandia.gov

Sarp Oral
Oak Ridge National Laboratory
oralhs@ornl.gov

ABSTRACT

In this paper, we develop a predictive model useful for output performance prediction of supercomputer file systems under production load. Our target environment is Titan—the 3rd fastest supercomputer in the world—and its Lustre-based multi-stage write path. We observe from Titan that although output performance is highly variable at small time scales, the mean performance is stable and consistent over typical application run times. Moreover, we find that output performance is non-linearly related to its correlated parameters due to interference and saturation on individual stages on the path. These observations enable us to build a predictive model of expected write times of output patterns and I/O configurations, using feature transformations to capture non-linear relationships. We identify the candidate features based on the structure of the Lustre/Titan write path, and use feature transformation functions to produce a model space with 135,000 candidate models. By searching for the minimal mean square error in this space we identify a good model and show that it is effective.

KEYWORDS

Petascale supercomputer, Output performance, Linear regression

1 INTRODUCTION

Supercomputers and their I/O systems are built to host HPC (High Performance Computing) applications. These applications perform a variety of analyses, experiments and simulations [4–7, 19] from different scientific domains. Typical HPC applications issue periodic bursts of output to the file system for intermediate results and checkpointing; these outputs may total a terabyte or more over a typical run of the application [4, 5, 7, 21]. US-DOE (Department of Energy) leadership computing facilities report that HPC applications generate hundreds of petabytes of science data per year and

estimate that this rate will exceed an exabyte per year by 2018 [16]. Trends suggest that HPC applications are likely to generate more and larger output bursts.

Consequently, understanding performance of output burst absorption is crucial for these codes. Many HPC applications are loosely synchronous or bulk synchronous: they execute a sequence of iterations (e.g., for simulation timesteps) interspersed by barriers. These applications often initiate a synchronous output burst between iterations, and then wait for the burst to complete before resuming computation for the next iteration. This pause provides a consistent output image for checkpoints, and in certain other cases when double-buffering requires too much memory to be practical. Therefore, CPUs are left idle during the synchronous burst. As a case study we consider XGC [5], an important code that simulates magnetic confinement of plasma in future fusion reactor designs (§2.1). In practice output times typically comprise 7-20% of XGC's total (wall clock) execution time.

The HPC community recognizes the importance of I/O output performance. There are many efforts to address it. For example, [3, 26] summarize I/O access patterns across scientific domains and supercomputing platforms; [22, 25, 40] investigate behaviors of petascale file systems under various access patterns and system conditions. Others propose techniques, tools and middleware systems to improve I/O performance by reducing metadata operations [23, 33], aggregating/striping/reordering data streams [8, 16, 20, 24], and other techniques [13, 32, 35]. These works on I/O performance range from quantitative analysis on various targets to optimization techniques at various levels.

This paper presents an analysis to derive principles from quantitative models and to specify tradeoffs of techniques across settings and conditions. A key obstacle to meeting this goal is the dynamic nature of our production supercomputer environment. Applications have full ownership of the compute nodes assigned to them, but the interconnect and I/O system are shared and provide no performance isolation. The resulting noise complicates the task of modeling or predicting I/O performance.

We report observations from Titan [13]—a production supercomputer at ORNL—and its Lustre parallel file system (Spider 2/Atlas) to show that although output bandwidth of an HPC file system is highly variable, for a given burst pattern the mean absorption rate across compute nodes and storage targets is surprisingly stable

HPDC'17, June 26-30, 2017, Washington, DC, USA
© 2017 ACM. 978-1-4503-4699-3/17/06...$15.00
DOI: http://dx.doi.org/10.1145/3078597.3078614

over time (§3). We show that this continuity makes it possible to model and predict output performance obtained at a given scale and configuration precisely and accurately (§4). In particular, we conclude:

- For typical well-configured output bursts in Titan the congestion effects are dominated by the primary interconnect, rather than by the I/O system itself.
- At large scale these congestion effects are dominated by self-interference on the compute interconnect rather than by contention from competing workloads. Impacts from competing workloads tend to revert to the mean over relatively short time scales—tens of minutes—so that it does not affect the average absorption rate over an execution (hours or more likely days or weeks).
- The impact of self-interference is determined primarily by the number of *I/O pipes* configured for the burst. An I/O pipe is a logical output path from a task (typically occupying one core of a compute node) to a specific storage target. Well-configured bursts spread their output loads across the storage system so that the target of each I/O pipe is distinct from all other targets in the burst.
- For Titan, output bandwidth at the storage system and the impact of self-interference in the interconnect are predictable from a simple model based on the number of I/O pipes. We gathered data from synthetic probing experiments that emulate output bursts with a variety of configurations and scales on Titan, and use this data to train a regression model to predict the performance of output bursts. We show that the resulting model is precise and accurate in practice (§5).

The output rate model provides useful insight into output behavior on a leadership-class production supercomputer, and can be helpful to auto-configure burst parameters such as striping width for best performance. Moreover, the output model enables *predictions of total application run time*, which can assist with supercomputer scheduling. ORNL requires that submitted jobs include an estimate of wall clock time for use by the scheduler, and kills jobs that exceed their estimates. For XGC and other key applications, good models exist for the computation time for the iterations themselves, but the lack of an I/O model leads researchers to make conservative estimates of job cost ("just double it"). A good model of I/O cost can yield much tighter estimates, which can reduce delays in the job queue and yield more efficient use of resources. These benefits occur in part because the system may schedule mission-critical jobs and maintenance tasks in advance, and it may delay dispatching a job whose estimated run time indicates that the job would conflict with an advance reservation.

Although our current study focuses on a petascale file system, we expect that our approach is also applicable to exascale systems. The current Titan machine approaches an exascale deployment.

2 OVERVIEW

Our benchmarks on Titan and on its predecessor Jaguar [40] show that output performance is highly variable due to contention in the machine over time and across groups of compute nodes, due to

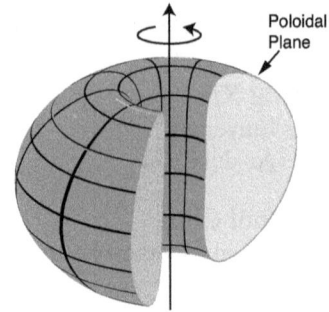

Figure 1: The XGC decomposition. A 3D tokamak is partitioned to D planes and a plane is partitioned to P subspaces. In an XGC run, DP tasks produce DP synchronous bursts for state snapshots on every T_1 iterations; D tasks represent D planes to produce three types of synchronous bursts for diagnostic analysis on every T_2, T_3, and T_4 iterations respectively.

transient system conditions resulting from the production workload. The delivered write bandwidth may be distributed across a wide range at small time scales (Figure 5). This makes it a challenge to predict output performance on production supercomputers. However, our benchmarks show that periods of severe congestion are generally of short duration; they are rarely more than tens of minutes—two to three orders of magnitude lower than application run times (e.g., days and weeks). As a result, the output burst times that an application observes across its entire execution are highly likely to regress to the mean. Therefore, in this study, we choose to model the *mean* output burst times as a basis to predict application performance (§3.2).

This section presents background to support two key points: (1) the mean write time is effective to address output behavior of a large group of scientific codes that write fixed-size bursts iteratively (§2.1); (2) we can predict mean absorption times for these output bursts based on data from synthetic benchmarks that isolate elements of the multi-stage write path across a range of I/O configurations (§2.2).

2.1 Output Behavior of Scientific Applications

It is widely observed from various supercomputer platforms that $50\% - 60\%$ of I/O requests are writes [2, 17]. This section discusses properties of write-intensive applications.

A large group of supercomputer applications are numerical analyses or simulations that compute over iterations or timesteps. We use XGC code as an example to illustrate their behavior.

2.1.1 XGC Code. XGC is a gyrokinetic particle-in-cell code used to simulate tokamak fusion reactor designs, focusing on the multiscale physics at the edge of the fusion plasma. An XGC run is a simulation for a given 3D tokamak—a magnetically confined torus—that is first decomposed to D poloidal planes with E particles in a plane, and then each plane is partitioned to P subspaces, each containing E/P particles. Figure 1 depicts the decomposition of a typical XGC run.

A run consists of DP identical tasks computing across L iterations and synchronizing at the end of each iteration. Each task runs as a process on a different core to solve a fixed set of gyrokinetic equations across iterations on particles in a subspace. Specifically, in each iteration particles are "pushed" by a governing gyrokinetic Hamiltonian equation and gathered onto F grid points of a discrete grid, where the gyrokinetic Poisson or gyrokinetic Maxwell's equations are solved. The computation time for each iteration (t_c) is fixed and predictable from (D, E, F, P).

During the run, each task produces a burst (B_1) as its state snapshot at the end of every T_1 iterations; a fixed set of D of the DP tasks produce summary outputs for the D planes ($D < P$), generating three types of bursts (B_2, B_3, B_4) for diagnostic analysis at the end of every T_2, T_3 and T_4 iterations respectively. For all four types of bursts, the data for each burst is stored as a file with a unique file name. When writing a burst, the entire execution is stalled until all data reaches disks.

The burst size of B_1 is bounded by the number of particles in a subspace (E/P): it preserves fixed-size byte-level data for the grid particle distribution function and numerical values of features (e.g., electric potential, plasma density, temperature) of particles in a subspace. The burst sizes for $B_2 - B_4$ are bounded by the number of grid points reported by the set of D tasks (F/D): it contains numerical values of features of particles on grid points. During an XGC run, particles may die or move, but in most cases any data imbalance across snapshots or grid points is ignorable: the burst sizes of $B_1 - B_4$ are constant and predictable. We observed in practice that for XGC runs common per-core burst sizes of state snapshots range from 500MB to 1.2GB; for diagnosis outputs the burst sizes range from 1MB to 400MB.

In an XGC run, E and F are given parameters as part of a problem setting; $D, P, L, T_1 - T_4$ are configurable parameters; t_c and burst sizes of $B_1 - B_4$ are predictable when the above-mentioned parameters are determined; all parameters are fixed and known before the run starts. Thus, the end-to-end execution time of a run (t_{run}) can be computed by summing up times consumed by computation and four types of bursts across iterations.

Besides t_c, if write times of $B_1 - B_4$ are also predictable, t_{run} can be estimated before a run. The prediction result can help scientists control the cost of their write operations. For example, scientists usually want to keep the time consumption for state snapshots within 10% of the execution time of an application run. But we observed from XGC production runs that the state snapshot cost varies from 7% to 20% of the entire application execution time. Therefore, given the predicted compute time and output times the state snapshot cost can be controlled by choosing T_1 appropriately.

2.1.2 Properties of Iterative Codes. XGC is representative of a large group of *static iterative scientific codes* that take iterative computation structures and produce periodic and predictable bursts [21, 22]. In general, these applications perform iterative scientific simulations on a static multi-dimensional space and produce one or more types of fixed-size bursts periodically.

Another group of scientific codes, e.g., AMR (Adaptive Mesh Refinement) [1], may vary computation space across iterations and produce different size bursts at different iterations accordingly. We call this group of codes *dynamic iterative scientific codes*.

This study focuses on output performance prediction and optimization for static iterative scientific codes. The principles also apply to dynamic codes to the extent that their burst sizes are fixed and predictable.

Similar to our analysis on XGC code in §2.1.1, presume that each run consumes t_c computation time on each of L iterations and produces a B_i type of burst on every T_i iterations ($i = 1, 2, ...$). We observed from the production supercomputer Titan and report in §3.2 that although output performance of the file system is highly variable, the mean write time (t_{B_i}) of the burst type B_i is fixed and predictable. As a result, the end-to-end execution time (t_{run}) of an application run can be predicted.

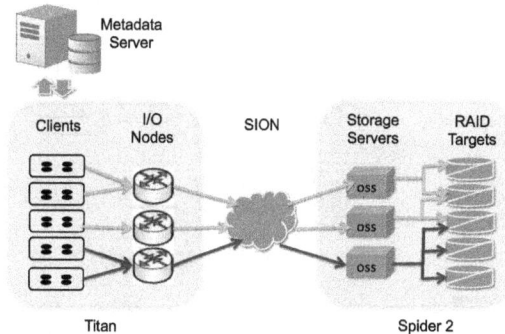

Figure 2: Titan and the Lustre File System (Spider 2)

2.2 Titan and its Lustre File System

Our target environment is Titan, the 3rd fastest supercomputer in the world. Titan is a Cray XK7 supercomputer hosted at the Oak Ridge Leadership Computing Facility (OLCF) and serving scientists in disciplines such as climate science, chemistry, molecular science, and materials science. Titan's file system, called Spider 2, is based on Lustre, an object-based parallel file system software that is deployed on ~75% of the top 100 systems [36]. Spider 2 has 32 PB of data storage and above 1TB/s peak I/O bandwidth [31]. This section summarizes Titan/Spider 2 based on materials from [13, 30, 39, 40].

Figure 2 depicts the write path of Titan and Spider 2. Titan is composed of 18,688 compute nodes; these nodes are connected by a 3D torus interconnect; each node has a 16-core CPU and a GPU: it runs the Lustre software and serves as both a Metadata Client (**MDC**) and an Object Storage Client (**OSC**).

A Metadata Server (**MDS**) stores metadata of files and objects (e.g., file namespaces and attributes, object IDs) on RAID devices, called Metadata Targets (**MDTs**). A Lustre file system is a single namespace maintained by one MDS on one or more MDTs. As described in §2.1, for scientific codes a write operation produces a group of synchronous bursts with each burst stored as an independent file. Thus, for each operation compute nodes (clients) only communicate with MDS for $file\_create()$, $file\_open()$ and $file\_close()$ at the start and the end of the operation.

Compute nodes access Spider 2 via I/O nodes (routers) that are evenly distributed through the torus interconnect. Titan is configured to connect a compute node to a fixed group of "closest" I/O nodes in the torus by a fine-grained routing policy [18]. Thus, an output operation with more compute nodes is highly likely to spread across more I/O nodes.

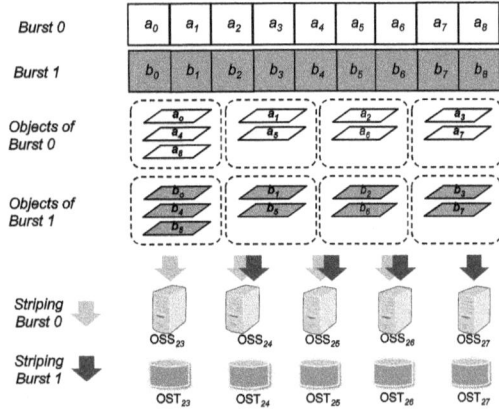

Figure 3: Striping Bursts/Files for a Write Operation. Users set *stripe_size, stripe_width* and *starting_OST*. Each burst is partitioned into a sequence of chunks with *stripe_size*-byte per chunk; the chunks are distributed round-robin across a fixed set of *stripe_width* objects (Formula 3); the sequentially-numbered bursts are assigned with a sequence of *starting_OSTs* (Formula 2). In this example, the *starting_OST* sequence is $\{OST_{23}, OST_{24}, ...\}$.

.

I/O nodes link Titan's compute nodes to the Lustre Object Storage Servers (**OSSes**) via a Scalable I/O Network (SION). Each OSS manages 7 Object Storage Targets (**OSTs**), each a RAID array direct-attached to an OSS. To balance the load across OSSes, Spider 2 maps sequentially-numbered OSTs across OSSes in a round-robin fashion. Let M and N represent the total number of OSSes and the total number of OSTs in Spider 2: $N = 7 \times M$. The M OSSes are numbered as $(OSS_0, ..., OSS_i, ..., OSS_{M-1})$; the N OSTs are numbered as $(OST_0, ..., OST_j, ..., OST_{N-1})$. Based on the mapping policy, OST_j is attached to OSS_i:

$$i = j \bmod M \quad (1)$$

For a write operation, each burst is stored as a Lustre file on one or more OSTs: a file is an interleaving of one or more data *objects* with each variable-sized object stored on a different OST. Lustre allows a job to configure three parameters to customize striping: *stripe size, stripe width* and *starting OST*: it first partitions a file into a sequence of *stripe_size*-byte data chunks, then spreads them in a sequence of *stripe_width* OSTs from the OST numbered *starting_OST*. In the simplest scheme, all files created by the job start on the same *starting_OST* and are consequently stored on the same sequence of *stripe_width* OSTs. Alternatively, a job may use an MPI-IO primitive to stagger the starting OSTs by offsetting each *starting_OST* by the number of the process that creates the file, as shown in Figure 3. Consider a job with P processes that produces P files $(f_0, ..., f_i, ..., f_{p-1})$, one from each process, and takes OST_* as f_0's *starting_OST*. According to this policy, f_i starts at the jth OST:

$$j = (* + i) \bmod N \quad (2)$$

OSSes and OSTs used in a write operation. According to Formula 2, we can compute the numbers of OSTs and OSSes used in a write operation (Formula 4 and 5). Consider an output pattern

that: (1) has P bursts with burst size K; (2) configures *stripe_size, stripe_width* and *starting_OST* as S, W, OST_* respectively; (3) applies the *starting_OST* policy in Formula 2. According to Formulas 1 and 2, the number of OSTs used per burst (N_{per}), the numbers of OSTs (N_{used}) and OSSes (M_{used}) used for this operation are given by:

$$N_{per} = \begin{cases} \lceil K/S \rceil & \text{if } \lceil K/S \rceil < W \\ W & \text{otherwise} \end{cases} \quad (3)$$

$$N_{used} = \begin{cases} P + N_{per} - 1 & \text{if } P + N_{per} - 1 < N \\ N & \text{otherwise} \end{cases} \quad (4)$$

$$M_{used} = \begin{cases} N_{used} & \text{if } N_{used} < M \\ M & \text{otherwise} \end{cases} \quad (5)$$

This study builds models to predict output performance on Titan/Atlas2: one of two equal-size partitions of Spider 2. Each partition consists of an MDS with an attached MDT, 144 OSSes and 1008 OSTs, and is configured in default as: *stripe_size*=1MB, *stripe_width*=4, and a randomly chosen *starting_OST*. We adopt the *starting_OST* policy addressed by Formula 2, and use Formulas 4 and 5 accordingly to build and evaluate models (§4 and §5).

3 OUTPUT BEHAVIOR ON TITAN

This section discusses burst absorption behavior of the Titan I/O system (§2.2), focusing on the metadata service and the stages of the data write path. The summary helps us to build a quantitative understanding of output behavior of a production petascale filesystem, which serves as a basis to model output performance of these filesystems.

3.1 Metadata Behavior

We summarize the logs of Spider 2's two metadata servers (MDS1 and MDS2), collected by MDSTrace [27] and reporting 14-day traces from Sept.10 to Sept.23, 2016. There are 3470 log files with 1735 files per metadata server. Each log file reports a trace sampled over a 60-second interval, giving the total number of requests, the number of requests per operation, the max/min request processing time, and the top ranked application by the number of requests [27]. We expect that the logs have sufficient coverage to capture the metadata behavior for most applications at OLCF.

Table 1 summarizes the logs. We conclude that: (1) The MDS load is balanced: each receives ~28K requests/minute (median) and ~32K requests/minute at the maximum. (2) The metadata cost is low and consistent in general: only one logged request had a processing time over 30 seconds, with 99.5% of requests completing within 6.09 seconds on MDS1 and within 0.9 second on MDS2 respectively. (3) The metadata load is diverse: sometimes it is dominated by a single application; sometimes it is shared by concurrent loads. (4) The *file_open()* requests are bursty and often dominate the metadata load: the median numbers of *file_open()* are 14.9K/minute on MDS1 and 21.6K/minute on MDS2 respectively. In some intervals the *file_open()* requests comprise more than 99% of the overall metadata requests.

In this study, we used a synthetic benchmark that stresses file create/open and file writes on Titan/Atlas2 to train and validate

Metadata Server	# Requests			Max request processing time (unit:sec)			# file_open()			#Requests from *the top ranked app*		
	max	*Q0.995*	*median*	*max*	*Q0.995*	*median*	*max*	*Q0.995*	*median*	*max*	*Q0.995*	*median*
MDS1	32K	30.6K	28K	16.62	6.09	0.01	30.2K	25.1K	14.9K	29.1K	27.7K	6.2K
MDS2	32.6K	32.2K	27.8K	567.05	0.90	0.006	32.2K	31.9K	21.6K	31.6K	30.9K	1.1K

Table 1: Metadata Behavior on Spider 2. This table summarizes the logs of the MDS1 and MDS2 metadata servers of Spider 2, focusing on four parameters: the total number of requests, the max request processing time, the number of requests for *file_open()*, the top ranked application by the number of requests. For each parameter, we report the max, quantile 0.995 and the median. In summary, the load on the metadata service is balanced and diverse; and response times are small in most cases.

the models. Under heavy load we observed a maximum *file_open()* time=585.38 seconds. As summarized above, this high response time is rare in practice. The goal of our study is to build a predictive model for expected output behaviors in practice with low benchmarking cost. Therefore, we discard the instances that take beyond 30 seconds for *file_open()*. We return to this topic in §5.3.

3.2 Output Behavior of the Other Stages

We conducted profiling experiments using a statistical benchmarking methodology proposed in [40]. This section sketches the methodology, the experiments and relative conclusions.

3.2.1 Statistical Benchmarking Methodology. The output behavior is derived from a set of experiments, each with a sequence of identical IOR *runs* based on *an experiment setting* consisting of a job script and an IOR configuration file. The job script gives the resource requirements (e.g., the number of nodes) and the job execution instructions specifying how to perform a sequence of IOR executions with varying sets of parameter values (Table 2) within the run. A set of parameter values is a *configuration set*. Each run consists of a sequence of identical *rounds*: a round consists of a sequence of IOR executions; each execution is an *instance* that measures the time for a synchronized output burst. The instances in a round have different configuration sets. Therefore, an experiment produces a set of instances for a configuration set, with one instance from each round. These instances run at different times and perhaps on different sets of compute nodes. Algorithm 1 presents the template of the job execution instructions.

Algorithm 1 The job script for IOR executions in an experiment
---
1: **number of Rounds:** Rounds = 1, 2, 3, ..., r
2: **Parameter 1:** $P_1 = \{p1_1, p1_2, ..., p1_i, ..., p1_l\}$
3: **Parameter 2:** $P_2 = \{p2_1, p2_2, ..., p2_j, ..., p2_m\}$
4: **for** Round: $1 \rightarrow r$ **do**
5:    **for** P1: $p1_1 \rightarrow p1_l$ **do**
6:       **for** P2: $p2_1 \rightarrow p2_m$ **do**
7:          execute $IOR -p1_i - p2_j$
8:          sleep 3
9:       **end for**
10:    **end for**
11: **end for**

3.2.2 Experiments. For each experiment, we use IOR as a burst generator: it coordinates P processes from m compute nodes with n cores each ($P = m \times n$) to write P bursts to disks. Each process runs on a different core and produces a burst of size K as a

new file with *stripe_width=W*. For each instance, we synchronize bursts before *write_start()* and measure the time from the minimum of *write_start()* to the maximum of *write_end()* among bursts. As discussed in §2.2, Lustre-based file systems support three configurable parameters: *stripe_size*, *stripe_width* and *starting_OST*. We found and reported in [40] that *stripe_size* doesn't affect output performance for its values in 1MB − 32MB, or leads to performance degradation for the values above 32MB. Thus, we choose 1MB as *stripe_size* and assign a randomly chosen OST as *starting_OST* across instances for all configuration sets in all experiments.

We conducted six experiments with varying parameters m, n, K, W (Table 2). The first five experiments ran on Titan and Widow1 [12, 13] from Jan. to Dec. 2013 and produced overall 116 configuration sets with 600 instances per set from 200 runs; the sixth experiment (*client-OST pairs 2*) ran on Titan and Atlas2 (§2.2) from May to June 2015 and produced 3 configuration sets with 1545 instances per set from 103 runs. We take two measures per instance: the aggregate bandwidth and the *effective bandwidth*. We assign an instance an effective bandwidth by normalizing its bandwidth to the maximum bandwidth received by identical instances from the same configuration set. The maximum bandwidth (*effective bandwidth=1*) represents the achievable bandwidth of the set under ideal conditions. We ran six types of experiments:

(1) Saturation of a client measures output performance from a single client to multiple storage targets (OSTs), varying burst sizes and the number of targets.

(2) Saturation of an OST probes the behavior of a single OST, in which processes from coordinated clients focus bursts on the same OST, varying the number of clients and burst sizes.

(3) Saturation of an OSS investigates the behavior of a single OSS by stressing the OSTs attached to it by varying the number of clients and burst sizes.

(4) Performance of Striping explores compute node performance variations on *stripe_width*. In this experiment, we vary burst sizes and *stripe_width*.

(5) Client-OST pairs 1 probes behavior of independent pipes by varying the number of pipes (client-OST pairs).

(6) Client-OST pairs 2 extends (5) by varying burst sizes.

3.2.3 Results and Conclusions. We report the benchmarking results in Figure 4 and Figure 5, and draw four major conclusions.
1. Performance Variability and Stability. We observed from all of the 119 configuration sets that the effective bandwidth varies significantly from instance to instance. However, Figure 4 suggests that the mean performance of each set converges rapidly to a steady state. It suggests that the mean output performance

Experiments	Performance-correlated Parameters			
Name	#nodes (m)	#cores (n)	burst_size (K)	stripe_width (W)
Saturation of a client	1	2, 4, 6, 7, 8, 10, 12, 14, 16	64MB, 256MB, 1GB, 4GB	1
Saturation of an OST	2, 4, 8, 16, 32, 64, 128	1	64MB, 256MB, 1GB	1
Saturation of an OSS*	2, 4, 7, 8, 14, 16, 28, 32, 56	1	7GB, 14GB, 28GB	1
Performance of striping	1	16	60MB, 240MB, 960MB	2, 4, 6, 8, 10, 12, 16, 32, 64
Client-OST pairs 1	50, 100, 200, 300, 336	1	64MB	1
Client-OST pairs 2	1008	1	16MB, 256MB, 4GB	1

Table 2: Varying parameters for the experiments. In an experiment, a varying parameter has multiple values. Each specific value set of varying parameters {m, n, K, W} is a *configuration set* (defined in §3.2.1) . This table presents overall 119 configuration sets from 6 experiments. *In Experiment *Saturation of an OSS*, each burst size reports the aggregate burst size across all engaged compute nodes.

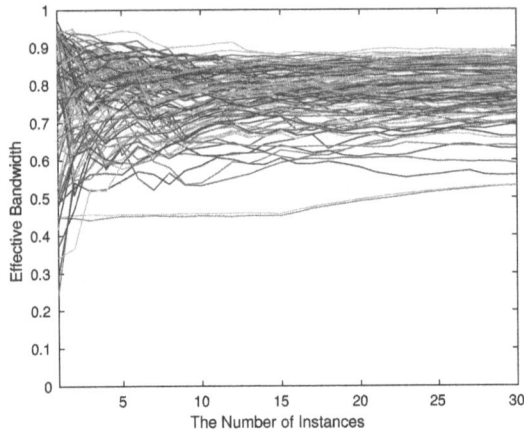

Figure 4: The Mean Effective Bandwidth across 119 configuration sets. Each line presents the data of the first 30 instances from one configuration set. In a line, each y value represents the mean effective bandwidth of the first x instances. It suggests that the mean performance converges to a steady state rapidly for all sets.

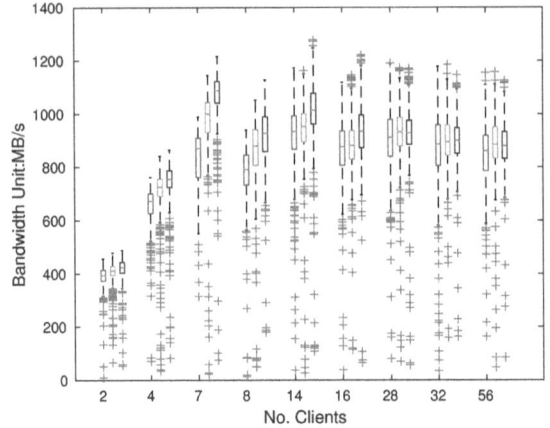

Figure 5: The Boxplots[1] of Experiment (3). In this figure, the x-axis represents the varying number of nodes; each x value has 3 boxplots reporting the bandwidths of 7GB, 14GB and 28GB aggregate burst sizes (see Table 2) from left to right respectively. It indicates that output performance is non-linearly related to the number of nodes and the burst size.

of scientific codes (§2.1) is stable and consistent after a few write operations/iterations.

2. Performance-correlated Parameters. Figure 5 presents the boxplots[1] of Experiment (3). It shows that output performance varies on m, K (Table 2). Experiments (1) and (4) (not reported) suggest that output performance also varies on n and W. We also categorized the effective bandwidths of specific *starting_OSTs* across 119 configuration sets, but we did not find a correlation between output performance and *starting_OSTs*. We conclude that output performance of Lustre-based file systems is correlated to m, n, K, W, as well as *stripe_size* (§3.2.2).

3. Behavior of Non-linearity. Figure 5 also suggests that when adding more clients or writing larger bursts, output bandwidth grows rapidly at the start, increases more and more slowly beyond a modest number of clients, and then declines after the saturation point. We also observed similar performance declines from other experiments (not reported), indicating that this behavior corresponds

---

[1]Each boxplot depicts the quartiles of the bandwidths of instances of a configuration set in an experiment: the bottom, the middle bar and the top of the box represents 0.25, 0.5 and 0.75 quartiles respectively; the box contains the middle 50% of samples (called *the interquartile range*, or IQR); the bottom and the top bars below and above the box report the sample bandwidths at the low and high 1.5 ×IQR respectively, the dots on both sides depict outliers.

to the peak bandwidth capacity of the hardware on individual stages. It suggests that output performance of multi-stage supercomputer file systems is likely to be non-linearly related to the performance-correlated parameters: feature transformation techniques [15] should be considered for models.

4. Noise. Figure 4 also shows that different configuration sets present different mean effective bandwidths. Sets that run during periods of high contention may receive lower mean effective bandwidths. By summarizing the 119 configuration sets, we find that: (1) the 119 configuration sets receive the mean effective bandwidths ranging from 0.52 to 0.89. (2) the noise is inversely correlated to the aggregate burst size ($\frac{1}{m \times n \times K}$): larger bursts tend to receive higher bandwidth. (3) the noise is positively correlated to m: sets with more compute nodes tend to receive lower effective bandwidth.

4 MODELING OUTPUT PERFORMANCE OF PETASCALE FILESYSTEMS

This section presents how to build performance predictive models for the target file system. In summary, we use machine learning techniques to model the end-to-end burst absorption time for various output patterns and I/O configurations. In a model, a time

Feature Name	Metadata Cost ($t_{metadata}$)	Titan Cost (t_{titan})		SION Cost (t_{sion})	Spider 2 Cost ($t_{spider2}$)*		Noise Cost (t_{noise})
		Node Cost (t_{node})	Router Cost (t_{router})		OSS Cost (t_{oss})	OST Cost (t_{ost})	
Feature Value	$m \times n$	$\frac{m \times n \times K}{m}$		$m \times n \times K$	$\frac{m \times n \times K}{M_{used}}$	$\frac{m \times n \times K}{N_{used}}$	$\frac{m}{m \times n \times K}$

Table 3: Features for the Output Performance Prediction Model. In this table, all features are addressed by the performance-correlated parameters (§3.2): $\{m, n, K, W\}$, following the definitions in Table 2. Moreover, both *Titan Cost* and *Spider 2 Cost* can be addressed by two types of features alternatively; *Noise Cost* is an optional feature. *: the feature value of $t_{spider2}$ is $\frac{m \times n \times K}{N_{used}}$.

represents the mean of write times (§3.2) of a configuration set (§3.2.1) across times, iterations and various system conditions.

We design features according to performance-correlated parameters (§2.2 and §3.2), transform them to address potential non-linear relationships between features and burst absorption time, introduce a semi-random sampling method to build training set, and propose a systematic modeling methodology to search for the best model from a linear model space.

Although the results are limited to the current Titan deployment and configuration, the selected features, methodology, and sampling method are applicable to other Lustre deployments. Other features may be important for alternative file system structures, but we expect our results to be representative of other parallel file systems in which individual write bursts spread evenly across their selected storage devices.

4.1 Features for a Multi-stage Write Path

In this study, a model describes burst absorption time as a function of *features* (independent variables). We choose features that reflect performance variations of individual stages of the target environment on performance-correlated parameters (§3.2).

Consider an output pattern of a program on a supercomputer that runs P processes/threads on m nodes with n cores per node: $P = m \times n$. The P processes produce P synchronous bursts with burst size K, each process traveling through the write path and eventually residing on disks as an independent file. The pattern is configured as: *stripe_width* = W (§3.2.2 and §3.2). Each specific value set for $\{m, n, K, W\}$ is a a *configuration set* (§3.2.1).

Therefore, a write operation of this configuration set produces $m \times n$ files and overall $m \times n \times K$ size of data. The data travels through stages of the write path: its end-to-end time can be computed by summing up its time consumption on separate stages (features). We list the features below and also present them in Table 3.

Metadata Cost ($t_{metadata}$) is positively correlated to the number of files produced by the configuration set: $t_{metadata} \sim m \times n$.

Titan Cost (t_{titan}). Figure 2 shows that the target write path has two stages in Titan: the compute nodes and the I/O nodes (routers). The number of used I/O nodes is determined by the number of used compute nodes (§2.2). Accordingly, we can design two types of features to address t_{titan}: (1) one feature: t_{titan}; (2) two features: t_{node} and t_{router}. All of these 3 features can be estimated by $\frac{m \times n \times K}{m}$.

SION Cost (t_{sion}) is positively correlated to the aggregate burst size: $t_{sion} \sim m \times n \times k$.

Spider 2 Cost ($t_{spider2}$). Figure 2 depicts two stages in Spider 2: OSSes and OSTs. The number of used OSSes (M_{used}) is determined by the number of used OSTs (N_{used}) (§2.2). Therefore, $t_{spider2}$ can be considered as two types of features: (1) one feature: $t_{spider2}$;

(2) two features: t_{oss} and t_{ost}. We can approximate $t_{spider2}$ and t_{ost} by $\frac{m \times n \times K}{N_{used}}$, and t_{oss} by $\frac{m \times n \times K}{M_{used}}$. Here, M_{used} and N_{used} can be computed for m, n, K, W from Formulas 4 and 5.

Noise Cost (t_{noise}). Since our target system is a production supercomputer, we consider the noise cost as an optional feature (§3.2): $t_{noise} \sim \frac{m}{m \times n \times K}$.

We can build a predictive model from any candidate feature set that combines these independent choices for features of the four stages in the target system: two choices for the Titan stage, two for the Spider 2 stage, and two for the optional Noise feature (include it or not). Therefore, there are 8 candidate feature sets. For example, we can choose a candidate feature set with 4 features: $\{t_{metadata}, t_{titan}, t_{sion}, t_{spider2}\}$, or a set with 5 features by replacing t_{titan} with t_{node} and t_{router}, or a set with 6 features by adding t_{noise}.

4.2 A Semi-random Sampling Method

A good training set for modeling output performance of a target system should cover the effects of varying key features. This section proposes a semi-random sampling method to build the training set with low cost and that satisfies three goals: (1) covers various configuration sets; (2) captures non-linear behaviors on the target machine (§3.2); (3) separates the stable behaviors of the configuration sets from the noise of samples in a production deployment.

To achieve these goals, we apply the statistical benchmarking methodology (§3.2). We use IOR as the burst generator, design a set of *model experiments*, and follow the experiment script template in Algorithm 1, with a few changes:

1. In an instance, we synchronize bursts before *file_open()* and measure the time from the minimum *file_open()* to the maximum *file_close()* among bursts.

2. We set *the number of Rounds*=1, fix m, and vary the other three performance-correlated parameters (Table 2): n, K and W.

3. For n, K, W in a setting, we produce a sequence of random values per parameter under certain constraints: (1) for n, we produce a fixed number of non-repeating random numbers in $1-16$. (2) for K and W, we first choose a value range, then partition the range into several continuous intervals, then produce a random number per interval (details in Table 5). This process yields configuration sets that are both representative and random.

4. For each configuration set, we produce a minimum number of instances to achieve its steady state by making the approximation on the mean observed time with some reasonable confidence interval. After a configuration set reaches its steady state, we take the mean across the observed times of its instances and consider the set with its mean time (t) as *a sample* for model training and validation.

Feature Transformation Function	$()^1$	$log()$	$()^{2/3}$	$()^{3/4}$	$()^{3/2}$
Transformed Feature	$m \times n$	$log(m \times n)$	$(m \times n)^{2/3}$	$(m \times n)^{3/4}$	$(m \times n)^{3/2}$

Table 4: Feature Transformation Functions. We use 4 types of common transformation functions (row 1, column $3 - 6$). Therefore, for each feature, e.g., Metadata Cost (row2), we produce 5 types of *transformed features*: its original feature and other 4 features transformed by 4 transformation functions respectively.

4.3 A Systematic Modeling Methodology

In this section, we search for the best predictive model from a linear model space built on top of the 8 candidate feature sets (§4.1) with feature transformation.

4.3.1 Feature Transformation. Feature transformation, also called *feature engineering*, represents a group of methods (functions) that transform a feature to new features for addressing the underlying nonlinear relationships between features and the target. In this study, we use this technique to depict the potential nonlinear relationships observed from the target environment (§3.2). For each feature across the 8 candidate feature sets, we take its original form and also apply 4 common transformation functions on it. Thus, for each feature we produce overall 5 types of *transformed features*, shown as Table 4.

A predictive model is built on *a transformed feature set*. Since each feature has 5 transformed features, each of the 8 candidate feature sets produces $5^{\wedge \#features}$ models, in which *#features* represents the number of original features in the feature set. In summary, we search for the best model from a model space with overall 135,000 candidate models.

4.3.2 Training a Model. This section presents how to train a model by using machine learning techniques. Consider a transformed feature set that consists of y transformed features $\{TF_1, TF_2, ..., TF_y\}$. For the target t', we build the linear model as:

$$t' = \alpha_0 + \sum_{j=1}^{y} \alpha_j \times TF_j \qquad (6)$$

α_0 is the intercept, α_j is the coefficient of TF_j. In this study, training a model means locating $< \alpha_0, \alpha_1, \alpha_2, ..., \alpha_y >$ for a transformed feature set $\{TF_1, TF_2, ..., TF_y\}$. Presume that a training set has x samples and transformed set is $\{TF_1, TF_2, ..., TF_y\}$. We use *LinearRegression()* method from scikit-learn toolkit [34] to train the model.

The most intuitive approach is to feed the training set directly to *LinearRegression()*, yielding a value set for $< \alpha_0, \alpha_1, \alpha_2, ..., \alpha_y >$. We adopt two techniques to improve result quality: *10-fold cross validation* [15, 34] and mean square error (*MSE*).

10-Fold Cross Validation is an important technique to evaluate model accuracy. It partitions the training set into 10 equal-size subsets with 9 subsets merged for training and the last one used as the *validation set*: it produces the intercept and coefficients for a model by training the merged 9 subsets and receives a model accuracy measurement by testing it on the validation set. In our

study, the entire cross validation process repeats *LinearRegression()* 10 times on the same training set by rotating the validation set across its 10 subsets; for each *LinearRegression()*, it produces a value set for $< \alpha_0, \alpha_1, \alpha_2, ..., \alpha_y >$ and also receives an accuracy measurement. Therefore, a trained model has 10 value sets for $< \alpha_0, \alpha_1, \alpha_2, ..., \alpha_y >$ and 10 accuracy measurements. We choose *MSE* as the accuracy metric and take the mean values for both intercept/coefficients and *MSE* for the model, shown as Formulas 7 and 8. In the Formulas, i represents the ith *LinearRegression()* outputs in a model training process.

$$< \alpha'_0, \alpha'_1, ..., \alpha'_y > = < \frac{\sum_{i=1}^{10} \alpha_{i0}}{10}, \frac{\sum_{i=1}^{10} \alpha_{i1}}{10}, ..., \frac{\sum_{i=1}^{10} \alpha_{iy}}{10} > \qquad (7)$$

$$MSE' = \frac{\sum_{i=1}^{10} MSE_i}{10} \qquad (8)$$

Mean Square Error is an error estimator that is widely used to quantify accuracy of regression models. Specifically, we use it to measure accuracy of each trained model: in the ith *LinearRegression()*, we feed the validation set to the trained model and get a prediction result set $< t'_1, t'_2, ..., t'_{\frac{x}{10}} >$. If the means of the observed times on the validation set are $< t_1, t_2, ..., t_{\frac{x}{10}} >$, then we compute the ith model accuracy metric: MSE_i, shown in Formula 9.

$$MSE_i = \sum_{j=1}^{\frac{x}{10}} (t'_j - t_j)^2 \qquad (9)$$

In summary, a trained model is composed of $\{TF_1, ..., TF_y\}$, $< \alpha'_0, \alpha'_1, ..., \alpha'_y >$ and MSE'.

Algorithm 2 Searching for the best model

1: **The Training Set**
2: **Candidate Feature Sets:** $\{t_{metadata}, ..., t_{spider2}\}, ...$
3: **Transformed Feature Sets:**..., $\{TF_1, ..., TF_y\}, ...$
4: **for** Candidate Feature Set: $1 \rightarrow 8$ **do**
5:     **for** Transformed Feature Set: $1 \rightarrow 5^{\wedge \#features}$ **do**
6:         *10-fold cross validation*
7:         The training set, *LinearRegression()*
8:         $\rightarrow < \alpha'_0, \alpha'_1, ..., \alpha'_y >, MSE'$
9:         **if** $MSE' < MSE_{min}$ **then**
10:             $\{TF_1, ..., TF_l\}^* = \{TF_1, ..., TF_y\}$
11:             $< \alpha'_0, \alpha'_1, ..., \alpha'_l >^* = < \alpha'_0, \alpha'_1, ..., \alpha'_y >$
12:             $MSE_{min} = MSE'$
13:         **end if**
14:     **end for**
15: **end for**

4.3.3 Searching for the Best Model. For each pair of trained models, we select one model as better if its MSE' is smaller than the other. Following this rule, we search for the best model with minimum MSE' from a linear model space with 135,000 candidate models (§4.3.2).

Scale (m)	Cores per Node (n)	Burst Size (K)	stripe_width ((W))
1, 2, 4, 8, 16, 32, 64, 128, 256, 512, 800	8 from 16	1MB—5MB, 6MB—25MB, 25MB—100MB, 101MB—250MB, 251MB—500MB, 501MB—1024MB, 1025MB—2560MB	1—4, 5—8, 9—16, 17—32, 33—64
1, 2, 4, 8, 16, 32, 64, 128	4 from 16	2561MB—5120MB, 5121MB—7680MB, 7681MB—10240MB	1—4, 5—8, 9—16, 17—32, 33—64

Table 5: Template for the small-scale and medium-scale samples following the sampling method in §4.2. The setting in row1 produces 11 model experiment settings: each examines on m nodes, varies n cores as 8 non-repeating random numbers in $1 - 16$, changes K on 7 random numbers with each from one of 7 continuous intervals, and alters W on 5 random numbers with each from one of 5 continuous intervals. Therefore, each setting in row1 produces $8 \times 7 \times 5$ samples; the setting in row2 follows the same rule and has 8 model experiment settings, each producing $4 \times 3 \times 5$ samples.

Consider the best model has l features: $\{TF_1, ..., TF_l\}^*$, $< \alpha'_0, \alpha'_1, ..., \alpha'_l >^*$ and MSE_{min}. At the initial state, $\{TF_1, ..., TF_l\}^* = \{\}$, $< \alpha'_0, \alpha'_1, ..., \alpha'_l >^* = <>$, $MSE_{min} = +\infty$. The searching process is shown as Algorithm 2.

5 EXPERIMENTS

This section evaluates our systematic machine learning analysis on Titan/Atlas2. We collected measures for IOR bursts with varying parameters for use as a dataset for training and validation. These bursts ran on Titan at scales up to 16K cores (1000 nodes) from Aug. 2016 to Jan. 2017.

5.1 Experiment Data

Output bandwidth is a scarce resource on supercomputers; large scale write operations are expensive. To generate models with low cost, we chose to focus on training models with *small-scale* writes (≤ 128 nodes) and testing them on *medium-scale* writes (256—800 nodes) supplemented with a modest set of measures from *large-scale* writes (=1000 nodes) with representative output patterns.

Consequently, we produce experiment data according to two templates: (1) for the small-scale and medium-scale samples, we follow the semi-random sampling method (§4.2) and choose intervals for n, K, W, focusing on typical output patterns and I/O configurations observed from production use; (2) for the large-scale samples, we use output patterns characteristic of production codes, including XGC (§2.1.1), PlasmaPhysics, Turbulence1, Turbulence2 and AstroPhysics reported in [21]. We produced overall 3578 samples. Tables 5 and 6 present details of the two templates respectively.

5.2 Model Evaluation

This section evaluates: (1) effectiveness of the features (§4.1), (2) usefulness of feature transformation (Table 4), and (3) accuracy of the model located by the systematic modeling methodology (§4.3).

To this end, we use a training set with 2720 samples produced by $1 - 128$ nodes according to the two settings in Table 5; we

Scale (m)	<cores per node, burst_size> ($< n, K >$)	stripe_width (W)
1000	<1, 59MB>, <4, 69MB>, <4, 4MB>, <4, 1024MB>, <16, 23MB>, <16, 121MB>, <16, 376MB>, <16, 750MB>, <16, 1280MB>	4, 5—100

Table 6: Template for the large-scale samples. This template mimics the output patterns of XGC and other sample production codes in [21], in which $< n, K >$ are given. We choose 2 *stripe_width* for each pattern: *stripe_width=4* (Titan's default configuration) and *stripe_width = a random number* in $5 - 100$ (typical configurations). This template produces overall 18 samples.

perform the systematic modeling methodology on 135,000 models across 8 candidate feature sets (§4.1) and pinpoint the model ($Model_{best}$) with MSE_{min}; we also process the methodology on 625 (5^4) models from the candidate feature set with 4 features and locate the best model ($Model_{local\_best}$) for the set; we train the model ($Model_{original}$) from the $Model_{best}$'s candidate feature set and with all original features. In summary, we address three models: $Model_{best}$, $Model_{local\_best}$, $Model_{original}$, shown in Table 7. Besides presenting models, Table 7 also reports the cost consumed to generate a group of models and select the best from the group: for $Model_{best}$ and $Model_{local\_best}$, the cost includes the time to train all models from the space of 135,000 candidate models and the space with 625 models respectively; for $Model_{original}$, the cost is the time to train the single model.

We use *relative true error* (ϵ) to quantify model accuracy. If the observed mean write time of the ith sample is t_i and its prediction result is t'_i then its ϵ_i is:

$$\epsilon_i = \frac{t'_i - t_i}{t_i} \qquad (10)$$

Thus, $\epsilon_i > 0$ suggests that t_i is over estimated; $\epsilon_i < 0$ suggests that t_i is under estimated; $\|\epsilon_i\|$ quantifies prediction accuracy: smaller $\|\epsilon_i\|$ indicates higher accuracy. We focus on two thresholds: $\|\epsilon\|=0.2$ and $= 0.3$.

We evaluate $Model_{best}$, $Model_{local\_best}$ and $Model_{original}$ on 4 test sets, plot the results in Figures 6 and 7, and draw 4 major conclusions below.

1. The identified features are effective predictors of output burst performance. Figure 6 shows that, for a model on a test set with $t \geq 5$, 63.28% — 96.51% and 76.84% — 98.84% of samples report $\|\epsilon\| \leq 0.2$ and ≤ 0.3 respectively. Similarly, Figure 7 shows that, for a model with $t \geq 5$, 43.75% — 56.25% and 62.5%—75% of samples report $\|\epsilon\| \leq 0.2$ and ≤ 0.3 respectively. It suggests that all 3 models are generally accurate across all 4 test sets if a write operation takes ≥ 5 seconds: the features we choose are effective to capture output behavior of the target environment.

2. Feature transformation is useful. Figures 6 and 7 also suggest that $Model_{best}$ is generally more accurate than $Model_{original}$ for all 4 test sets: feature transformation is useful to address non-linear relationships between output performance and its features under linear regression.

3. The modeling methodology identifies good models. For $t \geq 5$, $Model_{best}$ is most accurate for all 4 test sets. Moreover, for $Model_{best}$ on a test set with $t \geq 5$ in Figure 6, 83.05% — 96.51%

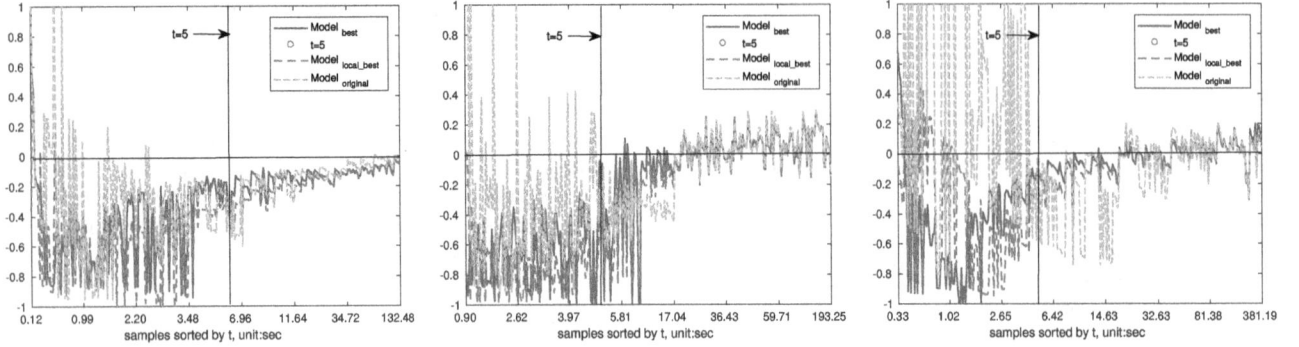

Figure 6: Model Evaluation. From left to right, 3 subfigures present accuracy of the models (Table 7) on 3 test sets produced by 256, 512 and 800 nodes separately by following the row1 template in Table 5. Each test set has 280 samples; in each subfigure, a line plots 280 error measures (ϵ) for a model on a test set; in a line, samples are sorted along the x-axis based on the observed mean write time (t). It suggests that, $Model_{best}$ is generally most accurate for all 3 test sets for $t \geq 5$.

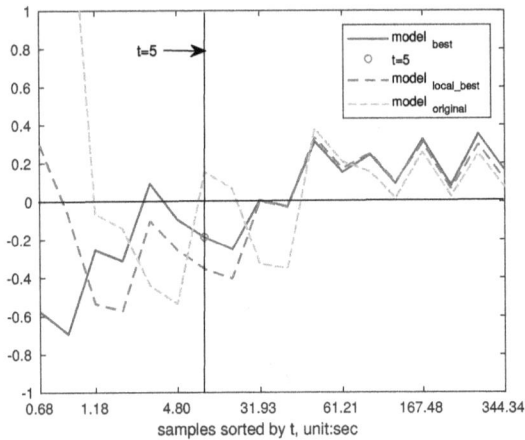

Figure 7: Model Validation on the large-scale samples. The test set has 18 samples; a line plots 18 error measures (ϵ) for a model; in a line, samples are sorted along the x-axis based on the observed mean write time (t). It suggests that $Model_{best}$ is generally most accurate.

and 89.83% − 98.84% of samples report $\|\epsilon\| \leq 0.2$ and ≤ 0.3 respectively; for $Model_{best}$ in Figure 7, 56.25% and 75% of such samples report $\|\epsilon\| \leq 0.2$ and ≤ 0.3 respectively. It suggests that the methodology locates the best model from the model space; the best model is highly accurate.

4. Limitations. When $t < 5$, all models are less accurate. This is likely results from two issues: (1) Titan is noisy. For short bursts, highly parallel writes are vulnerable to transient system conditions that are less likely to be reflected in the small-scale samples in the training set. (2) Error estimator biases to longer bursts. According to Formula 9, the model searching process searches for the model with minimum $\sum (t' - t)^2$. Therefore, it tends to identify models that perform well for samples with large t. We leave the followup study on this as our future work.

5.3 Metadata Anomaly

To address the expected behavior of Titan/Atlas2, we decided to discard the anomalous instances given how rarely they occur. An instance is considered anomalous if it consumes > 30 seconds on *file_open()* (§3.1). The 35,404 instances in our benchmark data showed 17 anomalous instances. These occurred across a range of configurations and scales (number of nodes, cores, and files) with no detectable pattern. It is possible that a larger dataset would reveal a correlation with scale. We leave a more detailed study for future work.

6 RELATED WORK

Related studies fall into three categories: quantitative I/O performance studies, novel techniques to improve performance, and I/O middleware systems.

1. I/O Performance Studies. Researchers started profiling supercomputer filesystems under production loads in the 1990s [28], [14],[29], [10], [9]. More recently, the Darshan team from Argonne National Lab [3, 26] investigates the I/O behavior of supercomputer platforms by analyzing logs and traces collected by continuous monitoring software installed on compute nodes. [40] and [37] adopt statistical benchmarking methods to analyze I/O behavior of parallel filesystem deployments, and identify factors that can slow down striped I/O operations. [22, 25] also study the I/O performance of Lustre-based file systems: [22] probes the application behaviors by analyzing server side I/O logs, while [25] explores factors inhibiting I/O performance on scientific codes with MPI-IO. Kim et al. [18] studies the combined application behavior on the server side by monitoring the performance of storage servers.

2. Techniques to Improve I/O Performance. Researchers have explored several techniques to improve the performance of Lustre-based file systems: multi-threading in the compute node client OSC [35], asynchronous journaling [32] in the server OSS, and fine-grained load balancing across I/O routers [13]. Another group of studies focuses on reducing the cost of metadata operations [23, 33].

Model Name	Cost	Intercept	$t_{metadata}$	t_{node} (t_{titan}*)	t_{router}	t_{sion}	t_{oss}	t_{ost} ($t_{spider2}$*)	t_{noise}
$Model_{best}$	44.46 minutes	0.65	-0.19	0.005	4.64^{-7}	1.00^{-9}	0.002	0.15	-0.58
			log()	()$^{3/4}$	()$^{3/2}$	()$^{3/2}$	()^{1}	log()	()$^{3/2}$
$Model_{local\_best}$	0.18 minute	3.04	-0.51	0.0004		1.65^{-5}		1.32^{-5}	
			log()	()^{1}		()^{1}		()$^{3/2}$	
$Model_{original}$	0.0003 minute	1.03	-0.001	0.0002	0.0002	-4.13^{-6}	0.003	-0.0004	-2.16
			()^{1}	()^{1}	()^{1}	()^{1}	()^{1}	()^{1}	()^{1}

Table 7: Three Trained Models defined in §5.2. In this table, features are defined in §4.1 and given in Table 3; $Model_{best}$ and $Model_{original}$ have the same 7 features with different feature transformation functions; $Model_{local\_best}$ has 4 features. For each model, we report its cost, intercept and features; for each feature (column 4-10), we report its name, coefficient (a numeric value) and feature transformation function (Table 4). *: $Model_{local\_best}$'s features.

3. I/O Middleware Systems. I/O middleware systems provide a high-level I/O API for applications and adapts I/O patterns and configurations automatically to improve I/O performance. ADIOS [8, 20, 24] is a widely used I/O middleware system for HPC applications on supercomputers. Our work is complementary to middleware systems: for example, they can use I/O system performance profiles and prediction results to guide their configuration choices and adapt I/O patterns.

Studies on cloud and data center workloads have investigated machine learning techniques to predict performance. For example, [38] and [11] adopt linear regression and SVD (*Singular Value Decomposition*) separately to predict end-to-end application execution time and drive co-scheduling choices. Compared to their works, we address an I/O system that provides massively parallel I/O for individual HPC applications, and apply a systematic modeling methodology for the multi-stage write path in a petascale I/O deployment under production load. To our knowledge our work is the first to apply machine learning regression models to analyze and predict I/O performance for HPC systems and applications.

7 CONCLUSION

Scientific codes generate periodic parallel output bursts in regular patterns. We propose a statistical approach to benchmark a production petascale I/O system and learn performance models that can predict output performance seen by applications. We show that accurate models can be learned based on a few key features of the deployment and I/O configuration parameters. Our premise is that accurate prediction models can guide configuration choices to reduce I/O cost, and also provide better information to the global scheduler, which can use this information to improve resource utilization.

The major obstacle to building the quantitative I/O analysis on petascale filesystems is the high degree of performance variability in production deployments. We find that although the output performance of petascale filesystems is highly variable, the mean performance for sufficiently large bursts is predictable.

This paper develops a regression approach to predict output performance of petascale filesystems under production load, focusing on the mean write time. We select and transform features to capture the properties of the target multi-stage write path and their impact on I/O performance. We introduce a semi-random sampling method to generate performance datasets to train the models

with low benchmarking cost. A systematic modeling methodology obtains the best model from a rich model space of features and transformations. The results suggest that the model is sufficiently accurate to predict performance for sufficiently large write bursts in practice. The key limitation is that small bursts are vulnerable to transient contention, and so are difficult to predict accurately.

8 ACKNOWLEDGMENTS

We are thankful to the anonymous reviewers and our shepherd Gabriel Antoniu for their invaluable feedback; to Choong-Seock Chang and Randy M. Churchill from PPPL for their help on understanding XGC; to Chris Zimmer and Matt Ezell from OLCF for their detailed explanations on Titan and Spider 2; to Norbert Podhorszki from ORNL and Philip Carns from ANL for their advice on I/O behavior of HPC codes; to Sayan Mukherjee at Duke for helpful suggestions on machine learning techniques; to Suzanne T. Parete-Koon at ORNL for her help on arranging Titan time for experiments.

This work was supported by the U.S. Department of Energy, under FWP 16-018666, program manager Lucy Nowell. The work used resources of the Oak Ridge Leadership Computing Facility, located in the National Center for Computational Sciences at the Oak Ridge National Laboratory, which is supported by the Office of Science of the Department of Energy under Contract DE-AC05-00OR22725. Sandia National Laboratories is a multi-program laboratory managed and operated by Sandia Corporation, a wholly owned subsidiary of Lockheed Martin Corporation, for the U.S. Department of Energy's National Nuclear Security Administration under contract DE-AC04-94AL85000.

REFERENCES

[1] M. Berger and J. Oliger. 1984. Adaptive mesh refinement for hyperbolic partial differential equations. *Journal of computational Physics* 53, 3 (1984), 484–512.
[2] P. Carns, K. Harms, W. Allcock, C. Bacon, S. Lang, R. Latham, and R. Ross. 2011. Understanding and improving computational science storage access through continuous characterization. *ACM Transactions on Storage (TOS)* 7, 3 (2011), 8–26.
[3] P. Carns, R. Latham, R. Ross, K. Iskra, S. Lang, and K. Riley. 2009. 24/7 characterization of petascale I/O workloads. In *Proceedings of 2009 IEEE International Conference on Cluster Computing (Cluster'09)*. IEEE, New Orleans, LA, 1–10.
[4] L. Chacón. 2004. A non-staggered, conservative, finite-volume scheme for 3D implicit extended magnetohydrodynamics in curvilinear geometries. *Computer Physics Communications* 163, 3 (2004), 143 – 171.
[5] C. S. Chang, S. Klasky, J. Cummings, R. Samtaney, A. Shoshani, L. Sugiyama, D. Keyes, S. Ku, G. Park, S. Parker, and others. 2008. Toward a first-principles integrated simulation of tokamak edge plasmas. *Journal of Physics: Conference Series* 125, 1 (2008), 012042.

[6] C. S. Chang and S. Ku. 2008. Spontaneous rotation sources in a quiescent tokamak edge plasma. *Physics of Plasmas* 15, 6 (2008), 062510.

[7] J. H. Chen, A. Choudhary, B. de Supinski, M. DeVries, E. R. Hawkes, S. Klasky, W. Liao, K. Ma, J. Mellor-Crummey, N. Podhorszki, R. Sankaran, S. Shende, and C. Yoo. 2009. Terascale direct numerical simulations of turbulent combustion using S3D. *Computational Science & Discovery* 2, 1 (2009), 015001.

[8] A. Choudhary, W. Liao, K. Gao, A. Nisar, R. Ross, R. Thakur, and R. Latham. 2009. Scalable I/O and analytics. *Journal of Physics: Conference Series* 180, 1 (2009), 012048.

[9] P. E. Crandall, R. A. Aydt, A. A. Chien, and D. A. Reed. 1995. Input/Output characteristics of scalable parallel applications. In *Proceedings of the ACM/IEEE Conference on Supercomputing (SC'95)*. ACM, San Diego, CA, 59–89.

[10] R. Cypher, A. Ho, S. Konstantinidou, and P. Messina. 1993. Architectural requirements of parallel scientific applications with explicit communication. In *Proceedings of the 20th Annual International Symposium on Computer Architecture (ISCA'93)*. ACM, San Diego, CA, 2–13.

[11] C. Delimitrou and C. Kozyrakis. 2013. Paragon: QoS-aware scheduling for heterogeneous datacenters. In *Proceedings of the 18th ACM International Conference on Architectural Support for Programming Languages and Operating Systems (ASPLOS'13)*. ATM, Houston, TX, 77–88.

[12] D. A. Dillow, G. M. Shipman, S. Oral, Z. Zhang, and Y. Kim. 2011. Enhancing I/O throughput via efficient routing and placement for large-scale parallel file systems. In *Proceedings of the 30th IEEE International Performance Computing and Communications Conference (IPCCC'11)*. IEEE, Orlando, FL, 21–29.

[13] M. Ezell, S. Oral, F. Wang, D. Tiwari, D. Maxwell, D. Leverman, and J. Hill. 2014. I/O router placement and fine-grained routing on Titan to support Spider II. In *Proceedings of the Cray User Group Conference (CUG'14)*. cug.org, Lugano, Switzerland, 1–6.

[14] G. R. Ganger. 1995. Generating representative synthetic workloads: an unsolved problem. In *Proceedings of the Computer Measurement Group Conference (CMG'95)*. CMG, Nashville, TN, 1263–1269.

[15] J. Han, J. Pei, and M. Kamber. 2011. *Data mining: concepts and techniques* (3 ed.). Morgan Kaufmann, Waltham, MA.

[16] Y. Kim, S. Atchley, G. Vallée, and G. Shipman. 2015. LADS: optimizing data transfers using layout-aware data scheduling. In *Proceedings of the 13th USENIX Conference on File and Storage Technologies (FAST'15)*. USENIX, Santa Clara, CA, 67–80.

[17] Y. Kim and R. Gunasekaran. 2014. Understanding I/O workload characteristics of a peta-scale storage system. *The Journal of Supercomputing* 71, 3 (2014), 761–780.

[18] Y. Kim, R. Gunasekaran, G. M. Shipman, D. A. Dillow, Z. Zhang, and B. W. Settlemyer. 2010. Workload characterization of a leadership class storage cluster. In *Proceedings of the 5th Petascale Data Storage Workshop (PDSW'10)*. ACM, New Orleans, LA, 1–5.

[19] S. Klasky, S. Ethier, Z. Lin, K. Martins, D. McCune, and R. Samtaney. 2003. Grid-based parallel data streaming implemented for the Gyrokinetic Toroidal Code. In *Proceedings of the ACM/IEEE International Conference on High Performance Computing, Networking, Storage and Analysis (SC'03)*. IEEE, Phoenix, AZ, 24–36.

[20] S. Kumar, J. Edwards, P.-T. Bremer, A. Knoll, C. Christensen, V. Vishwanath, P. Carns, J. A. Schmidt, and V. Pascucci. 2014. Efficient I/O and storage of adaptive-resolution data. In *Proceedings of the ACM/IEEE International Conference for High Performance Computing, Networking, Storage and Analysis (SC'14)*. ACM, New Orleans, LA, 413–423.

[21] N. Liu, J. Cope, P. Carns, C. Carothers, R. Ross, G. Grider, A. Crume, and C. Maltzahn. 2012. On the role of burst buffers in leadership-class storage systems. In *Proceedings of the 28th IEEE Conference on Massive Data Storage (MSST'12)*. IEEE, Long Beach, CA, 1–11.

[22] Y. Liu, R. Gunasekaran, X. Ma, and S. S. Vazhkudai. 2014. Automatic identification of application I/O signatures from noisy server-side traces. In *Proceedings of the 12th USENIX Conference on File and Storage Technologies (FAST'14)*. USENIX, Santa Clara, CA, 213–228.

[23] J. Lofstead, F. Zheng, S. Klasky, and K. Schwan. 2009. Adaptable, metadata-rich I/O methods for portable high performance I/O. In *Proceedings of the 23rd IEEE International Parallel & Distributed Processing Symposium (IPDPS'09)*. IEEE, Rome, Italy, 1–10.

[24] J. Lofstead, F. Zheng, Q. Liu, S. Klasky, R. Oldfield, T. Kordenbrock, K. Schwan, and M. Wolf. 2010. Managing variability in the I/O performance of petascale storage systems. In *Proceedings of the ACM/IEEE International Conference for High Performance Computing, Networking, Storage and Analysis (SC'10)*. ACM, Washington, DC, 1–12.

[25] J. Logan and P. Dickens. 2008. Towards an understanding of the performance of MPI-IO in Lustre file systems. In *Proceedings of the IEEE International Conference on Cluster Computing (CLUSTER'08)*. IEEE, Tsukuba, Japan, 330–335.

[26] H. Luu, M. Winslett, W. Gropp, R. Ross, P. Carns, K. Harms, M. Prabhat, S. Byna, and Y. Yao. 2015. A multiplatform study of I/O behavior on petascale supercomputers. In *Proceedings of the 24th International Symposium on High-Performance Parallel and Distributed Computing (HPDC'15)*. ACM, Portland, OR, 33–44.

[27] R. Miller, J. Hill, D. A. Dillow, R. Gunasekaran, G. Shipman, and D. Maxwell. 2010. Monitoring tools for large scale systems. In *Proceedings of Cray User Group Conference (CUG'10)*. cug.org, Edinburgh, 1–4.

[28] A. L. Narasimha Reddy and P. Banerjee. 1990. A study of I/O behavior of perfect benchmarks on a multiprocessor. In *Proceedings of the 17th Annual International Symposium on Computer Architecture (ISCA'90)*. ACM, Seattle, WA, 312–321.

[29] N. Nieuwejaar, D. Kotz, A. Purakayastha, C. S. Ellis, and M. L. Best. 1996. File-access characteristics of parallel scientific workloads. *IEEE Trans. on Parallel and Distributed Systems* 7, 10 (1996), 1075–1089.

[30] S. Oral, D. A. Dillow, D. Fuller, J. Hill, D. Leverman, S. S. Vazhkudai, F. Wang, Y. Kim, J. Rogers, J. Simmons, and R. Miller. 2013. OLCF's 1 TB/s, next-generation Lustre file system. In *Proceedings of The Cray User Group Conference (CUG'13)*. cug.org, Napa, California, 1–14.

[31] S. Oral, J. Simmons, J. Hill, D. Leverman, F. Wang, M. Ezell, R. Miller, D. Fuller, R. Gunasekaran, Y. Kim, S. Gupta, D. Tiwari, S. S. Vazhkudai, J. H. Rogers, D. Dillow, G. M. Shipman, and A. S. Bland. 2014. Best practices and lessons learned from deploying and operating large-scale data-centric parallel file systems. In *Proceedings of the ACM/IEEE International Conference for High Performance Computing, Networking, Storage and Analysis (SC'14)*. ACM, New Orleans, LA, 217–228.

[32] S. Oral, F. Wang, D. Dillow, G. Shipman, R. Miller, and O. Drokin. 2010. Efficient object storage journaling in a distributed parallel file system. In *Proceedings of the 8th USENIX Conference on File and Storage Technologies (FAST'10)*. USENIX, San Jose, CA, 143–154.

[33] K. Ren, Q. Zheng, S. Patil, and G. Gibson. 2014. IndexFS: scaling file system metadata performance with stateless caching and bulk insertion. In *Proceedings of the ACM/IEEE International Conference for High Performance Computing, Networking, Storage and Analysis (SC'14)*. ACM, New Orleans, LA, 237–248.

[34] scikit learn. 2016. scikit-learn:machine learning in Python. http://scikit-learn.org/. (2016). Accessed: 2016-08-29.

[35] G. Shipman, D. Dillow, D. Fuller, R. Gunasekaran, J. Hill, Y. Kim, S. Oral, D. Reitz, J. Simmons, and F. Wang. 2012. A next-generation parallel file system environment for the OLCF. In *Proceedings of the Cray User Group Conference (CUG'12)*. cug.org, Stuttgart, Germany, 1–12.

[36] E. Strohmaier, J. Dongarra, H. Simon, and M. Meuer. 2016. Top500 supercomputer sites. http://www.top500.org. (2016). Accessed: 2016-08-11.

[37] A. Uselton, M. Howison, N. J. Wright, D. Skinner, N. Keen, J. Shalf, K. L. Karavanic, and L. Oliker. 2010. Parallel I/O performance: from events to ensembles. In *Proceedings of the 24th IEEE International Parallel & Distributed Processing Symposium (IPDPS'10)*. IEEE, Atlanta, GA, 1–11.

[38] S. Venkataraman, Z. Yang, M. Franklin, B. Recht, and I. Stoica. 2016. Ernest: efficient performance prediction for large-scale advanced analytics. In *Proceedings of the 13th USENIX Symposium on Networked Systems Design and Implementation (NSDI'16)*. USENIX, Santa Clara, CA, 363–378.

[39] F. Wang, S. Oral, G. Shipman, O. Drokin, T. Wang, and I. Huang. 2009. Understanding Lustre filesystem internals. *Technical Report ORNL TM-2009*, 117 (2009), 1–80.

[40] B. Xie, J. Chase, D. Dillow, O. Drokin, S. Klasky, S. Oral, and N. Podhorszki. 2012. Characterizing output bottlenecks in a supercomputer. In *Proceedings of the ACM/IEEE International Conference for High Performance Computing, Networking, Storage and Analysis (SC'12)*. IEEE Computer Society Press, Salt Lake City, UT, 1–11.

TCP Throughput Profiles Using Measurements Over Dedicated Connections

Nageswara S.V. Rao, Qiang Liu,
Satyabrata Sen
Oak Ridge National Laboratory
Oak Ridge, TN 37831, USA
{raons,liuq1,sens}@ornl.gov

Don Towsley
Gayane Vardoyan
University of Massachusetts
Amherst, MA 01003, USA
{towsley,gvardoyan}@cs.umass.edu

Raj Kettimuthu
Ian Foster
Argonne National Laboratory
Argonne, IL 60439, USA
{kettimut,foster}@mcs.anl.gov

ABSTRACT

Wide-area data transfers in high-performance computing infrastructures are increasingly being carried over dynamically provisioned dedicated network connections that provide high capacities with no competing traffic. We present extensive TCP throughput measurements and time traces over a suite of physical and emulated 10 Gbps connections with 0-366 ms round-trip times (RTTs). Contrary to the general expectation, they show significant statistical and temporal variations, in addition to the overall dependencies on the congestion control mechanism, buffer size, and the number of parallel streams. We analyze several throughput profiles that have highly desirable concave regions wherein the throughput decreases slowly with RTTs, in stark contrast to the convex profiles predicted by various TCP analytical models. We present a generic throughput model that abstracts the ramp-up and sustainment phases of TCP flows, which provides insights into qualitative trends observed in measurements across TCP variants: (i) slow-start followed by well-sustained throughput leads to concave regions; (ii) large buffers and multiple parallel streams expand the concave regions in addition to improving the throughput; and (iii) stable throughput dynamics, indicated by a smoother Poincaré map and smaller Lyapunov exponents, lead to wider concave regions. These measurements and analytical results together enable us to select a TCP variant and its parameters for a given connection to achieve high throughput with statistical guarantees.

CCS CONCEPTS

•Networks →Network performance analysis; Transport protocols;

KEYWORDS

Transport protocols, TCP, dedicated connection, throughput profile, monotonicity, concavity, throughput dynamics, Poincaré map, Lyapunov exponent

HPDC '17, June 26-30, 2017, Washington, DC, USA
© 2017 ACM. 978-1-4503-4699-3/17/06...$15.00
DOI: http://dx.doi.org/10.1145/3078597.3078615

1 INTRODUCTION

Wide-area data transfers over dedicated connections are becoming increasingly important in a variety of scenarios, including multi-site cloud computing server complexes, High-Performance Computing (HPC) workflows, and distributed big data computing facilities [19]. In particular, memory-to-memory transfers are critical to applications such as computations coordinated over cloud servers at geographically dispersed sites, and on-going computations on supercomputers steered by remote analysis and visualization codes. To support such data transfers, network infrastructures, such as Department of Energy's (DOE) ESnet [8] and Google's Software Defined Network (SDN) [11], provide on-demand, dedicated connections. They are expected to provide predictable performance, thereby making it easier to achieve effective and optimized data transfers over them, compared to shared connections.

The dedicated connections play a particularly important role in data transfers between geographically distributed HPC sites, since they are unimpeded by other traffic. Within the DOE HPC infrastructure, special purpose Data Transfer Nodes (DTN) [7] are installed to take advantage of the dedicated OSCARS circuits [17] provisioned over ESnet. Furthermore, Lustre over Ethernet enables file systems to be mounted across long-haul links [2], thereby overcoming the 2.5 ms latency limitation of Infiniband [25]; this approach provides file access over wide area without requiring special transfer tools such as GridFTP [28], XDD [21, 30], or hardware IB range extenders [1, 16, 23]. It is generally expected that the underlying Transmission Control Protocol (TCP) flows over dedicated connections provide peak throughput and stable dynamics that are critical in ensuring predictable transfer performance. However, experimental and analytical studies of such flows are quite limited, since a vast majority of TCP studies focus on shared network environments [27]. More generally, TCP has been widely used for wide-area data transfers, including over dedicated connections. Sustaining high TCP throughput for these transfers requires parameter optimizations specific to dedicated connections. While these optimizations are somewhat easier, they are not simple extensions of the well-studied solutions developed for shared connections.

To gain insights into transport solutions for these dedicated transfers, we systematically collected throughput measurements and time traces for three TCP variants, namely, CUBIC [24], Hamilton TCP (HTCP) [26], and Scalable TCP (SCTP) [12], which are considered to be suitable for high-bandwidth connections. These iperf memory transfer measurements are intended to highlight the performance of TCP, and I/O and file systems are assumed to be of sufficient capacity so as not to impose additional constraints. We use dedicated physical connections and a suite of hardware-emulated

(a) throughput profile $\Theta_O(\tau)$

(b) time trace $\theta(\tau, t)$

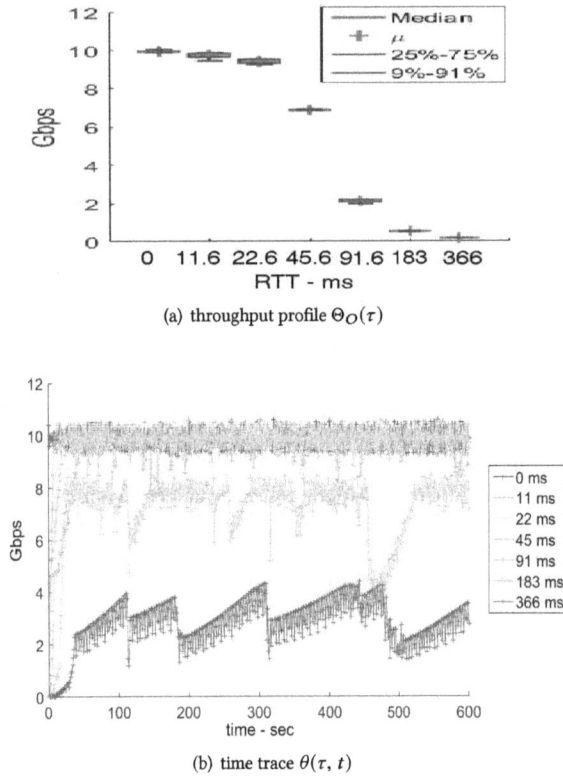

Figure 1: Throughput profile and time traces of Scalable-TCP

10 Gbps connections with 0-366 ms round trip times (RTTs). For a given configuration, hosts, TCP and connection parameters, let $\theta(\tau, t)$ denote the throughput at time t over a connection of RTT τ. Its average over an observation period T_O is called the *throughput profile*:

$$\Theta_O(\tau) = \frac{1}{T_O} \int_0^{T_O} \theta(\tau, t)\, dt$$

Fig. 1 shows representative plots of mean throughput profiles and time traces for a single STCP stream [12].

It is important to note from Fig. 1(a) that the throughput profile $\Theta_O(\tau)$ is *concave* for lower RTTs, but switches to *convex* for larger RTTs. Such dual-mode profiles are observed and analyzed in limited single TCP measurements in [22], but do not seem to be widely known. In this paper, we present extensive TCP measurements with multiple flows and varied buffer sizes, and also present analytical results that relate the extent of concave regions to these parameters and additionally to transport dynamics. From a practical perspective, the concave region is the most desirable characteristic because the throughput decreases slowly as RTT increases, and in particular is higher than the linear interpolation of the end points. In fact, such a profile is in stark contrast to (entirely) convex regions predicted by several TCP models [27], where the throughput decreases faster with RTT and is below the linear interpolation of the end points. Over the past decades, several detailed analytical models have been developed and experimental measurements have been collected for various TCP variants

[10, 20, 31]. Based on different loss models, these conventional TCP models provide entirely convex throughput profiles [15, 18, 27], and do not explain this dual-regime profile well. Our measurements demonstrate that both large host (TCP/IP and socket) buffers and more parallel streams expand the concave regions, in addition to improving the throughput. In another direction, throughput time traces exhibit rich dynamics as illustrated in Fig. 1(b), which are much more complex than periodic trajectories predicted by conventional transport models for dedicated connections with no external losses. These dynamics impact the throughput profiles in subtle ways as revealed by our application of Poincaré map and Lyapunov exponent methods from chaos theory [3]: at lower RTTs, higher throughput and smaller variations result in concave regions, and at higher RTTs, lower throughput and larger variations lead to convex regions. Similar and somewhat unexpected complex dynamics have been observed in User Datagram Transport (UDT) transfers [14], which were originally expected to have much smoother dynamics [9].

We propose a generic, coarse throughput model that abstracts the ramp-up (due to slow-start) and sustainment (due to congestion avoidance) phases of TCP and captures the qualitative trends observed in the measurements: (i) exponential ramp-up combined with sustained throughput leads to concave regions, particularly at low RTTs; and (ii) larger buffers and more parallel streams improve the average throughput and also expand the concave region. This model generalizes the single stream model with a fixed buffer size presented in [22]. We compute the Poincaré map of a throughput time trace that specifies the next transfer rate as a function of the current rate, and the Lyapunov exponent that specifies its rate of change. The Poincaré map of an ideal periodic TCP trajectory, predicted by existing models [27] for dedicated connections, is a simple 1-D curve [20]; but, several computed maps form scattered 2-D clusters with positive Lyapunov exponents. Such a 1-D map represents stable dynamics, but in the scattered map cases the nearby throughput values may widely diverge in the next step, indicating much richer dynamics [3]. The Poincaré map may determine critical properties of throughput profiles, and we show that stable throughput dynamics, indicated by a qualitatively compact map and small Lyapunov exponents, expand the concave region.

In addition to providing useful insights, these measurements combined with analytical results provide us practical transport solutions. A TCP variant and its parameters can be chosen using pre-computed throughput profiles to achieve high throughput for a given connection using its RTT, which can be incorporated into HPC wide-area infrastructures [19] and HPC I/O frameworks [5, 13]. Furthermore, throughput under this configurations can be estimated by interpolating the measurements with certain statistical guarantees without the knowledge of underlying joint error distributions of connections and host systems.

Various measurements and experimental configurations are described in Section 2. A generic throughput model is presented in Section 3, including illustrations of monotonicity and dual-regime concavity/convexity. The time traces and stability properties are discussed in Section 4. A method for selecting a transport method for a given connection and statistical guarantees of its throughput estimates are presented in Section 5. Conclusions are presented in Section 6.

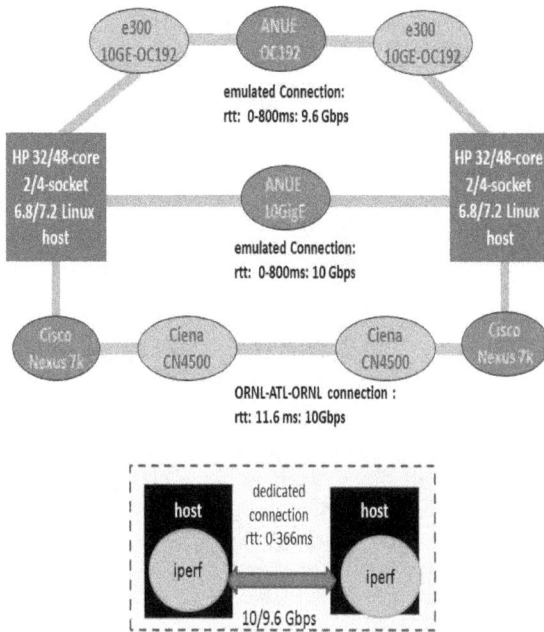

Figure 2: Testbed connections

and Asia; and the 366 ms RTT represents a connection spanning the globe.

TCP memory-to-memory throughput measurements and parameter traces are collected for three TCP congestion control modules using the *iperf* and *tcpprobe* kernel module. The number of parallel streams is varied from one to ten for each configuration, and throughput measurements are repeated ten times. The configuration for iperf includes transfer sizes of default (around 1 GB), 20 GB, 50 GB, and 100 GB. TCP buffer sizes are default, normal (recommended values for 200 ms RTT), and large (the largest size allowed by the kernel); and the socket buffer parameter for iperf is 2 GB. The net effects of these settings result in the allocation of 250 KB, 250 MB and 1 GB socket buffer sizes, respectively.

2.2 TCP Measurements

We compute the mean throughput profile by taking the mean of the average throughput rates from repeated transfer experiments conducted at specific τ values and numbers of parallel streams. The results are collectively shown in Figs. 3-6 for select configurations. From these plots, the overall trend can be easily observed: the mean throughput generally decreases with increasing RTTs, and increases with more streams.

In Fig. 3, mean throughput rates under three buffer sizes, namely, default, normal, and large, are plotted for HTCP with $f1\_sonet\_f2$ configuration. A larger buffer size significantly improves the mean throughput, especially for longer connections; for instance, throughput of 10 streams for 366 ms RTT improves from 100 Mbps to nearly 8 Gbps as the buffer size increases. The throughputs of CUBIC and STCP are very close to their HTCP counterparts. Unless otherwise specified, subsequent discussions primarily address performance with large buffers.

Figs. 4 and 5 show the mean throughput of STCP and CUBIC, respectively. For STCP, compared to SONET, the 10GigE ($f1\_10gige\_f2$) link improves the mean throughput for low-to-mid RTTs, especially for higher stream counts; the difference is less pronounced for CUBIC in the same RTT range, with little to no improvement for both versions under higher RTTs. On the other hand, transfer rates between hosts with Linux kernel 3.10 ($f3\_sonet\_f4$) are minimally affected by connection modality (OC192 or 10GigE) under most RTTs and somewhat worsened under 366 ms RTT using STCP. For CUBIC, changes are also seen mostly for high RTTs: while the cases with lower stream counts seem to benefit the most from the new kernel, more streams result in degraded performance just as with STCP. In what follows, we will focus on the $f1\_f2$ configurations.

So far, the TCP transfer size has been set to "default". When a fixed larger transfer size is imposed, the performances are quite different. In Fig. 6, each graph illustrates throughput as a function of number of streams and RTTs for different transfer sizes. Throughputs generally increase as a function of the transfer size, especially for larger RTTs. Recall that the average throughput is a weighted average between the ramp-up and sustainment phases; an increased transfer size effectively prolongs the sustainment stage, and thereby improves overall throughput. It is also interesting to note that with large transfer sizes, the throughput profiles (with increasing numbers of streams) become flatter for most RTTs, indicating the reduced effect of adopting multiple streams.

2 THROUGHPUT MEASUREMENTS AND PROFILES

We collected extensive TCP throughput measurements over the past two years, using three TCP variants, three buffer sizes, 1-10 parallel streams over connections of seven different lengths and two modalities, as shown in Table 1. Their throughput profiles share certain common qualitative properties in terms of monotonicity and concave/convex regions, which we summarize in this section; we do not, however, attempt to provide a comprehensive analysis of these large data sets.

2.1 Measurement Testbed

Measurements are collected over our testbed with four 32-core HP Linux workstations Feynman1 ($f1$) through Feynman4 ($f4$) with Linux kernel 2.6 ($f1,f2$) and Linux kernel 3.10 ($f3,f4$). Hosts with identical configurations are connected in pairs over a back-to-back fiber connection with negligible 0.01 ms RTT and a physical 10GigE connection with 11.6 ms RTT via Cisco and Ciena devices, as shown in Fig. 2. Two different physical modalities are represented by the 10GigE and SONET/OC192 connections. For the latter, 10GigE NICs are connected to a Force10 E300 switch that converts between 10GigE and SONET frames, and the OC192 ANUE emulator is in turn connected to WAN ports of E300, as shown in the top connection in Fig. 2. We use suites of emulated 10GigE and SONET/OC192 connections via ANUE devices with RTTs $\tau \in \{0.4, 11.8, 22.6, 45.6, 91.6, 183, 366\}$ ms. The lower RTTs represent cross-country connections, for example, between facilities across the US; higher RTTs 93.6 and 183 ms represent inter-continental connections, for example, between US, Europe,

Table 1: Configurations

option	parameter range
host OS	feynman1-2 (Linux kernel 2.6, CentOS 6.8), feynman3-4 (Linux kernel 3.10, CentOS 7.2)
congestion control	CUBIC, HTCP, STCP
buffer size	default (244 KB), normal (256 MB), large (1 GB)
transfer size	default ($\approx$ 1 GB), 20 GB, 50 GB, 100 GB
no. streams	1–10
connection	SONET-OC192 (9.6 Gbps), 10GigE (10 Gbps)
RTT	0.4, 11.8, 22.6, 45.6, 91.6, 183, 366 ms

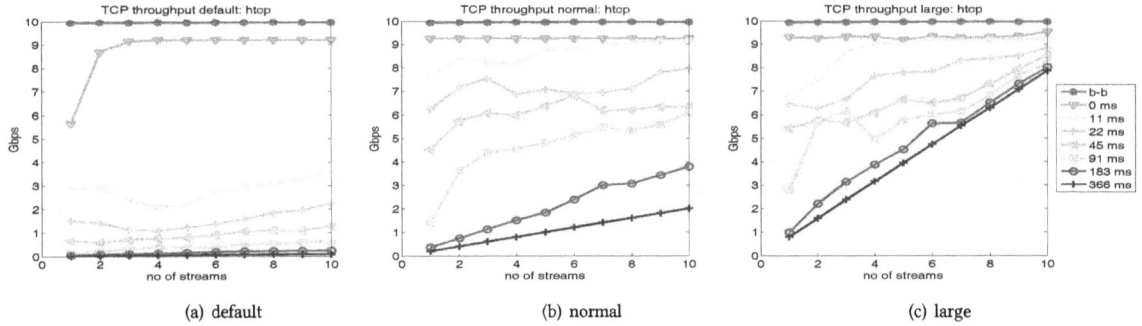

(a) default

(b) normal

(c) large

Figure 3: Throughput with variable RTTs, number of streams, and buffer sizes for HTCP with $f1\_sonet\_f2$ configuration

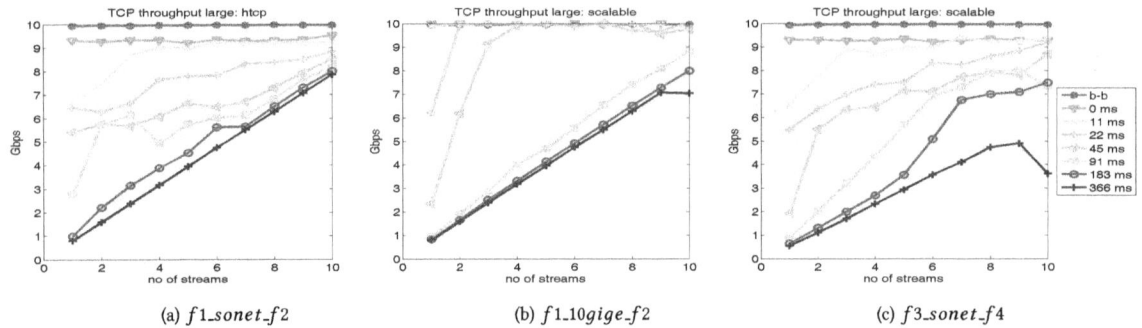

(a) $f1\_sonet\_f2$

(b) $f1\_10gige\_f2$

(c) $f3\_sonet\_f4$

Figure 4: Throughput with variable RTTs, number of streams, and configurations for STCP with large buffers

2.3 Profiles and Transitions

Throughput box plots for CUBIC with large buffers in Fig. 7 show that compared to SONET, 10GigE throughput rates in general exhibit less variation. More importantly, in both cases, using more streams not only increases the throughput, but also extends the concave region, as the convex region around larger RTTs with a single stream largely disappears with 10 streams. In addition, the buffer size also has a similar effect, namely, increased mean throughput and extended concave region. As seen from Fig. 8, for CUBIC with 10 streams over SONET, using the default buffer size results in an entirely convex profile; with the normal buffer size, a concave region (leading up to 91.6 ms) is followed by a convex region; finally, a large buffer extends the concave region all the way beyond 183 ms.

We compute the *transition-RTT* τ_T between concave and convex regions by regression fitting a pair of sigmoid functions, as illustrated in Fig. 9. Using the flipped sigmoid function $g_{a_1, \tau_1}(\tau) = 1 - \frac{1}{1+e^{-a_1(\tau-\tau_1)}}$, we fit concave-convex switch regression function

$$f_{\Theta_O}(\tau) = g_{a_1, \tau_1}(\tau)I(\tau \leq \tau_T) + g_{a_2, \tau_2}(\tau)I(\tau \geq \tau_T)$$

where $I(\cdot)$ is the indicator function, $g_{a_1, \tau_1}(\tau)$ is the concave fit, and $g_{a_2, \tau_2}(\tau)$ is the convex fit. The concave and convex portions of the regression model are ensured by constraining $\tau_2 \leq \tau_T \leq \tau_1$. We calculate the parameters a_1, τ_1, a_2, τ_2, and the transition-RTT τ_T by minimizing the sum-squared error (SSE) between the measured throughput values and the fitted model, defined as

$$\text{SSE} = \sum_{\tau \leq \tau_T} \left(\widetilde{\Theta}_O(\tau) - g_{a_1, \tau_1}(\tau) \right)^2 + \sum_{\tau \geq \tau_T} \left(\widetilde{\Theta}_O(\tau) - g_{a_2, \tau_2}(\tau) \right)^2,$$

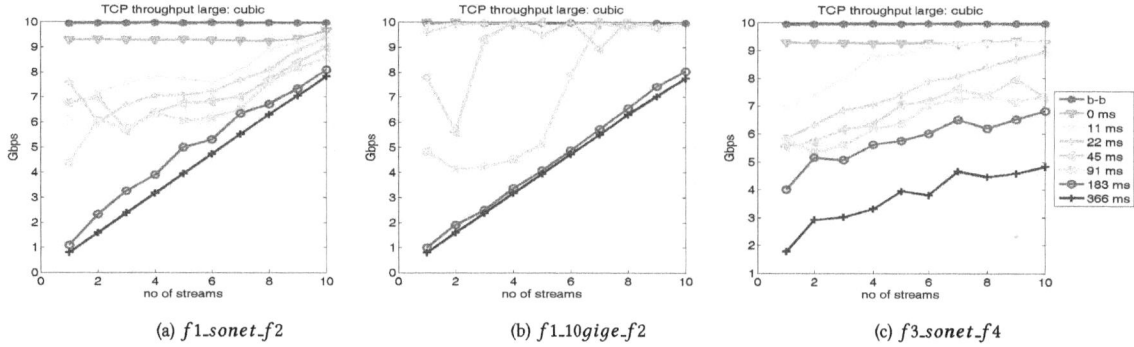

(a) $f1\_sonet\_f2$ (b) $f1\_10gige\_f2$ (c) $f3\_sonet\_f4$

Figure 5: Throughput with variable RTTs, number of streams, and configurations for CUBIC with large buffers

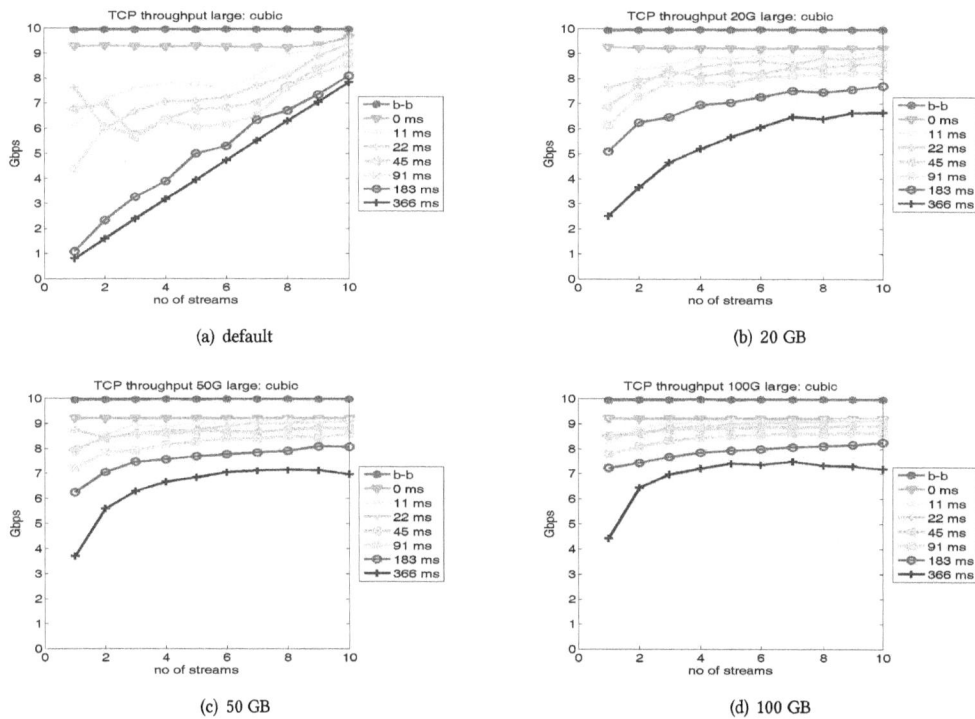

(a) default   (b) 20 GB

(c) 50 GB   (d) 100 GB

Figure 6: Throughput with variable RTTs, number of streams, and transfer sizes for CUBIC with large buffers and $f1\_sonet\_f2$ configuration

where $\widetilde{\Theta}_O(\tau) \in (0, 1)$ is the scaled version of the measured throughput values.

In Fig. 9, we demonstrate the fitted sigmoid models along with the measured throughput profiles for three different buffer sizes, with a single CUBIC stream over 10GigE. As mentioned earlier, the profile is entirely convex at the default buffer size, and consequently there is only a convex portion to the sigmoid fit. For normal and large buffer sizes, both the concave and convex sigmoid fits are present, respectively are shown with solid-blue and dashed-black curves. It is clear that τ_T increases, hence the concave region extends, as the buffer size is increased.

We repeat the regression model fit for 1-10 parallel streams and three congestion control modules. The overall variations of the estimated transition-RTT values w.r.t. number of parallel streams, buffer sizes, and TCP congestion control modules are shown in Fig. 10. For CUBIC, while using the default buffer size, the transition-RTT values increase from 0.4 ms for 1-3 parallel streams to 11.8 ms for 4 or more parallel streams. When the normal buffer size is used, the transition-RTT values remain consistently higher (at 45.6 ms, except for 2 steams) than those with the default buffer size, and further increase to 91.6 ms for 10 parallel streams. The τ_T estimates with the large buffer size show even larger values than both the default and normal buffer sizes; for example, 91.6 ms for 1-6 parallel

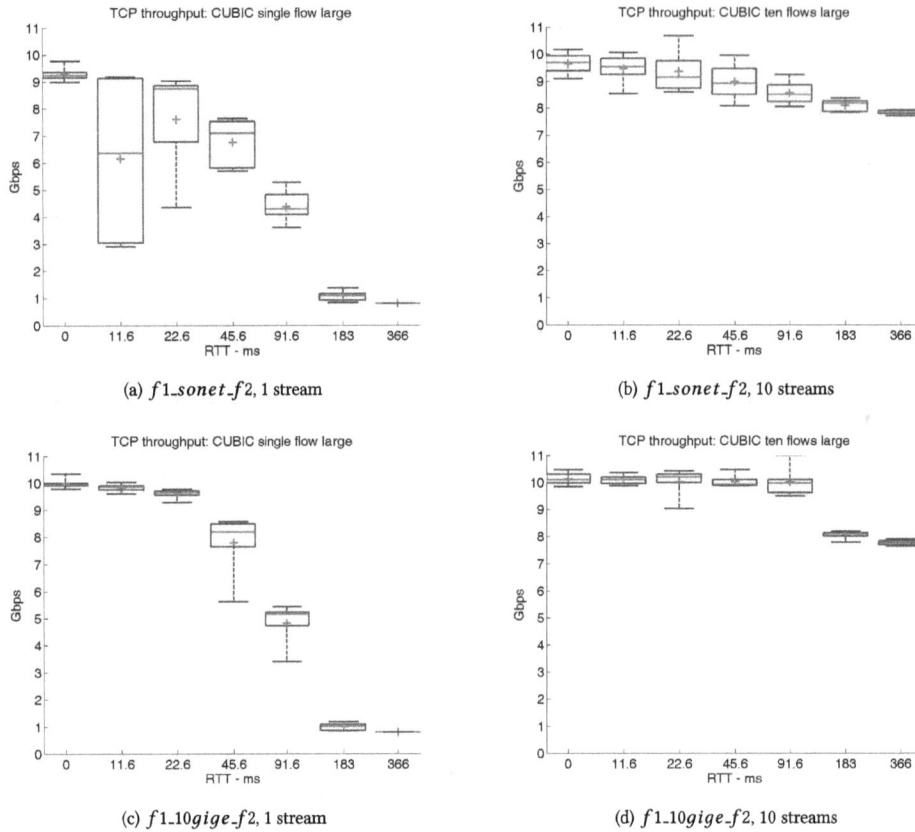

(a) $f1\_sonet\_f2$, 1 stream

(b) $f1\_sonet\_f2$, 10 streams

(c) $f1\_10gige\_f2$, 1 stream

(d) $f1\_10gige\_f2$, 10 streams

Figure 7: Throughput box plots with variable RTTs, stream counts, and configurations for CUBIC with large buffers

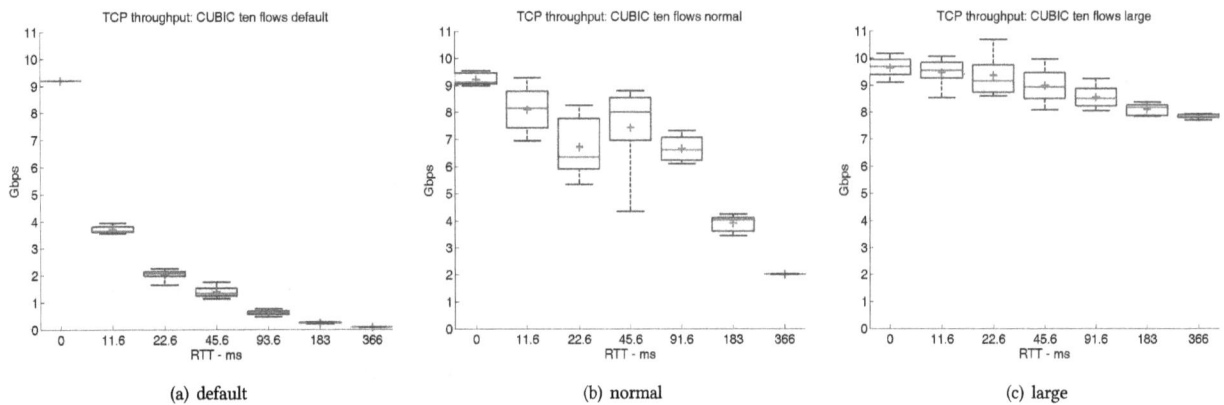

(a) default

(b) normal

(c) large

Figure 8: Throughput box plots with variable RTTs and buffer sizes for CUBIC with 10 streams and $f1\_sonet\_f2$ configuration

streams (except 2 streams) and 183 ms for 7 or more parallel streams. Similar increasing trends of the estimated τ_T values are also noted for HTCP and STCP, and thereby corroborate our inference that more streams and larger buffer sizes extend the concave region in addition to improving the throughput.

3 THROUGHPUT MODEL

We now present a generic throughput model[1] to explain the overall qualitative behavior observed in TCP measurements in previous section. A similar model has been presented for UDT in [14].

---

[1]This is a coarse or approximate model mainly aimed at explaining the concave-convex transitions in measured throughput profiles, and does not capture the complex, disparate congestion control details of TCP variants.

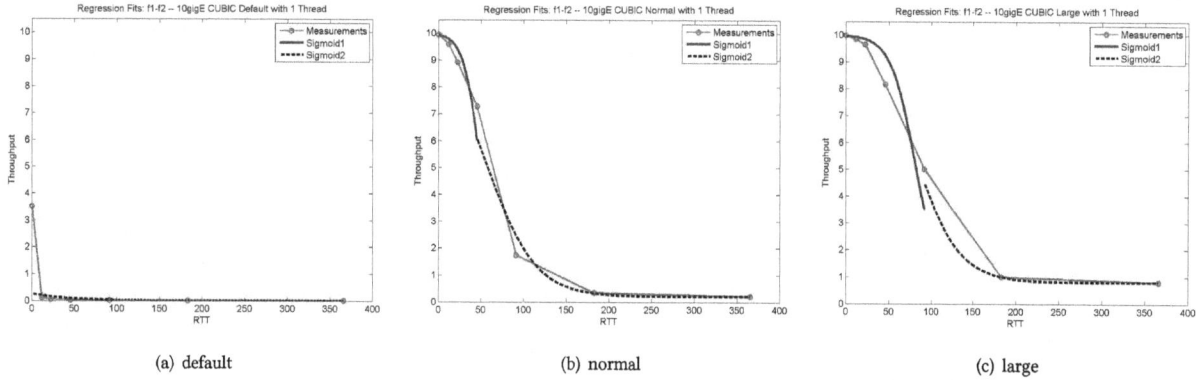

Figure 9: Sigmoid regression fits of throughput profiles with various buffer sizes for single stream CUBIC and $f1\_10gige\_f2$ configuration

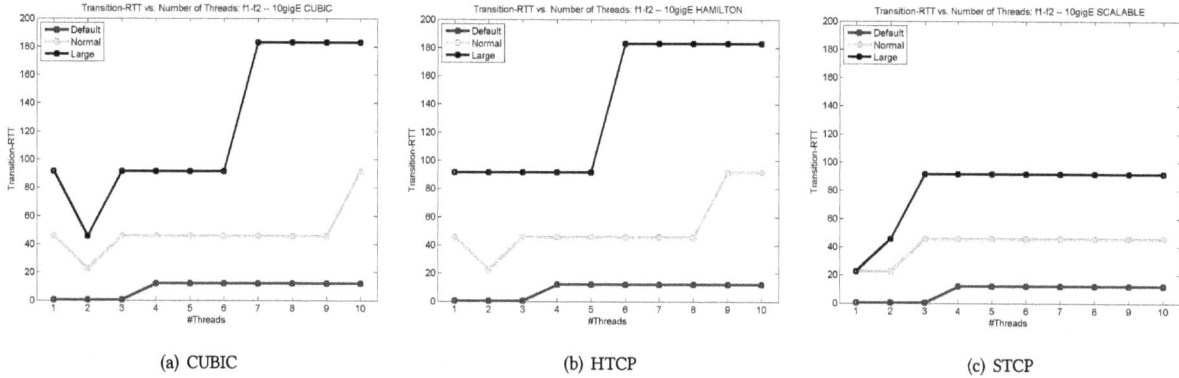

Figure 10: Transition-RTT estimates with 1-10 streams and various buffer sizes for CUBIC, HTCP, and STCP in $f1\_10gige\_f2$ configuration

3.1 Basic Throughput Model

The throughput profiles are determined by: (i) protocol parameters including version $V = C, H, S$, representing CUBIC, HTCP, and STCP, respectively, number of parallel streams n, and socket buffer size B allocated during measurements that is a result of cumulative effects of TCP/IP host and socket parameters at sending and receiving hosts; (ii) connection RTT, modality, and capacity, for example, 10 Gbps for 10GigE and 9.6 Gbps for SONET OC192; and (iii) settings of the measurement tool such as the duration and data transfer size for iperf. Let $\theta_V^{B,n}(\tau, t)$ denote the aggregate throughput at time t over a connection of RTT τ. These parameters may be explicitly used to denote the throughput profile as

$$\Theta_{V,O}^{B,n}(\tau) = \frac{1}{T_O} \int_0^{T_O} \theta_{V,O}^{B,n}(\tau, t)dt,$$

and selectively suppressed when evident from the context.

The throughput dynamics of a transport with fixed parameters over a connection with RTT τ and capacity C are characterized by two phases:

(a) **Ramp-Up Phase:** In the ramp-up phase, $\theta(t)$ increases for a duration of T_R until it reaches a peak $C_\tau^{B,n} \leq C$, which depends on B and n, and then switches to a sustained

throughput phase. The ramp-up phase corresponds to the slow-start of TCP, in which $\theta(t)$ increases exponentially as the congestion window $cwnd\ w(t)$ grows. The specifics of slow-start may vary among different TCP variants and their implementations. The average throughput in this phase is

$$\bar{\theta}_R(\tau) = \frac{1}{T_R} \int_0^{T_R} \theta(\tau, t)dt.$$

(b) **Sustained Throughput Phase:** Once throughput reaches the peak $C_\tau^{B,n}$, it is "sustained" using a mechanism which processes the acknowledgments, and infers and responds to losses. For TCP, this is the congestion avoidance phase that follows the slow-start, wherein $w(t)$ is incremented somewhat slowly by an amount specific to the TCP version. The average throughput in this region is

$$\bar{\theta}_S(\tau) = \frac{1}{T_S} \int_{T_R}^{T_R+T_S} \theta(\tau, t)dt.$$

In general, the average $\bar{\theta}_S$ lies below $C_\tau^{B,n} \leq C$ due to variations in $\theta(t)$ as shown in Fig. 1(b).

The average throughput is

$$\Theta_O(\tau) = \frac{T_R}{T_O}\bar{\theta}_R(\tau) + \frac{T_S}{T_O}\bar{\theta}_S(\tau) = \bar{\theta}_S(\tau) - f_R\left(\bar{\theta}_S(\tau) - \bar{\theta}_R(\tau)\right),$$

where $T_O = T_R + T_S$ and $f_R = T_R/T_O$. For a large observation period T_O with a fast ramp-up, typical in small τ settings, the qualitative properties of $\theta_S(\tau)$ directly carry over to $\Theta_O(\tau)$. For large τ, however, the ramp-up period can take significantly longer, for example, 10 seconds for 366 ms RTT (Fig. 1(b)), and the difference term $\bar{\theta}_S - \bar{\theta}_R$ modulates the behavior of $\theta_S(\tau)$ in determining that of $\Theta_O(\tau)$.

3.2 TCP Model for Dedicated Connections

A function $f(\tau)$ is *concave* [6] in interval I if for any $\tau_1 < \tau_2 \in I$, the following condition is satisfied: for $x \in [0,1]$

$$f(x\tau_1 + (1-x)\tau_2) \geq xf(\tau_1) + (1-x)f(\tau_2).$$

It is *convex* if $\geq$ in the above condition is replaced by $\leq$. A function is concave if and only if $\frac{df}{d\tau}$ is a non-increasing function of τ or equivalently $\frac{d^2f}{d\tau^2} \leq 0$. Using a simplified model, TCP memory-to-memory transfers for the special case of unlimited host buffers ($B = \infty$) and a single stream ($n = 1$) have been shown to have two basic regions [22]:

(a) *Concave Region:* For smaller RTTs, as the congestion window $w(t)$ crosses the slow-start threshold W_{SS}, $\theta(t)$ switches from exponentially increasing to a constant C (lower RTT plots in Fig. 1(b)). This behavior leads to the concave profile that we observed in measurements, as will be shown in the next section.

(b) *Convex Region:* For larger RTTs, $w(t)$ crosses W_{SS} before reaching $C\tau$, and its slower growth in the congestion avoidance model leads to losses (higher RTT plots in Fig. 1(b)) and a convex profile.

In most cases shown in the previous section, the profile is concave when RTT is small, and at transition RTT τ_T it becomes and continues to be convex as RTT increases. This behavior is in part a result of various host buffers being sufficiently large to fill up the connection to the near capacity C combined with the fast response of TCP congestion control at lower RTT. In this region we term the protocol to be *peaking at zero* (PAZ) since $\lim_{\tau\to 0}\Theta_O(\tau) \approx C$, as illustrated in Figs. 3, 4, and 6, particularly over the back-to-back connection.

Traditional TCP models, driven primarily by losses, lead to throughput profiles in the generic form $\hat{T}(\tau) = a + b/\tau^c$, for suitable constants a, b, and $c \geq 1$ [27]. These convex profiles (since $\frac{d\hat{T}}{d\tau} = -b/\tau^2$ increases with τ) are typical of large transfers and longer RTTs, and do not adequately account for transfers that lead to concave portions in the observed profiles.

3.3 Monotonicity of Throughput Profile

In the average throughput $\Theta_O(\tau) = \bar{\theta}_S - f_R(\bar{\theta}_S - \bar{\theta}_R)$, the ramp-up duration increases with τ and hence f_R increases. This condition is sufficient to show that in PAZ cases, the throughput profile decreases with RTT. Consider a best-case scenario of a sustainment phase such that $\theta_S(t) \approx C$, that is, B and n are sufficiently large, and TCP variant V is ideally responsive to RTT τ to completely

fill the connection capacity. Then $\Theta_O(\tau)$ decreases with RTT since $\bar{\theta}_R \leq C$, and $\bar{\theta}_S - \bar{\theta}_R > 0$. This property carries over to the more general case where $\theta_S(t)$ decreases with RTT, since the recovery time from losses increases and results in a lower $\bar{\theta}_S$. In general $\theta_S(\tau)$ decreases with τ in part as a result of TCP's self-clocking behavior that makes its response slower, which in effect enhances the monotonic decrease of $\Theta_O(\tau)$. There are two different ways such a decrease manifests, as will be shown in the next section: if B or n is sufficiently large, the decrease is slower and leads to the concave profile region, otherwise a faster decrease leads to the convex profile region. However, if throughput falls much below C after the ramp-up and has significant random variations, it is quite possible for $\Theta_O(\tau)$ to increase with respect to τ in certain albeit small regions (Fig. 8(b)), but our measurements show mostly decreasing profiles.

3.4 Multiple Flows and Large Buffers

We now consider a base case where the slow-start phase is followed by well-sustained throughput such that $\theta_S(\tau) \approx C$. For an exponential increase during the slow start of TCP, the throughput reaches C in $n_R = \log C$ steps, and the total data sent during T_R period is $2C$. Thus, we have $T_R = \tau \log C$, and $\bar{\theta}_R = \frac{2C}{\tau \log C}$, and

$$\Theta_O = \frac{2C}{T_O} + C\left(1 - \frac{\tau \log C}{T_O}\right).$$

Then, we have $\frac{d\Theta_O}{d\tau} = -C\log C/T_O$, a non-increasing function of τ, which shows concavity when throughput is maintained close to C. For a small τ, as shown in Fig. 1(b), TCP traces indicate smaller variations, which leads to $\bar{\theta}_S$ values around the peak C. However, for a large τ, deeper decreases in the traces lead to a lower $\bar{\theta}_S$, and in turn convex profiles as shown in Fig. 1(b).

Consider that throughput increases faster than exponential such that $T_R = \tau^{1+\epsilon}\log C$, for $\epsilon > 0$ as in the case of n TCP streams. Then,

$$\Theta_O^n(\tau) = \frac{2C}{T_O} + C\left(1 - \frac{\tau^{1+\epsilon}\log C}{T_O}\right)$$

and

$$\frac{d\Theta_O^n}{d\tau} = -C\log C/T_O(1+\epsilon)\tau^\epsilon,$$

which is a decreasing function of τ that leads to a concave $\Theta_O(\tau)$. On the other hand, for a slower-than-exponential increase, consider $T_R = \tau^{-\epsilon}\log C$, for a small $\epsilon > 0$. We have $\frac{d\Theta}{d\tau} = -C\log C/T_O(1-\epsilon)\tau^{-\epsilon}$, which is an increasing function of τ that leads to a convex $\Theta_O(\tau)$. Thus, the exponential increase ramp-up followed by sustained throughput, $\theta_S(t) \approx C$, represents a transition point for the profiles: either slower ramp-up or unsustained peak can result in convex profiles.

For buffer sizes $B_1 < B_2$, we have $\theta_S^{B_1}(\tau) \leq \theta_S^{B_2}(\tau)$, which leads to $\Theta_S^{W_1}(\tau) \leq \Theta_S^{B_2}(\tau)$. Thus, as the buffer size increases, the protocol operates closer to the PAZ region, which combined with suitably sustained throughput leads to a concave region. Then, the monotonicity of profiles implies $\tau_T^{B_1} \leq \tau_T^{B_2}$; that is, a larger buffer size results in an expanded concavity region, as indicated in Fig. 8(c).

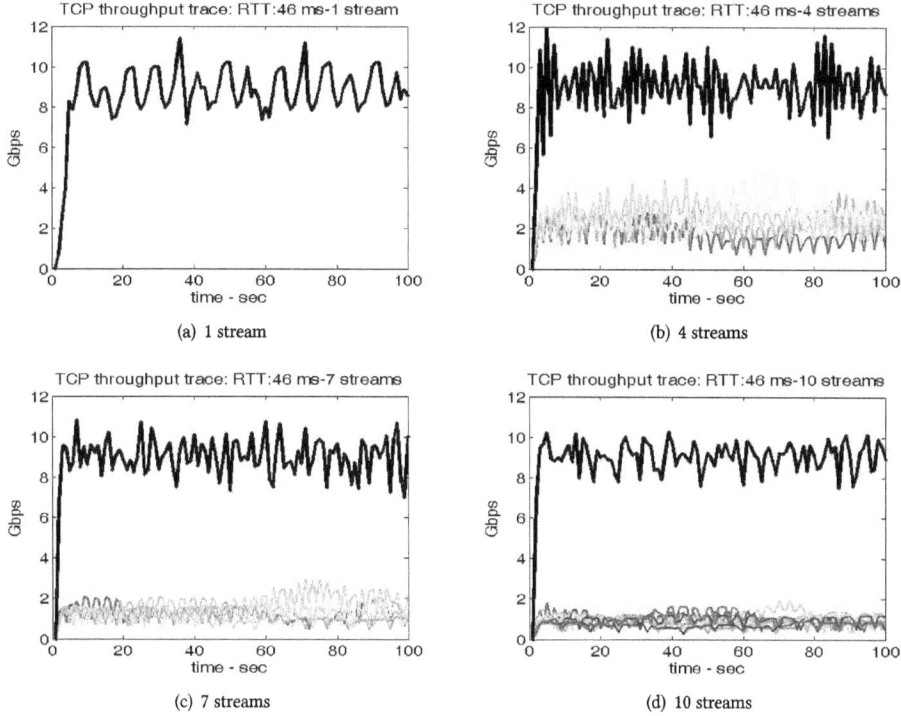

Figure 11: Throughput traces for CUBIC with $f1\_sonet\_f2$ configuration, large buffers, 45.6 ms RTT, and 1,4,7 and 10 streams

3.5 Concave Region Boundaries

The concave region is characterized by non-increasing derivative

$$\frac{d\Theta_O(\tau)}{d\tau} = \frac{d\bar{\theta}_S(\tau)}{d\tau} - f_R\left(\frac{d\bar{\theta}_S(\tau)}{d\tau} - \frac{d\bar{\theta}_R(\tau)}{d\tau}\right)$$
$$- \frac{df_R}{d\tau}\left(\bar{\theta}_S(\tau) - \bar{\theta}_R(\tau)\right)),$$

which is determined by $\bar{\theta}_S(\tau) - \bar{\theta}_R(\tau)$ and its derivative. Now f_R described in the previous section is almost linear in τ, and hence its derivative is constant. Consider that the derivatives are much larger such that effects of $\bar{\theta}_S(\tau) - \bar{\theta}_R(\tau)$ are not dominant; also, the throughput in the sustainment phase decreases faster than in slow-start, i.e., $\left|\frac{d\theta_S}{d\tau}\right| \geq \left|\frac{d\theta_R}{d\tau}\right|$. Then, the term $\left(\frac{d\bar{\theta}_S(\tau)}{d\tau} - \frac{d\bar{\theta}_R(\tau)}{d\tau}\right)$ is negative, which in turn makes the second term of $\frac{d\Theta_O(\tau)}{d\tau}$ a non-decreasing function of τ (since f_R is an increasing function of τ). Then, if $\left|\frac{d\theta_S}{d\tau}\right|$ is much higher, then the increase due to the second term amplified by f_R offsets the decrease in the first term, thereby leading to an overall convex profile. Increasingly large variations in the time traces lead to corresponding increases in $\left|\frac{d\theta_S}{d\tau}\right|$, and the profile consequently transitions to a convex region.

4 DYNAMICS OF THROUGHPUT TRACES

Time traces of throughput measurements provide more detailed information about the transfer processes than mean throughput profiles. Our main objective is to characterize their dynamics and stability as related to throughput profiles. We use tools from chaos theory, the Poincaré maps and the Lyapunov exponents (Section

4.1), to relate stability properties to throughput profiles, in particular, their concave and convex regions at peak throughputs (Section 4.2).

We generate throughput traces by sampling at one-second intervals for a total duration of 100 seconds. However, in contrast to measurements in Section 2, the transfer size here is not fixed, and a higher average throughput indicates a larger transfer size. Fig. 11 shows typical traces of CUBIC throughput over 45.6 ms RTT SONET, with large buffers and variable numbers of streams. In these plots, the thick black curves describe the aggregate transfer rates, whereas different colored curves are transfer rates for individual streams. As evident from these plots, while the per-stream transfer rate decreases with more streams, the aggregate rates across the cases appear to hover around 9 Gbps; in this case, the transfer size is around 100 GB for most cases, and the average throughput rates are more or less consistent with the mean profile shown in Fig. 6(d).

4.1 Poincaré Map and Lyapunov Exponent

A *Poincaré Map* $M : \mathfrak{R}_d \longmapsto \mathfrak{R}_d$ corresponds to a real-vector state $X_i \in \mathfrak{R}_d$ updated at each time step i such that $X_{i+1} = M(X_i)$ [3], and in our context, the sequence $X_0, X_1, ..., X_t$ corresponds to a throughput trace. Then, the Poincaré map generated from a throughput trace provides critical insights into the dynamics of the underlying transport method. Ideal TCP periodic traces lead to maps that form 1-D curves [20], and ideal UDT traces form 1-D monotone curves [14]. In general, the complex geometry of these maps, such as 2-D clusters, represents complex dynamics, since similar throughput values in the current step evolve into wildly

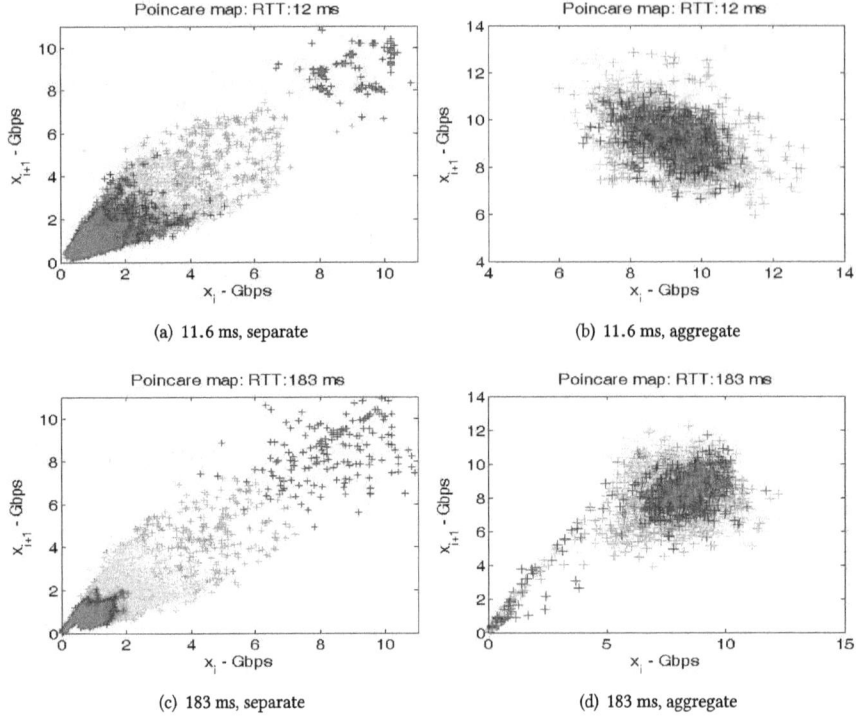

(a) 11.6 ms, separate

(b) 11.6 ms, aggregate

(c) 183 ms, separate

(d) 183 ms, aggregate

Figure 12: Poincaré maps for CUBIC with $f1\_sonet\_f2$ configuration, large buffers, and 11.6 ms vs. 183 ms RTTs

different ones in the next step. The trace of a Poincaré map M can be characterized by its *Lyapunov Exponent* $\mathcal{L}_M = \ln \left| \frac{dM}{dX} \right|$, which describes the separation of trajectories that originate from nearby states. The negative Lyapunov exponents correspond to stable dynamics and positive values represent exponentially divergence traces and possibly chaotic dynamics [3].

Fig. 12 displays the Poincaré maps for CUBIC with variable stream counts, large buffers, and 11.6 ms and 183 ms RTTs over SONET connections. In the plots labeled as "separate", per-stream Poincaré maps are plotted; more specifically, starting from the top right corner, each color represents an increasing stream count, from 1 all the way to 10 streams on the bottom left corner. Comparing Figs. 12(a) and (c), we observe that with single stream, the (red) 183 ms trace transfer rates occupy a much wider region than the 11.6 ms ones, indicating the larger variations – and the reduced average throughput – of the former. With 10 streams, though, per-stream transfer rates with 11.6 ms RTT become much larger than those in the 183 ms cases, as seen from the wider (purple) area.

On the other hand, in the aggregate transfer rate Poincaré maps in Figs. 12(b) and (d), the points are superimposed on top of one another with varying flow counts, forming a cluster that describes the sustainment stage. In particular, the 183 ms RTT case demonstrates the effect of a longer ramp-up stage by the points from the origin leading up to the cluster, absent in the 11.6 ms RTT case. Interestingly, the "tilts" of the two clusters appear different: whereas the 183 ms RTT cluster in Fig. 12(b) aligns more with the ideal 45° line, the 11.6 ms cluster tilts to the left, indicating a less stable profile of the corresponding time traces (even with overall higher

mean throughput rates). This can be further confirmed with the Lyapunov exponent plots shown in Fig. 13, where the points in the 183 ms case are more compact and closer to the zero line as opposed to the 11.6 ms case. In addition, both plots also reveal that using more streams can reduce the instability in aggregate transfer rates by pulling the Lyapunov exponents closer to zero.

4.2 Peak Throughput and Instability

The variations in throughput traces are a result of protocol dynamics, which in turn determine the average throughput. In particular, positive Lyapunov exponents play a critical role in determining the throughput of protocols that operate at peak throughput, since the diverging trajectories can only be below the peak and larger exponents lead to lower throughput. For throughput rate θ_S, let θ_{S-} be the corresponding sending rate in the previous Poincaré iteration, which is given by the inverse of the ideal Poincaré map at θ_S. Let $L(\theta_{S-})$ denote the corresponding Lyapunov exponent. Then the derivative $\frac{\partial \theta_S}{\partial \theta_{S-}} = e^{L(\theta_{S-})}$ could be large for positive Lyapunov exponents, e.g., those shown in Fig. 13. For fixed f_R and θ_R, we have

$$\frac{\partial \Theta_Q}{\partial \tau} = (1 - f_R) \frac{\partial \bar{\theta}_S}{\partial \tau} = (1 - f_R) \frac{\partial \bar{\theta}_S}{\partial \theta_{S-}} \frac{\partial \theta_{S-}}{\partial \tau},$$

which indicates the amplifying effects of positive $L(\theta_{S-})$. Consider two configurations C_1 and C_2 with Lyapunov exponents L_1 and L_2, respectively, such that $L_1 > L_2$, and $\bar{\theta}_S^1$ and $\bar{\theta}_S^2$ are their average throughput in sustainment phase, respectively. The trajectories of C_1 will have larger deviations than those of C_2, thereby leading to $\bar{\theta}_S^1 \leq \bar{\theta}_S^2$. This phenomenon is observed in Fig. 14 where there is an overall decreasing relationship between the Lyapunov exponent

(a) 11.6 ms

(b) 183 ms

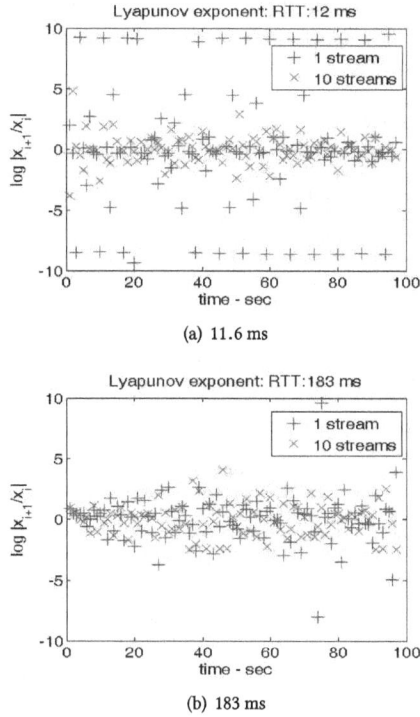

Figure 13: Lyapunov exponents for CUBIC over 11.6 ms and 183 ms RTT SONET and large buffers

and average throughput. Now by fixing $\bar{\theta}_S$, consider

$$\frac{\partial \Theta_O}{\partial \tau} = -\frac{\partial f_R}{\partial \tau}(\bar{\theta}_S - \bar{\theta}_R).$$

Since $\frac{\partial f_R}{\partial \tau} \geq 0$, the concavity of Θ_O is equivalent to the condition $\bar{\theta}_S - \bar{\theta}_R \geq 0$. Then, for a fixed configuration, the condition $\bar{\theta}_S^1 \leq \bar{\theta}_S^2$ in turn leads to $\{\tau : \bar{\theta}_S^1 \geq \bar{\theta}_R\} \subseteq \{\tau : \bar{\theta}_S^2 \geq \bar{\theta}_R\}$, which shows that configuration C_2 has a broader concavity region. Thus, lower throughput variations are desirable in addition to ramping up faster to reach peak throughput.

5 TRANSPORT SELECTION

Throughput profiles generated from the measurements can be used to select a configuration (V, n, B) based on RTT τ to achieve peak throughput as described next in Section 5.1. Furthermore, the corresponding throughput estimate $\hat{\Theta}_O(\tau)$ for this chosen configuration will be close to the actual peak throughput in a statistical sense with a high probability (as will be shown in Section 5.2).

5.1 Selection of Transport

Throughput profiles are generated by codes that sweep the parameters (V, n, B), and can be used as follows:

1. Determine RTT to destination using ping.
2. Use throughput profiles to determine a TCP variant and its parameters with the highest throughput if measurements are available at that RTT or by linearly interpolating the measurements otherwise.

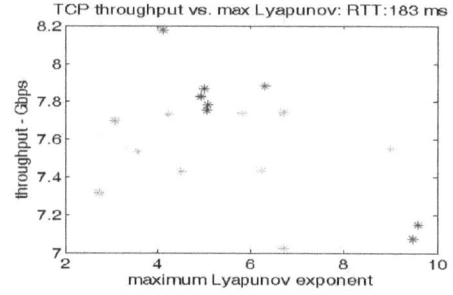

Figure 14: Average throughput vs. Lyapunov exponent for 10-stream CUBIC with 183 ms RTT SONET and large buffers

3. Load the congestion control module into kernel and set up the parameters.

Based on our measurements, this procedure selects STCP with multiple streams for smaller RTTs, which provides higher throughput compared to CUBIC, the Linux default.

5.2 Confidence Estimates

The throughput $\theta(\tau, t)$ is a random quantity whose distribution $\mathbf{P}_{\Theta_O(\tau)}$ is quite complex since it depends on the congestion control mechanism, and dynamics of the connection and host. We define the *profile regression* as

$$\bar{\Theta}_O(\tau) = E[\Theta_O(\tau)] = \int \Theta_O(\tau) d\mathbf{P}_{\Theta_O(\tau)},$$

which can be estimated based on measurements $\theta(\tau_k, t_i^k)$ at τ_k, $k = 1, 2, \ldots, n$, and times t_i^k, $i = 1, 2, \ldots, n_k$. It exhibits an overall decreasing trend with a concave region for $\tau \in [0, \tau_T]$ followed by a convex region for $\tau > \tau_T$. The throughput estimate, given by the *profile mean* $\hat{\Theta}_O(\tau)$, is computed using measurements as

$$\hat{\Theta}_O(\tau_k) = \frac{1}{n_k} \sum_{i=1}^{n_k} \theta(\tau_k, t_i^k)$$

at τ_k's and linearly interpolated between them. Note that $\hat{\Theta}_O(\tau)$, computed entirely using measurements, is indicative of the actual throughput at RTT τ, whose expected value is $\bar{\Theta}_O(\tau)$. We will now show it is indeed a good estimate of $\bar{\Theta}_O(\tau)$, in terms of expected error, and furthermore its performance improves with more measurements, independent of the underlying distribution $\mathbf{P}_{\Theta_O(\tau)}$.

Consider an estimate $f(.)$ of $\bar{\Theta}_O(.)$ based on measurements from a function class $\mathcal{M}$ of unimodal functions, which includes the dual-regime monotone throughput profiles as a special case. The *expected error* $I(f)$ of the estimator f is $I(f) = \int [f(\tau) - \theta(\tau, t)]^2 d\mathbf{P}_{\theta(\tau, t)}$, and the *best estimator* f^* is given by $\hat{I}(f^*) = \min_{f \in \mathcal{M}} I(f)$. The *best empirical estimator* $\hat{f} \in \mathcal{M}$ minimizes the empirical error

$$\hat{I}(f) = \frac{1}{n} \sum_{k=1}^{n} \frac{1}{n_k} \sum_{j=1}^{n_k} [f(\tau_k) - \theta(\tau_k, t_j)]^2,$$

that is, $\hat{I}(\hat{f}) = \min_{f \in \mathcal{M}} \hat{I}(f)$. Since $\hat{\Theta}_O(\tau)$ is the response mean at each RTT τ_k, it achieves the minimum empirical error. By using Vapnik-Chervonenkis theory [29], we have

$$\mathbf{P}\left\{I\left(\hat{\Theta}_O\right) - I(f^*) > \epsilon\right\}$$

$$\leq \mathbf{P}\left\{\max_{h \in \mathcal{M}} |I_D(h) - \hat{I}_D(h)| > \epsilon/2\right\}$$

$$\leq 16\mathcal{N}_\infty\left(\frac{\epsilon}{C}, \mathcal{M}\right) n e^{-\epsilon^2 n/(4C)^2}$$

where $\theta(\tau, t) \leq C$, and $\mathcal{N}_\infty(\epsilon, \mathcal{M})$ is the ϵ-cover of $\mathcal{M}$ under L_∞ norm. Due to the unimodality of functions in $\mathcal{M}$, their total variation is upper-bounded by $2C$, which provides us the upper bound ([4], p. 175):

$$\mathcal{N}_\infty\left(\frac{\epsilon}{C}, \mathcal{M}\right) < 2\left(\frac{n}{\epsilon^2}\right)^{(1+C/\epsilon)\log_2(2\epsilon/C)}.$$

By using this bound, we obtain

$$\mathbf{P}\left\{I\left(\hat{\Theta}_O\right) - I(f^*) > \epsilon\right\}$$
$$< 32\left(\frac{n}{\epsilon^2}\right)^{(1+C/\epsilon)\log_2(4\epsilon/C)} ne^{-\epsilon^2 n/(2C)^2}.$$

The exponential term on the right-hand side decays faster in n than other terms, hence for sufficiently large n it would be smaller than a given probability α.

In summary, the expected error $I(\hat{\Theta}_O)$ of the response mean is within ϵ of the optimal error $I(f^*)$ with a probability that increases with the number of observations. This performance guarantee is independent of how complex the underlying distribution $\mathbf{P}_{\Theta_O(\tau)}$ is. Thus, $\hat{\Theta}_O(\tau)$ is a good estimate of the actual peak throughput achievable at RTT τ independent of the underlying distribution, which is a complex composition of the effects of host systems and connection hardware as well as TCP/IP stack.

6 CONCLUSIONS

Wide-area data transfers in HPC infrastructures are increasingly being carried over dedicated network connections, driven in part by the expectation of high throughput and stable dynamics. In many cases, the underlying transport is provided by TCP for memory and file transfers, but its analyses and measurements over dedicated connections are limited, making it harder to assess its impact on application performance. To study the performance of TCP variants and their parameters for high-performance transfers over dedicated connections, we collected systematic measurements using physical and emulated dedicated connections. They revealed important properties such as concave regions and relationships between dynamics and throughput profiles. Interestingly, the dynamics are much richer than expected, as revealed by the Poincaré map and Lyapunov exponent estimates. We presented analytical results that identify RTT ranges corresponding to concave and high throughput profiles. The measurements and analyses enable the selection of a high throughput transport method and corresponding parameters for a given connection based on RTT.

Future directions include more detailed analytical models that closely match the measurements under packet drops and other errors with variable file and disk I/O capacities, particularly when they significantly impact TCP throughput dynamics. Also of future interest are enhancements of the current first-principle TCP models to explain the dual-mode throughput profiles by integrating dynamics parameters such as the Lyapunov exponents, and incorporation of throughput profiles into SDN technologies to select and set up suitable paths to match the transport protocols.

ACKNOWLEDGMENTS

This work is funded by RAMSES project and the Applied Mathematics Program, Office of Advanced Computing Research, U.S. Department of Energy, and by Extreme Scale Systems Center, sponsored by U. S. Department of Defense, and performed at Oak Ridge National Laboratory managed by UT-Battelle, LLC for U.S. Department of Energy under Contract No. DE-AC05-00OR22725.

REFERENCES

[1] Bay microsystems. http://www.baymicrosystems.com. Accessed: Apr. 2017.
[2] A. Aguilera, M. Kluge, , T. William, and W. E. Nagel. *HPC File Systems in Wide Area Networks: Understanding the Performance of Lustre over WAN*, pages 65–76. Springer Berlin Heidelberg, 2012.
[3] K. T. Alligood, T. D. Sauer, and J. A. Yorke. *Chaos: An Introduction to Dynamical Systems*. Springer-Verlag Pub., Reading, MA, 1996.
[4] M. Anthony and P. L. Bartlett. *Neural Network Learning: Theoretical Foundations*. Cambridge University Press, 1999.
[5] S. Atchley, D. Dillow, G. Shipman, P. Geoffray, J. M. Squyres, G. Bosilca, and R. Minnich. The common communication interface (CCI). In *19th IEEE Symposium on High Performance Interconnects (HOTI)*, Santa Clara, CA, 2011.
[6] M. Avriel, W. E. Diewert, S. Schaible, and I. Zang. *Generalized Concaviy*. SIAM, 2010.
[7] Science DMZ: Data Transfer Nodes. https://fasterdata.es.net/science-dmz/DTN. Accessed: Apr. 2017.
[8] Energy Sciences Network. http://www.es.net. Accessed: Apr. 2017.
[9] Y. Gu and R. L. Grossman. UDT: UDP-based data transfer for high-speed wide area networks. *Computer Networks*, 51(7), 2007.
[10] M. Hassan and R. Jain. *High Performance TCP/IP Networking: Concepts, Issues, and Solutions*. Prentice Hall, 2004.
[11] S. Jain, A. Kumar, S. Mandal, et al. B4: Experience with a globally-deployed software defined WAN. *SIGCOMM Comput. Commun. Rev*, 43(4):3–14, Oct. 2013.
[12] T. Kelly. Scalable TCP: Improving performance in high speed wide area networks. *Computer Communication Review*, 33(2):83–91, 2003.
[13] Q. Liu, J. Logan, Y. Tian, H. Abbasi, N. Podhorszki, J. Y. Choi, et al. Hello ADIOS: the challenges and lessons of developing leadership class I/O frameworks. *Concurrency and Computation: Practice and Experience*, 26(7):1453–1473, 2014.
[14] Q. Liu, N. S. V. Rao, C. Q. Wu, D. Yun, R. Kettimuthu, and I. Foster. Measurements-based analysis of performance profiles and dynamics of udp transport protocols. In *International Conference on Network Protocols*. 2016.
[15] M. Mathis, J. Semke, J. Mahdavi, and T. Ott. The mascroscopic behavior of the TCP congestion avoidance algorithm. *Computer Communication Review*, 27(3), 1997.
[16] Obsidian Research Corporation, http://www.obsidianresearch.com. Accessed: Apr. 2017.
[17] On-demand secure circuits and advance reservation system. http://www.es.net/oscars. Accessed: Apr. 2017.
[18] J. Padhye, V. Firoiu, D. F. Towsley, and J. F. Kurose. Modeling TCP Reno performance: A simple model and its empirical validation. *IEEE/ACM Transactions on Networking*, 8(2):133–145, 2000.
[19] S. Parete-Koon, B. Caldwell, S. Canony, E. Dartz, J. Hicky, J. Hill, et al. HPC's pivot to data. In *Cray User's Group Meeting*, 2014.
[20] N. S. V. Rao, J. Gao, and L. O. Chua. On dynamics of transport protocols in wide-area internet connections. In *Complex Dynamics in Communication Networks*. Springer-Verlag Publishers, 2005.
[21] N. S. V. Rao, Q. Liu, S. Sen, G. Hinkel, N. Imam, I. Foster, R. Kettimuthu, C. Q. Wu, and D. Yun. Experimental analysis of file transfer rates over wide-area dedicated connections. In *18th IEEE International Conference on High Performance Computing and Communications (HPCC)*, Dec. 2016.
[22] N. S. V. Rao, D. Towsley, G. Vardoyan, B. W. Settlemyer, I. T. Foster, and R. Kettimuthu. Sustained wide-area TCP memory transfers over dedicated connections. In *IEEE International Conference on High Performance and Smart Computing*, 2015.
[23] N. S. V. Rao, W. Yu, W. R. Wing, S. W. Poole, and J. S. Vetter. Wide-area performance profiling of 10GigE and InfiniBand technologies. In *Supercomputing Conference*, 2008.
[24] I. Rhee and L. Xu. CUBIC: A new TCP-friendly high-speed TCP variant. In *Proceedings of the Third International Workshop on Protocols for Fast Long-Distance Networks*, 2005.
[25] T. Shanley. *InfiniBand Network Architecture*, volume I and II. MindShare, Inc., 2003.
[26] R. Shorten and D. Leith. H-TCP: TCP for high-speed and long-distance networks. In *Proceedings of the Third International Workshop on Protocols for Fast Long-Distance Networks*, 2004.
[27] Y. Srikant and L. Ying. *Communication Networks: An Optimization, Control, and Stochastic Networks Perspective*. Cambridge University Press, 2014.
[28] GT 4.0 GridFTP. http://www.globus.org. Accessed: Apr. 2017.
[29] V. N. Vapnik. *Statistical Learning Theory*. John-Wiley and Sons, New York, 1998.
[30] XDD - The eXtreme dd toolset, https://github.com/bws/xdd. Accessed: Apr. 2017.
[31] T. Yee, D. Leith, and R. Shorten. Experimental evaluation of high-speed congestion control protocols. *Transactions on Networking*, 15(5):1109–1122, 2007.

AllConcur: Leaderless Concurrent Atomic Broadcast

Marius Poke
HLRS
University of Stuttgart
marius.poke@hlrs.de

Torsten Hoefler
Department of Computer Science
ETH Zurich
htor@inf.ethz.ch

Colin W. Glass
HLRS
University of Stuttgart
glass@hlrs.de

ABSTRACT

Many distributed systems require coordination between the components involved. With the steady growth of such systems, the probability of failures increases, which necessitates scalable fault-tolerant agreement protocols. The most common practical agreement protocol, for such scenarios, is leader-based atomic broadcast. In this work, we propose ALLCONCUR, a distributed system that provides agreement through a leaderless concurrent atomic broadcast algorithm, thus, not suffering from the bottleneck of a central coordinator. In ALLCONCUR, all components exchange messages concurrently through a logical overlay network that employs early termination to minimize the agreement latency. Our implementation of ALLCONCUR supports standard sockets-based TCP as well as high-performance InfiniBand Verbs communications. ALLCONCUR can handle up to 135 million requests per second and achieves 17× higher throughput than today's standard leader-based protocols, such as Libpaxos. Thus, ALLCONCUR is highly competitive with regard to existing solutions and, due to its decentralized approach, enables hitherto unattainable system designs in a variety of fields.

KEYWORDS

Distributed Agreement; Leaderless Atomic Broadcast; Reliability

ACM Reference format:
Marius Poke, Torsten Hoefler, and Colin W. Glass. 2017. AllConcur: Leaderless Concurrent Atomic Broadcast. In *Proceedings of HPDC '17, Washington , DC, USA, June 26-30, 2017,* 14 pages.
https://doi.org/http://dx.doi.org/10.1145/3078597.3078598

1 INTRODUCTION

Agreement is essential for many forms of collaboration in distributed systems. Although the nature of these systems may vary, ranging from distributed services provided by datacenters [16, 18, 59] to distributed operating systems, such as Barrelfish [56] and Mesosphere's DC/OS [46], they have in common that all the components involved regularly update a shared state. In many applications, the state updates cannot be reduced, e.g., the actions of players in multiplayer video games. Furthermore, the size of typical distributed systems has increased in recent years, making them more susceptible to single component failures [54].

Atomic broadcast is a communication primitive that provides fault-tolerant agreement while ensuring strong consistency of the

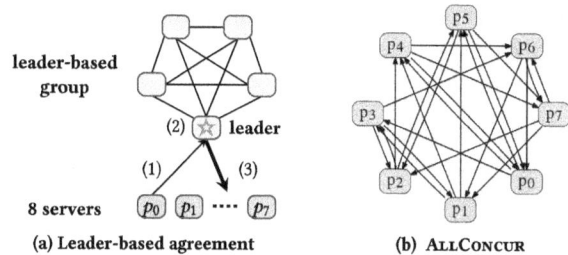

Figure 1: Agreement among 8 servers: (a) Using a leader-based group; three operations needed per update—(1) send; (2) replicate; and (3) disseminate. (b) Using a digraph G with degree three and diameter two [58].

overall system. It is often used to implement large-scale coordination services, such as replicated state machines [33] or travel reservation systems [59]. Yet, today's practical atomic broadcast algorithms rely on leader-based approaches, such as Paxos [37, 38], and thus, they may suffer from the bottleneck of a central coordinator, especially at large scale.

In this paper, we present ALLCONCUR[1]—a distributed agreement system that relies on a leaderless atomic broadcast algorithm. In ALLCONCUR, all participants exchange messages concurrently through an overlay network, described by a digraph G (§ 2.1). The maximum number of failures ALLCONCUR can sustain is given by G's connectivity and can be adapted to system-specific requirements (§ 4.4). Moreover, ALLCONCUR employs a novel early termination mechanism (§ 2.3) that reduces the expected number of communication steps significantly (§ 4.2.2).

Distributed agreement vs. replication. Distributed agreement is conceptually different from state machine replication (SMR) [36, 55]: Agreement targets collaboration in distributed systems, while SMR aims to increase data reliability. Moreover, the number of agreeing components is an input parameter, while the number of replicas depends on the required data reliability.

ALLCONCUR vs. leader-based agreement. We consider the agreement among n servers (see Figure 1 for $n = 8$). ALLCONCUR has the following properties: (1) subquadratic work, i.e., $O(nd)$, where d is G's degree (§ 4.1); 2) adjustable depth, given by G's diameter and fault diameter (§ 4.2.2); (3) at most $2d$ connections per server; and (4) server-transitivity, i.e., all servers are treated equally, which entails fairness. In contrast, typical leader-based deployments do not have all of the above properties. Figure 1a shows an example of leader-based agreement. Each server sends updates to the group's leader, which, for reliability, replicates them within the group; the replicated updates are then disseminated to all servers. In typical leader-based approaches, such as client-server

[1]Algorithm for LeaderLess CONCURrent atomic broadcast

gaming platforms, servers interact directly with the leader (for both sending and receiving updates). Although such methods have minimal depth and can ensure fairness, they require quadratic work and the leader needs to maintain n connections (§ 4.5).

Data consistency. AllConcur provides agreement while guaranteeing strong consistency. In particular, we focus on the strong consistency of state updates; thus, throughout the paper we use both request and update interchangeably. For strongly consistent reads, queries also need to be serialized via atomic broadcast. Serializing queries is costly, especially for read-heavy workloads. Typical coordination services [33] relax the consistency model: Queries are performed locally and, hence, can return stale data. AllConcur ensures that a server's view of the shared state cannot fall behind more than one round, i.e., one instance of concurrent atomic broadcast; thus, locally performed queries cannot be outdated by more than one round.

1.1 Applications and summary of results

AllConcur enables decentralized coordination services that require strong consistency at high request rates; thus, it allows for a novel approach to several real-world applications. We evaluate AllConcur using a set of benchmarks, representative of two such applications: (1) travel reservation systems; and (2) multiplayer video games.

Travel reservation systems are typical scenarios where updates are preceded by a large number of queries, e.g., clients check many flights before choosing a ticket. To avoid overloading a central server, existing systems either adopt weaker consistency models, such as eventual consistency [18], or partition the state [59], not allowing transactions spanning multiple partitions. AllConcur offers strong consistency by distributing queries over multiple servers that agree on the entire state. Each server's rate of introducing updates in the system is bounded by its rate of answering queries. Assuming 64-byte updates, AllConcur enables the agreement among 8 servers, each generating 100 million updates per second, in $35\mu s$; moreover, the agreement among 64 servers, each generating 32,000 updates per second, takes less than $0.75ms$.

Multiplayer video games are an example of applications where the shared state satisfies two conditions—it is too large to be frequently transferred through the network and it is periodically updated. For example, modern video games update the state once every $50ms$ (i.e., 20 frames per second) by only sending changes since the previous state [8, 9]. Thus, such applications are latency sensitive [7]. To decrease latency, existing systems either limit the number of players, e.g., ≈ 8 players in real time strategy games, or limit the players' view to only a subset of the state, such as the area of interest in first person shooter games [8, 9]. AllConcur allows hundreds of servers to share a global state view at low latency; e.g., it supports the simultaneous interaction of 512 players, using typical update sizes of 40 bytes [8], with an agreement latency of $38ms$, thus, enabling so called epic battles [10], while providing strong consistency.

In addition, AllConcur can handle up to 135 million (8-byte) requests per second and achieves 17× higher throughput than Libpaxos [57], an implementation of Paxos [37, 38], while its average overhead of providing fault-tolerance is 58% (§ 5).

Notation	Description	Notation	Description
G	the digraph	$d(G)$	degree
$V(G)$	vertices	$D(G)$	diameter
$E(G)$	directed edges	$\pi_{u,v}$	path from u to v
$v^+(G)$	successors of v	$k(G)$	vertex-connectivity
$v^-(G)$	predecessors of v	$D_f(G, f)$	fault diameter

Table 1: Digraph notations.

In summary, our work makes four key contributions:

- the design of AllConcur—a distributed system that provides agreement through a leaderless concurrent atomic broadcast algorithm (§ 3);
- a proof of AllConcur's correctness (§ 3.1);
- an analysis of AllConcur's performance (§ 4);
- implementations over standard sockets-based TCP and high-performance InfiniBand Verbs, that allows us to evaluate AllConcur's performance (§ 5).

2 THE BROADCAST PROBLEM

We consider n servers connected through an overlay network, described by a digraph G. The servers communicate through messages, which cannot be lost (only delayed)—reliable communication. Each server may fail according to a *fail–stop* model: A server either operates correctly or it fails without further influencing other servers in the group. A server that did not fail is called *non-faulty*. We consider algorithms that tolerate up to f failures, i.e., f-resilient.

In this paper, we use the notations from Chandra and Toueg [14] to describe both reliable and atomic broadcast: m is a message (that is uniquely identified); R-*broadcast*(m), R-*deliver*(m), A-*broadcast*(m), A-*deliver*(m) are communication primitives for broadcasting and delivering messages reliably (R-) or atomically (A-); and $sender(m)$ is the server that R- or A-broadcasts m. Note that any message m can be R- or A-broadcast at most once.

2.1 Reliable broadcast

Any (non-uniform) reliable broadcast algorithm must satisfy three properties [14, 29]:

- (Validity) If a non-faulty server R-broadcasts m, then it eventually R-delivers m.
- (Agreement) If a non-faulty server R-delivers m, then all non-faulty servers eventually R-deliver m.
- (Integrity) For any message m, every non-faulty server R-delivers m at most once, and only if m was previously R-broadcast by $sender(m)$.

A simple reliable broadcast algorithm uses a complete digraph for message dissemination [14]. When a server executes R-*broadcast*(m), it sends m to all other servers; when a server receives m for the first time, it executes R-*deliver*(m) only after sending m to all other servers. Clearly, this algorithm solves the reliable broadcast problem. Yet, the all-to-all overlay network is unnecessary: For f-resilient reliable broadcast, it is sufficient to use a digraph with vertex-connectivity larger than f.

Fault-tolerant digraphs. We define a digraph G by a set of n vertices $V(G) = \{v_i : 0 \leq i \leq n - 1\}$ and a set of directed edges $E(G) \subseteq \{(u, v) : u, v \in V(G) \text{ and } u \neq v\}$. In the context of reliable broadcast, the following parameters are of interest: the degree $d(G)$; the diameter $D(G)$; the vertex-connectivity $k(G)$; and the fault diameter $D_f(G, f)$. The *fault diameter* is the maximum diameter of G after removing any $f < k(G)$ vertices [35]. Also, we refer to digraphs with $k(G) = d(G)$ as *optimally connected* [20, 47]. Finally, we use the following additional notations: $v^+(G)$ is the set of successors of $v \in V(G)$; $v^-(G)$ is the set of predecessors of $v \in V(G)$; and $\pi_{u,v}$ is a path between two vertices $u, v \in V(G)$. Table 1 summarizes all the digraph notations used throughout the paper.

2.2 Atomic broadcast

In addition to the reliable broadcast properties, atomic broadcast must also satisfy the following property [14, 29]:

- (Total order) If two non-faulty servers p and q A-deliver messages m_1 and m_2, then p A-delivers m_1 before m_2, if and only if q A-delivers m_1 before m_2.

There are different mechanisms to ensure total order [19]. A common approach is to use a distinguished server (leader) as a coordinator. Yet, this approach suffers from the bottleneck of a central coordinator (§ 4.5). An alternative entails broadcast algorithms that ensure atomicity through *destinations agreement* [19]: All non-faulty servers agree on a message set that is A-delivered. Destinations agreement reformulates the atomic broadcast problem as *consensus* problem [6, Chapter 5]; note that consensus and atomic broadcast are equivalent [14].

2.2.1 Lower bound. Consensus has a known synchronous lower bound: In a synchronous round-based model [6, Chapter 2], any f-resilient consensus algorithm requires, in the worst case, at least $f + 1$ rounds. Intuitively, a server may fail after sending a message to only one other server; this scenario may repeat up to f times, resulting in only one server having the message; this server needs at least one additional round to disseminate the message. For more details, see the proof provided by Aguilera and Toueg [1]. Clearly, if G is used for dissemination, consensus requires (in the worst case) $f + D_f(G, f)$ rounds. To avoid assuming always the worst case, we design an *early termination* scheme (§ 2.3).

2.2.2 Failure detectors. The synchronous model is unrealistic for real-world distributed systems; more fitting is to consider an asynchronous model. Yet, under the assumption of failures, consensus (or atomic broadcast) cannot be solved in an asynchronous model [25]: We cannot distinguish between failed and slow servers. To overcome this, we use a failure detector (FD). FDs are distributed oracles that provide information about faulty servers [14].

FDs have two main properties: *completeness* and *accuracy*. Completeness requires that all failures are eventually detected; accuracy requires that no server is suspected to have failed before actually failing. If both properties hold, then the FD is *perfect* (denoted by $\mathcal{P}$) [14]. In practice, completeness is easily guaranteed by a heartbeat mechanism: Each server periodically sends heartbeats to its successors; once it fails, its successors detect the lack of heartbeats.

Guaranteeing accuracy in asynchronous systems is impossible—message delays are unbounded. Yet, the message delays in practical distributed systems are bounded. Thus, accuracy can be probabilistically guaranteed (§ 3.2). Also, FDs can guarantee *eventual accuracy*—eventually, no server is suspected to have failed before

actually failing. Such FDs are known as *eventually perfect* (denoted by $\Diamond \mathcal{P}$) [14]. For now, we consider an FD that can be reliably treated as $\mathcal{P}$. Later, we discuss the implications of using $\Diamond \mathcal{P}$, which can falsely suspect servers to have failed (§ 3.3.2).

2.3 Early termination

The synchronous lower bound holds also in practice: A message may be retransmitted by f faulty servers, before a non-faulty server can disseminate it completely. Thus, in the worst case, any f-resilient consensus algorithm that uses G for dissemination requires $f + D_f(G, f)$ communication steps. Yet, the only necessary and sufficient requirement for safe termination is for *every non-faulty server to A-deliver messages only once it has all the messages any other non-faulty server has*. Thus, early termination requires each server to track all the messages in the system.

Early termination has two parts: (1) deciding whether a message was A-broadcast; and (2) tracking the A-broadcast messages. In general, deciding whether a message was A-broadcast entails waiting for $f + D_f(G, f)$ communication steps (the worst case scenario must be assumed for safety). This essentially eliminates any form of early termination, if at least one server does not send a message. Yet, if every server A-broadcasts a message[2], it is *a priori* clear which messages exist; thus, no server waits for non-existent messages.

Every server tracks the A-broadcast messages through the received failure notifications. As an example, we consider a group of nine servers that communicate via a binomial graph [5]—a generalization of 1-way dissemination [30]. In binomial graphs, two servers pi and pj are connected if $j = i \pm 2^l (\mod n), \forall 0 \le l \le \lfloor \log_2 n \rfloor$ (see Figure 2a). We also consider a failure scenario in which p_0 fails after sending its message m_0 only to p_1; p_1 receives m_0, yet, it fails before it can send it further. How long should another server, e.g., p_6, wait for m_0?

Server p_6 is not directly connected to p_0, so it cannot directly detect its failure. Yet, p_0's non-faulty successors eventually detect p_0's failure. Once they suspect p_0 to have failed, they stop accepting messages from p_0; also, they R-broadcast notifications of p_0's failure. For example, let p_6 receive such a notification from p_2; then, p_6 knows that, if p_2 did not already send m_0, then p_2 did not receive m_0 from p_0. Clearly, both *A-broadcast()* and *R-broadcast()* use the same paths for dissemination; the only difference between them is the condition to deliver a message. If p_2 had received m_0 from p_0, then it would have sent it to p_6 before sending the notification of p_0's failure. Thus, using failure notifications, p_6 can track the dissemination of m_0. Once p_6 receives failure notifications from all of p_0's and p_1's non-faulty successors, it knows that no non-faulty server is in possession of m_0.

3 THE ALLCONCUR ALGORITHM

ALLCONCUR is a completely decentralized, f-resilient, round-based atomic broadcast algorithm that uses a digraph G as an overlay network. In a nutshell, in every round R, every non-faulty server performs three tasks: (1) it A-broadcasts a single (possibly empty) message; (2) it tracks the messages A-broadcast in R using the early termination mechanism described in Section 2.3; and (3) once

---

[2]The message can also be empty—the server A-broadcasts the information that it has nothing to broadcast.

Tracking digraph	INIT	⟨FAIL, p_0, p_2⟩	⟨FAIL, p_0, p_5⟩	⟨FAIL, p_1, p_3⟩	⟨BCAST, m_1⟩	time →
$g_6[p_0]$ server p_6 tracking m_0	p_0	p_0 → (p_1 p_2 p_4 p_5 p_7 p_8)	p_0 → (p_1 p_4 p_5 p_7 p_8)	p_0 → (p_1 p_4 p_7 p_8); p_1 → (p_2 p_3 p_5 p_6)	p_0 → (p_1 p_4 p_7 p_8); p_1 → (p_2 p_5 p_6)	
$g_6[p_1]$ server p_6 tracking m_1	p_1	p_1	p_1	p_1 → (p_0 p_2 p_3 p_5 p_6 p_8); p_0 → (p_4 p_7)	∅ (p_6 stops tracking m_1)	

(a)   (b)

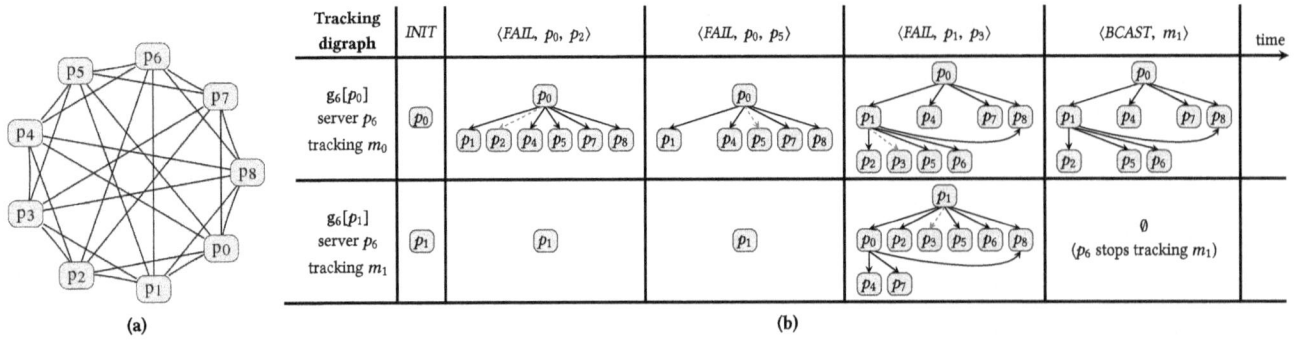

Figure 2: (a) A binomial graph. (b) Message tracking within a binomial graph. Messages are shown chronologically from left to right. Dashed edges indicate failure notifications; for clarity, we omit the edges to the root of the digraphs.

done with tracking, it A-delivers—in a deterministic order—all the messages A-broadcast in R that it received. Note that A-delivering messages in a deterministic order entails that A-broadcast messages do not have to be received in the same order. When a server fails, its successors detect the failure and R-broadcast failure notifications to the other servers; these failure notifications enable the early termination mechanism. Algorithm 1 shows the details of AllConcur during a single round. Later, we discuss the requirements of iterating AllConcur.

Initially, we make the following two assumptions: (1) the maximum number of failures is bounded, i.e., $f < k(G)$; and (2) the failures are detected by $\mathcal{P}$. In this context, we prove correctness—we show that the four properties of (non-uniform) atomic broadcast are guaranteed (§ 3.1). Then, we provide a probabilistic analysis of accuracy: If the network delays can be approximated as part of a known distribution, then we can estimate the probability of the accuracy property to hold (§ 3.2). Finally, we discuss the consequences of dropping the two assumptions (§ 3.3).

AllConcur is message-based. Each server p_i receives messages from its predecessors and sends messages to its successors. We distinguish between two message types: (1) ⟨BCAST, m_j⟩, a message A-broadcast by p_j; and (2) ⟨FAIL, p_j, $p_k \in p_j^+(G)$⟩, a notification, R-broadcast by p_k, indicating p_k's suspicion that its predecessor p_j has failed. Note that if p_i receives the notification and $p_k = p_i$, then it originated from p_i's own FD. Algorithm 1 starts when at least one server A-broadcasts a message (line 1). Every server sends a message of its own, at the latest as a reaction upon receiving a message.

Termination. AllConcur adopts a novel early termination mechanism (§ 2.3). To track the A-broadcast messages, each server p_i stores an array g_i of n digraphs, one for each server $p_* \in V(G)$; we refer to these as *tracking digraphs*. The vertices of each tracking digraph $g_i[p_*]$ consist of the servers which (according to p_i) may have m_*. An edge $(p_j, p_k) \in E(g_i[p_*])$ indicates p_i's suspicion that p_k received m_* directly from p_j. If p_i has m_*, then $g_i[p_*]$ is no longer needed; hence, p_i removes all its vertices, i.e., $V(g_i[p_*]) = \emptyset$. Initially, $V(g_i[p_j]) = \{p_j\}, \forall p_j \neq p_i$ and $V(g_i[p_i]) = \emptyset$. Server p_i A-delivers all known messages (in a deterministic order) once all tracking digraphs are empty (line 8).

Figure 2b illustrates the message-driven changes to the tracking digraphs based on the binomial graph example in Section 2.3. For clarity, we show only two of the messages being tracked by server p_6 (i.e., m_0 and m_1); both messages are tracked by updating $g_6[p_0]$ and $g_6[p_1]$, respectively. First, p_6 receives from p_2 a notification of p_0's failure, which indicates that p_2 has not received m_0 directly from p_0 (§ 2.3). Yet, p_0 may have sent m_0 to its other successors; thus, p_6 adds them to $g_6[p_0]$. Next, p_6 receives from p_5 a notification of p_0's failure—p_5 has not received m_0 directly from p_0 either and, thus, the edge (p_0, p_5) is removed. Then, p_6 receives from p_3 a notification of p_1's failure. Hence, p_6 extends both $g_6[p_0]$ and $g_6[p_1]$ with p_1's successors (except p_3). In addition, due to the previous notifications of p_0's failure, p_6 extends $g_6[p_1]$ with p_0's successors (except p_2 and p_5). Finally, p_6 receives m_1; thus, it removes all the vertices from $g_6[p_1]$ (i.e., it stops tracking m_1).

Receiving ⟨BCAST, m_j⟩. When receiving an A-broadcast message m_j (line 14), server p_i adds it to the set M_i of known messages. Also, it A-broadcasts its own message m_i, in case it did not do so before. Then, it continues the dissemination of each known message through the network—p_i sends all unique messages it has not already sent to its successors $p_i^+(G)$. Finally, p_i removes all the vertices from the $g_i[p_j]$ digraph; then, it checks whether the termination conditions are fulfilled.

Receiving ⟨FAIL, p_j, p_k⟩. When receiving a notification, R-broadcast by p_k, indicating p_k's suspicion that p_j has failed (line 21), p_i disseminates it further. Then, it adds a tuple (p_j, p_k) to the set F_i of received failure notifications. Finally, it updates the tracking digraphs in g_i that contain p_j as a vertex.

We distinguish between two cases, depending on whether this is the first notification of p_j's failure received by p_i. If it is the first, p_i updates all $g_i[p_*]$ containing p_j as a vertex by adding p_j's successors (from G) together with the corresponding edges. The rationale is, that p_j may have sent m_* to his successors, who are now in possession of it. Thus, we track the possible whereabouts of messages. However, there are some exceptions: Server p_k could not have received m_* directly from p_j (§ 2.3). Also, if a successor $p_f \notin V(g_i[p_*])$ is added, which is already known to have failed, it may have already received m_* and sent it further. Hence, the successors of p_f could be in possession of m_* and are added to $g_i[p_*]$ in the same way as described above (line 32).

Algorithm 1: The AllConcur algorithm; code executed by server p_i; see Table 1 for digraph notations.

```
Input: n; f; G; m_i; M_i ← ∅; F_i ← ∅; V(g_i[p_i]) ← ∅; V(g_i[p_j]) ← {p_j}, ∀j ≠ i

1  def A-broadcast(m_i):
2  │   send ⟨BCAST, m_i⟩ to p_i⁺(G)
3  │   M_i ← M_i ∪ {m_i}
4  │   check_termination()

5  def check_termination():
6  │   if V(g_i[p]) = ∅, ∀p then
7  │   │   foreach m ∈ sort(M_i) do
8  │   │   │   A-deliver(m)                          // A-deliver messages
       │
       │   /* preparing for next round              */
9  │   │   foreach server p_* do
10 │   │   │   if m_* ∉ M_i then
11 │   │   │   │   V(G) ← V(G) \ {p_*}              // remove servers
       │
12 │   │   foreach (p, p_s) ∈ F_i s.t. p ∈ V(G) do
13 │   │   │   send ⟨FAIL, p, p_s⟩ to p_i⁺(G)      // resend failures

14 receive ⟨BCAST, m_j⟩:
15 │   if m_i ∉ M_i then A-broadcast(m_i)
16 │   M_i ← M_i ∪ {m_j}
17 │   for m ∈ M_i not already sent do
18 │   │   send ⟨BCAST, m⟩ to p_i⁺(G)              // disseminate messages
19 │   V(g_i[p_j]) ← ∅
20 │   check_termination()

21 receive ⟨FAIL, p_j, p_k ∈ p_j⁺(G)⟩:
       │   /* if k = i then notification from local FD    */
22 │   send ⟨FAIL, p_j, p_k⟩ to p_i⁺(G)           // disseminate failures
23 │   F_i ← F_i ∪ {(p_j, p_k)}
24 │   foreach server p_* do
25 │   │   if p_j ∉ V(g_i[p_*]) then continue
26 │   │   if p_j⁺(g_i[p_*]) = ∅ then
       │   │   /* maybe p_j sent m_* to someone in p_j⁺(G) before failing */
27 │   │   │   Q ← {(p_j, p) : p ∈ p_j⁺(G) \ {p_k}}    // FIFO queue
28 │   │   │   foreach (p_p, p) ∈ Q do
29 │   │   │   │   Q ← Q \ {(p_p, p)}
30 │   │   │   │   if p ∉ V(g_i[p_*]) then
31 │   │   │   │   │   V(g_i[p_*]) ← V(g_i[p_*]) ∪ {p}
32 │   │   │   │   │   if ∃(p, *) ∈ F_i then
33 │   │   │   │   │   │   Q ← Q ∪ {(p, p_s) : p_s ∈ p⁺(G)} \ F_i
34 │   │   │   │   E(g_i[p_*]) ← E(g_i[p_*]) ∪ {(p_p, p)}

35 │   │   else if p_k ∈ p_j⁺(g_i[p_*]) then
       │   │   /* p_k has not received m_* from p_j         */
36 │   │   │   E(g_i[p_*]) ← E(g_i[p_*]) \ {(p_j, p_k)}
37 │   │   │   foreach p ∈ V(g_i[p_*]) s.t. ∄π_{p_*,p} in g_i[p_*] do
38 │   │   │   │   V(g_i[p_*]) ← V(g_i[p_*]) \ {p}    // no input

39 │   │   if ∀p ∈ V(g_i[p_*]), (p, *) ∈ F_i then
40 │   │   │   V(g_i[p_*]) ← ∅                        // no dissemination

41 │   check_termination()
```

If p_i is already aware of p_j's failure (i.e., the above process already took place), the new failure notification informs p_i, that p_k (the origin of the notification) has not received m_* from p_j—because p_k would have sent it before sending the failure notification. Thus, the edge (p_j, p_k) can be removed from $g_i[p_*]$ (line 35).

In the end, p_i prunes $g_i[p_*]$ by removing the servers no longer of interest in tracking m_*. First, p_i removes every server p for which there is no path (in $g_i[p_*]$) from p_* to p, as p could not have received m_* from any of the servers in $g_i[p_*]$ (line 37). Then, if $g_i[p_*]$ contains only servers already known to have failed, p_i prunes it entirely—no non-faulty server has m_* (line 39).

Iterating AllConcur. Executing subsequent rounds of All-Concur requires the correct handling of failures. Since different servers may end and begin rounds at different times, AllConcur employs a consistent mechanism of tagging servers as failed: At

the end of each round, all servers whose messages were not A-delivered are tagged as failed by all the other servers (line 9). As every non-faulty server agrees on the A-delivered messages, this ensures a consistent view of failed servers. In the next round, every server resends the failure notifications, except those of servers already tagged as failed (line 12). Thus, only the tags and the necessary resends need to be carried over from the previous round. Moreover, each message contains the sequence number R of the round in which it was first sent. Thus, all messages can be uniquely identified, i.e., $⟨BCAST, m_j⟩$ by (R, p_j) tuples and $⟨FAIL, p_j, p_k⟩$ by (R, p_j, p_k) tuples, which allows for multiple rounds to coexist.

Initial bootstrap and dynamic membership. To bootstrap AllConcur, we require a centralized service, such as ZooKeeper [33]: The system must decide on the initial configuration—the identity of the n servers, the fault tolerance f and the digraph G. Once AllConcur starts, any further reconfigurations are agreed upon via atomic broadcast. This includes topology reconfigurations and membership changes, i.e., servers leaving and joining the system. In contrast to leader-based approaches, where such changes may necessitate a leader election, in AllConcur, dynamic membership is handled directly by the algorithm.

3.1 Correctness

To prove AllConcur's correctness, we show that the four properties of (non-uniform) atomic broadcast are guaranteed (§ 2.2). Clearly, the integrity property holds: Every server p_i executes A-deliver() only once for each message in the set M_i, which contains only messages A-broadcast by some servers. To show that the validity property holds, it is sufficient to prove that the algorithm terminates (see Lemma 3.5). To show that both the agreement and the total order properties hold, it is sufficient to prove *set agreement*—when the algorithm terminates, all non-faulty servers have the same set of known messages (see Lemma 3.6). To prove termination and set agreement, we introduce the following lemmas:

LEMMA 3.1. *Let p_i be a non-faulty server; let $p_j \neq p_i$ be a server; let $\pi_{p_j,p_i} = (a_1, \ldots, a_d)$ be a path (in digraph G) from p_j to p_i. If p_j knows a message m (either its own or received), then, p_i eventually receives either $⟨BCAST, m⟩$ or $⟨FAIL, a_k, a_{k+1}⟩$ with $1 \leq k < d$.*

PROOF. Server p_j can either fail or send m to a_2. Further, for each inner server $a_k \in \pi_{p_j,p_i}, 1 < k < d$, we distinguish three scenarios: (1) a_k fails; (2) a_k detects the failure of its predecessor on the path; or (3) a_k further sends the message received from its predecessor on the path. The message can be either $⟨BCAST, m⟩$ or $⟨FAIL, a_l, a_{l+1}⟩$ with $1 \leq l < k$. Thus, p_i eventually receives either $⟨BCAST, m⟩$ or $⟨FAIL, a_k, a_{k+1}⟩$ with $1 \leq k < d$. Figure 3 shows, in a tree-like fashion, what messages can be transmitted along a three-server path. □

LEMMA 3.2. *Let p_i be a non-faulty server; let $p_j \neq p_i$ be a server. If p_j knows a message m (either its own or received), then p_i eventually receives either the message m or a notification of p_j's failure.*

PROOF. If p_i receives m, then the proof is done. In the case p_i does not receive m, we assume it does not receive a notification of p_j's failure either. Due to G's vertex-connectivity, there are at least $k(G)$ vertex-disjoint paths π_{p_j,p_i}. For each of these paths, p_i must

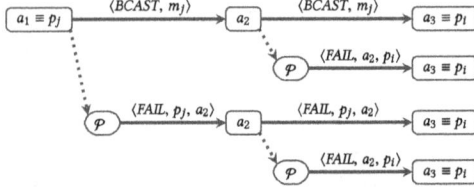

Figure 3: Possible messages along a three-server path. Dotted arrows indicate failure detection.

receive notifications of some inner vertex failures (cf. Lemma 3.1). Since the paths are vertex-disjoint, each notification indicates a different server failure. However, this contradicts the assumption that $f < k(G)$. □

COROLLARY 3.3. *Let p_i be a non-faulty server; let $p_j \neq p_i$ be a server. If p_j receives a message, then p_i eventually receives either the same message or a notification of p_j's failure.*

LEMMA 3.4. *Let p_i be a server; let $g_i[p_j]$ be a tracking digraph that can no longer be pruned. If $E(g_i[p_j]) \neq \emptyset$, then p_i eventually removes an edge from $E(g_i[p_j])$.*

PROOF. We assume that p_i removes no edge from $E(g_i[p_j])$. Clearly, the following statements are true: (1) $V(g_i[p_j]) \neq \emptyset$ (since $E(g_i[p_j]) \neq \emptyset$); (2) $p_j \in V(g_i[p_j])$ (since $g_i[p_j]$ can no longer be pruned); and (3) p_j is known to have failed (since $V(g_i[p_j]) \neq \{p_j\}$). Let $p \in V(g_i[p_j])$ be a server such that p_i receives no notification of p's failure. The reason p exists is twofold: (1) the maximum number of failures is bounded; and (2) $g_i[p_j]$ can no longer be pruned (line 39). Then, we can construct a path $\pi_{p_j,p} = (a_1, \ldots, a_d)$ in $g_i[p_j]$ such that every server along the path, except for p, is known to have failed (line 37). Eventually, p receives either $\langle BCAST, m_j \rangle$ or $\langle FAIL, a_k, a_{k+1} \rangle$ with $1 \leq k < d$ (cf. Lemma 3.1). Since p_i receives no notification of p's failure, the message received by p eventually arrives at p_i (cf. Corollary 3.3). On the one hand, if p_i receives $\langle BCAST, m_j \rangle$, then all edges are removed from $E(g_i[p_j])$; this leads to a contradiction. On the other hand, if p_i receives $\langle FAIL, a_k, a_{k+1} \rangle$, then the edge (a_k, a_{k+1}) is removed from $E(g_i[p_j])$ (line 36); this also leads to a contradiction. □

LEMMA 3.5. *(Termination) Let p_i be a non-faulty server. Then, p_i eventually terminates.*

PROOF. If $V(g_i[p]) = \emptyset$, $\forall p$, then the proof is done (line 6). We assume $\exists p_j$ such that $V(g_i[p_j]) \neq \emptyset$ and $g_i[p_j]$ can no longer be pruned. Clearly, $p_j \in V(g_i[p_j])$. Server p_i receives either m_j or a notification of p_j's failure (cf. Lemma 3.2). If p_i receives m_j, then all servers are removed from $V(g_i[p_j])$, which contradicts $V(g_i[p_j]) \neq \emptyset$. We assume p_i receives a notification of p_j's failure; then, $p_j^+(g_i[p_j]) \neq \emptyset$ (since $g_i[p_j]$ can no longer be pruned); also, $E(g_i[p_j]) \neq \emptyset$. By repeatedly applying the result of Lemma 3.4, it results that p_i eventually removes all edges from $g_i[p_j]$. As a result, $g_i[p_j]$ is eventually completely pruned, which contradicts $V(g_i[p_j]) \neq \emptyset$. □

LEMMA 3.6. *(Set agreement) Let p_i and p_j be any two non-faulty servers. Then, after ALLCONCUR's termination, $M_i = M_j$.*

PROOF. It is sufficient to show that if $m_* \in M_i$ when p_i terminates, then also $m_* \in M_j$ when p_j terminates. We assume that p_j does not receive m_*. Let $\pi_{p_*,p_i} = (a_1, \ldots, a_d)$ be one of the paths (in G) on which m_* arrives at p_i. Let k, $1 \leq k \leq d$ the smallest index such that p_j receives no notification of a_k's failure. The existence of a_k is given by the existence of p_i, a server that is both non-faulty and on π_{p_*,p_i}. Clearly, $a_k \in V(g_j[p_*])$. Since it terminates, p_j eventually removes a_k from $g_j[p_*]$. In general, p_j can remove a_k when it receives either m_* or a notification of a_k's failure; yet, both alternatives lead to contradictions. In addition, for $k > 1$, p_j can remove a_k when there is no path π_{p_*,a_k} in $g_j[p_*]$. This requires p_j to remove an edge on the $(a_1, \ldots, a_k)$ path. Thus, p_j receives a message $\langle FAIL, a_l, a_{l+1} \rangle$ with $1 \leq l < k$. Yet, since a_{l+1} received m_* from a_l, p_j must receive $\langle BCAST, m_* \rangle$ first, which leads to a contradiction. □

COROLLARY 3.7. *ALLCONCUR solves the atomic broadcast problem while tolerating up to f failures.*

3.2 Probabilistic analysis of accuracy

Algorithm 1 assumes a perfect FD, which requires the accuracy property to hold. Accuracy is difficult to guarantee in practice: Due to network delays, a server may falsely suspect another server to have failed. Yet, when the network delays can be approximated as part of a known distribution, accuracy can be probabilistically guaranteed. Let T be a random variable that describes the network delays. Then, we denote by $Pr[T > t]$ the probability that a message delay exceeds a constant t.

We propose an FD based on a heartbeat mechanism. Every non-faulty server sends heartbeats to its successors in G; the heartbeats are sent periodically, with a period Δ_{hb}. Every non-faulty server p_i waits for heartbeats from its predecessors in G; if, within a period Δ_{to}, p_i receives no heartbeats from a predecessor p_j, it suspects p_j to have failed. Since we assume heartbeat messages are delayed according to a known distribution, we can estimate the probability of the FD to be accurate, in particular a lower bound of the probability of the proposed FD to behave indistinguishably from a perfect one.

The interval in which p_i receives two heartbeats from a predecessor p_j is bounded by $\Delta_{hb} + T$. In the interval Δ_{to}, p_j sends $\lfloor \Delta_{to}/\Delta_{hb} \rfloor$ heartbeats to p_i. The probability that p_i does not receive the k'th heartbeat within the period Δ_{to} is bounded by $Pr[T > \Delta_{to} - k\Delta_{hb}]$. For p_i to incorrectly suspect p_j to have failed, it has to receive none of the k heartbeats. Moreover, p_i can incorrectly suspect $d(G)$ predecessors; also, there are n servers that can incorrectly suspect their predecessors. Thus, the probability of the accuracy property to hold is at least $(1 - \prod_{k=1}^{\lfloor \Delta_{to}/\Delta_{hb} \rfloor} Pr[T > \Delta_{to} - k\Delta_{hb}])^{n \cdot d(G)}$.

Increasing both the timeout period and the heartbeat frequency increases the likelihood of accurate failure detection. The probability of no incorrect failure detection in the system, together with the probability of less than $k(G)$ failures define the reliability of ALLCONCUR.

3.3 Widening the scope

A practical atomic broadcast algorithm must always guarantee safety. Under the two initial assumptions, i.e., $f < k(G)$ and $\mathcal{P}$, ALLCONCUR guarantees both safety and liveness (§ 3.1). In this section, we show that $f < k(G)$ is not required for safety, but only for liveness (§ 3.3.1). Also, we provide a mechanism that enables AllConcur to guarantee safety even when the $\mathcal{P}$ assumption is dropped (§ 3.3.2).

3.3.1 Disconnected digraph. In general, Algorithm 1 requires G to be connected. A digraph can be disconnected by either (1) removing a sufficient number of vertices to break the vertex-connectivity, i.e., $f \geq k(G)$, or (2) removing sufficent edges to break the edge-connectivity. Under the assumption of reliable communication (i.e., G's edges cannot be removed), only the fist scenario is possible. If $f \geq k(G)$, termination is not guaranteed (see Lemma 3.2). Yet, some servers may still terminate the round even if G is disconnected. In this case, set agreement still holds, as the proof of Lemma 3.6 does not assume less than $k(G)$ failures. In summary, the $f < k(G)$ assumption is needed only to guarantee liveness; safety is guaranteed regardless of the number of failures (similar to Paxos [37, 38]).

In scenarios where G's edges can be removed, such as network partitioning, a non-faulty server disconnected from one of its non-faulty successors will be falsely suspected to have failed[3]. Thus, the assumption of $\mathcal{P}$ does not hold and we need to relax it to $\Diamond\mathcal{P}$.

3.3.2 Eventual accuracy. For some distributed systems, it may be necessary to use $\Diamond\mathcal{P}$ instead of $\mathcal{P}$. For instance, in cases of network partitioning as discussed above, or for systems in which approximating network delays as part of a known distribution is difficult. Implementing a heartbeat-based $\Diamond\mathcal{P}$ is straightforward [14]: When a server falsely suspects another server to have failed, it increments the timeout period Δ_{to}; thus, eventually, non-faulty servers are no longer suspected to have failed. Yet, when using $\Diamond\mathcal{P}$, failure notifications no longer necessarily indicate server failures. Thus, to adapt Algorithm 1 to $\Diamond\mathcal{P}$, we need to ensure the correctness of early termination, which relies on the information carried by failure notifications.

First, a $\langle FAIL, p_j, p_k \rangle$ message received by p_i, indicates that p_k did not receive (and it will not receive until termination) from p_j any message not yet received by p_i. Thus, once a server suspects one of its predecessors to have failed, it must ignore any subsequent messages (except failure notifications) received from that predecessor (until the algorithm terminates). As a result, when using $\Diamond\mathcal{P}$, it is still possible to decide if a server received a certain message.

Second, p_i receiving notifications of p_j's failure from all p_j's successors indicates both that p_j is faulty and that it did not disseminate further any message not yet received by p_i. Yet, when using $\Diamond\mathcal{P}$, these notifications no longer indicate that p_j is faulty. Thus, both p_i and p_j can terminate without agreeing on the same set (i.e., $M_i \neq M_j$), which breaks AllConcur's safety. In this case though, p_i and p_j are part of different strongly connected components. For set agreement to hold (§ 3.1), only the servers from one single strongly connected component can A-deliver messages; we refer to this component as the *surviving partition*. The other servers are considered to be faulty (for the properties of reliable broadcast to hold). To ensure the uniqueness of the surviving partition, it must contain at least a majority of the servers.

Deciding whether to A-deliver. Each server decides whether it is part of the surviving partition via a mechanism based on Kosaraju's algorithm to find strongly connected components [2, Chapter 6]. In particular, once each server p_i decides on the set M_i, it R-broadcasts two messages: (1) a forward message $\langle FWD, p_i \rangle$; and (2) a backward message $\langle BWD, p_i \rangle$. The backward message is R-broadcast using the transpose of G. Then, p_i A-delivers the messages from M_i only when it receives both forward and backward messages from at least $\lfloor n/2 \rfloor$ servers. Intuitively, a $\langle FWD, p_j \rangle$ message received by p_i indicates that when p_j decided on its set M_j, there was at least one path from p_j to p_i; thus, p_i knows of all the messages known by p_j (i.e., $M_j \subseteq M_i$). Similarly, a $\langle BWD, p_j \rangle$ message indicates that $M_i \subseteq M_j$. Thus, when p_i A-delivers it knows that at least a majority of the servers (including itself) A-deliver the same messages.

Non-terminating servers. To satisfy the properties of reliable broadcast (§ 2.1), non-terminating servers need to be eventually removed from the system and consequently, be considered as faulty. In practice, these servers could restart after a certain period of inactivity and then try to rejoin the system, by sending a membership request to one of the non-faulty servers.

4 PERFORMANCE ANALYSIS

AllConcur is designed as a high-throughput atomic broadcast algorithm. Its performance is given by three metrics: (1) work per server; (2) communication time; and (3) storage requirements. Our analysis focuses on Algorithm 1, i.e., connected digraph and perfect FD, and it uses the LogP model [17]. The LogP model is described by four parameters: the latency L; the overhead o; the gap between messages g; and the number of processes (or servers) P, which we denote by n. We make the common assumption that $o > g$ [4]; also, the model assumes short messages. AllConcur's performance depends on G's parameters: d, D, and D_f. A discussion on how to choose G is provided in Section 4.4.

4.1 Work per server

The amount of work a server performs is given by the number of messages it receives and sends. AllConcur distinguishes between A-broadcast messages and failure notifications. First, without failures, every server receives an A-broadcast message from all of its d predecessors, i.e., $(n-1) \cdot d$ messages received by each server. This is consistent with the $\Omega(n^2 f)$ worst-case message complexity for synchronous f-resilient consensus algorithms [21]. Second, every failed server is detected by up to d servers, each sending a failure notification to its d successors. Thus, each server receives up to d^2 notifications of each failure. Overall, each server receives at most $n \cdot d + f \cdot d^2$ messages. Since G is regular, each server sends the same number of messages.

In order to terminate, in a non-failure scenario, a server needs to receive at least $(n-1)$ messages and send them further to d successors. We estimate the time of sending or receiving a message by the overhead o of the LogP model [17]. Thus, a lower bound on termination (due to work) is given by $2(n-1)do$.

---

[3]Note that if G is disconnected by removing vertices, a non-faulty server cannot be disconnected from its non-faulty successors.

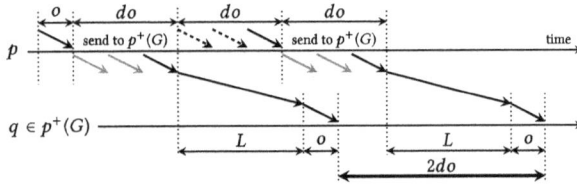

Figure 4: LogP model of message transmission in AllConcur for $d = 3$. Dashed arrows indicate already sent messages.

4.2 Communication time

In general, the time to transmit a message (between two servers) is estimated by $T(msg) = L + 2o$. We consider only the scenario of a single non-empty message m being A-broadcast and we estimate the time between $sender(m)$ A-broadcasts m and A-delivers m.

4.2.1 Non-faulty scenario. We split the A-broadcast of m in two: (1) R-broadcast(m); and (2) the empty messages $m_\emptyset$ travel back to $sender(m)$. In a non-failure scenario, messages are R-broadcast in D steps, i.e., $T_D(msg) = T(msg)D$. Moreover, to account for contention while sending to d successors, we add to the sending overhead the expected waiting time, i.e., $o_s = o + \frac{d-1}{2}o$. Note that for R-broadcast(m), there is no contention while receiving (every server, except $sender(m)$, is idle until it receives m). Thus, the time to R-broadcast m is estimated by $T_D(m) = (L + o_s + o)D$.

When the empty messages $m_\emptyset$ are transmitted to $sender(m)$, the servers are no longer idle; $T_D(m_\emptyset)$ needs to account for contention while receiving. On average, servers send further one in every d received messages; thus, a server p sends messages to the same successor q at a period of $2do$ (see Figure 4). In general, once a message arrives at a server, it needs to contend with other received messages. Yet, servers handle incoming connections in a round-robin fashion; processing a round of messages from all d predecessors takes (on average) $2do$, i.e., $2o$ per predecessor (see server p in Figure 4). Thus, on average, the message in-rate on a connection matches the out-rate: There is no contention while receiving empty messages, i.e., $T_D(m_\emptyset) = T_D(m)$.

4.2.2 Faulty scenario—probabilistic analysis. Let π_m be the longest path a message m has to travel before it is completely disseminated. If m is lost (due to failures), π_m is augmented by the longest path the failure notifications have to travel before reaching all non-faulty servers. Let $\mathcal{D}$ be a random variable that denotes the length of the longest path π_m, for any A-broadcast message m, i.e., $\mathcal{D} = \max_m |\pi_m|, \forall m$; we refer to $\mathcal{D}$ as AllConcur's *depth*. Intuitively, the depth is the asynchronous equivalent of the number of rounds from synchronous systems. Thus, $\mathcal{D}$ ranges from D, if no servers fail, to $f + D_f$ in the worst case scenario (§ 2.2.1). Yet, $\mathcal{D}$ is not uniformly distributed. A back-of-the-envelope calculation shows that it is very unlikely for AllConcur's depth to exceed D_f.

We consider a single AllConcur round, with all n servers initially non-faulty. Also, we estimate the probability p_f of a server to fail, by using an exponential lifetime distribution model, i.e., over a period of time Δ, $p_f = 1 - e^{-\Delta/MTTF}$, where $MTTF$ is the mean time to failure. If $sender(m)$ succeeds in sending m to all of its successors, then $D \leq \pi_m \leq D_f$ (§ 2.2.1). Thus, $Pr[D \leq \mathcal{D} \leq D_f] = e^{-n \cdot d \cdot o/MTTF}$, where o is the sending overhead [17]. Note

that this probability increases if the round starts with previously failed servers.

For typical values of $MTTF$ ($\approx$ 2 years [54]) and o ($\approx 1.8\mu s$ for TCP on our InfiniBand cluster § 5), a system of 256 servers connected via a digraph of degree 7 (see Table 3) would finish 1 million AllConcur rounds with $\mathcal{D} \leq D_f$ with a probability larger than 99.99%. This demonstrates why early termination is essential for efficiency, as for most rounds no failures occur and even if they do occur, the probability of $\mathcal{D} > D_f$ is very small. Note that a practical deployment of AllConcur should include regularly replacing failed servers and/or updating G after failures.

4.2.3 Estimating the fault diameter. The fault diameter of any digraph G is trivially bounded by $\left\lfloor \frac{n-f-2}{k(G)-f} \right\rfloor + 1$ [15, Theorem 6]. However, this bound is neither tight nor does it relate the fault diameter to the digraph's diameter. In general, the fault diameter is unbounded in terms of the digraph diameter [15]. Yet, if the first $f+1$ shortest vertex-disjoint paths from u to v are of length at most δ_f for $\forall u, v \in V(G)$, then $D_f(G, f) \leq \delta_f$ [35]. To compute δ_f, we need to solve the min-max $(f+1)$-disjoint paths problem for every pair of vertices: Find $(f+1)$ vertex-disjoint paths $\pi_0, \ldots, \pi_f$ that minimize the length of the longest path; hence, $\delta_f = \max_i |\pi_i|, 0 \leq i \leq f$.

Unfortunately, the problem is known to be strongly NP-complete [41]. As a heuristic to find δ_f, we minimize the sum of the lengths instead of the maximum length, i.e., the min-sum disjoint paths problem. This problem can be expressed as a minimum-cost flow problem; thus, it can be solved polynomially with well known algorithms, e.g., successive shortest path [3, Chapter 9]. Let $\hat{\pi}_0, \ldots, \hat{\pi}_f$ be the paths obtained from solving the min-sum disjoint paths problem; also, let $\hat{\delta}_f = \max_i |\hat{\pi}_i|, 0 \leq i \leq f$. Then, from the minimality condition of both min-max and min-sum problems, we deduce the following chain of inequalities:

$$\frac{\sum_{i=0}^{f} |\hat{\pi}_i|}{f+1} \leq \frac{\sum_{i=0}^{f} |\pi_i|}{f+1} \leq \delta_f \leq \hat{\delta}_f. \tag{1}$$

Thus, we approximate the fault diameter bound by $\hat{\delta}_f$. Then, we use Equation (1) to check the accuracy of our approximation: We check the difference between the maximum and the average length of the paths obtained from solving the tractable min-sum problem.

As an example, we consider the binomial graph example from [5], i.e., $n = 12$ and $p_j^+ = p_j^- = \{p_j : j = i \pm \{1, 2, 4\}\}$. The graph has connectivity $k = 6$ and diameter $D = 2$. After solving the min-sum problem, we can estimate the fault diameter bound, i.e., $3 \leq \delta_f \leq 4$. After a closer look, we can see that one of the six vertex-disjoint paths from p_0 to p_3 has length four, i.e., $p_0 - p_{10} - p_6 - p_5 - p_3$.

4.3 Storage requirements

Each server p_i stores five data structures (see Algorithm 1): (1) the digraph G; (2) the set of known messages M_i; (3) the set of received failure notifications F_i; (4) the array of tracking digraphs g_i; and (5) the internal FIFO queue Q. Table 2 shows the space complexity of each data structure. In general, for regular digraphs, p_i needs to store d edges per node; yet, some digraphs require less storage, e.g., binomial graphs [5] require only the graph size. Also, each tracking digraph has at most fd vertices; yet, only f of these digraphs may

Notation	Description	Space complexity per server
G	digraph	$O(n \cdot d)$
M_i	messages	$O(n)$
F_i	failure notifications	$O(f \cdot d)$
g_i	tracking digraphs	$O(f^2 \cdot d)$
Q	FIFO queue	$O(f \cdot d)$

Table 2: Space complexity per server for data structures used by Algorithm 1. The space complexity for G holds for regular digraphs, such as $G_S(n, d)$ § 4.4.

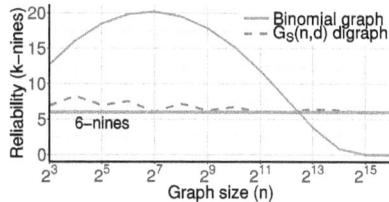

Figure 5: ALLCONCUR's reliability estimated over a period of 24 hours and a server $MTTF \approx 2$ years.

have more than one vertex. The space complexity of the other data structures is straightforward (see Table 2).

4.4 Choosing the digraph G

ALLCONCUR's performance depends on the parameters of G—degree, diameter, and fault diameter. Binomial graphs have both diameter and fault diameter lower than other commonly used graphs, such as the binary Hypercube [5]. Also, they are optimally connected, hence, offering optimal work for the provided connectivity. Yet, their connectivity depends on the number of vertices, which reduces their flexibility: Binomial graphs provide either too much or not enough connectivity.

We estimate ALLCONCUR's reliability by $\rho_G = \sum_{i=0}^{k(G)-1} C(n, i) \cdot p_f^i (1-p_f)^{n-i}$, with $p_f = 1 - e^{-\frac{\Delta}{MTTF}}$ the probability of a server to fail over a period of time Δ (§ 4.2.2). Figure 5 plots this reliability as a function of n. For a reliability target of 6-nines, we can see that the binomial graph offers either too much reliability, resulting in unnecessary work, or not sufficient reliability.

As an alternative, ALLCONCUR uses $G_S(n, d)$ digraphs, for any $d \geq 3$ and $n \geq 2d$ [58]. In a nutshell, the construction of $G_S(n, d)$ entails constructing the line digraph of a generalized de Bruijn digraph [23] with the self-loops replaced by cycles. A more detailed description that follows the steps provided in the original paper [58] is available in an extendend technical report [53]. Similarly to binomial graphs [5], $G_S(n, d)$ digraphs are optimally connected. Contrary to binomial graphs though, they can be adapted to various reliability targets (see Figure 5 for a reliability target of 6-nines). Moreover, $G_S(n, d)$ digraphs have a quasiminimal diameter for $n \leq d^3 + d$: The diameter is at most one larger than the lower bound obtained from the Moore bound, i.e., $DL(n, d) = \lceil \log_d (n(d-1) + d) \rceil - 1$. In addition, $G_S(n, d)$ digraphs have low fault diameter bounds (experimentally verified). Table 3 shows the parameters of $G_S(n, d)$ for different number of vertices and 6-nines reliability; the reliability is estimated over a period of 24 hours according to the data from the

$G_S(n, d)$	D	$DL(n, d)$	$G_S(n, d)$	D	$DL(n, d)$
$G_S(6, 3)$	2	2	$G_S(64, 5)$	4	3
$G_S(8, 3)$	2	2	$G_S(90, 5)$	3	3
$G_S(11, 3)$	3	2	$G_S(128, 5)$	4	3
$G_S(16, 4)$	2	2	$G_S(256, 7)$	4	3
$G_S(22, 4)$	3	3	$G_S(512, 8)$	3	3
$G_S(32, 4)$	3	3	$G_S(1024, 11)$	4	3
$G_S(45, 4)$	4	3			

Table 3: The parameters—vertex count n, degree d and diameter D—of $G_S(n, d)$ for 6-nines reliability (estimated over a period of 24 hours and a server $MTTF \approx 2$ years). The lower bound for the diameter is $DL(n, d) = \lceil \log_d (n(d-1) + d) \rceil - 1$.

TSUBAME2.5 system failure history [28, 54], i.e., server $MTTF \approx 2$ years.

4.5 AllConcur vs. leader-based agreement

For a theoretical comparison to leader-based agreement, we consider the following deployment: a leader-based group, such as Paxos, that enables the agreement among n servers, i.e., clients in Paxos terminology (see Figure 1a). The group size does not depend on n, but only on the reliability of the group members. Also, all the servers interact directly with the leader. In principle, the leader can disseminate state updates via a tree [32]; yet, for fault-tolerance, a reliable broadcast algorithm [12] is needed. To the best of our knowledge, there is no implementation of leader-based agreement that uses reliable broadcast for dissemination.

In general, in such a leader-based deployment, not all servers need to send a message. This is an advantage over ALLCONCUR, where the early termination mechanism requires every server to send a message. Yet, for the typical scenarios targeted by ALL-CONCUR—the data to be agreed upon is well balanced—we can realistically assume that all servers have a message to send.

Trade-off between work and total message count. The work require for reaching agreement in a leader-based deployment is unbalanced. On the one hand, every server sends one message and receives $n-1$ messages, resulting in $O(n)$ work. On the other hand, the leader requires quadratic work, i.e., $O(n^2)$: it receives one message from every server and it sends every received message to all servers. Note that every message is also replicated, adding a constant amount of work per message.

To avoid overloading a single server (i.e., the leader), ALLCONCUR distributes the work evenly among all servers—every server performs $O(nd)$ work (§ 4.1). This decrease in complexity comes at the cost of introducing more messages to the network. A leader-based deployment introduces $n(n-1)$ messages to the network (not counting the messages needed for replication). In ALLCONCUR, every message is sent d times; thus, the total number of messages in the network is $n^2 d$.

Removing and adding servers. For both ALLCONCUR and leader-based agreement, the cost of intentionally removing and adding servers can be hidden by using a two-phase approach similar to the transitional configuration in Raft [51]. Thus, we focus only on the cost of unintentionally removing a server—a server failure. Also, we consider a worst-case analysis—we compare the impact of a leader failure to that of a ALLCONCUR server. The consequence of a leader failure is threefold: (1) every server receives one failure notification; (2) a leader election is triggered; and (3) the new leader needs to reestablish the connections to the n servers. Note that the cost of reestablishing the connection can be hidden if the servers connect from the start to all members of the group. In ALLCONCUR, there is no need for leader election. A server failure causes every server to receive up to d^2 failure notifications (§ 4.1). Also, the depth may increase (§ 4.2.2).

Redundancy. The amount of redundancy (i.e., d) needed by ALLCONCUR is given by the reliability of the agreeing servers. Thus, d can be seen as a performance penalty for requiring a certain level of reliability. Using more reliable hardware increases ALL-CONCUR's performance. In contrast, in a leader-based deployment, more reliable hardware increases only the performance of message replication (i.e., less replicas are needed), leaving both the quadratic work and the quadratic total message count unchanged.

5 EVALUATION

We evaluate ALLCONCUR on two production systems: (1) an InfiniBand cluster with 96 nodes; and (2) the Hazel Hen Cray XC40 system (7712 nodes). We refer to the two systems as IB-hsw and XC40, respectively. On both systems, each node has 128GB of physical memory and two Intel Xeon E5-2680v3 12-core CPUs with a base frequency of 2.5GHz. The IB-hsw system nodes are connected through a Voltair 4036 Fabric (40Gbps); each node uses a single Mellanox ConnectX-3 QDR adapter (40GBps). Moreover, each node is running ScientificLinux version 6.4. The XC40 system nodes are connected through the Cray Aries network.

We implemented ALLCONCUR[4] in C; the implementation relies on *libev*, a high-performance event loop library. Each instance of ALLCONCUR is deployed on a single physical node. The nodes communicate via either standard sockets-based TCP or high-performance InfiniBand Verbs (IBV); we refer to the two variants as ALLCONCUR-TCP and ALLCONCUR-IBV, respectively. On the IB-hsw system, to take advantage of the high-performance network, we use TCP/IP over InfiniBand ("IP over IB") for ALLCONCUR-TCP. The failure detector is implemented over unreliable datagrams. To compile the code, we use GCC version 5.2.0 on the IB-hsw system and Cray Programming Environment 5.2.82 on the XC40 system.

We evaluate ALLCONCUR through a set of benchmarks that emulate representative real-world applications. During the evaluation, we focus on two common performance metrics: (1) the *agreement latency*, i.e., the time needed to reach agreement; and (2) the *agreement throughput*, i.e., the amount of data agreed upon per second. In addition, we introduce the *aggregated throughput*, a performance metric defined as the agreement throughput times the number of servers. Also, all the experiments assume a perfect FD.

In the following benchmarks, the servers are interconnected via $G_S(n, d)$ digraphs (see Table 3). If not specified otherwise, each server generates requests at a certain rate. The requests are buffered until the current agreement round is completed; then, they are packed into a message that is A-broadcast in the next round. All the figures report both the median and the 95% nonparametric

[4]Source code: https://github.com/mpoke/allconcur/commit/c09dee8f8f186ee7b2d4fdb23e682016eb3dbde8

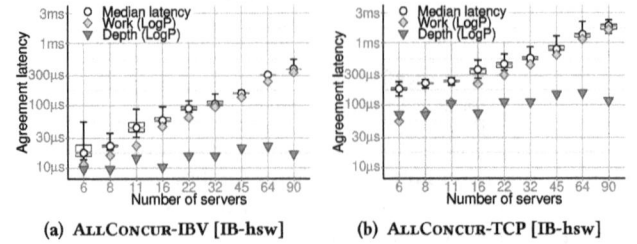

(a) ALLCONCUR-IBV [IB-hsw]　　(b) ALLCONCUR-TCP [IB-hsw]

Figure 6: Agreement latency for a single (64-byte) request. The LogP parameters are $L = 1.25\mu s$ and $o = 0.38\mu s$ over IBV and $L = 12\mu s$ and $o = 1.8\mu s$ over TCP.

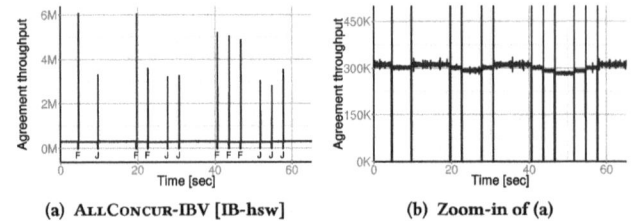

(a) ALLCONCUR-IBV [IB-hsw]　　(b) Zoom-in of (a)

Figure 7: Agreement throughput during membership changes—servers failing, indicated by F, and servers joining, indicated by J. Deployment over 32 servers, each generating 10,000 (64-byte) requests per second. The FD has $\Delta_{hb} = 10ms$ and $\Delta_{to} = 100ms$. The spikes in throughput are due to the accumulated requests during unavailability periods.

confidence interval around it [31]. Moreover, for each figure, the system used to obtain the measurements is specified in square brackets.

Single request agreement. To evaluate the LogP models described in Section 4, we consider a benchmark where the servers agree on one single request. Clearly, such a scenario is not the intended use case of ALLCONCUR, as all servers, except one, A-broadcast empty messages. Figure 6 plots the agreement latency as a function of system size for both ALLCONCUR-IBV and ALLCONCUR-TCP on the IB-hsw system and it compares it with the LogP models for both work and depth (§ 4). The LogP parameters for the IB-hsw system are $L = 1.25\mu s$ and $o = 0.38\mu s$ over IBV and $L = 12\mu s$ and $o = 1.8\mu s$ over TCP. The models are good indicators of ALLCONCUR's performance; e.g., with increasing the system size, work becomes dominant.

Membership changes. To evaluate the effect of membership changes on performance, we deploy ALLCONCUR-IBV on the IB-hsw system. In particular, we consider 32 servers each generating 10,000 (64-byte) requests per second. Servers rely on a heartbeat-based FD with a heartbeat period $\Delta_{hb} = 10ms$ and a timeout period $\Delta_{to} = 100ms$. Figure 7 shows ALLCONCUR's agreement throughput (binned into $10ms$ intervals) during a series of events, i.e., servers failing, indicated by F, and servers joining, indicated by J. Initially, one server fails, causing a period of unavailability ($\approx 190ms$); this is followed by a rise in throughput, due to the accumulated requests (see Figure 7a). Shortly after, the system stabilizes, but at a lower throughput since one server is missing. Next, a server joins the

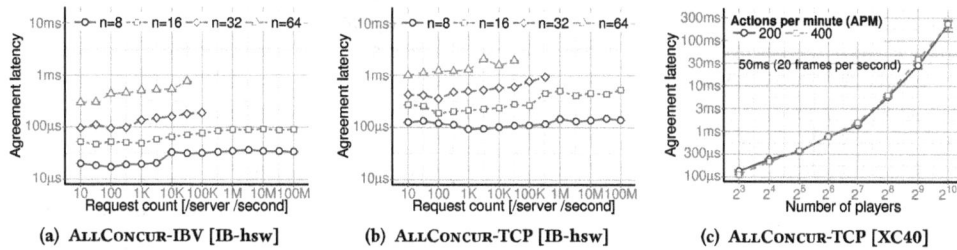

(a) ALLCONCUR-IBV [IB-hsw]   (b) ALLCONCUR-TCP [IB-hsw]   (c) ALLCONCUR-TCP [XC40]

Figure 8: (a),(b) Constant (64-byte) request rate per server. (c) Agreement latency in multiplayer video games for different APM and 40-byte requests.

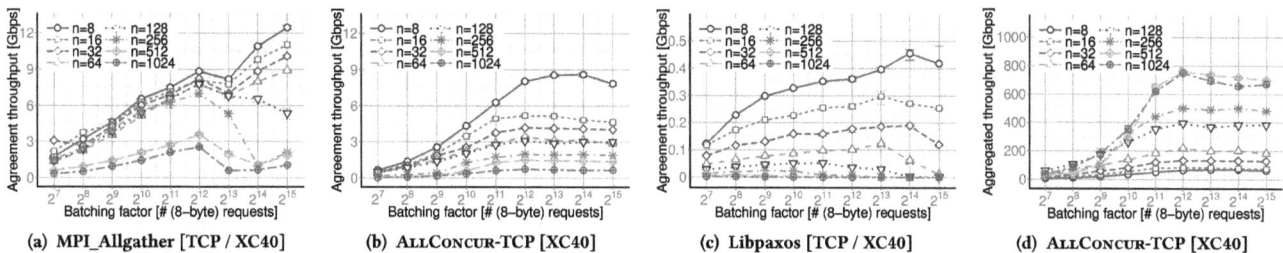

(a) MPI_Allgather [TCP / XC40]   (b) ALLCONCUR-TCP [XC40]   (c) Libpaxos [TCP / XC40]   (d) ALLCONCUR-TCP [XC40]

Figure 9: (a) Unreliable agreement vs. (b) ALLCONCUR vs. (c) leader-based agreement—batching factor effect on the agreement throughput. (d) Batching factor effect on the aggregated throughput.

system causing another period of unavailability ($\approx 80ms$) followed by another rise in throughput. Similarly, this scenario repeats for two and three subsequent failures[5]. Note that both unavailability periods can be reduced. First, by improving the FD implementation, Δ_{to} can be significantly decreased [22]. Second, new servers can join the system as non-participating members until they established all necessary connections [51].

Travel reservation systems. In this scenario, each server's rate of generating requests is bounded by its rate of answering queries. We consider a benchmark where 64-byte requests are generated with a constant rate per server r. Since the *batching factor* (i.e., the amount of requests packed into a message) is not bounded, the system becomes unstable once the rate of generating requests exceeds the agreement throughput; this leads to a cycle of larger messages, leading to longer times, leading to larger messages etc. A practical deployment would bound the message size and reduce the inflow of requests. Figures 8a and 8b plot the agreement latency as a function of r; the measurements were obtained on the IB-hsw system. By using ALLCONCUR-IBV, 8 servers, each generating 100 million requests per second, reach agreement in $35\mu s$; while 64 servers, each generating 32,000 requests per second, reach agreement in less than $0.75ms$. ALLCONCUR-TCP has $\approx 3\times$ higher latency.

Multiplayer video games. In this scenario, the state is updated periodically, e.g., once every $50ms$ in multiplayer video games [8, 9]; thus, such systems are latency sensitive. Moreover, similarly to travel reservation systems, each server's rate of generating requests is bounded; e.g., in multiplayer video games, each player performs a limited number of actions per minute (APM), i.e., usually 200 APM,

although expert players can exceed 400 APM [40]. To emulate such a scenario, we deploy ALLCONCUR on the XC40 system; although not designed for video games, the system enables large-scale deployments. Figure 8c plots the agreement latency as a function of the number of players, for 200 and 400 APM. Each action causes a state update with a typical size of 40 bytes [8]. ALLCONCUR-TCP supports the simultaneous interaction among 512 players with an agreement latency of $28ms$ for 200 APM and $38ms$ for 400 APM. Thus, ALLCONCUR enables so called epic battles [10].

ALLCONCUR vs. unreliable agreement. To evaluate the overhead of providing fault-tolerance, we compare ALLCONCUR to an implementation of unreliable agreement. In particular, we use MPI_Allgather [49] to disseminate all messages to every server. We consider a benchmark where every server delivers a fixed-size message per round (fixed number of requests). Figures 9a and 9b plot the agreement throughput as a function of the batching factor. The measurements were obtained on the XC40 system; for a fair comparison, we used Open MPI [26] over TCP to run the benchmark. ALLCONCUR provides a reliability target of 6-nines with an average overhead of 58%. Moreover, for messages of at least 2,048 (8-byte) requests, the overhead does not exceed 75%.

ALLCONCUR vs. leader-based agreement. We conclude ALLCONCUR's evaluation by comparing it to Libpaxos [57], an open-source implementation of Paxos [37, 38] over TCP. In particular, we use Libpaxos as the leader-based group in the deployment described in Section 4.5. The size of the Paxos group is five, sufficient for our reliability target of 6-nines. We consider the same benchmark used to compare to unreliable agreement—each server A-delivers a fixed-size message per round. Figures 9b and 9c plot the agreement throughput as a function of the batching factor; the measurements were obtained on the XC40 system. The throughput

---

[5]The $G_S(32, 4)$ has vertex-connectivity four; thus, in general, it cannot safely sustain more than three failures

peaks at a certain message size, indicating the optimal batching factor to be used. AllConcur-TCP reaches an agreement throughput of $8.6Gbps$, equivalent to ≈ 135 million (8-byte) requests per second (see Figures 9b). As compared to Libpaxos, AllConcur achieves at least 17× higher throughput (see Figure 9c). The drop in throughput (after reaching the peak), for both AllConcur and Libpaxos, is due to the TCP congestion control mechanism.

AllConcur's agreement throughput decreases with increasing the number of servers. The reason for this performance drop is twofold. First, to maintain the same reliability, more servers entail a higher degree for G (see Table 3), hence, more redundancy. Second, agreement among more servers entails more synchronization. Yet, the number of agreeing servers is an input parameter. Thus, a better metric to measure AllConcur's actual performance is the aggregated throughput. Figure 9d plots the aggregated throughput corresponding to the agreement throughput from Figures 9b. AllConcur-TCP's aggregated throughput increases with the number of servers and it peaks at $\approx 750Gbps$ for 512 and 1,024 servers.

6 RELATED WORK

Many existing algorithms and systems can be used to implement atomic broadcast; we discuss here only the most relevant subset. Défago, Schiper, and Urbán provide a general overview of atomic broadcast algorithms [19]. They define a classification based on how total order is established: by the sender, by a sequencer or by the destinations [14]. AllConcur uses destinations agreement to achieve total order, i.e., agreement on a message set. Yet, unlike other destinations agreement algorithms, AllConcur is entirely decentralized and requires no leader.

Lamport's classic Paxos algorithm [37, 38] is often used to implement atomic broadcast. Several practical systems have been proposed [11, 16, 34, 45]. Also, a series of optimizations were proposed, such as distributing the load among all servers or out-of-order processing of not-interfering requests [39, 44, 48]. Yet, the commonly employed simple replication scheme is not designed to scale to hundreds of instances.

State machine replication protocols are similar to Paxos but often claim to be simpler to understand and implement. Practical implementations include ZooKeeper [33], Viewstamped Replication [43], Raft [51], Chubby [13] and DARE [52] among others. These systems commonly employ a leader-based approach which makes them fundamentally unscalable. Increasing scalability comes often at the cost of relaxing the consistency model [18, 42]. Moreover, even when scalable strong consistency is provided [27], these systems aim to increase data reliability, an objective conceptually different than distributed agreement.

Bitcoin [50] offers an alternative solution to the (Byzantine fault-tolerant) atomic broadcast problem: It uses *proof-of-work* to order the transactions on a distributed ledger. In a nutshell, a server must solve a cryptographic puzzle in order to add a block of transactions to the ledger. Yet, Bitcoin does not guarantee *consensus finality* [60]—multiple servers solving the puzzle may lead to a fork (conflict), resulting in branches. Forks are eventually solved by adding new blocks. Eventually one branch outpaces the others, thereby becoming the ledger all servers agree upon. To avoid frequent forks, Bitcoin controls the expected puzzle solution time to

10 minutes and currently limits the block size to 1MB, resulting in limited performance, i.e., around seven transactions per second. To increase performance, Bitcoin-NG [24] uses proof-of-work to elect a leader that can add blocks until a new leader is elected. Yet, conflicts are still possible and consensus finality is not ensured.

7 CONCLUSION

In this paper we present AllConcur: a distributed agreement system that relies on a novel leaderless atomic broadcast algorithm. AllConcur uses a digraph G as overlay network; thus, the fault-tolerance f is given by G's vertex-connectivity $k(G)$ and can be adapted freely to the system specific requirements. We show that AllConcur achieves competitive latency and throughput for two real-world scenarios. In comparison to Libpaxos, AllConcur achieves at least 17× higher throughput for the considered scenario. We prove AllConcur's correctness under two assumptions— $f < k(G)$ and a perfect failure detector. Moreover, we show that if $f \geq k(G)$, AllConcur still guarantees safety, and we discuss the changes necessary to maintain safety when relaxing the assumption of a perfect failure detector.

In summary, AllConcur is highly competitive and, due to its decentralized approach, enables hitherto unattainable system designs in a variety of fields.

ACKNOWLEDGMENTS

This work was supported by the German Research Foundation (DFG) as part of the Cluster of Excellence in Simulation Technology (EXC 310/2) at the University of Stuttgart. We thank Michael Resch for support; our shepherd Samer Al Kiswany and the anonymous reviewers; Nitin H. Vaidya, José Gracia and Daniel Rubio Bonilla for helpful discussions; and Holger Berger for providing support with the InfiniBand machine.

REFERENCES

[1] Marcos Kawazoe Aguilera and Sam Toueg. 1999. A simple bivalency proof that t-resilient consensus requires t+1 rounds. *Inform. Process. Lett.* 71, 3 (1999), 155 – 158. https://doi.org/10.1016/S0020-0190(99)00100-3

[2] Alfred V. Aho, John E. Hopcroft, and Jeffrey Ullman. 1983. *Data Structures and Algorithms*. Addison-Wesley Longman Publishing Co., Inc., Boston, MA, USA.

[3] Ravindra K. Ahuja, Thomas L. Magnanti, and James B. Orlin. 1993. *Network Flows: Theory, Algorithms, and Applications*. Prentice-Hall, Inc., Upper Saddle River, NJ, USA.

[4] Albert Alexandrov, Mihai F. Ionescu, Klaus E. Schauser, and Chris Scheiman. 1995. LogGP: Incorporating Long Messages into the LogP Model—One Step Closer Towards a Realistic Model for Parallel Computation. In *Proc. 7th Annual ACM Symposium on Parallel Algorithms and Architectures (SPAA '95)*. Santa Barbara, CA, USA. https://doi.org/10.1145/215399.215427

[5] Thara Angskun, George Bosilca, and Jack Dongarra. 2007. Binomial Graph: A Scalable and Fault-tolerant Logical Network Topology. In *Proc. 5th International Conference on Parallel and Distributed Processing and Applications (ISPA'07)*. Niagara Falls, Canada. https://doi.org/10.1007/978-3-540-74742-0_43

[6] Hagit Attiya and Jennifer Welch. 2004. *Distributed Computing: Fundamentals, Simulations and Advanced Topics*. John Wiley & Sons.

[7] Tom Beigbeder, Rory Coughlan, Corey Lusher, John Plunkett, Emmanuel Agu, and Mark Claypool. 2004. The Effects of Loss and Latency on User Performance in Unreal Tournament 2003®. In *Proc. ACM SIGCOMM Workshop on Network and System Support for Games (NetGames '04)*. Portland, OR, USA. https://doi.org/10.1145/1016540.1016556

[8] Ashwin Bharambe, John R. Douceur, Jacob R. Lorch, Thomas Moscibroda, Jeffrey Pang, Srinivasan Seshan, and Xinyu Zhuang. 2008. Donnybrook: Enabling Large-scale, High-speed, Peer-to-peer Games. In *Proc. ACM SIGCOMM 2008 Conference on Data Communication (SIGCOMM '08)*. Seattle, WA, USA. https://doi.org/10.1145/1402958.1403002

[9] Ashwin Bharambe, Jeffrey Pang, and Srinivasan Seshan. 2006. Colyseus: A Distributed Architecture for Online Multiplayer Games. In *Proc. 3rd Conference on Networked Systems Design & Implementation (NSDI'06)*. San Jose, CA, USA. http://dl.acm.org/citation.cfm?id=1267680.1267692

[10] Blizzard Entertainment. 2008. WoW PvP battlegrounds. (2008). http://www.worldofwarcraft.com/pvp/battlegrounds.

[11] Romain Boichat, Partha Dutta, Svend Frolund, and Rachid Guerraoui. 2003. Reconstructing Paxos. *SIGACT News* 34(2) (2003).

[12] Darius Buntinas. 2012. Scalable Distributed Consensus to Support MPI Fault Tolerance. In *Proc. 2012 IEEE 26th International Parallel and Distributed Processing Symposium (IPDPS'12)*. Shanghai, China. https://doi.org/10.1109/IPDPS.2012.113

[13] Mike Burrows. 2006. The Chubby Lock Service for Loosely-coupled Distributed Systems. In *Proc. 7th Symposium on Operating Systems Design and Implementation (OSDI '06)*. Seattle, WA, USA. http://dl.acm.org/citation.cfm?id=1298455.1298487

[14] Tushar Deepak Chandra and Sam Toueg. 1996. Unreliable Failure Detectors for Reliable Distributed Systems. *J. ACM* 43, 2 (March 1996), 225–267. https://doi.org/10.1145/226643.226647

[15] F. R. K. Chung and M. R. Garey. 1984. Diameter bounds for altered graphs. *Journal of Graph Theory* 8, 4 (December 1984), 511–534. https://doi.org/10.1002/jgt.3190080408

[16] James C. Corbett, Jeffrey Dean, Michael Epstein, Andrew Fikes, Christopher Frost, J. J. Furman, Sanjay Ghemawat, Andrey Gubarev, Christopher Heiser, Peter Hochschild, Wilson Hsieh, Sebastian Ka nthak, Eugene Kogan, Hongyi Li, Alexander Lloyd, Sergey Melnik, David Mwaura, David Nagle, Sean Quinlan, Rajesh Rao, Lindsay Rolig, Yasushi Saito, Michal Szymaniak, Christopher Taylor, Ruth Wang, and Dale Woodford. 2012. Spanner: Google's Globally-distributed Database. In *Proc. 10th USENIX Conference on Operating Systems Design and Implementation (OSDI'12)*. Hollywood, CA, USA. http://dl.acm.org/citation.cfm?id=2387880.2387905

[17] David Culler, Richard Karp, David Patterson, Abhijit Sahay, Klaus Erik Schauser, Eunice Santos, Ramesh Subramonian, and Thorsten von Eicken. 1993. LogP: Towards a Realistic Model of Parallel Computation. *SIGPLAN Not.* 28, 7 (July 1993), 1–12. https://doi.org/10.1145/173284.155333

[18] Giuseppe DeCandia, Deniz Hastorun, Madan Jampani, Gunavardhan Kakulapati, Avinash Lakshman, Alex Pilchin, Swaminathan Sivasubramanian, Peter Vosshall, and Werner Vogels. 2007. Dynamo: Amazon's Highly Available Key-value Store. *SIGOPS Oper. Syst. Rev.* 41, 6 (December 2007), 205–220. https://doi.org/10.1145/1323293.1294281

[19] Xavier Défago, André Schiper, and Péter Urbán. 2004. Total Order Broadcast and Multicast Algorithms: Taxonomy and Survey. *ACM Comput. Surv.* 36, 4 (December 2004), 372–421. https://doi.org/10.1145/1041680.1041682

[20] Anthony H. Dekker and Bernard D. Colbert. 2004. Network Robustness and Graph Topology. In *Proc. 27th Australasian Conference on Computer Science - Volume 26 (ACSC '04)*. Dunedin, New Zealand. http://dl.acm.org/citation.cfm?id=979922.979965

[21] Danny Dolev and Christoph Lenzen. 2013. Early-deciding Consensus is Expensive. In *Proc. 2013 ACM Symposium on Principles of Distributed Computing (PODC '13)*. Montréal, Québec, Canada. https://doi.org/10.1145/2484239.2484269

[22] Aleksandar Dragojević, Dushyanth Narayanan, Edmund B. Nightingale, Matthew Renzelmann, Alex Shamis, Anirudh Badam, and Miguel Castro. 2015. No Compromises: Distributed Transactions with Consistency, Availability, and Performance. In *Proc. 25th Symposium on Operating Systems Principles (SOSP '15)*. Monterey, CA, USA. https://doi.org/10.1145/2815400.2815425

[23] D. Z. Du and F. K. Hwang. 1988. Generalized De Bruijn Digraphs. *Netw.* 18, 1 (March 1988), 27–38. https://doi.org/10.1002/net.3230180105

[24] Ittay Eyal, Adem Efe Gencer, Emin Gün Sirer, and Robbert Van Renesse. 2016. Bitcoin-NG: A Scalable Blockchain Protocol. In *Proc. 13th Usenix Conference on Networked Systems Design and Implementation (NSDI'16)*. Santa Clara, CA, USA. https://www.usenix.org/conference/nsdi16/technical-sessions/presentation/eyal

[25] Michael J. Fischer, Nancy A. Lynch, and Michael S. Paterson. 1985. Impossibility of Distributed Consensus with One Faulty Process. *J. ACM* 32, 2 (April 1985), 374–382. https://doi.org/10.1145/3149.214121

[26] Edgar Gabriel, Graham E. Fagg, George Bosilca, Thara Angskun, Jack J. Dongarra, Jeffrey M. Squyres, Vishal Sahay, Prabhanjan Kambadur, Brian Barrett, Andrew Lumsdaine, Ralph H. Castain, David J. Daniel, Richard L. Graham, and Timothy S. Woodall. 2004. Open MPI: Goals, Concept, and Design of a Next Generation MPI Implementation. In *Proc. 11th European PVM/MPI Users' Group Meeting*. Budapest, Hungary. https://doi.org/10.1007/978-3-540-30218-6_19

[27] Lisa Glendenning, Ivan Beschastnikh, Arvind Krishnamurthy, and Thomas Anderson. 2011. Scalable Consistency in Scatter. In *Proc. 23rd ACM Symposium on Operating Systems Principles (SOSP '11)*. Cascais, Portugal. https://doi.org/10.1145/2043556.2043559

[28] Global Scientific Information and Computing Center. 2014. Failure History of TSUBAME2.0 and TSUBAME2.5. (2014). http://mon.g.gsic.titech.ac.jp/trouble-list/index.htm.

[29] Vassos Hadzilacos and Sam Toueg. 1994. *A Modular Approach to Fault-Tolerant Broadcasts and Related Problems*. Technical Report. Ithaca, NY, USA.

[30] Debra Hensgen, Raphael Finkel, and Udi Manber. 1988. Two Algorithms for Barrier Synchronization. *Int. J. Parallel Program.* 17, 1 (February 1988), 1–17. https://doi.org/10.1007/BF01379320

[31] Torsten Hoefler and Roberto Belli. 2015. Scientific Benchmarking of Parallel Computing Systems: Twelve Ways to Tell the Masses when Reporting Performance Results. In *Proc. International Conference for High Performance Computing, Networking, Storage and Analysis (SC '15)*. Austin, TX, USA. https://doi.org/10.1145/2807591.2807644

[32] Torsten Hoefler and Dmitry Moor. 2014. Energy, Memory, and Runtime Tradeoffs for Implementing Collective Communication Operations. *Supercomput. Front. Innov.: Int. J.* 1, 2 (July 2014), 58–75. https://doi.org/10.14529/jsfi140204

[33] Patrick Hunt, Mahadev Konar, Flavio P. Junqueira, and Benjamin Reed. 2010. ZooKeeper: Wait-free Coordination for Internet-scale Systems. In *Proc. 2010 USENIX Annual Technical Conference (ATC'10)*. Boston, MA, USA. http://dl.acm.org/citation.cfm?id=1855840.1855851

[34] Jonathan Kirsch and Yair Amir. 2008. Paxos for System Builders: An Overview. In *Proc. 2nd Workshop on Large-Scale Distributed Systems and Middleware (LADIS '08)*. Yorktown Heights, NY, USA. https://doi.org/10.1145/1529974.1529979

[35] M. S. Krishnamoorthy and B. Krishnamurthy. 1987. Fault Diameter of Interconnection Networks. *Comput. Math. Appl.* 13, 5-6 (April 1987), 577–582. https://doi.org/10.1016/0898-1221(87)90085-X

[36] Leslie Lamport. 1978. The implementation of reliable distributed multiprocess systems. *Computer Networks (1976)* 2, 2 (May 1978), 95 – 114. https://doi.org/10.1016/0376-5075(78)90045-4

[37] Leslie Lamport. 1998. The Part-time Parliament. *ACM Trans. Comput. Syst.* 16, 2 (May 1998), 133–169. https://doi.org/10.1145/279227.279229

[38] Leslie Lamport. 2001. Paxos Made Simple. *SIGACT News* 32, 4 (December 2001), 51–58. https://doi.org/10.1145/568425.568433

[39] Leslie Lamport. 2005. *Generalized Consensus and Paxos*. Technical Report. https://www.microsoft.com/en-us/research/publication/generalized-consensus-and-paxos/

[40] Joshua M Lewis, Patrick Trinh, and David Kirsh. 2011. A Corpus Analysis of Strategy Video Game Play in Starcraft: Brood War. In *Proc. 33rd Annual Conference of the Cognitive Science Society*. Austin, TX, USA.

[41] Chung-Lun Li, Thomas S. McCormick, and David Simich-Levi. 1990. The Complexity of Finding Two Disjoint Paths with Min-max Objective Function. *Discrete Appl. Math.* 26, 1 (January 1990), 105–115. https://doi.org/10.1016/0166-218X(90)90024-7

[42] Tonglin Li, Xiaobing Zhou, Kevin Brandstatter, Dongfang Zhao, Ke Wang, Anupam Rajendran, Zhao Zhang, and Ioan Raicu. 2013. ZHT: A Light-Weight Reliable Persistent Dynamic Scalable Zero-Hop Distributed Hash Table. In *Proc. 2013 IEEE 27th International Symposium on Parallel and Distributed Processing (IPDPS '13)*. Boston, MA, USA. https://doi.org/10.1109/IPDPS.2013.110

[43] Barbara Liskov and James Cowling. 2012. *Viewstamped Replication Revisited*. Technical Report MIT-CSAIL-TR-2012-021. MIT.

[44] Yanhua Mao, Flavio P. Junqueira, and Keith Marzullo. 2008. Mencius: Building Efficient Replicated State Machines for WANs. In *Proc. 8th USENIX Conference on Operating Systems Design and Implementation (OSDI'08)*. San Diego, CA, USA. http://dl.acm.org/citation.cfm?id=1855741.1855767

[45] Parisa Jalili Marandi, Marco Primi, and Fernando Pedone. 2012. Multi-Ring Paxos. In *Proc. 42nd Annual IEEE/IFIP International Conference on Dependable Systems and Networks (DSN '12)*. Boston, MA, USA. https://doi.org/10.1109/DSN.2012.6263916

[46] Mesosphere. 2017. DC/OS. (2017). https://docs.mesosphere.com/overview/.

[47] F. J. Meyer and D. K. Pradhan. 1988. Flip-Trees: Fault-Tolerant Graphs with Wide Containers. *IEEE Trans. Comput.* 37, 4 (April 1988), 472–478. https://doi.org/10.1109/12.2194

[48] Iulian Moraru, David G. Andersen, and Michael Kaminsky. 2013. There is More Consensus in Egalitarian Parliaments. In *Proc. 24th ACM Symposium on Operating Systems Principles (SOSP '13)*. Farminton, PA, USA. https://doi.org/10.1145/2517349.2517350

[49] MPI Forum. 2015. MPI: A Message-Passing Interface Standard Version 3.1. (June 2015). http://mpi-forum.org/docs/mpi-3.1/mpi31-report.pdf

[50] Satoshi Nakamoto. 2008. Bitcoin: A Peer-to-Peer Electronic Cash System. (2008). http://bitcoin.org/bitcoin.pdf.

[51] Diego Ongaro and John Ousterhout. 2014. In Search of an Understandable Consensus Algorithm. In *Proc. 2014 USENIX Annual Technical Conference (ATC'14)*. Philadelphia, PA, USA. https://www.usenix.org/conference/atc14/technical-sessions/presentation/ongaro

[52] Marius Poke and Torsten Hoefler. 2015. DARE: High-Performance State Machine Replication on RDMA Networks. In *Proc. 24th International Symposium on High-Performance Parallel and Distributed Computing (HPDC '15)*. Portland, OR, USA. https://doi.org/10.1145/2749246.2749267

[53] Marius Poke, Torsten Hoefler, and Colin W. Glass. 2016. AllConcur: Leaderless Concurrent Atomic Broadcast (Extended Version). *CoRR* abs/1608.05866 (2016). http://arxiv.org/abs/1608.05866

[54] Kento Sato, Naoya Maruyama, Kathryn Mohror, Adam Moody, Todd Gamblin, Bronis R. de Supinski, and Satoshi Matsuoka. 2012. Design and Modeling of a Non-blocking Checkpointing System. In *Proc. International Conference on High Performance Computing, Networking, Storage and Analysis (SC '12)*. Salt Lake City, UT, USA. https://doi.org/10.1109/SC.2012.46

[55] Fred B. Schneider. 1990. Implementing Fault-tolerant Services Using the State Machine Approach: A Tutorial. *ACM Comput. Surv.* 22, 4 (December 1990), 299–319. https://doi.org/10.1145/98163.98167

[56] Adrian Schüpbach, Simon Peter, Andrew Baumann, Timothy Roscoe, Paul Barham, Tim Harris, and Rebecca Isaacs. 2008. Embracing diversity in the Barrelfish manycore operating system. In *Proc. Workshop on Managed Many-Core Systems*. Boston, MA, USA. https://www.microsoft.com/en-us/research/publication/embracing-diversity-in-the-barrelfish-manycore-operating-system/

[57] Daniele Sciascia. 2013. Libpaxos3. (2013). http://libpaxos.sourceforge.net/paxos_projects.php.

[58] Terunao Soneoka, Makoto Imase, and Yoshifumi Manabe. 1996. Design of a d-connected digraph with a minimum number of edges and a quasiminimal diameter II. *Discrete Appl. Math.* 64, 3 (February 1996), 267–279. https://doi.org/10.1016/0166-218X(94)00113-R

[59] Philipp Unterbrunner, Gustavo Alonso, and Donald Kossmann. 2014. High Availability, Elasticity, and Strong Consistency for Massively Parallel Scans over Relational Data. *The VLDB Journal* 23, 4 (August 2014), 627–652. https://doi.org/10.1007/s00778-013-0343-9

[60] Marko Vukolić. 2016. The Quest for Scalable Blockchain Fabric: Proof-of-Work vs. BFT Replication. In *Proc. IFIP WG 11.4 Workshop on Open Research Problems in Network Security (iNetSec'15)*. Zurich, Switzerland. https://doi.org/10.1007/978-3-319-39028-4_9

IOGP: An Incremental Online Graph Partitioning Algorithm for Distributed Graph Databases

Dong Dai
Texas Tech University
Lubbock, Texas
dong.dai@ttu.edu

Wei Zhang
Texas Tech University
Lubbock, Texas
X-Spirit.zhang@ttu.edu

Yong Chen
Texas Tech University
Lubbock, Texas
yong.chen@ttu.edu

ABSTRACT

Graphs have become increasingly important in many applications and domains such as querying relationships in social networks or managing rich metadata generated in scientific computing. Many of these use cases require high-performance distributed graph databases for serving continuous updates from clients and, at the same time, answering complex queries regarding the current graph. These operations in graph databases, also referred to as online transaction processing (OLTP) operations, have specific design and implementation requirements for graph partitioning algorithms. In this research, we argue it is necessary to consider the connectivity and the vertex degree changes during graph partitioning. Based on this idea, we designed an Incremental Online Graph Partitioning (IOGP) algorithm that responds accordingly to the incremental changes of vertex degree. IOGP helps achieve better locality, generate balanced partitions, and increase the parallelism for accessing high-degree vertices of the graph. Over both real-world and synthetic graphs, IOGP demonstrates as much as 2x better query performance with a less than 10% overhead when compared against state-of-the-art graph partitioning algorithms.

CCS CONCEPTS

•**Information systems →Graph-based database models; DBMS engine architectures; Distributed storage;**

KEYWORDS

Graph Database; OLTP; Graph Partitioning

1 INTRODUCTION

Graphs have become increasingly important in many applications and domains such as querying relationships in social networks or managing rich metadata generated in scientific computing [2, 8, 21, 38]. These graphs are typically large, hence hard to fit into a single machine. More importantly, even though some graphs may fit into a single server, they are often accessed by multiple clients concurrently, requiring a distributed graph database to avoid performance bottlenecks. For example, our previous work utilized property graphs to uniformly model and manage rich metadata

generated in high performance computing (HPC) platforms [6–8]. The rich metadata graph, as the example shown in [8], might not be particularly large (contains millions of vertices and edges), but still needs a distributed graph database to efficiently serve the highly concurrent graph mutations and queries issued from thousands of clients. In fact, a large number of distributed graph database systems have emerged for such task, like DEX [10], Titan [32], and OrientDB [23].

Similar to relational databases, distributed graph databases are designed to serve continuous updates while simultaneously answering arbitrary queries from many clients. They are different from another important set of systems, namely graph processing engines, like Pregel [20], GraphX [37], and X-Stream [27], which focus on performing individual analytic workloads on the whole graphs quickly. In many cases, existing research does not clearly differentiate them because the line between graph databases and graph processing engines is fuzzy. For instance, most graph databases can deliver graph computations through defining complex graph traversal; and many graph computation engines support analytic queries on dynamic graphs. However, regarding the use scenarios they are designed for, there are significant differences. Specifically, graph databases are designed for online transaction processing (OLTP) workloads like INSERT, UPDATE, GET, and TRAVEL. These operations are typically issued concurrently from multiple clients and expected to finish immediately. They normally only operate on a small portion of the graph. On the other hand, graph processing engines are designed for online analytic processing (OLAP) workloads, like running PageRank on the whole graph [24] or finding the community structure of social graph [11]. Those workloads are typically issued once in a while with enough changes made in the graph. They often operate on the whole graph and take a long time to finish. These differences lead to completely distinct performance requirements and also affect the design considerations of graph partitioning fundamentally. In this research, we focus on *graph partitioning algorithms for distributed graph databases*.

The first difference is the acceptable cost of time in graph partitioning. Since graph processing engines run analytic workloads on the whole graph which usually take a long time, they can afford to spend more time in partitioning to accelerate later computations. But, this is not the case for graph databases as each transaction is normally short. They have to finish fast and take effect immediately. The graph partitioning algorithms of distributed graph databases have to make per-transaction, online decision rapidly, whereas the ones for graph processing engines do not.

The second difference is the needed knowledge to partition a graph. In most graph processing engines, when the partitioning starts, the majority of the graph is already known. In fact, many graph partitioning algorithms heavily rely on such knowledge (e.g., vertex degree and its connectivity) to deliver an optimized partitioning. The best-known examples include METIS [16] and Chaco [14]. Although several recent studies (e.g., LDG [22, 30], Fennel [33]) can partition without knowing the whole graph, some local graph information is still necessary. For example, when a vertex is inserted, most of its connected edges should be known at that time. However, in distributed graph databases, vertices and their connected edges are normally inserted independently and concurrently from multiple clients. When the partitioning happens, it is common that neither the global nor the local graph structure is known. The graph partitioning algorithms should be able to work with limited knowledge about graphs, in which case, the existing partitioning algorithms may not be applicable or effective at all.

The third difference is the measurement of partitioning quality. The graph processing engines mainly run analytic tasks on the whole graph, so they are optimized for the best overall throughput. Most existing graph partitioning algorithms are designed for such a goal, which can be formulated as the k-way partitioning problem: 1) minimize "edge cuts" across partitions to reduce the communication cost; 2) maximize "balance" of partitions to avoid potential stragglers. However, these metrics do not necessarily generate good partitions for distributed graph databases. For example, if a graph consists of k equal size disconnected subgraphs, its best k-way partitioning should be just putting each subgraph to one server to achieve the minimized 'cut' and best 'balance'. However, from graph databases' perspective, if any of these subgraphs contains high-degree vertices, graph traversal starting from these vertices will be significantly slower due to the throughput bottleneck of a single machine. The graph partitioning algorithm should consider metrics for individual OLTP operation instead of the overall throughput.

In this paper, we introduce a new graph partitioning solution, namely *Incremental Online Graph Partitioning (IOGP)*, specifically designed for distributed graph databases. It makes per-transaction, online partitioning decisions instantly while serving individual OLTP operation. It adjusts the partitions incrementally in multiple stages based on the increasing knowledge about the graph. It achieves optimized performance for OLTP workloads like graph mutation and graph traversal comparing to the state-of-the-art practices. The contributions of this work are threefold:

- Propose the first (to the best of our knowledge) incremental (multi-stage), online graph partitioning algorithm for distributed graph databases.
- Design and implement the proposed algorithm that incorporates new vertices and edges instantly with limited resources.
- Conduct extensive evaluations of proposed partitioning algorithm on multiple graph data sets from various domains.

Please note that, even though many graph processing systems tend to accommodate large graphs into a single server to avoid network communications introduced by partitioning the graphs (for example, G-store compresses a trillion-edge graph into 2 TB and processes it using one server [18]), the graph size is not the only fundamental reason for partitioning graphs and deploying distributed graph databases. In many cases, the highly concurrent workloads issued from multiple/many clients, demand a distributed graph database to provide quality service to applications, even though the stored graphs are not that large.

The rest of this paper is organized as follows. Section 2 introduces the background for the proposed algorithm. Section 3 analyzes the performance model for graph databases as the basis of IOGP. Section 4 introduces the overview of the three-stage algorithm. In Section 5, more implementation details are introduced. Section 6 reports the evaluation results. Section 7 concludes this study and plans future work.

2 RELATED WORK

It has been well known that graph partitioning problem is NP-hard [13]. In fact, even the simplest two-way partitioning problem is NP-hard [12]. Hence, current widely-used algorithms are heuristic methods. Among them, one important category is called *multi-level* scheme. Examples include METIS [16], Chaco [14], PMRSB [1], and Scotch [25]. They first coarsen the graphs and cut them roughly into small pieces, then refine the partitioning and finally project the pieces back to the finer graphs. These algorithms can be parallelized for improved performance, such as ParMetis [17] and Pt-Scotch [4]. Although algorithms in this scheme are able to handle large graphs efficiently, they are not designed for dynamic graphs, whose vertices and edges are continuously changing. To apply the multi-level scheme to dynamic graphs, re-partitioning the graphs after a batch of changes is typically needed [28]. However, this re-partitioning is heavyweight (can easily take hours in large graphs [31]) and tends to process a batch of changes instead of transactional workloads on graph databases. In contrast, in this paper, we focus on lightweight online partitioning that conducts partitions while changes are streaming into the databases.

In recent years, several lightweight algorithms have been proposed. They partition a graph while performing a single-pass iteration on the data. They normally use some heuristics to decide where to assign current vertex (and all its connected edges), leveraging the local graph structure about vertex. Typical examples include linear deterministic greedy (LDG) [30] and Fennel [33]. However, as we have described in the previous section, in graph database cases, even such local information may not be available while performing partitioning. Another major drawback of such strategy is that each vertex is only assigned once even it might get new edges later. These new changes may deteriorate the previous partitioning. Although several extensions [22, 34] can partition graphs in several passes or iterations, they still suffer in graph database use cases, where vertices and edges are inserted continuously and independently.

Several recent works have introduced online partitioning algorithms for large-scale dynamic graphs, which are relevant to the proposed IOGP algorithm in this study. Vaquero et. al. [35] partitions the dynamic graphs while the processing workloads are running. It updates existing partitions continuously by migrating all vertices in each super-step of a Pregel-like graph batch computation framework. This introduces significant cost and long delay for handling the graph changes, which are acceptable for batch processing, but do not fit for our case. Leopard [15] proposes a partitioning algorithm and a tightly integrated replication algorithm for large-scale, constantly changing graphs. It borrows techniques from single-pass streaming approaches like Fennel, but improves it with a carefully designed replication strategy. The limitation of Leopard is that it is specifically designed for read-only graph computations to utilize a replication mechanism. Hence, not only graph database workloads do not fit it, but also many graph analysis tasks are not supported, like an analysis of finding single source shortest path. Compared to those algorithms, IOGP is designed to achieve much better performance on OLTP workloads (like accessing to or traveling from a given vertex).

3 MODELING AND ANALYSIS

3.1 Graph Database Model

In this study, we characterize the distributed graph databases with following features: 1) supporting directed graphs; 2) supporting bi-direction traversal, i.e., a vertex can access both its incoming or outgoing edges; and 3) supporting vertices and edges with queryable properties. In fact, these features are common in existing distributed graph databases.

Figure 1 shows a typical architecture of distributed graph databases. In this architecture, each physical server stores a part or a partition of the whole graph in its local *storage engine*. Servers can talk to each other through a high-speed network, and clients are linked with driver libraries to talk to servers. Since each vertex needs to access both its incoming and outgoing edges to enable bi-direction traversal, the storage engine will keep two edge lists as shown in Figure 1. Each server contains an OLTP execution engine to serve requests from clients. The graph partitioning components in both clients and servers cooperate to deliver partitioning. Based on this generic model, we will analyze key factors of OLTP operation performance, which leads to the design and implementation of IOGP described in the next section.

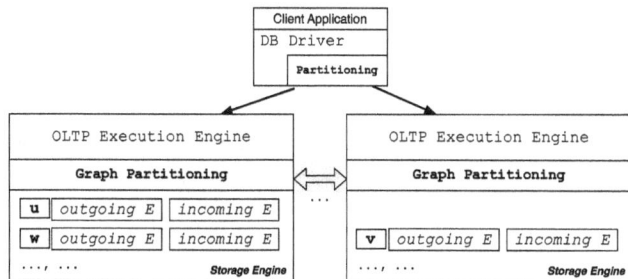

Figure 1: Graph database architecture overview.

3.2 Performance of Single-Point Access

The single-point OLTP operations in graph databases typically include INSERT, UPDATE, and GET. Their performance is largely impacted by whether the clients know the location of the vertex or edge: knowing the accurate location, clients can directly send requests to the server, saving extra cost for querying the location. This could cut the latency by half and double the throughput in many cases. To achieve such a "one-hop" mechanism, clients and servers need to share the same knowledge about current partitions. A widely adopted solution is to use a deterministic hash function,

which can be easily shared, to partition the graphs. Many existing distributed graph databases like OrientDB and Titan are using this strategy. Although its drawback is obvious: deterministic hashing does not learn the affinity of vertex connectivity leading to poor locality, its one-hop advantage still deserves considerations for better OLTP single-point access performance. *In this study, the proposed IOGP algorithm maximizes the chance of one-hop access by keeping clients and servers agreeing upon the locations for the majority of the graph.*

3.3 Performance of Graph Traversal

Efficiently supporting graph TRAVEL is a unique feature of graph databases and the key difference between graph databases and other storage systems like relational databases or key-value stores [36]. Figure 2(a) shows a sample graph and a traversal starting from vertex u. A traversal usually consists of multiple steps, each contains accesses of vertices and their neighbors in parallel, like those visits of v, w in step S_1.

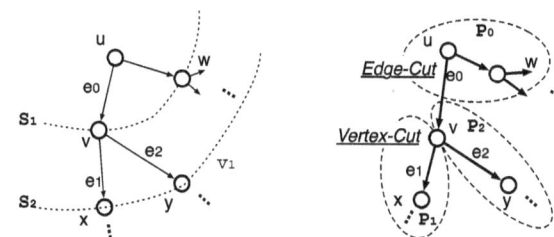

a) Graph travel example from u b) Graph with 3 partitions (P0,P1,P2)

Figure 2: Graph traversal analysis.

Graph partitioning is to place graph vertices and edges into different parts, stored on separate servers. In general, there are two ways to partition a graph as shown in Figure 2(b), i.e., the *edge-cut* and *vertex-cut*. Edge-cut tends to place the source vertex and its connected edges together. Since the destination vertices may be placed on a different server, their in-between edges will look like being cut. For example, u and its neighbors are placed this way and e_0 is cut between two partitions. On the other hand, vertex-cut tends to place the source vertex and its edges separately, so the vertex will look like being cut. For example, v is cut into two partitions as its edges e_1 and e_2 are stored separately shown in the figure.

In fact, regardless of edge-cut or vertex-cut, a 'cut' is introduced as long as two connected vertices are not stored together. For traversal, such a 'cut' simply means extra network communications between servers. Hence, all graph partitioning algorithms strike for minimizing these cuts to achieve better locality between vertices. *In this study, the proposed IOGP algorithm enhances the locality between vertices by leveraging a heuristic method to dynamically adjust vertex location.*

In addition, even with the same locality, vertex-cut and edge-cut can lead to different performance. For instance, if a vertex u has more than one million connected edges, which is highly possible in real-world power-law graphs, edge-cut will store all edges together with u. This will lead to long time for loading edges while accessing u. Comparatively, vertex-cut can assign these edges into multiple servers to amortize the workloads and deliver much better performance. On the other hand, if a vertex u has a small number of edges, splitting them into multiple servers introduces extra network communications, diminishing the benefit of parallelism. In such cases, which are quite often as most vertices in power-law graphs have a small number of edges, edge-cut is clearly a better choice. *In this study, the proposed IOGP algorithm considers the degree of a vertex during partitioning and chooses the better way to partition graphs accordingly.*

4 ALGORITHM OVERVIEW

The goal of the IOGP is to optimize the performance of OLTP operations in graph databases. The performance analysis in previous sections enlightens and rationalizes its design and implementation. Specifically, IOGP first leverages deterministic hashing to quickly place new vertices. This strategy enables one-hop access for most of the graph vertices by default. While more edges of a vertex are inserted, IOGP will adjust the location of the vertex to achieve better locality leveraging the increasing knowledge about the vertex connectivity. Until this step, the graph is still partitioned following the *edge-cut* partitioning. However, once a vertex has too many edges, IOGP will apply *vertex-cut* to increase the parallelism and further improve the traversal performance. In this way, IOGP manages to generate high-quality partitions while serving continuous OLTP operations. We summarize IOGP into three stages, namely *quiet stage*, *vertex reassigning stage*, and *edge splitting stage* respectively, and introduce them in more details below.

4.1 Quiet Stage

IOGP operates in quiet stage by default. At this stage, it places a new vertex into a server using the deterministic hashing function. All clients and servers share the same function to ensures the one-hop access. Following *edge-cut*, IOGP places new edges together with their incident vertices. Note that an edge $u \rightarrow v$ will be stored in both the outgoing edge list of u and the incoming edge list of v to enable the bi-direction graph traversal.

The problem of deterministic hashing is it does not consider the locality affinity of vertices. It is not a significant problem when a vertex does not have many edges, but would lead to problems while vertex grows. IOGP solves the problem in the *vertex reassigning stage* after knowing more about the vertex connectivity. In addition, as edge-cut may create hotspots if the vertices have too many edges, IOGP applies vertex-cut in the *edge splitting stage* to address this issue.

4.2 Vertex Reassigning Stage

In the quiet stage, vertices do not have enough connectivity information, hence random hashing is a good option. But, as more edges are inserted, more connectivity information is obtained. It is desired to leverage such knowledge to re-assign vertices to a better partition. The goal is straightforward: move a vertex to a partition that stores most of its neighbors while keeping all partitions balanced to avoid stragglers.

To determine which partition is the best choice, IOGP leverages the Fennel heuristic score [33], as shown in Equation 1. Here, P_i

refers to the vertices in the ith partition, v refers to the vertex to be assigned, and $N(v)$ refers to the set of neighbors of v. α and γ are adjustable parameters.

$$max\{|N(v) \cap P_i| - \alpha\frac{\gamma}{2}(|P_i|)^{\gamma-1}\} \qquad (1)$$

This heuristic takes a vertex v as the input and computes a score for each partition. Then, IOGP places v in the partition with the highest score. $|N(v) \cap P_i|$ is the number of neighbors of v in partition P_i. As the number of neighbors in a partition increases, the score of the partition increases too. To ensure balanced partitioning, the heuristic contains a penalty based on the number of vertices and edges in the partition ($|P_i|$). As the number increases, the score decreases.

In Fennel, such a heuristic score is calculated simply by scanning all neighbors of the vertices in each partition. The time cost is acceptable as Fennel is not designed for serving OLTP operations. However, such computation consumes too much time in our focused cases. To solve this issue, in this research we propose a new strategy to calculate it by maintaining edge counters continuously. More details are introduced in Section 5.

4.3 Edge Splitting Stage

In a power-law graph, degree of a vertex could be extremely large. As we have discussed, the *edge-cut* may lead to significant performance degradation. In IOGP, we introduce the edge splitting stage to handle it. Specifically, we propose to split edges of high degree vertices into multiple servers to amortize the loads. In the generic graph database model, each vertex contains incoming edges and outgoing edges. We consider them together as traversals may happen in both directions.

IOGP defines a threshold MAX_EDGES to decide when to split a vertex. If a vertex degree exceeds this number, IOGP will cut and split all its edges. The splitting is quite simple: IOGP will place an outgoing edge together with its destination vertex and place an incoming edge together with its source vertex. Figure 3 shows an example of splitting with three storage servers. In this example, u's edges need to be split to offload its loads. Initially, all edges (from 1 to 6) are stored with u on server 1. After splitting, they are assigned across all three servers according to the locations of their destination vertices. Note that the vertex u is not moved. The ones on server 2 and 3 are just Id index (shown in shadow pattern in the figure).

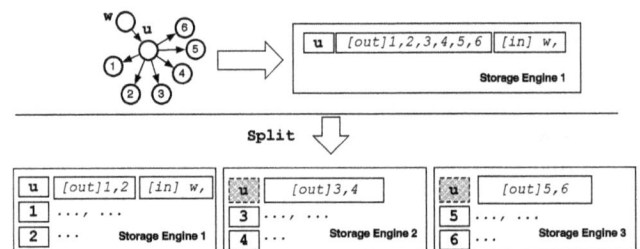

Figure 3: An edge splitting example

The locality does not change in this stage because an edge is moved to either its source or destination vertex without altering the locality. However, this will significantly improve the performance of accessing a high-degree vertex as these operations can be carried out in parallel across multiple servers. Also, concurrent edge mutations on that vertex can be offloaded to multiple servers for better performance.

5 ALGORITHM DESIGN AND IMPLEMENTATION

In the previous section, we briefly describe the three stages of IOGP. However, its implementation in distributed graph databases is non-trivial. A number of implementation challenges and various design trade-offs remain. In this section, we will introduce more design and implementation details.

5.1 IOGP Data Structure

IOGP introduces a series of data structures to achieve efficient online graph partitioning. These data structures are mainly counters, which record the states of vertices in each partition. They are stored in memory for quick access. In case of failures, they can be rebuilt from a full scan on the existing database.

- On the server currently storing vertex v, there is a $split(v)$ indicating whether its edges have been split or not.
- On the two servers that originally or currently store vertex v respectively, a $loc(v)$ records its accurate location. It only exists once IOGP reassigns the vertex, serving as a location service for the graph database.
- Each vertex v has maximum four edge counters to incrementally maintain its connectivity information. These counters may be stored on multiple servers.
    1) $alo(v)/ali(v)$ store the number of *actual local outgoing/incoming* edges of v. They count the outgoing/incoming edges whose destination/source vertices are also stored in local server, i.e., local neighbors. They only exist in server that actually stores v.
    2) $plo(v)/pli(v)$ store the number of *potential local outgoing/incoming* edges of v. These two counters exist in servers that do not store v. They count v's local neighbors if v has been moved back to local server.
- Each server also maintains a *size* counter, indicating its vertices and edges number.

Overall, those data structures are small. Each server only has one *size* counter. For each vertex v, the $split(v)$ and $loc(v)$ only exists on one or two servers, hence also scales well. But, the edge counters may exist on all servers: one server stores alo, ali and all others store plo, pli. If each counter takes 2 bytes, together they take 4 bytes per vertex on each server. This might lead to a problem if the entire graph database stores over a billion vertices, which will consume over 4GB memory on each server in the worst case. However, the real cases are much better than this worst scenario for two reasons: 1) vertices that enter *edge splitting stage* do not need edge counters anymore, and 2) the $plo(v), pli(v)$ potential counters only exist in servers that store v's neighbors. These significantly reduce the memory consumption in real-world power-law graphs.

In the evaluation section, we show more details about the memory footprints of these counters.

5.2 Quiet Stage Implementation

In the quiet stage, IOGP places vertices using the deterministic hashing function by default. Note that to support bi-direction traversal, inserting an edge like $e(u \rightarrow v)$ will lead to two insertions: one as the outgoing edge of u and the other as the incoming edge of v.

IOGP maintains *edge counters* for vertex reassignment. Initially, we set all counters to 0. Once a new edge $(u \rightarrow v)$ is inserted, two insertions are issued. On the server that stores the source vertex (s_u), after successfully inserting the edge as the outgoing edge of u, IOGP will check whether the destination vertex v is also stored locally. This check can be done instantly by examining the hash value of v and the existence of $loc(v)$ in local memory. If yes, the edge is local to both its source and destination vertices, hence it increases $alo(u)$ by 1 as this indicates the existence of actual locality. If not, it increases $pli(v)$, which means only potential locality is introduced for v. Note that, this pli counts for vertex v, which means that only v is moved back to this server in the future, then the actual locality can be obtained. Similarly, on the server that stores the destination vertex (s_v), counters are updated accordingly.

IOGP updates edge counters while serving vertex and edge insertions. The actual local edges (alo, ali) and potential local edges (plo, pli) are used in the vertex reassigning stage to calculate the best partition for a vertex efficiently.

5.3 Vertex Reassigning Stage Implementation

In the vertex reassigning stage, IOGP tries to reassign the vertex to a different server to enhance the locality. The first task of reassigning vertex is to calculate the best partition. According to the description in Section 4.2, instead of scanning the databases to obtain $|N(v) \cap P_i|$, IOGP leverages the edge counters to efficiently calculate the best location.

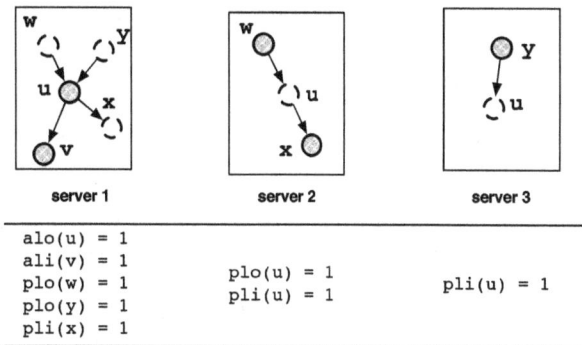

server 1	server 2	server 3
alo(u) = 1 ali(v) = 1 plo(w) = 1 plo(y) = 1 pli(x) = 1	plo(u) = 1 pli(u) = 1	pli(u) = 1

Figure 4: An example of partitions during vertex reassignment. Edge counters are shown.

Figure 4 shows a sample graph with 5 vertices and edges, partitioned into three servers. We also show their edge counters. Here, solid circles with colored patterns indicate actual existence of vertices in that server; dashed circles indicate the vertices do not exist, only their edges exist. As this figure shows, each edge actually is stored twice. For example, $e(u \rightarrow x)$ is stored in $server_1$ as an outgoing edge of u, and at the same time, stored in $server_2$ as an incoming edge of x.

In this example, only edge $e(u \rightarrow v)$ indicates the actual locality, which means that we have $alo(u) = 1$ and $ali(v) = 1$ on $server_1$. The other three edges only indicate the potential locality. The relevant edge counters are shown in Figure 4. These values are efficiently maintained in the quiet stage.

When IOGP reassigns a vertex, like u, it will compare whether moving u to another server will increase or decrease the score calculated from Equation 1. Specifically, moving u out of s_1 will certainly reduce the amount of locality on server s_1 by $2*(alo(u)_{s_1} + ali(u)_{s_1})$. We double it because the locality decrements come from both vertex u and its locally connected vertices. At the same time, moving u into another server s_j will increase its locality by $2 * (plo(u)_{s_j} + pli(u)_{s_j})$. The partition size $size$ on each server should also be calculated. IOGP will choose the partition s_i that obtains the largest positive value from following equation:

$$ra\_score_{s_i} = max\{2 * (plo(u)_{s_i} + pli(u)_{s_i})$$
$$- 2 * (alo(u)_{s_{cur}} + ali(u)_{s_{cur}}) \quad (2)$$
$$+ [size_{s_i} - size_{s_{cur}}]\}$$

This equation is derived from Equation 1 by choosing parameter $\alpha = 1$ and $\gamma = 2$. These parameters are also widely used in existing studies [15]. If we take Figure 4 as an example, vertex u would be reassigned to $server_2$ as its ra_score is 1.

5.3.1 Maintain IOGP Data Structure. Algorithm 1 shows how IOGP maintains the in-memory data structures while reassigning a vertex. When a vertex u is moved, the $loc(u)$ in the original server will be updated to its new location. Any further reassignment also updates the $loc(u)$ in the original server. This serves as a distributed location service for the graph database. A fresh client needs to ask the original server that stores u to retrieve its current location through querying $loc(u)$. Clients can cache the location for future requests. In addition, servers involved in this reassignment will update their $size$ counter accordingly.

In terms of updating the edge counters, vertex u's counters are updated first: 1) in the original server s_u, u's actual locality will turn into a potential locality; 2) on the target server s_k, u's potential locality will turn into an actual locality. In addition to updating u, it is more important to update vertices that are connected to u. Their actual localities are changed because vertex u is moved out or in. For example, in the original server (s_u), for all u's incoming edges, if their source vertices (src) are also stored in local server, we need to reduce their actual outgoing locality ($alo(src)$) by 1 because their destination vertex u is no longer in local server. This is also required for outgoing edges. The target server s_k performs similar updates except it will increase the localities. More importantly, every time a vertex u is reassigned, the edge counters of its neighbors also need to be updated. These updates are actually fast (as iterating u's incoming and outgoing edges in-memory) and overlapped with the actual data movement (described in Section 5.5).

5.3.2 Timing of Vertex Reassignment. The timing of reassigning vertices is critical to balance partitioning quality and overheads.

Algorithm 1 Maintain IOGP Data Structure

```
1:  ◇ Assign u from s_u to s_k
2:  if on server s_u then                      ▷ on source server s_u
3:      size -= 1;
4:      plo(u) = alo(u);
5:      pli(u) = ali(u);
6:      for e ∈ incoming(u) do
7:          if e.src stored in s_u then
8:              alo(e.src) -= 1;
9:      for e ∈ outgoing(u) do
10:         if e.dst stored in s_u then
11:             ali(e.dst) -= 1;
12:
13: if on server s_k then                       ▷ on target server s_k
14:     size += 1;
15:     alo(u) = plo(u);
16:     ali(u) = pli(u);
17:     for e ∈ incoming(u) do
18:         if e.src stored in s_k then
19:             alo(e.src) += 1;
20:     for e ∈ outgoing(u) do
21:         if e.dst stored in s_u then
22:             ali(e.dst) += 1;
```

This is especially true for the proposed online IOGP algorithm. We have observed that when a vertex has more edges, its connectivity becomes more stable, thus less reassignment is needed. This rationale is rather straightforward. For example, when a vertex has only one edge, a new edge may significantly change its locality affinity. But, if a vertex has 1K edges already, most likely a new edge does not make a significant difference. This observation and rationale lead to our design in IOGP: 1) deferring vertex reassignment until its connectivity stabilizes; and 2) reducing vertex reassignment frequency while more edges are inserted. Specifically, we consider until a vertex contains over REASSIGN_THRESH connected edges (both incoming and outgoing edges), a vertex reassignment attempt can be made. After a reassignment, we will check the possibility of another reassignment only after a similar amount of new edges are inserted. Assuming k=REASSIGN_THRSH, we check vertex reassignments when it reaches $[k, 2 * k, 4 * k, ., 2^i * k, ..]$ edges. This significantly reduces the number of reassignments for a vertex. For example, if REASSIGN_THRSH=10, for a vertex with 10,240 edges, the maximum number of movements is only 10. The choice and impact of REASSIGN_THRSH will be discussed in the evaluation section.

5.4 Edge Splitting Stage Implementation

The edge splitting stage is a key optimization of IOGP for high-degree vertices. It is mainly designed to amortize loads of accessing high-degree vertices and to improve the performance of operations like scan and traversal.

As described in the vertex reassigning stage, when a vertex is split, it may have already been reassigned multiple times. But, once a vertex enters into the splitting stage, it will never be reassigned again. IOGP will invalidate and free up all its edge counters to reduce the memory footprint. This strategy is chosen for two reasons. First, when a vertex is split across the cluster, statistically, its edges will be evenly distributed as their neighbors are randomly distributed through hashing. Hence, reassigning vertex will not significantly increase the locality anymore. Second, moving vertices that have been split also introduces unnecessary complexity. The algorithm needs to take extra care when a vertex is reassigned and its edges are already split, which may invalidate the edge counters.

Regarding updating the IOGP data structures, it is straightforward in the edge splitting stage. First, it updates $split(u)$ to the corresponding value. Second, it invalidates and frees up local edge counters of vertex u. It further frees up edges counters of u in other storage servers along with the edges movement. The sizes of u's incoming and outgoing edges will be updated accordingly.

5.5 Asynchronous Data Movement

In an IOGP-enabled graph database, there are two extra data movements introduced: vertex reassigning and edge splitting. Moving data synchronously while serving OLTP requests can cause potential performance issues. In IOGP, we optimize these data movements to be asynchronous to avoid blocking OLTP operations.

During edge splitting, once IOGP needs to split a vertex, it will update the in-memory IOGP data structures and add the vertex into the *pending splitting queue* in one transaction. Once this transaction finishes successfully, even without moving data yet, we start to reject new edges that should not be stored locally. Clients that issue edges insertions to a wrong server will be rejected with a notification indicating that the vertex has been split. Clients synchronize their statuses based on the replies and request the correct server again. Reassigning vertices is similarly handled. After determining the target server, it will update in-memory IOGP data structures, and then add the vertex into the *pending reassigning queue* in one transaction. The server will also stop serving requests about the vertex and notify clients to request the target server in the future. For both cases, the real data movement actions are implemented via a background thread, which periodically retrieves vertex v from the header of pending queues and handles the data movement for it. After data has been moved, the local copy will be removed afterward.

This asynchronous data movement mechanism is efficient, but may introduce a problem for read requests because the requested vertices or edges may be in an uncertain status while data movement takes place. They could be on the original server (copying is not started yet), on the new server (copying and deleting are finished already), or even on both of them (copying is finished but not deleting). To solve this, the clients need to issue *two* read requests concurrently for elements that are under movement: one request is sent to the original server, and the other one is sent to the new server. If both requests get results, the one from new server wins. Clients can learn whether the edge movement has finished or not based on the replies from new servers and avoid the extra requests in the future.

6 EVALUATION

6.1 Evaluation Setup

All evaluations were conducted on the CloudLab APT cluster [5]. It has 128 servers in total, and we used 32 servers as the back-end servers. Each server has an 8-core Xeon E5-2450 processor, 16GB RAM, and 2 TB local hard disk. All servers are connected through 10GbE dual-port embedded NICs. Unless explicitly stated, we used all 32 servers in experiments.

6.1.1 Dataset Selection. We used the popular SNAP dataset for real-world graph evaluations [19]. SNAP is a collection of networks from various domains, and most of them are power-law graphs. We show a representative selection of these graphs used in our evaluations and outline their properties and scales in Table 1.

Specifically, we selected graphs scaling from less than 200K edges to almost 100M edges to represent different stages of continuously growing graphs that graph databases serve. Although many graph processing frameworks are capable of processing graphs with these sizes (i.e., the number of edges or vertices) in a single server, we do consider distributed graph databases are still necessary for these graphs in practice. As our previous work has shown [6–8], a graph with millions of vertices and edges may be accessed by thousands of clients concurrently, hence demands graph partitioning and a distributed graph database solution. Additionally, the property graphs tend to have a rich set of queryable properties. They can easily be large enough (e.g., multiple KB) to make a graph with millions of vertices and edges not fit for a single machine.

In this evaluation, another reason we did not include tremendously large graphs is, unlike the offline graph partitioning algorithms or the underlying storage engines, the online algorithms like IOGP, are not sensitive to the size of the graph. Instead, they concentrate on the structures of the graphs (e.g., the connectivity). So we considered a diverse set of structures when selecting graphs from various domains in the datasets. Note that the SNAP dataset only contains graph structures. We attached randomly generated property, a 128K bytes key-value pair, on each vertex and edge.

Table 1: Selected graphs from SNAP dataset

Data Set	Domain	Vertex Num.	Edge Num.
as-Skitter	network	1,696,415	11,095,298
web-Google	web	875,713	5,105,039
roadNet-CA	geo	1,965,206	2,766,607
Loc-Gowalla	geo	196,591	950,327
amazon0302	purchase	262,111	1,234,877
amazon0601	purchase	403,394	3,387,388
ca-AstroPh	social	18,772	198,110
wiki-talk	social	2,394,385	5,021,410
email-EuAll	social	265,214	420,045
email-Enron	social	36,692	183,831
soc-Slashdot0902	social	82,168	948,464
Soc-LiveJournal1	social	4,847,571	68,993,773
cit-Patents	citation	3,774,768	16,518,948
cit-HepPh	citation	12,008	118,521

We also used synthetic graphs to evaluate IOGP. The synthetic graphs were generated using the RMAT graph generator [3] following the power-law distribution. We used the following parameters to generate an RMAT graph with 10K vertices and 1.2M edges: $a = 0.45, b = 0.15, c = 0.15, d = 0.25$. The graph is named as *RMAT-10K-1.2M*.

6.1.2 Software Platform. We evaluated IOGP on a distributed graph database prototype, namely SimpleGDB [29]. Its core has been used in several research projects and proven to be efficient [6, 7]. More importantly, its flexible design supports various graph partitioning algorithms and enables fair comparison among them.

SimpleGDB follows the generic graph database architecture shown in Figure 1. It uses consistent hashing to manage multiple storage servers in a decentralized way by mirroring Dynamo's approach [9]. This allows the dynamic growth (or shrinking) of the graph database cluster. Each server runs the same set of components including an OLTP execution engine, a data storage engine, and a graph partitioning layer. The OLTP execution engine accepts requests from clients and serves them. The storage engine organizes graph data such as vertices, edges, and their properties into key-value pairs and stores them persistently in RocksDB [26]. The graph partitioning layer is designed as a plugin to allow hackers to change algorithms without affecting other components, which largely simplifies the evaluation and the fair comparisons presented in this study. Another key feature of SimpleGDB is that it contains a server-side asynchronous graph traversal engine built based on study [6]. Through a server-side traversal, we are able to fully utilize the locality gained by graph partitioning algorithms.

6.2 Evaluation Results

6.2.1 Edge-Cut and Balance. We first compare the k-way partition metrics (i.e., edge cuts and partition balance) among IOGP and the state-of-the-art graph partitioning algorithms (METIS, Fennel, and Hash). Since METIS cannot efficiently work with OLTP workloads, to conduct the comparison, we actually ran METIS on the final graph once, assuming all vertices and edges were already inserted. Similarly, to conduct the fair comparison against Fennel, we assume that the graph is inserted in a way that a vertex and all its edges are inserted together. Their insertion order is chosen randomly. Results of the hashing and IOGP were conducted in an online manner following the same order as the datasets provided.

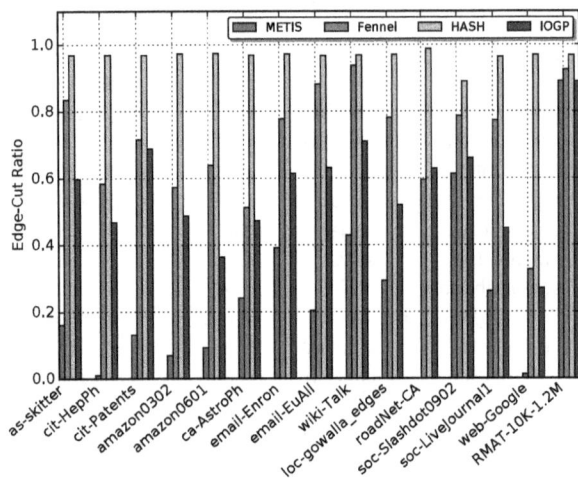

Figure 5: Edge-cut ratio comparison.

We plot the results of all graphs (described in the previous subsection) in Figure 5 and 6. Figure 5 shows the edge-cut ratio, calculated as the number of edge cuts over the total number of edges in a

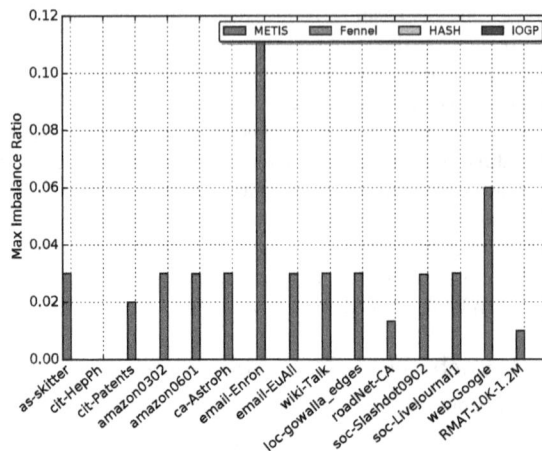

Figure 6: Partitions balance comparison.

graph. Figure 6 shows the imbalance ratio, calculated as the maximum difference among all partitions over the average partition size. Since Fennel, IOGP, and Hash achieve highly balanced partition, their imbalance ratios are almost zero for all cases. Their results cannot be seen in the figure. From these results, we have several observations. First, METIS achieves the best locality but worst balance among all tested algorithms. In the *web-Google* graph, it results in a partition with less than 1% edge-cut ratio, but over 6% imbalance. On the other hand, Hash results in the worst partitioning in all cases, but at the same time, provides excellent balance. Second, IOGP and Fennel are in between of METIS and Hash and their imbalance is small. In terms of edge-cut ratio, IOGP is better than Fennel in all tested cases. In many cases (e.g., *email-EuAll* and *wiki-Talk*), the difference is clear. These results confirmed that IOGP can obtain better vertex locality than the state-of-the-art streaming partitioning algorithms like Fennel, even using the same heuristic functions. The reason is quite straightforward. Fennel only assigns a vertex once when it is first inserted. But, IOGP may reassign a vertex multiple times during continuous insertions and hence have more chances to choose a better location for a vertex. We will show more detailed analysis in the next subsection.

6.2.2 Continuous Refinement of IOGP. As shown from the evaluations reported and discussed in the previous sub-section, IOGP achieves better locality than Fennel due to its ability to continuously refine the partitions. In Figure 7, we show how this happens in detail. The x-axis indicates the number of insertions that happened during constructing the graph. The y-axis shows current edge-cut ratio. We took a sample after every 10^5 insertions. We show the first $2 * 10^7$ insertions in this figure. The results confirm two important patterns that we leverage in IOGP: 1) the initial insertions changed the locality more significantly, and 2) graph becomes more stable while more edges are inserted. This is also why IOGP is designed to increase the REASSIGN_THRSH exponentially to reduce the frequency of reassignment.

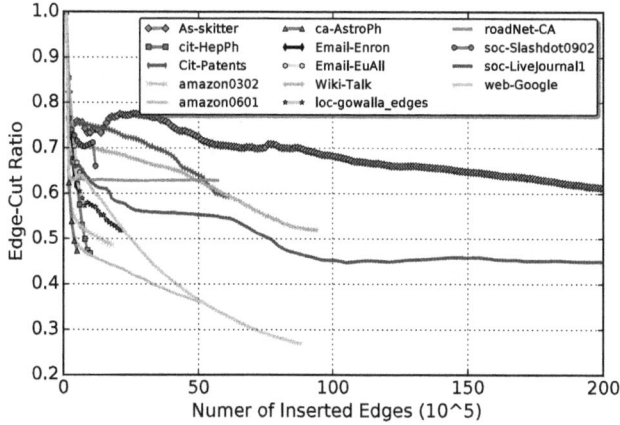

Figure 7: Changes of edge-cut ratio while inserting.

6.2.3 Vertex Reassigning Threshold.
We discuss the reassignment threshold (i.e., REASSIGN_THRSH) in this evaluation. Specifically, we constructed the whole graph multiple times using different reassignment thresholds and collected the edge-cut ratio of each round and the number of vertex reassignments. It is expected that a smaller REASSIGN_THRSH brings more overheads (i.e., more vertex reassignments), and generates better partitions (i.e., smaller edge-cut ratio). In fact, the best value for REASSIGN_THRSH should be different for separate graphs. In this evaluation, we tested a wide range of possible values to find the potential rules in choosing this value. Specifically, we iterated thresholds from 1 to 50 with an increase of 5 each step. All results are plotted in Figure 8.

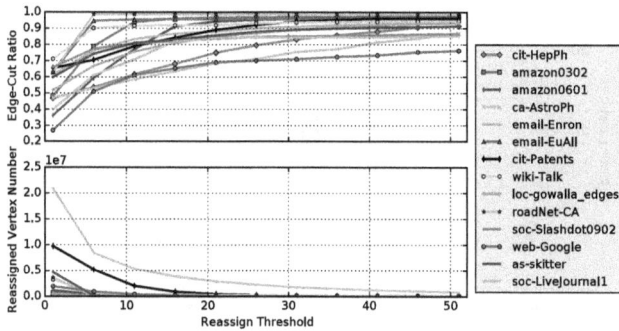

Figure 8: Edge-cut ratio and reassignment times.

The top sub-figure shows that the edge-cut ratio increases as the REASSIGN_THRSH become larger. More specifically, the increase is significant at the beginning and turns into flat afterward. This is because most of these graphs have a small average degree (according to Table 1), and they are more sensitive to threshold changes in the smaller end. Once the threshold became sufficiently large, their ratios became more stable. In the bottom sub-figure, we show how many times of the vertices are reassigned with different thresholds. As expected, a larger threshold reduces the number of vertex reassignments. From those results, we conclude that the best choice

of REASSIGN_THRSH should be near half of the average degree of the graph to strike a balance between achieving better locality and less vertex reassignments. This is an empirical result, like, 6 for *web-Google*.

6.2.4 Edge Splitting Threshold.
In IOGP, we split a vertex based on its degree to achieve the best traversal performance in the edge splitting stage. Although splitting edges into multiple servers saves time while loading data from disks, it does introduce extra network overhead to retrieve data from remote servers. It is important to find the best threshold to balance the disk and network latency. As we have described, the splitting threshold is relevant with both the hardware (disk speed and network latency), the scale of the distributed cluster, and the vertex degree. It is non-trivial to obtain a universally optimal setting. In this evaluation, we aim to build a general guideline of choosing the edge splitting threshold. It is desired to conduct similar evaluations before deploying IOGP on a specific system to obtain the optimal setting.

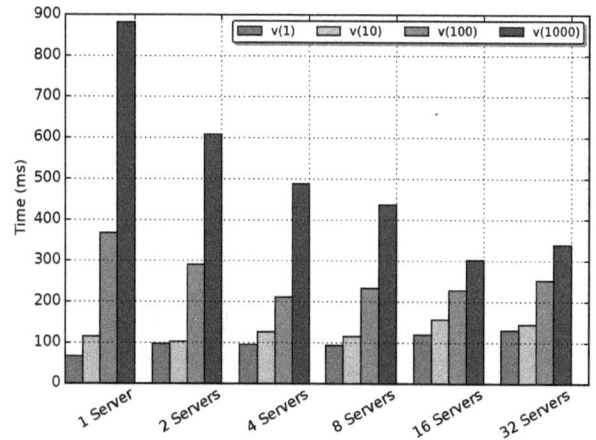

Figure 9: Scan performance with different degrees.

Specifically, we conducted a series of evaluations on various cluster scales (from $2 \rightarrow 32$ servers), towards different vertices with distinct degrees (from $1 \rightarrow 10^3$). Each edge is attached with 128KB randomly generated properties. The disk and network latency are fixed based on the hardware configuration of CloudLab APT cluster. For comparison, we measured the time cost of one-step traversal from these vertices in different cluster scales. The results are reported in Figure 9. The x-axis shows different scales in the evaluations, where 'k server(s)', indicates all edges are split among all of them. Note that the case of '1 server' means there is no edge-splitting. The y-axis shows the time cost of reading each vertex and its neighbors. There are four cases in total. From these results, we can draw several observations. First, low-degree vertices like $v(1)$ and $v(10)$ tend to obtain better traversal performance in smaller scale cluster. On the other hand, high-degree vertices achieve better performance in larger scale cluster. This also confirms our previous analysis. Second, each degree has its best scale. For example, for a vertex with 10^3 edges, the minimum time is obtained in '16 servers' cluster. For a vertex with 100 edges, '4 servers' cluster would be the best. This metrics can guide the deployment to choose the best MAX_EDGES for a specific cluster.

6.2.5 Memory Footprint of IOGP Data Structure. As we have discussed in Section 5, IOGP introduces a number of in-memory counters to facilitate partitioning process. Their memory footprints may limit the scalability of IOGP algorithms. In this evaluation, we examined the maximal memory footprint during constructing the graphs listed in Table 1. The results are plotted in Figure 10. The *x*-axis shows different graphs and the *y*-axis shows the maximal memory consumption (KB) across 32 servers. We also plot the 'Expected' memory footprint, which is calculated simply assuming each vertex *v* has two edge counters in each server. From these results, we can easily observe that, the actual memory consumption is much smaller than the upper-bound estimation, especially for those large-scale graphs. These results from real-world graphs clearly show that IOGP is practical in partitioning large-scale graphs.

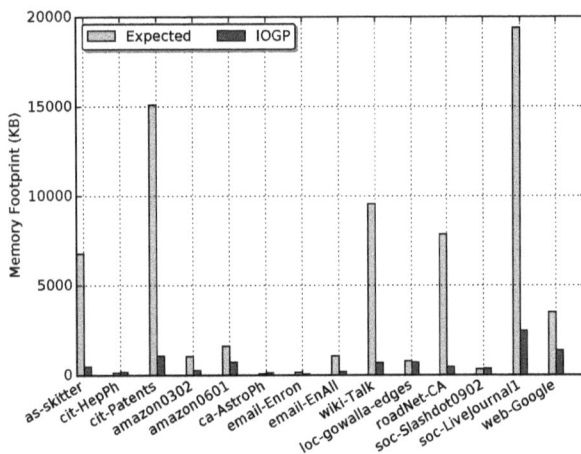

Figure 10: Memory footprint of IOGP.

6.2.6 Single-point Access Performance. As we have described, most graph databases use simple hashing strategy to deliver online graph partitioning. Hashing is fast and benefits single-point OLTP operations like INSERT most. Other graph partitioning algorithms including METIS and Fennel are expected to have much worse performance on insertions due to their offline nature. In this research, to study the benefit of IOGP, we compared its insertion performance with the best algorithm (hashing). Again, the evaluations were conducted in the 32-server SimpleGDB cluster. Figure 11 plots the insertion speed of IOGP and Hash algorithms. The performance was generated from a single client. As the results show, Hash always performs better than IOGP as expected, because there are overheads introduced by vertex reassigning and edges splitting. However, the difference is small and less than 10%.

6.2.7 Graph Traversal Performance. In this evaluation, we further compared the traversal performance of IOGP and Hash. As the most important OLTP operation in graph databases, graph traversal should obtain the best performance. This is achieved by less edge-cut ratio between reassigned vertices and higher parallelism

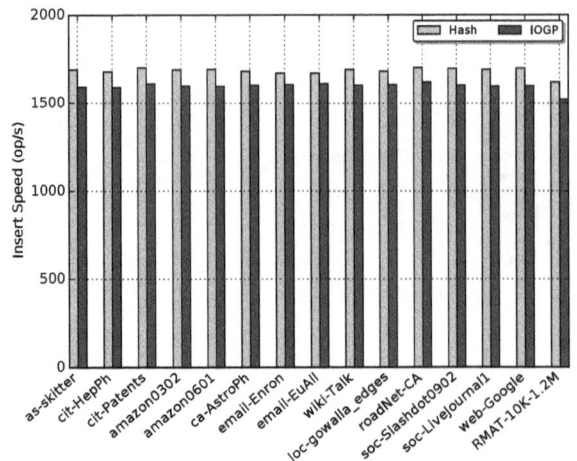

Figure 11: Insertion performance.

while accessing split high degree vertices. In this evaluation, all traversals started from the same set of randomly chosen vertices. Their average finish time is used for comparison. We evaluated graph traversal with 2, 4, 6, and 8 steps.

Due to the space limit, we cannot show the comparison results from all tested graphs. Instead, we chose a set of representative graphs based on the edge-cut ratio shown in Figure 5. Specifically, we selected two graphs that have the maximal edge-cut ratio difference between Fennel and IOGP (i.e. *web-Google* and *RMAT-10K-1.2M*) and two graphs that have the minimal edge-cut ratio difference (i.e. *soc-LiveJournal1* and *wiki-Talk*). We excluded METIS since it is not valid in streaming graphs to avoid unfair comparison.

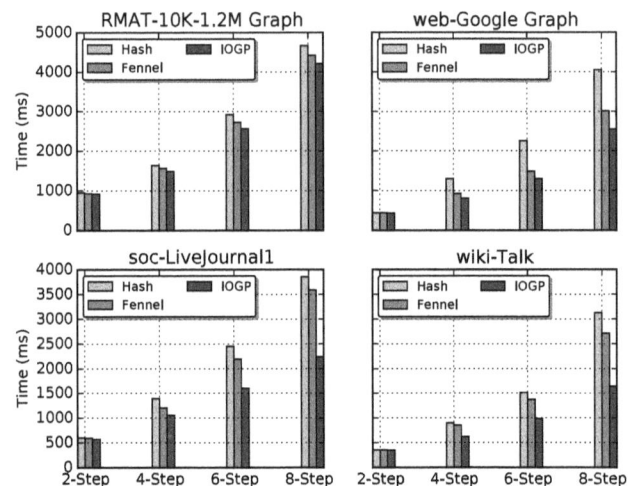

Figure 12: Graph traversal performance.

The results are plotted in Figure 12. As the results show, IOGP achieves clearly better traversal performance than Hash and Fennel for all cases. The performance gap also increases while more traversal steps are performed. These results demonstrate the advantage and importance of IOGP for future, more complex graph traversal requests. Additionally, we can observe that IOGP achieves more improvements on graphs with better edge-cut ratio. This observation recalls the importance of vertex locality in graph partitioning.

7 CONCLUSION & FUTURE WORK

In this study, motivated by the OLTP performance requirements of distributed graph databases, we have introduced an Incremental Online Graph Partitioning (IOGP) algorithm and have described its design and implementation details. IOGP adapts its operations among three stages according to the continuous changes of the graph. It operates fast, obtains optimized partition results, and generates partitioned graphs serving complex traversals well. We have also presented implementation details including in-memory data structures (e.g., edge counters) to deliver fast, online graph partitioning. Our detailed and concrete evaluations on multiple graphs from various domains confirmed the advantages of IOGP. From these evaluations, we are also able to draw important conclusions including the general guidelines of selecting its key parameters. We believe that IOGP has the great potential to be widely used as a graph partitioning solution for distributed graph databases. In the future, we plan to investigate and develop fault tolerance feature for IOGP, with a focus on rebuilding in-memory data structures efficiently when needed.

8 ACKNOWLEDGMENTS

We are thankful to the anonymous reviewers for their valuable feedback and our shepherd, Dr. Jay Lofstead, for his detailed and valuable suggestions that improved this paper significantly. This research is supported in part by the National Science Foundation under grant CNS-1162488, CNS-1338078, IIP-1362134, and CCF-1409946.

REFERENCES

[1] Stephen T Barnard. PMRSB: Parallel Multilevel Recursive Spectral Bisection. In *Proceedings of the 1995 ACM/IEEE conference on Supercomputing*.
[2] Peter J Carrington, John Scott, and Stanley Wasserman. 2005. *Models and methods in social network analysis*. Vol. 28. Cambridge university press.
[3] Deepayan Chakrabarti, Yiping Zhan, and Christos Faloutsos. 2004. R-MAT: A Recursive Model for Graph Mining. In *Proceedings of the 2004 SIAM International Conference on Data Mining*, Vol. 4. SIAM, 442–446.
[4] Cédric Chevalier and François Pellegrini. 2008. PT-Scotch: A tool for efficient parallel graph ordering. *Parallel computing* 34, 6 (2008), 318–331.
[5] CloudLab. 2017. https://www.cloudlab.us/. (2017).
[6] Dong Dai, Philip Carns, Robert B Ross, John Jenkins, Kyle Blauer, and Yong Chen. 2015. GraphTrek: Asynchronous Graph Traversal for Property Graph-Based Metadata Management. In *2015 IEEE International Conference on Cluster Computing*. IEEE, 284–293.
[7] Dong Dai, Yong Chen, Philip Carns, John Jenkins, Wei Zhang, and Robert Ross. 2016. GraphMeta: A Graph-Based Engine for Managing Large-Scale HPC Rich Metadata. In *Cluster Computing (CLUSTER), 2016 IEEE International Conference on*. IEEE, 298–307.
[8] Dong Dai, Robert B Ross, Philip Carns, Dries Kimpe, and Yong Chen. 2014. Using property graphs for rich metadata management in hpc systems. In *Parallel Data Storage Workshop (PDSW), 2014 9th*. IEEE, 7–12.
[9] G. DeCandia, D. Hastorun, M. Jampani, G. Kakulapati, A. Lakshman, A. Pilchin, S. Sivasubramanian, P. Vosshall, and W. Vogels. 2007. Dynamo: Amazon's Highly Available Key-Value Store. (2007).
[10] DEX. 2017. DEX. http://www.sparsity-technologies.com/. (2017).
[11] David Ediger, Jason Riedy, David A Bader, and Henning Meyerhenke. 2011. Tracking structure of streaming social networks. In *Parallel and Distributed Processing Workshops and Phd Forum (IPDPSW), 2011 IEEE International Symposium on*. IEEE, 1691–1699.
[12] Michael R Garey and David S Johnson. 2002. *Computers and intractability*. Vol. 29. wh freeman New York.
[13] Michael R Garey, David S Johnson, and Larry Stockmeyer. 1974. Some simplified NP-complete problems. In *Proceedings of the sixth annual ACM symposium on Theory of computing*. ACM, 47–63.
[14] Bruce Hendrickson and Robert Leland. 1995. *The Chaco user's guide: Version 2.0*. Technical Report. Technical Report SAND95-2344, Sandia National Laboratories.
[15] Jiewen Huang and Daniel J Abadi. 2016. Leopard: lightweight edge-oriented partitioning and replication for dynamic graphs. *Proceedings of the VLDB Endowment* 9, 7 (2016), 540–551.
[16] George Karypis and Vipin Kumar. 1998. A fast and high quality multilevel scheme for partitioning irregular graphs. *SIAM Journal on scientific Computing* 20, 1 (1998), 359–392.
[17] George Karypis and Vipin Kumar. 1998. A parallel algorithm for multilevel graph partitioning and sparse matrix ordering. *J. Parallel and Distrib. Comput.* 48, 1 (1998), 71–95.
[18] Pradeep Kumar and H Howie Huang. 2016. G-store: high-performance graph store for trillion-edge processing. In *Proceedings of the International Conference for High Performance Computing, Networking, Storage and Analysis*. IEEE Press, 71.
[19] Jure Leskovec and Andrej Krevl. 2014. SNAP Datasets: Stanford Large Network Dataset Collection. http://snap.stanford.edu/data. (June 2014).
[20] Grzegorz Malewicz, Matthew H Austern, Aart JC Bik, James C Dehnert, Ilan Horn, Naty Leiser, and Grzegorz Czajkowski. 2010. Pregel: a System for Large-Scale Graph Processing. In *Proceedings of the 2010 ACM SIGMOD International Conference on Management of data*. ACM, 135–146.
[21] Richard C Murphy, Kyle B Wheeler, Brian W Barrett, and James A Ang. 2010. Introducing the graph 500. *Cray User's Group (CUG)* (2010).
[22] Joel Nishimura and Johan Ugander. 2013. Restreaming graph partitioning: simple versatile algorithms for advanced balancing. In *Proceedings of the 19th ACM SIGKDD*. ACM, 1106–1114.
[23] OrientDB. 2017. http://www.orientechnologies.com/orient-db.htm. (2017).
[24] Lawrence Page, Sergey Brin, Rajeev Motwani, and Terry Winograd. 1999. The PageRank citation ranking: bringing order to the web. (1999).
[25] François Pellegrini and Jean Roman. 1996. Scotch: A software package for static mapping by dual recursive bipartitioning of process and architecture graphs. In *International Conference on High-Performance Computing and Networking*. Springer.
[26] RocksDB. 2017. http://rocksdb.org/. (2017).
[27] Amitabha Roy, Ivo Mihailovic, and Willy Zwaenepoel. 2013. X-stream: Edge-Centric Graph Processing using Streaming Partitions. In *Proceedings of the Twenty-Fourth ACM Symposium on Operating Systems Principles*.
[28] Kirk Schloegel, George Karypis, and Vipin Kumar. 1997. Multilevel diffusion schemes for repartitioning of adaptive meshes. *J. Parallel and Distrib. Comput.* 47, 2 (1997), 109–124.
[29] SimpleGdb. 2017. https://github.com/daidong/simplegdb-Java. (2017).
[30] Isabelle Stanton and Gabriel Kliot. 2012. Streaming graph partitioning for large distributed graphs. In *Proceedings of the 18th ACM SIGKDD international conference on Knowledge discovery and data mining*.
[31] Yuanyuan Tian, Andrey Balmin, Severin Andreas Corsten, Shirish Tatikonda, and John McPherson. 2013. From think like a vertex to think like a graph. *Proceedings of the VLDB Endowment* 7, 3 (2013), 193–204.
[32] Titan. 2017. http://thinkaurelius.github.io/titan/. (2017).
[33] Charalampos Tsourakakis, Christos Gkantsidis, Bozidar Radunovic, and Milan Vojnovic. 2014. Fennel: Streaming graph partitioning for massive scale graphs. In *Proceedings of the 7th ACM international conference on Web search and data mining*. ACM, 333–342.
[34] Johan Ugander and Lars Backstrom. 2013. Balanced label propagation for partitioning massive graphs. In *Proceedings of the sixth ACM international conference on Web search and data mining*. ACM.
[35] Luis M Vaquero, Felix Cuadrado, Dionysios Logothetis, and Claudio Martella. 2014. Adaptive partitioning for large-scale dynamic graphs. In *Distributed Computing Systems (ICDCS), 2014 IEEE 34th International Conference on*. IEEE, 144–153.
[36] Jim Webber. 2012. A Programmatic Introduction to Neo4j. In *Proceedings of the 3rd annual conference on Systems, Programming, and Applications: Software for Humanity*. ACM, 217–218.
[37] Reynold S Xin, Joseph E Gonzalez, Michael J Franklin, and Ion Stoica. GraphX: A Resilient Distributed Graph System on Spark. In *First International Workshop on Graph Data Management Experiences and Systems*.
[38] Yang Zhou, Ling Liu, Sangeetha Seshadri, and Lawrence Chiu. 2016. Analyzing enterprise storage workloads with graph modeling and clustering. *IEEE Journal on Selected Areas in Communications* 34, 3 (2016), 551–574.

Machine and Application Aware Partitioning for Adaptive Mesh Refinement Applications

Milinda Fernando
School of Computing,
University of Utah
Salt Lake City, Utah
milinda@cs.utah.edu

Dmitry Duplyakin
Department of Computer Science
University of Colorado
Boulder, Colorado
dmitry.duplyakin@colorado.edu

Hari Sundar
School of Computing,
University of Utah
Salt Lake City, Utah
hari@cs.utah.edu

ABSTRACT

Load balancing and partitioning are critical when it comes to parallel computations. Popular partitioning strategies based on space filling curves focus on equally dividing work. The partitions produced are independent of the architecture or the application. Given the ever-increasing relative cost of data movement and increasing heterogeneity of our architectures, it is no longer sufficient to only consider an equal partitioning of work. Minimizing communication costs are equally if not more important. *Our hypothesis is that an unequal partitioning that minimizes communication costs significantly can scale and perform better than conventional equal-work partitioning schemes. This tradeoff is dependent on the architecture as well as the application.* We validate our hypothesis in the context of a finite-element computation utilizing adaptive mesh-refinement. Our central contribution is a new partitioning scheme that minimizes the overall runtime of subsequent computations by performing architecture and application-aware non-uniform work assignment in order to decrease time to solution, primarily by minimizing data-movement. We evaluate our algorithm by comparing it against standard space-filling curve based partitioning algorithms and observing time-to-solution as well as energy-to-solution for solving Finite Element computations on adaptively refined meshes. We demonstrate excellent scalability of our new partition algorithm up to 262, 144 cores on ORNL's Titan and demonstrate that the proposed partitioning scheme reduces overall energy as well as time-to-solution for application codes by up to 22.0%.

CCS CONCEPTS

•Computing methodologies →Massively parallel algorithms;

KEYWORDS

domain decomposition; communication minimizing algorithms; energy efficient computing; AMR; FEM

1 INTRODUCTION

As we scale up to exascale machines, the cost of data movement and load-imbalance therein are a major bottleneck for achieving

HPDC '17, June 26-30, 2017, Washington, DC, USA
© 2017 ACM. 978-1-4503-4699-3/17/06. . . $15.00
DOI: http://dx.doi.org/10.1145/3078597.3078610

scalability [28] and energy and power efficiency [31]. These are dictated largely by how data (or tasks) are partitioned across processes. This motivates a need for better partitioning schemes for our most demanding applications. While we continue to build larger supercomputers, these come with increased parallelism and heterogeneity at the node as well as the cluster level. In all cases, minimizing load-imbalance and communication-costs as well as minimizing data-movement are critical to ensuring scalability and performance on leadership architectures. Additionally, the partitioning algorithms need to be architecture (*e.g.* bandwidth) and application-aware (*e.g.* data access pattern) and not simply divide the problem into equal-sized chunks across p processes. These are also important for reducing the energy footprint of our algorithms and making extreme-scale computing economically viable [31]. To be practical, such partitioning algorithms need to be optimal, i.e., with a $O(N/p + \log p)$ parallel complexity for partitioning N data across p processes, ideally with low constants [12].

Space Filling Curves (SFC) are commonly used by the HPC community for partitioning data [7, 10, 36] and for resource allocations [3, 32]. By mapping high-dimensional spatial coordinates (or regions) onto a 1D curve, the task of partitioning is made trivial. Locality, i.e., ensuring that regions that are close in the higher dimensional space are also close along the 1D curve, is guaranteed by the *ordering* of the curve, leading to different SFC, such as Morton, Hilbert, Peano, etc. The key challenge is to order the coordinates or regions according to the specified ordering, usually performed using an ordering function and sorting algorithm. This approach is easily parallelized using efficient parallel sorting algorithms such as SAMPLESORT [11]. This is the approach used by several state-of-the-art packages [5, 7, 10, 24, 36]. This approach either aims to get the ideal load balance ($N/p \pm 1$) or relies on the underlying sorting algorithm to load balance. In either case there is no expectation on the minimization of the communication costs beyond what is afforded by the locality of the SFC.

Our hypothesis is that an unequal partitioning that minimizes communication-costs significantly and is architecture and application-aware, can scale and perform better than conventional equal-work partitioning schemes. In this work, we test this hypothesis in the context of SFC-based partitioning and present novel sequential and distributed partitioning algorithms that minimize the overall time-to-solution as well as the energy-to-solution by minimizing communication costs in exchange for a (small) increase in workload imbalance. We evaluate energy-to-solution in addition to time-to-solution to ensure that the increased load-imbalance does not result in increasing the energy-cost of computations. Our approach is architecture and application-aware and will produce different partitions on different machines and for different applications.

Related Work. Load balancing and partitioning are critical when it comes to parallel computations. Generally partitioning involves equally dividing the work and data among the processors, reducing processor idle time and communication costs. The standard approach is to model the problem using a communication or data-dependency graph and partition the vertices of the graph into (roughly) equal-sized groups such that the weight of the edges crossing across processes is minimized. Graph partitioning is a NP-hard problem and most work focuses on heuristics to obtain good approximations. Several graph partitioning packages exist [9, 17, 22, 23, 37] but performance and parallel scalability is challenging, especially for applications requiring repeated partitioning, such as Adaptive Mesh Refinement (AMR). In many such cases, SFC are used as a scalable and effective partitioning technique [2, 5]. Note that several recent Gordon-Bell award winners have used SFC-based partitioning techniques for this reason [15, 18, 27, 30]. One of the main advantage of SFC based partitioning is the preservation of geometric locality of objects between processors. Depending on the SFC (i.e. Morton, Moore, Hilbert) that is used for partitioning, the amount of locality preserved differs [2]. Most SFC based partitioning—especially for adaptive meshing—use the Morton ordering that offers a good balance between the quality of partition and the efficiency of implementation.

There is a large literature of Space Filling Curve (SFC) based partitioning schemes. Several works have compared the clustering properties of space filling curves [1, 25] and concluded the superiority of Hilbert curves over the Morton curve. Gunther *et al*[13] demonstrated that using SFCs to build hierarchical data structures such as octrees minimizes data access time. Algorithms have been proposed for computing the (inverse) mapping between one and d-dimensional spaces [2, 6, 7] including indexing schemes for unequal dimension cardinalities [16], resulting in reduced communication costs. Other applications include multi-dimensional data reordering [20] and to speed up sparse matrix-vector multiplications [38] by improving cache-utilization. Several implementations of SFC-based partitioning algorithms are also available including Dendro [36], p4est [5] and Zoltan [8]. A thorough review of SFCs and their applications can be found in [2].

Contributions. While SFCs have been used for partitioning data for a long time and several efficient implementations exist, our algorithms produce better partitions and demonstrate the scalability and efficiency experimentally. *Our main contribution is the development of a new SFC-based partitioning algorithm that enables incorporation of a machine-model to produce high-quality partitions.* Our contributions in detail:

- **Method:** We present an algorithm that allows us to factor in the overall communication costs during SFC-based partitioning. We demonstrate that reducing load-imbalance is accompanied with increasing communication costs when performed in a top-down manner. By using a performance model to determine the tradeoff between work-imbalance and communication costs, we can determine the optimal partition that results in reduced time-to-solution for application codes. Our approach is also comparable in performance and scalability to existing SFC-based partitioning approaches.

- **Experimental Evaluation:** We conduct experiments to demonstrate the efficiency and scalability of our algorithm on ORNL's Titan up to 262,144 cores. We demonstrate that our algorithm reduces runtime by up to 22% while performing Finite Element computations. We also include energy measurements for resulting MATVEC operations on Cloudlab [29] and demonstrate similar 22% savings in energy-to-solution.

Organization of the paper. The rest of the paper is organized as follows. In §2, we give a quick overview of space filling curves and octree-based adaptive meshing. In §3 we describe the new partitioning algorithm, as well as justifications for trading minor load-imbalance for reduced communication costs. In §4, we discuss the experimental setup including the framework for measuring the energy costs related with a finite element simulation. In §5, we present results demonstrating the superiority of the new partitioning algorithm. Finally, we conclude with directions for future work.

2 BACKGROUND

The most common strategy for parallelizing algorithms is to partition data. The primary goal of the partitioning approach is to divide work equally (load-balance) and minimize the communication between processes. Geometry-based heuristics, such as the use of Space filling curves (SFC) are often the only choice when the data is complex and dynamic, such as for adaptive mesh refinement [2]. For this reason, we will primarily use adaptively refined octree meshes for illustrative purposes, although the proposed methods are equally applicable to other spatial partitioning problems, such as resource allocation[3, 32]. SFCs define a one-to-one mapping between an d-dimensional space and one dimensional space. Since, partitioning 1D data is trivial, such an ordering enables simple load-balanced partitioning of data. The minimization of communication is achieved by the clustering properties of the SFC. For applications where the data dependencies are geometrically local, SFC-based partitioning schemes are efficient, scalable and highly effective. We introduce notation used for the rest of the paper in Table 1.

While SFCs are defined primarily for coordinates, they can be easily extended to support regions, such as octants or elements, by having a notion of an *anchor* coordinate, say the smallest corner along all dimensions, and a measure of the size of the region, such as the level of refinement. In the context of octrees, firstly a discretization of the coordinates is specified by the maximum level of refinement, D_{max}. This allows for the coordinates to be stored as unsigned integers of length D_{max} bits. We will consider ordering for 3D regions specified using 4 values, the anchor (x, y, z) and the level $l \in [0, D_{max})$. As previously mentioned, the usual approach has been to define an ordering function using such coordinates and use existing parallel sorting algorithms such as SAMPLESORT. Since it is not straightforward to incorporate the machine-model into a parallel sorting algorithm like SAMPLESORT, we will first present a modified SFC ordering (and therefore partitioning) algorithm that

comm	MPI communicator
p	number of MPI tasks in comm
r	the task id (MPI Rank)
A	global: input elements or regions
A_r	local : input elements or regions local to task r
A_i	local : elements or regions in the ith bucket
N	global number of elements in A
$n = N/p$	local number of elements in A
l	refinement level of the curve or tree
R_h	SFC based permutation function
W_{max}	max. of work assigned to an individual processor
C_{max}	max. of data communicated
t_w	interconnect slowness (1/bandwidth)
t_s	interconnect latency
t_c	intranode memory slowness (1/ RAM bandwidth)

Table 1: *Notation used in this paper.*

Algorithm 1 TREESORT (Sequential)

Input: A list of elements or regions A, the starting level l_1 and the ending level l_2
Output: A is reordered according to the SFC.

```
1: counts[] ← 0                          ▷ |counts| = 2^dim, 8 for 3D
2: for a ∈ A do
3:     increment counts[child_num(a)]
4: counts ← R_h(counts)                  ▷ Permute counts using SFC ordering
5: offsets ← scan(counts)
6: A'[] ← empty
7: for a ∈ A do
8:     i ← child_num(a)
9:     append a to A' at offsets[i]
10:    increment offset[i]
11: swap(A, A')
12: if l_1 > l_2 then
13:     for i := 1 : 2^dim do
14:         TREESORT(A_i, l_1 − 1, l_2)    ▷ local sort
```

---

we will eventually extend to an architecture and application-aware, communication-minimizing partitioning algorithm.

2.1 Modified SFC Ordering

Let us consider the sequential case first. Instead of relying on a comparison based sorting algorithms such as quicksort or SAMPLESORT, one can instead opt to use a non-comparative sorting algorithm, such as the Radix sort [39]. If one considers the Most-Significant-Digit (MSD) Radix sort, then this is equivalent to a top-down construction of quadtrees or octrees, in 2D and 3D respectively. Bucketing the data (re-ordering) based ok the k-th bit of the x, y, and z coordinates, is equivalent to splitting the octree at the kth level. We call this algorithm TREESORT (Algorithm 1). A key difference between the standard Radix sort and TREESORT is that we need to re-order the buckets based on the SFC-curve. The complexity of the algorithm is not affected by the choice of SFCs. In case of the Morton Curve, the ordering is fixed, independent of the level. For cases where the ordering is based on the level, as in the case of Hilbert, these can be applied at this level with an $O(1)$ cost. Another advantage of this approach is that it traverses the tree in a depth-first fashion leading to good locality and cache utilization.

While it might seem like we have simply replaced SAMPLE-SORT with a Radix sort, there is an important reason for this. Because of the similarity to the octree construction, note that we get progressively closer to the optimal N/p load on each partition. It is this iterative nature of the Radix sort (induced partitions) that makes it appealing over comparison-based approaches like SAMPLESORT.

3 ARCHITECTURE-OPTIMAL PARTITIONING

Two desirable qualities of any partitioning strategy are load balancing, and minimization of overlap between the processor domains. SFC-based partitioning does a very good job in load balancing but does not permit an explicit control on the level of overlap. Ideally, we would like to have a perfectly load-balanced partition that also minimizes the overall communication. But this is usually not possible, especially for non-uniform work distributions such as for adaptively refined meshes. Additionally, it might not be possible

to minimize the load-imbalance and overall communication simultaneously. Since the cost of communication across inter-process boundaries depends both on the machine characteristics, say network bandwidth, as well as the application, i.e., the amount of data being exchanged per unit boundary, it is important to consider these aspects while partitioning data. Specifically, since the goal of most parallel codes is to minimize time-to-solution (and possibly energy-to-solution), it is important that the partition balances "equal assignment of work" with "overall communication cost" to achieve these goals. Clearly such a balance is dependent on both the machine-characteristics as well as the application's data-dependencies. In this section, we will incorporate these features into SFC-based partitioning.

Simple partitions, such as those producing relatively cuboid partitions have a smaller overlap compared with more irregular partitions, as might be produced by a SFC-based partitioning algorithm. In [35], we proposed a heuristic partitioning scheme based on the intuition that a coarse grid partition is likely to have a smaller overlap between the processor domains as compared to a partition computed on the underlying fine grid. This algorithm first constructed and partitioned a complete linear octree based on the data (equivalent to a standard SFC-based partitioning). This was followed by coarsening of the ocree and a second weighted partitioning of the coarse octree to get *simpler* partitioning. There are a few shortcomings of this approach. Firstly, this is a heuristic and there are no guarantees that the partition produced will be better than using the standard SFC-based partition. This is mainly due to the reliance on an external sorting function and the bottom-up (coarsening) fashion in which it operates. Secondly, the algorithm considers neither the machine-characteristics nor the application characteristics and will produce the same partition on different machines and for different applications[1]. OptiPart addresses these shortcomings. We will first present the distributed memory version of TREESORT, then demonstrate that decreasing the load-imbalance via this algorithm results in a monotic increase in overall communication costs, allowing users to specify a tolerance and reduce overall communication costs. We then develop a performance model to estimate the optimal tolerance to obtain the best time-to-solution for the specific machine and application.

---

[1] e.g. for the Poisson equation vs the wave Equation on the same mesh.

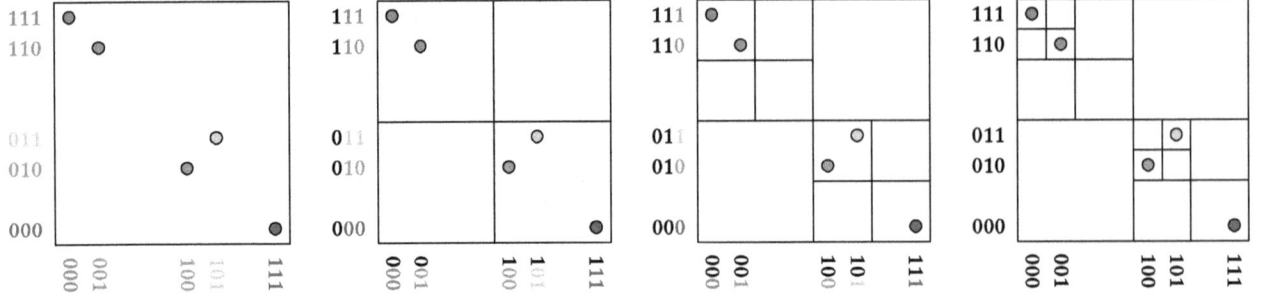

Figure 1: Equivalence of the MSD Radix sort with top-down quadtree construction when ordered according to space filling curves. Each color-coded point is represented by its x and y coordinates. From the MSD-Radix perspective, we start with the most-significant bit for both the x and y coordinates and progressively bucket (order) the points based on these. The bits are colored based on the points and turn black as they get used to (partially) order the points.

3.1 Distributed Memory TreeSort

Our modified SFC-ordering algorithm TREESORT operates in a top-down fashion. In this section, we propose a distributed variant of TREESORT that enables fine control over the load-balance and also enables reduction in communication costs in exchange for higher load-imbalance. The distributed algorithm proceeds as the sequential variant (§2.1), bucketing and partially sorting the data. Unlike the sequential TREESORT, we have to traverse the tree in a breadth first fashion, as the data needs to be distributed across processors. Note that at each level, we split each octant 8 times (for 3D), so in $\log_8 p$ steps we will have p buckets. A reduction provides us with the global ranks[2] of these p buckets. Here p is the desired number of partitions. Using the optimal ranks ($r \cdot N/p$) at which the data needs to be partitioned for process r, we selectively partition the buckets to obtain the correct partitioning of the local data. This is in principle similar to the approach used by algorithms such as histogramsort [33] and hyksort [34], except that no comparisons are needed for computing the ranks. The computational cost corresponds to the $O(N/p)$ bucketing required for each of the $\log_8 p$ levels. We also need p reductions and an all-to-all data exchange. Therefore the expected parallel runtime, T_p for the distributed algorithm is,

$$T_p = t_c \frac{N}{p} + (t_s + t_w p) \log p + t_w \frac{N}{p}, \tag{1}$$

where t_c, t_s, and t_w are the memory slowness (1/RAM bandwidth), the network latency and the network slowness (1/bandwidth), respectively. In our evaluation, we considered trees of depth 30 (so that the coordinates can be represented using unsigned int). Note that up to $8^6 = 262, 144$ buckets can be determined using six levels, so the cost of determining splitters to distribute the data across processors is significantly lower than other approaches. An analysis of complexities for popular distributed sorting algorithms can be found in [34].

While TREESORT is performed in place, the distributed version requires $O(p)$ additional storage to perform the reduction to compute the global splitter ranks. The additional storage as well as the cost of performing the reductions can be significant for large p, therefore we perform the splitter selection in a staged manner. We

[2]The rank here referes to the position of a element in a sorted array.

limit the maximum number of splitters to a user-specified parameter $k \leq p$. This also reduces the cost of the reduction to compute the global ranks of the splitters from $O(p \log p)$ to $O(k \log p)$. The expected running time for the staged distributed TREESORT is,

$$T_p = t_c \frac{N}{p} + (t_s + t_w k) \log p + t_w \frac{N}{p}. \tag{2}$$

Additionally, the all-to-all exchange is also performed in a staged manner similar to [4, 34], avoiding potential network congestion. We will now develop the algorithm further to automatically determine the best tolerance.

REMARK. *We will develop the distributed TREESORT algorithm further to balance work and communication costs based on the machine-model in §3.4. Therefore, for clarity of presentation, we are not presenting the pseudocode for distributed TREESORT. The pseudocode for OPTIPART is presented in Algorithm 3.*

3.2 Justification for Flexible Partitioning

An advantage of the distributed TREESORT algorithm is that we can specify a tolerance, *tol*, for the desired load-balance, i.e., stopping if the induced partitions are $r \cdot N/p \pm tolerance$ instead of the optimal $r \cdot N/p$. While it is possible to specify such a tolerance for samplesort variants [21, 33, 34], the advantage is limited to reducing the cost of computing the partition or ordering at the cost of reduced load-balance and will not provide any reduction in communication costs. SFC-based partitioning algorithms are likely to partition using the *finest* level octant, resulting is increased boundary surface, as the primary criterion is to equally divide the work (octants) amongst the processes. Our hypothesis is that, it should be possible to find a partition in close proximity to the optimally load-balanced partition, that has a lower inter-process boundary surface. This will enable users to get the partition with the minimum boundary surface, by specifying a tolerance on the equally-divided load. In case of TREESORT, specifying a tolerance, in addition to making the ordering faster to compute, the induced partition also has reduced communication costs (for subsequent computations, like numerical simulations) in exchange for the increased load-imbalance. This makes TREESORT attractive when the communication costs are high. If we consider the cost of communication to be 10x that of performing the work on one unit of data, then an increase of 20

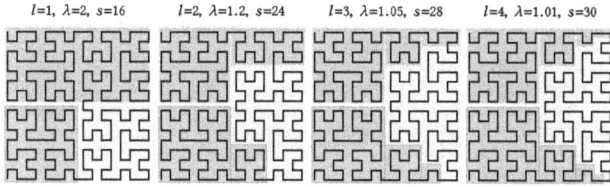

Figure 2: Illustration of the increase in communication costs with increasing levels of TREESORT. Partitions for the case of $p = 3$ are drawn with the boundary of the partition (s) and the load-imbalance (λ) given along with the level (l) at which the partition is defined. At each level, the orange partition (█) gets the extra load that is progressively reduced. The green partition ( ) gets the largest boundary that progressively increases.

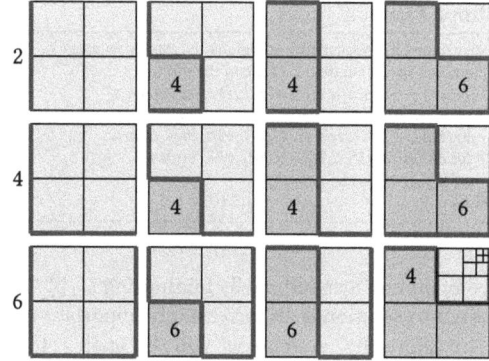

Figure 3: Demonstration that the communication costs are non-decreasing with increasing levels of TREESORT for most refinements and identification of the pathological case where the surface area decreases (bottom-right). The left column corresponds to initial boundaries (blue line) sharing 1, 2, and 3 faces of the quadrant (rows) that will be refined at level l. The remaining columns illustrate the change in surface area for the cases where 1-3 child nodes get added to the blue partition. The numbers represent the surface area of each case.

units of work resulting in a reduction of 5 units of data-exchange, would still provide savings of $5 \times 10 - 20 = 30$ units. This is a contrived example, but the key point is that even small reductions in data-movement over the network provide large savings in overall runtime.

By design, for the TREESORT algorithm the load-imbalance, $\lambda = \max(|W_r|)/\min(|W_r|)$ decreases with increasing l getting closer to the optimal value of $\lambda = 1$. However, as we increase levels, the boundary of the partition s is non-decreasing. This is illustrated in Figure 2 using a simple 2D partition using 3 processors. This allows the user to specify a tolerance, say 1%, which when reached will prevent further refinement, potentially reducing the inter-process boundary and thereby the communication costs of subsequent operations. Note that the claim is not for reducing the data-exchange cost during the reordering, but for subsequent operations that might be performed based on the partition.

The example in Figure 2 considers uniform refinement, but the result is also true for meshes with adaptive refinement, as would be the case for most numerical simulations. This is demonstrated in Figure 3. Here we consider the partition between two processors, and the specific element that will be refined at the next level. It can be seen that for all cases except one, the surface area of the partition is non-decreasing. The case where the surface area decreases is a case of extreme refinement, that will only occur if the last child has a significantly higher refinement compared to the other siblings. While this case appears to limit the effectiveness of the approach, it is important to realize that other more-expensive approaches like spectral bisection also fail for similar examples [26].

3.3 Performance Model

While having the user specify a tolerance for the load-balance in order to lower the communication costs allows for better performance, it does limit the portability of the method and makes it difficult when either the architecture or the data distribution changes. Ideally, we would like to automatically determine the optimum tolerance based on the application and the machine characteristics. As mentioned previously, the tradeoff is between the load and the communication costs across all machines. Additionally, the time for either stage will be dominated by the processor that has

the maximum load (W_{max}) or has to communicate the maximum (C_{max}) amount of data. We build a simple performance model to characterize the overall parallel runtime as a combination of these two terms. We further note that these times can be estimated using the network bandwidth ($1/t_w$) and the memory bandwidth ($1/t_c$)– for memory-bound computations. In other words the total runtime (T_p) can be characterized by the following equation,

$$T_p = \alpha t_c W_{max} + t_w C_{max}. \tag{3}$$

Here, α is indicative of the number of memory accesses performed per unit of work. For example, if the target application is a 7-point stencil operation, then α will be ~ 8. In general, this can be computed using a simple sequential profiling of the main execution kernel. While this model ignores aspects such as overlapping computation and communication, it is simple and can help us easily determine if given a set of partitions with different W_{max}, C_{max} which partition is likely to be the most efficient.

REMARK. *It is easy to modify (3) for a compute-bound application, and even use a simple profiling step to determine the right parameters for running a specific application on a specific architecture.*

We would also like to briefly discuss the model from the energy perspective, as there might be concerns that the increased load imbalance might increase the overall energy cost of the computation. For most modern cluster architectures, the overall energy will be strongly correlated with the overall runtime. Assuming an efficient processor architecture, the overall energy for the computation will not depend on the partitioning, as the sum of *work* will remain the same. The overall energy cost of communication will however be lower for the lowest total data communicated. This is what we aim for, i.e., a partition that gives the best runtime by balancing W_{max} and C_{max} and minimizes the total energy required

---

Algorithm 2 PartitionQuality

Input: A distributed list of elements or regions A_r, comm, splitters s,
Output: Predicted execution time T_p for current splitters s

```
1: bdyOctants ← computeLocalBdyOctants(A_r, s)
2: localSz ← size(A_r, s)
3: MPI_ReduceAll(bdyOctants, C_max, MPI_MAX, comm)
4: MPI_ReduceAll(localSz, W_max, MPI_MAX, comm)
5: T_p ← αt_c W_max + t_w C_max
6: return T_p
```

---

for the computation by additionally minimizing C_{max}. However, since energy-to-solution is an increasingly important metric for current and future HPC systems, we will also analyze the energy-to-solution in addition to time-to-solution while evaluating our new partitioning algorithm.

3.4 OptiPart: Architecture & Data optimized partitioning

Armed with our performance model, we can easily modify the distributed TreeSort to compute the optimal partition without having to guess the appropriate tolerance. We will use the memory and network slowness (t_c, t_w) based on the machine and will expect the user to provide the parameter α that is representative of the core computations. We call this algorithm OptiPart. The algorithm proceeds the same as distributed TreeSort , but instead relies on estimates of W_{max}, C_{max} for the current and next refinements and proceeds only if the runtime estimates (3) for the next refinement are lower than the current estimate. This does not change the complexity of the partitioning algorithm, requiring only $O(N/p)$ local work and a single reduction $O(\log p)$. OptiPart relies on a helper routine that computes the quality of the current partition, by doing a linear pass over the elements to determine the size of the local boundary. The pseudocode for this routine is given in Algorithm 2. Finally, the pseudocode for OptiPart is given in Algorithm 3. Note that the standard distributed TreeSort can be recovered by iterating till the work is equally divided instead of using Algorithm 2 to estimate the partition quality.

4 EXPERIMENTAL SETUP

Large scalability experiments reported in this paper were performed on Titan and Stampede. Titan, a Cray XK7 supercomputer at Oak Ridge National Laboratory (ORNL), has a total of 18,688 nodes consisting of a single 16-core AMD Opteron 6200 series processor, for a total of 299,008 cores. Each node has with 32GB of memory. It is also equipped with a Gemini interconnect and 600 terabytes of memory across all nodes. Stampede at the Texas Advanced Computing Center (TACC), is a linux cluster consisting of 6400 computes nodes, each with dual, eight-core processors for a total of 102,400 available cpu-cores. Each node has two eight-core 2.7GHz Intel Xeon E5 processors with 2GB/core of memory and a 3 level cache. Stampede has a 56Gb/s FDR Mellanox InfiniBand network connected in a fat tree configuration. In our largest runs we use a total of 262,144 cores on Titan.

4.1 Power Measurements

In order to quantify energy consumption tradeoffs, we provisioned two clusters on the CloudLab testbed [29]: *Wisconsin-8* – an 8-node

---

Algorithm 3 OptiPart

Input: A distributed list of elements or regions A_r, comm, p (w.l.g., assume $p = mk$), r of current task in comm,α,t_c,t_w,
Output: globally sorted array A

```
1:  counts_local[] ← 0, counts_global[] ← 0
2:  s ← TreeSort(A_r, l − log(p), l)           ▷ initial splitter computation
3:  default ← PartitionQuality(A_r, comm, s)
4:  current ← default
5:  while default ≥ current do
6:      counts[] ← 0                          ▷ |counts| = 2^dim, 8 for 3D
7:      for a ∈ A_r do
8:          increment counts[child_num(a)]
9:      counts_local ← push(counts)
10:     counts ← R_h(counts)                  ▷ Permute counts using SFC ordering
11:     offsets ← scan(counts)
12:     A'[] ← empty
13:     for a ∈ A_r do
14:         i ← child_num(a)
15:         append a to A' at offsets[i]
16:         increment offset[i]
17:     swap(A_r, A')
18:     MPI_ReduceAll(counts_local, counts_global, MPI_SUM, comm)
19:     s ← select(s, counts_global)
20:     default ← current
21:     current ← PartitionQuality(A_r, comm, s)
22: MPI_AlltoAllv(W_r, s, comm)               ▷ Staged All2all
23: TreeSort(A_r, 0, l)                        ▷ local sort
```

---

cluster in the Wisconsin datacenter consisting of nodes with 2x Intel E5-2630 v3 8-core Haswell CPUs (2.40 GHz), 128GB ECC Memory, and 10Gb Ethernet NICs, and *Clemson-32* – a 32-node cluster in the Clemson datacenter with each node having 2x Intel E5-2683 v3 14-core Haswell CPUs (2.00 GHz), 256GB ECC Memory, and a 10Gb Ethernet NIC. We configured the provisioned hardware into SLURM-based [32] cluster environments and ran a set of selected parallel jobs with 256 (on Wisconsin-8) and 1792 (on Clemson-32) MPI tasks.

During execution, we obtained on-board IPMI sensor information and recorded every machine's instantaneous power draw (in Watts) every second. As concluded in [14] and stated in a recent survey [19], power samples collected using IPMI are accurate enough as long as the temporal load-varying effects do not occur at the rate that is near the sampling rate. Accurate energy estimation is a difficult task for short-period jobs. The energy experiments reported in this work includes over 380 jobs that are between 2 and 14 minutes in duration–120 to 8400 samples–on these clusters. In our evaluation, with the aforementioned runtimes and the number of power samples we collected, we are convinced that we are able to draw reliable quantitative conclusions about the energy tradeoffs.

After job completion, we combined the recorded power traces with the job start and end timestamps from the scheduler and obtained per-job energy consumption estimates (in Joules). In addition to the total job consumption, we estimated the amount of energy consumed during the communication phase (i.e. matvec operation in FEM computations) of these jobs. In order to eliminate the impact of the dynamic CPU frequency scaling on our energy estimates, we disabled the dynamic scaling and set all CPU cores to run at 2.4 and 2.0 GHz on Wisconsin-8 and Clemson-32, respectively.

4.2 Implementation details

All algorithms described in this work were implemented using C++ using MPI. We tested the performance using randomly generated

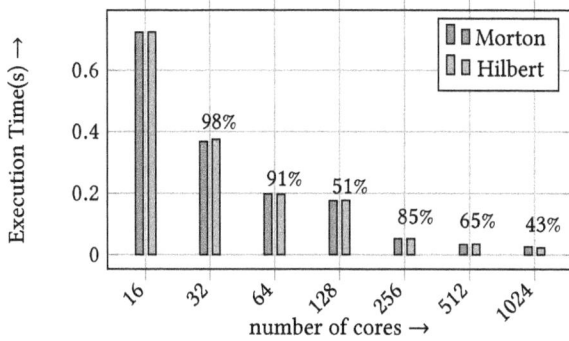

Figure 4: Strong scaling results for Hilbert & Morton based partitioning using a problem size of 16×10^6 elements on ORNL's Titan using core-counts from 16 to 1024. The parallel efficiency for each case (rounded) is listed above the bars.

octrees according to three distributions, uniform, normal, and log-normal. These were generated using the standard c++11 random number generators. No significant difference in performance was observed across the distributions, and therefore the distribution information has been suppressed for clarity of presentation. All results presented in this paper are for data generated according to the normal distribution. We implemented standard FEM computation on randomly generated octrees, focusing on matrix vector multiplication (matvec) for energy measurements. All the energy measurements are done in CloudLab (Wisconsin-8 & Clemson-32) cluster and all the other performance runs are done on ORNL's Titan and TACC's Stampede supercomputers.

5 PERFORMANCE EVALUATION

In this section we present results demonstrating the scalability and performance of OptiPart as well as the quality of the partitions produced. We will first demonstrate the scalability of OptiPart and its capability of partitioning large adaptive meshes efficiently. We will also compare its performance with standard SFC-based partitioning algorithms, primarily to demonstrate that OptiPart's performance is comparable to existing approaches. This is followed by detailed characterization of the partitioning qualities of the partitions generated by OptiPart in the context of a finite element computations on adaptively refined meshes.

5.1 Scalability

In this section we present both strong and weak scalability results carried out for OptiPart. Figure 4 shows the strong scalability results, using a fixed problem size of 16×10^6 elements, with increasing number of cores on ORNL's Titan. We present results for two popular space filling curves, Hilbert and Morton [2], to demonstrate that our algorithm is insensitive to the choice of the SFC. We obtain very good strong scalability with a parallel efficiency of ~ 43% for a 64x scaleup. We are able to partition 16 million elements in ~ 25 msecs across 1024 cores on Titan. We also present weak scalability results, in figure 5 up to 262, 144 cores on ORNL's Titan. We used a grain size of 10^6 elements per process for

16 to 262, 144 processes. In our largest run, we were able to partition 262 Billion elements in ~ 4 seconds across 262, 144 processes. Note that the increase in runtime is largely due to the increased cost of moving elements across the network (MPI_Alltoallv) whereas the partitioning algorithm demonstrate better scalability.

5.2 Comparison with SFC-based partitioning

In this section, we present a comparison between existing SFC-based partition schemes and OptiPart. Most existing SFC-based partitioning algorithms rely on parallel sorting algorithms such as SampleSort along with an ordering defined based on the SFC. In general, we would expect OptiPart to be slightly faster than a comparable implementation of SFC-partitioning relying on parallel sorting, as we terminate the splitter selection early. In this comparison, our primary goal is to demonstrate that incorporating the machine and application model does not adversely affect the efficiency or scalability of OptiPart compared to standard SFC-based partitioning. We compare against the SFC-based partitioning implemented in Dendro[36]. This implementation uses the Morton ordering along with SampleSort to partition data. This implementation was also used by the 2010 Gordon-Bell winner [27], and has been demonstrated to scale to leadership architectures. Since OptiPart produces different partitions for different machines, we performed this comparison on both ORNL's Titan as well as TACC's Stampede supercomputers using a grain-size of 5×10^6 elements. These results are presented in Figure 6. We can see that OptiPart has a small performance and scalability improvement over Dendro. This could be due to implementation differences, but the major take-away from this experiment is that it is possible to get application and architecture-aware partitioning without sacrificing performance or scalability.

5.3 Test application

Our target applications are solving Partial Partial Differential Equations (PDEs) using adaptive discretizations using the Finite Element method (FEM). In most computational codes, the basic building block is the matvec, a function that takes a vector and returns another vector, the result of applying the discretized PDE operator to the the input vector. Complex operations such an non-linear operators, time-dependent problems, and using iterative solvers to solve a linear system can all be represented as a series of matvecs. The communication as well as the compute pattern for most PDEs is characterized by the matvec. For this reason, we evaluate the effectiveness of OptiPart using a adaptively discretized Laplacian operator. This is equivalent to us solving a 3D Poisson problem with zero Dirichlet boundary conditions on a unit cube. In order to avoid any issues related to the convergence, we run all application comparisons using 100 matvecs using the standard partition produced by Dendro as well as the partition produced by OptiPart.

5.4 Improved performance for the matvec

In this section we present experiments demonstrating the reduction in time-to-solution and energy-to-solution for 100 iterations of the Laplacian operator using the OptiPart algorithm. All energy measurements were carried out in Clemson-32 (1792 cores) and Wisconsin-8(256 cores) in CloudLab cluster. Figure 7 shows the

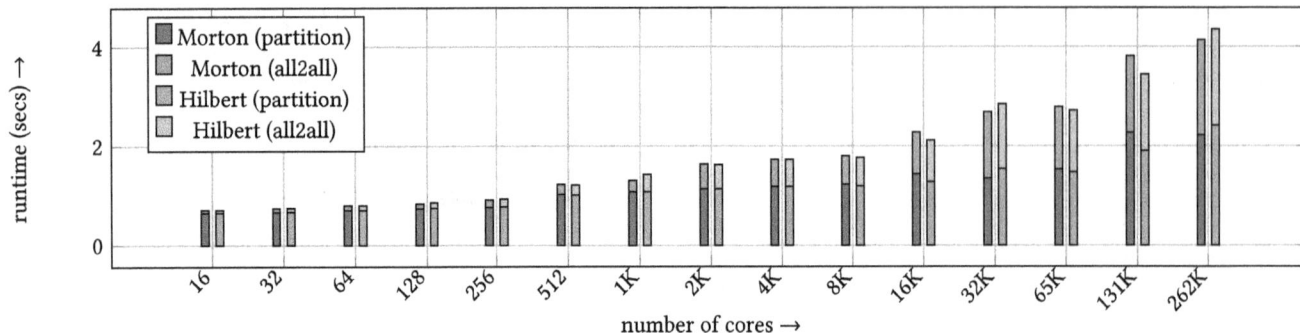

Figure 5: Total execution time for HILBERT & MORTON curve based partitioning scheme with a grain size of 10^6 elements (minimum of $16M$ & maximum of $262B$ elements), on ORNL's Titan with number of cores from 16 to 262, 144. The total time is divided into time for computing the partition (partition) and the cost of actually exchanging data (all2all).

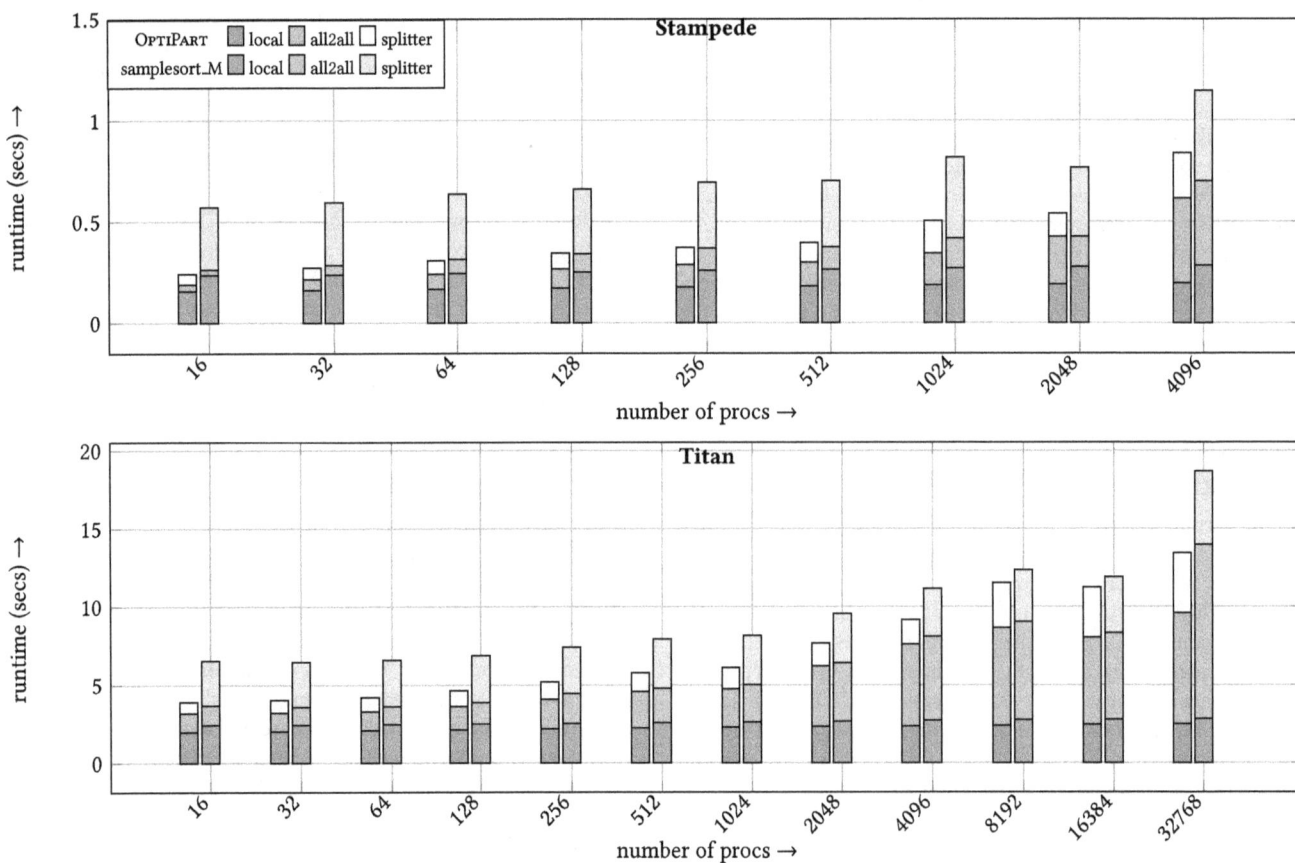

Figure 6: Weak scaling results breakdown (local sort, all to all, splitter calculation) for OptiPart & SampleSort in Dendro[36] with a grain size of 10^6 octants on Stampede (top) and on Titan (bottom) with a grain size of 5×10^6 octants. The scalability of OptiPart is better than SampleSort as show in above figure. Note that the performance and partitions produced by OptiPart are architecture specific, hence the differences between the results on Stampede and Titan.

runtime and energy consumption using an adaptive discretization with $179.2M$ elements on 1792 cores for different tolerances. Note that the energy and runtime are strongly correlated. Additionally, the Hilbert curve produces better partitions compared to the Morton

curve. Both curves show reduction in runtime as well as energy for tolerances > 0, indicating that our initial hypothesis is correct. Figure 8 shows the runtime and energy consumption of the same MATVEC operation for a smaller problem size of $95M$ octants on 256 cores (8 nodes). A closer look at the energy consumption across these 8 nodes for the best tolerance (0.3), shown in Figure 9, that while there is some variability in the energy consumption across the nodes, there is reduction in energy across all nodes. This is true for both the Hilbert and the Morton curves.

Optimal tolerance. We use the performance model, §3.3, to estimate the optimal tolerance. In order to validate our model and determine if it indeed was able to obtain the best partition, we compared our predicted runtime with the actual runtime using a brute-force run for all tolerance values. These results are presented in Figure 10 for the Hilbert curve. This comparison suggests that the overall time consumed by matvec operation is directly correlated with the maximum work assigned to an individual processor (W_{max}), the maximum amount of data exchanged for any two processors (C_{max}), the underlying architectural (t_c, t_w) parameters and the computational kernel of the application (α). Please note that OptiPart starts from a higher tolerance and progressively decreases this, i.e. in the plot it approaches the optimum from the right. For this example, OptiPart will not reduce the tolerance below 0.3 as the predicted runtime increases at this stage and will terminate the partition.

5.5 Quality of induced partitions

Our main motivation for developing architecture-aware partitioning algorithms, is to lower the communication costs and consequently reduce the time-to and energy-to solution for application codes. In this section, we analyze the partitions produced by OptiPart to understand the savings better. For FEM computations, processes need read-only access to information from neighboring processes–commonly referred as ghost/halo regions–in order to perform the matvec. The performance and scalability of the parallel code depends on both the number of processes that a process needs to communicate with as well as the total amount of data that it needs to send or receive. The communication pattern can be represented in the form of a communication matrix $\mathcal{M}$, where

$$\mathcal{M} = \begin{cases} m_{ij} & \text{if } p_i \text{ needs access to } m_{ij} \text{ elements on } p_j \\ 0 & \text{if no shared data between } p_i \text{ and } p_j \end{cases}$$

We can consider the number of non-zeros (NNZ) elements in the communication matrix $\mathcal{M}$ as a metric for communications cost between partitions since it captures the total number of messages that are exchanged during the computation. We use total amount of data communicated between partitions as another metric. We collect these metrics for a fixed problem size (fixed number of elements and number of processors) with varying tolerance value and evaluate how above mentioned metrics behave for the same input data.

Number of non-zeros (NNZ): We observed the effect of varying tolerance on the number of non-zeros in the communication matrix for $1B$ elements partitioned across 4096 processes. These results are shown in Figure 12. Note the scale difference of two graphs in figure 12 which is due to higher locality preserving nature of the Hilbert curve compared to the Morton curve. Figure 12 suggests that NNZ strictly decreases with increasing tolerance

value, but note that although we can reduce the NNZ with increasing tolerance value, this leads to increased load & communication imbalances (see Figure 11). In order to get optimal partitions (in terms of communication and energy) we need to find the tolerance value that does not disproportionately affect the work imbalance.

Total data communicated: Total data communicated during matvec operation in FEM computations is directly coupled with the overall communication cost of the partitions. Figure 12 shows the total data exchanged during 100 matvec operations for a fixed problem size on the CloudLab cluster. As expected we can reduce the total data exchanged by increasing the flexibility in the OptiPart implementation. Figure 12 demonstrates the superiority of Hilbert compared to Morton in terms of communication cost. The results for Hilbert empirically confirm our observations that the communication decreases with increasing tolerance. The kink in Morton in Figure 12 is likely due to the discontinuous partitions that are possible with Morton ; a case we did not consider in our discussions in §3.2.

6 CONCLUSIONS & FUTURE WORK

In this work we presented a new partitioning algorithm that by being architecture and application aware is able to reduce parallel runtime as well as overall energy consumption. The key idea is to assign unequal work to processes in order to reduce overall communication costs. By incorporating machine characteristics such as the slowness of memory and network as well as the applications characteristics we were able to develop a performance model that is able to predict the optimal tradeoff between reducing communication costs and increased load-imbalance. We demonstrated the scalability of the proposed partitioning algorithm up to $262,144$ cores on ORNL's Titan Supercomputer. We also demonstrated energy savings of up to 22% while using the new partition compared to standard SFC-based partitioning algorithms for performing FEM based matvec. Our code is available on github[3] so that other researchers can incorporate these methods in their codes. For future work, we would like to refine our performance model with additional information about the machine and the application, such as NUMA and memory access patterns. While the current work is developed in the context of SFC-based partitioning algorithms, the key ideas are applicable to other partitioning algorithms and will be the focus of future research. Specifically, we are working on incorporating architecture and application models while partitioning irregular applications.

ACKNOWLEDGMENTS

We thank the reviewers whose feedback greatly improved this paper. This work was supported in part by the National Science Foundation grants ACI-1464244 and CCF-1643056. This research used resources of the Oak Ridge Leadership Computing Facility, which is a DOE Office of Science User Facility supported under Contract DE-AC05-00OR22725 and the Extreme Science and Engineering Discovery Environment (XSEDE), which is supported by National Science Foundation grant ACI-1548562.

---

[3]https://github.com/orgs/paralab

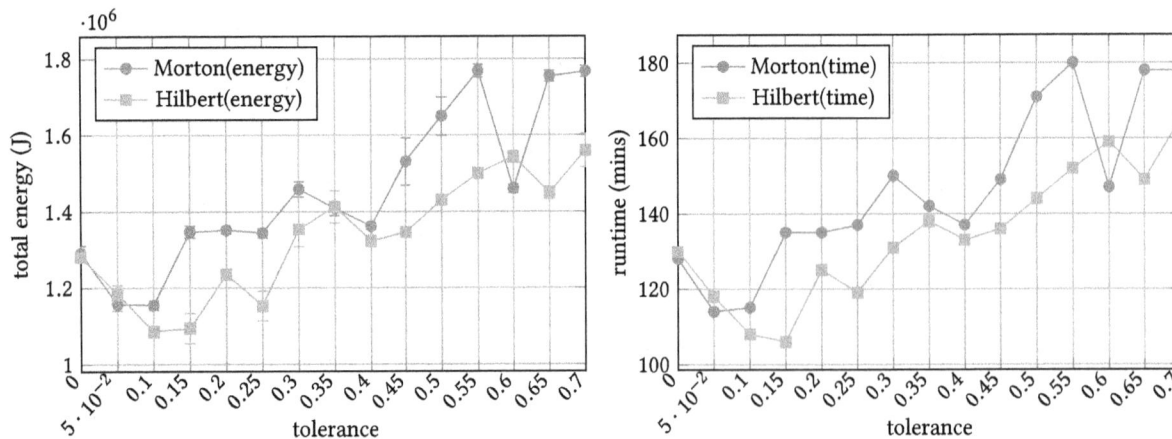

Figure 7: (left) Total energy & time consumption (right) for 100 iterations of MATVEC(distributed) operations, for HILBERT and MORTON curve based partitioning with initial element grain size with 10^5 with maximum depth (of octree) of 30 across 1792 MPI tasks on the Clemson CloudLab cluster.

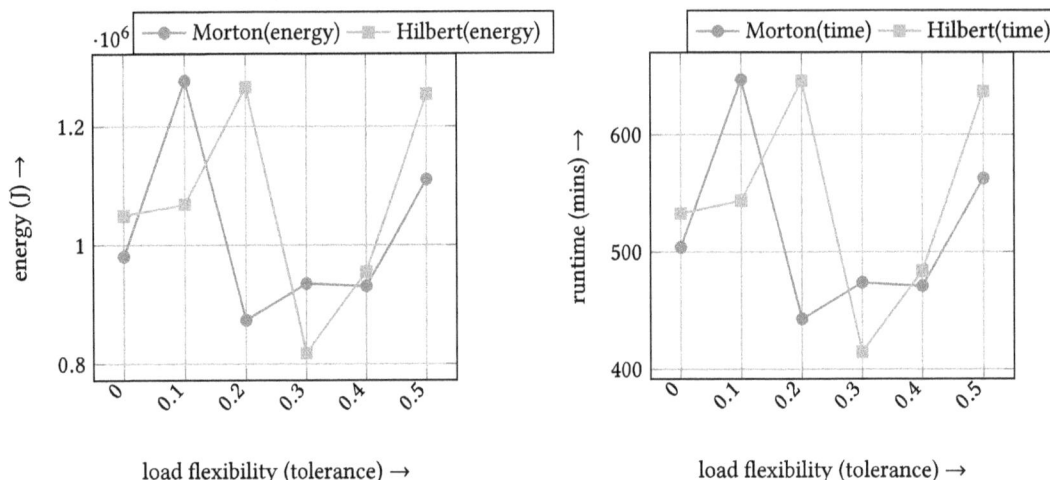

Figure 8: Comparison for MATVEC energy consumption based on HILBERT and MORTON based partitioning schemes for a mesh size of 95M nodes with 256 mpi with varying tolerance values in CloudLab Wisconsin cluster.

REFERENCES

[1] David J Abel and David M Mark. 1990. A comparative analysis of some two-dimensional orderings. *International Journal of Geographical Information System* 4, 1 (1990), 21–31.

[2] Michael Bader. 2012. *Space-filling curves: an introduction with applications in scientific computing.* Vol. 9. Springer Science & Business Media.

[3] Michael A Bender. 2006. Compute Process Allocator (CPA). *Urbana* 51 (2006), 61801.

[4] Jehoshua Bruck, Ching-Tien Ho, Shlomo Kipnis, Eli Upfal, and Derrick Weathersby. 1997. Efficient algorithms for all-to-all communications in multiport message-passing systems. *Parallel and Distributed Systems, IEEE Transactions on* 8, 11 (1997), 1143–1156.

[5] Carsten Burstedde, Lucas C. Wilcox, and Omar Ghattas. 2011. p4est: Scalable Algorithms for Parallel Adaptive Mesh Refinement on Forests of Octrees. *SIAM Journal on Scientific Computing* 33, 3 (2011), 1103–1133. DOI:http://dx.doi.org/10.1137/100791634

[6] Arthur R Butz. 1971. Alternative algorithm for Hilbert's space-filling curve. *IEEE Trans. Comput.* 4 (1971), 424–426.

[7] Paul M Campbell, Karen D Devine, Joseph E Flaherty, Luis G Gervasio, and James D Teresco. 2003. Dynamic octree load balancing using space-filling curves. *Williams College Department of Computer Science Technical Report CS-03* 1 (2003),

68.

[8] U.V. Catalyurek, E.G. Boman, K.D. Devine, D. Bozdag, R.T. Heaphy, and L.A. Riesen. 2007. Hypergraph-based Dynamic Load Balancing for Adaptive Scientific Computations. In *Proc. of 21st International Parallel and Distributed Processing Symposium (IPDPS'07).* IEEE. Best Algorithms Paper Award.

[9] Cédric Chevalier and François Pellegrini. 2008. PT-Scotch: A tool for efficient parallel graph ordering. *Parallel computing* 34, 6 (2008), 318–331.

[10] Karen D Devine, Erik G Boman, Robert T Heaphy, Bruce A Hendrickson, James D Teresco, Jamal Faik, Joseph E Flaherty, and Luis G Gervasio. 2005. New challenges in dynamic load balancing. *Applied Numerical Mathematics* 52, 2 (2005), 133–152.

[11] W. D. Frazer and A. C. McKellar. 1970. Samplesort: A Sampling Approach to Minimal Storage Tree Sorting. *J. ACM* 17, 3 (July 1970), 496–507. DOI:http://dx.doi.org/10.1145/321592.321600

[12] Ananth Grama. 2003. *Introduction to parallel computing.* Pearson Education.

[13] Frank Günther, Miriam Mehl, Markus Pögl, and Christoph Zenger. 2006. A cache-aware algorithm for PDEs on hierarchical data structures based on space-filling curves. *SIAM Journal on Scientific Computing* 28, 5 (2006), 1634–1650.

[14] Daniel Hackenberg, Thomas Ilsche, Robert Schöne, Daniel Molka, Maik Schmidt, and Wolfgang E Nagel. 2013. Power measurement techniques on standard compute nodes: A quantitative comparison. In *Performance Analysis of Systems and Software (ISPASS), 2013 IEEE International Symposium on.* IEEE, 194–204.

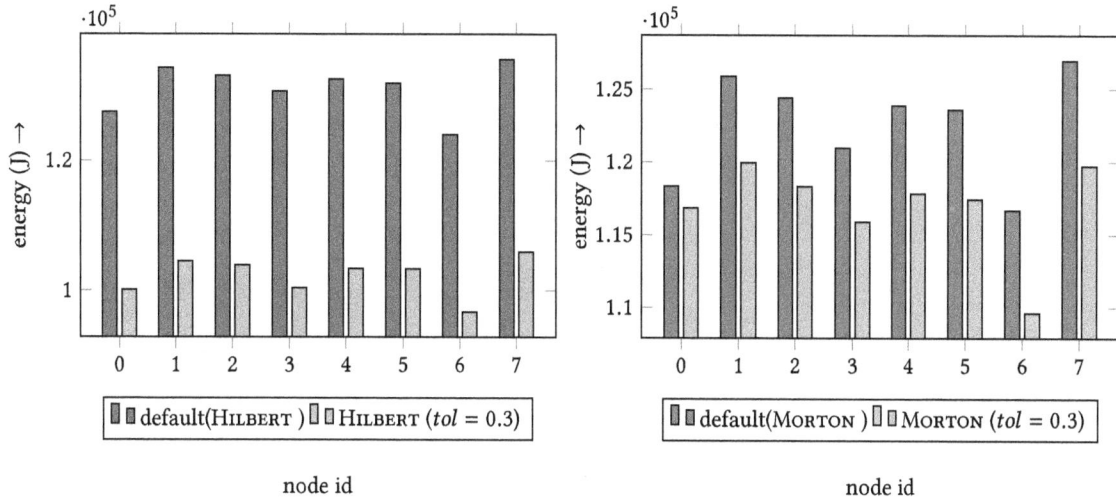

Figure 9: Energy consumed by each node while performing MATVECoperation , with ideal load balancing (for both HILBERT (left) and MORTON (right)) Vs. flexible load balancing with a tolerance of 0.3 for 95M mesh nodes with 256 mpi tasks in CloudLab8 node cluster.

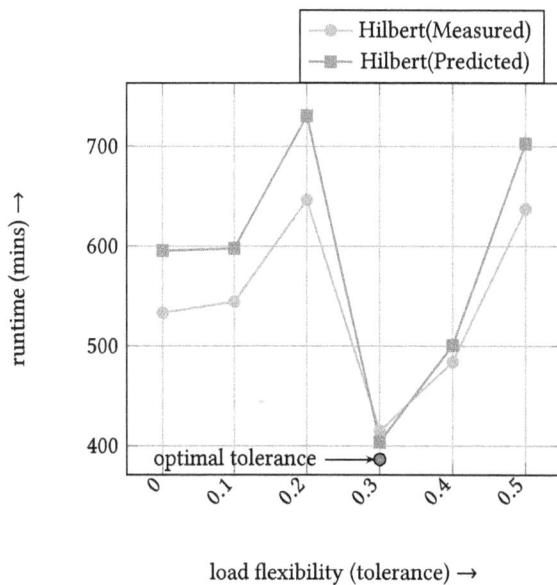

Figure 10: Total time consumed by the 100 MATVEC operations with 256 cores in Wisconsin CloudLab cluster and the interpolated execution time values for HILBERT and MORTON based partitioning, using the model $T_p = \alpha t_c W_{max} + t_w * C_{max}$. This implies the total time consumed during the MATVEC operation directly correlated with maximum amount of work assigned for each core and maximum amount of communication that each core has to carry out. The optimal tolerance that is computed by OPTIPART is highlighted in each figure. Note that OPTIPART starts from a higher tolerance and progressively decreases this, i.e. in the plot it approaches the optimum from the right.

[15] Tsuyoshi Hamada, Tetsu Narumi, Rio Yokota, Kenji Yasuoka, Keigo Nitadori, and Makoto Taiji. 2009. 42 TFlops Hierarchical N-body Simulations on GPUs with Applications in Both Astrophysics and Turbulence. In *Proceedings of the Conference on High Performance Computing Networking, Storage and Analysis (SC '09)*. ACM, New York, NY, USA, Article 62, 12 pages. DOI : http://dx.doi.org/10.1145/1654059.1654123

[16] Chris H. Hamilton and Andrew Rau-Chaplin. 2008. Compact Hilbert Indices: Space-filling Curves for Domains with Unequal Side Lengths. *Inf. Process. Lett.* 105, 5 (Feb. 2008), 155–163. DOI : http://dx.doi.org/10.1016/j.ipl.2007.08.034

[17] Bruce Hendrickson and Robert Leland. 1995. *The Chaco userfis guide: Version 2.0.* Technical Report. Technical Report SAND95-2344, Sandia National Laboratories.

[18] Tomoaki Ishiyama, Keigo Nitadori, and Junichiro Makino. 2012. 4.45 Pflops Astrophysical N-body Simulation on K Computer: The Gravitational Trillion-body Problem. In *Proceedings of the International Conference on High Performance Computing, Networking, Storage and Analysis (SC '12)*. IEEE Computer Society Press, Los Alamitos, CA, USA, Article 5, 10 pages. http://dl.acm.org/citation.cfm?id=2388996.2389003

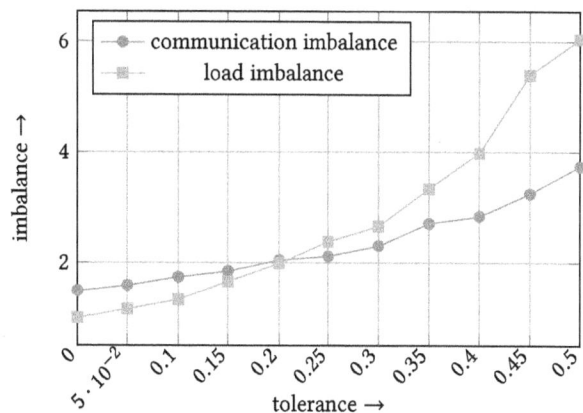

Figure 11: Load imbalance (work_max/work_min) and communication imbalance (bdy_max/bdy_min) plots for HILBERT curve based partitioning, with initial element grain size with 10^5 with maximum depth (of octree) of 30 across 1792 MPI tasks on the Clemson CloudLab cluster.

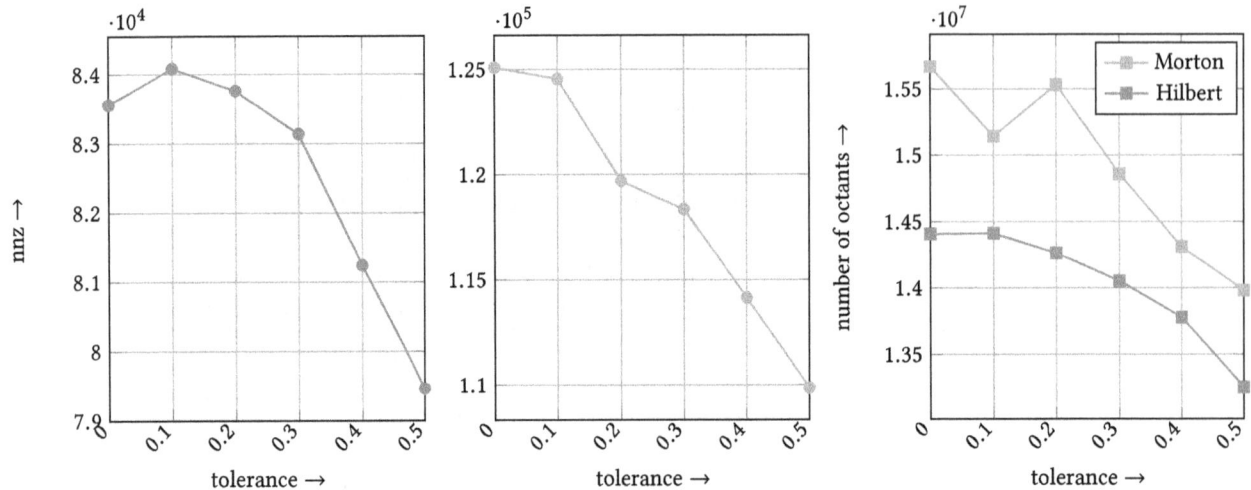

Figure 12: Comparison for number of non-zeros (nnz) elements in the communication matrix corresponding to perform MATVEC operation based on HILBERT (left) and MORTON (center) based partitioning schemes for a mesh size of 1B nodes with 4096 mpi tasks with varying tolerance values. Note that the scale difference between the axes in the plots, and for both partitioning schemes we can reduce the nnz (overall communication cost) by increasing the tolerance value. (right) Total amount of data communicated while performing 100 iterations of MATVEC in Wisconsin-8 in CloudLab with 25.6M elements and 256 cores with varying tolerance value.

[19] Chao Jin, Bronis R de Supinski, David Abramson, Heidi Poxon, Luiz DeRose, Minh Ngoc Dinh, Mark Endrei, and Elizabeth R Jessup. 2016. A survey on software methods to improve the energy efficiency of parallel computing. *International Journal of High Performance Computing Applications* (2016), 1094342016665471.

[20] Guohua Jin and John Mellor-Crummey. 2005. Using space-filling curves for computation reordering. In *Proceedings of the Los Alamos Computer Science Institute Sixth Annual Symposium.*

[21] L.V. Kale and S. Krishnan. 1993. A comparison based parallel sorting algorithm. In *International Conference on Parallel Processing, 1993,* Vol. 3. IEEE, 196–200.

[22] George Karypis and Vipin Kumar. 1995. Metis-unstructured graph partitioning and sparse matrix ordering system, version 2.0. (1995).

[23] George Karypis, Kirk Schloegel, and Vipin Kumar. 2003. Parmetis. *Parallel graph partitioning and sparse matrix ordering library. Version 2* (2003).

[24] Justin Luitjens, Martin Berzins, and Tom Henderson. 2007. Parallel space-filling curve generation through sorting. *Concurrency and Computation: Practice and Experience* 19, 10 (2007), 1387–1402.

[25] Bongki Moon, H.v. Jagadish, Christos Faloutsos, and Joel H. Saltz. 2001. Analysis of the Clustering Properties of the Hilbert Space-Filling Curve. *IEEE Transactions on Knowledge and Data Engineering* 13, 1 (2001), 124–141. DOI:http://dx.doi.org/10.1109/69.908985

[26] Alex Pothen, Horst D. Simon, and Kang-Pu Liou. 1990. Partitioning Sparse Matrices with Eigenvectors of Graphs. *SIAM J. Matrix Anal. Appl.* 11, 3 (1990), 430–452. DOI:http://dx.doi.org/10.1137/0611030 arXiv:http://dx.doi.org/10.1137/0611030

[27] Abtin Rahimian, Ilya Lashuk, Shravan Veerapaneni, Aparna Chandramowlishwaran, Dhairya Malhotra, Logan Moon, Rahul Sampath, Aashay Shringarpure, Jeffrey Vetter, Richard Vuduc, Denis Zorin, and George Biros. 2010. Petascale Direct Numerical Simulation of Blood Flow on 200K Cores and Heterogeneous Architectures. In *Proceedings of the 2010 ACM/IEEE International Conference for High Performance Computing, Networking, Storage and Analysis (SC '10).* IEEE Computer Society, Washington, DC, USA, 1–11. DOI:http://dx.doi.org/10.1109/SC.2010.42

[28] DOE report. 2010. The opportunities and challenges of exascale computing. (2010).

[29] Robert Ricci, Eric Eide, and CloudLab Team. 2014. Introducing CloudLab: Scientific infrastructure for advancing cloud architectures and applications. *; login:: the magazine of USENIX & SAGE* 39, 6 (2014), 36–38.

[30] Johann Rudi, A. Cristiano I. Malossi, Tobin Isaac, Georg Stadler, Michael Gurnis, Peter W. J. Staar, Yves Ineichen, Costas Bekas, Alessandro Curioni, and Omar Ghattas. 2015. An Extreme-scale Implicit Solver for Complex PDEs: Highly Heterogeneous Flow in Earth's Mantle. In *Proceedings of the International Conference for High Performance Computing, Networking, Storage and Analysis (SC '15).* ACM, New York, NY, USA, Article 5, 12 pages. DOI:http://dx.doi.org/10.1145/2807591.2807675

[31] John Shalf, Sudip Dosanjh, and John Morrison. 2011. Exascale computing technology challenges. In *High Performance Computing for Computational Science– VECPAR 2010.* Springer, 1–25.

[32] Leszek Sliwko and Vladimir Getov. 2015. Workload Schedulers-Genesis, Algorithms and Comparisons. *International Journal of Computer Science and Software Engineering* 4, 6 (2015), 141–155.

[33] E. Solomonik and L.V. Kale. 2010. Highly scalable parallel sorting. In *Parallel & Distributed Processing (IPDPS), 2010 IEEE International Symposium on.* IEEE, 1–12.

[34] Hari Sundar, Dhairya Malhotra, and George Biros. 2013. HykSort: a new variant of hypercube quicksort on distributed memory architectures. In *International Conference on Supercomputing, ICS'13, Eugene, OR, USA - June 10 - 14, 2013.* 293–302. DOI:http://dx.doi.org/10.1145/2464996.2465442

[35] Hari Sundar, Rahul Sampath, and George Biros. 2008. Bottom-up construction and 2:1 balance refinement of linear octrees in parallel. *SIAM Journal on Scientific Computing* 30, 5 (2008), 2675–2708. DOI:http://dx.doi.org/10.1137/070681727

[36] Hari Sundar, Rahul S. Sampath, Santi S. Adavani, Christos Davatzikos, and George Biros. 2007. Low-constant Parallel Algorithms for Finite Element Simulations Using Linear Octrees. In *Proceedings of the 2007 ACM/IEEE Conference on Supercomputing (SC '07).* ACM, New York, NY, USA, Article 25, 12 pages. DOI:http://dx.doi.org/10.1145/1362622.1362656

[37] C. Walshaw and M. Cross. 2007. JOSTLE: Parallel Multilevel Graph-Partitioning Software – An Overview. In *Mesh Partitioning Techniques and Domain Decomposition Techniques,* F. Magoules (Ed.). Civil-Comp Ltd., 27–58. (Invited chapter).

[38] Albert-Jan N Yzelman and Rob H Bisseling. 2012. A cache-oblivious sparse matrix–vector multiplication scheme based on the Hilbert curve. In *Progress in Industrial Mathematics at ECMI 2010.* Springer, 627–633.

[39] Marco Zagha and Guy E Blelloch. 1991. Radix sort for vector multiprocessors. In *Proceedings of the 1991 ACM/IEEE conference on Supercomputing.* ACM, 712–721.

Author Index

NOTES